Hammarskjöld

Dag Hammarskjöld, 1958

(photo: Pål-Nils Nilsson, collection of the Swedish National Library)

Hammarskjöld

A Life

Roger Lipsey

The University of Michigan Press

Ann Arbor

Copyright © by the University of Michigan 2013

Published in the United States of America by

The University of Michigan Press

Manufactured in the United States of America

⊗ Printed on acid-free paper

2016   2015   2014   2013   4   3   2   1

A CIP catalog record for this book is available from the British Library.

ISBN 978-0-472-11890-8 (cloth:alk. paper)

ISBN 978-0-472-02934-1 (e-book)

The title page graphic of monogram and crossed ice axes reflects Dag Hammarskjöld's book plate during the UN years.

Book Design: Bill McAllister

Cover Design: James Sarfati

Composed using the Archer and Garamond Premiere Pro font families.

For Jacob Needleman and Laurence Rosenthal
thought and music, music and thought

It is as one of my friends here has said: either you get very cynical—or *very* serious.

—Hammarskjöld correspondence, 1954

It may well be that the United Nations' effort will ultimately fail and, if so, S.O.S.

—Hammarskjöld correspondence, 1956

You fellows know there are those voyages that seem ordered for the illustration of life, that might stand for a symbol of existence.

—Joseph Conrad, "Youth"

Table of Contents

Illustrations

Frontispiece: Dag Hammarskjöld, 1958. *(photo: Pål-Nils Nilsson, in the collection of the Swedish National Library)*

1. Dag Hammarskjöld trekking in the Swedish far north. *(photo: Gösta Lundquist, in the collection of Nordiska Museet)*

2. Hjalmar Hammarskjöld, Dag's father. *(photo: private collection)*

3. Agnes Hammarskjöld with her son Dag. *(photo: private collection)*

4. The Hammarskjöld sons. (from left to right): Bo, Dag, Åke, Sten. *(photo: Swedish National Library)*

5. Axel Hägerström, professor of philosophy at Uppsala University. *(photo: private collection)*

6. Archbishop Nathan Söderblom, early mentor and family friend. *(photo: private collection)*

7. Greta Beskow in Hammarskjöld's photograph at his home in Brewster, New York. *(photo: Dag Hammarskjöld, in the collection of the Swedish National Library)*

8. Dag Hammarskjöld, secretary-general elect, and Trygvie Lie, outgoing secretary-general, at Idlewild Airport, New York, April 9, 1953. *(photo: Lisa Larsen/Time & Life Images/Getty Images)*

9. The oath of office, April 10, 1953. *(UN Photo/AK)*

10. Andrew W. Cordier, executive assistant to the secretary-general, standing to count votes in the General Assembly, October 14, 1958. *(UN Photo/YES)*

11. Dag Hammarskjöld with Ralph J. Bunche, Nobel laureate, undersecretary for special political affairs, October 13, 1955. *(UN Photo/ MB)*

12. Dag Hammarskjöld and Zhou Enlai, Beijing, January 10, 1955. Hammarskjöld's security guard, Bill Ranallo, stands between and behind them. *(UN Photo)*

13. The Room of Quiet, United Nations Headquarters. Designed in part by Dag Hammarskjöld, with a fresco by Bo Beskow. *(UN Photo)*

14. Dag Hammarskjöld and Martin Buber, Jerusalem, January 2, 1959. *(UN Photo/FS/gf)*

15. Patrice Lumumba, prime minister of the newly independent Republic of the Congo, late July 1960, at a meeting of the United Nations
Security Council. *(photo: Bob Gomel/Time & Life Images/Getty Images)*

16. Dag Hammarskjöld and Patrice Lumumba at United Nations Headquarters, July 24, 1960. *(UN Photo)*.

17. Hammarskjöld in Katanga, August 14, 1960. *(UN Photo/HP)*.

18. Unveiling of the sculpture Single Form by Barbara Hepworth, in
memory of Dag Hammarskjöld. United Nations Headquarters, June
11, 1964. *(UN Photo/Yutaka Nagata)*

19. Ben Shahn, *Portrait of Dag Hammarskjöld*, 1962. *(photo: Swedish
National Museum)*

Acknowledgments

This book has had and has needed many friends. In the United States, Tracy Cochran embraced the project early as both literary agent and adviser. Her unreasonable faith in the project and her publishing experience and fine intelligence have meant the world to me. In Sweden, my early and wonderful collaborator, Daniel von Sydow, translated Dag Hammarskjöld's Swedish correspondence and in many ways acted as a second self. Daniel's translations appear throughout this book. How can I thank him? His wife and son, Eva Lena and Jacob, offered hospitality and scholarship, so appreciated. Midway through the project I had the good fortune to be introduced in New York to Thord Palmlund, a person of wide and deep culture recently retired from the United Nations. Keenly aware of the Hammarskjöld legacy, he made this project his own as a wisely critical reader and a translator of additional materials. His comments on the near-final draft were invaluable. As I often write to him, thank you entirely.

I gratefully bring to mind Jack Zawistowski, the librarian at the Swedish National Library (Kungliga biblioteket), who assembled the large Hammarskjöld archive and for many years helped me and others find our way in it. Now retired, he was most generous. Others in Sweden who know my debt to them are Jan-Eric Ericson, Inga-Lill Hammarskjöld, Henning Melber, Olle Nordberg, and the team at AthenaFilm, especially Göran Gunér, who generously supports my wish to bring to American audiences their brilliant documentary film, *Visions of a Secretary-General: Dag Hammarskjöld and the United Nations 1953–1961*.

The late and much missed Sture Linnér deserves a special word: our meetings were unforgettable occasions. The death in summer 2012 of Sverker Åström, Hammarskjöld's colleague and friend, stirs the same sense of loss. He and Linnér were among those who knew Hammarskjöld best.

In Germany, I am grateful to Manuel Fröhlich for his friendship and encouragement. His recent book on Hammarskjöld's political ethics and his discovery and interpretation of important correspondence mark, to my mind, the beginning of a new exploration of the Hammarskjöld legacy by a new generation. Marie-Noëlle Little, who has published and interpreted two important bodies of Hammarskjöld correspondence, is very much a part of that new generation. Her encouragement and interest have heartened me.

At the Thomas Merton Institute in central Kentucky, where I had the benefit of a writing retreat, and at the nearby Abbey of Gethsemani, I think with fondness and gratitude of Sr. Kelly O'Mahony, Br. Paul Quenon, Fr. Mark Scott, and the hospitable Fr. Damien. Each of you advanced this book. Thank you. Who could fail to work in a disciplined way with Vigils at 3:15 in the morning, Vespers at 5:30 in the evening, and guesthouse supper at 6?

Others to whom I am most grateful in the United States are Susan Brandwayn, Rebecka Danielsson Deroche, Jenny Doyle, Dianne Edwards, Nicole Graf, Jessica Kirshner, Nicole Miozzi, Paula Plantier, Jane Kielty Stott, Anahit Turabian and her colleagues in the UN photo archive, Robertson Work, and Jeff Zaleski. Each of you knows the contribution you have made. I thank you. A special word of thanks is due Fenton Johnson, who read parts of the manuscript with kindness and acumen. James George, a retired Canadian diplomat, has time and again shared his memories of Hammarskjöld and of Lester Pearson; I have been so happy to converse with him, an old and dear friend. Douglas Burton-Christie, editor of *Spiritus: A Journal of Christian Spirituality*, was the first to publish a substantial essay drawing on my new research; that meant a great deal to me.

Three heartfelt acknowledgments: to Sir Brian Urquhart, Dr. Susan Williams, and Raymond Beier and his team at PricewaterhouseCoopers.

Sir Brian's magnificent biography of Dag Hammarskjöld "kept me on the rails," as Hammarskjöld liked to say, and his truth-telling voice in the United Nations Oral History Project provides unique insight. The firmness and clarity of his writings about Hammarskjöld, and about United Nations affairs in the decades after Hammarskjöld, set the standard. His laconic encouragement—"Keep at it"—helped me keep at it.

Susan Williams, author of the careful and courageous *Who Killed Hammarskjöld? The UN, the Cold War and White Supremacy in Africa* (2011), became a key friend at a later stage of this project. Her reading of the near-final draft, her encouragement, and our conversations have greatly touched and helped me. Dr. Williams was kind enough to introduce me to Hans Kristian Simensen, who has amassed an extraordinary documentation related to the tragedy at Ndola. His generosity and trust in sharing key documents have been, as a famous American liked to put it, "beyond category."

I salute Raymond Beier and his group at PricewaterhouseCoopers, with whom it was such a vivid exercise in thought and collegiality to work in the closing years of my business career. Without a quarter-century as a business writer, I doubt that I would have had sufficient perspective to approach the public aspects of Hammarskjöld's life and thought.

I am grateful to Thomas Dwyer, editor in chief of the University of Michigan Press, for recognizing this project at an early stage and bringing together a skilled team to publish with care and elegance. Key members of that team have been Paul Cohen and his colleagues at Epigraph Publishing Services. Sincere thanks to you all.

My scarcely conscious "imitation of Ananda Coomaraswamy" continues. This book is in many respects my version—experiential, biographical, immersed in our time and its people—of his learned study, *Spiritual Authority and Temporal Power in the Indian Theory of Government* (1942). His influence, no matter how far I stray, retains authority and beauty.

To my wife Susan, thanks beyond measure. The project was long. So fortunately, our marriage is longer.

All interpretations in this book are my own, and of course its errors. Those who have so generously helped took me to the threshold.

Roger Lipsey

Foreword

Asked by a friend why and when I became interested in Dag Hammarskjöld, I could find no beginning. There must have been one; I've walked with him for decades now, though I don't imagine he's noticed. He is long since gone. He was the second secretary-general of the United Nations, serving in the years 1953–61, formidable in his time, somewhat forgotten now. The publication of this book falls soon after the fiftieth anniversary of his death in an air crash while on duty in Central Africa. It was September 18th, 1961, in the dark of night, for reasons once explained as pilot error, now an open question. I must have read of his death in the newspaper. I could not have missed the wave of sadness that passed over much of the world. The sound of public life in early days after the fatal crash was stunned eulogy; many stepped forward to say what they felt, what they knew of the lost world leader. Even that left no trace on me. Hammarskjöld was not yet close.

Then *Markings* was published, first in Swedish in 1963, the following year in English translation. You may recall that this is Hammarskjöld's private journal, found on a bedside table in his New York apartment with a note leaving the decision to publish or not to a friend. It revealed a person whom scarcely anyone had known: a religious seeker taking his lead from Albert Schweitzer for ethics and from medieval Christian mystics for the conduct and direction of inner life. He proved to be Pascal-like in his critique of self and society, Montaigne-like in his questioning, Augustine-like in his need and willingness to chronicle his hard journey. He was a sufferer, a doubter, a discoverer; a man who had encountered transcendent warmth and solace at the edge of experience; an incisive, troubled, prayerful mind and heart at work on the deepest issues facing human beings.

With the publication of *Markings*, the portrait of Dag Hammarskjöld abruptly doubled in size and scope: there was the great statesman and peacemaker, the man of unshakeable integrity who had dueled with Khrushchev, negotiated with Ben-Gurion and Nasser, faced the wrath of de Gaulle, rebuked great nations, nurtured small nations, and kept something resembling order in what he called "this house," the United Nations. And there was another: a vulnerable, questing man of spirit, among his generational peers more like the martyred pastor Dietrich Bonhoeffer or the monk and author Thomas Merton than like his political peers. What they explored in seclusion, in prison and monastery, he explored in glare at the highest level of public life.

I read *Markings* soon after publication, and it went at once to the shelves of "real books" in my library—a select company to which I return, confident that they record fundamental truths and experiences with unrestrained eloquence, fearlessly. Occupying fewer shelves than you might think, they form neighborhoods. For example, there is a neighborhood for ancient Greek and Roman philosophy and another for translations of the Bible, plus the Greek New Testament and a general concordance. That neighborhood extends as far as Meister Eckhart, a key source for Hammarskjöld, and to a treasure of English medieval spirituality, *The Cloud of Unknowing* (again well known to Hammarskjöld—he cared enough for it to send a copy to David Ben-Gurion, prime minister of Israel, who was both a stubborn negotiating partner and a kindred spirit). Nearby are Pascal's *Pensées*, the *Mathnawi* of Rumi, the Gita and Upanishads, the Tibetan *Life of Milarepa*, early Chinese classics, Martin Buber's *Tales of the Hasidim*, and much else. What a feast of knowledge, of attention to reality, all familiar to Hammarskjöld.

His book fit right in. It was the personal record of a mind both ferocious and sensitive. Its "world" encompassed many worlds, from cool clouds of unknowing to hot zones of war. In 1954, after serving as United Nations secretary-general for a year or so, he described his world in much this way in the privacy of his journal. "Blood, grime, sweat, earth—where are these in your world of will?" And he continued: "Everywhere—the ground from which the flame ascends straight upward." The mutual dependence of inner and outer, lower and higher, ground and flame, is evident in these few poetic words echoing both Winston Churchill's wartime realism and the imagery of the Bhagavad Gita.

The evolving perspective of his journal from year to year recorded a struggle first to survive and then to be; to see without illusion both self and others; to know clearly, serve humbly, and lead firmly; to find understanding and renewal in stillness and prayer; and toward the end to accept the possibility of his own death in line of duty. He was a man inside out, and that struck me as just what is needed: he drew from within to understand and insofar as possible shape events. However, no short characterization of Hammarskjöld is likely to be complete enough. For example, what I've just written leaves out his thorough knowledge of diplomatic process, international law, and the history of nations. This inner-directed man was a connoisseur of externalities. If he was quick to find solutions or promising directions in hugely difficult circumstances—there were many in the course of his eight years as secretary-general—it was in part owing to the large world inside him, where new thoughts and glints of possibility could knock around freely and find a pattern that led on.

At times he would reach in public talks for words to describe his approach. If you listened well, you couldn't miss that they were provocative words, suggesting a perspective on action that left much unsaid. For example, in September 1953, early in his tenure as secretary-general in months when he seems to have been probing the limits of public expression, he said this to a New York audience: "We cannot mould the world as masters of a material thing. Columbus did not reach the East Indies. But we can influence the development of the world from within as a spiritual thing." No one, it seems, took him aside on that occasion to ask: "Kind sir, isn't that something of an overstatement? What really do you mean?" He had too few pupils.

All of this, and more, seemed to me a new heroism. Total, astute, and deliberate engagement with the world, total and deliberate engagement with an inner path, each carried out with no trace of laziness—and often enough with wit and enjoyment, once he found his footing. Was that not a kind of heroism? It offered a nearly impossible ideal to be remembered and appreciated as my generation and I stumbled on.

One of his interpreters, the Swedish poet Erik Lindegren, issued a warning some months after Hammarskjöld's death: "It would be a pity," he said to the members of the Swedish Academy, where he was invited to occupy Hammarskjöld's seat, now empty, "if Dag Hammarskjöld were turned into a model of virtue and unwillingly appeared as a moralizing shadow for future Swedish generations when they grow up. His life was lighter but also darker than that." As a young person, I almost certainly missed Lindegren's point: Hammarskjöld *was*, for me, a model of virtue. I was inspired by his attack on life, his attack on himself, his need to clarify and ready himself to serve without self-serving. His example decisively confirmed values that had touched me from other sources as well. If there was to be some whole, and something like a whole view, he was part of it. After reading *Markings*, I could not forget him.

In the 1960s, the first wave of writings about Hammarskjöld dealt mainly with *Markings*, often brilliantly. The mass of UN statements

xvi   Hammarskjöld | A Life

and documents, press conference transcripts, and public talks had not yet been assembled in one place, and a definitive biography in progress was not yet published. Two short biographies were in print, but a reader could be forgiven in the 1960s for thinking of Dag Hammarskjöld as a man of spirit, a Marcus Aurelius of our time, who did one thing or another for the United Nations, just as Marcus kept busy with boring wars on the frontiers of the Roman Empire while writing a most interesting book of personal meditations. It was a mistaken view of Hammarskjöld, but natural enough: his record of diplomatic accomplishment and reflections about world community were slipping into the past and no widely available, new publications filled the gaps.

That situation was remedied in the 1970s with the release of Brian Urquhart's masterful biography (*Hammarskjold*, 1972) and the four volumes of *Public Papers* (1972–75), compiled and edited by Andrew Cordier and Wilder Foote, both of whom, like Urquhart, had worked closely with Hammarskjöld. Now the pageant and effort of his life, and the exceedingly fine thought about peace, negotiation, the obligations of nations, and the grounds for hope, were laid before us.

Despite all that, his thought and example have not yet found a lasting place in our collective memory. There may be a detectable reason; I'll try in a moment to explore it, and, of course, he's not wholly forgotten. His name is on streets and plazas and schools nearly worldwide. *Markings* remains in print in English. Elsewhere in the world—notably Germany and Italy—revised translations have been published in recent years, and revised translations are signs of caring. There have been excellent books, especially in and around his birth centenary year, 2005, and a superb documentary film. Hammarskjöld's distinguished successor, Kofi Annan (UN secretary-general, 1997–2007), significantly contributed to that moment of remembering and interpreting his legacy. The Dag Hammarskjöld Foundation (Uppsala, Sweden) pursues topics in international development inspired by Hammarskjöld's late focus on newly independent nations, and it periodically sponsors lectures and publishes research on Hammarskjöld's life and contributions. A book published in 2011, Susan Williams's brilliant and thorough *Who Killed Hammarskjöld?*, sheds new light, as Hammarskjöld sometimes said, "in many directions."

All to the good. But if things run their current course, Dag Hammarskjöld will soon be remembered for the most part in two circles only: at the United Nations, where he is somewhat inescapable though somewhat forgotten, and among readers interested in spirituality who discover *Markings* and recognize it as a modern classic.

Why this eclipse, so much so that a writer such as myself feels that he is raising his hand in the dark, pointing unseen to an unseen person? The likely answer is disappointingly banal: he was ahead of his time. Well, then, as a culture have we caught up with him at last? Probably so. Having caught up, will we now pass him by without really noticing? I hope not.

Today the distinctive balance he found between wholehearted engagement with the needs of the world and wholehearted engagement in what he called "the journey inward" has become more recognizable. We call it engaged spirituality, and we learn it—at least in the abstract—from teachers, enlightened political leaders, and authors ranging from Henry David Thoreau in the nineteenth century to Gandhi, Martin Luther King Jr., and inspiring Buddhist teachers of our time, preeminently the Dalai Lama, leader of the long-suffering people of Tibet. Hammarskjöld was a man of the West through and through. He found inspiration, guidelines, and hints for the journey inward from Western and predominantly Christian sources, only to discover in his later years that the same sensibility existed in Asian religious cultures and in Judaism. By the end of his life, he had become—what are the right words?—a Christian to whom all the world's wisdom spoke as to an intimate. His intelligent and broad sympathies broke open any lingering narrowness; and that, in turn, made him a still more remarkable and faithful disciple of Jesus of Nazareth.

In his lifetime, Hammarskjöld did not wish to be known as a spiritual seeker; he preferred to be a tree judged by its edible fruit, not by its private ideas about treeness and its attraction to light. His edible fruit was in the realm of furthering peace with justice in the world and encouraging economic and social development, and for his accomplishments in this realm he was admired nearly worldwide. Where the rest is concerned, he preserved his privacy and, as noted earlier, left to a friend the posthumous decision to publish *Markings*. But by throwing *Markings* into the world after his death, he was surely putting a question: Does the approach he took matter? Does the journey inward, undertaken seriously and with bright energy, bear some relation to achieving a little more peace on Earth, a little more goodwill toward men and women?

Hammarskjöld could not live in some other way; his nature forced him to become a daily practitioner of what Socrates called the examined life and to turn in prayer toward his Lord. I do not think that he proposed himself as a model. He suffered too much, knew too well his own darknesses, just as he knew what he was capable of, and it was a very great deal. But through *Markings* he does propose something, asks something of later generations, leans our way. He gives away his secrets there: he churned what it is to be human, and what it takes to engage in intensive action without losing inner freedom, resourcefulness of mind, and kindness where sensible. The identical thing can and must be said of his public papers—the many UN statements, press conferences, talks at university gatherings, and so on. Although the situations out of which they emerged are long past, and the details of those situations may not long capture our interest, the essence of his thought and the principles he cared for have not aged. These sources also are strewn with questions and insights pointing in their own way to what Hammarskjöld once called "the laws of inner life and of action."

Pursuing knowledge of Dag Hammarskjöld's mind and methods, I've had the privilege of touching extraordinary objects. The physicality of archival research is worth a mention: documents are singular objects, passed from hand to hand and carrying the invisible trace of hands and intentions. To be permitted to touch them implies trust that one's own hands will leave only welcome traces. I'm thinking particularly of the typescript of *Markings*, preserved in the Royal Library in Stockholm, with its small *X*'s penned by Hammarskjöld between certain entries—a document in which he clearly invested a great deal of hope and furious sincerity. I'm thinking also of the draft Swedish translation on yellow legal pad sheets of Martin Buber's book, *I and Thou*, which Hammarskjöld was advancing during the last flight in Africa. Flung free from the crash, his briefcase with these papers remained intact. And then, preserved at Columbia University in the collection of his friend and chief of staff Andrew Cordier, a set of some forty handwritten notes they passed back and forth during UN meetings—sometimes to entertain each other during dull spells, sometimes to exchange substantively. Here is one, Hammarskjöld to Cordier: "The intervention was more effective than clear!"

May this book escape that judgment by proving to be, in your eyes, both effective and clear.

Roger Lipsey

1

Mr. Hammarskjöld

"You see," he once said, "even a very small dent may lead to a rift, and a rift may lead to an opening and you may break in through the wall. . . . The interesting thing is, is this a dent which may lead to a rift?"[1] He was speaking of the search for nuclear disarmament. A dent that leads to a rift is needed here also because Dag Hammarskjöld is all but forgotten. His star rises astronomically on special occasions and anniversaries, and declines until the next. Yet his wisdom and methods, and his focused verve in the face of difficulty, offer crucial guidance and inspiration for our time. Secretary-general of the United Nations for more than eight years (1953–61), he endowed the organization with new methods and dignity, and left a vivid written legacy that can speak powerfully to many now who carry public responsibilities or have in mind lives of service in communities large or small. A man of the mid-twentieth century and of the UN, he is more: a classic figure awaiting clarity of recognition.

A small but global tribe of political scientists, working diplomats, NGO participants, and scholars of literature and religion know the Hammarskjöld legacy well. They are aware of his struggles and achievements as secretary-general; he set the standard. They know the value of his political thought, which is as much an enduring reflection on the human condition as it is a response to specific circumstances. They are reinterpreting his politics, exploring the previously little-known record of his youth and early career in Sweden, gradually publishing his correspondence, and revising translations of *Markings*. To this audience that knows him well, I promise new perspectives and more than enough unfamiliar documents to reward their attention. A further promise: I will not rehash their work.

And then there are the Old Believers, men and women for whom their reading of *Markings* decades ago (and many times since) was a notable event of their lives. A surprise bestseller in the first year or so after its publication in English in 1964, *Markings* is a spiritual classic of the twentieth century. Although it has long since dropped off bestseller lists, it is likely to have a place in the canon of literature to which people far into the future will turn. Like the *Meditations* of Marcus Aurelius, it records the thoughts at quiet moments of an exceptional man engaged at the highest level of responsibility in world affairs. Like the *Confessions* of St. Augustine, it is an exhaustingly honest exercise in autobiography. And like Pascal's *Pensées*, its scope is vast, from unflinching observations of human nature—his own and others'—to moments of transcendent perception surely granted only to those whom the gods love. *Markings* was deliberately left unpublished in his lifetime. One person knew of it; no one had read it.

For these Old Believers, *Markings* is the treasure, and the rest—the immense work at the United Nations, the speeches and public writings ranging over so much of human experience—can be courteously ignored. Their attitude reverses the attitude typical of scholars and diplomats for whom the shattering self-interrogation of the journal, its intimate engagement with issues of faith, hope, and love, and its delight in refined literary expression—all that the Old Believers most care for—tend to mean little.

There is a third cohort: men and women of a certain age who remember Hammarskjöld with respect but without detail. Some seniors say, "Wasn't he a mystic? Why do I think that?" Others: "Yes, I remember him. That must date me." They would have seen covers of *Time* magazine that carried his portrait—the first, businesslike and direct in 1955 for the tenth anniversary of the United Nations, or perhaps the third, summer 1960, offering an icon-like allegory of the Congo Crisis: Hammarskjöld's face, softly lit with raised blue eyes, set against a mighty storm in the background. Members of this cohort might also remember something of his courageous handling of the Suez Crisis of 1956–57 and his later struggle with Nikita Khrushchev. And of course they recall his tragic death in an air crash in central Africa, mid-September 1961.

Readers and rememberers of such widely differing ages, interests, and levels of knowledge reflect the fact that Hammarskjöld left a dual legacy. That legacy has been difficult to assimilate. Had he been exclusively the outstanding diplomat and diplomatic thinker of his era, an immensely creative influence on the United Nations when the institution was young, that would have been, so to speak, just fine. Had he been exclusively a religious author, a sensitive explorer of human identity under modern conditions, he might have earned a place beside Dietrich Bonhoeffer, Martin Buber, Thomas Merton, and other engaged religious thinkers of our time—and that too would have been fine. But he was both. The record on both sides is powerful. Hammarskjöld's single act of multidimensional living challenges understanding.

But there is no reason to mistrust altogether how things fall out. Hammarskjöld is a man for *this* time. What he was, his thought, and his conduct of his high office can and should be an inspiration for our time. But new acts of understanding are needed. We must describe all this, name it, see its pattern, and that process of recovery has begun. A gifted political scientist, Manuel Fröhlich, recently published a study of Hammarskjöld's political ethics that takes a long step toward integrating the two sides of his legacy, the externally focused statesmanship and the internally directed inquiry into human being.[2] The public life led Fröhlich to *Markings*; from a point of departure in his university discipline, he set out to see Hammarskjöld whole and to project that larger understanding into today's global politics. This book takes the opposite course to the middle. It originates in an Old Believer's decades of familiarity with *Markings*, followed by curiosity about the ways in which the mind that shaped *Markings* operated in the world at large. But that curiosity was not wholly random. It was impelled by a question and led to another question.

Sanctuary and conflict

The first question turns on the notion of sanctuary. Sanctuary is an experience sought and needed in today's anxious world. It can be found in worship communities that value moments of quiet. It can be found in traditional liturgies—for example, in the spacious flow of Gregorian chant. It can be found in theaters, concert halls, and opera houses where art mirrors experience with love and insight. It belongs also to the meditation hall, now naturalized in the West although its roots are Asian. More than a few of us know the peaceful order of such spaces: the regular rows of cushions, the still figures of men and women seated in meditation, perhaps a sacred image on an altar. What a perfect place and means for learning to be human from the inside out.

But as one of Hammarskjöld's preferred authors, Hermann Hesse, taught with elegant precision in *The Glass Bead Game*, sanctuary is tied to the world. Joseph Knecht, leading member of a spiritual elite in Hesse's secluded fictional province of Castalia, discovers that he must descend into the world to be of service on terms, however humble, that worldly people value. Within days of his arrival he perishes, and the book concludes on that note. Having written an altogether satisfactory masterpiece in the preceding four hundred pages, Hesse leaves to us the issue of what happens next. What happens next is crucial.

Many know something of spirituality in the sanctuary of a spiritual community or in their privacy. But what becomes of it, how does it serve and find paths forward when it must return to the world—when it has duties? Does it enrich a man or woman's dedication to work? Does it strike deep roots in plain things or is it aloof? Does it touch life and allow itself to be touched only because there is no practical alternative? Does it learn from troubled circumstances and difficult people or does it long for the close of business so that it can go off on its own? Is it denatured by stress or does it somehow thrive? Does it make one more clear-sighted and strategic when strategy is needed—or hamper mobility by draping it in holy vestments, in slow ideas? Only Hammarskjöld and a very few others of our era can answer these questions—he best of all.

Hammarskjöld had a sense of sanctuary. He even sponsored the creation of a small sanctuary on the ground floor of the United Nations Secretariat building, the Room of Quiet, for which he wrote a beautiful short statement still available at the entrance (see pp. 326–27). By the time he became secretary-general, he was a man of profound inner life, a veteran of bitter internal wars and hard-won peace revealed in the pages of *Markings*. He was capable of new and authentic prayer. And during his years at the UN he became a renowned public figure, widely and justly admired for what those close to him described as his "lightning-like" capacity to understand challenging situations, foresee their possible lines of development, take measures, and persevere with agility and tireless attention. Further, what he said in many different forums, from the Security Council and General Assembly to press conferences and addresses worldwide, was an education in itself. There was little he hadn't thought about.

To approach the dual legacy of Dag Hammarskjöld, we'll do best to take things as he did, as they come along. We will join him in his diplomatic concerns without a glance toward the exit, toward sanctuary. There was no such glance in him. Long before the popularization of notions about being "here and now"—the value of living in the present— he had made that discovery on his own and ever after strived to stay put, just where he was, looking after present needs. However, when at last he had time for himself and returned to his long exploration of the inner dimensions of experience and the subtleties of literature and the arts, we should follow him there too, even to the edge of what he called "the unheard-of," where he encountered the sacred or found prayer. His commitment to the work of the United Nations was entire and wholehearted. He gave himself unsparingly. He was made for that. His commitment to an inner path was no less entire. He was made for that. How did these two intersect and reinforce each other? How did Hammarskjöld become able to carry the clarity and poise of the sanctuary into the world? What can be said of his way, without sentimentalizing or dismissing it?

Here and there in his writings are short versions of the answer to that question as he lived it from day to day. For example, in a letter of 1958 to the Swedish author Eyvind Johnson, he wrote: "The other day I was forced by a journalist to try to formulate my views on the main requirements of somebody who wishes to contribute to the development of peace and reason. I found no better formulation than this: 'He must push his awareness to the utmost limit without losing his inner quiet, he must be able to see with the eyes of others from within their personality without losing his own.'"[3] But the short version is too short. A book is needed.

No intellectual activity more ruthless

A second question grows out of the first. What is a political education? The question has an old-fashioned ring, as if Henry Adams has risen to ask it. Adams didn't fail to look at the issue—for example, in an autobiographical passage (written in his characteristic third person) reporting his response as a young man in Washington to turf battles in the administration of president Ulysses Grant. "The selfishness of politics was the earliest of all political education," he wrote. "Adams had nothing to learn from its study; but the situation struck him as curious—so curious that he devoted years to reflecting upon it."[4] The need for a political education and the uses of that education once acquired are so evident to some that the question hardly occurs; they just live it. But others, more idealistic or remote, come to it slowly as life thrusts them into positions of influence or leadership. Such people realize they have never deliberately explored the nature of political relationships and purposes, and have failed to construct a point of view. They have an inner compass, but events quickly show that it's incompletely marked and not always sensitive enough. As well, their maps don't reach far enough from home. "Here be monsters" starts just offshore. If they intend to serve a community rather than burden it with their inexperience, what do they need to understand? Challenging activities require discipline, but what discipline suits this particular challenge? What is a *principled* political mind? What is a *kind* political mind—a mind that recognizes and values kinships? What is a principled and kind political mind that is neither naïve nor irresolute?

Hammarskjöld is again among the few in our era who can answer the question. The education offered by Hammarskjöld won't appeal to people who entirely mistrust political processes and enter them unwillingly or enter largely for their own benefit. But it is perfectly suited to those who cannot abandon hope for common sense and goodness in the larger community and who for that reason willingly expose themselves to the hazards of political processes. "Politics and diplomacy are no play of will and skill," Hammarskjöld said to a university audience in 1955, "where results are independent of the character of those engaging in the game. Results are determined not by superficial ability but by the consistency of the actors in their efforts and by the validity of their ideals. Contrary to what seems to be popular belief, there is no intellectual activity which more ruthlessly tests the solidity of a man than politics. Apparently easy successes with the public are possible for a juggler, but lasting results are achieved only by the patient builder."[5] The education he offers is for patient builders.

Hammarskjöld knew a great deal about the history and theory of politics and diplomacy. He persisted in thinking of himself as "primarily a university man," as he once put it, although his life led elsewhere.[6] At times his learning would surface as if from an underground stream that generally flowed unnoticed. For example, just five months after he became secretary-general he gave a talk to members of the American Political Science Association in which he congenially showed his knowledge of their professional concerns and literature. "So the Secretary-General of the United Nations," he said in the stately third person, "is led into very wide fields which are under the reign of political science. In his efforts he may have to enter the world of *An American Dilemma* and the land of *The Lonely Crowd*, and he must give such knowledge its proper background in the broodings of the Toquevilles and Schumpeters."[7] The term "brooding" is in character. One can't know how another person thinks, but Hammarskjöld gives the impression of having thought as a whole from foot to crown of head, and of thinking with enough perseverance to capture even faint shreds of nuance. People brood about difficulties, and difficulties were by and large his lot during the UN years.

On another occasion, in the course of the ceaselessly tense Congo

Crisis of 1960–61, he and some colleagues hit a lull after midnight in his office when there was nothing to do but wait for a communication from Africa and improve the time by whatever means occurred to them. An interpreter sitting with the group remembered years later that "we were mostly discussing French medieval literature and medieval political theory, . . . an item of great interest to me and which, as it turned out, Hammarskjöld was a great expert in."[8] The choice of topic could, no doubt, have been something else, depending on the company and its interests. But the willingness to draw a free breath between urgencies, to dispel anxiety and restore perspective, is very like Hammarskjöld.

A close reader of many religious literatures who quietly converted some of their precepts into practice, he once commented at a gathering in his honor that "Bhagavad Gita echoes somewhere an experience of all ages and all philosophies in these words: 'Work with anxiety about results is far inferior to work without such anxiety, in calm self-surrender.' These are words of worldly wisdom which we can all share. But they also express a deep faith. We will be happy if we can make that faith ours in all our efforts."[9] He may not realistically have expected many to join him in that journey. The wisdom of the Gita may have seemed worldly and politically sound only to him, to Gandhi, to a few others. He would have known that it calls for a balance of hands-on and hands-off not so easy to attain. But it was well worth mentioning as an ideal: ideals hold the tent up and create a working space beneath them. For his part, Hammarskjöld infused an attitude of that kind into UN teams in which he directly engaged, such as the so-called Congo Club, the group of advisors meeting on that early morning in his thirty-eighth floor office in the Secretariat building.

A political education has its basis in experience. Hammarskjöld was insistent on this point. "All first-hand experience is valuable," he once wrote as part of a condensed primer of political wisdom, "and he who has given up looking for it will one day find—that he lacks what he needs: a closed mind is a weakness."[10] Even if one had a divine map that recorded everything people do, every move they are likely to make, some would find ways to somersault off the map and reappear in unexpected places with unexpected demands or apt proposals. A sound political education is, among other things, as opportunistic and agile as those somersaults: always in progress, never complete, it captures new details and insights on the fly and throws them into roughly the right place in an ever-changing, developing point of view. Perfect order isn't required, but liveliness and topicality are essential. "I don't think it will surprise you," he wrote to a fellow diplomat during the Congo Crisis, "to hear that we all manage to remain in good health and in good heart, catching as they pass those bricks which can be built into the structure and dodging, if we can, those that we fail to catch."[11]

In later chapters we'll look closely at Hammarskjöld's views of many elements of political process. But there is a point worth noticing now: he thought it crucial to follow and continuously absorb not only what others are and do, but also and just as crucially the same for oneself. He included himself at the negotiating table, adopted this inclusive vision of self and other on the understanding that a man or woman with responsibilities is prey to unseen motives in the absence of self-knowledge. *Markings* records his search for self-knowledge; he described the journal as "a sort of *white book* concerning my negotiations with myself—and with God."[12] But in public statements not closely tied to UN topics (for example, his surprisingly frequent talks at universities), he would sometimes draw attention to the need to know oneself in the root Delphic and Socratic sense.

This is rare. No one else in the public life of our era has so insisted on the point. As well, it clarifies the common ground between the questions about spirituality under fire and the dimensions of a political education for practical idealists. The two questions nearly become one. "Too often our learning, our knowledge, and our mastery," Hammarskjöld said to Amherst College graduates in the spring of 1954,

> are too much concentrated on techniques and we forget about man himself. . . . When I speak of knowledge in this context I do not mean the kind of knowledge which you can gain from textbooks, but the knowledge which you can derive only from a study of yourself and your fellow men, a study inspired by genuine interest and pursued with humility. The door to an understanding of the other party, with whom you may have to deal in business, in politics or in the international sphere, is a fuller understanding of yourself, since the other party, of course, is made fundamentally of the same stuff as you yourself.
>
> Thus, no education is complete, in a world basically united, which does not include man himself, and is not inspired by a recognition of the fact that you will not understand your enemy without understanding yourself, and that an understanding of your enemy will throw considerable light also on yourself and on your own motives.[13]

Markings explores in far more intimate terms the "study of yourself . . . , inspired by genuine interest and pursued with humility." At Amherst he was telling students in clear, impersonal words about a discipline long pursued, never abandoned, fundamental. In *Markings*, the sound is different, the topic the same:

> When you are irritated by his "pretentiousness," you betray the character of your own: it is *just as it should be* that he increases while you decrease. Choose your opponents. To the wrong ones, you cannot afford to give a thought, but you must help the right ones, help them and yourself in a contest without tension.[14]

This is one of the momentous entries in *Markings*. It exemplifies the rigor of Hammarskjöld's approach to himself, reflects the maturity of his practical political wisdom, and in its concluding thought reaches past predictable boundaries. Hammarskjöld's commitment to Christian teaching is evident in the notion of helping the opponent; psychological wisdom is evident in the acknowledgment that to help the opponent is also to help oneself; Asian wisdom—Gita comes to mind—is evident in the stunning notion of a contest without tension. But it makes little sense to break down the elements; these few words from *Markings* are whole. They inspire hope, while offering no reassurances.

I remain quite green

"The international civil servant must keep himself under the strictest observation," Hammarskjöld noted in a late talk that brought to a fine focus much of his experience at the UN.[15] He was passionate about the search for peace and justice, passionate about creating dialogue among adversaries, passionate about crafting durable solutions to prevent what the UN Charter calls "the scourge of war." But he spoke and wrote with deliberately dispassionate intelligence in his public role as chief servant of the Charter and UN member nations. Sir Brian Urquhart, his close colleague in the face of many challenges and author of the best biography we shall ever have of Hammarskjöld, has written that with one exception Hammarskjöld avoided rhetorical flourish and even the strict minimum of performance that helps to deliver public statements. On a General Assembly podium that has seen and heard every tone and gesture over the years, and some of the longest clocked speeches in history—Hammarskjöld once wrote to a friend that "here the good old river of oratory keeps rolling and rolling"[16]—he was quiet, clear, and purposeful. Even the exception cited by Urquhart, Hammarskjöld's afternoon response to a morning's worth of fierce attack by Nikita Khrushchev, is an exercise in contained fury.

While his public statements are polished and reasoned, Hammarskjöld's mind is creatively at work in them. We will often have occasion in later pages to hear what he said or wrote at the UN and for worldwide audiences; this is where much of his insight into politics and community is recorded. But what did he candidly think about political people and situations? What were his personal feelings about the dramatic encounters and crises that came one after another in the later years of his tenure as secretary-general? The answer to these questions is not in the public statements and writings, nor is it explicit in *Markings*, which, as all commentators have observed, makes no mention of specific people and circumstances, however much certain dated entries can be coordinated with events in the public life. But there is a third source: correspondence with people he trusted—certain family members, certain diplomats, Swedish officials whom he had known for years, writers, artists, and theater people, some of them in the much smaller circle of people on whom he relied for moments of warm conversation and simple living when circumstances permitted. His correspondents included a number of people whom he had met infrequently but with whom there were strong affinities. Among them, the Israeli philosopher Martin Buber and the British sculptor Barbara Hepworth come to mind; they were as much "his people," and he theirs, as any of his Swedish friends and close colleagues.

This correspondence remains largely unpublished. The selection in these pages won't remedy the absence of a volume of collected correspondence, but it permits us to hear a supple, expressive middle voice, midway between the public papers and the private intensity of *Markings*. That middle voice is evident, for example, in a letter to the Swedish painter, Bo Beskow, dating to March 1957, when Hammarskjöld had been working for months to replace Israeli forces in the Gaza Strip with a UN peacekeeping force. Though to a Swedish friend, the letter was in English. Hammarskjöld wrote and spoke with equal fluency in English, French, and German, and as a source of rest and renewal when time permitted, translated into Swedish difficult modern literature in all three languages. The choice of language for typed correspondence depended in part on which stenographer happened to be available in his office (handwritten correspondence to Swedish friends and associates is typically in their shared native language). To Beskow, with whom, among other things, he freely shared his interest in visual art, he wrote:

> One of the lasting experiences from the last months and weeks is that, with our so-called rising civilization, we do in no way see a decline in the art of lying. The modern media of communication, the modern entanglement of interests all over the world, have opened the door to a paradise for those who fight with words representing *mala fide* assumptions, false presentations, invidious comments, outright slander—and so on. If I were Hieronymus Bosch, I could paint a beautiful triptych in the colors of Hell and in celebration of this new Great Harlot.
>
> But why be bitter? At the same time you have the insistence on straight lines and simple facts, and simple rights, and I kind of feel that, like grass, this attitude, and its results, is more long-lived and more certain to endure than the sterile fancy flowers of the moment. Anyway, I take pride in belonging to the family of grasses, and I remain quite green in spite of a lot of trampling.[17]

The scope of these remarks is fully Hammarskjöldian: a candid, unhappy observation about the state of contemporary politics and the amplification of its worst features through the media; a subtle inventory of lies that seems to draw on his university training in law; an art-historical reference to a Dutch master remembered for his surreal vision of sins and sinners; reference to the Great Harlot (Revelations 17–19), reflecting Hammarskjöld's bottomless knowledge of the New Testament; then a marvelous shift of ground—"why be bitter?"—and steady, improvised movement toward a metaphor of disarming beauty. I belong to the family of grasses, and I remain quite green.

Thousands of conversations must have had this character through the UN years—trusting, far reaching, creative—but they are by and large lost. Friends and colleagues did what they could after Hammarskjöld's untimely death to record from memory the best of their conversations with him. We will draw on that legacy, and we have the letters. Here is another, written to a Swedish diplomat while the spring 1961 General Assembly was seized with the question of the Congo, still in crisis. As in the previous fall session, the Communist bloc, including Poland, was hammering away at Hammarskjöld's conduct of the United Nations intervention in the Congo.

During the present session I have superficial contacts with several whom
I have to place in the category MDP (Morally Displaced Persons). . . . I
rather pity them, but what is nauseating is this repetition of the experience
of decent Germans one met during the war, or in the late '30s, who were left
with little choice and hadn't the guts to break out. It must be a consolation
for the Poles that they are MDPs collectively, while in some of the other
delegations there are "loners" who must have a rather sad time.[18]

There is nothing here that he could or should have said aloud, yet the insights are vivid, permanently instructive, sadly funny. Czesław Miłosz's
classic book, *The Captive Mind*, offers in effect an extended commentary
on Hammarskjöld's perceptions as he listened to diplomats from the Soviet satellite nations in the General Assembly and met with them privately.

The personal correspondence does not undercut the public statements, as if he spoke more truly in private than in public. What he said
publicly he meant. He was a patient builder, not a juggler. There was
no more truthful statesman—but also none more discreet in a role that
requires the incumbent to earn and maintain the trust of all, including
those who are one another's bitter adversaries. Nearly the first words
from Hammarskjöld, when he met reporters in New York upon his
arrival from Stockholm on April 8th, 1953, to take office as secretary-
general, underscored the importance of separating public and private:

Of course, I—like all of you, like all engaged in diplomatic or political
activity—have my views and ideas on the great international issues facing us. But those personal views of mine are not—or should not be—of
any greater interest to you today than they were just a couple of weeks
ago. Those views are mine as a private man. In my new official capacity
the private man should disappear and the international public servant
take his place. . . .[19]

But the private man did not wholly disappear, after all; he shared his
personal views and feelings with trusted friends who never, as far as the
record shows, betrayed that trust.

Two further brushstrokes are needed to complete this sketch of the
correspondence, the middle voice. Deeply committed to what he called
private diplomacy—direct, personal exchange with the key figures in
disputes, sheltered from the media and any need to posture—Hammarskjöld used correspondence to continue confidential talks and work
toward sensible solutions. A letter to David Ben-Gurion, the fierce and

superbly intelligent prime minister of Israel, offers an example. The date is July 31st, 1956, just five days after Gamal Abdel Nasser, president of Egypt, had nationalized the Suez Canal. Several months earlier, the Security Council had asked Hammarskjöld to involve himself in the effort to restore adherence to the armistice already existing between Israel and Egypt. Responding at once, he invented the practice of shuttle diplomacy between Middle Eastern capitals and came to know well both Ben-Gurion and Nasser before nationalization of the canal plunged the region into a new, still more volatile situation. Hammarskjöld's letter of July 31st is a candid statement of working method and a plea for trust in a political environment that was as treacherous then as now:

> Please do not believe that I permit myself to be taken in by *anybody*, but realize, on the other hand, that I cannot work on the general assumption of people trying to double-cross me even when this runs counter to their own interest. Being afraid of being fooled to that extent, I would fool myself. I could then just as well stop all efforts, thus sacrificing the chance of getting the right thing—however small—because I was always fearing to get what is of no value.[20]

This is tough talk. It reflects the dangerous neighborhoods to which Hammarskjöld's work as secretary-general often took him. But it also reflects his strategy of identifying small zones of common ground between disputants, and then broadening the common ground until a sensible solution becomes acceptable or at least inevitable. "The right thing—however small" is that pailful of common ground.

Like us all, Hammarskjöld also used correspondence to encourage, to acknowledge kindnesses, to signal his existence from afar, to connect if only briefly with people he valued. One such person was Ahmed Bokhári, head of the Pakistani delegation to the United Nations when Hammarskjöld first met him. Hammarskjöld admired the breadth of background and ability of this unusual man, by training a professor of literature, an author and translator, who for some years had led the Pakistani delegation. He drew Bokhári into the Secretariat as Under-Secretary for Public Information.

In late 1953, Bokhári fell seriously ill. Still new to the UN, Hammarskjöld must already have forged a special relation with him. His letter wishing Bokhári a speedy recovery conveys genuine warmth in few words: "To me a talk with you, even when we had to talk shop, has always been an oasis where I felt the presence of live water close under the soil."[21] The concluding phrase suggests that Bokhári was among the few at the UN with whom Hammarskjöld more fully shared perceptions of the spiritual dimension of their work, the daily grind that cannot be abandoned and must be lifted. Gracefully acknowledging in his letter Bokhári's Muslim origin and image-world through the reference to an oasis, Hammarskjöld also speaks the language of Christianity in the lovely image of "live water," recalling John 4:7–15.

Later, during Bokhári's years in the public information office, Hammarskjöld sought his help to assemble talent and resources for the redesign of the Room of Quiet, the small meditation space that so interested him on the ground floor of the Secretariat building. Bokhári reached out to the American poet, Robert Frost, for lines that might be inscribed somewhere in the space. Frost's reply to Bokhári in a letter of April 19th, 1957, offered what the poet hoped would not be "too Orphic a dark saying" for the purpose:

> Nature within her inmost self divides
> To trouble men with having to take sides.[22]

But it must have been too Orphic a dark saying; Hammarskjöld is likely to have been uneasy with the notion that inmost Nature is divided. The lines weren't used. Professionally, Hammarskjöld was called to recognize and where possible heal divisions; this was his lifework, and men do take sides. But religiously and as a matter of experience he acknowledged one God. An entry in *Markings*, dating to 1955, transcribes a passage from the medieval mystic and preacher Meister Eckhart, reading in part: "'But how, then, am I to love God?' '. . . Love Him simply as the One, the pure and absolute Unity in which is no trace of Duality. And into this One, we must let ourselves fall continually.'"[23]

On the day of Bokhári's death, December 5th, 1958, Hammarskjöld's office circulated a touching notice. He himself is surely speaking in its dual acknowledgment of Bokhári's professional contributions and his commitment to "the possibility of a synthesis of great traditions." This internal notice, in which Hammarskjöld chose to record some essential thoughts, read in part as follows: "[Professor Bokhári's] rich and perceptive mind has left its strong mark in the Organization. He carried the dual heritage of Eastern and Western civilization. This gave him an unusual width of approach to those problems of our time with which the United Nations has to deal. He reflected in his personality the possibility of a synthesis of great traditions on which it is the task of our generation to build one world. He also knew in a deep personal sense the difficulties and tensions which must accompany such a process."[24]

We must be ready now to advance. This introductory chapter has something of the nature of a postage stamp collection. It offers miniature views of Hammarskjöld's person, mind, and methods, and his engagement at the UN. It means only to welcome you into his world—a world of relentless fact, of war and peace, reason and anger, yet within and alongside all that was a current of inspiration as pure as any in our time.

Hammarskjöld had hoped, after completing his second term as secretary-general, to return to Sweden, among other things to write a book that drew on his experience during the UN years. While at the UN, he knew he hadn't time for such a project and felt he hadn't enough distance. On this topic, toward the end of his life he wrote a note to Erik Lindegren, the Swedish poet already briefly mentioned:

> The mission and formula for our generation—I think I know them, perhaps I even live them. But I could not formulate them in a way that would help others. Perhaps I shall be able to do so one day when I can see what I experience every day in a more neutral perspective.[25]

2

Steep Swedish Hills

In nearly every young life the essential escapes. Family, education, friends, influences, and incidents can be documented. But the gifts and purposes deeply native to the person remain at least partially undisclosed until they deploy in the life and begin their work. This is obvious, hardly worth stating. But in the context of Dag Hammarskjöld's earlier years it bears repeating. The conditions of his early life, though materially comfortable, socially privileged, and educationally elite, should have defeated him. There were enough confusing psychological cross-currents to generate sterile excellence and recurrent personal misery, and no more than that. But within the visible matrix of opportunities and obstacles, there was an imperceptible: the person himself, the kernel of individuality. In time he broke through to become an authentically great human being, respected by millions and for good reason. Some deep discomforts have the blessed effect of keeping one awake, of turning life into an inquiry. In the "steep Swedish hills" of his youth—the words are from one of his late haiku poems[1]—and in the corridors of power in Stockholm during the first decades of his public life, Dag Hammarskjöld consolidated enough well-being, and enough love of the world, to go on.

A few weeks before the fatal air crash of September 1961, Hammarskjöld wrote a satisfyingly ironic and entertaining letter about autobiography to Jytte Bonnier, the wife of Sweden's major publisher, to whom he may have sent the draft of an indirectly autobiographical essay he had been working on that summer.

> Most autobiographical literature, in which the author forces himself to get over the natural inhibitions about personal matters, has the same theme: "Love me, and love me *as I am*"; therefore this urge to truly humiliating honesty, short of which the absolution would be without value. This was the old prayer of any honest man to his God. Now it is a prayer to public opinion, *und der Teufel steckt darin*. (An alternative explanation may, of course, be that the author considers himself such an important figure that the public is entitled to know all about him, but I doubt whether there have been many cases of such truly Promethean hubris).[2]

In this chapter and several to come, the project is to gain enough familiarity with the earlier years in Sweden to ground our understanding of Hammarskjöld's mind and methods. His contributions are not bound to his era and circumstances, but they root there and that needs to be acknowledged.

Light and warmth

Four buildings, richly symbolic, look at each other across the compact center of Uppsala, the Swedish university town where Hammarskjöld grew up and acquired much of his education. The massive sixteenth-century Vasa castle, rebuilt after a fire in the eighteenth, occupies a low but commanding hilltop some ten minutes by foot from the university. It is said to have been sited on higher ground than the nearby cathedral to teach the clergy a lesson. The Brick Gothic cathedral, seat of the Church of Sweden and its presiding archbishop, rises above the narrow, cobbled streets of the university quarter. Burial place of kings and queens, it is both grand and modest. While it doesn't aspire to compete with Chartres, it has the tangible self-respect and solemnity of centuries of use. The third structure, the Gustavinium, is one of the most eccentric and beautiful academic buildings in Europe. The remarkable feature is a rooftop addition sponsored by a seventeenth-century physician, Olof Rudbeck: a windowed, lantern-like structure housing one of Europe's earliest anatomical theaters, where the new demands of medical science were met by dissecting cadavers for an audience of medical students and courageous others. Balanced above this practical space is an oddly captivating, large copper sphere set on a narrow stalk, a Copernican statement about the world seemingly intended to teach a scientist's lesson to the cathedral's heaven-seeking spires. Inscribed with the hours and serving as the university sundial, the sphere is Time resolutely facing Eternity. These buildings talk with one another. Not far from the Gustavinium is the university library, known as Carolina Rediviva (Carolina Revived), a graceful foursquare nineteenth-century building replacing an earlier one, hence its charming Latin name. This is a peaceable structure: its design and placement teach no evident lessons apart from solidity and inevitability. These buildings within sight of each other—the seats of secular power and religious authority, the seat of aggressively pursued scientific knowledge, and the all-embracing library—collectively map the compact world into which young Dag was born. To learn, in Uppsala, was to learn from these sources. Dag would find teachers in them all.

The Vasa castle, resembling a taut scroll of brick stretched between massive cylindrical towers, overlooks not only the city but also nearby plains receding to the horizon. Founded by Gustav Vasa, the ambitious ruler who consolidated Sweden's independence from Denmark, this storied castle was the Hammarskjöld family residence for the many years in which Dag's father, Hjalmar, served as governor of the surrounding province of Uppland. Dag lived in the castle from the age of two until his departure for Stockholm at age twenty-five, in 1930, to complete a graduate degree in economics and launch his career. With a magnificently spacious central hall, wide stone staircases, and innumerable living and administrative spaces, the castle has seen many generations of kings and queens and many dramas, and it is certifiably haunted. A haiku written late in life by Dag must reflect the legend that Queen Kristina—seventeenth-century, brilliant, scholarly, unstable— occasionally makes the rounds:

> Night. Plains. An empty hall.
> In the window niche
> She waits for the sunrise.[3]

Dag Hammarskjöld was the last of four sons born to Knut Hjalmar Leonard Hammarskjöld (1862–1953) (fig. 2) and his wife Agnes née Almqvist (1866–1940). Among Dag's brothers, Bo, Åke, and Sten (fig. 4), it was with Sten—just five years older—that he would form the closest alliance as he grew up and with Bo when they had matured, but there would be many years when he was the only son at home. The family, so assembled, was the latest edition of what Dag in his maturity would describe as "generations of soldiers and government officials on my father's side" and "scholars and clergymen on my mother's side."[4] The Hammarskjöld family was of the old nobility; the warlike name, combining the words for "hammer" and "shield," was granted in 1610 to the meritorious first of that long line of soldiers and officials. Like many Swedes of his generation, Hammarskjöld paid no mind to aristocratic titles; in a letter of 1954 to a titled gentleman, an editor at Bonnier, he began, "Brother (I think we've cleared away the title business)."[5] Among Agnes's forebears, the one whom Dag particularly recalled was Carl Jonas Love Almqvist (1793–1866), a still-admired author, composer, and advocate of social reform who lived a richly disreputable life, including some fourteen years in the United States to avoid the consequences of a scandal at home.

"Where the one was light, the other is warmth," Dag wrote indirectly of his father and mother to a friend in 1930, in an early letter that provides valuable guidance about his experience of growing up.[6] It can be difficult to interpret photographs of nineteenth-century people, and of those even decades later who were shaped by nineteenth-century values. In men, the conventional mustache and whiskers and wing collars, the projection of position and propriety—in a word, the politics of the portrait—can defeat the effort to decipher a lively identity. In the surprisingly poignant photograph illustrated here, Hjalmar looks out through slightly skewed pince-nez spectacles with a half-aggressive, half-inquiring tilt of head and tension across his features: a man of high intelligence, intransigence, and contained melancholy. He seems in many other photographs a heavy, severe presence, and by all accounts that was true, although in the brilliant film documentary of Dag Hammarskjöld's life and achievements released for his birth centenary, there is a brief sequence in which the large father, accompanied by the still diminutive son, takes the boy's hand as they walk away from the camera in a wintry street.[7] Dag looks happy to know his father. Where mother Agnes is concerned, photographs reveal less than one looks for (fig. 3). She is said to have been the warmest of women, even effusive, but the photographic record delivers (with few exceptions) the generic woman of the era: heavy-set, groomed, posing, disconcertingly like one's own great-grandmother, as if all family photographs were interchangeable. During the UN years Dag kept in his New York apartment a photo showing himself as a marvelously cheerful boy with his well-pleased mother, accompanied by a separate small photo of his mother as a young woman. His eyes must have fallen on these images thousands of times, and they still speak. However, to discover more fully these two formidable individuals, both of whom exercised a lifelong influence on Dag, we must look elsewhere.

Hjalmar Hammarskjöld was one of the leading and, for a time, embattled men of his era in Sweden. A lawyer by training, he began his career as a professor in Uppsala but made his mark through a series of government positions and assignments that drew in part on his expertise in international law. He was appointed minister of justice in the short-lived government of 1901–2; became a member in 1904 of a new institution, the Permanent Court of Arbitration at The Hague; and in 1905 served as one of four Swedish representatives who negotiated the peaceful dissolution of the union between Sweden and Norway, an uneasy arrangement in place since 1814. At the time of Dag's birth on July 29th, 1905, Hjalmar was absent from home on this mission. Returning to Uppsala in 1907 as county governor, he established his family in the grand quarters set aside for the governor, the castle on the hill, and continued to build his reputation as a highly able jurist and problem solver, conservative in his views but not tied to any party.

In a governmental crisis pitting king against parliament that emerged at the beginning of 1914, Hjalmar was asked by the king to form a government after two other politicians failed to win enough support. It was thus his fate to be prime minister at the outbreak of the European war in August 1914. Sweden was committed to neutrality but hardly an unconcerned northern outpost where the carnage to the south could be waited out. Hjalmar used his high position both to safeguard Swedish neutrality and to try in vain to persuade the warring powers to stand down from what soon showed itself to be a new kind of disaster. But his efforts, as he once put it, not to say yes to all parties but to say no, eventually took their toll.[8] The imposition of food rationing in 1916 cost him his popular reputation—he was saddled with the name "Hungersköld"—while his refusal to enter into a trade agreement with Great Britain, favored by the influential foreign minister in his own cabinet, added to other disputes to cost him his political reputation. In 1917 he resigned as prime minister and retired to Uppsala, where he resumed his duties as county governor.

Despite the public view of him as authoritarian and unbending, he had loyal friends. In 1918, he was elected to membership of the Swedish Academy, whose duties include awarding the annual Nobel Prize in Literature. It was not a merely honorific appointment, consolation for the distressing end of his political career: Hjalmar had a great love of literature, had studied ancient languages and literature before taking the more practical route into law, and in later years would spend long hours exploring and translating Spanish and Portuguese poetry and transcribing regional Swedish folklore. Like Dag, when the son in turn became a member of the Academy, Hjalmar trolled the world's literatures for contemporary authors worthy of recognition. It should also be remembered that he served as a member of parliament in later years and was chairman of the Nobel Foundation in the years 1929–47. Hjalmar died less than a half year after Dag was named secretary-general of the United Nations; they had had time to discuss the matter.

This was not a man with whom many could be close, certainly not his son Dag, but he was a person from whom one could learn. In that revealing late-summer letter to a friend, Dag at age twenty-five painstakingly and rather ungenerously articulated what he then viewed as the good and bad reaching him from his father and the tradition embodied in his father. Dag's friend, Rutger Moll, had been staying with his mother in the same pension as Hjalmar, who often holidayed on his own. Rutger reported that Dag's father had been quite friendly. Dag replied, in a passage worth reading in full:

> Concerning the relations between father and son, mother and son, the son is perhaps less able than many others in the vicinity to shed light. Your fellow-guest and I think differently about nearly everything, and yet my views—in the deep sense of the word—are thoroughly based on his. And there probably is in me the seed of a nature much like his—a taciturn sense of responsibility, quite taut, blind to how easily it can damage and discard, apt to preempt the results of slow collaborative effort; an admiration for the drawn sword that disregards the value of negotiated results and will only accept victories won in open battle; the firm belief of the poor Swedish soldiering nobility in the State, which in the hands of strong men is a fit home for men—even if they're hungry; a certain shyness, which can lead to severe misanthropy and isolation, tied to a quality of ruthless candor grounded in the conviction that one has everything to gain, nothing to lose by letting people see you as you are, in the certainty that everyone in the end is no more than what he can—or cannot—make of himself. I said a seed. . . . It's a full-grown plant with its good and bad. I'm afraid that the closing words of your letter reflect your awareness of this and your—too benevolent—opinion as to how deeply it's already rooted in me. The problem for me—if I may prolong this confession—isn't how to spare myself from becoming tired and melancholy soil, sucked dry by the spiritual plant I've been describing, but rather how to integrate two human types within myself; for I have another inheritance which, in its streaming, explosive power, just as ruthlessly rips apart its bearer. This inheritance also has earned my jealous admiration. Where the one was light, the other is warmth. And who wouldn't want to integrate light and warmth?[9]

Marvelously searching, endlessly ambivalent, young Dag's analysis addresses not only the father but also prior generations of tough, dedicated

Hammarskjöld men. Despite the uneasiness declared in these lines with frightening clarity, in years to come Dag would be entirely loyal to his father and assure him companionship after the untimely death of his distinguished son, Åke, in 1937, and of his wife Agnes in 1940. (Åke might also have written that his "views—in the deep sense of the word" were based on his father's; responding to Hjalmar's early and passionate commitment to international law, he had become a judge in the Permanent Court of International Justice at The Hague.)

Many years and transformations later, Dag could pay simpler homage to the man who had transmitted to him firm values which his own life experience had confirmed. The occasion was a radio talk of late 1953. In his maturity, Dag could look past the oppressive and somewhat self-defeating traits he perceived in his father—and perceived as threats to his own well-being—to see the underlying excellence:

> From generations of soldiers and government officials on my father's side, I inherited a belief that no life was more satisfactory than one of selfless service to your country—or humanity. This service required a sacrifice of all personal interests, but likewise the courage to stand up unflinchingly for your convictions concerning what was right and good for the community, whatever were the views in fashion.[10]

At the end of the following year, 1954, it was Dag's responsibility to offer, as his inaugural address upon accepting membership of the Swedish Academy, an overview of the vision and achievements of his predecessor in Seat No. 17: his father. Such was the custom, although this was the first time that a son had been called upon to speak of his father. Like the Académie française on which it is modeled, the Swedish Academy is the defender of the language and composite author of the dictionary of record. A communion of writers, scholars, and cultural leaders entrusted with selecting the annual Nobel laureate in Literature, this elite setting offered Dag the company of seventeen other Swedish men of letters, including the Nobel laureate author Pär Lagerkvist (Seat No. 8), with whom he soon discovered a generation-spanning friendship. As was his wont, he took his duties seriously. A substantial correspondence with Academicians on the sometimes controversial or politically sensitive issue of identifying award candidates bears witness to his concerned approach. On Hammarskjöld's watch, Boris Pasternak was offered the Nobel Prize in Literature in 1958 (the Soviet government obliged him to decline), and the French poet and diplomat Saint-John Perse, was honored in 1960, primarily on Dag's initiative.[11] He also set in motion among his colleagues a close look at the works of John Steinbeck, awarded the prize in 1962.

Of the long and quite compelling Academy address honoring Hjalmar—edited in part, Hammarskjöld confessed, during tedious UN meetings—here we need only consider a few elements. Given its special audience and his lifelong love of literature, the address is naturally an exercise in style. To a UN staff member in New York he once remarked that a person who read nothing but UN reports would have "rather a curious mentality."[12] Speaking with his fellow Academicians, he could release from captivity the literary refinement and sensitivity to detail that became familiar to a larger public only with the posthumous publication of *Markings*. While the address is richly biographical, it is also a political analysis, an investigation of forces in conflict and the decisions of a man who did his best at a time when much of Europe was waging total war.

The very first image offered by Dag is of his father's empty chair, still turned toward a window overlooking one of Stockholm's public gardens, where jackdaws—members of the crow family—would endlessly quarrel to the "ironical amusement" of Hjalmar, who found in their behavior a close parallel to human affairs. Dag was acutely aware of his father's loneliness in later years, a trait passed intact from father to son as our later exploration of *Markings* will make only too clear. Dag also derived from his father a commitment to public service without party affiliation. "Personally," he said of his father, "he remained outside the parties all of his life."[13] This, too, was Dag's way.

About the horrendously difficult years of World War I, when Hjalmar's political career played itself out, Dag's words echo against his own experience of public life. In his father's conduct he finds the model for a fundamental value—maturity—which, on the evidence of *Markings*, reached vibrant fullness in Dag not long before he became secretary-general. His comments in the Academy address are part of a recurrent reflection on maturity whose light we will find in many places. It would be difficult to overstate the importance of the theme. Dag discovered maturity as a force, a surprising gift, an effective coherence, a clarity but also a capacity to respond. It proved to be a better thing than perfection, which eluded him like us all, because it allowed him at last to be both resolute and relaxed. It was the basis for a certain joie de vivre and, no less, an enriched way of thinking. In his view, it is not just a private resource; he often referred in public statements to the need for maturity among all parties to a negotiation. Where his father was concerned, he emphasized the principled independence of maturity. "A mature man is his own judge," Dag said of his father.

> In the end, his only firm support is being faithful to his own convictions. The advice of others may be welcome and valuable, but it does not free him from responsibility. Therefore, he may become very lonely. Therefore, too, he must run, with open eyes, the risk of being accused of obdurate self-sufficiency. As the war went on and difficulties increased, this was the fate of Hjalmar Hammarskjöld.[14]

Hjalmar is sparsely translated in English, but at least one text in English verifies the son's debt to the father. Stockholm was the site in late summer 1925 of an important international meeting, the Universal Christian Conference on Life and Work, convened with superior energy by the head of the Church of Sweden, Archbishop Nathan Söderblom, a close family friend of the Hammarskjölds' in Uppsala. Hjalmar had been unwilling to speak at the conference proper; advocating a strong military as the guarantor of neutrality, he didn't want to be closely associated with what appeared to him a predominantly pacifist gathering.[15] But he was willing to speak at a final luncheon in Uppsala under the auspices of the university, and did so very ably. He praised the conference, of course, and offered his perspective on its achievements, and then memorably shared thoughts that with little alteration might have been Dag's in later life. Hjalmar touched unknowingly on key elements of the life his son would live. "Man is an apprentice," he said,

> and an apprentice he will remain even after he has sought and found the powerful aid of divine guidance. But everything depends on the spirit in which he undertakes his apprenticeship. . . . Religion, faith, and Christianity all leave their mark on our work and enable men and peoples to reach nearer to the ideal which we dream of in our best thoughts and hopes. . . .
>
> The Conference has devoted great attention to international relations. . . . The commonwealth of nations possesses neither government, parliament, nor police.[16]

Dag, at age twenty, was doubtless in the audience.

In that late-summer letter to a friend, Dag spoke of the need to integrate light and warmth—light from his father, warmth from his mother

Agnes and the Almqvist lineage of clergy, scholars, and one immensely gifted poet. At age twenty-five he described that second inheritance in alarming terms: "in its streaming, explosive power, [it] just as ruthlessly rips apart its bearer." What did he mean? He was inexplicit; we must find our way on our own, but there are clues.

In his personal reflections of 1953–54—the radio talk in New York, the Academy address in Stockholm—Hammarskjöld spoke both indirectly and directly of his mother. "From scholars and clergymen on my mother's side," he said in 1953, "I inherited a belief that, in the very radical sense of the Gospels, all men were equals as children of God, and should be met and treated by us as our masters in God." This provocative statement asks for exploration. The first point—the equality of all as children of God—restates a familiar truth, recorded in a secular but impressive version in the Universal Declaration of Human Rights (United Nations, 1948): "All human beings are born free and equal in dignity and rights. They are endowed with reason and conscience and should act towards one another in a spirit of brotherhood." The second point is more difficult: "and should be met and treated by us as our masters in God." Objectively, all are equal as children of God, but experientially are we to meet others and treat them as our *masters*—in God? The meaning opens out a little in light of New Testament passages that bear on the relations between servants and masters.[17] The first Christians advised slaves and servants in their flock to "work hard and willingly, but do it for the sake of the Lord and not for the sake of men." In his highly condensed phrase, Hammarskjöld may be thinking more of the dedicated servant than of the master served. Is he saying that the legitimate needs of others exercise a special claim on us, so that from a certain perspective others are our masters and we their servants? That seems about right.

Are we closer now to identifying the "streaming, explosive power" to which he referred as a young man? Was he speaking of the radical impact on him of the Gospels, understood not as words on Sunday but as a living, transformative path? Be that as it may, Hammarskjöld's first spare mention of his mother at the outset of his years at the UN focuses on Christian teachings and the religious dimension of service. The Academy address offers a forthright word portrait. Dag makes the link with his father and goes on at once to speak of Agnes:

In 1890, [Hjalmar] founded a family of his own. In his wife he found a
determined faithfulness to personal ideals on a par with his own. Oth-

erwise, Agnes Almqvist was different from him in many respects. Her characteristics, which appear to me to reflect her family origin, had once emerged with particular clarity and with the somewhat frightening overtones of genius in the poet Carl Jonas Love Almqvist, a stepbrother of her father: a radically democratic view of fellow humans, "evangelic" if you like, a childlike openness toward life, an anti-rationalism with warm undercurrents of feeling. With these qualities, and the personal generosity toward both intimates and strangers to which it drove her, she introduced elements into Hjalmar Hammarskjöld's life which carry great weight.[18]

It scarcely need be said that she introduced elements also into Dag's life that carried great weight.

The polarity in the household was nothing short of astonishing. Where Hjalmar was cool, demanding, and often absent, Agnes was warm, receptive, and present. Where religion for Hjalmar was a respectable element in the lofty triad of God, King, and Country, for Agnes it was a guide to living and the warmth inside things. Where for Hjalmar the castle on the hill was a redoubt, a place apart, for Agnes it was the scene of lively gatherings such as the Tuesday nights she hosted for years and a traditional New Year gathering that assembled all segments of Uppland society.

The fourth son, Dag, was her favorite. For ever so long, he was her "little larva." The double diminutive promises trouble for the young man in question, but he seems to have come by this heart's name through his own enterprising interest in the biology of nearby gardens and woods. "As usual, Dag has nothing much to do," Agnes wrote when he was thirteen, "except make cages for peculiar larvae and feed them greenery, and collect animals from ditches like before."[19]

In 1922, when Dag was touring Central Europe with his brother Bo and his wife, Agnes wrote to him about a minor contretemps in the family. Perhaps somewhat jealous of their closeness, Hjalmar had teased her for writing to Dag on such large sheets of paper. This time, he said, he would write instead of Agnes. She continued in her letter to recount the incident:

> For you, my little larva, the little blue paper does not work. So here you have me on large paper. . . . Do you know, I who hardly ever show tears in front of father started crying when he offered to write you instead of

me. Writing to you is the most fun I have. Dag is the only one I really own on earth, the only one who cares about me. There you hear, my little larva, how much you mean to mother.[20]

Her larva was then seventeen years old. In the summer of 1931, when he was twenty-six, another letter records his mother's feelings:

> What would my life be without you, and what has it been since you were born? God knew what he was doing when He gave you to me, gave me my own little Dag—you have fulfilled what he intended for you. You have fulfilled your mission and you will continue until you prepare everything for my last resting place in the old Uppsala graveyard for those who sleep in its holy soil. You remember that we spoke about this one evening in the spring, and now I put it in your hands again. Then I know that everything will be fine.[21]

We need an eyewitness to look in on this family romance, which is surely making both armchair psychotherapists and licensed psychotherapists writhe. A highly intelligent witness is near at hand: Sven Stolpe, an exact age peer of Dag's, a friend for many years though by his own account not among the closest, and in later years one of Sweden's foremost writers. Stolpe's short book, *Dag Hammarskjöld: A Spiritual Portrait*, is pitch-perfect. "Agnes Hammarskjöld was her husband's opposite in almost every respect," he writes there. "She was warm and gushing; it was hard to tell at times whether she was laughing or crying; she had so overflowing and generous a heart that no one who came near her could avoid her eager—sometimes slightly ill-considered but always warm—solicitude."[22] He goes on to say that "Dag was a markedly virile person, entirely free from feminine traits of character; yet he had no difficulty in accepting his mother's kindly despotism and volubility."[23] Stolpe calls to the witness stand another close observer, Sten Söderberg, who reports that "Dag was his mother's gentleman-in-waiting, her page, her faithful and considerate attendant."[24] Someone not altogether on Dag's side described him a little later in life as "the stay-at-home daughter."[25] Friends of Dag's own age were well aware that his life in Uppsala was largely divided between academic study, at which he excelled, and dutiful attendance at home. A young and witty man, attending a party at the castle, heard Agnes say as Dag momentarily left the room, "When Dag leaves, the sun goes down." The young and witty man replied, "It would be better if Dag went out when the sun goes down."[26]

In that sense, Dag rarely went out. Some years later, when he was a rapidly rising star in the Swedish government, he continued to live with his parents, now in Stockholm. Nearly always joining them for dinner, he often brought a fresh bouquet of flowers to his mother. After dinner, as his friends well knew, he would return to the office and continue his work into the early morning; he needed little sleep. That single lighted window in the darkened government building where he worked while so many others played or helped their children with homework was a singular feature in Stockholm at the time. Some would look up from the street and know that Dag was at his desk.

But this image takes us too far ahead. We should turn back to the castle and Dag's student years, which were by no means forlorn through and through or defined exclusively by the distant father and engulfing mother. There is more in the sky than sun and moon. All difficulties duly noted, it remains evident that Hjalmar contributed richly to his son's development as a social thinker and potential leader: evening table talk must have ranged over the whole of human affairs from the sophisticated perspective of a senior political leader, a man convinced that effective international law and innovative international institutions offer the only hope of peace. All difficulties duly noted, Agnes surely gave Dag the internal basis for a caring emotional life, for sharing with others the good and the bad, for daring to view the human condition with the mind and heart of faith.

During his later years at the UN, Hammarskjöld formed a friendship with John Steinbeck, to whom he was introduced by Bo Beskow. As Steinbeck was setting off on a world tour, he asked his friend's advice: What should he keep in mind? What is most important? "Sit on the ground and talk to people. That's the most important thing," Hammarskjöld responded.[27] This, from one of the world's subtlest and most experienced diplomatic leaders, is surely in keeping with what Agnes had hoped as she clumsily, faithfully reared her son.

For all good things, man needs help

"For all good things, man needs help." These simple words conclude the first chapter of the *Meditations* of Marcus Aurelius, in which he thanks mentors by name for lessons and values they passed on. Some of Hammarskjöld's early mentors and grounding experiences find their place in the pages that follow. For many good things, he too needed help.

Hammarskjöld's last literary effort, somehow pursued at the request of the Swedish Tourist Association during lulls in the Congo Crisis, is an essay-length evocation of life in and around the castle in Uppsala: the changing seasons, ice-skating and tobogganing nearby, customs such as marches and festivals that brought townspeople and students to the castle through the cycle of the year.

> In the small hours after the spring ball, the couples make their way up the hill. If the air is mild you see them lying there in the grass, in evening dress, ready for the sunrise. Perhaps it is Ascension Day. In the early-morning air Whitsun chorales are heard from the cathedral towers. They reach only faintly across to Castle Hill.[28]

Similarly, a haiku sequence in *Markings*, dating to 1959, called simply "From Uppsala," condenses into the sparest of poetic forms Hammarskjöld's recollections of places, persons, and events of his youth. The Vasa castle and its somewhat neglected gardens offered Dag the most splendid playground imaginable. Nearly as thick and dark as a Crusader fortress, the castle captured and fed his imagination. Some of the haiku are written from the perspective of a castle dweller looking out:

> Dawn in the east. From the wide plain
> Blue sacrificial smokes
> Go straight up.[29]

It is the young man's view from a castle window—but the older man's theme of sacrifice, transforming the placid agricultural plain around Uppsala into a visionary landscape.

Even more captivating than the castle, the grounds and gardens were young Dag's botanical-zoological workshop. Beginning to learn the Latin names of plants by age six, as one of his brothers admiringly reported, he became a clear-eyed explorer of all things that grew or padded, hopped or crawled within sight of the castle. As Dag would have known from an early age, Carl Linnaeus, originator of the taxonomy for plants and animals still in use (genera, species, etc.), was an Uppsala person, the professor of botany at the university in the mid-eighteenth century. One of Linnaeus's whimsical inventions was a petal clock, based on observation of the different times of day at which flowers opened. A haiku "from Uppsala" records Dag's own investigation along these lines as a young person:

> In the shadow of the castle
> The flowers closed
> Long before nightfall.[30]

It is again the young man's observation, the older man's perception of a certain heaviness and melancholy in the vicinity of the castle.

Young Dag, whom some expected to become a botanist, took Carl Linnaeus as a permanent role model, separated only by time. He kept in his New York apartment during the UN years a framed reproduction of the well-known painting of Linnaeus dressed in rustic Laplander's clothing. Like Linnaeus, and throughout his life, Hammarskjöld loved both the minute details and the vastness of landscape. Like Linnaeus, he found spiritual renewal and adventure in the Swedish far north, the mountainous region of the ancient Sami people, reindeer herders. And it was to Linnaeus that he dedicated a major literary effort, a 1957 address delivered to the Swedish Academy.[31] In that complex spoken essay, Hammarskjöld evoked the mind, methods, and experiences of Linnaeus in a way that reflected more than admiration and brotherhood—it reflected sameness, as if these two identities were one. "With the creative power of the poet," Hammarskjöld said of Linnaeus, "he showed us how better to capture and hold the elusive experience of the moment in the net of language. . . . A great naturalist guided the author, but a great poet permitted the scholar to peer into the secret council chamber of God."[32]

A year earlier, in 1956, an entry in *Markings* points again, though more secretly, to the permanence of Linnaeus in Hammarskjöld's inner life. The entry is characteristically austere, learned in the academic sense yet acutely self-questioning:

> My devise—if any:
> Numen *semper* adest.
> In that case: if uneasy—why?[33]

A devise is a personal or familial motto, words taken to heart, presumably for a lifetime. The Latin translates as "The divine is *always* present" or "*always* enters in," almost certainly borrowing the notion of the numinous from Rudolf Otto's classic book *The Idea of the Holy*, which Dag read hungrily as a young man. But that is not the only source. Old father Linnaeus also had a devise, inscribed in a prominent place in his home: *Innocue vivite, numen adest*. It is a line from Ovid's *Art of Love*: "Live innocently; the divine is present." Hammarskjöld's updated version abandons the notion of innocence—he viewed neither himself nor his fellow human beings as wholly innocent—to focus solely on the presence of God always and everywhere.[34] In that case, if uneasy—why? The truth of faith—numen *semper* adest—grappled in his mind with the truth of experience, in which God is so often in hiding.

Even in a life as tightly wound as young Dag's—wound around rigorous academic study, Hjalmar's insistence on excellence, and Agnes's needy nature—there were zones of relaxation and unscripted experience. The most important, warm friendships and adventurous trekking in the far north, sometimes coincided. Two Swedish scholars have recently published and interpreted a trove of correspondence between Dag in his university years and his two closest friends, Jan Waldenström and Rutger Moll.[35] They conducted their friendships with nineteenth-century fervor, used one another as critical listeners to test views, share doubts, search for direction, laugh and complain, and create their personal pantheon of literary gods—Flaubert, Emerson, Conrad, and Dreiser among them, as these young men were already multilingual and voraciously inquiring. Together they hammered out their values. All three were brilliant; their letters are often prodigious. Dag's letter about light and warmth was written to Rutger.

Dag and Jan spent a semester at Cambridge in the fall of 1927, where Dag attended the lectures of the renowned economist J. M. Keynes. Their time in England was an idyll, as Dag vividly recalled in a nostalgic letter written—as it happens, some ten days before his death—to a couple with whom he had felt entirely at home:

> Thirty-four years ago I came as a very green post-graduate student to Cambridge. . . . I remember . . . the simple warmth with which you approached life and its manifold problems, the atmosphere of deep quiet in your "wayside" home in the Michaelmass sun under the big trees with the scent of lavender, fragrant and clean, outside and inside. I remember your morning prayers and the moments when you let music interpret your deep faith. You gave me a home during the short time I stayed in Cambridge and you gave me impressions and experiences which have been with me ever since.[36]

It seems improbable that this pastoral letter, filled with peaceful memories, could have been written from the "heart of darkness," at a time when the Congo Crisis was about to explode again with new violence. Yet it was. Hammarskjöld had acquired the ability to focus on the immediate task in all dimensions, factual, emotional, and more. This was a value or practice he cared for and, as we'll see, in his private journal he called himself to it.

After Dag and Jan's return to Sweden, they would begin their letters to one another with English endearments—"darling," "dear"—which they must have heard all around them while in England. It was apparently a standing joke between them, but Dag had written in August 1927 to Rutger about his feelings for Jan: "I regard him as 'mine'—in a few years or perhaps sooner. It won't be long."[37] How to interpret this? What does that bit of punctuation imply, around the strong word "mine"?

Hidden in Hammarskjöld's extensive personal library is an inscription in a handsomely bound first edition of Joseph Conrad's *Lord Jim*. It reads: "'There are wonders in true affection. It is a body of enigmas, mysteries and riddles, wherein two so become one as they both become two. I love my friend before myself and yet methinks I do not love him enough.' England hösten 1927."[38]

England, autumn 1927. The passage is taken from Sir Thomas Browne's *Religio Medici* (II.6), a seventeenth-century text that both Dag and the author of the inscription—most likely Jan—must have valued. The inscription speaks to idealistic warmth between friends. Thelin interprets Dag's apparently homoerotic sentiment—"I regard him as 'mine.' . . . It won't be long"—as an expression of youthful intensity rather than homosexual desire. The correspondence shows that Jan would turn to Dag on occasion for advice on sorting out his girlfriends. In an extended note to himself, dating perhaps to 1930, Dag at age twenty-five distinguished between true friendship and relationships "colored with sensuality":

> Complete friendship is the experience of striving together toward authenticity in life. Just here arises that mutual trust which is a measure of the worth of a man and [the basis for] complete authenticity in dealings with one another. From all this, great affection is born, which can never be exclusive like love and degenerate friendship, and never colored with sensuality—that great affection which, for the other as for oneself, makes it possible to be oneself.[39]

It seems clear that Dag, Jan, and Rutger, passionate friends who embarked on life with a thousand questions to share with one another, were not lovers. But the presence or absence of intimacy in Hammarskjöld's later life will need exploration. This much can be said at once: he rarely experienced later the spontaneous, emotionally freewheeling intimacy he enjoyed with these two comrades. There were rich personal friendships—with the painter Bo Beskow and his wife Greta, with Leif Belfrage and his wife, also Greta, with trusted Swedish colleagues such as Henrik Klackenberg, Sverker Åström, Per Lind, Sture Petrén, and still others. He often enjoyed the company of the great and wise of the world—celebrated thinkers, writers, artists, and theater people with whom he found the searching dialogue, ready wit, and exploration of the arts that served as a counterpoint to his responsibilities at the UN. At the UN itself, there were rich friendships with certain colleagues who were thinkers, lovers of life in breadth and depth, stimulating individuals, some of whom recognized his religious perspective on life and, without trespassing, threw lines across from their inner lives to his. The strongest examples are his Australian colleague George Ivan Smith; his Swedish colleague in the Congo Crisis, Sture Linnér; and the distinguished Indian diplomat Rajeshwar Dayal and his wife Susheela, all of whom we will meet in later pages. But never again, as Dag and his friends entered on their careers and lost close touch with each other, would there be quite the same serious, whacky, glorious intimacy with others. There would be no mate; there would be friends.

Hammarskjöld's characteristic personal restraint, the distance that prompted even some close UN associates to write after his death that he might know you, but you never quite felt you knew him, closed over him at some point when the early friendships had run their course. That restraint would disappear with chosen friends and colleagues during his years at the UN. John Steinbeck knew him by this warmer light: "He was neither cold, cool, dispassionate nor neutral," Steinbeck wrote in the days after Hammarskjöld's death. "He was a man passionate about what he was doing."[40] Hammarskjöld understood how to "sit on the ground and talk to people" with curiosity and delight, just as thoroughly as he understood how, when necessary, to keep his own counsel as secretary-general. We know through *Markings* the questing inner life beneath the ordered surface. But the loneliness that periodically filled him with sorrow in later years has a root somewhere here, in the transition from Uppsala to Stockholm, from university life to government service. At the age of twenty-eight—just twenty-eight—he wrote a letter to Sven Stolpe that should have been written by a much older man:

> For all of us, no doubt, existence acquires an increasing chill as we grow older. To "go one's own way" now means surely more than ever to go that way alone. . . . Of course, one can run with the herd and find warmth among others, but can this be done without sacrificing what is more important?[41]

From Uppsala and later from Stockholm, Dag and his friends traveled when they could to the distant north, the region perceived to this day by Swedes as other, elsewhere, magical. He became an able mountaineer and technical climber, cross-country skier, and in time (like his father before him), a loyal supporter and official of the Swedish Tourist Association. He acquired a cartographer's knowledge of the far north and wrote of it, typically for Tourist Association publications, with a keen Linnaean eye for botanical detail.[42] In his youth he was fortunate to come briefly under the mentorship of Nils Thomasson (1880–1975), a boulder of a man, Sami by birth and conviction, whose photographs of northern life and landscape have become part of Swedish legacy. A three-day trek with Thomasson must have added to Dag's confidence in his ability to travel the steep Swedish hills and may have initiated his lifelong practice of nature photography, strengthened in later years by friendship and treks with Gösta Lundquist, an outstanding nature photographer for whom during the UN years he wrote a preface to a book of photographs.[43] The Sami were the first quite "other" people he had encountered. There would be many more in later years. Of that encounter he wrote late in life, "Sami culture demands respect and the Samis' nature induces affection."[44] Among his Sami friends he counted Andreas Labba, a herdsman, guide, and chronicler of his people's experience whom he hosted once in New York. He persuaded Labba in the early 1940s to become a writer. The result, in time, was an extraordinary book.[45]

The mountains became his retreat, sometimes with friends, sometimes on his own—retreat from pressures of work, society, and family, retreat into a world that cleansed and clarified. An entry in *Markings* for 1951, two years before he became secretary-general, reflects some part of what he found above the Arctic Circle:

> Lean fare, austere forms,
> Brief delight, few words.
> Low down in cool space
> One star—
> The morning star.
> In the pale light of sparseness
> Lives the Real Thing,
> And we are real.[46]

The poem suggests the extent to which Hammarskjöld acquired a sense of the sacred not only from religious literature and from those around him for whom Christianity was alive, but also from experience in Nature. The perception of the real, faithfully recorded here, cuts through theory and ideals to make itself known as the first fact. Later in 1951, Hammarskjöld made at least two further journeys to the north, each an occasion of religious discovery. In summer he wrote of "the sacrament of the arctic summer night," in autumn of "the opening bars in the great hymn of extinction."[47]

As secretary-general, Hammarskjöld had no time to revisit the north country, but it remained with him. In 1957 he scanned back through decades of memory in an article published in the Swedish Mountain Club Annual. "The mountains provide a new solitude," he wrote, "in the shared tasks of hiking and climbing, shared adventure and experience of beauty. A new solitude in a companionship hard to achieve in another environment . . ."[48] It wasn't solitude for its own sake or in fearful withdrawal; it was solitude for the sake of more acutely perceiving "the Real Thing" and to be real alongside it. Toward the end of his life he prepared an anthology of texts on Lapland by many authors, including his own essays and one by his father. It was published in the year after his death with a striking photograph on the cover: the solitary figure of Dag, climbing stick in hand, making his way up the snowy flank of a mountain. The landscape is formidably abstract, the figure both alone and at home (fig. 1).[49] This is one of the iconic images of the man. It doesn't say all there is to say.

In his years as secretary-general, mountaineering served as a recurrent metaphor. It allowed him to convey a great deal about process and attitude without reference to the specific facts, typically confidential, of current problems or missions in progress. With news reporters in 1954, for example:

> I think that those of you who have tried [mountaineering] will agree with me that it has more than one object lesson to teach us. For example, this one: don't move without knowing where to put your foot next, and don't move without having sufficient stability to enable you to achieve exactly what should be the next step. One who is really serious in his determination to reach the top does not gamble by impatiently accepting bad footholds and poor grips. His keen awareness of . . . the goal is expressed in his concentration on the immediate problems, which if not properly solved would render all talk about the top empty daydreams.[50]

At the intersection of Hägerström and Söderblom

There are further strands to follow in Hammarskjöld's earlier years before we reach the event in April 1953 that changed and clarified his life: his election as Secretary-General of the United Nations. The capital letters in his future title suggest something about the transition to a formidable role in world affairs from service in the background to a small, resourceful country. If these early chapters are a compact Bildungsroman—the story of an education—we should remember throughout the trials to come, some of which cannot help but make him seem awkward and unpromising, that we are tracing the development of one of the great ones. We would know little of his trials, had he not wished us to know by permitting publication of *Markings*.

Studies came so naturally to young Dag that the topic seems scarcely worth raising: he rocketed through, earning more diplomas in more fields than anyone can be expected to earn. Entering Uppsala University at the age of eighteen after thorough schooling at the "gymnasium" level, he completed in 1925 a bachelor of arts degree with honors in linguistics, literature, and history—the first of four demanding courses of study and degrees. Following his father's example, he moved on from humanistic study to professional preparation by spending the next three years in the economics department and earning the equivalent of a master's, with somewhat middling honors. Despite the fact that some of his professors declined to award him the loftiest honor for his academic work in economics, he would prove in later years to be an effective practical economist and become, in effect, their government-based colleague. In two further years at Uppsala, Dag earned a bachelor of laws in 1930, and could then confidently turn toward Stockholm and government service. His first assignment—analyzing the factors causing high unemployment—provided data for his doctoral dissertation, defended in 1933. His studies do not seem to have been sealed off from one another. For the rest of his life he read literature in four languages and, until he left Uppsala, must have attended university lectures of interest while pursuing formal programs in economics and law.

There was, of course, a price to pay for this extraordinary academic performance. Dedicating himself to study and to his role as the son at home, with scarcely any slack for improvisation and social life, he wrote to Jan in May 1926, "It's amazing, how horribly alone you can feel in this city, where you know an endless number of contemporaries. . . . I've had the deeply rooted feeling that my presence is not only a matter of indifference to some, but even less than that, a minus."[51] Later in the year, Dag sent much the same message to Rutger: "I lead at present what you could call an awfully dry life."[52] But it can't have been hopelessly dry. In 1929, he was elected leader of his student association, the Uppland Nation (all Uppsala University students belong to one or another regional "nation"). The miserable "minus" of 1926 must have found his way by then to general regard among his peers, if not to a carousing night life that in any case had no appeal. A heartening photograph of young Dag shows him vigorously addressing members of the Uppland Nation.

Among his professors was an exacting philosopher, Axel Hägerström (1868–1939), one of two presiding and contrary geniuses of those years in Uppsala. Hägerström taught a value of lifelong importance to Hammarskjöld and a value he soon rejected. The value accepted was intellectual rigor. Even his comments for the press on mountaineering bear witness to a systematic mind taking note of elements in sequence, missing nothing of importance, drawing it all into a satisfying whole—and that may have been a largely ad lib performance. The value rejected was Hägerström's demolition of what he called metaphysics, which included the religious perspective of medieval Christian mystics whom Hammarskjöld had begun to read in these years. In the spring of 1928, he reported to Rutger on his extracurricular reading—"only edifying literature, if you will . . . Thomas à Kempis and Eckhart—quite sporadically and quite in bits and pieces."[53]

We're fortunate to have in English a selection from Hägerström's philosophical writings.[54] The frontispiece photograph from that volume, well worth reproducing here (fig. 5), returns us imaginatively to a distant world of fierce Scandinavian thinkers and artists—Kierkegaard, Ibsen, Strindberg, Munch. Hägerström belongs with them. The streets of Uppsala must have shaken as this slender man swept by. The appeal of Hägerström's writing and teaching for the nonspecialist is the intensity with which he explored what he called "metaphysical religiosity" in order to do away with it. He had mastered medieval Scholastic thought, pored over Eckhart and others in order to slay it all. One could have few better guides to the intellectual foundations of Christian mysticism until he goes on the attack. He is the nondrinker who knows everything there is to know about wine, the missionary who has mastered Aztec thought. "This reality, so familiar to our souls," he wrote, "this Mighty

One, is nevertheless . . . nothing but a creation of our own confused thought."[55] "One thing is clear. . . . Every interpretation of a spirit-life in the world, every idea of the spiritual in and for itself . . . as a power active in the world, is false at its root. . . . Every attempt to base a knowledge of reality on the foundation of spiritual experience . . . is by its very nature bound to be unsuccessful."[56]

There are signs in Hammarskjöld's early writings that he absorbed some of Hägerström's language and method. In that extended note to himself from about 1930, from which we have already drawn, he wrote, "To wish to become a man means to choose a certain 'I' and to form oneself on that basis."[57] This is Hägerström-like. Karl Birnbaum, in his study of Hammarskjöld's earlier years, attributes something of the mature Hammarskjöld's ability to face facts to his training in Hägerström's school.[58] Still, Dag was tempted to write a defense of Christianity against Hägerström's assaults in collaboration with Sven Stolpe, the future writer and Catholic educator whom he first met at Uppsala in 1930.

Hägerström was one of two contrary geniuses in Uppsala whose minds touched Hammarskjöld. The other was the archbishop and head of the Church of Sweden, Nathan Söderblom (1866–1931) (fig. 6), member of the Swedish Academy from 1921, winner of the Nobel Peace Prize in the year of his death. Anyone who explores Hammarskjöld's early biography encounters Söderblom in passing. He and his family were great friends with the Hammarskjöld family; the children played and grew up together. Because the archbishop had the same birthday as Agnes—and because they were fond of each other—they were known as "the twins."[59] My own first encounter with Söderblom, apart from brief mentions in the Hammarskjöld literature, was misleading. Above a landing in a chilly stairway of the Vasa castle hangs an enormous formal portrait, depicting the clergyman in full ecclesiastical vestment—a confection of velvet, lace, and embroidered symbol—miter firmly on head, crosier firmly in hand. It is a statement of office that gives no hope of meeting a man. A Jesuit writer, not altogether friendly, once recorded the archbishop's "remarkable partiality for the miter and the crosier" on solemn occasions.[60] However, exploration of Söderblom in his independence, rather than as a footnote to another narrative, quickly reveals a remarkable individual, beyond doubt one of Hammarskjöld's mentors in depth. His delight in the traditional theater of the church seems wholly forgivable.

Söderblom preaching cut a formidable figure: "a strong square man with . . . flowing blond hair. . . . The voice is light yet strong and allowing for variations of nuances. It can beat against the pillar opposite with a mighty roar, and change into the finest piano, without one word being incomprehensible. This man has the inner fire of a leader and commands supremely all means of rhetorical art."[61] Thus an eyewitness in 1926, the year after Söderblom's greatest exploit, the ecumenical Christian conference in Stockholm that brought together, by count, six hundred delegates from thirty-seven nations and thirty-one denominations for nine days of meetings, during which 115 prepared addresses were translated and distributed in advance, 180 extempore contributions and speeches were minuted, 36 sermons were preached from Stockholm's pulpits, and who knows how many hymns were sung from a hymnal published for the occasion at the archbishop's request and under his editorship.[62] The prodigious energy and powers of persuasion and organization underlying the conference were Söderblom's. Young Dag, participating as a French translator, could not have taken it all in—no one could—but he must have attended a steady sequence of events and returned to Uppsala for the closing ceremonies and his father's talk.

The impulse behind this immense conference wasn't just the wish to forge greater mutual understanding among all churches of the West and East willing to send senior representatives. (The Roman Catholic Church had declined the invitation. Söderblom famously commented at the conference that "two men are gathered here," John the apostle and Paul the disciple, but "the third man, Peter, the spokesman of the disciples, still tarries.")[63] Ecumenical unity mattered to Söderblom, but it wasn't all that mattered. The conference was what it was because World War I had been what it had been. Söderblom viewed effective Christian churches as a necessity in a world that now pinned its hope for peace and justice on a new international entity, the League of Nations. "The League of Nations needs a soul, a spirit, . . . else it becomes a dead mechanism," he wrote after the conference, "a soul that creeps into this newly created and strange organism, but if it is not a Christian soul, unconditionally subjecting itself to right and righteousness, the soul easily becomes a devil."[64] He had no naïve aspiration to "sacralize" politics but argued that "even politics needs moral principles."[65] Söderblom was tireless in teaching his global parish about the links between political ends and means and spiritual values. He won the Nobel Peace Prize in 1931 for his efforts.

Locally, the archbishop's parish included a young man whom he had known from infancy, received in his home countless times, and engaged in countless conversations as the two families, Söderblom and Hammarskjöld, led parallel lives in Uppsala. Years later, at an American meeting of the World Council of Churches, an outgrowth of Söderblom's ecumenical movement, Hammarskjöld's host politely offered to inform him about the council's history. Hammarskjöld replied, "Oh, I know all about that! I was brought up under Söderblom."[66]

To be brought up under Söderblom meant absorbing from an early age the pastor's conviction that society without a spiritual compass is adrift and in peril. It meant witnessing remarkably successful efforts to give institutional and communal expression to that conviction through the 1925 conference and other initiatives. It meant learning Bible from a man of faith who was also a well-published scholar of religious ideas. And it meant being long in the neighborhood of a Christian for whom the spiritual enterprise was vivid, real, and somewhat uncharted; one had to find one's way. "Nobody else can tell me what my calling is," Söderblom preached in 1909. "But we find it, we are in the midst of it. Here is something that must be done. Well, let me try."[67] Söderblom was not one of those preachers who are absent from their words. He was also not just an activist, darting off into good works without a glance at the inner life. As a young pastor, in 1893, he had been visited by a powerful experience of the Holy Spirit, and such encounters confer at best—as for him—a larger sensibility (not narrow dogmatism), greater warmth (not chilly expectations of others), and a flexible, living axis (not stony certainty) around which life can develop.[68] He could speak, as one who knew, of what he called *innerlighet*, warmth of heart touched by spirit.

The intellectual and spiritual riches offered to those around him went even further. Söderblom had found in the new philosophy of Henri Bergson, especially in the notion of creative evolution, a fresh way of thinking about the interdependence of insight and service.[69] Both Bergson's influence and this view of service as a way of discovery sparked over from Söderblom to Hammarskjöld. With an aphoristic power equal to Ralph Waldo Emerson's, Söderblom spoke his mind: "Take reality seriously. Grasp it so firmly that it opens its eyes."[70] And in a talk with students in 1911, he shared thoughts that would be central to Hammarskjöld in his maturity: "In God's Kingdom you can see nothing so long as you are standing as a mere spectator; only those who serve God fully and self-sacrificingly can perceive God's will."[71]

There was team play among most of the adults around young Dag for his religious education. Hjalmar, for his part, is likely to have left the matter largely to the discretion of the archbishop, whom he trusted. Hjalmar's specialty was the political education of his sons and their grounding in international values. But Agnes Hammarskjöld and Anna Söderblom, the archbishop's wife, were highly interested parties. For Dag's confirmation, Agnes gave him a copy of a late medieval work, *The Imitation of Christ* by Thomas à Kempis (ca. 1380–1471), which would become in Dag's maturity one of few books he read always; it was at his bedside at home, among his papers when he traveled. Söderblom must also have had a hand in calling it to Dag's attention. "What is it that unites us?" asked Söderblom in his book on Christian fellowship. "The answer is: the imitation of Christ. It certainly ought to be a sufficient communion that we all, collectively and individually, wish honestly to follow in the footsteps of the Master."[72]

A woman of intellect and charm, and author of several books (including one about those strange creatures, the Americans), Anna Söderblom was someone to whom young Dag could turn. He once complained to her about the superficiality of French literary study at the university: "I had thought that I was going to learn about ideas and their travels through the ages and not waste time on the love affairs of authors." Mrs. Söderblom responded, wisely, that he might want to read the *Pensées* of Blaise Pascal.[73] It took. Pascal's range of observation and form of thought, his religious perspective and lucidity about human affairs, were fundamental to the development of Hammarskjöld's mind and sensibility, even to his developed literary style. Many years later, in the week between receiving word of his nomination as secretary-general and departing for New York, Hammarskjöld took time to visit Anna Söderblom in Uppsala.

When one looks at Dag Hammarskjöld's family and education, at those who gathered around to help, at the opportunities abundantly on offer at the university, one can't help but reflect that it was *nearly* perfect if the purpose was to give a strong start in life to someone very like Dag Hammarskjöld. It can't be denied that his earlier years sowed bitter problems he would have to face in middle years. But Hammarskjöld left Uppsala for Stockholm in the fall of 1930 with an extraordinary education, an international perspective, a sensibility touched by Christian teachings of rare vitality, and a love of the outdoors that could be relied on to renew him. The apprenticeship was not yet complete. It had force-fully, delicately begun.

Many years later, in 1956, Hammarskjöld offered his own valediction of those years in Uppsala. The occasion was a commencement address at Upsala College in East Orange, New Jersey, where he received an honor-ary degree. "The Uppsala tradition," he said,

> ... reflects a heritage which I feel has something to give to our world of today. . . . In doing so I am not referring to any country or people but to a spiritual legacy beyond such boundaries.
>
> At their best the representatives of this legacy show the quiet self-assurance of people firmly rooted in their own world, but they are, at the same time and for that very reason, able to accept and develop a true world citizenship. At their best they are not afraid to like the man in their enemy and they know that such liking gives an insight which is a source of strength. They have learned patience in dealings with might-ier powers. They know that their only hope is that justice will prevail and for that reason they like to speak for justice. However, they also know the dangers and temptations of somebody speaking for justice without humility. They have learned that they can stand strong only if faithful to their own ideals, and they have shown the courage to follow the guidance of those ideals to ends which sometimes, temporarily, have been very bitter. And, finally, their spirit is one of peace.[74]

The language is so understated and the thought flows so easily from point to point that one could miss the wide ground covered. The lessons of Uppsala at every level—political, spiritual, human—found supple and lasting expression in Dag Hammarskjöld.

3

You Asked for Burdens

Hammarskjöld in Stockholm is a study in promise. The professional economist emerged, increasingly an expert among experts with ever-growing responsibility for issues of the national economy. Alongside and within him, the literate spiritual seeker continued to mature and question. As he often said, he was uneasy. His education was unfinished. Rapidly acquiring systematic professional knowledge for his new role in life, he toiled also toward that elusive thing, self-knowledge. In the northern wilderness he encountered from time to time another dimension of experience, intrinsically religious; Nature spoke. He continued to read widely and hungrily, as if the acts of self-decipherment in literature were necessities for his own maturing awareness. For such a person, the world of day-to-day work is at times a burden but more often a welcome shelter. The routines of professional life and teamwork with valued colleagues provide a secure frame of reference, and there is unmistakable joy in doing things well. In that steady context, an identity in search of itself may have the time and circumstances to unfold.

In the fall of 1930, Dag moved with his parents to an apartment overlooking Humlegården, that highly civilized park in Stockholm with bickering jackdaws, home of the Swedish National Library where his personal papers and many of his books would years later be preserved.[1] Hjalmar retired from government service at roughly the moment Dag entered government service as a humble assistant secretary in a committee studying the unemployment situation and looking for solutions. He was bright, just twenty-five, and untried.

Hammarskjöld's professional life in Swedish government service was so specialized in its issues, methods, and vocabulary that we can scarcely discuss it at length without losing one another in terrain that belongs to trained economists; it is their challenge and attractive intellectual puzzle, typically no one else's. Fortunately, university-based economists and central bankers claimed their share of the Hammarskjöld birth centenary in 2005 by publishing the first thorough treatment of his career prior to his election as secretary-general.[2] That publication demonstrated how little had been previously documented and explored about his working life through this long stretch of years. We need to know something of all that. It was the context for much else, and richly furnished.

The Swedish civil service, which he now joined, adhered to long traditions of excellence, integrity, and distance from party politics, all of which earned his loyalty and admiration. In later years at the United Nations, he would apply lessons learned in Sweden to the international civil service for which he would then be responsible. Franklin D. Scott, author of a standard history of Sweden, has written that the Swedish civil service provided opportunities somewhat like those offered in Great Britain by the military and the church. He points to a further parallel: "Swedish officials had the chance to work for the community without the turmoil and uncertainty of political strife or the competitiveness of business. The civil service in Sweden had, in brief, something of the nimbus of the courts in the United States."[3]

The political leadership throughout Hammarskjöld's years in government service was, more often than not, exceptional. A group of able and innovative men gathered under the banner of the Social Democratic party in the mid-1920s and came to power in 1932. With few breaks, they remained dominant for decades. They were practical, undogmatic socialists, and Hammarskjöld was comfortable among them although he never joined their party or any other and, as we shall see, experienced a generation gap. Architects of the welfare state that remains to this day a signature Swedish creation, the Social Democrats included a long-serving prime minister (1932–46), Per Albin Hansson; a sociologist and financial expert, Ernst Wigforss, who would quickly emerge as Hammarskjöld's mentor, superior, and friend; and Östen Undén, a future foreign minister who would also be mentor, superior, and friend in later years. Gunnar Myrdal, some seven years Hammarskjöld's senior, soon to be famous as an author and social critic and ultimately a Nobel laureate, was nearby both as an advisor to government and as a young professor at the university where Dag began working toward a doctorate in political economy. There were, as well, other resourceful thinkers in both government and university, participants in the celebrated Stockholm School of Economics, founded in 1909—an institution whose views broadly speaking anticipated Keynesian economics. They kept Sweden stable and reasonably prosperous through the worldwide depression of the 1930s and helped shape the postwar welfare state.

Like several of his young colleagues, Hammarskjöld used the data and

insights he collected in his first post with the committee on unemployment as the topic of his doctoral dissertation, defended in November 1933,
under formal public questioning by Professor Myrdal and a colleague. His
thesis, "The Dissemination of Business Cycles: A Theoretical and Historical Study," did not receive highest honors although Myrdal, after a forceful
debate, made sure that the defense itself received high honors. A Swedish
professor of economics has recently written that the thesis is "known for
its abstruseness and little read,"[4] but Hammarskjöld's middling achievement as an academic economist cast no shadow over his progress as a practical economist: he was entrusted with more and more responsibility. For
several years after completing his dissertation, he taught at the university
and published learned articles on topics in political economy. Through
much of his career in Sweden, he would occasionally debate government
economic policy in the pages of professional journals. But in the end he
preferred government to the academy.

Ernst Wigforss, who befriended Hammarskjöld upon his arrival in
government, pondered in later years why an academic career never clicked
for his protégé. Despite appearances, Wigforss perceived in Hammarskjöld a "man of action"[5] who wished to influence events. "It belongs to
the picture of the young Dag Hammarskjöld," wrote Wigforss, "that he
was obviously alien to the thought of devoting himself professionally to
science. For somebody who stood between science (or teaching) and politics as the only temptresses at the crossroads—with virtue and lust equally
distributed on both sides—it was surprising to find a scientific head so
little tempted by an academic career."[6] But he was, after all, the son of a
former prime minister and heir to a long tradition of national service. As
well, there was scarcely any gap between government and the academic
world, where political economy was concerned: the best minds from both
worlds were keenly interested, available, and cooperatively at work.

There was another point, recalled by Hammarskjöld's friend Sven
Stolpe, who had witnessed the public defense of his doctoral thesis.
When Stolpe expressed admiration for the proceedings, Dag demurred
in the sharpest of tones:

> I don't share your opinion of the debate; from an intellectual point of
> view it was just a circus, with a dialectical tight-rope act as the main
> item. The ritual seemed to me morally inferior. . . . I disagree with you
> even more strongly about the intellectual level of us economists. What
> may support your impression is the extroversion, the ease in public,

which results from training in political discussion and administration
and which gives economists the air of intellectual strength.[7]

But Stolpe also detected that Hammarskjöld's pride had suffered. He was
accustomed to unqualified recognition of high achievement; anything
less was a blow.

The early reverses of outstanding people deserve a close look. Inex-
plicably, doors close. But others open, as if providence or fate has at its
disposal both an irreversible no and invitations. There was no lack of
invitations in government service. By the spring of 1934, Dag's brother
Bo, also in government service, could write to their brother Åke, then at
the International Court of Justice in The Hague, that "Dag goes from
strength to strength. His reputation, as a theoretician as well as a practitioner, is very great and widespread. They are already fighting for him
and it will probably get worse."[8] Wigforss had drawn him into the Ministry of Finance as a second undersecretary, and he quickly found himself
in a small circle of Wigforss confidants, working toward a new approach
to economic planning. But Ivar Rooth, governor of the Riksbank, the
Swedish central bank, had noticed young Hammarskjöld and, needing
an economist on staff, took steps to transfer him. Meanwhile, the unemployment committee still required his participation. For a short while
there were three competing employers within the government, and his
time was meted out somewhat clumsily.

Initially, our young hero found the bank tedious—"started full-time at
the bank—naturally with nothing to do," "days without end," "work-day
consumed by the usual *petits riens*"—but matters soon sorted themselves
out.[9] Rooth almost at once trusted him to represent the bank at a meeting
in Basel, and early in 1935 he was given responsibility for a multinational
study of central banks that took him to many countries in Western Europe. He was twenty-nine. His diplomatic career had begun, disguised for
the moment as an exercise in central banking.[10] In the summer of 1935,
he was promoted to a permanent post in the Riksbank, which quickly
proved to be impermanent. A half year later, what some have described
as a tug of war between the bank and the Ministry of Finance resolved
when he accepted a full-time position as state secretary in the Ministry
of Finance, reporting to Wigforss. He remained in that post until 1945.
But the bank would claim his time and attention in due course: in 1941,
Hammarskjöld returned as chairman of the Board of Governors of the
Riksbank while retaining his role at the Ministry of Finance.

In memoirs written many years later, Wigforss recorded that some of his colleagues doubted the wisdom of appointing a man just thirty years old, no matter how able, to a highly responsible position in his ministry. Perhaps the position should be shared with an older, more experienced person? Wigforss notes that Dag declined to divide the position "after having consulted his father. Old Hjalmar Hammarskjöld seems to have been short and determined as usual. Either the whole thing or nothing at all."[11] And so it was the whole thing.

The Riksbank centenary volume suggests that Hammarskjöld's major accomplishment in the 1930s, from his post at the Ministry of Finance, was a 1937 budget reform to which he contributed key organizing concepts.[12] By 1938, he was "the uncontested budget authority."[13] However, he was not just a coldly analytic expert. Wigforss recognized and valued Dag's "ability to win people over personally, thus leveling opposition and fulfilling overall a leading task in a large organization."[14] Certainly, the technical expertise was there. Wigforss is again the best observer: "His ability to convey in a clear and concentrated way the essentials of a message made it a pleasure to follow his presentation of reports—if you were alert and interested enough to follow him. But it was as with the study of mathematical truths. If you hadn't understood the preceding part, there wasn't a great deal to be enjoyed in the continuation."[15]

Though he resembled his father in many ways, Dag had his mother's social conscience. Wigforss interpreted in political terms: "After a few years of cooperation in the ministry," he wrote, "you could not very well be altogether mistaken when it came to each other's reactions to fundamental social issues, and it was rather obvious that Hammarskjöld did not fit into any of our existing political parties. . . . In order to label him, in spite of that, I chose the classification 'Tory democrat,' a much modernized Tory democrat. His emotional attitude to people and class differences did not seem to be far from my own, and he seemed to regard a democratic equalizing policy as natural."[16] Wigforss was delighted with his protégé: "The balanced judgment, the balance between different aspects of a great natural talent, is probably the greatest impression I keep from many years of cooperation with Dag Hammarskjöld."[17] If Wigforss was the teacher in most respects, Hammarskjöld took the lead in one respect: always a voracious reader, he would recommend books of interest to his superior and weave into their world of work signs and echoes from elsewhere. Wigforss was grateful.

We must soon release the professional dimension of Hammarskjöld's years in Stockholm to explore how he felt about life and what he cared for, but it would be best to complete the curriculum vitae. Too little is now documented about his experience in the war years when Sweden, alone among Scandinavian countries and nearly alone in Europe, maintained its independence and neutrality—neutrality insofar as possible. German troops were permitted to cross Sweden by rail; war-critical iron ore and ball bearings were traded with Germany; banking facilities and safekeeping were available to the Nazi regime; and there were other concessions for the sake of keeping the Germans at bay. A few incidents involving Hammarskjöld, then serving as both a key central banker and key policy maker in the Ministry of Finance, have come to light. For example, he participated in a Swedish commercial mission to England in 1943, during which the rude treatment meted out to him and his colleagues left no doubt about the British attitude toward Swedish neutrality. "At present," they were told by a future governor of the Bank of England, "Sweden is probably the most unpopular country in Europe and in many quarters you will no doubt be regarded as spies."[18] Despite wartime conditions, the "spy" took time to browse London's bookstores and acquire a copy of T. S. Eliot's *Dry Salvages* and other works.[19] It would fall to him and a few coworkers, after the war, to repair Sweden's trade relations with the Western allies, work out a modus vivendi with the Soviet Union, and restore international confidence.

As chairman of the Riksbank Board of Governors, 1941–48, Hammarskjöld is said to have enjoyed the complete confidence of Ivar Rooth, himself a highly able individual who would serve in 1951–56 as the second managing director of one of the great postwar institutions, the International Monetary Fund. A member of the board during Hammarskjöld's tenure recalled that Hammarskjöld was "sometimes referred to as 'the real Governor of the Riksbank,'" and went on to write that "the situation at the time demanded strong, energetic leadership by the Riksbank: Dag Hammarskjöld had the will and the capacity to exercise such a leadership. Ivar Rooth . . . treated him with the utmost loyalty; he knew that in Hammarskjöld he had a supporter and friend. The cooperation between the two was the very best."[20]

In his dual role as a leading central banker and trusted member of Wigforss's finance ministry, Hammarskjöld was called upon during the war years to provide his share of leadership in dangerous circumstances.

That he did well, and shone particularly in diplomatic missions, is reflected in a sequence of postwar appointments. Serving in 1946 as an international representative attached to the Ministry for Foreign Affairs and becoming in 1949 an undersecretary in the ministry, he entered the prime minister's cabinet in 1951 as a minister without portfolio, charged with managing international issues in finance and economics. He had become "the principal actor behind Sweden's position in the postwar world of trade and money."[21] He now entered scenes that will be increasingly familiar to readers: the Paris Conference, spring 1947, which launched the Marshall Plan to provide seed money for economic recovery in Europe; ongoing meetings in Paris of the Organization for European Economic Cooperation (OEEC), which administered Marshall Plan funds; helping to secure Sweden's participation in the Bretton Woods agreements on international monetary management (1951); and ultimately the United Nations, where he served as vice-chairman of the Swedish delegation to the General Assembly in 1951, and acting chairman in 1952.

There are signs here and there that Dag and his closest colleagues enjoyed their work and retained just enough irreverence. For example, a discreet exchange of scrawled notes between Dag and his friend and colleague, Sture Petrén, survives among more solemn documents. In September 1950, side by side at what must have been an appallingly dull meeting, they did their best to cheer each other up. The exchange begins with a fantasy about orienteering, a competitive wilderness sport still popular in Sweden that involves finding your way from designated point to point. At each station a referee stamps your map; the idea is to reach the finish line first. "My association," writes Dag about the speaker then holding forth, "—an orienteering race in marshy terrain. 'Hullo, this is a brand-new pool,' he says, when the rest of us thought it was the same pool we all just got soaked in." Petrén: "*Yes*. Aren't we like two birds with their feathers all ruffled up, sitting on a telegraph line and looking at the traffic below?"[22] Hammarskjöld's correspondence with Petrén during the UN years is, as we shall see, candid, realistic, free, often warmed by humor. He was one of the trusted friends.

The Riksbank volume makes clear that Hammarskjöld's tasks in the immediate postwar period were crucial for the future of the nation: "Sweden was caught in a difficult political situation. It was maneuvering to participate in 'Western' economic and political cooperation while at the same time trying to maintain a neutral stance between 'East' and

'West.' Much of this delicate maneuvering was performed by Hammar-skjöld."[23] The general editors of the Riksbank volume consider that here he made his "most important contributions as a Swedish civil servant, not least in restoring Sweden's credibility with the victors and promot-ing our integration in the new world that was emerging after the war."[24] Wigforss felt that it was at the OEEC, where Hammarskjöld became known for integrity and intellectual resourcefulness, that the foundation was laid for his nomination as secretary-general of the United Nations.[25] Sture Linnér, a close colleague and friend during the Congo crisis, con-firms this view and underscores that at the OEEC Hammarskjöld often worked on behalf of Europe rather than Sweden—Sweden received no Marshall aid—and those at the table with him were well aware of his large sense of duty.[26] At the time of his nomination and election in the early spring of 1953, he was unfamiliar to the public and in the broad diplomatic arena, but he had impressed a small circle of influential people, among them Anthony Eden, the long-serving foreign secretary of the United Kingdom and later prime minister, who is said to have been the first, with the French diplomat Henri Hoppenot, to mention Hammarskjöld as a candidate.

As a member of the Swedish cabinet in 1951–53, Hammarskjöld at last had responsibilities that broke through the confines of trade relations and economic recovery. Joseph Lash, a journalist on the UN beat and author of the first Hammarskjöld biography (written with his subject's cooperation, written very well), tells one of the best stories in this regard. In summer 1952, the Russians created a serious diplomatic incident when their fliers shot down a number of Swedish planes over the Baltic. Hammarskjöld's boss, the foreign minister, was on holiday in Italy; he himself had to be fetched by military aircraft from Lapland, where he was hiking. For days he and two colleagues represented Swe-den in a sharp diplomatic exchange that made the morning headlines in Stockholm.[27] It was not his last encounter with Soviet aggressiveness.

Henrik Klackenberg, a colleague in the government, became a loyal friend to Hammarskjöld in the war years and after. His recollections, pub-lished in several places, are as valuable as Wigforss's. The professional work of the two men must have overlapped, and they did things together after hours—squash at a local club, seasonal weekend bicycle trips and cross-country skiing in the countryside around Stockholm, rambles on foot in the city. They talked things over. Klackenberg was aware of his friend's interest in religion and detected the interior battle in Dag between the "philosophical hardening" he had received "in Axel Hägerström's school" and his persistent reading in "religious experiential psychology." Their conversations ranged over the works of William James, Ernest Renan on Christianity, Rudolf Otto's *The Idea of the Holy*, C. G. Jung, and no doubt much more; these are the topics Klackenberg recalled years later.[28]

In later years he also recalled that at the foreign ministry Hammarskjöld had surrounded himself with able colleagues, but "it wasn't a brain trust, he was his own brain trust." He went on to say that Hammarskjöld had "almost the wisdom of an old man" though he was Klackenberg's senior by only a few years. When he shared this view with Dag, "it wasn't taken as a compliment."[29] Klackenberg dispels any notion that his friend was a withdrawn or rigid sort of person: "I remember chiefly his moral stature and incorruptible justice, his integrity and whole-hearted commitment, and his never-failing sense of responsibility vis-à-vis the task. Yet emphasis on these traits should not suggest an eternal, forbidding morality. On the contrary he had devastating charm. His colleagues readily became his personal friends. But least of all in the portrait of Dag Hammarskjöld should one lose sight of the gently considerate, somewhat diffident friendliness."[30]

Once, toward the end of winter, they were standing beside a waterway in Stockholm and watching the ice break up. Klackenberg recalled their conversation vividly: "When the nights for a long time had been too short and the years in the finance department had been long, there could be a sigh about how life feels like a squirrel wheel and longing for a more humane existence—which would never come. 'One is like a seal that has a hard time getting its head above water between the ice floes to breathe,' he once said. Mostly he got on well with this life."[31] When Hammarskjöld left Swedish government service, he was remembered. Charmingly, one of his successors at the finance ministry insisted on using the same coat hook that Hammarskjöld had used.[32] It must have had charisma.

Hammarskjöld himself offers little retrospection on these years in his professional life, but in his correspondence with Wigforss two points are clear: he never fully identified with Wigforss and his generation of socialist nation builders, although he loyally served them, and he was enormously grateful for the training he had received as a member of the Wigforss inner circle. Responding in 1950 to the first volume of Wigforss's memoirs, he sent over an illuminating note. "I envy you a little," he wrote.

It is—after all—a much cleaner world you describe than the one met by people born in my years. What strikes me most, and what I never saw so clearly in our discussions, is the disastrous decay of values during the quarter-century that divides us. Without stooping to dramatize, if I were to compare the public debate of ideas I have experienced and the one you describe, I would compare the environment of values where the former took place to a bombed-out city, in which the inhabitants are happy to be able to join shattered ruins into a temporary shelter with no consideration for connection, plan, or permanence.[33]

Wigforss's own commentary sheds additional light: "[Hammarskjöld's generation] was skeptical, without illusions; they had seen the whole mass of traditional values fall. We who were some 25 years older could still seek shelter in what looked like a collective belief."[34] Yet Hammarskjöld as secretary-general articulated with classical clarity, as if arguing an eternal thesis, the need for faith in humanity. Traditional values had not lost their grip on him, although he reinterpreted them in light of new circumstances and his own search for meaning. For this also he owed some debt to Wigforss. In the rushed days of early April 1953, after being notified of his nomination to be secretary-general, he dealt with a few loose ends in Sweden and contacted certain friends, Wigforss among them, before leaving for New York:

Dear E. W.

It is hard for me, in the pressing circumstances that these days have become mine, to answer your letter in the way I would wish and do justice to the renewed feeling of owing you a great debt of gratitude which these days have given me. Now it will have to be just a few words to say that your letter made me very happy by the light it cast also on your view of the long time I was allowed to attend your school. Your belief in the future and your capacity to say yes to humanity is an inspiration I need now more than ever.[35]

Close readers of Hammarskjöld will at once recall his struggle, evident in *Markings*, to find his own durable yes in the face of life circumstances that could feel, despite appearances, comfortless and desolate. "How seldom growth and blossom / How seldom fruit," he wrote in his journal in 1950, at a time when his career was dynamic and poised to become more so through appointment to the prime minister's cabinet. Three years later, on the eve of taking up his duties at the UN, there is another sound:

For all that has been: thanks!
To all that shall be: yes![36]

Discovered through trials and illuminations we should now explore, his yes was not just a personal attitude confined to private life. It had enough vigor and stability to guide his work at the United Nations—as he rather promised his old mentor Wigforss in that grateful note.

Search of another kind, 1925–1949

In its published form, Hammarskjöld's private journal, *Markings*, is a work of literature deliberately shaped by its author. The epigraph on the title page of the surviving typescript leaves no doubt of that: citing the contemporary Swedish poet Bertil Malmberg, Hammarskjöld records that "only the hand that erases can write the true thing."[37] The original journal, however extensive, has not come to light and is assumed to have been destroyed after serving Hammarskjöld as a source for the edited typescript. But the erasing hand was not moved by self-flattery or justification. *Markings* is a crushingly honest exploration of what it is to live; to have mind, heart, and body; to be thrown into this world; to decipher experience; to carry burdens and face weaknesses a little wisely; to find something approaching inner peace; to glimpse a larger pattern, and somehow serve the good. What was ragged and difficult in the original journal surely remains ragged and difficult in the published version, however much Hammarskjöld with his acute sense of style may have altered a verbal rhythm or reordered entries here and there to clarify a point. Similarly, what was pure, dreamt, or prayed remained pure, dreamt, and prayed. We can know very little about how and what he edited as he drew long years of journal keeping into a literary whole, but the result gives the impression of being only lightly reworked. We have in *Markings* what he wished us to have, carefully typed for the most part on a somewhat ink-clogged, older typewriter he used at home (documents from the office were elegantly produced). This is his Bildungsroman, the story of an education.

The year divisions in the typescript are clearly marked, 1925–30, followed by a long gap, then 1941–42, 1945–49, and thereafter a continuous annual sequence through late summer 1961. Hammarskjöld had premonitions in the course of 1960–61 that he might be swallowed up in the violence of the Congo Crisis then under way; later pages of *Markings* bear vivid witness to those premonitions. He must have put aside time to set the manuscript in order. As we shall see, he wasn't certain that it should be published, but he must have wanted it clean and ready. The entries are invariably brief; the longest may be two pages typed at most, the shortest no more than a few words. The years we're now ready to explore, 1925–49, encompass only some thirty pages in a book of more than two hundred pages, and the absence of entries for the 1930s and the war years 1943–44 is noticeable. But we'll find in those thirty pages early signs of his commitment to the examined life and a vivid prelude to the crisis and resolution of 1950–52, when the man we know as Hammarskjöld in his maturity at last found his footing.

1925–1930: I am being driven forward

Markings begins and ends with poems so like each other in theme and tone that the later must have been written with the earlier in mind—but which is the later one? Entitled "Thus it was," the opening poem may well be a late addition, written by the older Hammarskjöld to capture the essence of the younger man's aspiration and anxiety. The title gives weight to this speculation. There is a further scrap of evidence to suggest that the poem found its place only when Hammarskjöld was setting the typescript into something like final order: the poem is typed in sharper, less clogged characters than much else, matching the handful of other fully retyped pages—again suggesting that it was positioned late in the process, and perhaps also written or revised late in the process. Be that as it may, the poem reflects the spiritual quest and quest for self-knowledge to which *Markings* is dedicated, and it speaks with maturity.

> I am being driven forward
> Into an unknown land.
> The pass grows steeper,
> The air colder and sharper.
> A wind from my unknown goal
> Stirs the strings
> Of expectation.
>
> Still the question:
> Shall I ever get there?
> There where life resounds,
> A clear simple note
> In the silence.[38]

In spare modern version, the poem embraces the traditional imagery of the questing hero of epic and folk tale. The hero is driven forward—the quest as much a matter of destiny as of chosen enterprise—through an unknown land toward an unknown goal. The rigors of ascent are increasingly harsh, as in the northern wilderness Hammarskjöld knew so well. Though a communicating wind from the unknown goal encourages him to persevere, he doesn't know whether he is capable of completing the quest. Were he to find his way, he has some sense of what awaits him: a realm where life rings out (Sw. *klingar ut*) as a clear simple note in the silence. Climbers know that sound in the call of an isolated bird above the timberline. Notably, the questing hero is alone; there are no companions for either journey or destination, and the goal is expressed in the language of Romantic nature poetry and, close by, of Christian mysticism. And so the very first words of *Markings* clear a space for an internal adventure undetectable in the facts and circumstances of the brilliant career thus far chronicled.

It won't be possible or even wise to notice in these pages every engaging feature of *Markings*. This is not a work of literary criticism. But we need to notice foreshadowings, revelations large and small, moments of edgy self-knowledge, patterns that move past a single entry into the larger life. In the first few pages that follow the poem, representing no doubt the mature Hammarskjöld's cull from an early journal, and with more extensive retyping (therefore, editing?) than in later pages, certain themes are launched that remain central: loneliness, the need for self-sacrifice, the nearness of death, lessons from wilderness trekking, a habit of measuring personal experience by an inner ethic that scans attitude as closely as action. And then, a suffering encounter with sensual beauty, as if the journal keeper's effort to evoke perfect beauty in perfect words rescues him from touch, from falling in love.

In these early pages we should look more closely at just two further entries, each echoing into the future. The first:

> What you have to attempt—to be yourself. What you
> might achieve—to become a mirror in which, according
> to the degree of purity you have attained, the greatness
> of life will be reflected.[39]

At some point between the ages of twenty and twenty-five, Dag conceived this wish wise beyond his years. He couched it in compressed, severely dialectical terms: On one hand, he wishes to be himself, by which he must have meant free from social imitativeness, free to experience and manifest in ways native to him, psychologically mobile and unafraid. On the other hand, he wishes something else unlike all this:

to mirror the greatness of life with all possible purity. For the Christian tradition in which Hammarskjöld had been raised, and which he would rediscover and reclaim as his own in later years, the notion of purity implies a scouring—deliberate abandonment of much that might once have seemed to be oneself. Hammarskjöld recorded in a journal entry for 1955, well into his tenure as secretary-general, a brief passage from one of the honored texts that presided over his maturity, *The Imitation of Christ*. As noted earlier, Dag's mother had given him a pleasant edition of this book on the occasion of his religious confirmation, which was an important rite of passage in the Sweden of that day.[40] The edition he actually read in later life was of his own choosing: a French translation dated 1719. Just why he preferred an antique edition is a topic for later pages. The passage from Thomas recorded in *Markings* states in traditional terms the aspiration young Dag had adopted as his own. "The purer the eye of her attention," wrote Thomas,

> the more power the soul finds within herself. But it is very rare to find a soul who is entirely free, whose purity is not soiled by the stain of some secret desire of her own. Strive, then, constantly to purify the eye of your attention until it becomes utterly simple and direct.[41]

We must be closer now to understanding Dag's early statement of purpose. In what seemed a severe dialectic—push and pull between unlike forces—there was a missing middle term identified by Thomas, and in turn by the mature Hammarskjöld, as attentive living. To fulfill the seemingly paradoxical aspiration to be oneself and yet reflect with purity the greatness of life needs an engine in the middle, a reliable strategy or practice. Young Dag surely found pointers toward practice in the traditional literature of the spirit, but pointers only, often somewhat vague, more focused on aspiration and result than on the long stretch between, where the actual living gets done.

There are something like miracles in the life of Dag Hammarskjöld. Among the first is that he worked out for himself a practice of self-observation, or what he later called "conscious self-scrutiny," that set him on a path toward living his chosen values: to be himself, to mirror the greatness of life. Was Dag somehow able to convert broadly stated, traditional Christian teachings into a precise, modern code? Did he find in Professor Hägerström's intellectual rigor or Archbishop Söderblom's warm self-inquiry models of the examined life? Was Blaise Pascal, one of

the most acute observers of human nature, the teacher here? Dag's sense
of Christian duty is much like that of Thomas à Kempis, his lucidity and
irony much like Pascal's. We know that he read them both with gratitude
and recognition, and had with him in Africa at the time of his death in
1961 a compact edition of Thomas. However all this may be, the earliest
pages of *Markings* leave no doubt of his commitment to self-observation
as the natural path to self-knowledge and means of purifying the eye
of attention. It seems best to leave these terms open and somewhat
undefined for the moment. Later pages of *Markings* will show us what
they mean in practice, and there is no persuasive reason to adopt defini-
tions from beyond the borders of Hammarskjöld's life and sensibility,
however much it may be true that readers familiar with the traditional
Buddhist teaching of mindfulness or G. I. Gurdjieff's twentieth-century
teaching of self-observation need not reach far for parallels. There is no
sign whatever that he knew of Gurdjieff, and his discovery of an affinity
with Buddhism largely coincided with a world tour he made as secretary-
general in 1956.

The second early entry of exceptional interest confirms that Hammarskjöld had begun in his twenties to look at his experience with the
peculiar ruthlessness that came to be a hallmark of his practice of self-
observation.

> To be sure, you fence with a foil. But in the loneliness of yesterday—
> Did you not play with poison?[42]

Said to have been a capable gymnast, young Dag would have known
something of fencing. Here he refers to the foil with a buttoned tip,
which inflicts no injury. But he observes that loneliness drove him to
make what must have been a poisonous remark to someone who had
expected to spar with harmless weapons—with good-natured wit. This
is the first of many entries in *Markings*, to the very last years, in which
Hammarskjöld traces the corrosive influence of loneliness in his life and,
on occasion, celebrates moments of fellowship and love. The movement
of self-observation, more ready in later years to capture scarcely visible,
complex patterns, is clear-sighted enough in this early entry to note the
link between a dark emotion and a spoiled action. The observation is
recorded, it seems, in the spirit of a memo to self: no analysis, no advice
to the erring human who happens to be oneself, just the moment of self-
perception recorded in a minimum of words.

To mirror with purity the greatness of life is a phrase with two possible meanings. It can point to receptivity to all that is great and good in life with as little distortion as possible, as if one were called to be a keen, appreciative witness. It can point as well to a more difficult aspiration: to embody that greatness and goodness, to be the bearer of it. The meanings are linked. But it seems fair to say that Hammarskjöld in these early years has a sense of destiny with no object. There is an unknown land, prelude to an unknown goal. But a promising wind reaches him.

1941–1942: Gaze steadfastly at the vision

After a gap of some eleven years for which there are no journal entries, young Dag's early statement of purpose evokes an enriched echo in the brief set of entries for the middle war years, 1941–42.

> The more faithfully you listen to the voice inside you, the better you will hear what is sounding outside. And only he who listens can speak. Is this the starting point of the road towards the union of your two dreams—to be allowed in clarity of mind to mirror life and in purity of heart to mold it?[43]

This central aspiration, now cast in the words of a man thirty-six or thirty-seven years old, reflects what Wigforss had seen in him: the wish of a man of action to influence the course of events. Hammarskjöld's search to understand purity in the privacy of the inner life and its shaping power—if any—in the rough-and-tumble of external life is supported in these years by his fierce practice of self-observation. The "stain of secret desires," to which Thomas à Kempis and much of Christian tradition alerted him, is a recurrent theme in these pages of *Markings*, although not the only theme: the journal records a many-sided search, not a self-punishing exercise in contrition. The secret desires are not predominantly sexual at this point in his life—just one entry touches on that theme ("You cannot play with the animal within you without becoming wholly animal").[44] The stains he observes most closely are insistent self-centeredness and recurrent indifference to others, traits he encounters as grave hindrances: there can be neither clarity nor purity where they dominate. A search of the kind undertaken by Hammarskjöld burns. It burns owing to what one discovers in oneself and burns to find a new quality of being—burns with self-doubt, burns with longing. It cannot really be otherwise, but between these psychological forces something new can appear in encouraging flashes.

We are witnessing a gifted soul deeply engaged in its own education. The vision is rarely comforting or pleasant. "Isn't the void surrounding you when the noise ceases," he notes, "your just reward for a day devoted to preventing others from neglecting you?" "How can you expect to keep your powers of hearing," he asks, "when you never want to listen?" "Praise nauseates you," he acknowledges, "but woe betide him who does not recognize your worth."[45]

One might think, why bother to look so closely when it causes such pain? What, if anything, relieves these anguished encounters? In response to the first question, we can refer back to Hammarskjöld's expression of purpose: "to be allowed in clarity of mind to mirror life and in purity of heart to mold it." There is a price for such a thing, and he chose to share with us—though only after his death—some record of the price he had found it necessary and possible to pay. In response to the second question, we can detect in certain journal entries for these years new dimensions of experience.

The first dimension is a new sensitivity to others. "Openness to life," he writes in these years, "grants a lightning-swift insight into the life situation of others."[46] There is no anguish in this report; it is factual. Words much like "lightning-swift" would be used by two of his closest collaborators at the UN, Brian Urquhart and Ralph Bunche, to describe his quickness of mind in later years. But initially he discovered for himself that the inner struggle he had entered upon with such dedication grants vivid receptivity to others. This discovery is confirmed and enlarged by the words that open this section: "The more faithfully you listen to the voice inside you, the better you will hear what is sounding outside." Dag has discovered a reciprocity between digging deeper into himself and clearer perceptions of other people—an insight that would prove fundamental for his later life.

> Our inmost creative will intuits its counterpart in others, experiences its own universality—and thus opens the way to knowledge of that power of which it is itself a spark within us.[47]

And so this man who takes himself so severely to task for flashes of selfishness and indifference also experiences flashes of extraordinary linkage, in which his own and others' deep life is experienced as a continuity without barriers, a spark of some greater fire. And this too is factual; it is a matter of observation.

Discovering a new capacity for relationship, Hammarskjöld in these years is also discovering new depth in himself—discovering "the fleeting light in the depth of our being":

> The road to self-knowledge does not pass through faith. But only through the insight we gain by pursuing the fleeting light in the depth of our being do we reach the point where we can grasp what faith is. How many have been driven into outer darkness by empty talk about faith as something to be rationally comprehended, something "true."[48]

There is a tight weave among the internal discoveries of these years. Here Hammarskjöld links insight into the depth of human being to the possibility of a deep and grounded assent to religious faith, not as a set of doctrines held to be true but as a direct experience. This points to the third new dimension of Hammarskjöld's sensibility in these middle years: a passage toward mature religious faith.

Self-observation has shown him his waywardness, the imprint of self-centeredness even on attempts to pray: "Your cravings as a human animal," he notes, "do not become a prayer just because it is God whom you ask to attend to them." "That God should have time for you, you seem to take as much for granted as that you cannot have time for Him."[49] Despite their bitter cast, these journal entries signal that in Hammarskjöld's midthirties religious sensibility takes a more central place in his inner life. As always, he observes the internal distortions and distractions that are the common lot of most human beings, but his awareness of shortcomings does not call a halt to the search. In one striking entry, he evokes the vast simplicity of the Lord's Prayer, records something of what *could be*—and recognizes his confusion:

> "Hallowed be Thy Name." When all your strength ought to be focused into one pencil of light pointing up through the darkness, you allow it to be dissipated in a moss fire where nothing is consumed, but all life is suffocated.[50]

Through a metaphor reflecting his wilderness experience, he records what nearly everyone who prays or meditates can acknowledge: the mind's reluctance to concentrate. Even the Lord's Prayer can lose its way in the smoke.

In these years when a religious temperament reasserts itself, the Lord rises above him as a reality beyond measure. His growing self-knowledge makes him acutely vulnerable: "When we are compelled to look ourselves in the face," he writes, "then He rises above us in terrifying reality, beyond all argument and 'feeling,' stronger than all self-defensive forgetfulness."[51] But the imperative from within to continue looking is stronger than the dread provoked by doing so. When all becomes silent around you, and you recoil in terror, . . . gaze steadfastly at the vision until you have plumbed its depths."[52]

In a life that threatens to be unstable, a life in which *too much* is seen yet driven by rampant thirst for knowledge, sources of stability are urgently needed. We recognized at the beginning of this chapter that day-to-day professional work—useful to society, sometimes challenging and innovative, in the company of worthwhile colleagues—would ground Hammarskjöld through these inwardly tumultuous, risky years in Stockholm. But there is another source of stability of an altogether different order: Christian faith, the riches of Judeo-Christian scripture and wisdom literature, the possibility of prayer and a slowly growing capacity to dwell within in peace, to find sanctuary in stillness and silence. For the moment the Lord may tower above as a fearsome presence—may take the form of the angry Lord of Jeremiah 30:24 or a wrathful deity, as Buddhist tradition puts it—but wrath is only one of the faces of God. Hammarskjöld begins in these years to conduct his life in sight of God. This is a vast stability. It provides an ancient, steady context, increasingly life giving and life preserving as he comes to know it.

In these war years, soon after the loss of his mother in 1940, Hammarskjöld rediscovers the nearness of death—a theme already evident in the earliest pages of his journal. That nearness is now recognized as another source of stability through its power to settle one down and bring one back to core values. He frames this insight in terms that recall the Congo setting of Joseph Conrad's novella *Heart of Darkness*, which he knew well. With his incomparable appreciation of the ambiguities of human nature and conduct, Conrad was among Hammarskjöld's teachers in earlier years and in effect a companion-at-arms in later years. In his New York apartment he kept a framed portrait etching of Conrad.[53]

> There is only one path out of the steamy dense jungle where the battle is fought over glory and power and advantage—one escape from the snares and obstacles you yourself have set up. And that is—to accept death.[54]

At this stage of his education we are encountering in Hammarskjöld a striving that has become largely unfamiliar in our culture. His practice of self-searching has a disconcertingly heroic dimension, as if we were reading fragments from an account of the early struggles of a Christian desert father. The outer life as a rapidly rising government man and the inner life as a seeker of self-knowledge in a steadily consolidating religious context seem to have no middle term, no easy place for everyone to get together and enjoy themselves. There are hints of an emerging maturity capable of looking deeply within, capable of meeting others with warm understanding, capable of prayer. But this is a life under tension. It could resolve in several different ways.

1945–1949: To let go and fall

Most of the preceding entries from *Markings* reflect indoor activities—indoor and even further within, as if the intense transactions of Dag Hammarskjöld with himself have been wholly internal matters of the mind and heart. The beginning of the next section of *Markings* seems to promise more of the same. An opening exploration of superficial choices made "out of curiosity or wonder or greed" raises the possibility of quite different choices: "casting anchor in the experience of the high mystery of life, and consciousness of the talent entrusted to you which is your 'I'."[55] Hammarskjöld's recognition of the mystery of life and his aspiration to cast anchor in that mystery, which must mean to make a durable relation, are good signs for the future. Where there is a sense of mystery, there are less likely to be hard condemnations or rigidities. Mystery is a floating sort of thing, a blessedly loose organization that allows life to find its way.

But the real burden of this section of *Markings* and of these years in Hammarskjöld's inner life lies elsewhere. He begins to ramble in the city—or more likely now finds his rambles important enough to record. By hindsight, it can seem strange that the life of the city and its multitude of incident have found no earlier place in the journal, but much is now conveyed through a series of vignettes in which, among other things, he seems to be testing his abilities as a writer. "Soaked, dark, woolen garments. Watchful, defensive glances. Tired mouths. It is late." This from an account of a Zen-like experience, an awakening, to which we will return in a moment. "In the mirror-world of the water, pale olive against pewter, the bare branches of an alder tree . . . " This from an evocation of winter landscape. He is already a skilled photographer, and each of these spoken images has the framed concision of a photograph. "Photography taught me to see," he wrote in 1958.[56]

The entries for 1945–49 are not the darkest in the journal, but they are a rehearsal for darkness. In just seventeen pages there are accounts of three suicides that Hammarskjöld happened to witness, a near-fatal car accident, two immensely unhappy episodes involving colleagues in government service, and a predominantly dark meditation prompted by the seagulls in Stockholm's dockyards, "well-nourished carrion birds who feel so much at home among us all."[57] (One of Hammarskjöld's first biographers, Emery Kelen, reports what seems to be a *fourth* suicide attempt, in which Dag and his friend Henrik Klackenberg successfully intervened.)[58] We need a key to understand something of all this—and need to remember that we're speaking of a soul in motion, not at standstill. The key may lie in a well-told vignette in *Markings* that opens with world-weary sophistication, moves quickly into fierce self-confrontation, and closes with a glimpse of a way forward. "What is one to do on a bleak fall day," he asks, "but drift for a while through the streets—drift with the stream?"[59] Hammarskjöld describes himself as a passive object aimlessly floating in the streets of Stockholm as the grey light of November falls, "but the twilight brings no promise of mitigation or peace." He looks into the faces of passers-by in "the gray ditches of the streets" and finds there no more than he finds in himself: "atoms in whom the radioactivity is extinct, and force has tied its endless chain around nothing."[60]

At this sagging moment, he recalls a powerfully optimistic verse from the contemporary poet, Erik Blomberg: "That one may be translated into light and song." He suddenly longs for freedom from the self-image, forged "by social ambition and sheer force of will," which dominates and isolates him:

> To let go and fall, fall—in trust and blind devotion. Toward something else, someone else.
> To take the risk—

He avidly searches the faces of those passing him in the streets as if he might discover that someone else, but in the mean light of a November nightfall he sees only variations on his own meanness. Outer climate and inner feeling are identical: *snåla*—mean or ungiving. Like himself, these people haven't taken the risk. The scene he records could be a circle in Dante's inferno for those who risked too little in their lives, who could not let go and fall.

But he is not quite done. The journal entry concludes with spare words that reset the scene, as if he had failed until now to notice a door leading on from it. The vision is again somewhat Dantesque:

> Into the fulfilling death of self-surrender each one goes alone. And on this
> side of it one will never find the way to anyone who has passed through it.[61]

Where are we now? To what he has led us? Toward an abstraction, perhaps not fully understood, not fully furnished with experience—yet
promising, provided one hasn't set one's heart on pleasure: the fulfilling
death-in-life of self-surrender. Surrender to what? For now that remains
unclear or unstated, as does the hope, scarcely audible, of fellowship with
others who have taken the risk of self-surrender. However possible it may
be in later years to be "translated into light and song," the emotional key-
note in these years is not of that kind. One fears for him. The brilliant
government man, the thoroughly capable man, is at risk.

It seems evident that he was thinking of suicide. There are too many accounts
of suicides witnessed in these years for us to view them as random notes in a day-
book. A colleague is dragged out to sea by a strong undertow—perhaps a suicide,
perhaps unlucky. A beautiful young woman abandons herself to muddy shallows
and insistently tries to drown until she succeeds. On shore, where rescuers try to
revive her, she becomes a fallen statue, attractive in her nakedness to Dag as witness, and immensely distant. In the third incident, a young man shoots himself in
the head, and Dag senses the hold of otherness even on the living: "That eternal
'Beyond,'" he writes, "which can separate us from those chosen by death long
before the bullet hits the temple."[62] Some years later, in 1952, he writes explicitly
in his journal about the temptation of suicide. The passage foreshadows the next
chapter, which explores the years of sharpest inner turmoil while his career continued to soar. "Fatigue dulls the pain," he writes,

> but awakens enticing thoughts of death. So! *That* is the way in which
> you are tempted to overcome your loneliness—by making the ultimate
> escape from life. —No! Death must be your final gift to life, not an act
> of treachery against it.[63]

Even at the height of his work at the United Nations, he occasionally has
to talk himself out of recklessly putting himself in harm's way. "Do not
seek annihilation," he notes down in 1957. "It will find you. Seek the way
that makes it a fulfillment."[64] His physical courage was recognized by his
UN colleagues. In 1956 he deliberately traveled a dangerous line of demarcation between Egyptian and Israeli forces as a sign to all concerned
that there must be no further bloodshed. In 1960 he negotiated at length
by radio from an airplane in flight with the unpredictable leader of the
Katanga secession in the Congo. It was unclear whether his plane would

be authorized to land, turned away, or shot out of the sky. He had the courage and steadiness of an experienced mountaineer.

Throughout the immediate postwar period, there was of course more than melancholy, longing, and loneliness on the inside of this life whose externalities were so impressive. This was a tormented soul, but not lacking in resources. As we know, he drew a sense of well-being from Nature, the sense of a potent reality to which he belonged. Even during his unhappy ramble through the urban dockyards of Stockholm, where he was struck by the predatory behavior of seagulls, he responded also to "the swell, the salt tang, and the awakening breeze."[65] That awakening breeze would carry far into him as the years passed.

The point of a wintry narrative in his journal about the "watchful, defensive glances" and "tired mouths" of fellow citizens waiting in a pharmacy is not just their unhappiness. The point is a sudden awakening. Looking past weary customers, he catches sight of the elderly pharmacist, whose warm yet contained way of being abruptly transforms his perceptions. He conveys that transformation in a brief poem:

> Here and now—only this is real:
> The good face of an old man,
> Caught naked in an unguarded moment,
> Without past, without future.[66]

Does this journal entry record his initial discovery of the here and now, without past, without future, alive with possibility? In any case, here he introduces the theme. It would become central in years to come.

He was studying scripture. Guided by Albert Schweitzer's writings, he had engaged in a return to the sources of Christian faith and to the source person, Jesus of Nazareth. That effort moved through time, slowly accumulating insight and purpose, personal confidence and the breadth of faith. But there was another movement, more difficult to describe—a sudden arrival in reality, which also tasted of revelation. Recall the wilderness poem of 1951, which concludes:

> In the pale light of sparseness
> Lives the Real Thing
> And we are real.

Hammarskjöld's praise of the elderly pharmacist also evokes that movement, a tumble into reality as if one has snapped awake or suddenly landed on one's feet just where one is. His mature understanding of time and process, so vastly useful and effective in his role as secretary-general, included a subtle recognition of immediacy, the here and now in which all things occur. "To let go and fall, fall," he wrote, "Toward something else, someone else." There would never be "someone" in this life, a companion in full intimacy, although there would be friends. But there would be something and someone of another order. Through hard trials, many still to come, he was learning to fall with trust and devotion.

We shouldn't move past these years in Hammarskjöld's inner life without acknowledging two late entries. The first is a simple, firm expression. It has the force of a credo or promise: "No rest which is not rest for all, no stillness until all has been fulfilled."[67] Within the private turmoil of this life, there is nonetheless a steady dedication to community, joined to a sense of destiny that has yet to find its object. The word "stillness" (Sw. *stillhet*) may seem strange here; it is almost certainly a sign that he is reading Meister Eckhart, the fourteenth-century preacher and mystic whose writings would be among the presiding documents of his maturity. In one of his earliest—and rare—religious statements as secretary-general, he would speak of the hidden but, to his mind, crucial link between stillness and service to others (see pp. 177–78).

The record of these difficult years, 1945–49, ends with a characteristically merciless self-observation: "You asked for burdens to carry— And howled when they were placed on your shoulders."[68] Just beyond that occurs the first acknowledgment in *Markings* of Hammarskjöld's deepening sense of discipleship toward "the carpenter's son," as he once called Jesus. With a sharp sense of drama, he recalls passages in Matthew 16:13–28 and Mark 8:27–35, when Jesus at a place called Caesarea Philippi spoke of the sufferings that lay ahead and taught in words never forgotten: "If any man would come after me, let him deny himself and take up his cross and follow me. For whoever would save his life will lose it; and whoever loses his life for my sake will find it" (Matthew 16:24–25).

In the pages of his journal, Hammarskjöld calls out to that moment of teaching and acknowledges that he has heard:

> O Caesarea Philippi: to accept condemnation of the work ahead as its fruit and premise, to accept this when one recognizes and chooses it.[69]

4

The Fire of Clear Eyes: 1950–1952

Strange to say, we can know more of this statesman's inner experience in the years just prior to his election as secretary-general than we can readily know of his life as a government official. Much of his day-to-day work occurred behind closed doors and, while archival minutes may exist, the issues in them would for the most part no longer compel attention. He was not a colorful figure in those years, a Churchill flaring with wit and restless initiative, creating headlines at will. But we can't leave the matter there. Were there no approachable record of Hammarskjöld's earlier political thought, the breadth and firmness of his thinking as soon as he became a public figure would seem to spring from nowhere, as if he had been privately rehearsing. In reality, he had been publicly rehearsing for years as a senior diplomat in Swedish and international economic affairs and, in 1952–53, as acting chairman of the Swedish delegation to the General Assembly—flying in, it seems, when the Swedish foreign minister leading the delegation had to be elsewhere.[1] He does not appear at any point to have spoken on behalf of the delegation, but he surely looked around, listened to the flood of oratory, and formed a preliminary view of the UN at work.

What he had understood in those preparatory years became widely evident only after his election as secretary-general. It seems right to say that no one apart from Swedish friends and colleagues, and those who worked with him at international meetings, had some inkling of the breadth of his political philosophy, integrity, capacity for dialogue, and strategic acumen. Had his full range been better known, he would not have been elected secretary-general. The Big Powers would only compromise their separate interests around someone believed to be safe—a reliable, apolitical administrator. Hammarskjöld himself may have had little idea of his own range. There was rebirth ahead.

In 1951–52, Hammarskjöld felt moved to publish three articles on political issues.[2] They are predominantly impersonal, even bureaucratic in style and content, offering little evidence of the public figure he would become. Much in them could serve mainly as a foil illustrating the extent to which he changed. But of the two published in 1951, "The Civil Servant and Society" explores terrain that would compel his interest to the end, and there are signs of the warmly inquiring, humanistic view of later years. One of his last elaborate public statements as secretary-general was an address at Oxford in May 1961 on virtually the same topic, under the title "The International Civil Servant in Law and in Fact."[3]

In the opening paragraphs of the 1951 piece, he deprecatingly describes what is to follow as "marginal reflections on a personal problem"—doubtless the friction he experienced as a high government official unaffiliated with any party. The article has a mixed nature, for the most part dry and insistently analytical, but with engaging zones and a thought-provoking conclusion where Hammarskjöld pleads, in effect, for a political philosophy based on Albert Schweitzer's value of "reverence for life." As secretary-general he would often evoke values. In this essay predating the UN years, he explores the boundary where personal values may conflict or cohere with official service in a role that calls for objectivity.

The fundamental position he takes about civil service in political contexts is straightforward. It would prove to be lasting:

> The basic and obvious commandment in the code of the civil servant is that he serve the community and not any group, party, or special interest. This by no means implies that he should be—or even that it is best that he be—politically indifferent, but it does imply that, however deeply engaged he may be in politics, as an *executive civil servant* . . . he must not work for his political ideals *because they are his*. On the other hand, if he wishes to express his political views, his position as a public official does not in itself cut him off from the right of every citizen to influence the development of the community by political activity according to his own judgment. His own political judgment can outweigh his duty as a civil servant only if he finds that the view he holds represents a communal interest about which varying opinions cannot prevail on objective grounds.[4]

During the UN years, Hammarskjöld pointedly did not express personal political judgments in public—until the last year or so, when ad hominem attacks from the Soviet bloc forced him to respond as an individual. In private correspondence and messages to trusted colleagues, he willingly shared strong opinions about political leaders and situations but rarely came out swinging or sought private revenge for public misdeeds. Speaking with the press in Moscow in 1956, he stated his position: "I regard myself as a little different from ordinary politicians, as I am the servant of 76 nations representing the most varied political philosophies and outlooks. This does not of course mean that I am completely neutral and have no point of view of my own"[5]—this by way of apologizing in advance if his remarks were something less than newsworthy.

One further point about objectivity is worth retaining from the 1951 article. Hammarskjöld writes there of a "type, not unimportant for political development, who in his political work has the individualist's need for an unconditional examination of all questions and suggestions on their merits without being captured by special interests."[6] This was his type.

In light of Hammarskjöld's future, a passage of importance occurs at the end of the article where he explores—as he writes, "for personal reasons"—the political impact of Schweitzer's principle of reverence for life. The personal reasons were very real: as an adolescent he had spent time with Schweitzer when he came to Uppsala in the spring of 1920 at the invitation of Archbishop Söderblom to give a series of lectures, one of which publicly stated for the first time the principle of reverence for life. To visit the Söderblom family was, in effect, to visit the Hammarskjöld family living closely alongside. In 1953, Hammarskjöld reconsidered Schweitzer's influence. "The two ideals which dominated my childhood world," he said, "met me fully harmonized and adjusted to the demands of our world of today in the ethics of Albert Schweitzer, where the ideal of service is supported by and supports the basic attitude to man set forth in the Gospels."[7]

The analysis Hammarskjöld offered in 1951 of a political ethic based on Schweitzer's thinking is large and, if such a thing is possible, drily inspirational:

> It is tempting to . . . illustrate how an . . . attitude rooted in the moral scale of values . . . can gain . . . expression [when it] does not find a natural outlet in party activity. As everyone knows, Schweitzer has summed up his ethical views in the formula: "reverence for life." . . . The question is . . . the general political orientation one can expect from those persons, surely numerous, who could make Schweitzer's saying their own.
>
> One of [its] first products . . . is a respect for historical practice built up through generations of effort and of attempts to find solutions to problems. Here we encounter a markedly conservative feature. Another result is that political actions will be governed by respect for the individual, which may result on the one hand in the greatest possible

liberty for him to shape his life as he chooses, and on the other in social justice in the form of equal rights and equal opportunity for all. It is on this latter point that liberal and social-radical elements find common ground. Finally the ethic exemplified by Schweitzer finds expression in the subordination of private interests to the whole: a moral obligation firstly to the community, in the sense of nation; secondly to that larger community represented by internationalism. This view, in all its modes of expression, is bound to be characterized by a respect for the convictions of others which is difficult to reconcile with the brilliant one-sidedness of the born party-man.

To the superficial observer this blend of conservative, liberal, social-radical and international elements may appear eclectic in the extreme. If so, it is because he fails to see that these elements have not been dragged together from different directions, but have grown out of the same basic view which, so far from indicating any desire to have a finger in every pie, or an inability to choose, leads on the contrary to having no home in any political party.[8]

The characteristic elements here, so evident in later years, are Hammarskjöld's recognition of common ground where none is obvious, his analytic flair, and his reliance on principle as a guide and unifying force. There is a fourth characteristic, a certain kindness or large decency. Hammarskjöld wasn't sentimental, but he was most certainly a humanist. Evident in virtually any entry for these years in *Markings*, his humanism had not yet found its public voice at the time he wrote the three Swedish articles. Although the private journal has seemed, to many observers, remote from Hammarskjöld's public life, the person he allowed himself to be there would come to the rescue of the public man and endow that public man with warmth.

What was the color palette of Hammarskjöld's developed humanism? In part that is clear in his elaboration of Schweitzer's view of communal welfare, though a few years later he would say it more simply, with more feeling. His humanism drew on close attention to what human beings do and to what we are, to our obstacles, struggles, and contradictions no less than our potential and achievements. It drew on his own woundedness: he could not stand apart as if unscathed. It drew on his sustained sense of surprise and inquiry into the odd, precious phenomenon of intelligent life. It viewed human life as a quest, a work in progress on every level, in which individual integrity and initiative are critically needed. It included cultural, spiritual, and religious dimensions without pinning the human project to a restrictive ideology. It gave a central place to the notions of human dignity and inalienable rights. And Janus-like it looked toward both past and future while finding reality, and opportunity, only here and now. A few months after becoming secretary-general, Hammarskjöld said: "The intensity of a man's faith in life may be gauged by his readiness to say yes to the past *and* yes to the future, to recognize the good he has inherited while being ready to accept change."[9]

Markings, 1950–1952

We could find parallels for these immensely difficult years in Hammarskjöld's personal life. The traditional Hindu notion of *tapasya* stands first in line. Literally "heat," it designates the austerities and sufferings to which the spiritual seeker must typically submit at some long stage on the way to liberation. *Tapasya*, writes A. K. Coomaraswamy, "might well be described as a raising of the spiritual potential to the sparking point."[10] Hammarskjöld knew the experience, although perhaps not the word. "Let everything be consumed in the fire of clear eyes," he wrote in what might have been mid-1950, "in the hope that something of value may be left which can be washed out of the ashes."[11]

He knew also Dante's experience of losing his bearings *"nel mezzo del cammin di nostra vita,"* midway along life's road, and finding himself in a dark wood, no longer knowing which way to turn: "Ah, how hard it is," read Dante's famous lines, "to tell what that wood was. . . . It is so bitter that death is hardly more so."[12] And at moments in these long years Hammarskjöld knew what Blaise Pascal knew just past the midpoint of his life through a direct experience of God's presence. "From about half past ten at night until about half past midnight," Pascal recorded,

FIRE.

GOD of Abraham, GOD of Isaac, GOD of Jacob
not of the philosophers and the learned.
Certainty. Certainty. Emotion. Joy. Peace.[13]

There are still other parallels—for example, in the way of inner poverty, harsh prelude to illumination, prescribed by the sixteenth-century Roman Catholic teacher, St. John of the Cross. Hammarskjöld knew his writings well and adopted his definition of faith as "the union of God and the soul," words periodically recalled in *Markings*.

But in the end we do best to set him free of known patterns to enter his own dark wood, to struggle toward a basis for well-being when none seemed very evident—to map out a world and reliable points of reference, zones of self and relationship needing attention, traps uncovered and examined for what they teach, sources of light and calm and the taste of happiness. Behind the reticent but pleasant façade of the cabinet minister and diplomat, a man had gone in search of himself. He understood that little time remained to steady his life and discover its meaning.

The characteristics of these years are alternation and breakthrough: alternation between illumination and despair, clarity and confusion, fellowship and loneliness; self-acceptance in a larger pattern of faith, service, and striving—and self-loathing in light of the poor, conceited, strapped thing one is. Beyond and within this often painful alternation there would prove to be certain fixed points, beautiful and encouraging, which made themselves known to him at quiet times in the city and during treks in the Swedish far north when his senses came more vividly alive. As well, there were solicitations from beyond or beneath the conscious mind; he began to remember and attend to his dreams, which could speak with strange authority. Three themes, then: the misery and pettiness of what one is—and not infrequently what others are; the warmth and promise of life, touched by an intuition of destiny that defeated his sense of defeat; and periodic recognitions of what he called "the unheard-of," the unfathomable greatness of a world in which God *is*, as he once put it. If the word "God" is opaque for some readers, then words he used late in life—"someone or something"—will do just as well.[14]

The impressionistic entries for these years in *Markings* make a jagged graph: lows and highs succeed each other without intervening middle values; stunning breakthroughs to inner peace and understanding leave no apparent trace, predict nothing about the character of succeeding entries. But there is nonetheless a steady discipline, abandoned neither at top nor bottom of his volatile experience in these years, the discipline to which he gives the name "conscious self-scrutiny."[15] Through good and bad, Hammarskjöld practices the Socratic discipline of the examined life as if his life depends on it, and that may have been factually so. From this point forward in *Markings*, if not earlier, the book joins a distinguished literature. It brings to mind the genial tone of Socratic self-inquiry; the bitter self-rejection of St. Paul ("I do the very thing I hate," Romans 7); the lucidity of Pascal's inquiry into self and other; on occasion the aphoristic edginess of La Rochefoucauld; and more still. Hammarskjöld's destination was unknowable, but he journeyed now with conscious self-scrutiny—at times seasoned with good humor, more often stark.

1950: From the storm center

Hammarskjöld as a social animal, striving and drifting among other social animals, is a recurrent theme. "The lap dog disguised himself as a lamb," he writes in 1950, "but tried to hunt with the wolves."[16] As readers we grasp at once that we are in a careerist, competitive milieu. But who, pray tell, is the lap dog? And why is the lap dog so befuddled that it disguises as the classic prey of wolves? That doesn't promise a happy ending. And is this deluded, aspiring lap dog Mr. Hammarskjöld or someone else? Often in entries for these years we don't know, and the answer when in doubt is probably "all of the above." This much is certain: what he saw in himself he saw in others, and vice versa. There are, of course, many entries specifically focused on his own person and conduct. "Out of indifference, ignorance, consciousness of an audience (were it only your own reflection in the mirror)—out of such reasons I have seen you take a risk or assume a responsibility."[17] On the same page he writes of "a blown egg" that floats nicely and "sails well on every puff of wind" but has no substance, no interior.[18] Is he speaking of himself or of another? A little further on, he clearly takes himself to task: "At any rate, your contempt for your fellow human beings does not prevent you, with a well-guarded self-respect, from trying to win their respect."[19]

A longer entry in the course of 1950 may best summarize Hammarskjöld's observations of the social animal—vain, self-serving, quick to compromise, not without aspirations—which he knows himself and others to be. It brings to light, as well, the great counterpoint to all that: conscious self-scrutiny.

> On whatever social level the intrigues are begun and the battle fought, and whatever, in other respects, the external circumstances may be, when what is at stake is his own position, even the "best head" unfailingly exhibits his naïveté. The possible tricks are so few. He who pursues such a course becomes as blind and deaf as the mountain cock courting his hen—especially at those moments when he imagines he is being most

astute. A grace to pray for—that our self-interest, which is inescapable, shall never cripple the capacity for conscious self-scrutiny with a sense of humor, which alone can save us.[20]

Were *Markings* nothing more than a confession of error it would be a small book but, as we have recognized in previous chapters, there is much more. The first four entries for 1950, serving as a gateway to the strenuous learning that lies ahead, announce themes and experiences of another order. The first recalls a transcendental promise, embedded in the words of an old Swedish hymn read aloud by Hammarskjöld's mother at every New Year: night is drawing nigh, with its threats and unknown forces, but in the end "where I am, there ye may be also." This lovely Gospel promise (John 14:3) could not be more reassuring or heartwarming. However, what follows at once in the next entry is alternation: a storm of self-doubt, a purple passage contrasting an imagined high-operatic death scene with the daily anguish and sense of "unspoken judgment hanging over his life," to which Hammarskjöld felt vulnerable, and by which he felt condemned.[21]

What follows is again alternation. A beautifully conceived poem draws on traditional spiritual ideas but also, perceptibly, on direct experiences of another quality of life and consciousness. The poem introduces and, with a clear sense of category, orders some of the key insights that will in time steady his life and equip him for challenges on a much larger stage.

> The chooser's happiness lies in his congruence with the
> chosen,
> The peace of iron filings obedient to the forces of the
> magnetic field—
> Consciousness emptied of all content,
> In restful harmony—
> This happiness is here and now,
> In the eternal cosmic moment.
> A happiness in you—but not yours.[22]

There is no stability here, no lasting coherence. Alternation resumes. Nonetheless, there is an inventory of possible sources of stability and coherence: obedience to a higher pattern, a state of awareness corresponding to the spacious emptiness of mature meditation, that alertness to the here and now which many spiritual traditions and poets describe as the place of encounter of time and eternity—and alongside all this, a quality of happiness notably impersonal, "in you—but not yours." These elements will move to the core of Hammarskjöld's full maturity to meet and fuse with other elements. But that time has not yet come: the very next entry speaks of "the anguish of loneliness" bringing "blasts from the storm center of the anguish of death," and of the little that may be "salvaged . . . from the nothing which some day will have been your life."[23]

The source of greatest agony in these years was loneliness. It would never quite cease. Hammarskjöld understood and accepted his loneliness in various ways as time went on, but understanding hadn't the power of permanent remedy. He would learn to accept solitariness—no wife and family, no close partner—as a practical condition of his wholly dedicated life as secretary-general. He would find it a natural though unhappy consequence of a certain shyness that had never been wrung out of him by some happy encounter in love. He would highly value the camaraderie that developed with UN colleagues as they pursued massively challenging tasks together. It slayed loneliness. And he would sometimes perceive loneliness in a warmer light as aloneness, consecrated and vibrantly aware. Among the entries in *Markings* for 1950, he describes what could be a Sami herdsman or the poet Bertil Ekman, who died young during a trek in the Norwegian wilderness: "He is one of those who has had the wilderness for a pillow, and called a star his brother. Alone. But loneliness can be a communion."[24] It remains that the Swedish words *ensam* and *ensamheten*, lonely and loneliness, recur throughout his journal. This is not a theme we can dismiss; in the next chapter we'll look more closely.

The alternation continues throughout 1950. "Like the bee," he writes, "we distill poison from honey for our self-defense—what happens to the bee if it uses its sting is well known."[25] Who won't hear in these words both bitter self-recognition and a pervasive sense of futility? Even ordinary nastiness is self-defeating. But there is also the counterpoint, the other melody, as when he writes of "the huge elementary mistake, the betrayal of that within me which is greater than I—in a complacent adjustment to alien demands."[26] In these years of *tapasya*, of heat building toward ignition, Hammarskjöld is aware of something axiomatic and uncorrupted within himself as perhaps within all human beings, however much it may be out of reach. "Vulgarity, lust, pride, envy—and longing," he writes.[27]

He prays, and in later years truly becomes a man of prayer. But in these years of harshest inner trial, prayer like all else is subject to doubt. "When the conflicting currents of the unconscious create engulfing whirlpools," he writes, "the waters can again be guided into *one* single current if the dam sluice is opened into the channel of prayer—and if that channel has been dug deep enough."[28] These are the years of digging; the channel is still shallow, though he knows how much it's needed. Some months later, he returns indirectly to the theme of prayer in a reflection about belief and unbelief. The alternation between darkness and light gathers in a single entry:

> God does not die on the day when we cease to believe in a personal deity, but we die on the day when our lives cease to be illumined by the steady radiance, renewed daily, of a wonder, the source of which is beyond all reason.[29]

We must try later to understand the place and fruitfulness of religious faith in Hammarskjöld's life—but for now it's enough to allow the drops to accumulate, the moments when he speaks from there and to there.

It is exhausting to read Hammarskjöld at this stage of his life, and exhausting to be Hammarskjöld. But there is no need here to accompany every alternation in these troubled years that broke and rebuilt him. "Is life so wretched?" he asks toward the end of 1950. "Isn't it rather your hands which are too small, your vision which is muddied? You are the one who must grow up."[30] Reasonable, quietly voiced insights of this kind show up here and there in these still early pages of *Markings*, and one knows that he'll be all right. On one hand he is often forlorn:

> How seldom growth and blossom
> How seldom fruit[31]

On the other hand he has no end of courage, as in this passage again from 1950, echoing in a contemporary voice his seventeenth-century mentor, Pascal:

> These wretched attempts to make an experience apprehensible (for my sake? for others?)—the tasks of the morrow—Y's friendship or X's appreciation of what I have done: paper screens which I place between myself and the void to prevent my gaze from losing itself in the infinity of time and space.
>
> Small paper screens. Blown to shreds by the first puff of wind, catching fire from the tiniest spark. Lovingly looked after—but frequently changed.
>
> This dizziness in the face of *les espaces infinis*—only overcome if we dare to gaze into them without any protection. And accept them as the

reality before which we must justify our existence. For this is the truth
we must reach to live, that everything *is* and we just in it.[32]

The conclusion returns us to the direct awareness he seems to have first
discovered in the Swedish far north: everything *is*, and we just in it.
Like Pascal, he recognizes dizzying infinity, scrappily hidden by "paper
screens"; and like Pascal he has the courage—or wishes for the courage—
not to forget that this is our common condition as human beings on a
small planet for a short time.

What is most difficult to convey from entries for these years in
Markings is not the critique of self and other, the weariness in society,
the loneliness, but rather the liberating moments that restore hope and
promise. Although deeply in character, they can seem out of character
and short of context because they have hidden causes well below the
surface. He is searching awkwardly, sufferingly, toward active religious
faith, uncluttered perception, a life of service—toward the release of his
immense gifts without debilitating drag. This multifaceted search opens
him to others with a warmth and willingness that his aversions, however
insistent, haven't hollowed out. If there was little open debate between
his parents, whom he identified as light and warmth—intellectual clarity and love of humanity—that debate is ignited now in a single soul at
times scarcely able to bear it.

Hammarskjöld's *Markings* has become a source of quotable quotes
in our day; do an Internet search and take in the harvest. Our journey
through 1950 now brings into view lines that have been engraved on
rocks in public parks and probably printed on refrigerator magnets.
However, just the first two lines, strong on their own, have become so
familiar. As the poem moves on it darkens, touched by the isolation of its
author, who had no one with whom to share and correct, test and rejoice
in the quest reported in these lines—hence his notion that the seeker
necessarily withdraws from the company of others.

> The longest journey
> Is the journey inwards.
> He who has chosen his destiny,
> Who has started upon the quest
> Toward his own ground
> (Is there such a ground?)
> He is still with you,

But outside the fellowship,
Isolated in your feelings
Like one condemned to death
Or one whom imminent farewell
Prematurely dedicates
To the loneliness which is the final lot of all.

Between you and him is distance,
Uncertainty—
Concern.

He will see you
At greater and greater distance,
Hear your voices fading,
Fainter and fainter.[33]

Apart from the memorable first lines, the jewel embedded in the poem is the firm recognition that henceforth there is and will be a quest for the ground of being. That the poet doubts whether some ultimate ground exists scarcely matters; he has no doubt of the rightness and, for him, the necessity of the inward journey. This has nothing to do with politics or the diplomatic life, it is personal; but the firm commitment recorded here to a quest that does not meet the eye and confers no obvious advantage in daily life provides a foundation for firmness and perceptiveness in years to come on the public stage. The language used here—especially the notion of the ground—derives from Hammarskjöld's now steady reading of the medieval Christian mystics, two of whom he mentions in a revealing comment during the UN years. "The counterpoint," he wrote to a friend, "to this enormously exposed and published life is Eckhart and Jan van Ruysbroeck. They really give me balance and a—more and more necessary—sense of humor. My salvation is to 'take the job damned seriously but never the incumbent'—but it has its difficulties. The roads to a basic conviction that in the deepest sense is religious can be most unexpected."[34] Readers familiar with the writings of Eckhart and Ruysbroeck may wonder at Hammarskjöld's ability to derive a sense of humor from their vast, lively, but scarcely lighthearted texts. Perhaps there is a parallel to the advice once received by an abbot, newly elected to his post, from an older colleague: "If you must be an abbot, then be a laughing abbot." An unshakeable core of religious faith and experience may allow abbots and secretaries-general to look at human folly and set things a little more right with a light touch.

We can now gather our belongings and take leave, for the moment, from this difficult year 1950; later we'll return briefly to assemble, from texts of this and the two years that follow, a better understanding of Hammarskjöld's persistent loneliness. As 1950 drew to a close, he was deepening his commitment to a life of service so thorough and focused that what he perceived as his own flawed person might after all find its place. He was revising his approach to relationship with others: "'Treat others as ends, never as means,'" he recorded in his journal from the writings of Immanuel Kant, "And myself as an end only in my capacity as a means . . . so that my *whole* being may become an instrument for that which is greater than I."[35]

He was also acknowledging, if anything more deeply, the primal reality of the present moment as the steady place, the sole place.

> It is *now*, in this very moment, that I can pay for all that I have received. The past and its load of debt are balanced against the present. And on the future I have no claim.
>
> Is not beauty created at every encounter between a man and life, in which he repays his debt by focusing on the living moment all the power which life has given him as an obligation? Beauty—for the one who pays his debt. For others, too, perhaps.[36]

That "perhaps" remains: he is unsure of the possible transaction, but he knows its location and has tasted something of the freedom—from past burden, future hope—that it requires.

The last entry for the year shows him engaged in a heartfelt moment of contact with another person: "What was required of me was to experience [his] reality not as an object but as a subject."[37] But Hammarskjöld's time of *tapasya*, of scorching trial, is not yet over.

1951–1952: The mirror and the doorway

There is a pattern in these years, as if light were repeatedly thrown against a wall: much light, in flashes, and more walls than can easily be counted. The alternation continues. As does Hammarskjöld's practice of conscious self-scrutiny, weighted as before toward ruthless recognitions of the lonely careerist, though that is far from the only theme. "As a climber," he writes in this self-critical vein, "you will have a wide sphere of activity even after, if that should happen, you reach your goal.

You can, for instance, try to prevent others from becoming better qualified than yourself."[38] Yet there is also guileless contact with others: "Before an important decision," he writes, "someone clutches your hand—a glimpse of gold in the iron-gray, the proof of all you have never dared believe."[39] What is it he never dared believe? Is it the possibility of generous, uncalculated warmth in the course of ordinary days—not set off in some better land, as a Mendelssohn song puts it, but here and now? As well, there are stunning insights that reach past solitude and loathing to another way of being: "To exist in the fleet joy of becoming," he writes in 1951, "to be a channel for life as it flashes by in its gaiety and courage, cool water glittering in the sunlight—in a world of sloth, anxiety, and intrusiveness. To exist for the future of others without being suffocated by their present."[40] The first insight here is free, courageous, mobile; it uncovers a way to be that doesn't hinder itself. The afterthought is promising in its commitment to service—but fastidious. To embrace the future of others, surely one has to touch and be touched by what they are at present and let them in: someone clutches your hand. Hammarskjöld remains at war with himself.

The war is conducted in skirmishes through these years. We can make order among the skirmishes, and it will serve us well to do just that, provided we keep in mind the source material: flashes of insight, contradictory fragments, a house of uneven cards. This, on the surface. Underneath, as we have already recognized, there is something else, steady and clear, to which Hammarskjöld is making his way. He acknowledges as much at the end of a midyear entry for 1951, which we'll have reason to explore in full on a later page: "Prevented by the duties of life on the surface from looking down into the depths, yet all the while being slowly trained by them to descend as a shaping agent into the chaos, whence the fragrance of white wintergreen bears the promise of a new belonging."[41] As in other memorable passages of *Markings*, Hammarskjöld draws on his experience of the sights and scents of the northern wilderness to put elusive meaning into words. His perception that the duties of life on the surface are a training for an incomparably greater role—to descend as a shaping agent into the chaos of human affairs—forecasts that there might after all be a link between what we identified as sanctuary some pages ago and the demands of public life.

We should remember that these were years of outstanding worldly achievement: he became a Swedish cabinet minister in 1951, soon assigned interim leadership of the Swedish delegation to the United Nations. He stood nearly at the summit of government, while within him two ways of being engaged in unseen warfare. From their sharp combat some new identity might emerge, but the outcome was wholly uncertain. All this he records in his private journal. It safeguards a fragile order; he writes to survive. He doesn't believe in his success, but what was there to believe in? "Never let success hide its emptiness from you," he had noted down in 1950, "achievement its nothingness, toil its desolation. And so keep alive the incentive to push on further, that pain in the soul which drives us beyond ourselves. Whither? That I don't know. That I don't ask to know."[42]

At some point in 1952, Hammarskjöld finds himself thinking at length about the personal application of a pair of metaphors—the mirror and the doorway—encountered in a film released a few years earlier, Jean Cocteau's *Orphée*. "Is my contact with others anything more than a contact with reflections?" he asks. "Who or what can give me the power to transform the mirror into a doorway?"[43] Intimacy continues to escape him except in the briefest of flashes. The unwilling self-enclosure continues. Again and again he finds vivid metaphors for his dilemma; though he cannot put it behind him, he knows the terrain. In one session of journal writing he draws inventively, but with utmost pain, from Swedish folklore: "The ride on the Witches' Sabbath to the Dark Tower where we meet only ourselves, ourselves, ourselves."[44] As in a mirror or multiplicity of mirrors. On another occasion he sees all too well the hidden poverty of his life: "Work as an anesthetic against loneliness, books as a substitute for people—! You say you are waiting, that the door stands open. For what?"[45] At least as ably as any well-educated person of his time, he could apply to his distress a range of psychological categories, but he is unwilling to settle the matter in that way. In a passage expressing that refusal, there is another emphatic repetition like "ourselves, ourselves." He draws a particularly subtle verbal portrait of an unnamed person, possibly a government colleague with abilities and contradictions somewhat like his own, and concludes as follows: "My friend, the popular psychologist, is certain of his diagnosis. And he has understood nothing, nothing."[46] The vehemence here surely reaches past the unnamed subject of this portrait to his own person. If we have any doubt on that score, it is settled by a late entry in *Markings* for 1951, where he returns to the theme: "How easy psychology has made it for us to dismiss the perplexing mystery with a label which assigns it a place in the list of common aberrations."[47] Facing himself and uncertain where honesty leads, Hammarskjöld insists on using means native to him and trusted, and only those means: the practice of conscious self-scrutiny, the understanding of human nature bred in him by decades of reading masterworks of Swedish, French, English, and German literature, the guidance offered by scripture and long Christian tradition, a maturing custom of prayer that opens a felt dialogue.

Markings in these troubled years is not only a furnace fired by *tapasya*, it is also a convenient archive of lessons learned. One such, quoted to me as his watchword by an American chief executive, reads as follows: "Only he deserves power who every day justifies it."[48] This was a concern that remained with Hammarskjöld, recurring in still richer form in 1955, some two years into his service as secretary-general: "Your position never gives you the right to command. It only imposes on you the duty of so living your life that others can receive your orders without being humiliated."[49] He was a lifelong explorer of the relations of power/responsibility/accountability/humility, in numerous ways and on numerous occasions, never relinquishing his interest. In these years just prior to UN service, he wrote a compressed fable: "Once upon a time, there was a crown so heavy that it could only be worn by one who remained completely oblivious to the glitter."[50] In this realm—call it maxims—there is much to be found in *Markings*. Some are obvious—"Never, 'for the sake of peace and quiet,' deny your own experience or convictions"[51]—though not necessarily easy. Others are remarkably subtle, little rebuses that spin in the mind as lasting questions:

> Mixed motives. In any crucial decision, every side of our character plays an important part, the base as well as the noble. Which side cheats the other when they stand united behind us in an action?
>
> —When, later, Mephisto appears and smilingly declares himself the winner, he can still be defeated by the manner in which we accept the consequences of our action.[52]

Some observations give the impression of standing apart from all else, as sudden discoveries or perceptions that delight him to know and record. "The aura of victory that surrounds a man of good will," he writes in the course of 1951, "the sweetness of soul which emanates from him—a flavor of cranberries and cloudberries, a touch of frost and fiery skies."[53] However much Hammarskjöld feels imprisoned in these years, such perceptions coming from who knows where send solace: perhaps, after all, he will not always fight the same interminable battles, turn in the same airless circles. Although he has not yet found steady footing, he too is a man of goodwill.

He is in search of his raison d'être, of purpose that transcends his personal misery and draws the elements of the strange puzzle into a life-sustaining pattern. About this he has no doubt. He knows, as well, that the object of his search calls for integrity and discretion: "How far," he writes in 1951, "both from muscular heroism and from the soulfully tragic spirit of unselfishness which unctuously adds its little offering to the sponge cake at a *Kaffeeklatsch*, is the plain simple fact that a man has given himself completely to something he finds worth living for."[54] He knows that the search for meaning is fundamental, existential: "That our pains and longings are thousandfold and can be anesthetized in a thousand different ways is as commonplace a truth as that, in the end, they are all *one*, and can only be overcome in *one way*. What you most need is to feel—or believe you feel—that you are needed."[55] He catches glimpses of terrain ahead in which his sense of isolation and futility could find a life-changing answer—but at what price, and is the price beyond his powers of payment? "Fated or chosen," he continues in the passage just cited, "—in the end, the vista of future loneliness only allows a choice between two alternatives: either to despair in desolation, or to wager so heavily on its 'possibility' that we win the right to life in a fellowship transcending the individual. But doesn't choosing the second call for the kind of faith which moves mountains?"[56] However things may turn out, faith is assigned a large role. His emphasis on possibility and the otherwise puzzling quotation marks around that word has its ultimate source in the Gospels: "With men this is impossible, but with God all things are possible" (Matthew 19:26).

Hammarskjöld is measuring the price to be paid for recognizing and accepting one's "true destiny" at a time, in 1951, when his true destiny must have appeared to be nothing more—and admittedly, nothing less—than a sequence of positions at the top of the Swedish government, and perhaps later in international institutions focused on economics and finance. Instinctively he rejects that path. "Dare he, for whom circumstances make it possible to realize his true destiny, refuse it simply because he is not prepared to give up everything else?"[57] The intensity of this language suggests that something more is working its way through him than reflection about his own life and its troubled juxtaposition of worldly success and intimate sorrow.

A young man, adamant

In our era of science and secular humanism at one end of the spectrum and religious fundamentalism at the other, an act of imagination may be needed to enter into the experience of a deeply thoughtful seeker for whom discovering and living a relation with God was central to his effort to come to terms with himself. For some of us, faith is a fiction that matters not at all. For others it is an invisible force capable of moving mountains in the world at large and of creating exquisite internal sensitivity. Those who do not have religious faith or something much like it (for example, the meditator's conviction that human awareness possesses unexplored clarities and depths) may feel distant from any pattern in which faith has a place. For them, Dag Hammarskjöld's religious search can seem a waking dream. Similarly, those for whom faith is a closed system may experience his lifelong quest and individual insights as a departure from soundness, tolerable in a man of his stature, nonetheless off course. Both attitudes will close Hammarskjöld out.

Some lives need vast context: mineral, vegetable, animal, human, divine. They need history, traditions, literature, music, visual art, all of which strike them as urgent messages, good news. And within that vast context, they need contact: for such people it is not enough to think things through; they need experience that registers on body and feeling because only that is convincing and transforming. Henry David Thoreau was of this kind. "Contact! contact!" he wrote in the powerful concluding pages of *The Maine Woods*. Hammarskjöld was of this kind and had more than a little in common with Thoreau (a topic for the next chapter).

Despite the turmoil of his intimate ordeal in 1950–52, certain insights and loyalties ensured Hammarskjöld's survival and almost imperceptibly gained in strength. The most central was his renewed sense of himself as a disciple of Jesus. Whatever his warmly religious mother taught him, whatever the brilliant archbishop taught him, whatever he absorbed from the person and writings of Albert Schweitzer had long since passed deep inside—and was largely overlooked during his university years when the skeptical philosophy of Axel Hägerström dominated Hammarskjöld's generation. But now he is reengaging with familiar texts such as the *Imitatio Christi* of Thomas à Kempis and almost certainly intensifying the "long read" of Meister Eckhart that accompanies him for the rest of his life. The Gospel teachings of Jesus and the narrative of the Passion offer him both guidance for the conduct of life and a concept of self-sacrifice that becomes crucially important for him.

At some point, perhaps in the winter of 1951, Hammarskjöld records the result of what must have been an extended private contemplation of the life and Passion of Jesus. In the longest continuous passage of *Markings*, he writes from an intimate perspective, as if Jesus were a contemporary and the events preceding his betrayal are just now unfolding, therefore needing fresh interpretation. The passage is an act of assimilation through which Hammarskjöld draws close to the sacred narrative, as if he were a nearby observer. It acknowledges Jesus as a hero making fateful choices, not merely as an officiant in a scripted mystery play. It sifts key moments for their meaning and, insistent on knowing what was thought and felt, novelistically reads the minds of participants in the drama. It dwells on the idea of possibility and of selfless fidelity to the greatest possibility, however dimly perceived, however heavy the possible consequences. It may be that the *imitatio Christi*, the aspiration to take up one's cross and live a wholly dedicated life, begins here for Hammarskjöld. The passage would suffer from abridgment. Here it is in full:

> A young man, adamant in his commitment to life. The one who was nearest to him relates how, on the last evening, he arose from supper, laid aside his garments, and washed the feet of his friends and disciples—an adamant young man, alone as he confronted his final destiny.
>
> He had observed their mean little play for his—his!—friendship. He knew that not one of them had the slightest conception why he had to act in the way that he must. He knew how frightened and shaken they would all be. And one of them had informed on him, and would probably soon give a signal to the police.
>
> He had assented to a possibility in his being, of which he had had his first inkling when he returned from the desert. If God required anything of him, he would not fail. Only recently, he thought, had he begun to see more clearly, and to realize that the road of possibility might lead to the Cross. He knew, though, that he had to follow it, still uncertain as to whether he was indeed "the one who shall bring it to pass,"

but certain that the answer could only be learned by following the road to the end. The end *might* be a death without significance—as well as being the end of the road of possibility.

Well, then, the last evening. An adamant young man: "Know ye what I have done to you? . . . And now I have told you before it comes to pass. . . . One of you shall betray me. . . . Whither I go, ye cannot come. . . . Will'st thou lay down thy life for my sake? Verily I say unto thee: the cock shall not crow. . . . My peace I give unto you. . . . That the world may know that I love the Father, and as the Father gave me commandment, even so I do. . . . Arise, let us go hence."

Is the hero of this immortal, brutally simple drama in truth "the Lamb of God that taketh away the sins of the world"? Absolutely faithful to a divined possibility—in that sense the Son of God, in that sense the sacrificial Lamb, in that sense the Redeemer. A young man, adamant in his commitment, who walks the road of possibility to the end without self-pity or demand for sympathy, fulfilling the destiny he has chosen—even sacrificing affection and fellowship when the others are unready to follow him—into a new fellowship.[58]

I would not say that this passage is brilliant as literature; it has a harsh sincerity. But it is brilliant in its search for the human texture of the Passion, brilliant in its perception of possibility as a magnet drawing life forward, brilliant in its understanding of the need for courage and clarity.

Hammarskjöld's recurrent focus on possibility is striking; as if it were a lighted object, the word acquires a substantiality it often lacks. He seems to be pondering not only the destiny of the young man adamant, but a much closer one, his own. He glimpses in the Gospel of John a sequence of recognitions: possibility dawns at first as a purely internal "assent to a possibility in his being"; later Jesus "begins to see more clearly . . . the road of possibility" stretching before him, though he needn't take it; and finally he is "absolutely faithful to a divined possibility" and willing to "walk the road of possibility to the end"—perhaps toward immense suffering, certainly toward what Hammarskjöld enigmatically calls "a new fellowship." We have encountered his concern with fellowship in earlier pages, and will encounter it again. We have heard him say that the person who seeks the ground of being necessarily withdraws from fellowship. But here that isn't so: fellowship of some unstated, mysterious character awaits Jesus and, by extension, disciples who follow his way to the end.

When *Markings* was posthumously published in Sweden in 1963, some Scandinavian journalists reacted vehemently, accusing Hammarskjöld of a Christ complex, of delusively believing himself to be a Christ figure. In a Scandinavian culture increasingly secular as the twentieth century moved on, the attitude of Christian discipleship, and the acute form of discipleship traditionally called the imitation of Christ, seemed to some readers alien, even mentally unbalanced. Other critics and readers rapidly came to the rescue to shed light on the nearly forgotten context in Christian tradition from which Hammarskjöld derived hope and nourishment. (See chapter 17 for an account of this war of words.) A more recent exploration by Hans Küng, the very brilliant, rebellious Catholic priest and teacher, puts the issue with remarkable clarity:

> [Jesus] is for believers the living authoritative embodiment of his cause. In all that he is, in all that he said, did and suffered, he personifies the cause of God and the cause of humanity. And so he calls us to discipleship. For some this is too lofty a word, and in its challenge almost alarming. But do not let us misunderstand what discipleship means. Certainly the living Christ does not call merely for adoration without practical commitment, nor simply for us to say "Lord, Lord" or "Son of God, Son of God." But neither does he call us to literal imitation. It would be presumptuous to want to imitate him. No, he calls for personal discipleship, not in imitation but in correlation, in *correspondence*. That means that I commit myself to him and pursue my own way in accordance with his direction—for each of us has his or her own path to follow.[59]

Hammarskjöld would almost certainly have accepted every word here; this is what the imitation of Christ means, though there is no need to retire the traditional expression, *imitatio Christi*, with its centuries-old root in Thomas à Kempis, whom he read faithfully during the UN years.

There are two further entries concerning Jesus and the Passion in these pages of *Markings* for 1951. They have something of the character of afterthoughts, once the main lines of perception have been laid down. In the first and more important of the two, he confronts the possibility of mixed motives, an issue to which we know he was vigilantly alert:

> Assenting to his possibility—why? Does he sacrifice himself for others, *yet for his own sake*—in megalomania? Or does he realize himself for the sake of others? The difference is that between a monster and a man. "A new commandment I give unto you: that ye love one another."[60]

I do not think that Hammarskjöld is questioning Jesus's motives here, although that is the form taken by the entry. He is in his own camp, looking at his own possibility of selfless discipleship. The monster and the man dwell within, he has been observing them for years, and perhaps only the force of the new commandment cited from John 13:34, which bears on discipleship, can resolve their relations favorably: "A new commandment I give to you, that you love one another; even as I have loved you, that you also love one another. By this all men will know that you are my disciples, if you have love for one another."

This is Mr. Hammarskjöld, aet. 46, a Swedish government man, capable of close calculation of interests including his own, struggling to put his destiny, whatever it might be, under the sign of a new commandment.

It comes as a surprise that in later pages of *Markings* and in his public life Hammarskjöld does not frequently refer to Jesus. On occasion, yes—for example, in a beautiful short prayer of 1956 in the privacy of his journal, in which Jesus is addressed as "brother":

> *Before* Thee, Father,
>   In righteousness and humility,
> *With* Thee, Brother,
>   In faith and courage,
> *In* Thee, Spirit,
>   In stillness.[61]

Before, with, in: it is a map of spiritual contact that converts the traditional dogma of the Trinity into intimate experience. But this still lies ahead; it is not yet won, and it seems unlikely that such perceptions are ever definitively won—they are moments in a life. In future years the teachings and example of Jesus would never become for Hammarskjöld merely rote points of reference. His keen sense of discipleship remained a largely private matter. In the prayers recorded in *Markings* he almost always addresses God as "Thou," without distinction of Persons.

Through the UN years as Hammarskjöld traveled worldwide, met thoughtful people, and read in non-Western literature and scripture, his spiritual horizons widened. He came to admire—and to explore both in his journal and in public settings—the language and imagery of the early Chinese classics, Buddhism, the Bhagavad Gita, Judaism, and Rumi. He recognized the convergence of wisdom, not in every detail but in sufficient detail. He acknowledged with his Pakistani colleague Ahmed

Bokhári "the possibility of a synthesis of great traditions on which it is the task of our generation to build one world," and knew all too well "the difficulties and tensions which must accompany such a process." On principle, one would hope that in his position of global influence and responsibility he would find his way to something resembling a universal spirituality drawing on world traditions, and this is in fact what occurred. Yet he began as a Christian, lived as a Christian, and had with him on his last journey to the Congo a copy of the *Imitatio Christi*.

Dreams and awakenings

Men and women who search for the ground of being have decisions to make along the way. One such is to decide whether to admit—as food for thought, crumbs of guidance—whatever can be remembered of dreams. For some, dreams are negligible. For others, they are irresponsible. For still others, they represent a dazzling zone where what we are as individuals encounters what we are as members of an ancient race or as exiles from some larger, mysterious whole with which the dreaming mind connects. Hammarskjöld was a willing dreamer, or at least became one during these difficult years when every clue counted. Where he is concerned, the category "dreams" needs to be elastic enough to include waking visions that seem occasionally to have swept through his mind (the word "sweep" is his own) and left messages, sometimes poignantly beautiful, sometimes full of foreboding and unease.

Hammarskjöld's perhaps instinctive decision was to admit. He had noticed the indicative power of dreams, of the mind when it abandons common grammar and syntax to become a strange acrobat. Hammarskjöld had loved poetry throughout his life, and dreams are a spontaneous poetry, signed by oneself as author yet curiously other. Such paradoxes interested him. They shed light on hidden frontiers between one state of mind and another, one state of being and another; they shed light on identity. The existence and meaning of frontiers in the inner life became important to him in these years; the words "at the frontier" in some entries in *Markings* signal the beginning of rare adventures in understanding. "Where does the frontier lie?" he asks in an entry for mid-1951, and continues:

> Where do we travel to in those dreams of beauty satisfied, laden with significance but without comprehensible meaning, etched far deeper

on the mind than any witness of the eyes? Where all is well—without fear, without desire.

Our memories of physical reality, where do they vanish to? While the images of this dream world never grow older. They live—like the memory of a memory.[62]

Immediately after this questioning text, as if to substantiate what he means, he recounts three dreams that arc through a redemptive sequence from darkness (with a glimmer of light) to images of mixed promise and foreboding and, at last, to gentle dawn in the wilderness and a wide, welcoming vista seen from an open slope. He would, of course, have noticed this pattern and wished to set it down; it is far from a random selection. *Markings* even in these years of ordeal records the journey of a sophisticated individual in search of sure direction and fulfillment, and when things fall into place he is not slow to recognize that it's so.

The sequence of dreams serves as the preface to Hammarskjöld's account of an inner experience of surpassing beauty. Does respect for dreams—richly meaningful ones—help to open the mind or spirit to further possibilities? No clue in *Markings* answers this question, but we should no longer think of Hammarskjöld as predominantly a constricted person, warring with demons and likely to lose. Something more now emerges, a capacity for vision that breaks through the common ceiling and sees far. I cannot account for this breakthrough; it follows no logical A to B. Yet it is characteristic of the man as we shall come to know him in later years. After the dream sequence, he sets down words that we have already in part encountered:

Now. When I have overcome my fears—of others, of myself, of the underlying darkness:

at the frontier of the unheard-of.

Here ends the known. But, from a source beyond it, something fills my being with its possibilities.

Here desire is purified into openness: each action a preparation, each choice a yes to the unknown.

Prevented by the duties of life on the surface from looking down into the depths, yet all the while being slowly trained by them to descend as a shaping agent into the chaos, whence the fragrance of white wintergreen bears the promise of a new belonging.

At the frontier—[63]

There are familiar values here, but also new ones not previously encountered. We know something of his discovery of the present moment, here and now. But little in earlier pages of *Markings* prepares us for the simple clarity of his declaration, "I have overcome my fears." We know something of his awareness of frontiers, but here we find his first, by no means last, reference to "the unheard-of." I have counseled with Swedish and American friends concerning the proper translation and possible sources in literature of Sw. *det oerhörda*, literally the unheard-of. One might translate it as "the unfathomable"; the new Italian translation of *Markings* opts for "the imponderable," *l'imponderabile*. All choices point back to a book that Hammarskjöld read closely as a young man, Rudolf Otto's *The Idea of the Holy*, but only in a general way, and no doubt also to Meister Eckhart, but only in a general way. This is Hammarskjöld's word, then, best translated as "the unheard-of."

Up to a point, he characterizes the frontier of the unheard-of. "Here ends the known. But from a source beyond it, something fills my being with its possibilities." There is a clue here: the return to the notion of possibility, so dominant in the passage about the young man adamant. Whatever the unknown possibilities may prove to be, they belong to a renewed world in which inner striving and outer striving at last cohere — and may well be governed, at least in part, by the "new commandment." At the frontier of the unheard-of, rules and energies differ. There is no indifference or weariness. Consciousness is keen, feelings affirmative and vastly alive. Possibilities not even considered from day to day become central, and they can be articulated. Here "desire is purified into openness: each action a preparation, each choice a yes to the unknown." Ordinary acts of living become full of significance and promise; transformation is possible; even a new belonging might dissolve that chronic sense of not really belonging anywhere. The old round of yes and no, private misery and public success, vanishes at the frontier of the unheard-of. There is an intervention from well past that frontier. Yet nowhere in this remarkable account does Hammarskjöld use the word "God." Whatever stands waiting on the other side of the frontier is unknown. He experiences strictly on its own terms what can justly be called a moment of true mysticism or transcendent vision. He is a learned innocent arrived in God's world. He has no words but his own for what he sees and feels.

"Each choice a yes." Generations of readers of *Markings* have been moved by Hammarskjöld's discovery of his unconditional yes at the beginning of the UN years. He sets a new standard for yes. We'll look later at those pages of *Markings*. Most readers have sensibly assumed that Hammarskjöld's unreserved yes emerged in response to the extraordinary opportunity he was offered at the United Nations. The evidence here suggests that it's not quite so. A second source of his simple, stunning capacity to affirm lies in a visionary experience that must have swept through him at some time during yet another year of personal torment, 1951.

There are precedents, none closer than the seventeenth-century mathematician Blaise Pascal's visionary session, mentioned early in this chapter. But we decided to view Dag Hammarskjöld's experience in the singular, as a separate adventure. It is unkind to smudge across from one fine thing to another.

Now you know

We need to find our way out of this chapter but, as if it were a crowded cocktail party, there are still a few conversations worth our time before reaching the door. The year 1951 seems to close a little more peacefully for Hammarskjöld; one would think that inevitable after such an experience. But the pain of loneliness doesn't diminish for long, and like physical pain it competes for attention. That summer and fall he must have gone trekking in Lapland. He writes beautiful lines about "the sacrament of the arctic summer night: an odor of ice and bursting buds,"[64] and some months later evokes "autumn in Lapland." That passage continues:

> The warm rain-laden east wind rushes down the dried-up river bed. On its banks, yellowing birches tremble in the storm.
>
> The opening bars in the great hymn of extinction. Not a hymn to extinction or because of it. Not a hymn in spite of extinction. But a dying which is the hymn.[65]

In the presence of Nature, which earlier that year he reverently described as "great Nature," Hammarskjöld is adept at removing barriers and entering into communion. He knew himself to be nearly blind to the natural scene if he was thinking too much—and as awake as can be when he was quietly aware, a living seismograph. During the UN years he would strive to empty his awareness of personal concerns in order to perceive others—fellow diplomats, political adversaries, and of course friends—in a receptive, uncluttered way. "Here desire is purified into openness," we have heard him say, and we understand through these words that he had unusual inner resources and cared to develop them further. That was partly an internal religious process, partly a challenge to conscious self-scrutiny—and partly a matter of hiking. The following entry from *Markings* is somewhat analytically expressed, but if we read patiently we'll see that its topic is the ground rules for communion.

> The extrahuman in the experience of great Nature. This does not allow itself to be reduced to an expression of our human reactions, nor can we share in it by expressing them. Unless we each find a way to chime in as one note in the organic whole, we shall only observe ourselves observing the interplay of its thousand components in a harmony outside our experience of it as harmony.
>
> Landscape: only your immediate experience of the detail can provide the soil in your soul where the beauty of the whole can grow.[66]

He had the heartfelt goal of preserving this quality of awareness, a treasure from Lapland, during his life in cities among people. "To preserve the silence within," he writes in 1952, "—amid all the noise."[67] It wasn't merely a romantic ideal; good evidence in later years shows that he worked on it.

Despite every effort and discovery, every prayer that did and didn't find its way into *Markings*, periodic waves from what he once called "the storm center of death" continue to wash through him. As we know, he considers suicide and rejects it: "No! It may be that death is to be your ultimate gift to life: it must not be an act of treachery against it."[68] He ponders "this bleak world of mine" and "asks for the absurd: that life shall have a meaning. . . . I dare not believe, I do not see how I shall ever be able to believe: that I am not alone."[69] And as if life refuses to leave him fixed in one place, light or dark, he returns on another memorable occasion to "the frontier of the unheard-of."

> Now you know. When the worries over your work loosen their grip, then this experience of light, warmth, and power. From without—a sustaining element, like air to the glider or water to the swimmer. An intellectual hesitation which demands proofs and logical demonstration prevents me from "believing"—in this, too. Prevents me from expressing and interpreting this reality in intellectual terms. Yet, through me

there flashes this vision of a magnetic field in the soul, created in a timeless present by unknown multitudes, living in holy obedience, whose
words and actions are timeless prayer.

—"The Communion of Saints"—and—within it—an eternal life.[70]

This altogether striking passage gathers up many themes we have been
following: the visionary capacity based in a deeply religious sensibility, the argument with himself even here, the surpassing beauty of what
is seen, the longing for fellowship. His transformation of worn words
in the Apostles' Creed (the Communion of Saints) into direct vision
is remarkable.

Fellowship was now making its approach, not precisely in a community of saints, but would a community of nations do? "Pray," he wrote
toward year-end 1952, "that your loneliness may spur you into finding
something to live for, great enough to die for."[71] As events unfolded, it
wasn't he who found it; he was found.

5

Monastic Enough?

Consider two scenes. It is late March, 1953. Dag Hammarskjöld, known to few reporters covering UN affairs, has just been nominated by the Security Council as the next secretary-general. A UN press officer calls a hasty press conference to convey the bare essentials of Hammarskjöld's background for tomorrow's papers. He runs through various official positions—chairman of the Board of Governors of the Bank of Sweden, state secretary in the Department of Finance, vice-chairman of the Swedish delegation to the United Nations—when, according to an eyewitness, "a voice from the crowd broke in loudly: 'And a fairy!'"[1]

The next scene is quieter. At some point in 1954, a society journalist visited Hammarskjöld's newly furnished apartment on the Upper East Side in New York to research a short illustrated article on his taste. At the time he was still a new man in town and an object of discreet curiosity. It wasn't remotely Hammarskjöld's style to publicize his personal life, but in his first year as secretary-general he seems to have been experimenting with communications—what helps, what might be tried, what does no harm. This visit would have been in the harmless category. The journalist discovered that, apart from a few family antiques, his taste ran to austere contemporary Scandinavian furnishings, and the overall color scheme was subdued though with bright woolen carpets here and there. What was there to report? The journalist must have looked disappointed. There is no record of their conversation, but at much the same time a UN photographer showed up to have a look, and she also was disappointed. Hammarskjöld turned to her with a remark that echoes well beyond its immediate context: "Monastic enough for you?"[2]

Coming upon this life now long after Hammarskjöld's passing, we have choices to make. We can apply to him the intrusive standards—half Freud, half paparazzi—of today's culture, as if we have the right to know how he spent his nights. We can turn away from all such considerations as a matter of elementary respect for privacy. Or we can do our best to adopt a third approach, neither voyeuristic nor disembodied, that advances this book's concern to shed light on Hammarskjöld's internal composition and lifework. Private and public intersect at some points, as he acknowledged by authorizing his literary executor to publish *Markings*. It is clear that his recurrent loneliness in the years just prior to his UN service was both a severe personal misery and a powerful inducement to "find himself," to know what he was about. Loneliness entered into the deep equations he would write as he lived, above all his aspiration to serve selflessly and his engagement with a spiritual dimension that puts personal sufferings in a new perspective.

There are two dimensions here, political and personal. Politics first. Eyewitnesses from Hammarskjöld's era have pointed to two smear campaigns in the course of his tenure as secretary-general. Widely spaced in time and differently sourced, they were equally intended to damage him at a time when homosexuality was closeted. Allegations could harm a public career, facts could ruin one. The tragic fate of Alan Turing, the English mathematician of overwhelming genius, founder of computer science, unfolded at just this time: subject in 1952 to a criminal prosecution in England for homosexuality and given the choice of prison or chemical emasculation, he chose the latter and ended his life two years later. The years between Turing's suicide in 1954 and the knighting of Elton John, the magical British musician, in 1998 saw vast changes in society and law in Great Britain and many other countries.

The reporter's rude comment at that initial press conference stemmed from the first whisper campaign, launched by the outgoing Norwegian secretary-general Trygve Lie and his loyal lieutenants—this according to Lie's own, relatively sympathetic biographer. A complex figure with redeeming virtues, Lie can easily seem a rough prelude to Hammarskjöld, but this commandingly stout, politically outspoken individual, serving as secretary-general in the years 1946–52, took the United Nations from early days through chaotic Cold War disputes to the completion of the UN's vast and beautiful headquarters buildings in Manhattan. This was hardly a small achievement.

He did not go gently when the time came. Shunned and ignored by the Soviet Union and its allies after the UN involved itself as the combatant in the Korean War, he had served with difficulty after June 1950, through what was to be a three-year extension of his term in office. A replacement was needed. According to George Ivan Smith, Hammarskjöld's trusted colleague and friend, Lie and his circle did what they could to derail Hammarskjöld's nomination or, failing that, undermine his reception before he arrived to take up his duties.[3] They are said on good evidence to have organized a classic smear. The chronicler of Lie's UN career, James Barros, provides detail:

> For Lie the selection of Hammarskjöld was traumatic. . . . He undoubt-edly had hoped that the stalemated negotiations on a successor would lead to his reappointment. . . . Lie's vilification of his successor, which can only be called sordid, now commenced. At his politest, he observed that Hammarskjöld would allow the office's political functions to "wither." . . . He observed to [Lester Pearson, president of the General Assembly, that] Hammarskjöld would be nothing more than a clerk. Lie hit his nadir when he circulated a rumor that Hammarskjöld was a homosexual, although there is not a shred of evidence to prove the al-legation. For example, he approached the Greek representative, Alexis Kyrou, and queried whether he was going to support the "fairy." . . . Unfortunately, the rumor lingered. It was not one of Lie's finest hours.[4]

So there we have the charming word, "fairy," a relic from the prehistory of social changes that have ensued since those years.

When Hammarskjöld arrived in New York on April 9th to take up his duties, Lie met him at the airport. Some traditional photographs were taken: the two men cordially greeting one another, Hammarskjöld making an initial statement to the press corps—images of that kind. But another photograph was preserved over the years by the editors of *Life* magazine, presumably because they perceived in it something more than an awkward gesture lasting an instant (fig. 8). It *is* an awkward gesture on Lie's part, but also covertly menacing. He must have meant to direct Hammarskjöld's attention to their left but his thumb became entangled in Hammarskjöld's suit, yielding the image of an intrusive hand placed over Hammarskjöld's middle and heart.

Intrusion took more than one form. When Hammarskjöld moved in-to temporary quarters arranged for him by the UN in the posh Waldorf Towers—the search for a suitable apartment had just begun—a UN secu-rity person rang the US State Department to report that Hammarskjöld was "shacked up" with some young man. The young man in question was Per Lind, a Swedish foreign ministry colleague whom Hammarskjöld particularly trusted, there to help him make the transition to the UN. The State Department is said to have reacted with indignation over the telephone call, and a small posse of senior UN diplomats, at last fed up, called a private meeting with Trygve Lie to insist that he close down the campaign of slander or suffer nasty personal consequences which lay within their administrative scope to arrange.[5]

Brian Urquhart, Hammarskjöld's eminent biographer and close colleague, has commented several times and without equivocation about the smear campaigns. One of those comments bears on this early period:

> Stupid or malicious people sometimes made the vulgar assumption that, being unmarried, he must be homosexual, though no one who knew him well or worked closely with him thought so. When he was confronted, in the first month of his Secretary-Generalship, with the rumors to this effect then being put about by his predecessor, Hammarskjöld remarked that if there had been any element of truth in the story, he would not, and could not in the prevalent state of public opinion on the question of homosexuality, have accepted the office.[6]

One of Hammarskjöld's early interpreters recorded a somewhat similar conversation: "When a close colleague thought it only fair to warn Hammarskjöld of the rumors, he replied quite simply with an emphatic disclaimer: 'Before God, they are untrue.'"[7] A related incident occurred in 1954 or '55, when a young member of Hammarskjöld's staff felt duty-bound to report to him that an American gossip magazine had run an article claiming that the secretary-general "has four handsome body-guards" and had tossed off an innuendo on that basis. It wasn't remotely true: he had inherited from Trygve Lie one security guard and had the warmest of relations, nearly familial, with Bill Ranallo, his wife and children. By his own account, the young staff member said to Hammar-skjöld, "Excuse me sir, did you hear this, did you see this?" "Yes," he said. "Well, Victor, it's like this. I don't care what they write." I said, "I would sue them." "Yes, and why?"[8] He was not indifferent to the rumors; they hurt. But he knew enough not to reinforce them by responding.

The second smear campaign occurred during the Suez Crisis of fall 1956 through winter 1957, when two permanent members of the Security Council, Britain and France, conspired with Israel to launch a surprise attack on Egypt. G. I. Smith, always firm in defense of Hammar-skjöld, recalled that era years later in a letter to the editor of *The Times* of London, in which he took issue with a mid-1980s BBC documentary on diplomacy which yet again cited the rumor. Smith wrote, in part:

I do know how, for political reasons, such a rumor was spread by officials of one of the States involved in the Suez affair. I was at the time Director of External Relations at the UN and received from our information centers newspaper clippings about UN affairs. Suddenly one week's coverage from Paris contained a batch of stories, so similar in content and phrase as to make it obvious that the stories in the various journals came from the same source in the same week. The burden of them was that Hammarskjöld was a homosexual and in an alleged T. E. Lawrence tradition had such affection for Arabs that he favored their interests against those of Israel. . . . I felt obliged to show Hammarskjöld the clippings. He read them and said, "Imagine the state of mind of people who can write such stories."[9]

We catch Hammarskjöld's tone here, close to his tone with the staff member clutching a copy of *Hush Hush* magazine: weary, philosophical, even slightly compassionate.

Among the sources for the French smear campaign may have been a remarkably unsavory character, Fernand Legros, who claimed in print many years later to have had an affair with Hammarskjöld before the UN years and to have lived for some period, like a house cat, comfortably planted in Hammarskjöld's New York apartment. He also claimed to have been in the Congo and to have been warned off by the CIA from flying in the doomed airplane carrying Hammarskjöld to a peace negotiation. No one else has recorded any of this; surely someone would have seen him somewhere?

Yet this nonsense has had an impact. His claims found literary permanence of a sort in a 1976 biography of Legros written by Roger Peyrefitte, a prolific, brashly homosexual author with a taste for scandal real and imagined, who put allegations about Hammarskjöld in the first pages of the book so that no reader would miss them.[10] Those pages— part of the sanctity of literature, after all—almost certainly explain why the entirely undocumented allegations of Legros, relayed by Peyrefitte, still occasionally turn up on the Internet, passed from believing author to believing author. Legros's life story must have appealed to Peyrefitte as an example of modern picaresque, a nasty one. First a dancer, then an art dealer, Legros formed a partnership with the legendary art forger Elmyr de Hory, sold masses of fake paintings particularly to wealthy American collectors, and eventually served jail time in France for the profitable fraud. On his side, Peyrefitte seems to have outworn his welcome both in the nascent gay rights movement and in literature. An obituary (d. 2000) recalled "his often ludicrous fabrications, though they were always delivered with great style and conviction, and with an effrontery that was amusingly malicious."[11] We need a motive, don't we, if this is a mystery thriller? In the 1930s Peyrefitte had a career in French diplomacy which foundered twice: he was dismissed for homosexuality in 1940, reinstated by the collaborationist Vichy government, dismissed again after the war as a collaborator, and though cleared of the second charge, was by then a successful author who preferred not to rejoin the postwar diplomatic service. Was he jealous of Hammarskjöld's renown as a diplomat? Is that the motive behind the thriller, apart from whatever mean pleasure or profit he and Legros derived from claiming to "out" Hammarskjöld fifteen years after his death? And then, the French in general, led by President de Gaulle, didn't much like "Monsieur H."

There was, all the same, a little fun to be had around Hammarskjöld's status as a confirmed bachelor. For example, a journalist long on the UN beat, Pauline Frederick, whom Hammarskjöld held in high regard, once had a private chat with him, which she later recalled:

> I said to him one day, "You know, Mr. Secretary-General, if you would only take a strong stand on some of these controversial issues that are coming up, you'd give us reporters something to do, we'd be able to report." And he said, "Well, I feel this way: that I'm the parents of a wayward son, who do not scold the son while he is in the midst of the crisis, but wait until that passes, and before he gets involved in another one, they try to reason with him, and explain the facts of life." And I asked, "Well, how does a bachelor know about these things?" And he said, "I have nieces and nephews."[12]

On occasion, society twittered in a pleasant way. Early in his tenure at the UN, the *New York Times* plunged cheerfully into the topic of Mr. Hammarskjöld's perceived problems as a host: "Single women who have hopes of being picked by the United Nations' new chief, a bachelor, to help him preside at official parties are out of luck. Any hostess selected by Secretary-General Dag Hammarskjöld must be married, and her husband should be present to signify his consent and approval. This word was passed on today by the United Nations' top authority on the subject, Count Jehan de Noue, Chief of Protocol. Since Mr. Hammarskjöld already has indicated a preference for informality, M. de Noue feels that the question of a hostess may not soon arise."[13] At least that much was settled early.

We should call to the witness stand two gay men whom Hammarskjöld counted among his friends: Sverker Åström, a Swedish diplomat who had worked with him in Sweden and later saw him from time to time at the UN, and W. H. Auden, the Anglo-American poet who was a not infrequent guest at Hammarskjöld's table in New York and later cotranslator of *Markings*. We'll have reason to consult Auden again in this chapter, but for the time being we should be aware of thoughts he published two months after Hammarskjöld's death. Speaking of the life of a UN secretary-general—the one he knew or presumably anyone in the office—he noted that "the many political enemies he is bound to make will keep close watch on his private life in the hope of finding some weakness or irregularity they can use as a weapon against him. Hammarskjöld accepted personal isolation as a necessary condition of his post, but he needed will power to maintain it. Though he would never have complained to others—he was completely free from self-pity—he was, I believe, a lonely man, not a self-sufficient one."[14] Recognizing that these lines can be interpreted in various ways, I believe that Auden never referred to Hammarskjöld as gay, though he surely decrypted with ease every signal, intended and unintended, that passes between gay men. As we'll soon see, in his translation Auden very occasionally "wrote into" *Markings* homoerotic sentiments that are absent from the Swedish original. Swedish authors have faulted him for this and many other shortcomings, and Auden's biographer, acknowledging the errors, has explained that Auden often inserted signs of his own preoccupations into texts where in-group friends would discover and understand them.[15] On his side, writing in 1959 to a Swedish friend, Hammarskjöld expressed a superbly urbane, rather disappointed view of Auden:

> With Auden I still have good contact (he commutes between New York, Oxford, and his farm in Niederösterreich). We are in fact really good friends—in the way it's possible at all to be friends with Auden, who covers his brilliant intelligence and sensibility behind a mask, amply moistened by the local strong brews and a professorial bonhomie that fends off attempts at searching discussion.[16]

On balance, we haven't gained much insight into the issue at hand by considering Hammarskjöld's relations with Auden, though Auden's insight about the vulnerability of the secretary-general to scandal has been worth collecting.

Sverker Åström's witness could not be clearer. Ten years younger than Hammarskjöld, a Swedish diplomat entrusted for many decades with highly responsible roles at home and abroad, he is said to have informed his government superiors that he was gay in order to avoid the possibility of blackmail but "came out" publicly only at the age of 88, long since retired, and for a time joined his name to Swedish gay rights efforts. In these late years he has written and spoken about Dag Hammarskjöld, to whom he reported in the years just prior to Hammarskjöld's UN service. Åström has categorically stated that Hammarskjöld was not gay, and just as categorically stated that they were good friends who took weekend trips together in the early 1950s in Hammarskjöld's beat-up Citroën. They would visit sites of historical interest. They would walk in the woods and discuss great issues at great length. If Åström seriously felt that his admired friend's reputation needed protection, his strategic sense as a diplomat would surely have guided him away from recounting such memories. In an interview with me several years ago, he offered a thoughtful and candid response: "You can ask the question of what kind of sexuality he did have. I don't know if he had sexual relations with women, but I'm certain he had no sexual relations with men. I happen to be homosexual myself, and that makes one more observant, but I couldn't observe any sign of that, which would have been quite natural if we were both homosexual. . . . You know, he was reading all the time and had read several of the novels of Jean Genet, and he would discuss them—but without any nuance of personal interest."[17]

Åström likes to tell a story about mountaineering in the northern wilderness with his intrepid colleague and friend. It was a long trip to a distant place (Hammarskjöld had written to a friend and government colleague just before setting out: "If nothing occurs, I hope to go north the day after tomorrow together with Åström and a like-minded climbing partner. I am then cut off from modern means of communication for about a fortnight.")[18] It is irresistible to record here Åström's published account of a hair-raising exploit and its tranquil aftermath:

> In the summer of 1950 I hiked in the mountains with Dag and the great photographer and outdoors expert, Gösta Lundqvist. We climbed Sulitälma. The peak is reached via a twenty-meter-high sheer

cliff. Dag and Gösta swung themselves up. Then they threw me down a rope and, with death clutching at my heart, I crawled my way up. Later, we pitched camp below the mountain. Hammarskjöld and Lundqvist gathered some damp firewood. I made pancakes over a smoking fire. Hammarskjöld suggested we recite poems from memory. After Lundqvist and I had ripped through the two or three verses we knew, Dag carried on for about an hour, quoting Swedish and foreign poetry while the fire died down and the light summer night dimmed.

Hammarskjöld placed high moral demands on himself and others. The prime value was unconditional honesty. Just as his intellectual brilliance could make those around him feel both stupid and gifted, so could his moralistic attitude be both stimulating and guilt-provoking. You were unable to remain indifferent.[19]

There is no sign here of torrid passion, every sign of good fun and good-natured challenges among friends. Any online photograph of Sulitälma, an awesome rocky peak in a glacial region, will persuade you that Åström had good reason to feel "death clutching at his heart." The third climber, Gösta Lundquist, was a formidable photographic chronicler of the landscape and people of the Swedish far north. Hammarskjöld wrote the foreword to his *Lappland*, published in 1954, soon after Lundquist's untimely death.[20]

In the preceding effort to assess politically motivated rumor, it hasn't been possible or sensible to exclude all personal reflections. But we should turn now to the other aspect, the strictly personal. Was it Rabbi Menachem Mendel of Kotzk—the brilliant pessimist of nineteenth-century Jewish life in Poland—who said there is nothing as whole as a broken heart?

In the unicorn stable

Here is a sample invitation written by Hammarskjöld to his good friend and colleague, the Swedish lawyer and diplomat Sture Petrén, in early November 1956 when the Suez Crisis had just moved on from angry talk to a surprise attack on Egypt. It is a sample in the sense that it stands in for quite a few such invitations extended by Hammarskjöld to close friends coming to New York, where he ran a credibly authentic Swedish household with the help of Swedish staff who looked after food and comfort. "During this wildest of periods," he wrote to Petrén,

> with two permanent Council members engaged in an unrighteous "shooting war" against another member state, it is difficult to collect oneself for

letter writing. Therefore, just a line to tell you with what joy I'm looking forward to your arrival on the 20th of November. You are not allowed to disappoint me by seeking other abode than the unicorn stable . . . !

When you come, I will in suitable portions share the most peculiar of laws—of which decisive sections have been written in the last few days. One would like to weep, faced with this *Eloge à la folie*. My only possibility to avoid death by moral strangulation and really help the idea of the Organization you will find in the attached little speech.[21]

"The unicorn stable"—it was a pleasantry in passing, a witty reference to his apartment in New York City. But there is an undercurrent of meaning. During the UN years, Hammarskjöld adopted two symbolic images as something like totems, significant images that spoke to him of his worldly role and his private person. He would lightly write or speak of them with a very few friends and coworkers, and had statuettes of both figures. The Egyptian god Anubis was a recurrent topic in letters exchanged with his friend, the poet and diplomat Saint-John Perse. Hammarskjöld would emphasize the maieutic role of the jackal-headed god—his role as midwife to births of all kinds, including (as far as Hammarskjöld was concerned) the birth of peace and reason among nations. They were, of course, aware of the other role of Anubis, as leader of souls after death into the underworld, and sometimes felt constrained by political events to evoke that aspect. The unicorn was something else again. An exquisite imagined creature like a horse with a single horn on its forehead, a goat's beard, and cloven hooves, it figures in two beautiful tapestry cycles exhibited at The Cloisters in New York and the Musée de Cluny in Paris; Hammarskjöld would have known them. This solitary creature, belonging to some other world of purity and beauty, never mates.

It was the other totem. Among his intimates he made no secret of his regard for it. His security guard, Bill Ranallo, gave him a silver statuette of a unicorn, which he kept on one of his desks. All this was fun, a way of acknowledging his bachelor life without being heavy about it. But in the seclusion of his private journal, a haiku poem dating to October 1959 makes explicit the unicorn's meaning for him:

> Because it never found a mate
> Men called
> The unicorn perverted.[22]

Best to read these few lines alongside another haiku written a few months earlier, at a time when Hammarskjöld was finding in this compact poetic form a way of remembering the past, giving shape to insights, resting from public work. Haiku was to Hammarskjöld as golf is to some serious players: an exercise of utter concentration on a small object, temporarily freeing them from preoccupation with larger objects.

> Denied any outlet,
> The heat transmuted
> The coal into diamonds.[23]

In the first of these brief poems he identifies with the unicorn and privately expresses his distress over the rumors that surfaced with the political tide, whenever adversaries believed that underhanded personal attack would reduce his command of the scene. Some friends, writing about him in later years, have commented that he never seemed to seek a mate. Sven Stolpe, the firmest of friends in the Swedish years, put this well:

> In Dag, whom I admired and liked more than anyone else of my generation, there was so vast and unsatisfied a need of tenderness that he not seldom appeared to be in real distress. He was masculine all through; there was nothing effeminate in his nature. He was not afraid of women, and could speak expertly on feminine beauty; yet I sometimes felt that for all his polite talk at parties he never visually discriminated between a shapely woman and, say, a sofa or a chair.[24]

Hammarskjöld's experience as he recorded it in *Markings*, of course selectively, has a texture somewhat different than Stolpe interpreted as a friendly observer. Certainly, the vast and unsatisfied need of tenderness was very real. What Stolpe may have missed is that, though reticent, Hammarskjöld was a full-bodied, sensual person who could be struck by longing and desire. But the coal buried deep had no outlet; it could not but become a diamond. What is a diamond, in this realm of allusion and metaphor? Is it clarity, brilliance, and durability purchased at high cost—at the cost of intimacy? Are we in the realm of monastic discipline, not by formal vow but by force of character and circumstance?

In the troubled years 1950–52, as during the UN years, Hammarskjöld would occasionally record encounters or perceptions that shook him, often in the context of his debate with loneliness. Among those encounters, only a few involve women; many more bear witness to the personal truth he expressed in 1950 in these hard words: "Hunger is my native place in the land of the passions."[25] One of the few references to feminine beauty reveals his sensuality, his willingness to be intoxicated by the sheer beauty of things seen:

> A line, a shade, a color—their fiery expressiveness.
> The language of flowers, mountains, shores, human bodies:
> the momentous interplay of light and shade, the aching beauty of a neckline,
> the grail of the white crocus on the alpine meadow in the morning light—
> words in a transcendental language of the senses.[26]

But this universal appreciation of sensual life, rich in scope, is not a marriage proposal. Where that is concerned, he had conceded at some point in years prior to the UN that he would be unable to overcome his reticence. There is an extraordinarily sad but realistic entry in *Markings* toward the end of 1952:

> Incapable of being blinded by desire,
> Feeling I have no right to intrude upon another,
> Afraid of exposing my own nakedness,
> Demanding complete accord as a condition for a life together:
> How could things have gone otherwise?[27]

I do want to insist on the overlooked reality that Hammarskjöld, single and destined to remain so, was a man of passions, no stranger to sexual longing though deeply puzzled by it, checkmated rather than mated. As in his reflections on "a line, a shade, a color," he was apt to immerse that longing in larger contexts. He was aware of the rescuing maneuver, if that is what it was. Here, for example, is an entry in *Markings* from 1951:

> So rests the sky against the earth. In the dark stillness of the tarn, the forest opens its womb. As a husband embraces his wife's body in faithful tenderness, so the bare ground and trees are embraced by the still, high light of the morning.
>
> I feel pain, a longing to share in this embrace, to be absorbed, to share in this encounter. A longing like carnal desire, but directed toward earth, water, sky, and returned by the whispers of the trees, the fragrance of the soil, the caresses of the wind, the embrace of water and light. Content? No, no, no—but refreshed, rested—while waiting.[28]

In one of his best short works of the mid-1960s, Thomas Merton, the Trappist monk and author, came to a virtually identical insight when he was a hermit living in the woods at some distance from his monastery. "One might say," he wrote, "I had decided to marry the silence of the forest. The sweet dark warmth of the whole world will have to be my wife. Out of the heart of that dark warmth comes the secret that is heard only in silence, but it is the root of all the secrets that are whispered by all the lovers in their beds all over the world."[29]

On occasion, Hammarskjöld felt himself drawn into the turmoil of desire unanswered, seemingly unanswerable. At some point in the difficult months preceding the Suez Crisis of 1956–57—a period demanding the utmost from him—there occurred a surcease of some kind. And he noted in the privacy of his journal: "In the suction of the vacuum, created when a strain upon the nerves ceases but the nerves have not yet relaxed, the lust of the flesh gets its chance to reveal the loneliness of the soul."[30] On an earlier occasion, he insisted on the universality of the human body in terms that distance it from the particulars of passion and desire: "The body: not a thing, not 'his' or 'hers,' not an instrument of action or desire. In its utter nakedness—Man."[31] A true thought from a certain perspective, but incapable of settling once for all the misery of loneliness.

Yet there were times of inner peace, and people who conferred peace and happiness. During the UN years Hammarskjöld developed the warmest of friendships with a Swedish painter, Bo Beskow (1906–89), and his wife, Greta. On rare occasions when he was free to holiday in Sweden, he would join them at their seaside home in Skåne, a beautiful region of southern Sweden, and he trusted them to find and furnish a nearby farmhouse for him where he intended to retire and write; it has since become the Hammarskjöld Museum at Backåkra. The couple also visited and stayed with him in New York when Bo was working on a mural for the Room of Quiet at United Nations headquarters. There is a rich correspondence between Hammarskjöld and Beskow, in which the secretary-general once memorably responded to the artist's inquiry about his well-being, his need for the simple, good things of life. The letter dates to November 1955:

> You ask where is human warmth? Everywhere and nowhere. In my situation in life I suppose this is part of the price of the stakes, that you are able to give yourself wholly and without reservation only if you don't steal, even in the smallest degree, from someone else: really to "die" in the evangelical sense, which is so frighteningly realistic as a description of the situation of man—can at certain times force you to this paradoxical egoism. ("Who is my mother and my brother, etc., etc.") Instead I have the light and easy warmth of contact with friends such as Greta

and yourself, or, for example, the Belfrages—or Bill [Ranallo]: a kind of comradeship under the same stars where you ask for nothing and receive so much. When I see other possibilities (like yours), I can feel a short pain of having missed something, but the final reaction is: what must be, is right.[32]

Hammarskjöld was a lifelong photographer; his camera accompanied him. For that reason we have a further object to add toward understanding him: his photograph of Greta Beskow, young and utterly beautiful, taken at his weekend home in Brewster, New York (fig. 7). The image is surely not a snapshot, a casual record from a pleasant day; it carries some larger message.[33] It reveals the photographer's vast appreciation of this woman, who represented "the other possibility" and who, with her husband and child, offered the warmth of unconditional friendship and a home to a man who had dedicated his life in other directions.

Monastic enough?

"For one who has responded to the call of an unknown but possible achievement," Hammarskjöld wrote in 1955,

> loneliness may be obligatory. Such loneliness, it is true, may lead to a communion closer and deeper than any achieved by the union of two bodies, but your body is not going to let itself be fobbed off by a bluff: whatever you deny it, in order to follow this compelling call, it will claim back if you fail and claim back in forms which it will no longer be in your power to select.
>
> It is not we who seek the Way, but the Way which seeks us. That is why you are faithful to it, even while you stand waiting, so long as you are *prepared*, and act the moment you are confronted by its demands.[34]

Surely we now have enough elements before us to bring this exploration to a close. Hammarskjöld's solution to the enigma of destructive personal loneliness was to immerse his person in a much larger world—the world of nations and peoples, which he served; to immerse himself in a much larger cause—the cause of peace in a menaced and scarcely stable world; and to immerse himself at length in a large dialogue through religious faith, prayer, and a kind of reverent curiosity which guided him into realms best known to monastics and mystics. Add to these engagements his knowing love of the arts and a circle of friends with whom he could explore the fine points of a book, a play, an operatic performance, music, dance, painting or sculpture—and this often with poets and novelists, theater directors, performers, artists. The solution was not unshakeable. It conferred no permanent immunity to desperate loneliness, which would recur from time to time. But it was dignified and enriching, and it released his genius.

Why, really, was Hammarskjöld lonely? Marc E. Vargo, in his recent book *Noble Lives: Biographical Portraits of Three Remarkable Gay Men*,[35] offers in a most respectful and sensitive manner the conclusion that some readers will undoubtedly have reached: given Hammarskjöld's family history, reinforced by his own and familial expectations of high accomplishment in public life, he may have been homosexual without knowing or acknowledging it, and abstained from sexual intimacy. Vargo recognizes that he uncovered no new evidence; he uses fewer documents than we have used here. Unlike Peyrefitte and Legros, he makes no wild assertions.

Men closest to Hammarskjöld—Åström, Stolpe, Urquhart, George Ivan Smith, others—will have none of that. The person they knew was obviously a "man's man"; he had no intimate women friends and until the UN years periodically roamed the northern Swedish wilderness with men who enjoyed its challenges. But none of his UN colleagues or Swedish friends perceived him as gay.

Sture Linnér, Hammarskjöld's trusted Swedish colleague who was the senior UN figure in the Congo in later 1961, briefly left his post in August to confer in New York and at Hammarskjöld's pleasant country home in Brewster. At some point they took a break from work. Linnér continues:

> We were bathing in a little lake on his country estate north of New York on a bright summer day, floating around on rubber rafts and staring up into the sky. Hammarskjöld was no fan of small talk. Suddenly he said, "If you were to recommend three books you think I might not have read, which ones would you suggest?" So we talked about that. And then, after a silence, he said, "Have you heard rumors about my alleged homosexuality?" I said that of course I had—but probably much less than most of my colleagues because they know that we are not only colleagues but friends. "Well," he said, "what do you think?" I said, "Frankly, Dag, I never thought about it. It's a problem that is no problem for me. Had I ever noticed any peculiar appointment or favoring of anyone in the UN system that could not be explained apart from some very special personal relation, then I would have reacted, but I have never seen a trace of such a thing." He replied, "Let me just tell you that there is

no ground for these rumors. I want you to know that." I said, "Thank you for your confidence. I take note of that." And then I said, "You indirectly raise an issue that interests me very much: why are you not married?" He said, "I'll come back to that on another occasion—I don't feel like talking about it now. But the occasion will come when I'll open my heart to you." He kept his word. Sometime later he told me that he had had a love. I know who she was, he told me her name and background. And she preferred somebody else. She went along with him for a while but then chose somebody else. Hammarskjöld said that, after that, he couldn't envision marrying anyone else. She was so wonderful.[36]

This summertime conversation makes evident that Hammarskjöld had been lastingly afflicted over the years by the smear campaigns.

Posthumously, Auden did him no service by mistranslating a number of sensitive passages in *Markings*. In the passage we know about the mirror and doorway, dated 1952, Hammarskjöld returned to the theme of the unheard-of to rephrase it in terms of personal hesitation:

"At the frontier of the unheard-of—" Aware of the *consummatio* of the deep-sea dive—but afraid, by instinct, experience, education, for "certain reasons," of putting my head under water, ignorant, even, of how it is done.[37]

But Hammarskjöld didn't write the coy "for certain reasons," which implies a secret—why not the secret of homosexuality? His word there is Sw. *hänsyn*, meaning "consideration" or "discretion." Similarly, in a pair of passages from 1950 on friendship, Sw. *vänskap*, Auden substituted for "friendship" the word "love," in this way converting the second passage into a forlorn commentary on a misunderstanding with an unidentified man with whom there was a love relation.[38] Accurately translated, the passage *can* be read in that way, but nothing obliges the reading; according to his friends, Auden tilted it his way because he was having difficulties with his own long-term partner at the time he was translating.

But this is Auden, after all—a strong poet capable of unique insights and expression. Despite his lapses as a translator, he can advance our understanding. Writing surely of himself in a book review of 1941, but with a resonance that reaches other lives, not least Hammarskjöld's, he offered this remarkable thought:

The so-called traumatic experience is not an accident, but the opportunity for which the child has been patiently waiting—had it not occurred, it would have found another, equally trivial—in order to find a necessity

and direction for its existence, in order that its life may become a serious matter. Of course it would be better if it could do without it, but
unconsciously it knows that it is not, by itself, strong enough to learn to
stand alone: a neurosis is a guardian angel; to become ill is to take vows.[39]

"In order that life may become a serious matter." With this insight Auden
returns us in contemporary terms to the nineteenth-century Kotzker
rebbe's truth: there is nothing as whole as a broken heart. We may never
indisputably know what innate characteristic or early trauma gave rise
to Dag Hammarskjöld's recurrent and sometimes devastating loneliness,
existing side by side with his immense capacity to understand others'
situations, assess human predicaments in creative ways, and resourcefully
set courses of action. We may never quite know what caused him "that
pain in the soul which drives us beyond ourselves," as he wrote in 1950.[40]
We can surmise this or that; it may or may not be so. But even if we could
be quite sure—if new evidence dropped from the skies or from unexplored archives—that wouldn't matter.

Why? Because he was so much like a monastic that we owe him the respect
and absence of intrusive inquiry we willingly grant a monk. What does it
matter if a monk is by nature straight or gay? What matters is his dedication,
his service, his radiance, his suitedness to what he undertakes. We know that
he has chosen not to relate to others through sexual intimacy—and think no
more of it; it's a choice made, not in the least our concern.

There was one other so like Hammarskjöld that we should recall him.
Ralph Waldo Emerson left behind the perfect description of his younger
friend, Henry David Thoreau, another dedicated journal keeper, learned
outdoorsman, and practitioner of a politics of integrity. The description
appears in the eulogy spoken at Thoreau's funeral in 1862, later printed
and read far and wide.

> Henry Thoreau remains erect, calm, self-subsistent, before me, and I
> read him not only truly in his journal, but he is not long out of mind
> when I walk, and, as today, row upon the pond. He chose wisely no
> doubt for himself to be the bachelor of thought and nature that he was,
> —how near to the old monks in their ascetic religion! . . . Perhaps he
> fell—all of us do—into his way of living, without forecasting it much,
> but approved and confirmed it with later wisdom.

Much the same thought occurred a century later to the monk Thomas
Merton as he considered the life and example of Albert Camus. In the

mid-1960s, Merton could no longer locate the monastic spirit exclusively behind cloister walls; it was a much larger thing, it found its people and touched them—and they in turn touched others. "Are people like Camus," he wrote, "the true monks of our day? Is monasticism to be really found in an external commitment to certain formal sacrifices and an institutional and ritual life or in the kind of solitude, integrity, commitment that Camus had?"[41]

This is the company in which we should recognize Dag Hammarskjöld. There is no counterfactual Hammarskjöld arriving unscathed at the UN. The one who factually arrived had been tested and refined in an unseen ordeal that never disclosed its full meaning to him: glimpses, yes, certainties, no. Even at the very end of 1952, as we know, he could write in the privacy of his journal: "What I ask for is absurd: that life shall have a meaning. . . . I dare not believe, I do not see how I shall ever be able to believe: that I am not alone."[42] The brilliant aristocrat equipped with multiple diplomas, recruited from the height of Swedish government and international economic planning, charming, urbane, immensely able, had a whole, broken heart. And to this we owe some part of his breadth and humanity.

As secretary-general, he did not make a fetish of achieving perfect solutions to political problems; he could be satisfied with small, meaningful advances if large, dramatic advances were not to be had. In a public talk of 1955, he articulated this line of thought in a way that tells us as much about himself as about his political philosophy:

> Every individual lives out his life to the accompaniment of many unsolved problems and few ages have succeeded in achieving a final solution of the problems which have faced them. A partial settlement may be arranged at one time; a more general settlement may be reached at a later date; frequently all that is possible is to maintain the existing state of affairs until the evolution of time brings a more favorable opportunity.[43]

6

Possibility Never Touched Upon

The process was a bizarre blend of systematic negotiation and jerky improvisation. Trygve Lie's resignation speech in the General Assembly on November 10th, 1952, set in motion a diplomatic merry-go-round that revolved and slowed, and revolved again through late March of the following year, when Dag Hammarskjöld was nominated by the Security Council and quickly endorsed by the General Assembly. His election surprised everyone. He hadn't even been a dark horse candidate, lingering and longing nearby while the advocates of other candidates had it out with one another. Like others in diplomacy he was aware of the selection process, but it was of no personal concern. He was not among the candidates under consideration; no one had privately spoken with him, and when his candidacy came up events moved so quickly that none of the principals quite had time, or thought to take time, to sound him out. Among the diplomats at the center, most of whom knew only his resume, there was some unstated calculation that if asked he couldn't say no. How strange. His name wasn't floated until March 23rd, well into a seemingly endless series of East-West stalemates that the very able Lester B. Pearson of Canada, then serving as president of the General Assembly, described as threatening to make the United Nations look ridiculous.[1] On April 10th, a youthful man, unfamiliar, courtly and contained, took the oath of office and turned to the General Assembly for the first time: "Ours is a work of reconciliation and realistic construction."[2] It was a new voice.

This chapter, like many to follow, is threaded on the narrative of Hammarskjöld's years at the UN. You will not find here a step-by-step diplomatic history; no challenge is intended to the classic account by Brian Urquhart. We will always know the essentials of Hammarskjöld's working context— problems faced, relationships engaged, ideas generated, solutions set in motion—and we'll continue to follow his thoughts as he recorded them in *Markings* and in correspondence with trusted friends. But biography now enters a larger stream and can no longer be our sole concern.

From the beginning he had a swarm of ideas. It is sometimes said, and I believed, that Hammarskjöld's first year and more in office were largely dedicated to administrative issues, in-house matters urgent but dull in comparison to what came next. That no longer seems well interpreted. From the very beginning, when he made a quietly remarkable statement to the press upon arrival in New York on April 9th to take office, he was *thinking* in the most active way imaginable—thinking about the values and structure of the United Nations, thinking about its foundational Charter, thinking about problems left unresolved by his predecessor, thinking about the history and political culture that had given rise to the United Nations and in which the Organization, as he often called it, remained embedded. All of this was not a cold exercise. His thinking was suffused with felt values and insights, and it began to revitalize especially the central Secretariat after the difficulties endured since early 1950.

Brian Urquhart and others have pointed out that Hammarskjöld's tenure at the UN began under a lucky star. Stalin's death on March 5th, 1953, opened the possibility of greater understanding between the Western democracies and the Soviet bloc; the new Eisenhower administration in the United States was promising; and on July 27th the Korean War armistice agreement, in force to this day, was signed, ending a conflict that had had dramatic consequences for the UN, not least the Soviet bloc's refusal to acknowledge or work with Trygve Lie. These fortunate changes were one element of context for a nearly tangible effort of thought—as if thought, like wind and sunlight, can move and nurture. Institutions large and small need the refreshment of thought. Otherwise, they easily become brittle, abstract, or dated. The needed quality of thought is neither brittle nor abstract; it is accompanied by personal commitment and a steady gaze. It was this that Hammarskjöld brought to the UN, not as a drily calculated strategy but as an expression of his identity; it simply represented who he was, in action. A clear analysis that solved a nasty problem, comments at a staff meeting, statements to the press with a particular ring to them, a commemorative gathering, a guest lecture, a New Year message over UN radio—it added up.

It is not enough to think. Thoughts must be stated and routed effectively to find homes in other minds. The twentieth-century master of political storytelling was without doubt Winston Churchill. One of his morale-building strategies during World War II—so in character it hardly seemed a strategy—was to recite the narrative of current events in the House of Commons or on BBC radio, always conveying by tone and pace that he knew the outcome in advance, that all the horror, setbacks, and striving were appointed stations on the way to inevitable victory. This brilliant, beneficent seduction was recognized at the time; midwar in 1943, *Punch*'s parliamentary journalist described Churchill as "the Grand Story-Teller of Britain."[3] Hammarskjöld was a very different man, but what he had to say and its cumulative impact were something like: he retold the story, enriched his listeners' and readers' sense of its cultural moorings and ethical substance, refreshed the values that make the United Nations central to the fate of humanity, measured grave risks and hopeful possibilities, called his listeners to a sense of participation. He was more soft-spoken than Churchill and made no use of the weapons of showy speakers—no long weighty pauses, no dramatically voiced perorations, little or no physical drama. In the course of time there were grand statements, even campaigns in which he had to maintain an intense stream of communication. But there were many more undramatic statements which, closely heard or read, conveyed a new clarity and impulse. There is a border between values and realities where they mix a little. He moved with ease there. Like his handwriting—compressed, charged with energy, a jet stream on the page—his spoken words and choice of images almost invariably possessed quiet force. About his handwriting, a journalist hosting a friendly "roast" for Hammarskjöld commented in 1958: "On the authority of the author, I might say that it looks the same backwards and forwards. And he acknowledges that at least in appearance it has some resemblance to Arabic."[4]

The example of Christopher Columbus appealed to Hammarskjöld's imagination through the mariner's voyage into the unknown, westbound to an unanticipated destination. In a public talk of September 1953, he evoked Columbus, not for the last time, in a way that parsed attitudes toward the UN and, Churchill-like, mixed high romance with a bluntly realistic strike of the gong at the end. His regard for Columbus must have caught someone's attention: at the first United Nations Day Concert he organized (annually on October 24th), he received the gift of a beautifully detailed model of the mariner's flagship, the *Santa Maria*, which found its way to his mantelpiece at home. That September he had said:

> On the seas we sail we have to face all the storms and stresses created by the ideological, economic, and social conditions of our world. Aboard this new *Santa Maria* we have to meet the impatience of those sailors who expect land on the horizon tomorrow, also the cynicism or sense of futility of those who would give up and leave us drifting

impotently. On the shores we have all those who are against the whole expedition, who seem to take a special delight in blaming the storms on the ship instead of the weather. Well, let us admit that this comparison with the crew of Columbus soon after he set sail on the *Santa Maria* has some truth also in its negative implications. We have still to prove our case.[5]

This must be an inventory of people and attitudes encountered since April, fitted with a watchmaker's skill into a single image.

April 1953: Possibility never touched upon

On the first of April, 1953, Hammarskjöld sent a telegram to his superior, Östen Undén, foreign minister of Sweden and fellow cabinet member:

> According to communication from New York, the Security Council has tonight decided, by 10 votes and one abstained, to nominate me for Secretary-General. Possibility never touched upon in personal conversations. Have agreed with Erlander on discussion in government Wednesday. Grateful your reaction.
>
> Hammarskjöld[6]

Tage Erlander was the long-serving prime minister; Undén was both colleague and friend, in whom Hammarskjöld had found a last valued mentor in the Swedish government. The government decided that very day to release him from duty to take up his new post at the UN.

The nomination process, confined to the Security Council with its small membership of permanent members and rotating membership of smaller nations, had been a frustrating Cold War exercise. Among candidates seriously considered, there were future prime ministers, a future Nobel laureate, men and a woman—Nehru's sister, Vijaya Lakshmi Pandit—with records of distinguished UN service.[7] Some political leaders warmly remembered to this day, such as Lester Pearson of Canada and Paul-Henri Spaak of Belgium, were among the more durable candidates. But none prevailed. The Western democracies and the Soviet Union could not come to terms. Just out of sight of the stately horseshoe-shaped table at which the Security Council met, ragged hallway conversations among the most influential members and messages to and fro with home governments kept the issue unresolved and nearly beyond resolution. There were dazzlingly fine calculations on one side and the other of who might accept what, in what sequence, and why. Pearson was right: it was faintly ridiculous. Trygve Lie is said not to have minded; he would have accepted a draft return to office, had the Western allies and his adversary, the Soviet Union, turned to him in an hour of need.

Hammarskjöld was known to Anthony Eden, Churchill's long-serving foreign secretary (and a future prime minister who would disastrously collide with Hammarskjöld over Suez). They had worked together, and Hammarskjöld had impressed Eden, at the postwar Organization for European Economic Development. Eden suggested his candidacy to the permanent UN representative of Great Britain, Gladwyn Jebb, who knew Hammarskjöld slightly, and he in turn mentioned him to the French representative, Henri Hoppenot, who knew Hammarskjöld not at all but would later become a friend. The Americans and Russians each had just enough knowledge of Hammarskjöld to consider him a viable compromise candidate. Urquhart provides an earthy account of the situation: "They went searching around all over the place," he recalled in an oral history session, "and, by pure accident, picked up somebody who was exactly the opposite to what everybody wanted. They thought they'd got a safe, bureaucratic civil servant, non-political, and they got Hammarskjöld. It will never happen again; nobody's ever going to make that mistake twice."[8]

Other witnesses have recorded much the same thing. Emery Kelen, one of Hammarskjöld's first biographers, wrote that "his reputation was that of a brilliant economist, an unobtrusive technician, and a Swedish aristo-bureaucrat."[9] A senior European diplomat recalled that the so-called Great Powers wanted "a careful and colorless official" who would focus on administrative issues.[10] Pauline Frederick, a journalist we have already encountered, said that "he was not a well-known figure. . . . The fact that neither the United States nor the Soviet Union would oppose Dag Hammarskjöld for this important post meant that they assumed, as everybody else did, that he would not make waves as Secretary-General Trygve Lie had done. In other words, he would not involve himself in political issues that either of them would be opposed to. As a consequence, there was not much controversy, not any as a matter of fact."[11]

In the night of March 31–April 1, Hammarskjöld received a call from a journalist in Stockholm: "We understand you've been designated secretary-general of the United Nations." In UN circles, his reply is famous: "This April Fool's Day joke is in extremely bad taste: it's nonsense!"[12] Urquhart's exhaustive research uncovered why it was that a stray journalist had been first to contact him: a member of the Security Council had slipped out of the meeting to go to the restroom, happened to run into a correspondent, and told him the news—an elementary diplomatic error, but there it was. Other calls from journalists soon convinced Hammarskjöld that the nomination was real, the Swedish mission in New York confirmed at 3:00 in the morning, and an official communication soon arrived from the Security Council, chaired at the time by the Pakistani representative, Ahmed Bokhári. Recognizing that to convey this stunning news without any preparation whatever fell somewhere between haphazard and rude, Bokhári included a cordial message in the Council's cable: "In view of the immense importance of this post, more especially at the present time, members of the Security Council express the earnest hope that you will agree to accept the appointment if, as they hope and believe, it is shortly made by the General Assembly."[13] Little more than a week later, welcoming Hammarskjöld to his new post in a speech before that body, Gladwyn Jebb had the good humor to describe the new secretary-general with due sympathy as having been "unexpectedly pitchforked into this unruly political arena."[14]

After a night's thought, the requisite government discussion, and conversations only some of which have left a trace, Hammarskjöld replied by cable to Bokhári: "With strong feeling personal insufficiency I hesitate to accept candidature but I do not feel that I could refuse to assume the task imposed on me should the Assembly follow the recommendation of the Security Council by which I feel deeply honored."[15]

There is little record of what Hammarskjöld was doing toward the end of March 1953. But there was one touch of magic. The artist Bo Beskow tells the story with characteristic warmth. Hammarskjöld had spoken with him for the first time a few months earlier because a formal portrait was needed, no doubt for a gallery of senior government figures of the kind that dignifies many nations' administrative buildings. Beskow's reputation as a portraitist must have been strong enough at the time to attract Hammarskjöld's attention. They met and liked one another; sittings began in March. During those sessions they conversed, and among other things speculated about the selection of Trygve Lie's successor. Beskow suggested that Hammarskjöld himself would be an excellent candidate. Reply: "Nobody is crazy enough to propose me—and I would be crazy to accept."[16] Then came April 1st.

Hammarskjöld was back in his chair at the studio early that afternoon. Beskow writes: "I opened a fresh bottle of sherry and we talked for two hours."[17] He drove him later to the Foreign Office for his first press conference as secretary-general designee. So far, so plain—but there was nonetheless magic: though Beskow finished the portrait, he saw that it had been invalidated by events. Reversing the central metaphor of Oscar Wilde's *Dorian Gray*, to the painter's keen eye Dag Hammarskjöld was no longer the same man. "The portrait was more or less finished," Beskow recalled, "as a portrait of the man he was when I met him, not as the man he turned out to be. I would say that he matured almost overnight, being suddenly able to use and develop the whole range of his unique qualities."[18] The painting did have an afterlife—it must have been a topic for teasing between sitter and artist. A few years later, Hammarskjöld mentioned it in a letter to a Swedish friend: "It could amuse Gertrud [the correspondent's wife] to hear that Bo Beskow now does not think much of his painting of me. He wants to do it again . . . with no ambition to endow me with the dignity fit for the Bank of Sweden."[19]

Other witnesses to these days of change add light and color. Both in interview and in a published memoir, Sverker Åström reported along the same lines as Beskow, though with a diplomat's knowledge and sense of irony.

> When he got the offer, I had dinner with him, and he was extremely hesitant about whether he should accept it. Then he phoned the prime minister and got his permission to accept the offer. I warned him that this was a great sensation in the world, Stockholm would be filled with international journalists, and he would need to hold a press conference. The following day there was indeed a press conference in the foreign ministry, and I had the impression that he had spent the night reading ten books about the United Nations because he answered all questions in the most expert manner imaginable. Not only did he know the facts about the United Nations, but he had also mobilized during the night an immense personal interest in the idea of the United Nations, which I know he hadn't had the day before. . . . He had never shown any real enthusiasm for the United Nations.[20]

This from the interview. In his memoir, Åström thinks further about Hammarskjöld's changed attitude: "[It] would fit with a characteristic feature of his intellectual equipment which held that if a new fact cannot easily be accommodated in a certain pattern of thinking, you simply give the pattern a new definition and expand the frame of reference. Most important for him at the decisive moment was surely that he understood he had been given the role of his life, the task that he gradually came to understand as his special assignment and calling."[21] Gunnar Jarring, a Swedish diplomat and head of mission at the UN during some of Hammarskjöld's years, must also have been nearby at this time. Urquhart records Jarring's recollection: "[Hammarskjöld's reaction] could best be described as an agony of doubt: 'Do I really have to accept? Isn't there somebody else who would be available?' . . . But as soon as his cable of acceptance had left Stockholm, his agony disappeared as if by . . . magic. There was no hesitation, no irresolution. He had decided to accept and had pledged himself to the United Nations."[22]

These are enlightening reports: Beskow insightful, Åström worldly wise and in the end simply wise, Jarring precise. But we should look beyond them to Hammarskjöld's own words. In the few days he had in Sweden before departing for New York, he made a point of reconnecting with old friends and advisors. We know that he called on Anna Söderblom, widow of the archbishop whose personal warmth and example had taught Dag early lessons about the forces that contribute to international understanding. On his side, Wigforss wasn't surprised by the good fit between his protégé and the UN assignment. He had long thought of him as an intellectual *and* man of action who hadn't yet found his terrain. In his memoirs, published in the 1950s, Wigforss completed that thought: "In the international arena, in pursuit of peace and collaboration between peoples, [Hammarskjöld] found an outlet for a desire for action which never before had been able to be released. At the same time one seems to gather that in this endeavor he found something of an ideology that the skeptic in him had lacked before."[23]

Much will be revealed by entries for 1953 in *Markings*, but—perhaps perversely—I would like us first to find strong signs elsewhere of the change that came upon Hammarskjöld when, in his own words, he was "catapulted without previous soundings, indeed, without any prewarning" into the post of secretary-general.[24] One strong sign lies in the difference in tone between a statement for Swedish and UN radio made on April 8th, before his departure for New York, and the statement he made upon arrival in New York. His words in Stockholm are tentative, self-effacing—and dull. One can't quite detect him in the words; they are all right, but nothing like a message. After his flight over the Atlantic, the tone changed. He was still modest, as was only proper in the circumstance and true to his ideals, but what he had to say is compelling. At the end of his remarks he evoked a rugged experience he knew well—mountaineering—to convey metaphorically not just thoughts but energy, direction, feeling. A. M. Rosenthal, the distinguished *New York Times* writer and editor who established a strong rapport with Hammarskjöld, reported in his paper that the New York statement was written in flight.[25] There is no reason to doubt that; he probably asked. From a mythic perspective, which needn't be wholly disregarded, Hammarskjöld's flight from Stockholm to New York, from old life to new, was transformative. In flight he was nowhere, neither here nor there, and something invisible occurred. In Stockholm he had said,

> My great hope is, of course, the one shared by people all over the world that we are going to a period of less tension and less fear. Of course to that I would add that it would make me very happy if the United Nations could play its part in that development as the peace instrument which it was intended to be. That would give an extraordinary meaning to the work I am going to do. . . . I wouldn't like to say anything about myself, but it is quite obvious that for me this is a great challenge. It is a situation in which one wants to do one's very best and even more than one's best for the mere chance of making a contribution—a small one, of course, but after all a contribution—to the development which is highly desirable.[26]

He sounds exactly like the self-effacing bureaucrat whom the United States and Soviet Union thought they were hiring. In New York, he had a great deal more to say, touching on a number of issues. The first was to make a sharp distinction between the international public servant he was to become and the private man who now stood before the press gathered at the airport. "Of course, I—like all of you, like all engaged in diplomatic or political activity—have my views and ideas on the great international issues facing us. But those personal views of mine are not—or should not be—of any greater interest to you today than they were just a couple of weeks ago. Those views are mine as a private man. In my new official capacity the private man should disappear and the international public servant take his place." This is a theme to which he would return, forcibly in the sense that he knew he would soon be dealing with a privacy issue left unresolved by his predecessor, but also naturally because he cared very much to establish a boundary between his future public role and whatever might be left of privacy.

He went on to define that public role in terms implying that his approach would differ from his predecessor's, who in his later years in office had publicly taken sides on grave issues between member nations. Hammarskjöld's initial vision of the secretary-general's role put all the emphasis on behind-the-scenes activity. "The public servant is there in order to assist, so to say from the inside," he said, "those who take the decisions which frame history. He should—as I see it—listen, analyze, and learn to understand fully the forces at work and the interests at stake, so that he will be able to give the right advice when the situation calls for it. Don't think that he—in following this line of personal policy—takes but a passive part in the development. It is a most active one. But he is active as an instrument, a catalyst, perhaps an inspirer—he serves."[27] This is remarkably well expressed, and he would prove to be a master at what he later called quiet diplomacy, but it captures only a fraction of the activities of the secretary-general as he would shape the office.

Thus far in "this first meeting on American soil," as he rather grandly put it, Hammarskjöld was operating within a predictable frame of reference. He had been a Swedish civil servant for decades, knew from experience the tensions between public and private, and had refined the practice of quiet diplomacy at countless international meetings after World War II. But he moved past safe thoughts in his concluding words. He must have known that he needed now to hammer home a memorable point in a memorable way. This was no longer rehearsal. If he was to speak and be heard, this was the time to get started. He constructed a compelling metaphor around mountain climbing—easing into it modestly with a touch of humor, and then disclosing.

> In articles recently published it has been said that I am interested in mountaineering. That's true. But I have never climbed any famous peaks. My experience is limited to Scandinavia where mountaineering calls more for endurance than for equilibristics, and where mountains are harmonious rather than dramatic, matter of fact . . . rather than eloquent. However, this much I know of the sport, that the qualities it requires are just those which I feel we all need today: perseverance and patience, a firm grip on realities, careful but imaginative planning, a clear awareness of the dangers but also of the fact that fate is what we make it and that the safest climber is he who never questions his ability to overcome all difficulties.[28]

This is the first sighting of the swarm of ideas to come. In one sentence it assembles eight values, demonstrates intellectual command and freshness of mind likely to be equal to the challenges ahead, projects confidence without pride, and asserts a view—"fate is what we make it"—to which he would often return in years to come. There was nothing deterministic in his approach, no displacement of responsibility from human beings to seemingly fixed conditions that leave no initiative or choice.

Returning to Sweden in mid-May to wind up certain affairs, Hammarskjöld gave a press conference in which he again spoke briefly but tellingly of values. "When we met here last time," he said to the journalists, many of whom could recall how tentative he had been,

> I told you about my hesitation, a hesitation which would have prompted me to say no to the new post, if I had felt that I had any right to do so. If, on that occasion I had had my present—rather intense—experience of all there is for a Secretary-General to be done in the UN and for the UN, and if I had had my present knowledge of those who have dedicated themselves to the UN venture and of the spirit in which they work, my hesitation concerning my own qualifications would have been the same. But my feeling of what a privilege it is to have a chance to do this job would certainly have overshadowed everything else. A soldier may react when unexpectedly drafted. But once in the fight for what he finds to be essential values in this life of ours, he is just happy.[29]

There is soul-satisfying simplicity in the closing words—"he is just happy"—and all requisite sophistication and realism elsewhere in this loaded sentence: he knew full well that there would be fights in which essential values would be at stake. It was with a philosopher's slight distance and a preacher's call for participation that he referred to "this life of ours."

On April 10th, 1953, Hammarskjöld took the oath of office as secretary-general. The scene in the General Assembly (fig. 9) displayed, for an eloquent instant, the order and stillness of a Byzantine icon: Hammarskjöld and Lester Pearson, president of the General Assembly, at center, flanked by ranks of solemn, uniformly dressed vice presidents and committee chairs, male from one end to the other. So light and slender that he scarcely seemed to touch the floor, Hammarskjöld pronounced the oath while at the opposite side of the rostrum Trygve Lie, frowning and heavy, betrayed his dissatisfaction. The three chairs behind are empty for the moment; the leftmost chair in years to come would be Hammarskjöld's.

Like the UN Charter, the oath of office mattered crucially to Hammarskjöld; together they set his course. He seems to have carried a small typed version of the oath whenever he traveled; it was found after the fatal air crash in Africa between the pages of his traveling copy of Thomas à Kempis's *Imitation of Christ*. It was a bookmark, but more. We should know its brief text:

> I, Dag Hammarskjöld, solemnly swear to exercise in all loyalty, discretion and conscience the functions entrusted to me as Secretary-General of the United Nations, to discharge these functions and regulate my conduct with the interests of the United Nations only in view, and not to seek or accept instructions in regard to the performance of my duties from any government or other authority external to the Organization.

After administering the oath, Lester Pearson—in future, an important and trusted colleague—said a few cordial words of welcome and turned the occasion over to the new secretary-general.

Hammarskjöld's maiden speech must have elicited good listening from the representatives of the member nations and journalists who would relay his message and manner to a global public. Entrusted with the most influential post in the diplomatic world, he was all but unknown. He opened with plain words of acknowledgment—"With humility I accept an election expressing a confidence in me which I have still to justify"—and went on to evoke the values of loyalty, devotion, and integrity that he had encountered in the Swedish civil service and in postwar European councils, values closely echoing the oath of office. All of this was wholly appropriate but had not yet flared into a striking statement. That came quickly:

> Ours is a work of reconciliation and realistic construction. This work must be based on respect for the laws by which human civilization has been built. It likewise requires a strict observance of the rules and principles laid down in the Charter of this Organization. My work shall be guided by this knowledge.[30]

It is a sequence of declarations, set side by side as if by a mason. The UN enterprise is "a work," the sober term summoning a sense of dedication and due procedure. It is a search for reconciliation; it must be constructive and realistic in its aims and means; it must respect the Charter, which Hammarskjöld would have been reading in depth since his nomination; and it must acknowledge the guidance of "the laws by which human civilization has been built." This last, pure Hammarskjöld, widens the context and points in several directions. It surely refers to the importance he gave to the rule of law and to the need for a robust body of international law. But his words point elsewhere, as well. He asks his listeners to remember the long narrative of human successes and failures, and to draw lessons for the present. He asks for active memory—and as we'll see in a moment, returns to that theme as he closes. It may be that there is one further element here, unstated but implied: his respect for Henri Bergson's concept of "creative evolution," a cautiously optimistic view of positive forces at work in nature and history which can be temporarily deflected or defeated but have a way of persisting.

In a graceful gesture toward the American host of the United Nations, Hammarskjöld now chose to quote from the Gettysburg Address the powerful passage where Lincoln calls on "the living" to be "dedicated here to the unfinished work" begun by the sacrifices of those who had recently fought and died for freedom. Hammarskjöld had in mind World War II, out of which the United Nations had arisen. There is "a great task remaining to us," Lincoln had said, and Hammarskjöld echoed.

Having brought to mind one of the greatest wartime speeches, with its suffering ideals and call to duty, Hammarskjöld turned at the end toward another memory. Easter had been celebrated that year on April 5th, less than a week earlier.

> In concluding, may I remind you of the great memory just celebrated by the Christian world? May I do so because of what that memory tells us of the redeeming power of true dedication to peace and goodwill towards men? We are of different creeds and convictions. Events and ideas which to some of us remain the very basis of our faith are elements of the spiritual heritage of man which are foreign to others. But common to us all and above all other convictions stands the truth once expressed by a Swedish poet when he said that the greatest prayer of man does not ask for victory but for peace.[31]

Calling the member nations to a renewed sense of purpose, he again called them to memory. Events or persons vividly remembered confirm identity, unite us with those who have come before, and radiate wisdom or warning. As Sverker Åström has already told us, Hammarskjöld himself had formidable powers of memory. Memory created within him a kind of internal atmosphere; there are unmistakable signs that this was so. He knew when he was pioneering, when there was no precedent, but knew also how to draw on the past for courage, guidance, and a sense of large belonging.

Hammarskjöld's maiden speech at the United Nations, soft-spoken enough to be easily overlooked, placed him within the circle; "our work," he had said. He could no longer be viewed as an unknown outsider or awkward newcomer. Whoever he was, he had taken the place offered him.

No one is permitted to write about the transition from Trygve Lie to Dag Hammarskjöld without calling attention to a moment at the airport on April 8th, when Lie welcomed his successor to what he called "the most impossible job in the world."[32] The phrase stuck, if not with Hammarskjöld then with journalists, one of whom checked back with him a month later. A French reporter asked, "Mr. Lie told you that you were undertaking the most impossible job in the world. Now, after working here some weeks, do you subscribe to that view?" Hammarskjöld responded: "No, it is not an impossible one. It is one which represents quite an extraordinary kind of challenge, and it is very easy to make a mess of it. But that is not exactly the same as saying that it is impossible. On the other hand, I very well understand his feelings after seven years of this special kind of *travail*."[33]

Maturity: Among other things

> "—Night is drawing nigh—"
> For all that has been—thanks!
> To all that shall be—yes![34]

The reader can't help but look with astonishment at these opening lines in *Markings* for 1953. The biographer looks with bewilderment. Were the lower lines, among the most quoted in *Markings*, actually written at the start of the year? Because his jubilant affirmation is joined to his customary recollection of the rather melancholy verses of a hymn read by his mother at the turn of the year, we could take the view that he made an abrupt transition, for reasons unreported in *Markings*, from pervasive anguish at the end of the previous year to *this*. That may be so. But more likely he made an editorial decision at a later date to dedicate the whole of his journal for this year of years to his response to the vast change in his life. "Only the hand that erases can write the true thing," he had stated on the first page of the edited journal; perhaps that hand erased much that seemed trivial in light of the events of April.

Entries in *Markings* for 1953, few in number, rich in substance, occupy just five printed pages. Of those pages, two may well have been written in the week between April 1st and Hammarskjöld's departure for New York on April 7th, reflecting a time of furious readjustment. If Bo Beskow's suddenly obsolete portrait of Hammarskjöld represents how the week started, the following entry dated April 7th—dated entries are rare and deliberate—shows its conclusion. It is a passage transcribed from Thomas à Kempis's *Imitation of Christ*, Hammarskjöld's trusted late medieval guide to living a Christian life in depth. To explore a point we would otherwise miss, you will find here both a translation and the seventeenth-century French recorded in *Markings* from Hammarskjöld's rare edition of Thomas, published in 1689. Readers familiar with French will see at a glance that certain spellings are of another era.

> Their lives grounded in and sustained by God, they are incapable of any kind of pride; because they give back to God all the benefits He has bestowed on them, they do not glorify each other, but do all things to the Glory of God alone.[35]

> Estant fondez et affermis en Dieu, ils ne peuvent en aucune sorte estre superbe; & parce qu'ils rendent à Dieu tous les biens dont il les a comblez ils ne reçoivent point de gloire les uns des autres; mais ils ne desirent que celle de Dieu seul. (Thomas II:10)[36]

Why did Hammarskjöld read and painstakingly transcribe antique French when the text was available in any number of modern translations from the original Latin? One can only speculate; he left no account. But this could be true: the older French language and typography restored Hammarskjöld to a world in which Thomas's strict ethic and monastic austerity—so like his own—were at home. In modern translation, Thomas can easily sound prudish, narrow, unfit for our tumbling world. In the French of three hundred years ago, he is a native speaker of native things: the fit is perfect. Hammarskjöld found both instruction and intimate echo in the 1689 edition of the *Imitatio Christi* he is said to have kept by his bedside.

Taking up an old theme with new urgency, Hammarskjöld spent some part of the week before leaving for New York reconsidering the basis for a life of service—for prominence without pride, action without deliberate or unconscious self-serving. Earlier in the week (this is how I understand the timing, there can be no certainty), he had recorded a most demanding thought: "Goodness is something so simple: always to live for others, never to seek one's own advantage."[37] And perhaps a day or two later, he again used few words to capture the starkest of thoughts: "Not I, but God in me."[38] These entries and others later in the year make clear that Hammarskjöld's working solution to the challenges of prominence and action was religious. It relied on a vivid sense of living with others by the light of traditional ethics under the love and scrutiny of God—a God experienced as wholly transcendent yet also present within us and potentially active. So stated, the model seems dry. It was anything but dry. It called for keen awareness of concrete detail, keen awareness of ceaseless change and the flicker of a numinous presence not wholly revealed, not wholly absent. "Not I, but God in me" is not an assertion; it is a prayer.

So much had happened suddenly. During the week that remained to him in Sweden, he found himself interpreting the sequence of events as an act of divine providence striking his life with ruthless objectivity:

> When in decisive moments—as now—God acts, it is with a stern purposefulness, a Sophoclean refinement. When the hour strikes, He takes what is His. What have *you* to say? —Your prayer has been answered, as you know. God has a use for you even though what He asks doesn't happen to suit you at the moment. God, who "abases him whom He raises up."[39]

After reaching New York and assuming his new post, Hammarskjöld continued to explore the larger meaning of the events in which he was now a willing captive. He was asking, for example, in what sense am "I" taking action?—and answering, "He who has nothing can give nothing. The gift is God's—to God."[40] He was asking in what sense am "I" subject to God's will?—and answering, "I am the vessel. The draught is God's. And God is the thirsty one."[41] These words can seem strange in the broad daylight of thought, but they may find an echo in the far background of feeling. As well, we should remember Hammarskjöld's situation. He didn't need philosophical nuance to guide him at this time; he needed unshakeable truth recognized by feeling and faith.

Hammarskjöld's personal insights at this time would not perceptibly affect his outward actions; they conferred relaxation and acceptance, quickness and fluidity—but all this, so crucially important, would not have met the eye of new colleagues or journalists. They were small shifts or gleams at the center of himself, markings on an unseen compass. He wasn't striving to erase himself from the equation, as if some wise ghost could act in his stead. He knew perfectly well that we are each responsible for ourselves and that our lives are our terrain. Entries in *Markings* later in the year refer with precision to personal challenges: "If only I may grow: firmer, simpler—quieter, warmer."[42] He was following his experience. Faithful to his practice of conscious self-scrutiny, he was watching for key features and feelings. He noted, for example, "the humility which comes from others having faith in you."[43] Perceptions of this order are often just a flash in time, but the light they shed can reach far.

Hammarskjöld's traditionally religious solution of the riddle facing him—how to accept and execute a role of high leadership with all of one's powers, boldly, yet as a servant—is not the only possible solution; it was his, deeply in character. He was deriving insights from Judeo-Christian teachings and Thomas à Kempis's vision of the imitation of Christ by ordinary, striving human beings. Thomas could teach him, for example, that "he who has surrendered himself to it knows that the Way ends on the Cross—even when it is leading him through the jubilation of Gennesaret or the triumphal entry into Jerusalem."[44] These words in *Markings* convey Hammarskjöld's intuition from the beginning that "the most difficult job in the world" was very possibly both a Way—an enterprise with spiritual dimensions—and a route toward suffering and early death. Conceivably he also had in mind his remarkable countryman, Count Folke Bernadotte, assassinated five years earlier in Jerusalem while on a mission of mediation for the UN.[45] UN service in the field has never been safe service. In July 1953, when the calendar of events at the UN required Hammarskjöld to say a few words at the rededication of a memorial plaque for Bernadotte, he took the occasion to identify Bernadotte as a hero of the United Nations, its first, and to restate the values in whose service he had died.[46] Hammarskjöld understood and respected the need for heroes, for the accumulation of valid legend; it was part of the story and storytelling.

There are enough resources in our philosophical, political, artistic, and even managerial cultures to permit serious people to strive under other inspirations for sustained excellence in a spirit of service. I have a friend, for example, who leads an NGO, a nongovernmental organization. Before meetings likely to require a great deal of him he often listens to recordings of Schubert's music. Schubert's genius for creating ordered beauty and for summoning emotion, Schubert who died at the age of thirty-one, is quite enough to remind him in depth of the small thing we are and the greatness of what is possible. Music offers my friend a circumscribed but dynamic context for the psychological forces and interpersonal issues worked through by Hammarskjöld in quite other terms. The result is roughly the same: renewed awareness of something far greater than oneself, realistic acknowledgment of others' mastery, willingness to play one's role to the extreme limit of one's ability. At a staff gathering in 1958 to celebrate the beginning of his second term in office, Hammarskjöld recalled his state of mind at the start of his first term: "I knew only one thing," he said, "and that is that nobody can do more than is in his power, and I had only one intention and that was to do that much."[47]

In the revolutionary week between notification in Stockholm and departure for New York, two further understandings dawned. We have already noticed that he discovered his "yes," an unreserved affirmation and acceptance of self and situation and the future, come what may. Scarcely detectable in preceding years, this heartfelt "yes" was to be a steady force in years to come. Now he writes, "To be free, to be able to stand up and leaving *everything* behind—without looking back. To say *Yes*—."[48] Somewhat later in the year, he looked again at the dimensions of "yes" and experienced its redemptive power:

> To say Yes to life is at one and the same time to say Yes to oneself.
>   Yes—even to that element in one which is most unwilling to let itself be transformed from a temptation into a strength.[49]

This is depth psychology, as if one has fished in vain for years and suddenly draws from the empty sea a magical fish, the very one that one somehow knew was there. This is Christianity at work, its long emphasis on sin and redemption suddenly becoming experience. And this is surely just a momentary flash of perception—of the kind that sheds light and warmth well past the isolated moment.

There was a second insight, no less life-changing than the first: an abrupt recognition of his own maturity and readiness. Beskow has prepared us through his observation that Hammarskjöld seemed to have matured "nearly overnight." Hammarskjöld's insights into the dimensions and central importance of maturity clarified much in his own experience but also much in his diplomatic work; the threads from the one to the other were quickly woven. Few if any leaders in modern public life have offered such an attractive understanding of maturity as a crucial asset at all levels; we will often encounter it in one or another form, suited to the circumstances he was addressing. But the initial insight was purely internal, occurring in the week of transition from Stockholm to New York:

> Maturity: among other things—not to hide one's strength out of fear and, consequently, live below one's best.[50]

> Maturity: among other things, a new lack of self-consciousness—the kind you can only attain when you have become entirely indifferent to yourself through an absolute assent to your fate.
>
> He who has placed himself in God's hand stands free vis-à-vis men: he is entirely at his ease with them, because he has granted them the right to judge.[51]

Striking here is Hammarskjöld's repeated use of the phrase "among other things," nicely translating Sw. *också* (related to English "also"). He was thinking widely and had insights, any one of which could be drawn out for a closer look; and his inquiry was ongoing, the sum of insight was growing. What is maturity? These lines in *Markings* set inquiry in motion without closing it off. At a watershed moment he turned to himself and discovered someone different, much like the person there before but more coherent, more resourceful, freer to reflect and respond without being trapped in personal labyrinths. It was an unexpected encounter with surprising competence, surprising willingness, surprising order in spite of all else, supported in Hammarskjöld's experience by faith in God. In a letter of 1956 to a fellow member of the Swedish Academy about the explorer Sven Hedin, he returned to the theme of fearlessness: "Another point I would like to discuss with you sometime," he wrote, "is the importance of the religious relation for [Hedin's] 'fearlessness.' I know quite well what I am talking about. The thing is far less simple than it may seem. And that fearlessness could be rather hard-earned."[52]

All of this is rigorous. It emerged from Hammarskjöld's encounters with the raw experience of life and with the religious tradition he had made his own. But he noticed another shade of maturity: a child's freedom and joyousness. "Maturity," he wrote after what must have been some months at the UN. "Among other things, the radiant serenity of play in the moment for the child, who takes it for granted that he is at one with his playmates."[53] We know that he had despaired about relationship and suffered a recurrent sense of harsh isolation. But here, and in a remarkable entry in *Markings* dating to early 1954 (we'll see it later), he acknowledged a new experience much like a child's fearless joy in companionship and shared activity—and defined it as an aspect of maturity. We can whirr back to the gospel texts where Jesus admonishes the disciples to "become as little children" (Matthew 18:1 and elsewhere); Hammarskjöld would have known those texts from his earliest years. But that doesn't feel relevant here. He was transcribing not from tradition but from life experience. "This little republic," as he described the UN at the beginning of November 1953, quickly came to be his home, with all that home implies at best for well-being and warm relations.[54]

There is more still about maturity in *Markings* for these months of 1953, but we have seen enough to know what we need to know. It was often true of Hammarskjöld that what he had understood internally, as episodes in his private spiritual search, reappeared in public talks in words and thoughts that retain the force they had acquired within him, though with no sign of their origin in his personal life of inquiry. He externalized the concepts just a little, just enough; adapted them to new contexts. "Maturity" became, for example, "maturity of mind" or a related expression. "Faith," as we shall later see, often became faith in humanity or in the future. Insofar as possible, he worked out in his inner life—in a "rather hard-earned" way—the characteristics and potential of human nature, therefore the potential for peaceful relations at the level of nations. The leap may seem wide, but he interposed very little between what persons are, for good or ill, and what nations do, for good or ill. He was, of course, acutely aware of impersonal, rules-driven bureaucracies—he worked daily with member nation and UN bureaucracies—but he was convinced that individuals at every level, from national leaders to members of the public at large, are responsible in varying degrees for what occurs, and that what occurs billows out from what we are. A few years later, when he was reading regularly in the poet Ezra Pound's translation of early Chinese classics that explore the links between spirituality and political order, he would come upon richly expressed passages saying much the same thing: "One humane family can humanize a whole state," he would read. "One courteous family can lift a whole state into courtesy; one grasping and perverse man can drive a nation to chaos."[55]

In 1953, Hammarskjöld like many others viewed the United Nations as a work in progress. The organization was not mature; it had some chance of maturing. "The United Nations is a positive response by the world community to the fundamental needs of our time," he wrote in his first annual report, published in July. "Its record should be judged against this background. Its efforts are significant insofar as they show the growing maturity of the Organization as an instrument by means of which the nations can solve conflicts threatening the natural evolution of the world community."[56] The thought here again reflects Hammarskjöld's respect for Henri Bergson's notion of creative evolution. For Bergson, as for Hammarskjöld, there was a possible, a desirable, a "natural" evolution implicit in current circumstances. From the first, in his years at the UN, Hammarskjöld had a good deal of clarity about the possibilities and path forward of the community of nations. He had, as well, clarity about obstacles that deflect the possible into dangerous or inhumane alternatives. His sense of the long movement of events made itself felt some years later in a letter to the famed Swedish writer and Nobel laureate, Pär Lagerkvist—much his elder, a fellow member of the Swedish Academy with whom he had a surprisingly candid, searching correspondence. "The unique, totally undeserved gift I have been given," he wrote to Lagerkvist, "is the opportunity to engage in a decisive way in one of the greatest experiments of mankind and of this era. It is incredible to know that everything you can do, insofar as possible, to bring this experiment to maturity, even if it should fail, contributes to laying the foundation of something that has to succeed in the end."[57]

Hammarskjöld also understood in terms of maturity the demands placed on himself and his colleagues in the UN Secretariat. At a staff meeting in Geneva in early December, he again evoked the theme in a statement that has lost none of its energy or relevance: "The weight we carry is not determined by physical force or the number of people who form the constituency. It is based solely on trust in our impartiality, our experience and knowledge, our maturity of judgment. Those qualities are our weapons, in no way secret weapons, but as difficult to forge as guns and bombs."[58]

7

This Little Republic

On May 9th, just one month after taking office, Hammarskjöld wrote a compelling report on the feel of his new life to close friends Leif and Greta Belfrage. "Of this [the UN] I somehow cannot tell," he began.

> It remains too preposterous—both evil and encouraging. The Thousand and One Nights—but the Thousand and One Nights with the Sermon on the Mount as a counterpoint. No, you cannot understand me; this must sound quite mad and still it is true.
>
> For the most part people have been incredibly kind and it has all gone well in a way I haven't at all deserved. There is wind in the sails, and the boat answers to the helm. So far–! But still, even though I now know what it is (and it is worse than I thought), in an unreasonable way I still feel safe and secure. It is all somehow going "right," and then you neither ask nor are you afraid.
>
> The annoying thing is something superficial: the shortage of time itself and the enormous physical wear and tear. I can't see it stretching far into the future without wonder. But to each day its sorrow.[1]

We can readily understand Hammarskjöld's recall of the Sermon on the Mount, but what did he have in mind where the swirl of tales in the *Arabian Nights* is concerned? Surprisingly, we don't have to guess. In a letter written a week earlier to his brother Bo, with whom he maintained a warm exchange through the UN years, he launched the analogy with vivid detail. He was writing from the Waldorf-Astoria Hotel in New York, temporary personal quarters with his transition staff.

> That you haven't heard from me is entirely due to a harder workload than I have experienced since the first winter of the war. I have so far ... had to go on an 18-hour basis without break, and that doesn't make one a great letter writer.
>
> All of this remains a sort of Arabian Nights. Just as cruel and vulgar on the one hand, but also as humanly rich and—I dare say—touching and bewitching. Destiny—if that is what we should call it—has so far been unbelievably kind: everything has gone decently beyond all

reasonable limits—but you are surrounded by wolves and skiing with blind trust across glacial crevasses over a very thin snow bridge! As resolutely independent as I have preferred to be—in both directions [presumably toward the United States and Soviet Union]—I expect the big crash anytime. But they are careful with me; I am still politically a rather precious object.[2]

The "precious object" had naturally set to work at once. Trygve Lie was not untidy in the way he left matters, though he himself untidily lingered for some weeks on the thirty-eighth floor and needed a vigorous farewell celebration to accept that it was time to move on. Hammarskjöld took immediate steps to connect with the Secretariat staff. In a gesture remembered even years later, he made a point of going to all departments, shaking hands with something like four thousand people and offering a warm hello. He also made a point of eating in the staff cafeteria whenever possible rather than in lofty privacy and released the secretary-general's private elevator for general service. Small gestures, large meaning.

He must have recognized early that he had inherited from Lie a number of altogether outstanding high officials, most notably Ralph Bunche (Nobel Peace laureate, 1950) and Andrew Cordier, who became his right and left hands, wholly trusted aides and advisers (figs. 10, 11). One doesn't think of them as Lie's men; they are remembered with Hammarskjöld, but for years they had both worked closely and well with Trygvie Lie and like him had participated in drafting the UN Charter at the San Francisco Conference, 1945. Ralph Bunche (1904–71) deserves a larger place in American history than he has so far been granted. Though he was the friend of US presidents, he gave the best of himself to the United Nations rather than directly to his country. This may have conferred some remoteness, as if he were part of a different narrative. One of his biographers, Charles P. Henry, professor of African American studies at the University of California, Berkeley, records another remoteness: the uneasy relations between Bunche, thoroughly assimilated into the mainstream, and other prominent African Americans who were struggling against racism as representatives of their community. It was their problem, not his; Bunche never forgot his roots and remained active in the civil rights movement. Nonetheless, he "became a victim of his own success," Henry writes.[3] Be that as it may, he was an African American of vast attainment, a trailblazer in public life.

Orphaned rather early and raised in modest circumstances by his grandmother in Los Angeles, Bunche had intellectual and athletic gifts in overwhelming abundance. Doors opened. A summa cum laude graduate of UCLA and class valedictorian, he went on to Harvard where he earned a doctorate in political science in 1934. Over the next years he taught at Howard University, did anthropological field work in Africa, contributed to journals of ideas, and worked with the Swedish economist and sociologist, Gunnar Myrdal, on his groundbreaking book of 1944 on American racism, *An American Dilemma*. (We have already encountered Myrdal as the principal examiner of Hammarskjöld's doctoral thesis.) In the US State Department during the war, Bunche became expert on what was then called dependent area affairs, which led in time to his leadership at the UN in assisting the transition from colonial status to independence among emerging nations in Asia and Africa. Accepting in 1946 what would prove to be lifelong employment at the UN, he served as chief aide in 1948 to Count Folke Bernadotte, the UN mediator charged with negotiating an end to the war that had broken out between Israel and surrounding Arab countries immediately after Israel achieved nationhood. When Bernadotte was assassinated in Jerusalem in September of that year, Bunche succeeded him and, through marathon negotiations staged in greater safety on the island of Rhodes, completed Bernadotte's mission. The world was grateful. The Nobel Peace Prize was well placed on him; he was the first person of color to be so honored.

In August 1954, Hammarskjöld appointed Bunche to be one of two undersecretaries for special political affairs (the other a Soviet diplomat). It was a catchall title; in practice the word "special" meant large scale, intricate, risky. Bunche was already involved in everything most difficult that Hammarskjöld and the Secretariat undertook, but his new responsibility turned his attention outward from administrative issues to the world. "Of all his senior UN colleagues," Urquhart has written, "Hammarskjöld probably regarded Bunche alone as his intellectual equal and as a person of equivalent stature to himself."[4] Urquhart must have added "probably" because, after all, there were others, notably Lester Pearson of Canada and Rajeshwar Dayal of India. Urquhart also records that Bunche "was one of Hammarskjöld's few professional associates who frequently dined with him at his . . . apartment . . . in New York."[5] Ralph Bunche was Urquhart's long-term superior at the UN; Urquhart's biography of him is both a richly detailed document and an homage.[6]

Andrew Cordier (1901–75) is more difficult to characterize. Though he served in prominent positions for much of his life and, as coeditor of the *Public Papers* of Trygvie Lie, Dag Hammarskjöld, and U Thant remains central to how we understand their UN careers, he has left a lighter trace in the record than Bunche. A large man in all respects, he served for many years as Hammarskjöld's executive assistant—in effect, his chief of staff—and, in a brief though fateful episode, as the senior UN figure in the Congo. He is said to have had a masterful understanding of the UN and its people, and there seem to have been standing jokes about his expertise in parliamentary procedure; no one could dodge past him. "If Andy did not exist," Hammarskjöld once said, "he would have to be invented. I need send him only a brief message knowing that he will not only immediately interpret its political and diplomatic essence, but he will call in the heads of all delegations capable of playing some part in the development, and he will give each of them precisely the ingredient needed for their role."[7] As with Bunche, Hammarskjöld could be entirely frank with Cordier, and something in the sparkle and trust of their relationship prompted Hammarskjöld to pithy insights, some of his best. For example, in a memo to Cordier written in the course of his efforts to calm the Middle East in the spring of 1956, Hammarskjöld wrote:

> We happen to be those on the spot, and we have to play ball with both guts and prudence. . . . What should I tell you more about the negotiations? . . . Let us pray to God that some fool will not throw us back now— or that other fools will not believe that what is achieved entitles them to turn their back to the desperate problems of this part of the world. . . . If we are to get further ahead, it will have to be in fertile darkness. . . . Perhaps you have to have been a participant in the development during the last fortnight to appreciate how the United Nations has functioned as a screen between us and—maybe—catastrophe. These are strong words, but I believe that they are justified. That should give us all satisfaction and encouragement to new efforts: once you go head first into it, even the most impossible task may show unexpected opportunities.[8]

After leaving UN service, Cordier became dean of the School of International Affairs at Columbia University and was asked to step in as president of the university during the student revolt in 1968. He served in that role on an acting basis for two years. His decades of UN experience—listening, persevering, acting with clarity—stood the university in good stead during that uniquely troubled period. Cordier's voluminous papers, now in the university library, have unexplored depths. He preserved every scrap of paper he possibly could from his UN years. Failing that, we wouldn't know that he and Hammarskjöld like mischievous students passed notes back and forth during lulls or enormities in the course of meetings. Hammarskjöld once passed him an archly astute note, no doubt while Mr. X was still speaking from the rostrum: "X is—to say the least—timid and wobbling, which in practice may make him too stiff by way of over-compensation." Hammarskjöld and Cordier were in every sense friends and colleagues.

Hammarskjöld's experience of collegiality at the UN was, in its intensity and trust, new to him. In *Markings*, most likely in early 1954, he explored the stunning comradeship discovered in the company of Bunche, Cordier, and others, all unnamed. There are two such entries. The first is compact; it asks for close reading. The second is expansive and vivid. Both rely on imagery of the sea and sailing, which came easily to Hammarskjöld's mind. We think of him as a mountaineer, but we must be missing something: he knew how to sail and liked to tramp along beaches with his camera. Hammarskjöld spent a year-end 1953 holiday week in Marathon Key, Florida—as good a beach as one can find, and he wrote to his brother Bo that he got some sailing in.[9]

> Salty and wind-swept, but warm and glittering. Staying in step under the fixed stars of the task. How many personal failures are due to mistrust of this harmony between human beings, at once strict and gentle.
>
> With all the powers of your body concentrated in the hand on
>   the tiller,
> All the powers of your mind concentrated on the goal beyond
>   the horizon,
> You laugh as the salt spray catches your face in the second of rest
> Before a new wave–
> Sharing the happy freedom of the moment with those who share
>   your responsibility.
> So—in the self-forgetfulness of concentrated attention—the door
> opens for you into a pure living intimacy,
> A shared, timeless happiness,
> Conveyed by a smile,
> A wave of the hand.

Thanks to those who have taught me this. Thanks to the days
which have taught me this.[10]

"At once strict and gentle": Yet again, in the first passage, he explores the
imprisoned misery of personality and, an evolving discovery, the liberation that can occur through *livsnärheten*, literally "closeness to life" (the
Swedish expression well captured by "pure living intimacy"). The misery
fades; it was in part an artifact of loneliness. But the harmony is both
strict and gentle: the need for rigor is never far from his thoughts. The
second passage, one of the most beautifully shaped in *Markings*, is a celebration. Much of what he knew of living at its best is here: concentration, self-forgetfulness, gratitude, the vivid present moment, the worthy
challenge faced with trusted others—and the slight austerity of good
feeling without dramatics (a smile, a wave of the hand). In these entries,
Hammarskjöld was evoking beach days and sailing at Marathon Key—in
what company I don't know, apart from his security aide Bill Ranallo—
but the scope is larger: it encompasses the voyage of the United Nations
and his shipmates there.

Speaking at a dinner in his honor in mid-September 1953, Hammarskjöld drew a distinction almost apologetically, a distinction relevant to
this chapter and several following. The apology may also be needed. He
had mentioned at least once before this talk a comment that must have
tickled him: an early characterization of him in the *New York Times* as an
"unashamed intellectual."

> Recently a distinguished New York newspaper found me to be an "un-
> ashamed intellectual." It is not because of any desire to live up to this
> standard that I propose to talk with you tonight of certain basic ideas
> and principles rather than of the specific issues and grave difficulties
> with which the General Assembly and the Members of the United Na-
> tions will be wrestling in the weeks ahead.[11]

As we set out to follow Hammarskjöld at the UN, we reach an early fork in
the road: either to follow him into the nearly infinite detail of the challenges he faced or to stay predominantly with the ideas and attitudes through
which he renewed the UN, redefined the nature of international community, and developed a vision of leadership suited to the interdependent
world of his day and ours. In other words, we need to choose, not rigidly or
exclusively, between "specific issues and grave difficulties" and "basic ideas
and principles." He was not one, nor should we be, to avoid conflict and

complexity. "No institution," he said toward the end of 1953, "can become effective unless it is forced to wrestle with the problems, the conflicts, and the tribulations of real life."[12] No institution, no person, and no book. Our trajectory lies between ideas and incidents, in clear view of both.

The unappeasable aggressor

Hammarskjöld took office at a generally promising time, but all the same he faced an immediate and nasty situation. His first fourteen months in office overlapped US senator Joseph McCarthy's last fourteen months of fame and power. The repressive, mercilessly destructive witch-hunt for "Communist subversives" in the US government, led by McCarthy and his political allies, had found its way into the UN Secretariat, which in principle was and is an independent, international entity sheltered from the domestic politics of any member nation. FBI agents had nonetheless been on site at UN headquarters since January 1953, interviewing and fingerprinting under an order issued by president Harry Truman before leaving office, which authorized loyalty investigations of all US personnel working in international organizations. For reasons that Trygvie Lie thought pragmatically acceptable though not beyond criticism, he had opened the door to the FBI.

Writing in the *New York Times* in January 1952, US Supreme Court Justice William O. Douglas vividly conveyed the atmosphere of the McCarthy era. He wrote with declarative force and bitter clarity. "The Communist threat inside the country," he wrote,

> has been magnified and exalted far beyond its realities. Irresponsible talk by irresponsible people has fanned the flames of fear. Accusations have been loosely made. Character assassinations have become common. Suspicion has taken the place of goodwill. Once we could debate along a wide range of inquiry. Once we could safely explore to the edges of a problem, challenge orthodoxy without qualms, and run the gamut of ideas in search of solutions to perplexing problems. Once we had confidence in each other. . . . Fear has mounted—fear of losing one's job, fear of being investigated, fear of being pilloried. This fear has stereo-typed our thinking, narrowed the range of free public discussion, and driven many thoughtful people to despair.[13]

This was America at the time, the nation just past the broad terraces of UN headquarters.[14] In the month before Justice Douglas's article, the chairman of the Senate Foreign Relations Committee had warned that "the United Nations should not become a haven for disloyal Americans or for espionage," and a New York grand jury had concluded a secret investigation without bringing charges but issuing an inflammatory public statement that alleged "infiltration into the United Nations of an overwhelmingly large group of disloyal United States citizens."[15] There was no evidence for such a large claim; a handful of cases had come to light through previous investigations, a handful of American personnel had resigned or been let go by decision of the secretary-general. If the situation Hammarskjöld had inherited was worse than he had imagined, this issue woven of obsession, fear, and self-aggrandizement must have been part of what he had in mind. In a letter some years later, he referred in passing to what he called "McCarthy-ish hysteria"; the phrase must reflect his view at the time he came directly to grips with it.[16] A letter of January 4th, 1954, addresses the McCarthy era in broad terms. Hammarskjöld wrote: "Bear . . . in mind how limited my possibilities are to speak frankly. But there are certain themes you cannot escape: one is the inconsequence in the formation of American public opinion. These people who are to bless us with 'a world without fear' and themselves lack moral courage. These people who preach righteousness to the world and apply such capricious justice to themselves."[17] It was an angry letter, and the fit is perfect to McCarthy-ish hysteria.

With the help of in-house committees expert in various areas, Hammarskjöld approached the problem diplomatically through a well-studied series of clarifications. He explored and freshly articulated the status and obligations of all Secretariat personnel, Americans included. He looked closely at the appropriate treatment of personnel information provided by a government in relation to the secretary-general's obligation under the Charter to make independent decisions. He reaffirmed a judicial review process already available within the UN. And he revised regulations to give legal force to his findings. By these means he and his colleagues successfully eliminated the FBI presence from the building and ensured that nothing of the kind would again tempt a member nation. Managing the "specific issues and grave difficulties" with thoroughness, legal acuity, objectivity, and humanity, he persuaded the Secretariat staff of all nations that he could be counted on to defend and advance their legitimate interests and welfare. They now knew of him that he was friendly, although often formal, and that he was fierce in the pursuit of common sense and justice.

The intrusive US investigations touched close to home: Ralph Bunche had been dragged into it in the month before Hammarskjöld took office and for another year was periodically obliged to face accusers and defend himself before being wholly exonerated and left in peace. Like many thoughtful Americans, particularly in the Depression years of the 1930s, Bunche had briefly associated with a number of organizations later listed by the US government as Communist fronts and had looked at the bearing of Marxist thought on the race problem in America.[18] There were other, more recent data points in his dossier. One of his subordinates at the UN had pleaded the Fifth Amendment in testimony before the Senate Internal Security Subcommittee; Lie later dismissed him from UN service. And Bunche at the State Department had worked for Alger Hiss, who was accused in 1948 of being a Soviet spy and convicted in 1950 of a related charge for which he served jail time. Formerly a central figure in US diplomacy, Hiss had served as secretary-general of the United Nations Conference in San Francisco, 1945. His case had received headline attention and served as a springboard in 1950 for McCarthy's campaign against the State Department. Had he influenced Ralph Bunche?

In March 1953, Bunche was called to meet with the leaders of a Senate committee for questioning. One of them, senator William Jenner, was a McCarthy loyalist convinced that "a ruthless political action group [is] determined to destroy the honor [of] America. . . . Like a cancer growing wild, it ignores all . . . restraints. . . ."[19] Soon after their meeting, Bunche addressed him by letter:

> I would have taken it for granted that my long record of service to my country, and my public utterances, written and oral, throughout my adult career, were more than adequate testimonial to my unqualified loyalty to my country and to my unwavering devotion to the American way of life. . . . Senator Welker . . . suggested that perhaps it would have been wiser not to have done some of the things I did in the thirties. Seen from today's perspective that may be true. But in the thirties the common and urgent enemy of peace and freedom was Hitler and his Nazi creed. Today it is communism alone. The lines now are much more sharply drawn, and the perspective of each of us is much simpler and clearer.[20]

In January 1954 began a period in Bunche's life described by Urquhart as "painful and Kafkaesque."[21] Fulfilling high-level UN duties by day, he spent some of his nights filling out an interrogatory from the Senate committee, and no doubt many more consumed by anxiety. The right-wing press and radio, fueled by leaks from Washington, kept the charges against him in front of their audiences. It was a shoddy reward for one of the foremost Americans of his time. Walter Lippmann, the liberal columnist who with his wife became a friend of Hammarskjöld's, described Joseph McCarthy, and by extension his allies, as "the unappeasable aggressor."[22] It was true; there was madness in his treatment of people. At a committee hearing on May 25th, 1954, Bunche faced two witnesses who for reasons of their own made false accusations; they were later convicted of perjury. He spent that evening with President Eisenhower at a dinner honoring the emperor of Ethiopia. Eisenhower had never lacked complete confidence in him.[23] There is much more detail, but we can leave it there: a horror story in the American grain of its time. In August of that year, as noted earlier, Hammarskjöld announced Bunche's appointment as undersecretary for special political affairs. He retained that post throughout Hammarskjöld's years in office.

So much for the cruelty and vulgarity of the *Thousand and One Nights*. What of the Sermon on the Mount? He could have meant a number of things by that expression. It could refer to his own sensibility—he who heard both the words of Thomas à Kempis ("Their lives grounded in and sustained by God, they . . . do all things to the Glory of God alone") and UN debates. This seems likely; this was his nature. It could also mean that he perceived in the swirl of events and mix of motives at the UN a scene in which ancient values and acquired wisdom sought their just influence. He said as much on United Nations Day, October 24th, 1953, to a gathering of invited guests with whom he apparently met before the general festivities. Despite his indifference to cocktail parties and such, Hammarskjöld was a gifted organizer of festive events. It was a social craft he practiced with improvisatory ease and obvious delight, and he knew how to make use of festive events for larger purposes. It was this, I think, that made them important to him. On that first of many UN Days he set in motion, he said in part:

> This is the first year that our home among you has been ready to receive you in this way on United Nations Day. These modern buildings, in a symbolic way, reflect a quality inherent in the organization and role of the United Nations in world affairs. These buildings are modern in design, but they reflect close adherence to many well test-

ed architectural and engineering principles. They combine, in that sense, the old and the new. The real value of the United Nations and its capacity to respond effectively to contemporary needs rests upon the wisdom with which it combines the present and the past. . . . The United Nations introduces a new element in political life. But it is wrong, in my judgment, to say that the United Nations is entirely new. It borrows much from past human experience and is a response in a very major sense to developing human needs. When one views the existence of the United Nations in this sense it takes its own appropriate place—a natural and normal place—in the evolution of human society.[24]

This little republic

He would have done it anyway, I'm sure, but American hysteria about loyalty gave Hammarskjöld a pressing reason to restate the role and obligations of international civil servants. Doing so was crucial to establishing a sound relation with Secretariat employees; he needed to make clear what he expected of them in keeping with the Charter. The Charter was the constitutional bedrock of the organization, therefore his bedrock. Just as crucial was to reach a better understanding with member nations, which offered staff members to the Secretariat and other UN branches. In the introduction to the first annual report for which he was responsible, August 1953, Hammarskjöld wrote with understated displeasure, "The place . . . of a truly international civil service, free from all national pressures and influences, should be recognized, not only in words, but in deeds. [This] has [not] yet been given the significance which it should have in the policy of the governments of Member States in relation to the United Nations."[25]

This sounds formal and dull; large organizations and the language of their annual reports are naturally a bit stiff in the legs. But behind Hammarskjöld's concern to restate the identity of the international civil servant was a passionate vision of what could and must be. He viewed the UN as centrally necessary if there was to be anything approaching peace, justice, and aid without strings attached between countries with wealth and those in need. He viewed the men and women who enacted UN programs and initiatives as specially placed in the world, bound by a larger calling, however much that calling was now in need of restatement. In the swarm of ideas he brought to the UN, this was among the first.

An international civil service was assembled by the League of Nations under the guidance of Sir Eric Drummond, its long-serving secretary-general for whom Hammarskjöld more than once expressed sincere admiration. "I have had very much to learn," he said in the course of a 1956 press conference in Australia,

> from the way in which Sir Eric Drummond built up the international secretariat. In the whole field of international politics, one of the most radical innovations was the creation . . . of the notion of an international secretariat as something lifted above all national contexts. That was a creation by Sir Eric Drummond. I admire the way in which he gave it body and weight. We have had to repeat the experiment. In doing so, I personally learnt very much from both the difficulties and the principles of the first experiment.[26]

But the League's failure left the radical innovation hanging while the world made war. Hammarskjöld was certain of the need for a highly effective international civil service: a cadre of individuals serving the common good, committed to an objectivity that could at times be costly, answering not to nations but to the "internation," in our era the United Nations. The elements aren't severed from one another. The founding nations, fifty-one in all, progressively joined by many others, wrote and ratified the UN Charter; the UN was their creation. Decisions taken by the decision-making bodies of the UN and implemented by the Secretariat reflect the will of the member nations. International civil servants do not cease to be citizens of their native countries; that is not expected of them. Retaining their identities as Swedes, Americans, Russians, Egyptians, in principle they acquire a new identity, as well: detached from national agendas, responsive exclusively to the "internation," thinking for the whole, acting for the whole.

There is here both a shining ideal and a great need for realism, as Hammarskjöld well knew. His youthful experience of World War I and of his father's ordeal as prime minister, and later his own and his family's disillusionment over the failed League of Nations, made him cautious about shining ideals. We can recall lines from that striking letter of 1950 to his mentor, Ernst Wigforss—written just five years after World War II had ended—in which he compared the sensibility of his generation to "a bombed-out city, in which the inhabitants are happy to be able to join shattered ruins into a temporary shelter." And yet . . . he had ideals for which he cared enormously, and he drew on them to inspire his fellow international civil servants. The balance in him between ideals and factual recognitions was always interesting. Often he was plainly factual. Just as often he voiced challenging ideals. During a visit in late May to the UN staff in Geneva, where the League's buildings now served as the European headquarters of the UN, ideals and realism mingled in a most poignant way when he spoke with his colleagues: "Although perhaps profiting from wider support of the common man than our predecessors [at the League of Nations], we have to work in a much harsher climate. Where our predecessors dreamt of a new heaven, our greatest hope is that we may be permitted to save the old earth. Behind that hope, however, are now rallied all peoples of the world."[27]

The task ahead was twofold: to redefine the status and duties of the international civil servant—a factual task requiring committee work, negotiation, revised regulations—and to infuse that identity with freshly recognized dignity and purpose. Both aspects had to be widely communicated to Secretariat staff, the officials of member nations, and the press and public. Once status and duties were clear, the rest could follow. Already by May 1st he promised the staff that "the principles on which the independence of our Secretariat is founded will be staunchly defended and firmly applied."[28] At a press conference in Geneva on May 22nd, he offered a more detailed look. He spoke of the basis on which everything else could be built.

> Let me stress what you know, that the members of the staff are international civil servants. It starts from the Secretary-General and it is true of all the rest. That means that there is one loyalty and that is . . . to the international organization and not to anybody else. . . . When going through these matters I must say that I have become more and more convinced that the rule has to be applied in a very strict way, in so strict a way in fact, that I really regard it as essential that members of the staff should abstain from all participation in political activities in their own country or other countries, which are not strictly . . . their duty as members of the staff of the UN, that is to say, what does not follow from instructions from the Secretary-General and the UN. That is a very strict rule and goes very far. Well, I think you will understand this in view of the fact that what is most essential in the present world situation is that the Secretariat should enjoy the full confidence of all Member Governments.

It is rather difficult for any member of the staff to engage in political activities in his own country or other countries without running the risk of getting into situations of conflict. Such conflicts will reflect on the governments' view of the neutrality and objectivity of the Secretariat, and what one member of the staff does may in this way have an influence on the confidence in the Secretariat in general. . . . I think that it would be to pay far too high a price if through any laxity, any wish to be liberal in the approach to Secretariat members' activities, we were running the risk of losing . . . the very basis of our operations—that is, the confidence of all parties concerned. . . .

I may add . . . , in order to avoid misunderstanding, that my experience is that the best international civil servant is the one who, while being loyal and 100 percent loyal to the Organization, is not an internationalist in the sense that he has lost his roots in his own country.[29]

He was interesting on this last point, love of country. At a lunch with political scientists in September, when the loyalty issue was still grinding forward, he returned to it:

In the United Nations Secretariat we have nearly sixty different nationalities represented. None of us can make ourselves entirely free from our own background, and why should we? Is not the national accent and the national experience very often a great asset in international cooperation? . . . [But] . . . it is necessary to find ways to make the national elements an asset, to overcome . . . divisive influences, and try to create a unity in which the diversity of the national backgrounds of the members of the administration is fully respected and preserved, but in such a way as to be an asset. . . . I am sure it must be evident to you how difficult and challenging a problem this is.[30]

Hammarskjöld himself retained what links he could in Sweden. He spent brief holidays there; they were infrequent. He purchased a home in southern Sweden as we know, but renovations and furnishing were necessarily left in the hands of friends. He "did business" from Stockholm when that made sense, as it would in 1956 when he needed a discreet diplomatic connection to the People's Republic of China. He remained a vice president of the Swedish Tourist Association and at the end of 1954 accepted membership of the Swedish Academy. Like the Tourist Association, the Academy was apolitical, although it could use its privilege of conferring the Nobel Prize in Literature to stir things up, as it did in 1958 by naming Boris Pasternak at a time when the Soviet government was hounding him over his politically provocative novel, *Doctor Zhivago*.

Hammarskjöld sometimes longed for home. "You might guess how much I would like to come to Sweden," he wrote in summer 1958 to Pär Lagerkvist, his honored colleague in the Swedish Academy, "and how warmly I then would hope to get a chance to talk to you in peace and quiet. Now the Middle East has smashed all plans."[31] And it was a prominent Swedish newspaper man, Herbert Tingsten, who somehow got under his skin more than any other. Tingsten had already declared himself an adversary when Hammarskjöld was a Swedish cabinet minister. By August of the year we're exploring, 1953, he wrote something—was it a personal letter to Hammarskjöld or an editorial?—that elicited a lively defense. We can reconstruct what he must have said from Hammarskjöld's letter in reply. "I can criticize," Hammarskjold wrote,

> and I do criticize, what is said and done by Member Governments, very firmly, behind closed doors in direct contact with the Governments concerned, but I win the right to do so by abstaining from voicing those opinions in the same way publicly. . . . The very delicate and, I feel, sound tactics I have to develop in these respects must be difficult to appreciate from the outside; I have myself had to make quite a few discoveries concerning what are the possibilities—and what are the limits to those possibilities—for a frank and independent expression of views from the Secretary-General.[32]

Tingsten must have wanted more visible, audible fireworks. Unless events called for fireworks, that wasn't Hammarskjöld's way. He preferred lasting fires that shed light.

We know enough now to move on. Hammarskjöld asked of each party to the issue—his own staff, member nations—to come to a new recognition of boundaries. He understood that there was a price to pay. "I have to ask of staff members to sacrifice part of their normal rights as private citizens. I feel I am right in doing so [in] . . . the interest of preserving the Secretariat as a body enjoying the full and unreserved confidence of all Member Nations."[33] On the other hand, as he wrote in the July 15th annual report, "on this basis the international civil service should be left free from national pressures of any sort. Only if this is so will the secretariats be able to render the service necessary to world organization."[34] By early September the difficulties weren't fully resolved and would perhaps always need tending and mending, but he encouraged his Secretariat colleagues to acknowledge progress.

> Sometimes, when I look ahead, the problems raised by our need to develop a truly international and independent Secretariat seem to me to be beyond human capacity. But I know that this is not so. There is no reason for despair. On the contrary, the very immensity of the task should serve as an inspiration; we are in the fortunate position of pioneers. Even if it will not be for us . . . ever to reach a stage where we can say, as it was said on the Seventh Day, that the world is good, even if we would have to leave our world with wide areas still unexplored and uncharted, we have a chance to map out some new land and to leave what we are working at a little bit less imperfect than it was when we started.[35]

Metaphor and symbol mattered to Hammarskjöld. A lover of the arts and literature, and a practiced writer both in the privacy of his journal and in the public arena, he used metaphor and symbol to convey the felt aspects of things or to place them in a mobile network of values. It was in this spirit, I believe, that within weeks of taking office he began referring to the United Nations as "this house."[36] Part of his language to the end, this first surfaced in a press conference covering our very issue, the international civil servant. "I have very strong feelings," he said, "about the necessity for every member of the staff to keep entirely free from any political engagement which is not in harmony with our position here in this house."[37] What were the boundaries of the house he had in mind? It was certainly the UN buildings; he had a strong sense for their physical mass and vast meeting halls and maze of offices. But it was also the organization as a whole. The word was resonant when he used it; it still catches the mind. It reflected a householder's familiarity and pride of place, and no doubt his wish that all UN staff feel at home and all embassies and visitors feel welcome. It reflected a sense of order, as if the UN with its worldwide reach and responsibilities was nonetheless a manageable household. He would use the expression in both utterly serious and pleasantly offhand ways. Speaking in 1955 with reporters about a high-level private dinner he had attended, he observed that "my job normally is around here in the house."[38] While in the text he wrote in 1957 for the Room of Quiet, the meditation room on the ground floor of the Secretariat building, he spoke of "this house, dedicated to work and debate in the service of peace." Sometimes his feel for things tied the word to the world: in February 1960, just returned to New York from a trip across the African continent, he described his visits with government officials as "on the whole, a household operation."[39] In all usages, it was an attractive, relaxing expression.[40] It had the same unpretentiousness and power as something else he said in his early months of UN service. He was giving a talk at a dinner in his honor, hosted by a university group. He must have felt that he was among learned people—he was freely referring to the Bhagavad Gita, Tao Te Ching, and other sources, weaving a richly complex version of the UN at work, its values and attitudes. And then he invited his listeners to return to "our working hypothesis of somehow living together."[41] It was so true, and so simple.

In early September 1953, Hammarskjöld expressed to his many colleagues at the Staff Day celebration his developing vision of their shared identity. Relying on yet another metaphor, he summoned the image of a company of fellow workers moved by a force from within and united by friendship. There was magical intent in his words; by summoning the image, he surely wished to summon or strengthen the reality.

> In a sense the Secretariat of this organization is a little republic of its own—like a people with its own rights, its own obligations, its own traditions and its own human problems. . . . The spirit of unity should be strong and positive . . . , a spiritual force which carries the group forward. . . . This positive feeling is not born out of nothing. . . . We have to go out of ourselves, we have to open our minds to the problems of our colleagues, we have to make friends, and in order to do so, we have to act as and be good friends ourselves.[42]

A right of initiative

The UN Charter identifies the secretary-general as "the chief administrative office of the Organization," charged also with carrying out functions that may be entrusted to him by the General Assembly, the Security Council, and other centers of authority within the UN. Further, under Article 99, "The Secretary-General may bring to the attention of the Security Council any matter which in his opinion may threaten the maintenance of international peace and security." The substance of Article 100 appears in the secretary-general's oath of office: the Secretary-General "shall not seek or receive instructions from any government or from any other authority external to the Organization," and each member nation undertakes "to respect the exclusively international character of the Secretary-General and the staff and not to seek to influence them." Article 101 assigns responsibility to the secretary-general to appoint Secretariat staff and dwells on the need for "the highest standards of efficiency, competence, and integrity" in staff members, taking precedence over a secondary need to recruit staff "on as wide a geographical as possible." And that, essentially, is all. The "job," as we have heard him say, addressing all the hopes and anguish of the world, is grounded in these simple premises.[43] It is both administrative and political—the administrative role largely hidden from public view, the political role ultimately public in impact although often pursued through what Hammarskjöld called quiet diplomacy.

Hammarskjöld frequently referred to the Charter and did his best to ensure that the diplomatic community kept it in mind; it was not to become old parchment. At a talk in London toward the end of the year, he spoke with particular eloquence: "The Charter is at once a supreme standard against which the worth of the policies of governments must always be measured and an evocative force constantly summoning these policies in more positive and constructive directions."[44] An evocative force: this is sophisticated language and thinking. Implicitly it conceives of the human community as awash with influences, some for the good, some destructive, all of them soliciting or summoning attention. The power of the Charter, however much overlooked or defied, was that all member nations had signed up; it was and is their common credo. Its opening words were contributed by the sole American woman in the US delegation to the San Francisco conference, Virginia Gildersleeve, in cooperation with her aide, Elizabeth Reynard. They remain evocative and summoning to this day: "We the peoples of the United Nations, determined to save succeeding generations from the scourge of war, which twice in our lifetime has brought untold sorrow to mankind. . . ." Gildersleeve was the long-serving dean of Barnard College, the women's division of Columbia University in New York City.[45]

"I cannot find," Hammarskjöld said in September 1953, "any part of my present task more challenging than the one which consists in trying to develop all the potentialities of that unique diplomatic instrument which the Charter has created in the institution called the Secretary-General of the United Nations."[46] From the beginning of his tenure,

he had been looking at the role as four-sided: administrative responsibility across the entire UN organization; confidential diplomatic
contacts with all delegations; the political role codified in Article 99,
which implies more than is strictly stated in its wording; and a role
unmentioned by the Charter, though crucially important, of public
communication. At a press conference in Geneva in late May, he spoke
of his political responsibility:

> The right of initiative of the Secretary-General is fairly well defined
> in the Charter. . . . I feel very strongly that the rights entrusted to the
> Secretary-General are rights which should be used when the situation
> calls for it. . . . It should be recognized that there exists a right of initia-
> tive which goes beyond the Charter, subject to the condition that any
> such initiative . . . has to be exerted with the greatest tact and judgment.
> If it is not done in that spirit, it may do more harm than good. . . . To
> sum up: What I feel is that there is, first of all, the right of initiative es-
> tablished in the Charter, but that there is also a moral right of initiative
> which goes beyond the Charter. It is, however, entirely the responsibil-
> ity of the Secretary-General that such a moral right of initiative can
> be exerted and what he does has to be done with the greatest tact and
> considerable judgment.[47]

In mid-September, in a talk from which we have already heard in part,
he clarified what he meant by a moral right of initiative requiring tact,
judgment, and not least, ironclad discretion.

> I do not conceive the role of the Secretary-General and the Secretariat
> as representing what has been called a "third line" in the international
> debate. Nor is it for him to try and initiate "compromises" that might
> encroach upon areas that should be exclusively within the sphere of re-
> sponsibility of the respective national governments.
>
> On the other side I see the duty of the Secretariat to form, in the
> first instance, a most complete and objective picture of the aims, mo-
> tives, and difficulties of the Member Nations. Acting in that knowledge,
> it is our duty to seek to anticipate situations that might lead to new
> conflicts or points of tension and to make appropriate suggestions to
> the governments before matters reach a stage of public controversy. Be-
> yond this, the Secretary-General should express with full frankness to
> the governments concerned and their representatives the conclusions at
> which he arrives on issues before the Organization. These conclusions

must be completely detached from any national interest of policy and based solely on the principles and ideals to which the governments have adhered as Members of the United Nations.[48]

He concluded his comments on this theme with a metaphor that remains provocative:

> Thus you see that I conceive the Secretariat and the Secretary-General in their relations with the Governments as representatives of a secular "church" of ideals and principles in international affairs of which the United Nations is the expression.[49]

This was a concept of the UN, and of the secretary-general's role within it, which must have intrigued, and perhaps haunted, him for years. It could easily lead to rigidity and righteousness—traits in diplomacy he abhorred. Nonetheless, there was something to the idea, and he wasn't the only one to whom it had occurred. At a meeting in Rome in 1958, Pope Pius told him, "Vous êtes mon homologue laïque" (You are my lay counterpart), and Hammarskjöld once lightly said to W. H. Auden that to be secretary-general of the United Nations was much like being a secular pope.[50] At a staff gathering in 1958, to mark the beginning of his second term in office, Hammarskjöld responded to their warm praise in part with words that ambiguously discard the notion—and as well the notion of "a little republic"— yet move toward something not wholly unrelated: "We are no Vatican, we are no republic, we are not outside the world—we are very much in the world. But, even within the world, there can be this . . . sense of belonging, this deeper sense of unity. I hope that we are on our road to that sense."[51]

Hammarskjöld perceived the UN as a moral force when its decisions and actions conform to the values of the Charter and the Universal Declaration of Human Rights, and he perceived the holder of his office as uniquely placed with a mandate to exercise some part of that moral force. Throughout his UN years he didn't shy away from the notions of moral force and responsibility. Speaking at a university commencement exercise in 1954, he said, "It is our duty to feel moral responsibility for a war in a remote part of the world as strongly as we would feel for a war in which we ourselves, or those dear to us, were directly threatened in a physical sense."[52] To members of the first peacekeeping force, deployed to the Suez Canal in 1956, he said over UN Radio that they represented "the front line of a moral force which extends around the world."[53] His talk had been written for him by Ralph Bunche, who with Brian Urquhart was directing the operation; it reflected their shared views.

And yet he would sometimes, and quite publicly—for example, with journalists—take the pieces apart: his role as secretary-general, UN decisions, moral urgencies. The result could be cleansing. It reopened the question, scoured away residues of sentimentality and routine thinking in his own mind or his listeners'. "For my own part," he said to the press corps in 1956, during what he called a "free-lance discussion," "I think that neutrality may be moral, that neutrality may be immoral, that lack of neutrality may be moral, that lack of neutrality may be immoral—it all depends on factors which are not strictly linked to the definition."[54] His comments were a Rubik's Cube for the mind, a set of spinning surfaces. On another occasion one of his favorite journalists, Pauline Frederick, asked a leading question: "Mr. Secretary-General, do you feel that the United Nations would have greater influence and impact on the world if there were stronger emphasis in the UN organs on moral condemnation of wrongdoers?" Hammarskjold found the bait interesting. "I am perhaps not a moralist," he replied. Joseph Lash, another journalist with whom he had a fine rapport and who later wrote the first biography of Hammarskjöld, wouldn't let him off the baited hook. "Sir, a moment ago you made a very intriguing statement when you said you were not a moralist. May I follow that up—I assume a moralist in a certain context—and ask, if UN decisions do not register moral judgments, what should be the purpose of UN decisions?" Hammarskjöld withdrew into his most gnomic redoubt: "They register judgments," he replied, "and I hope they are moral."[55] The topic came up from time to time in his friendly duels with reporters; many seem to have recognized that it was interesting. In August 1957, during a relaxed press conference, he was a good deal less gnomic. "Let me for one second—as we are likely to have some time for this kind of philosophical discussion as other matters don't seem too pressing—try to explain what I mean. In my case, on one side I wear the hat of the secretary-general, and on the other hand I am a human being like anybody else. In the first capacity I do not feel like moralizing. In the second capacity I may try to convert my fellowmen. You see that I keep the two functions apart. The second element, the human element, is the one which I think can reconcile you to my general statement that the Secretary-General should not try to be a moral prophet."[56]

But all such distinctions duly recognized, Hammarskjöld as secretary-general *was* a moral force, and everyone well disposed toward him—a very large but not static majority throughout his career—acknowledged that this was so. At a dinner in the fall of 1954, he spoke to the issue in broad terms without reference to himself: "The moral power exerted through the United Nations can become very great indeed. It has already influenced the course of history on some occasions—so far too few, alas. In the end such moral force can have the final word in deciding the issue of war or peace."[57]

To return for a moment to our initial theme, Hammarskjöld's evolving understanding of his office, in March 1954 he remarked with the summarizing force so characteristic of him that

> Article 99 is all right, but it does not go far enough. Article 99 entitles the Secretary-General to take the initiative in the Security Council when he feels there is a threat to peace and security; but the real significance is not that he is entitled to take that kind of initiative, the real significance is that this Article does imply that the Governments of the UN expect the Secretary-General to take the independent responsibility, irrespective of their attitude, to represent the detached element in the international life of the peoples. . . . Sometimes he will have to voice the wishes of the peoples against this or that government.[58]

To represent the detached element in the international life of the peoples—from an institutional perspective, this was the high calling of his office. From a personal perspective, this is surely close to what the young Hammarskjöld had in mind, many years earlier, when he wrote privately of his wish "to be allowed in clarity of mind to mirror life and in purity of heart to mold it." That was a religious presentiment, a young man's yearning. The mature man now surveyed a field and office in which such language had no place, but the underlying attitude, hidden behind openness to others and efficiency in all things, still guided him.

Interdependence

The idea of interdependence would have reached Hammarskjöld from many sources. It had been explored up to a point in economics and philosophy, institutionalized in the frail but pioneering League of Nations, recognized by the first generations of environmentalists, and reborn as a founding concept of the United Nations. It was a current

in Christian thought from the Sermon on the Mount, which can be
read as a guide to peaceful community, to John Donne's classic lines,
"No man is an island, entire of itself . . . I am involved in mankind." It
was axiomatic in the thought of Mahatma Gandhi. But even without
sources, Hammarskjöld would have had to place the idea at the center of what he was beginning to say both in public forums and at the
UN. He and all understood that a world still recovering from the last
war and now threatened by weapons of mass destruction needed to
recognize global interdependence. The first detonations of hydrogen
bombs nearly framed Hammarskjöld's early months in office—by the
United States in November 1952, the Soviet Union in August 1953.
"The United Nations exists because a shrinking world, in which no nation or group of nations can live any more unto itself alone, has made
world organization necessary for the purposes expressed in the Charter"[59]. This from the introduction to the July 15th annual report. His
language remembers John Donne's.

By mid-July 1953, Hammarskjöld had begun working out an an-
thropology of sorts, reflecting the varied attitudes he was encountering.
We have already looked at several rich examples; here is another, more
extended, from a talk at a luncheon with the UN press corps. Responding to unnamed parties whose "dark prophecies" predicted the imminent
death of the UN, Hammarskjöld inventoried the attitudes that impede
interdependent action. His language is colorful, rather entertaining;
nonetheless, he is marking off points on a continuum to which he had
obviously given much thought.

> I have in mind all those who react instinctively against international
> ventures for the very same reason which makes them or their neigh-
> bors react unfavorably against people from other places. There are
> others who may recognize the need for an international approach to
> the problems of the world of today, but who have never really accept-
> ed the risks involved, and for that reason pull back the very moment
> the international sea gets rough. . . . And I think also of those who
> have accepted the necessity of an international approach and the risks
> involved but who, when troubles start piling up, get scared and are
> reduced to defeatist passivity, despairing about the future as fright
> makes them blind to existing possibilities to overcome the immediate
> difficulties. Rereading the other day the French author Paul Valéry,
> I found a phrase that in a very pointed way covers the attitudes to

which I have referred. He talks about those who drown rather than swim under the conditions imposed by the water: *"ceux qui préfèrent se noyer à nager dans les conditions de l'eau."* . . . It expresses the simple truth that, when trying to change our world, we have to face it as it is. Those are lost who dare not face the basic facts of international interdependence. Those are lost who permit defeats to scare them back to a starting point of narrow nationalism. Those are lost who are so scared by a defeat as to despair about the future. For all those, the dark prophecies may be justified. But not for those who do not permit themselves to be scared, nor for the organization which is the instrument at their disposal in the fight—an instrument which may be wrecked, but, if that happens, would have to be, and certainly would be, recreated again and again.[60]

Hammarskjöld's command of English was more than good enough for him to know that the word "scared," used often here, is a childhood word implying cowardice, ducking for cover, disorderly flight. "Fright" has some dignity, "fear" also. "Scared" has none. He must have been quite fed up with things he had been hearing. He would return in public talks to the issue of fear, which he knew to be one of the main obstacles on the way toward global interdependence. He didn't view it in the abstract; he understood it as an intimate trait of individual human beings, magnified by nations and their leaders into what he would later in the year call "walls of ice."[61] And he viewed the UN—and his own office—as responsible for doing whatever possible to eliminate unnecessary fear from international life. In Washington, DC, that fall, he spoke directly to this aspect of the issue.

> The United Nations has to activate in its support people's urge to live together and work together in peace and decency. For that reason the United Nations has to try and create a new awareness of human and national interdependence. In order to be able to do so it will have to understand what makes so difficult the development of such an awareness. It will have to understand—and challenge—the fear that motivates so much of human action, the fear that is our worst enemy but which, somehow, seems to taint at least some corner of the heart of every man.[62]

The inquiry of *Markings* into the heart of man and the inquiry here audibly overlap: the one nourishes the richness and aptness of the other. The words have an authority secretly earned through Hammarskjöld's attention to himself as he lived. "The United Nations has to try and create a new awareness." The thought remains provocative. It asks a great deal.

We need to read Hammarskjöld thematically or musically. Themes such as fear and interdependence recur over the years in variations, set to the music of a given time and circumstance. Sometimes he could be wonderfully offhand, as with the press in 1955, discussing Asian affairs: "You as journalists know very well that one of the most curious and most upsetting features about the present world situation in the East is that everybody is afraid of everybody."[63] At other times he drew about himself the most rigorous sense of speech and meaning, as if in our scrappy world of unfinished projects something precise needed to be said. I am thinking, for example, of a few words from a talk of October 1953: "The nerve signals from a wound are felt at once all through the body of mankind."[64]

In that talk he dwelt on another aspect of interdependence: multilateral diplomacy, the diplomacy practiced by sixty member nations at the time he took office. It had been used before, initially at the Congress of Vienna in 1813–15, which shaped post-Napoleonic Europe, and tried again by the League of Nations. Hammarskjöld thought it both necessary and interesting.

> A first and major change in diplomatic techniques . . . might be described as the multilateral element. I do not mean to suggest that bilateral diplomatic contacts and negotiations have lost their old importance, only that they prove insufficient. In a world of interdependence means must be devised for a broadening of the approach so that the interests of a group of nations or of the community of nations are given their necessary weight. . . . Undoubtedly, there are some who still dislike the idea of a group of political representatives from countries far from the storm center passing judgment on the actors in the drama and making recommendations for a solution of conflicts. But is that not a true expression of a very real interdependence?[65]

Hammarskjöld had a benign attitude toward regional political and economic groupings, "provided," he said, "they are developed with full recognition of the essentially universal interdependence of our world and do not attempt to make of regional groupings an extension of exclusive nationalism."[66] This is just what occurred, to Hammarskjöld's complete displeasure, in 1954 when the United States used a regional Latin American grouping, the Organization of American States, as a shield against the Security Council's desire to take up the topic of a coup organized by the CIA in Guatemala. We'll look further at that story. Hammarskjöld's benign remarks come from a mid-December talk in London, from which we might draw one further set of thoughts on interdependence before moving on—though the theme will musically recur. He measures here both need and challenge. His reasoning, as so often, is progressive; its logic builds.

> We know that world interdependence is inescapable. And world interdependence requires world organization. We know that the fact that we have been catapulted, as it were, into a world of close neighborhood without the necessary historical preparation to be good neighbors makes effective world organization a problem of supreme difficulty. The United Nations is a young institution. . . . Of course we must use discretion, we must avoid overloading a young institution. . . . But on [the] great issues we should not use other approaches. . . . We must not let the United Nations become a mere hostage to the conscience of the Member States, a shrine at which obeisance is paid at the appropriate seasons while the real action goes on elsewhere.[67]

The thinking remains active and alive to this day; we are not in the museum of ideas.

One of the canards about Hammarskjöld that lodged in some minds as he made his way through more than eight years of UN service was that he had the secret agenda of converting the organization into a world government. Even Thomas Kanza, a generally sensible and insightful Congolese official, his country's first UN ambassador, wrote retrospectively that "it might be said that [Hammarskjöld's] whole life had been dedicated to making the UN secretariat-general the basis of a world government. . . . [This was his] secret ambition."[68] Already in his first year in office, Hammarskjöld must have noticed notions of a "super-state" floating around among influential people interested in or frightened by the UN and its position in world politics. In mid-September 1953, he directly addressed the question.

> Applied in international life today, we might say that the United Nations represents ideals at least professed by all nations, but that it is not a super-state trying to impose on people any "right" way of life or any

way of life different from one freely chosen by the people. On the contrary, it seeks as the repository and voice of a common heritage of ideals to penetrate the life of states in their international relations and to influence their conduct toward a wider realization of those ideals.[69]

Nowhere detectable in this early statement or many to come is a purpose, uncountenanced in the UN Charter, to develop the organization into a super-state. It is probably a measure of Hammarskjöld's effectiveness, and the Secretariat's, as "the detached element in the international life of the peoples," that he was regarded by some as too ambitious. The UN needed substantial authority to fulfill some reasonable portion of its mission; it took a growing number of initiatives in many domains from high diplomacy to agriculture. But it was not a government, and Hammarskjöld knew better than anyone its chartered scope and his own.

He was inexhaustible on the topic of interdependence. He practiced it, encouraged it, knew its challenges. "It is not always so easily accepted," he said at a talk in Washington, DC, in spring 1954, "that . . . interdependence does not recognize any ideological or racial barriers. It embraces Capitalists, Communists, and Socialists; Catholics, Protestants, and Jews; Hindus, Moslems, and Buddhists; black, brown, yellow, and white skins; and many more variations in beliefs, appearance, and ways of life besides."[70]

8

A Swarm of Ideas

The emphasis on ideas and attitudes in the preceding chapter could give the false impression that Hammarskjöld was functioning as a sort of Plato in the palace of the Sicilian tyrant—a thinker and preacher otherwise unengaged. That was of course not so. His political wisdom and practical abilities were engaged at every level, from entering for the first time into Middle East diplomacy to taking on a local New York tyrant, Robert Moses, over the grave issue of parking permits in the UN garage. In that dispute he applied his best international manner with a slight New York accent: "I am sure Mr. Moses knows that I am happy to see him here for lunch now in order to settle this dispute, and that I shall always be responsive . . . to such man-to-man settlements of questions that may arise."[1] That was fun, at least in retrospect.

By the end of 1953, he knew virtually everyone he needed to know in the UN, and virtually everyone in the Secretariat, delegations, and overseas branches knew him. He was meeting regularly with the UN press corps on cordial terms and developing a point of view about public communications, which he understood to be very much a part of his job. He had the loyalty question well in hand and had persuasively redefined the duties and dignity of the international civil servant. He had put great effort into preparing the late summer and fall meeting of the General Assembly. He had launched an internal study aimed at streamlining the Secretariat by positioning departments and people more productively and flexibly. In 1954, the program would deliver a revised organizational structure and savings of a million dollars at a time when that represented a substantial sum even for a large organization. He was something of an onlooker where the armistice that ended the Korean War was concerned. His office served primarily as a "letter box" for communications between belligerents, writes Urquhart, but his public comments, both explicit and allusive, provided thoughtful perspectives.

Just at year's end two major issues reached his desk: the peaceful uses of atomic energy and—an issue from which he would never be wholly free again—the Middle East. The first was initiated by US president Dwight Eisenhower before the General Assembly on December 8th in a celebrated speech now known as "Atoms for Peace."² Soon after the president's appearance, Hammarskjöld sent him a brief note of thanks: "I want to register again my profound feelings of satisfaction and appreciation for your presence and for your historic address. . . . It is this type of collaboration in approaching the baffling problems that confront us in our present-day world that offers the best prospect of a favorable outcome."³ Eisenhower's initiative would lead to a genuinely productive event under UN auspices at Geneva in August 1955, an international conference on the peaceful uses of atomic energy. The second issue, in the Middle East, was to set the terms of a conference between Jordan and Israel under the armistice agreement in place between them, after a severe episode of border violence. Hammarskjöld's first diplomatic démarches in that theater were widely approved: they were modest and impartial and, though they didn't solve the problem, they built trust.

In mid-August, the *New York Times* correspondent for UN affairs, A. M. Rosenthal, published an extensive interview with Hammarskjöld.⁴ It reads like a relaxed encounter between people who had already come to trust one another. This was the article that described Hammarskjöld, to his amusement, as a "practicing, unashamed intellectual. . . . For him the-other-side-of-the-coin is not a cliché but a way of life." They spoke of Hammarskjöld's conviction that "some day the United Nations will come alive in the consciousness of men." "It's a conviction," he said, "that has to do with, well, church words, with a belief in a bond of morality and decency. There is a simple basic morality that motivates most people. The great moment is the moment of realization in people that their desire for decency exists not only in their own groups but in others. It is a difficult thing to get across, but it does get across. Some day, I know it, people will realize that the UN is a reflection of that desire." Naturally, there was discussion of his role. "The secretary-general has to be available," he said. "That's not an oblique, diplomatic word. It means that here sits a man who the delegations know can be used to check their own opinions against the opinions of other countries, who will pass on to other delegations not their confidences but the conclusions he has drawn from them, who perhaps can advise, who perhaps is in a better position to judge than any single delegate. . . . It is an immensely important thing—the job, not the man—because in this split, this damned world split, there is nothing to take its place. . . . You know, people don't mind taking advice. But they don't like being publicized as taking advice.

A question of tact." Hammarskjöld also offered a deprecating but vivid personal commentary: "I am what I am. I am cast in a European mold of understatement. I do not wish to use, ever, one word that to my friends, or to myself, would sound false. A colorless sort of prophet, maybe." At the end of the conversation, he offered a new metaphor: "The UN is a mold that keeps the hot metal from spilling over."

I'm not sure just when Hammarskjöld moved into his apartment at 73 East Seventy-Third Street in the Upper East Side of Manhattan—then and now, an elegant address in a quiet neighborhood. There is correspondence with a former director of the decorative arts division of the National Museum of Sweden who was helping him find or commission furnishings. He had settled in by May 1954, when he wrote to his good friend Sture Petrén, "The apartment is now in order, at last, with the world's sweetest and most competent Swedish butler-cook couple. So, now I can really offer my distinguished—and this autumn expected—Monseigneur all facilities."[5] He acquired early the country house in Brewster, New York, something more than an hour's drive north; it assured him of peaceful weekends when possible, woods to hike in, a sizable pond at the edge of the property. A mid-November note from the wife of his security guard thanked him for a weekend loan of the house; the family had had a good time.

In mid-August Hammarskjöld wrote to his brother Bo, "Here it's extremely hard work and also rather trying on the nerves."[6] A month later the tenor hadn't changed. Writing again to Bo, he remarked in passing about the spectacular Staff Day celebration a few days earlier, where the guest performers were wonderful—Danny Kaye than whom none was funnier, Ezio Pinza than whom no opera star was grander, and Marian Anderson, the African American contralto celebrated both as a singer and as a champion of racial justice.

> Here is no end of drama. The responsibility you're forced to take practically on your own is so enormous that it actually dulls you: you don't have the strength to realize that decisions can be final as to whether we have war or peace, and for the UN's ability to survive. In such a situation it's actually relaxing to have to act as *compère* for Danny Kaye and others. (By the way, a very nice and rewarding experience. D. K. is an exceptionally intelligent and serious gentleman in private.)
>
> As you understand, under these conditions I have to switch off all complications and worries on the private front. You cannot be divided, and you cannot manage both. Otherwise everything here is fine.

The news about Papa is what could be expected. I feel very sorry
for him.[7]

When Hammarskjöld had left Stockholm for New York, his father's health
and mental condition were already failing. He died on October 12th;
Hammarskjöld immediately joined his family in Sweden for the funeral.
The elder Hammarskjöld's rapid decline had been difficult to bear, his
death no doubt more so. A few days after his father's passing, while in Sweden for the funeral, Dag expressed his anguish by letter to Petrén, nearly
his age peer and a member of the transition team, by then disbanded: "I
thought that dark moment in New York in April," he wrote,

> to which you were the only witness, was for me the end of the father-son
> problem. Recent days have shown that I was *very* wrong in that regard:
> there is so much left for me to sort out for myself. For instance, the way
> my father now more than ever represents all of the people, better, stron-
> ger than I, who believe in me in the very peculiar task I have been given.
> That hardly makes it easier.
> ... When are you coming to NY? You know the room stands ready.[8]

Microcosms and macrocosms

At the United Nations Day concert in October 1953—there would
be concerts yearly throughout his tenure—Hammarskjöld felt confident enough of his standing with the large and varied audience that
had assembled to release his thought in an intermission talk. His trust
in his audience was little short of amazing. The program he had chosen for performance by the New York Philharmonic and other forces
juxtaposed high classical and modern music: the choral movement of
Beethoven's Ninth Symphony, which he could be sure all would appreciate, and a complete performance of "The Harmony of the World"
by the German American composer Paul Hindemith, a symphony premiered just a year earlier. Beethoven would be heard each year, soon
in complete performances, the Hindemith just this once, and almost
certainly with two purposes in mind: to set before the UN community
the sound and something of the essential feelings of the world at that
time, and to give Hammarskjöld a basis for certain ideas he wished
to express. Written in an individual harmonic language painstakingly
worked out by the composer, Hindemith's music was a daring choice.
It would have struck many listeners as strange: few pitches fall quite

where the ear expects them. That unfamiliarity wouldn't have troubled Hammarskjöld, who when time permitted approached new art with deepest curiosity, as if something of importance was being explored and expressed now, not just centuries ago. His interest in new art was part of his pact with our time.

Hammarskjöld often strove to elevate the image of the United Nations, to place it in a world of ideas where it could shine a little despite the organization's day-to-day engagement with innumerable earthbound details. All of those details taken together had a certain meaning: what was it? He cared very much to restate that meaning on occasions such as UN Day. Hindemith's theme of the harmony of the spheres gave him, so to speak, his chapter and verse, and to illuminate it he drew from the seventeenth-century writings of Dr. Thomas Browne, one of the great and intricate authors in the English language. Nothing there to stop Hammarskjöld—as a young man he was already reading Browne—and he was obviously determined that nothing there should stop his listeners. Referring to several parts of the world represented in his UN audience, he eased into his theme:

> In his Symphony of the World, Paul Hindemith has tried to express in the universal language of music the ancient belief in a basic harmony of the Universe. We find this belief in old India, we meet it again in Greece, we are familiar with its echoes in the writings of the prophets of Israel. Let me quote here a later author whose words seem to me to be a fitting comment on this concert.
>
> About 1635, Thomas Browne wrote . . . : "There is musick where ever there is harmony, order, proportion: and thus far we may maintain the musick of the Spheres; for those well ordered motions, and regular paces, though they give no sound on to the ear yet to the understanding they strike a note most full of harmony." – In music "there is something of Divinity more than the ear discovers: it is an Hieroglyphical and shadowed lesson of the whole world, and creatures of God; such a melody to the ear as the whole World, well understood, would afford the understanding. . . ."
>
> These words yield their full meaning, reveal their human implications when we add to them this further quotation from Browne: "There is no man alone, because every man is a Microcosm, and carries the whole World about him."

Having bravely introduced this fascinating but difficult text to an audience with perhaps a minority of native English speakers, and not one speaker of seventeenth-century English, Hammarskjöld was duty-bound to clarify and link it with the work at hand, the United Nations.

> In words that are no better than Browne's, but perhaps closer to our common language of today: behind the simple harmonies of music, which may be grasped by our senses, we see dimly a greater harmony—a harmony of the whole World—that should resound also in the small world of man, in the limited sphere of our own life.

> We are far from Browne's simple concept of the world. We may find it difficult to share his humble faith. But can we escape his conclusions? His is a hope for harmony in the world of men that should be valid for all times. The demand this hope places upon us may even have a deeper significance for us than for our predecessors. There is no man alone. There is no escape from the duty to create harmony in that microcosm in which we, every one of us, are at the center. Whatever the development of the concepts of the Universe, whatever the changes in our faiths and creeds, our responsibility in this respect has certainly not decreased since the time when Browne wrote, or since the old days when the first dreams about a world of harmony took shape in the East.

> Thus, an old philosophy of the Universe and the music which it has inspired . . . are linked to essential elements in our own personal lives—but likewise in our lives as men and women responsible to our neighbors, to society, and to history.

> It is not presumptuous to say that those elements are present in the background also of the work which is carried on—or should be carried on—in and by the United Nations. In our preoccupation with the outward forms, the established procedures, the publicity, and the immediate issues which attract our attention from day to day, we may tend to forget that at the very basis of this Organization is the will of all peoples to create a world of harmony. The United Nations in its fundamental purpose is one of the means by which it is possible for all of us, starting with and in our own lives, to work for that harmony in the world of man which our forefathers were striving for as an echo of the music of the Universe.[9]

This was Hammarskjöld's "Hieroglyphical and shadowed lesson" for the community, some six months after taking office. Though its news is timeless, it was issued as a press release. I have no idea whether his message was heard; surely some were moved by the scale of his vision.

Some would have heard his rigorous charge—"There is no escape from the duty to create harmony"—and his characteristic insistence on rooting larger possibilities in the quality of individual lives rather than in the collective: "It is possible for all of us, starting with and in our own lives, to work for that harmony in the world of man." Like the chorus master in ancient Greece who intrigued Diogenes the Cynic, he may have been deliberately setting the note too high so that average choristers, coming in lower, would hit the right note. But the atmosphere he created of dignity and striving was tangible. As if this wasn't enough, after he had spoken and the concert resumed, everyone could delight in the last movement of Beethoven's Ninth Symphony, which carried Hammarskjöld's main point home in both music and word.

> Alle Menschen werden Brüder,
> Wo dein sanfter Flügel weilt.

> All men become brothers,
> Where Your gentle wing abides.

This was the macrocosm—universal ideas, deep feelings that can surface in response to great music or exceptional words.

Through the closing months of 1953, there was also, and far more prominently, the microcosm of daily work. Hammarskjöld had a way of thinking about issues that moved in two directions: toward an immediate or eventual improvement and toward the principle guiding whatever practical steps struck him as appropriate. There is a long and distinguished history of manuals of diplomacy from the Italian Renaissance to *Satow's Diplomatic Practice*, first edition published nearly a century ago, now in its sixth revised edition. Had he lived longer, Hammarskjöld might have made a contribution to the literature, but as matters stand there is a manual in fragments throughout his public papers and key elements of that unwritten manual even in *Markings*. The swarm of ideas which he brought to the UN at once and from year to year is in part this material. A sentence or paragraph here or there, linked in theme to a sentence or paragraph elsewhere and perhaps from some years later—this we can discover and assemble. Hammarskjöld's political thought aerates much of what he said and did.

In a talk he gave in late November 1953, as so often thinking about the effects of fear, he said: "Fear of being misled should never be per-

mitted to mislead us into false positions."[10] He was commenting on the
political negotiations that followed the Korean armistice agreement of
July 27th. Subtle Hammarskjöld—but schematic; one would like to hear
more, and there is more from a very different moment. In the spring
and summer of 1956, he was negotiating separately with the president
of Egypt, Gamal Abdel Nasser, and the prime minister of Israel, David
Ben-Gurion, to restore their countries' adherence to the terms of an armistice. It wasn't easy; there was endless mistrust between the two leaders. On July 31st, Hammarskjöld sent a letter to Ben-Gurion from which
we have already seen a few lines. Here it is again nearly in full, owing to
its interest throughout:

> Please do not believe that I permit myself to be taken in by *anybody*, but
> realize, on the other hand, that I cannot work on the general assump-
> tion of people trying to double-cross me even when this runs counter to
> their own interest. Being afraid of being fooled to that extent, I would
> fool myself. I could then just as well stop all efforts, thus sacrificing the
> chance of getting the right thing—however small—because I was always
> fearing to get what is of no value. . . .
>
> I do, of course, make a moral distinction between attacker and attacked,
> but under the law which I have to apply, also actions by the attacked may be
> open to serious criticism. To use means beyond the needs of an emergency
> may, also under . . . [the] law of the tradition to which we belong, be an of-
> fence even where the action in itself is considered morally justified.[11]

Illustrating how one fragment of the unwritten manual links to others, Hammarskjöld here gives a compelling formulation to another key
method he practiced: the search for common ground, no matter how
skimpy it may initially be. A few months into 1954, in the context of a
dispute between Israel and Jordan over water rights, he spoke of the need
"to map the ground so that we can see if there is any common ground
on which Secretariat action would be indicated and wise." A journalist
asked, "Common as between whom?' Hammarskjöld responded: "Common where there is a harmony between the interests concerned. . . . For
example, it may be quite possible that there are points . . . where an Israeli
interest and an Arab interest, because of some development, happen to
coincide because it happens to fit in with the plans on both sides. If that
is so, . . . it obviously would be nonsensical not to try to get it down and,
at least, to get somewhere."[12]

Another example of the weave of ideas links a comment of mid-September 1953 to an aphoristic statement of 1955 and a Swedish anecdote. If we were building a memory palace, we would probably place these three elements in a room designated Interdependence and stack them in a niche under a sign reading "Like-minded club—not a good idea."

> As you all know, the United Nations Charter is based on what I may call a working hypothesis. This is that all the great nations and groups of nations must belong to it if it is to succeed. . . . We know that this hypothesis is being challenged, and challenged not only by those who do not yet fully understand and accept the essential interdependency of our world today, but also by truly internationally minded people animated by the most serious desire to build a better world. Yet it seems to me that the idea of the United Nations as a club to which only the like-minded will be admitted, in which membership is a privilege and expulsion is the retribution for wrongdoing, is totally unrealistic and self-defeating.[13]

A compelling point, with a corollary mentioned two years later in an entirely different context: the need for a quite new attitude that isn't second nature to most people. It has to be acquired through the force of experience. "I feel," he said, "that what very many people call negative sides—the talking, the conflicts, the flux of events, the uncertainties about outcomes and so on and so forth—are not negative sides but positive sides."[14] This in turn ties to a charming anecdote he told in June 1953: "What I just said reminds me of a story from my home country, and I ask you to excuse my telling it. A very prominent church-leader in the last century, who was not strictly orthodox, was accused of taking certain liberties in his way of preaching the Gospel. He gave a reply which has become famous: 'If the Devil tells me that two and two equals four, I will just say that the guy is right.' This approach to truth is one which I think we should all make ours."[15]

Hammarskjöld introduced early at the UN and in talks with the press and public what would prove to be a recurrent reflection about time and timing. The basis of his point of view was entirely practical; he closely followed the course of events and the effectiveness of interventions. His allegiance to Henri Bergson's vision of creative evolution may have provided a thin theoretical framework, but for the most part he was reading circumstances directly. "Time is . . . a great healer," he commented in mid-September 1953, and "playing for time" is an important element in the tactics we must follow in these days of crisis, anxiety, and frustration. We all have a tendency to regard the situation as it exists at any single moment as a lasting one, forgetting that we ourselves and the societies which we form are all subject to the law of change. . . . Conflicts, not only in human life, but also in the life of nations, are often never resolved, but simply outgrown. Often in history situations have arisen where people were saying, as it is sometimes being said now, that they could neither live together nor fight each other down, and in spite of that, the world has moved on and the situation of despair has become past history.[16]

It wasn't always about patience; sometimes rapid assessments and prompt action were essential, as events such as the Suez Crisis and the call for help from the Congo would prove in later years. He was ready to seize the moment when there was a moment to be seized. Nonetheless it was often about patience: "Impatience is a useful goad," he observed a few months later, "but a very poor guide. There are times when it is political wisdom, in the best sense, to mark time."[17] Most colorfully, in response to an Asian journalist's question as to whether the UN would ever realize its potential, he responded: "If the elephant walks and walks in the right direction, we should not be impatient. It does not move too quickly, but we shall certainly arrive at a goal."[18]

Hammarskjöld was of two minds about our ability to "master our world," as he put it. Speaking with a group of American political scientists in mid-September 1953, he insisted that mastery is simply necessary, given the dangers and promise of our world. "The ultimate challenge to the political sciences—and to us all—is whether man shall master his world and his history or let himself be mastered by a world and a history which after all is made by man. There cannot be more than one reply to this question. Man must master his world, but in order to do so, he must know it."[19] On the other hand, in a talk given just a few days later to a different group, he took a somewhat different view. This talk also provides the first sign that Hammarskjöld refreshed his thinking and gathered insights from ancient Chinese texts that characteristically blend political and spiritual wisdom. We should revise our timetable of diplomatic literature to extend much farther back in time than the Renaissance.

In the classical Chinese collection of poetic philosophy, *Tao-Te-King*, ascribed to Lao-Tse, it is said somewhere that whoever wants to grip the

world and shape it will fail, because the world is a spiritual thing that cannot be shaped. . . . The history of mankind is made by man, but men partly
make it blindly. No one can foresee with certainty what will emerge from
the give and take of the forces at work in any age. For that reason history
often seems to run its course beyond the reach of any man or nation. We
cannot mould the world as masters of a material thing. Columbus did
not reach the East Indies. But we can influence the development of the
world from within as a spiritual thing. . . . You cannot grip the world and
shape it as a material thing. You can only influence its development if you
recognize and respect it as a thing of the spirit. . . . No state, no group of
states, no world organization, can grip the world and shape it, neither by
force, nor by any formula of words in a Charter or a Treaty. There are no
absolute answers to the agonies and searchings of our time. But all men
and women of good will can influence the course of history in the direction of the ideals expressed in the Charter.[20]

No less persuasive than the previous statement, this applies the ancient
Taoist perspective directly to current circumstances and institutions.
But is Hammarskjöld trying to have it both ways? Are we to "master our
world" insofar as we "know it"—the words implying an active, somewhat
unhesitating attitude—yet refrain from "gripping the world"? This last
sounds ham-handed, possibly brutal. But if we can only exercise influence
by respecting the world as "a thing of the spirit" and in light of ideals codified in the UN Charter, what scope for action does that suggest? Puzzling.
I believe that here Hammarskjöld is thinking his way through a paradox
built into the experience of interdependence, in search of a middle position from which one approach or the other or some blend of both can be
adopted, depending on circumstances. He seems to be thinking aloud.

A month later, at a gathering in New York Hammarskjöld was unable
to attend owing to his father's death, Ralph Bunche read the short statement he would have delivered, had he been available. It speaks to that
middle position.

To say yes to the future does not mean a mere acceptance of change. We
must seek to prove our ability for dealing with change and to be instruments for constructive change. We have learned to master the ever-flow-
ing rivers; we must learn to master the flow of change itself. We have
to understand the changes that are taking place and their underlying
causes. Statesmanship—the statesmanship required of all of us—means

to anticipate the need for change, and by anticipating to influence the direction that we wish our civilization to take.[21]

Statesmanship occupies the middle position; understanding and accurate anticipation are its hallmarks. But mastery remains a key concept and mood, even taken to the point of analogy with major feats of engineering—building dams, redirecting rivers. Hammarskjöld retains the notion of influence, but the engineering metaphor tilts back toward "gripping the world." The balance is reset by thoughts he shared at a press conference a few months later, in February 1954.

> A good driver makes only slight movements of the wheel in order to give direction at the critical moment, and I must say that the United Nations political activity is not one where we keep fussing around and talking a lot, having day-to-day contacts and so on. It is a question of remaining wide awake and, so to say, saying our word in the way which seems to us to be appropriate to give that touch to the wheel which helps to keep the car on the road. In any case, there is no one else to say that word, to give that touch to the wheel.[22]

I don't want to give the impression that Hammarskjöld was working away at these ideas and pursuing them separately from day-to-day experience. It seems rather that he periodically read the tea leaves, reviewed recent experience, and on the many occasions when he spoke—press conferences, public talks, UN deliberations—reported on things lately seen, insights lately gained. Themes recurred because they were evident in the work at hand. His talks were something like a parallel journal, not personal like *Markings* but no less thoughtful. I suspect that a touch to the wheel conveys Hammarskjöld's ideal. But the UN with his guidance also needed at times to accelerate, turn sharp corners, find the way forward in conditions of stress and violence.

He had been thinking, of course, about peace and war. Fought under the flag of the United Nations, the Korean War was winding down when he took office. The July 15th annual report referred to "new hope for the early conclusion of an armistice in Korea"; on July 27th that hope was realized.[23] A month earlier, in a UN Radio address, he was already asking the UN community to think about a new sort of war outcome.

> The United Nations action in Korea marks the first attempt in history to meet aggression with unified force under an international standard. . . . We must adapt ourselves to accept such unfamiliar developments as a

war which ends without total victory for any party but only for a principle. Such a victory, although it may not be considered as satisfactory by those who still believe in the unconditional surrenders of old wars, is a full vindication of those brave men who have sacrificed their lives for this principle.

. . . A victory of the kind I have in mind will have to be followed by a peace without vengeance. The United Nations Charter provides for all manner of actions to repel aggression, but it makes no provision for the ultimate punishment of the aggressor, once the fruits of an attempted aggression have been taken from him. . . . It does not foresee the use of force to secure the fruits of victory in terms of land and power.[24]

Sweden had participated in the Korean war effort by setting up and staffing an evacuation hospital at Pusan that is said to have treated more than twenty thousand people.[25] It seems likely that before entering UN service Hammarskjöld would not have given a very great deal of thought to the war; he would have followed the news, perhaps taken special interest through government channels in the welfare and contributions of the Swedish hospital staff. But now he was responsible not for the armistice and related negotiations but rather for saying something true. He needed to speak for the United Nations, of which seventeen member nations had contributed fighting forces. The occasion was a dinner in New York, in November 1953, where he shared the podium with former US president Harry Truman. The secretary-general was to receive an award on behalf of the soldiers who had fought and died under the flag of the United Nations. Hammarskjöld had no military experience and his country, once aggressive like other European kingdoms, had fought no war since it had participated in defeating Napoleon. With the talk he gave on this occasion, Hammarskjöld in effect accepted that the United Nations and therefore he himself had a place in the history of twentieth-century violence and the effort to curb it. Though his prior life and his country's choices offered no great preparation for the role, he could not be silent. The most eloquent moment was the simplest:

Our purpose is peace, nothing but peace.

"Nothing that happens in the future," he continued, "can blemish the service and the sacrifice that has been rendered by the United Nations soldiers in Korea. . . . Each and all of the governments and peoples now share a heavy responsibility. When the soldiers have done their part and

the guns are silenced, the task of creating a solid basis for peace begins."
And here he issued a warning: "The men who fought in Korea have giv-
en us the possibility of a new beginning on this task in that part of the
world. Should we, by any failure in wisdom, in firmness of faith, or in
clarity of purpose, fumble this opportunity, then the verdict of history
upon us would justly be contemptuous."[26] This was Hammarskjöld: clear
about the moral stakes, clear also about the pragmatic way forward. In
that regard, he issued a further oblique warning against the opportunism
of the South Korean leaders, apparent since the cease-fire: "In negotiating for peace we must not permit any hope of other fruits of our efforts
to vitiate our position or to distort our tactics."

He had an active notion of peace. Peace is not the absence of war; it is
an engagement. This thinking again took shape during his early months in
office. Speaking at City Hall in New York in late October, he shared his view.

> Peace is not a gift that comes to us without effort. Peace is an achieve-
> ment attainable only for those who are willing to work for it and to
> make the sacrifices it may call for.
>
> Peace is not just the passive state of affairs in a world without war.
> It is a state of living devoted to action in order to build a world of pros-
> perity and equity where occasions for conflicts either disappear or are
> quickly challenged if they arise.
>
> In our own lifetimes we have seen two world wars fought to their
> bitter conclusions. Each has brought in its wake new tensions, new ha-
> treds, new fears as well as worldwide distress. The United Nations is a
> reply to the challenge presented by those experiences.[27]

Peace is "a state of living devoted to action": this is the core thought.

Among the ideas Hammarskjöld introduced in these early months,
one further cannot be overlooked. He often spoke of the need for faith,
by which rarely in public talks he meant his own religious faith but
rather faith in humanity, faith in the future, faith in oneself as an able
contributor. A characteristic expression along these lines—there are
many—is from a mid-October talk: "Today, as so often in the past, we
need a rediscovery of courage and of faith in man by leaders on every
level of the social scale, in every walk of life, from the local community
to this Assembly Hall of the United Nations."[28] The difference between
this and a cliché is that he meant it and lived it, and he found many
varied ways of restating this truth over the years ahead. One of the most

startling and best occurred in a year-end talk in London at the Royal Albert Hall, a vast circular auditorium suited for large events. He might not have known that in 1890 Henry Morton Stanley, the explorer of the Congo and first link in a chain of injustices that led to the Congo Crisis of 1960, had no doubt enthralled an audience there with his tales of adventure. After gracious tributes in various directions, Hammarskjöld took as his text—without specifying that he was doing so—lines in the New Testament Letter of James about faith and works. The Protestant Reformers and Roman Church had battled over these words; theologies had been constructed and demolished around them, and through it all they had remained quite perfect, stated with force and simplicity in James 2:14–24. Hammarskjöld could count on many in his audience to know them, as he would have known them from his youth. "Faith by itself, if it has no works, is dead," James wrote. "But someone will say, 'You have faith and I have works.' Show me your faith apart from your works, and I by my works will show you my faith. . . . A man is justified by works and not by faith alone. . . . As the body apart from the spirit is dead, so faith apart from works is dead."

Much here for a secretary-general to work with. "The United Nations is faith and works," he said,

> —faith in the possibility of a world without fear and works to bring that faith closer to realization in the life of men. . . . Its successes and its failures are the end result and the measure of the faith and works of all the peoples of its Member nations. . . . The works are as important as the faith and the faith, embodied in the United Nations, will not find the expression that the world needs so desperately without a living and developing institution that commands respect and loyalty from the peoples and the governments of the world in steadily growing measure.[29]

His words traced a line from the genius of early Christian thinking to the promising genius, the hoped-for genius, of the world's newest embodiment of common sense.

The laws of inner life and action

By now we may nearly have forgotten who he is. There has been so much outward address, so many people to encounter and issues to manage, so many carefully worded talks given in the effort to restate the meaning of the United Nations that we might logically conclude that Dag

Hammarskjöld had passed, not without relief, from his former world of prolonged inner questioning and bursts of discovery to a new world of problem solving and public communications. It wasn't so. For example, alongside his many touching and easily grasped public statements about the need for faith, at some point in the early months at the UN he recorded in his journal a complex personal reflection. It too is about faith.

> Except in faith, nobody is humble. The mask of weakness or of Phariseeism is not the naked face of humility.
>
> And, except in faith, nobody is proud. The vanity displayed in all its varieties by the spiritually immature is not pride.
>
> To be, in faith, both humble and proud: that is, to *live* that in God I am nothing but God is in me.[30]

It must derive for the most part from self-observation—his practice of conscious self-scrutiny. He would have witnessed episodes of false humility and, at the other extreme, nonsensical vanity; would have witnessed, as well, profound steadiness and clarity when he returned to the real geometry of his life, based on this earth and among people, looking upward and inward toward God in faith. He would have seen much of this also in others, in men and women of genuine integrity, in men and women terribly impressed with their international duties and standing.

The concluding entries for the year in *Markings* leave no doubt that Hammarskjöld, the faithful seeker and observer, had not lost touch with himself in the world of the Thousand and One Nights, although he moved easily in this new world and now influenced it—or gripped it, depending on circumstances. He wrote:

> Your life is without a foundation if, in any matter, you choose on your own behalf.

And as we have read in earlier pages:

> The humility which comes from others having faith in you.[31]

There remains one major document to explore from this moment in his life and career. At the time it was apparently little noticed, although UN communications treated it as news and issued the full text, two pages, to the press and public. In November Hammarskjöld accepted an invitation from Edward R. Murrow, one of America's most celebrated journalists, to speak on his radio program, *This I Believe*. Murrow's guests, typically well known, were asked to share with listeners their credo, the beliefs by which they lived, the goals they cared most for. At the time Hammarskjöld joined him for those few minutes, Murrow and his colleagues may already have been preparing the famous television program, broadcast on March 9th, 1954, which fiercely attacked Senator McCarthy by the blameless means of compiling film footage of McCarthy in action and drawing obvious conclusions; the program contributed substantially to McCarthy's fall from power.

In that fall season, Hammarskjöld seems to have been exploring the boundaries of communication. To what degree, in what ways could his private concerns enrich his public communications? His talk at the UN Day concert, October 25th, approached some boundary beyond which he couldn't expect people to follow—arguably, he went too far. I take it to be true, as Urquhart writes, that his beautifully constructed credo was little acknowledged. What is clear is that he decided in future not to reveal so much. The churning energy of his private search for meaning and inner peace contributed in years to come to the power of many of his public statements—those in which he explored values, paths toward sound purposes, obstacles blocking the way. But the Murrow statement marks the far edge of public communications of this kind. Henceforth, he would confine such things to his journal and to a very few relationships.

Here is the Murrow text in full. A wonder, it exists also as an audio file, Hammarskjöld speaking, at a website dedicated to the radio program.[32]

> The world in which I grew up was dominated by principles and ideals of a time far from ours and, as it may seem, far removed from the problems facing a man of the middle of the twentieth century. However, my way has not meant a departure from those ideals. On the contrary, I have been led to an understanding of their validity also for our world of to-day. Thus, a never abandoned effort frankly and squarely to build up a personal belief in the light of experience and honest thinking has led me in a circle: I now recognize and endorse, unreservedly, those very beliefs which once were handed down to me.
>
> From generations of soldiers and government officials on my father's side I inherited a belief that no life was more satisfactory than one of selfless service to your country—or humanity. This service required a sacrifice of all personal interests, but likewise the courage to stand up unflinchingly for your convictions concerning what was right and good for the community, whatever were the views in fashion.

From scholars and clergymen on my mother's side I inherited a belief that, in the very radical sense of the Gospels, all men were equals as children of God, and should be met and treated by us as our masters in God.

Faith is a state of the mind and the soul. In this sense we can understand the words of the Spanish mystic, St. John of the Cross: "Faith is the union of God with the soul." The language of religion is a set of formulas which register a basic spiritual experience. It must not be regarded as describing, in terms to be defined by philosophy, the reality which is accessible to our senses and which we can analyze with the tools of logic. I was late in understanding what this meant. When I finally reached that point, the beliefs in which I was once brought up and which, in fact, had given my life direction even while my intellect still challenged their validity, were recognized by me as mine in their own right and by my free choice. I feel that I can endorse those convictions without any compromise with the demands of that intellectual honesty which is the very key to maturity of mind.

The two ideals which dominated my childhood world met me fully harmonized and adjusted to the demands of our world of today in the ethics of Albert Schweitzer, where the ideal of service is supported by and supports the basic attitude to man set forth in the Gospels. In his work I also found a key for modern man to the world of the Gospels.

But the explanation of how man should live a life of active social service in full harmony with himself as a member of the community of the spirit, I found in the writings of those great medieval mystics for whom "self-surrender" had been the way to self-realization, and who in "singleness of mind" and "inwardness" had found strength to say yes to every demand, which the needs of their neighbors made them face, and to say yes also to every fate life had in store for them when they followed the call of duty, as they understood it. "Love"—that much misused and misinterpreted word—for them meant simply an overflowing of the strength with which they felt themselves filled when living in true self-oblivion. And this love found natural expressions in an unhesitant fulfillment of duty and in an unreserved acceptance of life, whatever it brought them personally of toil, suffering—or happiness.

I know that their discoveries about the laws of inner life and of action have not lost their significance.[33]

We could spend too much time exploring this text. It is like a microscope with three magnifications, one lens penetrating through time to the parental home, another to the middle years of doubt, still another clarifying mature attitudes and honored sources. However, the long penultimate paragraph, more allusive than any other, asks for an interpretive look. The unnamed medieval mystics would have to be Meister Eckhart, Jan van Ruysbroeck, and Thomas à Kempis, this last not so much a mystic as a teacher of monastic attitudes and an ethic of humility and love. From Ruysbroeck's amazing exposition of flows in *The Spiritual Espousals*, which Hammarskjöld was almost certainly reading late in 1953, he might well have constructed his own report on love as the overflow of strength of those who live in true self-oblivion. "God is a sea," wrote Ruysbroeck, "ebbing and flowing, ceaselessly flowing into each one of His elect, according to the needs and worth of each. He draws back again all men to whom He has given in heaven and in earth, with all that they have and all of which they are capable. And from such men He demands more than they can achieve. . . . [The] enlightened, loving man flows out to all men in charity in heaven and on earth."[34] Hammarskjöld would not have missed this exceptional passage, of which these few words only suggest their content. As for Meister Eckhart, he was always in the background; in later years in *Markings* he will come to the fore.

The most important observation about Hammarskjöld's words is that they are an interpretation. Other readers would not derive the same thoughts from the same sources or assemble them in the same way. The medieval mystics were teaching Hammarskjöld how to be Hammarskjöld, how to pass from concentrated religious experience and a rigorous view of personal conduct to the life he was now living—and how to do this, or let it be done, with the warmth of love in light of the simple, compelling affirmation he had discovered: Yes. If you look back at the text, you'll find Yes hidden in it.

What we learn here of Hammarskjöld was long in preparation. His friend Sten Stolpe sheds an interesting light: "In 1936," he recalled, "when I attempted to draw him into a certain group of Christian workers, he replied: 'I envy you, if you possess what you believe you possess. But so far it is in a more hidden community that I seek the innermost reality of life.'"[35] It would prove to be the community of the medieval mystics, distant in time but not in impact on him.

Hammarskjöld wrote in February 1954 to his brother Bo: "I am very glad that you and [his wife] Signe understood my 'This I believe' statement. It goes deep and is probably the clearest synthesis so far of my present and past."[36] He is speaking as a writer with rights of revision and further exploration; there could be other syntheses to come. Some months later, in a note to his friend Bo Beskow, he still had the Murrow credo in mind: "The pages of 'This I believe' that you happened to see are not polite statements but deeply engaged ones, partly in self-criticism."[37]

Hammarskjöld finished out the year with a UN Radio message to the UN community in New York and abroad. He returned in it to a theme he never tired of restating: the rootedness of large political facts in the intimate facts of each one's life.

> Our work for peace must begin within the private world of each one of us. To build for man a world without fear, *we* must be without fear. To build a world of justice, *we* must be just. And how can we fight for liberty if we are not free in our own minds? How can we ask others to sacrifice if *we* are not ready to do so?
>
> Some might consider this to be just another expression of noble principles, too far from the harsh realities of political life properly to be made the theme of this New Year's message. I disagree. Only in true surrender to the interest of all can we reach that strength and independence, that unity of purpose, that equity of judgment which are necessary if we are to measure up to our duty to the future, as men of a generation to whom the chance was given to build in time a world of peace.[38]

He had spoken at the end of his credo of "the laws of inner life and of action." Stated in that way, it sounds remote, though provocative. Stated as it is in this year-end message, it is not remote at all. It is modeled on his own striving.

9

It Takes Life to Love Life

Something in Hammarskjold's year-end message offended his industrious Swedish gadfly, Herbert Tingsten. The classic photo of Tingsten—vide Wikipedia—makes him look like a heavy in a 1940s film noir, but that may be misleading. As editor-in-chief of a major newspaper, *Dagens Nyheter*, Tingsten could and did pursue Hammarskjöld throughout the UN years, all the while exchanging occasional letters with him and seeing him time and again in New York, as if all were well. Hammarskjöld read Tingsten's columns, though they could infuriate him; he expected more support at home. But the rough treatment—we'll see a key example—surely heightened his vigilance, and in that sense their unarmed, long-distance combat did no harm. In the early days of 1954 he sent Tingsten the letter we've read about American hypocrisy (see p. 142). There were other thoughts in it:

> Allow me to send you a personal New Year greeting, somewhat saltier than the one that has caused concern at the D. N. [*Dagens Nyheter*].
>
> Lord knows there is not one day without "messages" or many weeks without "statements" from me. And it's not easy to keep high standards .... The worst thing about the sentence quoted by the D. N. is that I meant what I said—and that it had a specific object, misunderstood by no one here. It was a matter of criticism, not of edification. I think you would understand that better after some time here.
>
> But apart from this, consider that a poor devil who has to preach every Sunday might prefer to express his feelings in the kind of forum available to you.
>
> A happy and pugnacious New Year![1]

Hammarskjöld makes light of his role as the public voice and mind of the UN, but in reality he knew its importance and gave it his all. He turned down many opportunities—Andrew Cordier recorded that in his first year he received 120 invitations and accepted just 30—but there must have been almost always a talk in the works for either UN or public meetings.[2] There was some speechwriting capability at his disposal, but I don't detect other minds and hands in his talks about the human condition and the need for community; they are all of a piece, all bear his stamp.

The year 1954 was on the whole kind to him. As we'll see, *Markings* reflects a quieter season, more green tea than strong coffee, until early December when a great diplomatic challenge suddenly appeared. Throughout the year he was working nonstop, but that had long been his style. To his brother Bo he described "a workday—without breaks—that normally goes from 9 a.m. to 1 o'clock at night and even more, and a constant demand for unheard-of concentration (and very thick skin)."[3] In January through May, his desk calendar reflects innumerable meetings identified as "reorg"—the reorganization of the Secretariat and UN structure as a whole, set in motion the previous year.[4] In the Middle East, he was unable in the early months of the year to bring Israel and Jordan together under mutually agreed conditions to reaffirm their armistice agreement, just as he was unable, owing to a Soviet veto in the Security Council, to provide an on-site engineering team to evaluate a controversial Israeli hydroelectric and irrigation project under way at the Jordan River despite Syrian opposition. Blocked by the Security Council decision, for the first but not last time he untangled the strands of the situation and decided to institute, for purposes of the Secretariat only, an engineering study that would provide him a basis for knowledgeable participation in debate and decision at some later point. This in-house study team even dispatched to the site an advisory group—again strictly for Secretariat purposes, but the gain in knowledge paralleled what could have been accomplished by a positive Security Council decision. It was a clever solution, and no one seemed to mind.

On a larger scale, preparations were under way for a multinational conference at Geneva (April 26–July 20, 1954), intended to hammer out a political settlement for the two Koreas now that a cease-fire had been signed and to open discussion about restoring peace in Indochina. This was the era of the climactic battle at Dien Bien Phu between French colonial forces and Ho Chi Minh's Viet Minh, a fifty-five-day agony that ended during the Geneva conference with Ho Chi Minh's victory. The United Nations did not have an explicit role in the conference, attended by the belligerents and their allies, but both Dien Bien Phu and the conference were much in people's thoughts through that period. Conditions were slowly gathering for the Vietnam War.

A Guatemalan coup in June, covertly organized by the CIA to unseat a left-leaning government and install a government with which the

United States could be comfortable, occasioned another disappointing round of activity for Hammarskjöld. The vulnerable Guatemalan government had called for a meeting of the Security Council on June 19th, an act that brought Hammarskjöld into conflict with US policy and Henry Cabot Lodge Jr., the US ambassador. Urquhart notes that this was Hammarskjöld's first clash with a member nation. Lodge was an impressive individual, later to be a trusted colleague and friend, but at this point he was manipulating all available levers to avert a Security Council debate and define the Guatemalan issue as strictly a regional matter best taken up by the Organization of American States. He succeeded with the help of Latin American governments that needed to remain in the good graces of the United States. The Guatemalan government fell on June 27th. In his midsummer annual report, Hammarskjöld returned to this topic in cool but unmistakable terms:

> Developments outside the organizational framework of the United Nations, but inside its sphere of interest, do give rise to certain problems . . . . In the short view, other approaches than those provided by the United Nations machinery may seem more expedient and convenient, but in the long view they may yet be inadvisable. . . . For example, the importance of regional arrangements in the maintenance of peace is fully recognized in the Charter and the appropriate use of such arrangements is encouraged. But in those cases where resort to such arrangements is chosen in the first instance, that choice should not be permitted to cast any doubt on the ultimate responsibility of the United Nations.[5]

One further matter was on the agenda, but developing slowly and without Hammarskjöld's direct participation at the early stages: work toward the "Atoms for Peace" conference called for by Eisenhower. In the course of 1954, the United States and the Soviet Union in private talks agreed to a conference in August 1955, and the General Assembly (autumn 1954) voted to create an International Atomic Energy Agency—still very much with us—and asked Hammarskjöld to chair an advisory committee to plan the conference. To Hammarskjöld's lasting satisfaction, the committee included scientists from many countries, including two Nobel laureates, one of whom was the wise and witty I. I. Rabi of Columbia University. Urquhart writes that "the planning for the scientific conference went forward with exemplary speed and soon became a competitive exercise in the declassification of scientific material by East and West."[6] In a talk many years later, Rabi recalled the advisory committee's atmosphere: "Our committee became like a club where the members learned to respect and trust one another. Our trust was never misplaced or betrayed. As a result the committee could do its work with the utmost expedition and objectivity to the astonishment of expensive and sophisticated diplomats."[7] It was the first such club around Hammarskjöld. Others to come had participants who would report along the same lines, as would Hammarskjöld. Something in his nature favored and delighted in small circles of dedicated people.

Though he had told his brother about endless hours and work, he had nonetheless begun to consolidate such a circle of friends in New York and found time to attend theater, opera, ballet. Among the very many working dinners at his apartment for Secretariat colleagues, senior members of delegations, and visiting government leaders, he also found time for evenings with friends from other worlds—literary, artistic, theatrical, and Swedish friends passing through. He had obviously, and quickly, been deemed an interesting fellow by cultural leaders in New York. He attended opera from time to time at the invitation of Rudolf Bing, who was for many years director of the Metropolitan Opera. He attended ballet at the invitation of Lincoln Kirstein, cofounder and codirector of New York City Ballet. Kirstein would prove in later years to be a heartfelt supporter of Hammarskjöld at times when words of encouragement counted. Kirstein introduced him to the Anglo-American poet W. H. Auden, later the cotranslator of *Markings*, who was often enough a guest to dinner. And there were others: Arthur H. Sulzberger (publisher of the *New York Times* throughout Hammarskjöld's tenure at the UN), Walter Lippmann and his wife (he was a widely read, liberal columnist), Saint-John Perse (French poet and diplomat with whom Hammarskjöld maintained a rich correspondence), and eventually Carlotta O'Neill (the playwright Eugene O'Neill's widow), John Steinbeck (the famed American novelist), and more still. Even Greta Garbo emerged from hiding once to attend a particularly choice dinner party with theater people.[8]

Urquhart was comical on the subject of Hammarskjöld and Garbo, the two most celebrated Swedes in New York. In an oral history session he commented, "Hammarskjöld had on the whole surprisingly good public relations because he was rather like Greta Garbo. He was a mysterious, interesting man, obviously engaged in very important matters in a slightly lonely, heroic way. . . . He had just that element of obscurity and mystery that really fascinated people. The press was never bored with him."[9] Garbo was something of a point of reference for Hammarskjöld too. Writing in May 1955 to Uno Willers, director of the National Library of Sweden, who would prove most helpful in arranging private and unnoticed sessions with Chinese diplomats, Hammarskjöld commented on his need to avoid reporters during a planned summer visit to Sweden: "I hope that you don't believe I'm turning shy in some kind of Garbo style: I think I take [public attention] with a sufficient quantum of good humor, but I would like to find some way of avoiding . . . absurdities."[10] All this being said, Hammarskjöld's circle of friends helps explain why he could write from New York in mid-August 1955 to a Swedish colleague: "Outside the windows Hurricane Connie rages and the contrast to the sunny days in Europe is very great indeed. However, it is very good to be back. Funny, in spite of very deep roots in Sweden, this is after all the place where at present I feel most at home."[11]

The fight knows no end

In the course of 1954, Hammarskjöld made the transition from a predominantly administrative role, naturally with diplomatic concerns, to a predominantly diplomatic and political role, naturally with administrative concerns. Ralph Bunche witnessed the transition: "His interest and immersion in political problems soon began to leave him less and less time for the administrative aspects of his responsibilities, and both his attention to and interest in them steadily diminished. It also soon became clear that he would not be lacking in political initiative backed by courage. . . . It cannot be said that Dag Hammarskjöld displayed any reluctance about being carried in this direction, and he never seemed to be sorry about becoming more and more exclusively a 'political man.' Quite the contrary."[12] With dry wit, Hammarskjöld said of his office in mid-March: "The Secretary-General plays a somewhat peculiar role in this Organization. In a certain sense he is just a secretary; in another sense he is necessarily much more."[13]

It took American universities a little while to notice him, but once they did he was a sought-after speaker at commencements and other occasions. He gave three commencement addresses in 1954 and a talk at Columbia University. As well, at the start of the year he spoke to a gathering of academics and administrators where he stated with candor, veiled by formality of style, his delight in connecting with the university scene. "The opportunity you have given me of meeting with you, the representatives of higher education and research in this country, is most welcome and meets a deep need. This is the case also because, both personally and in the light of my family background, I have always considered myself, and still have the ambition so to be, primarily a university man."[14] It was nostalgia for a life he hadn't chosen, but not only that: he was still rethinking the United Nations, his own topic of higher education and research. His activity was in part parallel to the academy's and, although perhaps not so intended, the honorary doctorates he received from a number of institutions were recognitions of a certain kind of scholarship.

Five university occasions in one year can't be a random selection; he must have been looking for that audience. Hammarskjöld's themes in this round were the condition of the world community and the individual human condition, the urgent need for the United Nations and its further development, the scope and limits of his own role, values worthy of trust and essential to progress, attitudes that make peace with justice more possible. His themes recurred as if inscribed on a rotating prayer wheel. Some years later, at a time when he was privately reading in classic Chinese literature and could already look back on years of effort, he shared with an audience a passage that particularly moved him. It was a description of a band of peacemakers active at a war-torn period in Chinese history.

> Constantly rebuffed but never discouraged, they went round from state to state helping people to settle their differences, arguing against wanton attack and pleading for the suppression of arms, that the age in which they lived might be saved from its state of continual war. To this end they interviewed princes and lectured the common people, nowhere meeting with any great success, but obstinately persisting in their task, till kings and commoners alike grew weary of listening to them. Yet undeterred they continued to force themselves on people's attention.[15]

For the moment he had no reason to feel that he was forcing himself on public attention in the United States or elsewhere. Eventually he had some trouble with kings and such, but commoners never failed to welcome him.

Brian Urquhart has said and written more than once that Hammarskjöld was not a dramatic public speaker. One has only to listen online to the recording of his statement for Edward R. Murrow's radio program to confirm that he spoke without flourishes, as if ideas, images, and logic have a native force with which one shouldn't tamper.[16] As we have heard

Hammarskjöld tell the *New York Times*, he was satisfied to be "a colorless sort of prophet, maybe"; it was a matter of policy as well as a preferred personal style. A prophet nonetheless. No less than his actions, his words on the page, circulating as press releases, defined and sustained some real part of hope and clarity of direction in his era. Toward the end of 1955, no doubt during the fall General Assembly when oratory in five languages was in full flood and he was confined to his high supervisory seat, he turned in his private journal to the topic of language used and abused. There are few more strident entries; some speaker or tag team of speakers must have pushed past his limit of tolerance.

> *Respect for the word* is the first commandment in the discipline by which a man can be educated to maturity—intellectual, emotional, and moral.
>
> Respect for the word—to employ it with scrupulous care and an incorruptible heartfelt love of truth—is essential if there is to be any growth in a society or in the human race.
>
> To misuse the word is to show contempt for man. It undermines the bridges and poisons the wells. It causes us to regress down the long path of human evolution.
>
> "But I say unto you, that every idle word that men speak . . . "[17]

Perhaps the force of his words redressed the balance. It would have been in this spirit that he undertook his round of university talks in 1954.

The first stop was a meeting in Cincinnati of the academic grouping now known as the Association of American Colleges and Universities. As almost always, he offered early in his talk a fresh statement of the mission of the United Nations. On the surface, such compact but surprisingly comprehensive statements are models of straight thinking and declarative language, as well they ought to be. Beneath the surface, there is something else—a summoning or incantatory intent, as if to state clearly what *should be* is a step toward realizing it in practice. A somewhat hidden foundation in feeling or faith confers power on his elegantly rational discourse. "The United Nations," he said in Cincinnati,

> is the most ambitious effort so far made to translate into practical realities the old dream of an international community where nations and peoples are living together—in full recognition of mutual problems and rights—not as citizens of a super-state, but as members of a free association so constituted as to provide a frame inside which humanity may achieve an orderly and balanced progress in peace.[18]

Thinking further about this model, Hammarskjöld drew an analogy to university life in medieval Europe. Looking south from medieval Sweden to the magical gathering of teachers and students at the University of Paris, he offered a sweet vision of free association and intellectual inquiry supported by religious values which, as he put it, sanctified the pursuit of truth. Reaching further still, he proposed that values of that order, embedded in "aspirations and hopes" rather than specifically religious forms, can and should influence efforts today toward a world at peace. What was so very difficult to construct in his era—and in ours—finds, in his view, a provocative antecedent in an era when students and teachers felt themselves to be "citizens of one world." It was an interesting line of thought, meant to stir and refresh old ideals applicable to the present.

> As members of colleges and universities, you belong to a fraternity which transcends national boundaries—a community of the spirit and of the search for truth. In the Middle Ages, students from Sweden often walked the long way down to Paris to sit at the feet of Thomas Aquinas and other great teachers. They were but a few of the many, who, from all corners of the Western World of those days, gathered together and regarded themselves as citizens of one world, though all around them the conflicts among cities and states and peoples made Europe an extreme example of disunity. . . . Those students . . . were not only members of a fraternity in search of truth. They were also animated by a faith in the ultimate aims of the life of man; they were citizens of a *Civitas Dei*. The liberal education of free individuals can and should bear in mind those aspirations and hopes which sanctify the search for truth as well as our efforts to build a world of law and order.[19]

The medieval scene as Hammarskjöld conceived it translates easily to the Cold War era and the hope he invested in thoughtful people of all countries. There is no program here, no simplistic agenda. But there is an expression of hope that universities and their scholars and students, by virtue of what they are and what they care for, would help to reduce what he had already called "walls of ice" and would later call "walls of mistrust," which divided the world. This must explain why he chose to speak so often at large, influential universities: he wanted them to recognize the United Nations as *their* project also. He wanted them to help.

Hammarskjold introduced on this occasion a theme—emerging nations—that would become a major concern of his later years in office. The passage from the original 51 UN member nations to today's roster of 193 nations began during his tenure. In early 1954 he hadn't yet deeply engaged with this issue in practical terms, but he was thinking. Ralph Bunche, long responsible for the Trusteeship Council that dealt with the affairs of emerging nations, must have been a sound mentor, and UN headquarters in New York would have offered Hammarskjöld conversations with ambassadors of member nations in this category, from Afghanistan at the top of the alphabet (admitted 1946) to Yemen (admitted 1947).

> From the point of view of one engaged in international politics, the awakening of the peoples of the former colonial and underdeveloped countries is one of the great challenges of our time.... Along with a thirst for knowledge of the modern industrial techniques of the Western World, the peoples of Asia and Africa are experiencing a rebirth of interest in their own cultures and a deep preoccupation with the problems of their own identity and of their place in the world. The results of this awakening will be shared by material help as well as by the intellectual and spiritual guidance that our own experience and maturity will enable us to provide.[20]

His reference to Western experience and maturity suggests bias. If so, he rebalanced later in the talk by recalling Albert Schweitzer, to whom he had long looked: "For good reasons, Albert Schweitzer has called it a betrayal of the very idea of civilization to claim priority and predominance for any special national variety of civilization." And rebalanced yet again: "The educator knows that sympathetic understanding and tolerance of diversity in the world does not mean a weakening of personal conviction or of devotion to truth as he sees it."[21] In 1959, after traveling widely in South Asia, he returned to this topic with conviction in a letter to a friend: "A *great* experience: how much more mature and fine the Asiatic art of living is compared to ours. Evidently you have to accept the thought that everything is an illusion, before you can master the whole scale of reality with ease, style, seriousness, and happiness. What does it then matter if you are poor, politically ignorant or threatened."[22] This little canon of good things—ease, style, seriousness, and happiness—comes close to defining what he cared for.

The next stop in Hammarskjöld's tour of the academy was the University of Pennsylvania for a midwinter commencement. Here he rethought a theme we have already encountered—the individual's inner life as the ultimate cause of peace or war—and tied it to a melancholy assessment of human nature.

It is . . . said that our time is the age of the decisive fight between freedom and tyranny. It is true that such a fight is going on. But it has always
been fought and I don't believe that I could justifiably be called a pessimist for expressing my belief that this fight will never be over. It will
go on, generation after generation, as long as human beings are human
beings. Furthermore, this is basically not a struggle between political
systems and ideologies, but a struggle within and for the hearts of men,
including our own. There is a Swedish proverb which says that it is always easy to agree on fighting the devil when you have him painted on
the wall. But we can never forget that the real devil may also be within
ourselves and all the more dangerous for not being recognized.[23]

It was another moment when the perspective of *Markings* intersected with
and spoke through a public talk. That was to occur more than once in the
course of his efforts this year to articulate the UN's mission and ground it
in intimate human experience no less than in larger political realities.

At the University of California, Berkeley, in the spring, he went after
the topic with something approaching anguish, although his delivery
was no doubt calm. At the end of the following passage from that talk
he refers to brainwashing, to which some prisoners of war in the Korean conflict had been subjected by their North Korean captors. It was a
particular horror of that time—horrible in itself, and deeply unsettling
because it had shown the fragility of identity.

Morally, the findings of modern psychology and the thought of modern
philosophers should have made us better equipped to tackle our problems. So should the development of democracy, and of liberal institutions as tools of democracy. . . . But for all this "progress," are we really
better than our forerunners? When we are ridden by fear, do we not experience as often as before, brutal or mean reactions? Do we not seek to
pass the burden of our responsibility over to innocent scapegoats? Do
we not forget the sufferings of our neighbor? Do we not covet his possessions? And when we think of brainwashing and mental torture, what
must we say of such fruits from the tree of psychological knowledge
applied in a refinement of evil—to kill the man instead of the body.[24]

In Hammarskjöld's political world, fear is the root of all evil. After this
partially biblical summation of error, followed by an equally severe assessment of the gap between the fund of knowledge available and the
poor use we make of it, he continued that "the demands put to us *must*

be met—if our civilization is to survive," and opened the topic of "practical means to cope with the situation." The issue, as he stated it, was to translate knowledge—good knowledge, sound knowledge—into practice. And his theme was the willingness to tinker patiently and at length.

> I do not believe that any ready-made solutions can be found or that we can avoid a painful period of trial and error in the elaboration of the necessary tools. It will undoubtedly be a slow process requiring much patience, registering many shortcomings and mistakes, suffering serious setbacks. But I am sure that such a process will ultimately yield results if approached and conducted in the right spirit.
>
> The right spirit. From what I have said it is obvious that the first thing required is patience, the patience inspired by a firm faith in our ability to reach the goal. But we need more than patience in the passive sense. We need perseverance, of the kind that equips us not to take defeats to heart, in the knowledge that defeats are unavoidable, and that if our efforts do not seem to get results, it may be because we have not yet applied the necessary degree of perseverance.[25]

So far he has not said a word about the United Nations. Now he feels ready to speak of its centrality. In the foregoing it turns out that he has proposed an attitude toward the UN.

> The United Nations was set up in response to the collective needs to which I have referred. It is an attempt to give a first rough constitutional form to the fact of world interdependence. It is an approach to the problem of world organization for a still anarchic world community.
>
> By regarding the United Nations in this pragmatic way, I feel that we will be more just in our appraisal both of its achievements and of its failures. We will look at the achievements as the first modest yield we have been able to reap from our efforts, and we will look at the failures as natural and unavoidable in such a pilot venture, where we learn as much from the mistakes as from the positive experiences.[26]

The seemingly endless stalemate and menace of the Cold War and the Arab-Israeli conflict must have been the sources of one of Hammarskjöld's most heartfelt insights, repeated always in new words to kings and commoners alike: the healing power of time. Toward the end of the talk at Berkeley, he put it this way:

> History has many lessons to teach about apparently irreconcilable conflicts. Terrible wars have been fought in the past because people thought

that they could not live in the same world together, or because they thought their beliefs were in head-on collision with those of their neighbors. Then, with time, they found that it was not only possible but necessary to make a working compromise that allowed for the differences. They found that it was not only possible but necessary to accept the principle of diversity in human society. Time itself is a great healer and situations that seem to defy solution can be lived with until that day when the evolution of human affairs may bring a more favorable opportunity.[27]

How often he would say this; how often it would be needed.

A month later on the East Coast, at Amherst College, Hammarskjöld outdid himself. He seems to have been happy to have a "verse" as a point of departure, in this case lines from Walt Whitman: "All Peoples of the globe together sail. . . ." Happy also to remember biblical words or situations demonstrating that sound insight has a long history; in this instance he recalled the Pharisees in the time of Jesus and drew from their example the admonition that "self-righteousness and intellectual self-sufficiency produce a rigidity which is the best ally of our adversaries because it blinds us both to our own weakness and to their strength."[28] He described true idealism as flexible, self-interest as rigid even when "dressed in the mantle of false idealism," and tied this back to Walt Whitman's certainty that all peoples "sail the same voyage, are bound to the same destination."

That said, Hammarskjöld felt ready to formulate the key point he had in mind: "Ultimately this flexibility is but a reflection of our insight into the essential unity of all mankind." It was the credo of a negotiator committed to discovering common ground, without loss of integrity, in situations where there appears to be none. The idea is pure and self-evident, but he didn't perceive it as too heavenly for use. However lofty and impractical it may seem, Hammarskjöld put the greatest possible emphasis on this idea. From time to time it can seem as if he alone, and perhaps a handful of others in each generation, would be capable of guiding by certain ideas and practices he proposed. The rest of us will stumble on at lower altitudes and somehow find our way. That was not his view. "I firmly believe," he said, "that we shall survive . . . , both morally and in the literal physical sense, only if we give full recognition to the fundamental and overriding unity of mankind."[29] This he wasn't willing to compromise.

Although these remarks toward the beginning of his talk remain provocative, the heart of the talk lies a little further on where, yet again, the perspective of *Markings* coincides with what he perceived as crucial in political life: self-knowledge on the personal level, knowledge of humanity at the level of study and career.

> Too often our learning, our knowledge, and our mastery are too much concentrated on techniques and we forget about man himself. . . . When I speak of knowledge in this context I do not mean the kind of knowledge which you can gain from textbooks, but the knowledge which you can derive only from a study of yourself and your fellow men, a study inspired by genuine interest and pursued with humility. The door to an understanding of the other party, with whom you may have to deal in business, in politics or in the international sphere, is a fuller understanding of yourself, since the other party, of course, is made fundamentally of the same stuff as you yourself.
>
> Thus, no education is complete, in a world basically united, which does not include man himself, and is not inspired by a recognition of the fact that you will not understand your enemy without understanding yourself, and that an understanding of your enemy will throw considerable light also on yourself and on your own motives.[30]

No one else in public life at the time was saying anything of this kind. Even today it remains new. He could have said more about the practical meaning of "a study of yourself . . . pursued with humility." But that would have prematurely opened the pages of *Markings*, and it was still a work in progress. Further, the approach to private self-knowledge and vigilant public participation recorded in his journal is, so to speak, the *kind of thing* he meant, but each person would of necessity have to find his and her own way. He was a serious and informed Christian with roots in the mystical and monastic literature. As well, he learned from other traditions, notably the early Chinese. That formula would suit perhaps few in his audience. But the point was made in his talk, and made clearly. No doubt, some heard. How to respond in our own time to Hammarskjöld's "teachings"— this passage has that character—is a question worth holding in mind as we move through further chapters in his life.

Reaching the end of his talk, Hammarskjöld again made clear his frame of reference: international affairs. "We must seek a fuller knowledge of man himself," he said,

> —a knowledge that will more nearly match our mastery of science and of techniques. Only in proportion as we close this gap shall we be able to diminish the dangers of fear and suspicion and of the irrational be-

havior that follows from them. This will be no affair of a few months or a few years, of course—a kind of war against fear and hate ending with conclusive victory as the reward of successful effort. Only if we should fail in our faith in human brotherhood might there be something resembling a conclusive end of the struggle—and that would be the destruction of our civilization. No, the signal of success will never be a final victory. It will be found rather in the stamina to continue the struggle, and in the preservation and the strengthening of faith in the future of man.[31]

That would have provided an elegant conclusion. But instead he chose to end by recalling the words of an American poet which have no political content at all. They are a simple, memorable call.

We must have "life" in that sense of the word which Edgar Lee Masters once gave to it when he had an old woman say in his *Spoon River Anthology*: "It takes life to love Life."[32]

He was thinking of a poem in which a ninety-six-year-old woman, speaking from beyond the grave like all other voices in the book, looks back and scolds the young people she had known:

What is this I hear of sorrow and weariness,
Anger, discontent and drooping hopes?
Degenerate sons and daughters,
Life is too strong for you—
It takes life to love Life.

Hammarskjöld gave voice only to the affirmative closing line; it meant what he meant. He must have read Masters recently, as part of moving in.

The last stop in Hammarskjöld's tour of universities in 1954 was Columbia to speak at a festive bicentennial gathering in October. It was again a formidable talk, from which we might draw just two passages. The first is a particularly deft assessment of the balance between national sovereignty and global interdependence.

The fact we have to face squarely is that the diversity of the nations makes world government still impossible, while the interdependence of nations has already made world organization necessary. Our knowledge of the past, and the results of our new knowledge in the present, combine to force us to find a middle road: a world organization respecting the sovereignty of nations—a middle road on which we can move, slowly but surely, towards that world community which for our civilization is the only alternative to disaster.[33]

The second, paying homage to the British in World War II, ends with his conviction that peacemakers should not expect what he termed, at Amherst, "final victory"; there will be other fruits, but not that. "In the Battle of Britain," he said,

> that fortress of freedom was held by a few brave men. On the wider fron-
> tiers of freedom of thought and knowledge they had, during the dark years,
> many comrades, fighting under the law of honesty with courage as their
> shield and intelligence as their only weapon. That fight knows no end.[34]

The language here is oddly allusive, as if shaped by an undisclosed thought. It wouldn't surprise me if he had in mind the fate of Sweden in World War II—neutral for the sake of survival, under the thumb of Nazi Germany, its representatives treated with suspicion by the Allies. Were he and his colleagues and fellow citizens "fighting under the law of honesty with courage as their shield," armed only with intelligence? Be that as it may, he shared his conviction and experience that the fight for peace with justice knows no end.

The flame ascends

It is odd how trivia, with the passage of time, acquire patina. Consider this undated, comical shred from those years at the UN:

> Mr. Vaughan
>   Various delegations hope to see an appropriate *hair-brush* in the
> proper place at the Delegates' entrance. It is a request modest in scope
> although curious in substance. I guess we should agree.
>
>   Dag

Written on a bit of paper, it was one of the small things Hammarskjöld's chief of staff, Andrew Cordier, collected alongside larger things. One can nearly see the secretary-general's inquiring eyes take in some poor fellow dispatched by a delegation to make the request, and nearly measure the light-years of distance from which he contemplated this "request modest in scope although curious in substance." And complied. In a world where the fight knows no end, there is some need for hairbrushes.

In the privacy of his journal, Hammarskjöld had begun 1954 as was his custom with a line from the hymn his mother read at New Year: "*snart stundar natten,"* soon night approaches, but added to it the first of many prayers to come: "Let me finish what I have been permitted to begin. Let me give all without any assurance of increase."[35] From this year on, *Markings* becomes Hammarskjöld's personal Book of Common Prayer. He read regularly in the Anglican Book of Common Prayer, especially its superb translation of Psalms, from which he would occasionally transcribe verses into his journal. Characteristically, he owned and used an edition published in 1762, a relic of time past. Reading scripture (and the medieval wisdom of Thomas à Kempis) was for him a consoling, instructive return to origins, symbolized but also made real by antique editions. This seems a sensible interpretation, although he said nothing about it.

Among many reflections of many kinds recorded in *Markings*, prayer now had its recurrent place to the end. Writing down a prayer, letting it advance in its own way and words, and in its own time, became a practice. He might not have called it that, but he acknowledged that he was following what he called "a spiritual discipline,"[36] practiced and explored in ways to which *Markings* is the key. I don't think that his act of writing recorded words found earlier and remembered later. It is likely to have had a richer role, as if the first words written down, in an intuitive process of discovery, created the need and possibility to know what came next. Sometimes his prayers end abruptly, as if whatever came next he didn't know or couldn't say. The unfinished has its eloquence. At other times his prayers are beautifully finished.

Among the four prayers he recorded in 1954, the second (here abridged) is especially memorable.

> Thou who art over us,
> Thou who art one of us,
> Thou who *art*—
> Also within us,
> May all see Thee—in me also,
> May I prepare the way for Thee,
> May I thank Thee for all that shall fall to my lot.
>
> . . .
>
> Give me a pure heart—that I may see Thee,
> A humble heart—that I may hear Thee,
> A heart of love—that I may serve Thee,
> A heart of faith—that I may abide in Thee.[37]

Bernhard Erling, a dedicated translator and interpreter of *Markings*, must be right to read the first three lines as trinitarian, addressed in turn to Father, Son, and Holy Spirit; the fourth also, giving location to the Holy Spirit. Hammarskjöld's prayer evokes the highest possible standard of conduct and radiance in life. It is supplication, not assertion. It is daring.

Prayer is an act of faith and feeling. At some point in the year Hammarskjöld found himself reflecting about the nature of faith. He began as a man of learning, citing a formula in the writings of the sixteenth-century mystic and teacher St. John of the Cross which must have closely matched his own experience. But he didn't remain a cool-minded man of learning for very long: his meditation led quickly to the solitude of Jesus in the garden of Gethsemane, a time and place of anguish by which Hammarskjöld felt intimately addressed.

> "Faith is the union of God and the Soul."
>
> Faith *is*: it cannot, therefore, be comprehended, far less identified with the formulae in which we paraphrase what is.
>
> –*en una noche oscura*. The Dark Night of the Soul—so dark that we may not even look for faith. The night in Gethsemane when the last friends left you have fallen asleep, all the others are seeking your downfall, and *God is silent*, as the union is consummated.[38]

Themes of inner life work through him for months and years. He returns here to thoughts broached in the Edward R. Murrow talk of last November, where he said that "The language of religion is a set of formulas which register a basic spiritual experience. It must not be regarded as describing, in terms to be defined by philosophy, the reality which is accessible to our senses and which we can analyze with the tools of logic." The primacy of the experience of faith—as indescribable as the taste of salt or tea, except to say that salt is salty and tea is tea-like—has again struck him, but he is looking now with the eyes of an ascetic at the price to be paid for it. In this sunny year, 1954, the image of Gethsemane is already inscribed in him. He would return to it in the last, immensely difficult months of his life when the Congo Crisis was consuming his attention and well-being. The passage here makes us understand that for Hammarskjöld authentic faith is unconditional; it does not require the reassuring and validating experience of God's presence. On the contrary, it takes shape in dark and solitary circumstances when all reassurance is withdrawn. And yet once shaped it becomes a force for the good across "the whole scale of reality," to recall words we have heard from him. Do not ask this man to keep things simple for us, but trust him to work toward what a late friend of mine called "the true truth," deeper truth free of conventional thinking or sentiment.

He knew of a shift in overall awareness. It was implicit in texts of Meister Eckhart and others of that era whom he read, but to read is one thing, to enter the terrain another, and he entered.

> To be governed by that which comes alive when "we" have ceased to live—as interested parties or know-it-alls. To be able to see, hear, and attend to that within us which *is* there in the darkness. And the silence.[39]

It would seem to be exclusively a report from his remoteness, from the most private times when quietness could take the lead, when day-to-day identity may cede to another. We are in the realm of being—of faith *is*, of that which *is* in the darkness and silence inside, a realm of direct perception. But it has its uses. Hammarskjöld must have already been discovering at this time insights he shared with others only in 1958, and only when caught by surprise. A reporter from the internal newsletter of the UN Secretariat rather diffidently approached him in January of that year to interview him. As published in *Secretariat News* for February 14th, their exchange was wide ranging. Just at the end, a question so compelled Hammarskjöld's interest that he returned to it a few days later in a personal letter to a Swedish friend, which we looked at briefly in chapter 1.

> Reporter: One last question, Mr. Hammarskjöld. What, in your opinion, are the main qualities that an international official should possess?
>
> Hammarskjöld: Well, that is a difficult question to answer straight away. You should give me a little while to think about it. First off, however, I would say that a heightened awareness combined with an inner quiet are among these qualities. Also, a certain humility, which helps you to see things through the other person's eye, to reconstruct his case, without losing yourself, without being a chameleon.[40]

A little later, as we know, Hammarskjöld wrote as follows to his friend:

> The other day I was forced by a journalist to try to formulate my views on the main requirements of somebody who wishes to contribute to the development of peace and reason. I found no better formulation than this: "He must push his awareness to the utmost limit without losing

his inner quiet, he must be able to see with the eyes of the others from within their personality without losing his own."[41]

There are invisible realities here: inner quiet, awareness pushed to the limit, a certain humility, seeing from the other's point of view without losing oneself. This is a jerky inventory, but useful toward grasping how much is engaged. To speak of this integrated movement of awareness and kinship as "mindfulness"—a term now common which Hammarskjöld may have encountered but to my knowledge didn't use—is to miss its singularity. Better to think of it as something Hammarskjöld advised, something he had mastered or very nearly, something very good. The two passages make clear that Hammarskjöld approached the diplomatic day, the day of the peacemaker, as an exercise in awareness and contact, and did so without calling attention to his approach.

There is something more in *Markings* for 1954: a new and quite different encounter with what he called "the unheard-of." He first wrote in 1951 of reaching "the frontier of the unheard-of." "Here ends the known," he added. It was a perception grounded in his religious life. He returned to the phrase in the last entry of that year, viewing it in light of an episode in the novel he preferred to any other, Joseph Conrad's *Lord Jim*. There he speculated that "the unheard-of" could be a state or moment of complete self-acceptance that acknowledges all the good and harm one has done in one's life.[42] He used the phrase a third time in an entry for 1952, already explored; in that entry he is again "at the frontier" and acutely aware of his unwillingness to cross over. We know also that he did sometimes cross over.

Throughout these recorded experiences the unheard-of is real; so too is the frontier—real to the mind and heart, which are what matter here. But he writes, it seems early in 1954:

> Then I saw that the wall had never been there, that the "unheard-of" is here and this, not something and somewhere else,
>
> that the "sacrifice" is here and now, always and everywhere—
> "surrendered" *to be* what, in me, God gives of himself to himself.[43]

This is surprising, as if an unyielding riddle has suddenly resolved. The density of traditional religious insight, made his own in these few words, gives pause. Until now, he has experienced the "unheard-of" as sealed behind an inner barrier, inviting but remote. Similarly, he finds that he has placed the possibility of selfless sacrifice at some distance, not flesh of his flesh but an ideal to be sought. Now, at a moment when, as he writes, "I saw," the two spiritual realities reveal themselves as here and now, part of the immediate fabric of life. Understood and experienced in a new way, sacrifice dissolves the wall, which was a commanding illusion. The remote and closed realm of the sacred and the familiar world of work, relationships, and striving more nearly coincide. Another entry in *Markings* for this year provides perspective:

> Blood, grime, sweat, earth—where are these in your world of will? Everywhere—the ground from which the flame ascends straight upwards.[44]

Here Hammarskjöld distinguishes between earthbound difficulty and the flame of spiritual insight, but the two are intimately related: one is the other's fuel, one sheds light on the other. A year later, in what must be the most quoted words in *Markings*, he would restate this thought in its definitive form—no further revision necessary:

> In our era, the road to holiness necessarily passes through the world of action.[45]

All such perceptions, for most people and perhaps also for Hammarskjöld, are flashes of clarified understanding that influence one's sense of the possible and subtly offer an altered way of being, more generous without calculation, wiser without pretension. The direct experience fades—how could it not?—but it leaves a trace. Spiritual seekers of Hammarskjöld's temperament tend to deal in such traces; they collect and store them, do their best not to forget them, cement them even awkwardly into the foundation of what they are and what they wish.

Something more should be said about his new understanding of surrender and sacrifice. Surrender is a concept, a "part of speech" in spiritual discourse, with a long history. It is central to the Lord's Prayer—Thy will be done—and integral to the literature of religious practice, Christian and other. Thomas Merton, the Cistercian monk and author still much read, was among those who found the concept in accounts of the fourth- and fifth-century Desert Fathers and other sources, and did his best in his writings to ensure that it remained available to his contemporaries.[46] That has worked out quite well. A short while ago, a retired abbot who trained as a monastic novice with Merton was asked from the audience at a conference to state, if he didn't mind, what he regarded as most essential in contemplative practice. He took his time to answer and responded: "I can only say what Merton said: desire and surrender."

Sacrifice, as Hammarskjöld understands it here, deserves the quotation marks he gives it because it is not all loss or misery—far from it. Surrender insofar as possible of what is trivial, self-serving, and driven in oneself is surely a sacrifice, but it can allow to some degree what he had wished and implored from the beginning of his UN service: "Not I but God in me"—not my little person, patrolling for advantage and fearing others, but a free intelligence truly serving. The sacrifice—such a frightening word— is really just a "sacrifice" allowing all things to be touched by something more. From Hammarskjöld's perspective, sacrifice is a constituent of a life well lived, a life of depth, intention, and the ability to "contribute to the development of peace and reason" (remembering the letter we considered a few pages ago).

None of this is easy, is it? To walk alongside Hammarskjöld in these years we need to be nearly as versatile as he was. We are drawing lines from what is clear and easily grasped in his thought—for example, "[The international official] must push his awareness to the utmost limit without losing his inner quiet"—to its fine roots in his deepest privacy.

It wasn't easy for Hammarskjöld, either. These entries in his journal memorialize moments of perception, clarities that enter the stream of life and undergo testing and change. For a moment or longer he experienced the unheard-of, the unfathomable presence of the divine here and now. This is remarkable, it is granted to few. But then, some weeks or months later, he felt constrained to note:

> The "unheard-of"—to be in the hands of God.
> Once again a reminder that this is all that remains for you to live for—and once more the feeling of disappointment which shows how slow you are to learn.[47]

If he needed a reminder, it means he forgot. No harm done—human beings forget and remember. His impression of being tested must have been daily or nearly so. The stakes were high, his demand on himself equally high. In the following entry, also from 1954, he seems to have been in a conversation with himself that suddenly finds its way to the page:

> Certainly God tempts—with "equality," with every virtue that allows itself to be used for other purposes than his glory. The more he demands of us, the more dangerous the raw material he has given us for our efforts. Thank him—also for the key to the Gates of Hell.[48]

On the desk was Anacreon

This atmospheric phrase from the beginning of Hammarskjöld's inaugural lecture at the Swedish Academy (December 1954) says much
about his father and the culture shared by father and son. As you may
recall, it was a memorial lecture: elected in March 1954 to occupy the
Academy seat previously held by his late father, Dag conformed to custom by giving an inaugural lecture about his predecessor. During the
days surrounding his father's funeral in October, he had returned to his
father's apartment and took in how things had been left. The statuette
of Anacreon, a riotous ancient Greek poet with incorrigible appetites
and a way with words, obviously struck him by its suggestion of permanence and memory, perhaps even its hint of hidden cheerfulness in
his father's nature.

Despite a minor difficulty with its timing, the election delighted
Hammarskjöld. It was news in mid-March 1954, and the UN press
corps didn't neglect to congratulate him. "I must say that I'm still rather
split on this issue," he replied, "because I've not quite digested this piece
of news. . . . It seems to be so entirely out of line with my type of life, my
being an international civil servant and so on. On the other hand, feeling very strongly our national traditions, I must say that nothing could
have moved me more or given a finer expression to the things I want
maintained outside the political sphere in my own country."[49] Within
days of receiving the news, he wrote to his brother Bo:

> The Academy. You are right: I am not happy about the election *now*.
> However, faced with the question of acceptance and with one hour to
> myself, I came to the conclusion that I had to say yes. Only once . . .
> has somebody declined. There is no objection in principle. In a few
> years I can function fully, and the commemorative speech is not an in-
> surmountable burden. And this: even if I were critical of Papa, would I
> . . . be right to shy away from a unique opportunity to interpret author-
> itatively his inmost concerns? However, I expressed a reservation in my
> answer to Österling [Anders Österling, author, permanent secretary of
> the Academy] regarding the commemorative speech. That reservation
> prompted a letter from Österling in which he warmly pleaded for a
> commemorative speech of the "portrait" type, not a "life." . . .
>   It has been a strange and dramatic year for me, now reaching the
> anniversary of the UN election. With Papa's departure in the center it

is surrounded by the two elections. The new UN year begins in a politically overheated atmosphere. Thank goodness, without deserving it I have inherited good nerves and, so far, a patient constitution.[50]

Election to the Swedish Academy would give Hammarskjöld a new circle of friends, some of whom came to mean a great deal to him, and an anchorage in Swedish life from which he was beginning to feel separated. Responding to a letter of congratulation in mid-April, he wrote, "I am happy to be able to have this particular link with Sweden now that I am in most other respects 'denationalized.'"[51] To Sten Selander, an Academician with whom he would have the best of relations, he responded in a similar vein: "One thing gives me undivided joy: the contact with you, Ingvar Andersson, Martinson, and others in this living connection. And the emigrant existence is after all limited in time. The commemorative speech presents problems which, however, I don't think will be so difficult to solve. More troublesome is that I most probably will find time both to read and to write but will hardly have time for a review yielding a safe perspective on many things that are combustibly close to me. But enough about that. Thanks again for the greeting of welcome."[52]

Later in the spring, he began writing his inaugural address. Given his UN agenda, the process was patchy but he managed. To Sture Petrén he wrote, "During flights and boring meetings I 'work' on the Academy speech—a fascinating but doubtless delicate task."[53] As we noted in an earlier chapter, the result was refined, thoroughly researched where facts were needed, elegantly expressed, rich in sensitive renderings of direct memories. There is no need to turn back at length to that talk, but we should remember its steady voice.

> Hjalmar Hammarskjöld was one of those who are firm in their roots and firm in their faith, those whose changing fates may well deepen the convictions and directions of their early years, but not change them. They may be transported far from their original setting, but their roots are never cut off. In that sense, his life ended where it began. . . . What gave an inner unity to his life was that in the period of revolutionary development through which he lived, he remained faithful to his past, faithful also to *the* past. By easily discernible intermediate stages, this faithfulness bridged the span to a far earlier era, seventeenth-century Sweden, when the throne, the altar, and the sword formed a terse triad in which a nation found its melody.[54]

The talk was extremely well received by his new peers. Later he couldn't resist relaying to Petrén some comments overheard. "The most pleasant, *really* pleasant remark: Lagerkvist to Gullberg: This was of *very* high literary standard. Gullberg to Lagerkvist: Yes—among the finest that will be in the Acts of the Academy. I am truly happy over these . . . judgments from the vantage points represented by L. and G. How far from the night editors."[55] Pär Lagerkvist was the world-renowned novelist who has already entered this narrative, Hjalmar Gullberg a poet and essayist whom Hammarskjöld held in high regard. And "night editors" was probably Mr. Tingsten.

Who was poised to pounce. Hammarskjöld saw his editorial just days after publication of the Academy talk in December. Tingsten's title was snide, "Hammarskjöld as a way of life," but he did come up with a description of two temperaments, borrowed from the Irish author Joyce Cary, which Hammarskjöld found interesting.

> Secretary-General Dag Hammarskjöld's speech on his father, former Prime Minister Hjalmar Hammarskjöld, has been given much praise. One can understand that and agree to much of it. The speech is well written, spiced with some words of emotion, some expressions of artistic elegance, but at no point affected or extravagant. The delightful vagueness that so often has served Mr. Hammarskjöld is . . . less obvious than in other cases. The weakness, the distortion, if you will, lies deeper. . . .
>
> Joyce Cary writes in his description of modern politics about men who have "grace" and of mere administrators, men of justice and order. By grace is not meant anything good in itself but imagination, a passion to improve, the longing for something great and good in the future; grace, the inner light, could lead astray just as well as considerations based on solid and approved norms, but it inspires those who change the world. This perspective . . . is totally lacking in the . . . the two Hammarskjölds. The will to work as a civil servant, with given even if unclear . . . instructions, is so imperative that other ways of action are forgotten or hidden. . . .
>
> Civil servants like that . . . are needed everywhere, they can be called the salt not of the earth, but of states. The dangers, or rather temptations, that threaten them, are obvious. A blend of skepticism and conceit, to which conviction and enthusiasm are something suspicious and naïve. . . . A concentration on technical skill, making performance an end in itself. . . . It is amusing to gain . . . insight, even if unintended, into this way of life.[56]

Hammarskjöld again chose to respond in a private letter. The gravitational link between these two men is surprising, as if the journalist couldn't free himself from growling negativity toward the statesman, and the statesman couldn't free himself from explaining matters to the journalist. At one point Hammarskjöld nearly perjures himself in his letter, and there is only a minor jab at his tormenter:

> It is with real interest that I have just read your editorial about my Academy speech. To a great extent you hit the mark—not least in the reference to Cary's distinction between men of "grace" and men of "order." It is again—on the more masculine level—the story of Martha and Mary. My father—and I—belong to Martha's prosaic breed. What I hoped to show among other things was that that line of life also has its deep pathos and unavoidable tragedy. . . . You are also all too right in what you say about the temptations to which men of order are subject—temptations we all fall for, do we not (with inhumanity as a consequence).
>
> Perhaps it could be of interest that thinking about my father and his problems to a great extent has forced me to reconsider. It was 43 years between us—and what years! When he was alive, conflict dominated. Now, not least in light of current experiences, I find easier ways, I believe genuine, to empathy. . . . Besides, a mature man has so much in him that is seemingly contradictory that a comprehensively balanced picture needs far greater perspective than I, or anybody, possesses.
>
> Warmest wishes for the New Year. You escape "messages" this year—I have other things to do.[57]

I don't think that any reader of this book could agree with Hammarskjöld that he belonged exclusively to "Martha's prosaic breed," that he was strictly a man of order lacking inspiration and creativity. Two days later even Hammarskjöld didn't agree. As he made clear in a note to Petrén, Joyce Cary's stimulating notion of order and grace had continued working its way through him. He wrote on the eve of his departure for China to continue what had already proved to be the most difficult diplomatic challenge to date of his UN service, and he had both Peking and Tingsten in mind (best to stay with the outdated spelling, Peking, for Beijing, because it appears everywhere in the record of events about to engage Hammarskjöld). "Now we shall take the leap to Peking," he wrote.

> Fourteen tough days—with a very uncertain aftermath. How many at home realize that *this* is "politics"? That in a role like *this* you are

whole—both a man of "order" and a man of "grace," to speak with
Herbert Tingsten. When will H. T. and others discover that there are
those who can never take sides on behalf of anything but their own
conviction of what is right and that they are certainly not mercenaries but live under stricter laws than others: "A mature man is his own
judge." Forgive this philosophy—you get a bit thoughtful at a moment
like this, when for the second time in my life for a moment something
of the destiny of us all lies in my hands.[58]

Something of the destiny of us all

Hammarskjöld had a striking ability to describe the United Nations to
his many audiences in a way that conferred dignity on the often harsh
debates in the Security Council and General Assembly. "We can look
at the Organization as a body where ideologies are permitted to clash
inside the wider framework of a fundamental unity of purpose for peace.
Utilized in this way the United Nations can shorten our road to a world
without fear."[59] But there was another UN, scrappy, chaotic, subject to
improvisations by heavily armed adversaries, in which ideologies weren't
"permitted to clash" but collided hard in unexpected ways that threatened regional or world peace. He was acutely aware of both realities. If
he was so admired as time went on, it was in part because he could bring
the two realities closer together.

There was an odd moment in August 1954 when the two realities
were more than usually side by side and out of touch. He had the opportunity on August 20th to "preach to the choir," thanks to an invitation from the World Council of Churches to address its meeting
near Chicago. As we noticed briefly in chapter 2, the council was an
outgrowth of the ecumenical work of archbishop Nathan Söderblom of
Uppsala, the recipient of the Nobel Peace Prize who influenced Hammarskjöld's youth. Hammarskjöld could not have been more at home
with its membership. He was among serious, open-minded Christians;
he had the opportunity to explore aloud the role not only of Christian
churches but of all mainstream religions in the effort to reach toward a
world without fear; and he could use religious language without being
misunderstood or offending.

At virtually the same moment—two days earlier, on August 18th—
the United States delegation at the UN had fired an angry salvo in a
war of words with the People's Republic of China (PRC) that remotely

threatened to become a shooting war. The potential casus belli was China's capture and detention of the eleven-man crew of a B-29 shot down over Chinese territory immediately adjacent to North Korea, where they had been dropping propaganda leaflets; they had been serving in the United Nations Command. Four other American pilots were also being held, and all were at risk of being tried for espionage rather than treated as prisoners of war. From the beginning the United States had regarded Communist China as an enemy. Since the Chinese civil war had brought Mao Zedong to power in 1949 and forced his adversary, Chiang Kai-shek, to retreat from the mainland to Taiwan, where he established the Republic of China (ROC), Joseph McCarthy and like-minded US politicians had blamed hidden Communists in the US State Department for what they called "the loss of China." It was a bitter issue much in public view; it had cost reputations and careers. US troops fought Chinese troops in brutal episodes of the Korean War, and the United States counted the ROC as an ally under its protection. Due in part to US influence, the ROC occupied not only a UN seat but also a permanent seat in the Security Council, while mainland China was excluded until 1971. At that time, after a vote in the General Assembly, mainland China replaced Taiwan.

On August 18th, Henry Cabot Lodge Jr., head of the US delegation, issued a public statement conveying the American view of the imprisonment and investigation. "The fifteen American fliers held illegally by Red China as 'political prisoners' should be a matter of grave concern to all civilized people. . . . The Chinese Communists should understand that just as they cannot shoot their way into the United Nations, they cannot blackmail their way by holding innocent prisoners as hostages in a game of political warfare. This is one more indication that Red China remains totally unfit for a seat in the United Nations, whose Charter is devoted to peace and common justice."[60] Clearly the United States perceived the threatened trial of its military personnel as a tactic in a rough game, with UN membership as the stake.

Hammarskjöld would have been aware of the US broadside, but the UN was not yet "seized of the issue." He remained on course, joining the church gathering on August 20th to express the ideals of the UN in words that retain relevance and energy. At one point he adopted an almost chant-like insistence, as if there is no substitute for certain words and the ideas they carry; they simply have to sink in.

> The United Nations stands outside—necessarily outside—all confessions, but it is, nevertheless, an instrument of faith. As such it is inspired by what unites and not by what divides the great religions of the world . . . . It may be said of the United Nations that what is required from the Organization—and from the governments and peoples therein represented—is a renewed faith, a faith renewed every day, expressed in a never abandoned, everyday newly initiated, responsible action for peace. . . . There is . . . in the international field, a need for practical action . . . . But . . . there is also a need for inspiration . . . .[61]

In front of this particular audience, he explored on the basis of a Gospel passage an attitude that deeply interested him: insofar as possible, to combine inner calm and faith with the very greatest effort to advance the work at hand, even when there is no evidence that events are falling out well. We have heard him express this once before in terms adopted from Hindu scripture. *Markings* was not distant; even the idea of surrender finds its place in what he now said.

> In the Sermon on the Mount it is said that we should take no thought of the morrow—"for the morrow shall take thought for the things of itself. Sufficient unto the day is the evil thereof." Can anything seem farther from the practical planning, the long-term considerations typical of political life? And yet—is this not the very expression of the kind of patience we must all learn to show in our work for peace and justice? Mustn't we learn to believe that when we give to this work, daily, what it is in our power to give, and when, daily, we meet the demands facing us to all the extent of our ability, this will ultimately lead to a world of greater justice and good will, even if nothing would seem to give us hope of success or even of progress in the right direction.
>
> Certainly, the words about the evil of the day and the things of the morrow do not mean that our actions should not be guided by a thoughtful and responsible consideration of future consequences of what we do. But they do mean that our work for peace should be pursued with the patience of one who has no anxiety about results, acting in the calm self-surrender of faith.[62]

At times I imagine Hammarskjöld as a trapeze artist walking a cable at great height with a long pole in hand to maintain balance. At one end of the pole his dedication, idealism, and discipline. At the other the rough reality of what we have heard him call a "still anarchic world community." He reported something like this, although in other terms, in a letter of October 1954 to his old colleague and friend, Sverker Åström:

> There is no end to what I would like to tell you. The experience continues to be extraordinary, but does not exactly tend to increase my appreciation for the motives animating people in politics: vanity, personal interest and "if-you-help-me-I-will-help-you" ideas, with a sad unwillingness to look beyond the next few months. The result is curious. I guess it could turn you rather cynical, but the psychological effect on me and my highly appreciated closest friends in the Secretariat seems to be exactly the opposite.[63]

10

Un Chinois aux Yeux Bleus

During a New York season of their theater company, the famed actor Jean-Louis Barrault and his wife, Madeleine Renaud, were invited by Hammarskjöld's French chief of protocol to bring their troupe to UN headquarters to perform *Le Misanthrope*. It was March 1957, well after the events we're about to explore. After lunch *à quatre* with the secretary-general on the day of the performance, the chief of protocol turned to Barrault. What did he think of his host? "The answer came in a flash: 'Un Chinois aux yeux bleus.'"[1] A Chinese with blue eyes.

On November 24th, China announced that the eleven airmen from the downed B-29, plus two other Americans—CIA agents captured separately—had been sentenced to prison terms. The fate of the other four American pilots was unclear. The United States immediately protested, and the majority leader of the Senate raised the threat of a naval blockade of China unless the airmen were freed. Taking a less bellicose line, President Eisenhower promised unceasing efforts to have the men released and called on the United Nations to take a hand in freeing these soldiers who had been serving in the United Nations Command in Korea. In those very days the United States also completed and signed a mutual defense treaty with Chiang Kai-shek's ROC, thereby signaling its disregard for Maoist China's contention that Taiwan was part of mainland China. Relations between the United States and the People's Republic of China were dismal in the aftermath of the Korean War: at the Geneva Conference, summer 1954, John Foster Dulles, US secretary of state, had refused to shake hands with Zhou Enlai, premier of the PRC. The handshake didn't matter so much, it was just angry theater made for media. But relations between the vast countries represented by the two men did matter.

On December 4th, a letter from Lodge to Hammarskjöld asked the UN to act. With Hammarskjöld's participation, a meeting of US diplomats with representatives of the fifteen other nations that had participated in the United Nations Command immediately convened to develop a response. Within a few days it became clear that Hammarskjöld would be the right choice to negotiate with Chinese officials if a negotiation could be arranged. Under Article 98 of the UN Charter, which broadly entitles the secretary-general to "perform such . . . functions as are entrusted to him" by major units of the UN, Hammarskjöld could play many roles.

After an all-night discussion with Sture Petrén, who happened to be his houseguest, Hammarskjöld made up his mind to accept the assignment, were the General Assembly to authorize it. That white night discussion became, for Hammarskjöld, an integral part of the legend of this period when he would later recall it. "You were there from the beginning one late Monday night when I worked my way to the conviction that I had to go myself to Peking," he would in time write to Petrén.[2] Urquhart records that he organized a similar all-night discussion with lawyers deeply versed in international law; Hammarskjöld was famously able to go with little sleep during urgent events, and sometimes asked as much of others. In the days just before passage of the General Assembly resolution on December 10th, he met with senior diplomats privately and saw to it that the resolution included language that gave him considerable latitude. Those key words authorized the secretary-general to undertake the mission "by the means most appropriate in his judgment."[3]

Immediately after passage of the resolution, which condemned China for its actions and called on the secretary-general to initiate "continuing and unremitting efforts" to free the captives, Hammarskjöld exchanged cables with the Chinese premier Zhou Enlai (1898–1976), whom he had never met. He deliberately refrained from forwarding the text of the resolution, not that Zhou would have difficulty receiving it from other sources. This was the first originality in Hammarskjöld's approach and a sign of its overall character to come. "Taking into consideration all facts and circumstances," he wrote to Zhou, "the Secretary-General must, in this case, take on himself a special responsibility. In the light of the concern I feel about this issue, I would appreciate an opportunity to take this matter up with you personally. For that reason I would ask you whether you could receive me in Peking . . . ," and he suggested a date before New Year or soon after. Urquhart writes that the text of this cable was released to the media, while a confidential cable to Zhou pointed to the "extraordinary nature of the initiative, this being the first time that the Secretary-General of the United Nations personally visits a capital for negotiations." Hammarskjöld had taken the precaution of communicating at once, directly, and personally with Zhou, rather than passing his messages through slower channels and giving time for a crust of interpretation to accumulate. It was unclear how Zhou would respond, but Hammarskjöld had seen no alternative to putting at some risk the prestige of the United Nations and of his office. There was an unspoken calculation: Mao Zedong's government wanted a seat as a UN member nation, and to ignore the secretary-general would likely delay admission.[4] But the weight of that consideration was unknown—perhaps meaningless in the severe current climate, perhaps meaningful.

On December 17th, Zhou responded, "In the interest of peace and relaxation of international tension, I am prepared to receive you in our capital, Peking, to discuss with you pertinent questions. We welcome you to China. Please decide for yourself the date of your visit and inform us of your decision." The dates were soon settled (January 5–10). Recently returned from Stockholm, where he had both given his Academy lecture and arranged a confidential channel with Zhou through the Chinese Embassy in Stockholm, Hammarskjöld left for Peking on December 30th by way of talks with government leaders in London, Paris, and New Delhi.

Hammarskjöld's negotiating strategy, known later as "the Peking formula," was daring and fragile: it would be effective only if it suited Zhou to disregard reality and embrace the intelligent illusion he was offered. The reality was that the General Assembly had dispatched Mr. Hammarskjöld. A further reality was that China owed nothing to a world body which vigorously excluded it. The intelligent illusion—probably offering the sole hope of negotiation—was a well-publicized assertion by Hammarskjöld that he was traveling to Peking not at the request of the General Assembly but in his individual capacity as secretary-general, in order to meet the independent responsibility for international peace assigned to his office by the Charter. Cordier and Foote, editors of Hammarskjöld's public papers, refer broadly both to "independent responsibilities" and to "the philosophy" of the Charter.[5] It was all very broad, very necessary, ingenious. And quite in Zhou Enlai's style. The meeting meant enough to China's interests for him to accept this civilized theater. It could only be helpful to assess the secretary-general and through him the United Nations, and to share Chinese perspectives with an influential world leader.

Hammarskjöld's contacts with the press in the weeks prior to his departure for Peking, and for months afterward, were an insistent exercise in discretion. He seemed to find the exercise engaging; it called for concise distinctions in defense of carefully drawn boundaries. "I beg you to excuse me," he said at a press conference in Stockholm, "if I find it necessary to keep down to bare facts and to avoid all comments of a general nature or anything that might in any way complicate the situation. . . . I hope you'll excuse me if I do not go into anything that *will* happen and will be satisfied if I tell you what *has* happened, and I will not speculate in any way on what *may* happen."[6] Where possible, he gave richer responses and projected a philosophy of negotiation that remains attractive. At the same press conference, someone asked whether he had "any real suggestion how to ease the tensions in the Far East." His initial response was noncommittal—"Anybody's guess"—but when the journalist persisted, he did better: "I don't think anybody has suggestions which he can carry with him. We're living in a fluid world, history is fluid, and to have preconceived ideas in any direction is just to sacrifice that flexibility which is a matter of course in diplomacy generally."[7]

Upon his return to New York, at a press conference on December 22nd he continued the same line. "Speculation about possibilities, outcomes, success, all that kind of thing . . . is not of any help in this story. . . . To succeed means to realize the possible."[8] But late in the session a journalist put a question probably intended to shake out of him an indiscreet comment. Hammarskjöld's handling of the incident remains interesting:

Question: By undertaking this trip to Peking under the instructions of the Assembly do you not feel that the head of the world Organization is now going to Peking to kneel somehow before Mr. Zhou Enlai for the release of the thirteen Americans?

The Secretary-General: I do not get your point.

Question: I mean do you not feel that there is a kind of humiliation for the United Nations, which is a belligerent Organization with the Chinese, to go to China to beg them or ask them to release the thirteen Americans?

The Secretary-General: I am not going anywhere to beg anybody for anything. I am going to bring up a situation which in my view calls for mutual consideration with the background to which I can refer in the General Assembly resolution.

Question: I gather, though, that Mr. Zhou Enlai replied that he wished to discuss pertinent questions.

The Secretary-General: So do I.

Question: Could you tell us whether you are willing to discuss other matters than the question of the prisoners which was specified by the resolution?

The Secretary-General: Well, it all depends upon what you mean by the word "discuss." I feel that you put into that word exchanges of views coming very close to negotiation. And if that is what you put into the word "discuss," I can only point out to you that the Secretary-General in this context acts under a specific authorization which is limited to one set of problems.[9]

Between Hammarskjöld's return to New York from Stockholm on December 21st and his departure for Peking on the 30th, practical preparations and consultations filled the agenda. Nonetheless, it was something of a pause in the forward motion of events; he had time to write a few letters, to open his journal to a fresh page. *Markings* has only three entries from December 10th forward, but each is telling. No doubt late in the evening of December 10th, when so much had already occurred, he found his way to the Book of Common Prayer and transcribed the concluding lines of Psalm 62, giving his own emphasis to words by which he must have felt especially addressed:

> God spake once, and twice I have also heard the same: that power belongeth unto God;
>   and that thou, Lord, art merciful: for thou rewardest every man according to his work.

Why did he focus on the words "God spake once"? As he would say, "Anybody's guess"—but it may reflect how vividly he experienced the General Assembly's charge to him, as if at the core of that body's response to an undeniable injustice with a real human cost he heard the echo of something more. The lines as a whole reflect his faith that, though power belongs to God, there may be mercy for those who give their best. The inscrutable balance between providence and hard work returned to his mind from time to time while this long diplomatic initiative advanced; his correspondence touches on the theme. Under the watchful eye of a global public that perceived the uniqueness and daring of the operation, Hammarskjöld returned privately to the faith and texts by which he guided. Two weeks later on Christmas day, much closer to departure, he recorded an injunction in his own words that captures something of the essence of those lines from Psalm 62:

To have faith—not to hesitate![10]

We have not seen passages from Psalms earlier in *Markings*. Hereafter they are frequent; he seems to return more regularly to Psalms than to any other part of the Bible. Their poetic vision and the elegance of the English translation he used must account for some of their appeal. As in his own prayers, they address God as Thou: episodes in an intense conversation, they teach the daring attitudes one can take with God in conversation. They have stunningly beautiful, tranquil passages about the human condition. But beyond all this, and perhaps most crucially, they are dramas of encounter that know every joy and sorrow, every liberation and entrapment, every celebration and suffering. Readers of Psalms find in them their own wishes, hopes, and fears raised and clarified, shown in their universality as the common, astonishing lot of all human beings. This book became Hammarskjöld's companion as he reached the center of his career and his opportunity for unusual service. He seems to have commented only once from a reader's perspective on the Psalms, in a letter of August 1955 where he described them as exemplifying "the extreme spirituality which found its first mature expression in, for example, the Psalms (If I take the wings of the morning, etc.)."[11]

Hammarskjöld's correspondence in the last few days of the year looks forward to Peking, backward to Stockholm and the Academy. To Sten Selander, now a brother in the Academy, he recorded the larger meaning for him of membership and reminisced about a gathering of that august company at Bourse House, its venerable meeting place in Stockholm, where the great minds looked into a small matter.

Brother,

A week after the Academy I am sitting here on the East River with my hands full of documents and itineraries of an impossible mission—around the world in 14 days, four of which in Peking to be defense counsel for 11 American officers! . . . My father would be skeptical.

From time to time, however, I think back to the Academy evening with greater and greater gratitude. When did I last feel so much "at home" as there, and in your circle? Politically denationalized, geographically almost always in airplanes, with missions in which a Chinese boy would have as much weight as those closest to me, I will have to look for an ever firmer and safer foothold in a tradition of mind reflected in the whisky glasses at Börshuset during the meditation concerning "why there are lice," but most of all perceptible in the warmth, openness, and interests that created the atmosphere around the long table.[12]

Two days later, writing to his friends Leif and Greta Belfrage, he offered a compact assessment of his situation on the eve of departure:

> Things have been shaping up fairly well, but in spite of all due preparation, the mission to Peking remains one of the most extraordinary experiments in modern diplomacy. Again I can only say that firmly anchored in a "must" as I am, I cannot ask of myself anything more than to do my very best—"success," whatever that means, will then have to follow or not follow.[13]

In a letter to his brother Bo on the day of departure, December 30th, he covered much ground, including afterthoughts about the unforgotten Mr. Tingsten. To understand the concluding irony in this letter, we need a lesson in Swedish culture: Grönköping is a fictional town created by the Swedish humorist Albert Engström (d. 1940), who used it as a mirror of Swedish life.[14] Everything in Grönköping is *very serious* and the politicians are pompous folk who speak and write in an old-fashioned bureaucratic style. Carrying on Engström's heritage, a weekly satirical magazine, *Grönköpings Veckoblad*, remains a fixture in Sweden. Hammarskjöld wrote:

> Everything here is in good shape for this strangest of journeys—around the world in two weeks including four days in Peking. Now all I can do is jump. If Tingsten and others at home could see that *a negotiation like this is politics*—in quite another sense than the petty bickering between Ohlin and Erlander [Bertil Ohlin was the opposition leader, Tage Erlander the long-serving prime minster]. Talking about Tingsten, the article amused me since, in spite of attacks and insinuations, it showed a first dawn of understanding . . . and . . . a first retreat where both Papa and I are concerned. But otherwise nothing could be more indifferent to me than his little private drama—a Jupiter in an academic Grönköping Olympus.[15]

The two protagonists, Hammarskjöld and Zhou, would have done their homework about one another. Our briefing book today is richer than the one to which Hammarskjöld would have had access, largely thanks to Gao Wenqian's superb political biography, *Zhou Enlai: The Last Perfect Revolutionary*, published in 2007. As well, the story is now fully told to

Zhou's death in 1976, while at New Year 1955 the PRC had existed for scarcely five years. The simplest finding is that the two men were surprisingly alike. Each was a mandarin of his culture. Prompted by ideals and a love of humanity that counted for more than mandarin fastidiousness, each had dived into the world of action. Henry Kissinger's description of Zhou many years after the Hammarskjöld-Zhou encounter could be of Hammarskjöld: "equally at home in philosophy, reminiscence, historical analysis, tactical probes, humorous repartee . . . [he] could display an extraordinary personal graciousness. . . . One of the two or three most impressive men I have ever met."[16] As we'll see, to a trusted friend Hammarskjöld wrote much the same, though with a sharper edge, in the weeks after the Peking negotiation.

Zhou was the orphaned son of a family that for generations had produced scholar-officials. Thanks to his easily recognized potential, he received an excellent education, including some years at a Chinese preparatory school modeled on Philips Andover Academy in Massachusetts. In years to come, he would rely on Confucian values, loyalty to the revolution, and precision of mind to see him through the turmoil of the long civil war and the deadly in-fighting around Mao that never ceased. As a young man he traveled widely to further his education—to Japan, Britain, France, and Germany—and acquired Western languages along the way. He was a natural statesman, not a natural revolutionary, but he became a revolutionary. He joined the Chinese Communist Party in 1922 while in Europe with other Chinese students, both men and women; it struck him as offering the best chance of improving the lot of the Chinese people. Immediately after his return to China in 1924, he immersed himself in political and military affairs. Zhou's schooling for his later role as the premier and senior diplomat of the PRC was intensive, many sided, and drastic. From his first maturity, working with passionate, driven colleagues, he was nearly always faced with life-or-death questions, with aggressions and retreats, with controlling or losing control of immense political and military forces, and this to the very end.

Zhou met Mao Zedong (1893–1976) for the first time in 1926, at the time when the Chinese Communists and Chiang Kai-shek violently parted ways. Mao was a wholly different man, of peasant stock, a brilliant and intuitive military leader, not a statesman, a revolutionary through and through. He was anti-Confucian; his lifelong instinct was to burn up the old, be it text or temple or social order.[17] And yet the two men forged a political partnership that would endure, with mishaps and tension, for a half-century. At an early stage in their relation, Zhou was in a position to protect Mao, who was regarded by the central Communist military command as unreliable and out of step with the agreed strategy. Zhou recognized Mao's indispensable excellence in military affairs and saw to it that he was brought in from the margin to the center. At that time and on one other occasion, Zhou had the upper hand—facts never forgotten or forgiven by Mao, according to Gao Wenqian. However, in later years Zhou subordinated himself to Mao and worked as invisibly as possible to preserve order and shelter good people from Mao's abrupt and deadly wrath. Never fully trusting him, Mao was jealous in later years of Zhou's domestic standing as the widely admired premier and of his international renown as a sophisticated, interesting diplomat, but he couldn't do without him. On his side, Zhou recognized the murderous folly of certain of Mao's national policies and personal vendettas against able colleagues, but he saved his own skin by helping to implement or failing to oppose them. Still, there was more to it than self-preservation. Gao Wenqian cites a maxim from ancient Chinese philosophy that speaks to another motivation: "Even when the emperor is errant, the minister must be loyal."[18] With Gao Wenqian's guidance, we cannot but perceive Zhou as a tragic figure, a well-meaning man with a vision of peaceful national development serving a gifted but violent master. To survive as premier and avoid the purges that took down so many of his old comrades-at-arms, he had to compromise and abase himself time and time again. In his last years, suffering from bladder cancer and denied timely treatment by Mao, who controlled even those strings, he declined slowly and painfully, filled with remorse toward colleagues still living whom he had betrayed. He was able to apologize to some of them. At his death, the entire nation dared to mourn publicly, despite instructions to the contrary. Mao chose not to attend his funeral.

Hammarskjöld and Zhou met at a time when two events that have become part of worldwide collective memory had not yet unfolded—the Great Leap Forward launched by Mao in 1958, which distorted the rural economy and led to millions of deaths, and the Cultural Revolution initiated in 1966 by Mao and the circle around his wife Jiang Qing, which subjected the country to a government-sponsored civil war of young against old. Among Zhou's last acts was to reinforce the position of Deng Xiaoping, who after Mao's death led the country away from political turmoil toward stability and economic development. Hammarskjöld's briefing book and his conversations with members of the Republic of China's UN delegation would nonetheless have told him quite enough to prepare for his meeting with one of the principal founders of the new Chinese state.

At some point on the day of departure, December 30th, he took time to record in his journal, from Psalms, an expression of faith that could reach around the world:

> If I take the wings of the morning and remain in the uttermost parts of the sea; even there also shall thy hand lead me.[19]

A brain of steel

Accompanied by a small team, Hammarskjöld reached Peking on January 5th. He had invited only his personal assistant Per Lind, Ahmed Bokhári of the UN Public Information office, his secretary and security guard, a British expert on international law, and a Swedish translator skilled in Chinese. Neither Hammarskjöld nor the Chinese had made any effort to help the UN press corps find their way to Peking; it was to be a quiet, private negotiation, although photographers and newsreel people were on hand at designated times. Daily afternoon meetings left time in the morning for Hammarskjöld to visit the sights. He did so with immense enjoyment.

All authoritative accounts of the negotiation published in the West stem primarily from an aide-mémoire written after the fact by Hammarskjöld, as was his custom, in which he detailed virtually every point of importance.[20] The negotiation had the clarity of a card game played for high stakes by two men of outstanding intelligence and observational powers. Their hands were radically different: China had hostages and the assertive pride of a new nation with a revolutionary program, Hammarskjöld had much of the world's good wishes behind him and could influence world opinion. Not least, later if not sooner, he could help the PRC toward UN membership.

Hammarskjöld initially restated that he had come to China under his obligation as secretary-general to work toward the relaxation of international tensions rather than under instructions from the General Assembly. This was the "Peking formula," which Zhou found adequate. They agreed to examine the facts and circumstances of the capture and treatment as spies of the eleven crew members aboard the downed B-29, and did so at length. They found scarcely any common ground. For example, the Chinese court had interpreted certain communications equipment on board the plane as specific to spy missions, while Hammarskjöld had verified that the equipment was standard on many aircraft, including one he had flown to reach China. Zhou asserted that the crew of the B-29 had included a "trained agent"—to which Hammarskjöld replied that the crew, flying over unfamiliar terrain, had recruited an airman with previous experience of it. Hammarskjöld laid out the case in international law for treatment of the air crew as prisoners of war; Zhou stood by the findings of the Chinese court which had sentenced them as spies. The cases of the four other pilots did not come under close examination, as Zhou stated that the men were soon likely to be deported, and the two captured CIA agents were not on the agenda.

But it wasn't a dialogue of the deaf. Hammarskjöld made clear that even if they couldn't agree on facts and their interpretation, and without putting in question the Chinese court's right to convict, there remained an option: in the interest of relaxing international tensions, to "trust that [China] will reach its *final* conclusion in a spirit of justice and fairness—before [its] own conscience."[21] At that level, Zhou could respond. The conversation had already proved to have two levels: utter disagreement at the level of fact, tentative willingness at the level of conciliation and gesture. In the end, Zhou offered some assurance that a formula focused strictly on relaxing tensions might lead to early release, other conditions permitting.[22] It was not a guarantee and said nothing about timing, but his assurance was crucially important to Hammarskjöld. He might not have come to China in vain.

After their discussion of the airmen, Hammarskjöld agreed with Zhou to take up other matters of concern to the Chinese, although he made clear that for the most part his role could be only to listen and comment in broad terms: he couldn't answer for the views of UN member nations. He expressed his own conviction that the mainland Chinese government, representing one quarter of the world's population, should be a member nation, but he also stated the obvious: it would take time (as indeed it did—until 1971, a year Zhou lived to see). On the topic of the United States' guarantee of Taiwan's security, Zhou pointed out with what must have been grave wit that his government had not reciprocally guaranteed the security of Hawaii. And on they went through the many issues dividing the new China from the West. They looked at the fear each had of the other, which Hammarskjöld described to Zhou as a "tragedy of errors" much like the plot of the Chinese opera they had seen the night before, in which—as he put it in the aide-mémoire—"two men were fighting each other in the dark, each of them believing that he had been threatened by the other man."[23] They concluded their meeting with a brief, bland statement to the press that did nothing to satisfy public curiosity or offer substantive hope; there was no mention of the airmen. However, its closing sentence held vague promise: "We feel that these talks have been useful and we hope to be able to continue the contact established in these meetings."[24]

Among photographs taken of Hammarskjöld and Zhou together, and of Hammarskjöld visiting the sights, one is haunting (fig. 12). It is the 10th of January, the eve of departure. The two statesmen have been speaking daily with one another since Hammarskjöld's arrival on the 5th. Now they stand side by side—with Bill Ranallo, Hammarskjöld's security man, just behind and between them. Turned slightly toward one another, they mirror each other, smiling in much the same way, joining their hands in much the same traditionally Chinese manner. Here is our "Chinois aux yeux bleus." Despite their inability, not unexpected, to agree about facts on the ground, they had almost inaudibly agreed that something could be done to ease the situation. In the course of their long conversation, good chemistry had drawn them together and given Hammarskjöld a wealth of impressions of an ancient political culture for which he had sympathy and admiration. He was, in practice, already proficient in its ways—it was more a matter of temperament than of tactics—but in Zhou he had encountered a skilled native practitioner. In later years he would read in that culture, take general guidance from it, and quote it publicly from time to time; it spoke to him, and on occasion for him, with an ancient voice. In 1957 he would write to Ezra Pound, translator of several classic texts of Chinese political philosophy: "It may amuse you to hear that your Confucius, especially *The Unwobbling Pivot*, is one of the books to which I have most often returned during the past years when most policy-making has been of a kind somewhat different . . . from the one our Chinese friends recommended."[25] By "our Chinese friends" he meant Confucius and his circle.

Hammarskjöld left China more jubilant than he could possibly show to press or public. The outcome still hung by a thread; it depended on unknowable factors within the Chinese government and on the public conduct of American political leaders, which was unpredictable. Although he and Zhou would never meet again, they remained in periodic communication over the next eight months, during which the hopes raised by their meeting slowly worked their way through.

The laconic joint communiqué given to the news media before his departure from Peking, and an equally flat statement at the Hong Kong airport, caused Hammarskjöld some grief as he made his way back to New York. The press and political responses were incredulous: hadn't anything positive occurred? Upon arrival on January 13th, he felt constrained to say something more, though he had little latitude. "My visit to Peking," he said at the airport, "was a first stage in my efforts to achieve the release of the eleven airmen and other United Nations Command personnel still detained. I feel that my talks with Mr. Zhou Enlai were definitely useful for this purpose. We hope to be able to continue our contact. The door that has been opened can be kept open, given restraint on all sides."[26] These themes of the open door and the need for restraint dominated his press conference the next day, slightly though not harmfully upstaged by an earlier public statement from US Ambassador Lodge, with whom he had already spoken. On the basis of Hammarskjöld's discussion with him, Lodge had expressed confidence that the airmen would be released.

At the press conference, in response to a round of applause, he improvised one of the sweetest remarks he ever made: "It was kind of you to applaud. There is no reason for such applause. If I have done what I hope I have done, that is part of what I should do."[27] Intriguingly circular, touchingly awkward, a string of monosyllables, this was a small sign of the beginning of his large effort to assimilate what had occurred. Incomplete as they were, the events and contacts had implications for the UN and his office. "I do have the unique advantage," he said to the reporters, "of having listened to and having seen a little bit from the inside the working of the mind of the other party. . . . This comes into the picture as something rather important which I have to digest, which I have to put into my picture of the world."[28] And as we shall see, Peking also had implications for him personally as a man striving to understand what makes it possible for things to fall into place in a distinctly right way. Unlike Ambassador Lodge, he was careful to offer no certainties:

> I have not myself said that I was optimistic. I used another expression. I
> said that the door was open and could remain open with due restraint.

I have said that I hoped to be able to continue contacts. That is a temperature somewhat lower than that reflected in the word "optimism." . . . It is obvious that [it] is a rather tender plant when you open talks of this type and under a blast of strong emotional reactions which, so to say, wreck the basis laid in one respect or another—that is to say, introduce an element of propaganda on either side—the other one would of course find it rather difficult to continue.[29]

The tender plant in Hammarskjöld's care was almost immediately exposed to withering blasts. Careful diplomacy transacted between two poised men had now entered a much larger, less stable context. Although the American authorities had set the adventure in motion, they proved unwilling to place full trust in Hammarskjöld's diplomatic effort and increased the tension between the United States and China. Some of their actions were necessary; many of their words and attitudes were almost certainly unnecessary. On January 17th—Hammarskjöld might by then have just recovered from jet lag—the Republican Senate Majority Leader, William Knowland, let it be known that he considered Hammarskjöld's efforts "a failure by any standard or yardstick," and a day later Secretary of State Dulles told reporters that the United States was standing aside while the UN tried to work the problem through, but he said, "I don't think that can go on forever."[30] Forever had so far lasted two weeks. Dulles and Lodge disregarded Hammarskjöld's advice as to how best to respond to a humanitarian gesture he had negotiated with Zhou: family visits to the imprisoned airmen. Hammarskjöld felt intuitively that the prisoners might well be released to accompany their family members home—an intuition confirmed months later, after the fact, by a Polish diplomat with inside knowledge of Chinese intentions.[31] The Americans loudly rejected the Chinese offer of family visits, described it as propagandistic trifling with the feelings of the families, and objected to Hammarskjöld's management of the fall-out from their decision. He had sent a "personal" note to Zhou about the whole matter; well, said Lodge, there isn't any "personal" here.

There was more and worse, if the goal was to get the airmen home. Hammarskjöld and the UN had been asked to intervene on behalf of the airmen because relations among Mao's China, Chiang Kai-shek's China, and the United States could hardly have been more choked. In summer 1953, Taiwan had deployed substantial armed forces to a pair of islands in the Taiwan Strait, Quemoy and Matsu, and the PRC had begun bombarding them from the mainland. On December 2nd, as noticed earlier, the United States and Taiwan entered into a mutual defense pact which didn't at the time refer to the Strait, but in response to intensified skirmishes between the combatants, the United States resolved in late January to protect islands under Taiwanese control if threatened by invasion. It stationed US Air Force bombers on Taiwan and put the redoubtable Seventh Fleet on full alert. The crisis in the Taiwan Strait was also brought to the Security Council with the intention of calling for a cease-fire, and an effort was made to invite to the UN a diplomatic representative from mainland China. None of that worked out, and all parties to the crisis settled by mid-February for the angry, periodically violent status quo.

Was this a way to free airmen? It was obvious that their release—if they were to be released—would have to await a quieter moment, but Hammarskjöld and Zhou continued their private exchange of communications in the spirit established at Peking, and Hammarskjöld did what he could to keep the issue of the airmen out of the media. By the end of January he also found time to begin writing thoughtfully to a few friends about Peking and its rocky aftermath; he seems to have used those letters, like his journal, to clarify the meaning of his experiences. To Uno Willers, director of the Swedish National Library and a most helpful insider who offered, as needed, discreet venues for Hammarskjöld to meet the Chinese ambassador in Stockholm, he wrote very fully. The letter calls for a quick lesson in Swedish geography, furnished at the end.

> You are right in saying that I have had an extraordinary opportunity of experiencing history in the making and there is obviously more forthcoming. The mission to Peking is not only unique in diplomatic history but also unique as a human experience. It is a miracle that everything went well, because the risks we were taking were extraordinary; but it did—in every detail. The contacts with Zhou Enlai and with this very foreign world made an enormous impression on me, and I would wish that other policy-makers had got it. What is so appalling is the basic lack of realism as to assumptions on which very much of Western policy is built.
>
> And now I am thinking not only of the situation in China, but of China's role in Asia and of the position of the present regime in Peking. It is a little bit humiliating when I have to say that Zhou Enlai to me appears as the most superior brain I have so far met in the field of foreign politics. Of course, that does in no way mean that I have found a wider area of agreement than I anticipated, but it does mean that policymak-

ing without taking into account his personal qualities is likely to lead to disaster. As I said to one of the Americans: Zhou is so much more dangerous than you imagine because he is so much better a man than you ever admitted.

Big international history in the making, the registration of why things succeed and the enormity of the mistakes made, give me a curious perspective on our domestic problems and on the noise concerning the lack of wisdom of such and such a note or statement. Of course you can drown if you maneuver, no matter how skillfully, on Mälaren, but it is rather amusing when such maneuvering is discussed as if it were a question of sailing on the Pacific . . . .[32]

Lying west and north of Stockholm, Lake Mälaren is a vast body of water with a complex shoreline giving the impression of many lakes linked together; one could spend weeks exploring its shoreline towns, castles, and wilderness. Hammarskjöld takes an easy swipe here at Swedish politics, as in an earlier letter where he was letting off steam about Tingsten. I suspect that "one of the Americans" was Lodge, with whom it could matter that he reappraise Zhou Enlai. Nautical metaphors seem to have been on Hammarskjöld's mind in this period. A few weeks later he wrote to a friend, "It's very 'rough sailing' here—but it won't do you any harm, and even if you get wet, the boat isn't leaking—so everything's all right."[33] "Rough sailing" is in English, the rest in Swedish. He was in top form.

In a letter nearly two weeks later to Bo Beskow, the painter with whom he could freely share poetic visual impressions, he wrote more intimately and added vivid details to his portrait of Zhou:

China was a fantastic experience, and since then I am somehow more mature than before. It was splendid and harrowing, infinitely remote and yet infinitely real. This applies to both the country (landscape), the atmosphere in Peking (that magnificent camp of the nomad princes who came down from the desert across the narrow mountain range—a camp with endlessly repeated rhythms of weighted tent-roofs), and to Zhou Enlai himself (with a brain of steel, blood on his hands, stern self-discipline, and a very warm smile).

This goes also for the unreal voyage "around the Earth in 7 days." Not forgetting the human and political problems when suddenly I was alone holding the knife. Such a situation relieves you of the last traces of an "I" which later does its utmost to push forward again!

> My working team was first class. Bill was great and he saved the morale both of my professors and of the others when the wind blew so sharply that only the most open, simple human sense of humor and warmth could prevent frostbite.[34]

The professors would have been Bokhári, a Pakistani who went wryly on record about the unacceptably cold Peking winter, and the Oxford professor of international law who joined the party in London. And Bill was Bill, the American security guard who, with his family, had become an intimate of Hammarskjöld's. Bill once wrote a birthday greeting to his boss to express his wish to help him "always in allways."[35]

There is a third letter from this time, to his brother Bo, in which Hammarskjöld steps back from the drama to identify the crucial gain already achieved, no matter what might later come to pass:

> The four weeks after my return from Peking have been a very hectic time. A lot of things were lagging behind—and the China issues became bigger and bigger and more charged. You are right in what you write about the influence of the latest events on the Peking results—in terms of externals. What *really* was won, a normalization of the connections with this quarter of humanity, remains—happily enough, no matter how little popular this is in certain circles. And within reasonable time I probably will get the pilots out, too, but they will have to take it a bit easier here in the USA.
>
> The experience . . . has . . . forced me to a considerable amount of re-thinking. . . . The whole episode has given both the organization and my position noticeably greater weight. The closing of the books is thus favorable.[36]

Give your all to this dream

For a moment we too might close the diplomatic books to return to a personal question that had occurred to Hammarskjöld before leaving for Peking. It can seem a hopelessly abstract, unanswerable question, better left unasked: who is the doer? But it wasn't abstract for him. For him and others a little like him, it is a nagging koan, sometimes the grain of sand in the nicely cooked spinach, sometimes a source of wonder. It touches on real things: proficiency in one's chosen calling, comfort with oneself. People who work this question through feel the pull of two elemental needs. They need to discover and live an inner attitude that permits the full positive expression of their identity and their wish to serve. And they need to discover and live an inner attitude that allows high achievement to wash through them without feeding self-importance and clogging their ability to respond freely. It's a large program; Hammarskjöld had been engaged with it for years and would remain so. It doesn't seem to be something that can be settled once for all. It needn't be defined or lived as a religious question; it has enough breadth to accommodate other perspectives, but Hammarskjöld experienced it in that way.

In his correspondence we have come upon traces, like the faint, curling patterns in a nuclear cloud chamber, of this private concern. To Beskow we have heard him say, "Suddenly I was alone holding the knife. Such a situation relieves you of the last traces of an 'I' which later does its utmost to push forward again!" To Uno Willers he wrote, "It is a miracle that everything went well, because the risks we were taking were extraordinary; but it did—in every detail." Unmistakably we are reading that he had passed through a time of heightened challenge and heightened awareness in which his ordinary experience of "I" yielded to another identity—himself through and through, yet keen, poised, and resourceful to a most unusual extent, as if helped. He knew something of this change in awareness and ability from the deeper experiences he occasionally recorded in his journal, but negotiating for the freedom of the airmen was far from the safety of solitude. His two worlds had coincided. And as he wrote, he felt more mature now. Reclaiming its rights, the ordinary sense of "I" crowded back, but his experience could not help but leave new indications on his compass.

In *Markings* itself, early entries for the year are undated but participate in the exploration evident in these letters.

> On a really clean table cloth, the smallest speck of dirt annoys the eye.
> At high altitudes, a moment's self-indulgence may mean death.[37]

His analogies are to banquet and mountain, but they point toward Peking and lessons learned there. After Peking he returned to his fundamental truths. "Before Thee in humility, with Thee in faith, in Thee in stillness," he wrote at this time in his journal, each element both a truth of his inner world and a gesture, an act of alignment.[38] One still feels the almost tangible veil of privacy drawn around these quiet affirmations.

Hammarskjöld made no public mention of the airmen's fate until an April 5th press conference, just after the United States had acceded to a request made by Zhou Enlai, through Hammarskjöld among others, for the return of seventy-six Chinese students who had been awaiting exit visas. That had warmed the atmosphere a little, though Hammarskjöld resisted a journalist's effort to link it with the airmen's possible release. He responded in a vaguely promising way to pointed questions: "Contacts which mean something in substance are being continued. I would not continue those contacts if I did not feel that they served a useful purpose."[39] Reserved, diplomatic. A few days later (April 11th), back in what he once called the "still anarchic world community," Taiwan's secret service, using technology provided by the CIA, attempted to assassinate Zhou Enlai. An agent planted a time bomb on a flight Zhou was expected to take from Hong Kong to the Bandung Conference in Indonesia, to which delegates from twenty-nine Asian and African countries were then converging. The conference laid groundwork for the so-called Non-Aligned Movement of nations seeking to inject a coherent third voice into the endless standoff between the Western democracies and the Soviet bloc. It appears that Zhou knew of the plot and made other travel arrangements; there was also talk of an emergency appendectomy, which delayed his departure. The airplane crashed with only three survivors. Mao's China at once blamed Chiang Kai-shek's China and the United States for the incident, though an investigation took some time to assemble the facts. Asked somewhat later in a press conference about the incident, Hammarskjöld refused to speculate. Surprisingly, the assassination attempt did not derail the effort to free the airmen.

In what might have been summer 1955, Hammarskjöld set down a thought in his journal:

> You are dedicated to this task—as the sacrifice in a still barbarian cult, because of the Divine intention behind it. It is a feeble creation of men's hands—but you must give your all to this dream, for that alone anchors it in reality.[40]

Though the entry isn't tied to a specific event, it may well represent a general reflection during an elaborate June gathering in San Francisco, celebrating the tenth anniversary of the founding of the United Nations. In content and mood—remarkably bitter—Hammarskjöld's words may reflect his attitude toward events such as the assassination attempt and the rough sailing of recent months. On June 27th, a striking portrait of Hammarskjöld appeared on the cover of *Time*.

You can intensify an intensification

The press corps on April 19th badly wanted news. Faithful to his policy of public restraint, Hammarskjöld could offer little more than a comparison between diplomacy and cooking. "When one prepares soup," he averred, "it is sometimes part of that preparation to take the soup off the fire. That may also be the case in this special kind of field. There are times when one furthers the purpose of negotiation by not sitting at the table all the time. . . . If there is an interval of silence, even such an interval may result in a wider perspective, greater calm, and lesser heat."[41] When he wasn't saying much, at least he was interesting. Later in April he conferred secretly with the Chinese ambassador in Stockholm when he was there for a meeting of the Swedish Academy. He found the exchange encouraging but in public still had little to say. At a New York press conference on May 5th, he offered a crumb: "The contacts are not only continued but, if anything, intensified." A reporter found this turn of phrase intriguing.

> Question: You just said "intensified." How have they been intensified?
>
> The Secretary-General: Will you leave a few family secrets to me?
>
> . . . .
>
> Question: Sir, I do not know what comes after "intensify." Would you explain what is the next word that can be used.
>
> The Secretary-General: You can intensify an intensification.[42]

That must have been fun. Of such episodes his reputation was built as one who could seem to say a great deal without revealing a thing. He loved the game, and so did the press. He drew lines of discretion wherever needed and managed to keep journalists entertained if not in the know until fuller disclosure suited his purpose.

The mood changed. US Ambassador Lodge went out of his way on the day after this press conference to praise Hammarskjöld's conduct of the Peking mandate; he grasped that events were turning in a positive direction. But Hammarskjöld had new reason for dismay when, on May 20th, he read in the *New York Times* that Sweden's ambassador to the Soviet Union had called on Zhou Enlai in Peking, possibly in the role of what the newspaper called a "volunteer mediator."[43] The article also noted that a senior Indian diplomat, V. K. Krishna Menon, was passing through Peking. The Swedish visit incensed Hammarskjöld at once; the

Indian visit incensed him later. The Swedish maneuver struck him as an unrequested, clumsy interference in a delicate process at a time when he had specifically asked that there be nothing of the kind. He fired off a letter to Leif Belfrage in the Swedish Foreign Office, and another to the trespassing Swedish ambassador, Rolf Sohlman. To Belfrage he wrote about "political innocence in a state of rare purity":

> The enclosed press clipping comes from the second page of today's issue of the *New York Times*. So *that* source of added confusion had to be added to the general picture, for no other reason than Sohlman's curiosity—or is there any other reason? The timing of the visit is perfect—at the same time as Krishna Menon and as my follow-up of the Stockholm démarche.
>
> Outside Stockholm, and Moscow not excluded, the least unfavorable comments will be that this is an example of political innocence in a state of rare purity. In less informed circles the waves of speculation may run high; I do not know if I shall try to explain as nobody would believe me, and it may be preferable that people think that Sohlman had a mission when he has made himself look like one of the rats running to Hameln after having listened to the flute player of Bandung.
>
> Although the Swedish interest in this matter may be said to be none of my business and although the interest I represent need not guide you, I feel that I should go on record in the Foreign Office with this reaction.[44]

Hammarskjöld included in his note a copy of the following letter to Ambassador Sohlman:

> What is done is done, what has happened has happened. Therefore it can seem pointless to say anything more about your visit to Peking—especially since the fact that Chinese radio was ordered to publicize your visit to Zhou Enlai is comment enough.
>
> Even so, I want to tell you that this matter gave me a couple of days of worry. . . . What's more, I was genuinely sad: this is obviously the importance a colleague and countryman—not to say a friend—attaches to a serious request from the one who has to pull the wagonload at the UN. If this experience were symptomatic of other people's reactions to a similar request, the possibilities of action of the secretary-general really would be slim.[45]

On May 29th, China released the four American fliers who from the beginning seemed to have the best chance. This time it was Krishna Menon's turn to step in front of Hammarskjöld. V. K. Krishna Menon

(1896–1974) was a special fellow. Born in south India, tall and slender with strong features not easily forgotten, he completed his education in London and was admitted to the English bar in 1934. A direct colleague of Nehru's in the struggle for Indian independence, he served as leader of the Indian delegation to the UN throughout Hammarskjöld's tenure while occupying other posts at home, notably minister of defence (1957–62). All of which doesn't capture the man. He holds, I believe to this day, the record for longest speech delivered before the Security Council, eight hours. He was trouble for Hammarskjöld because he was interfering and self-aggrandizing—but also trouble at times for his Indian colleagues. Nehru's formidable sister, Vijaya Lakshmi Pandit, who served as president of the General Assembly early in Hammarskjöld's tenure, has written that Krishna Menon was "a brilliant and versatile man [of] overpowering ambition, which he sometimes tried to hide under a cloak of pseudo-humility. He was like a Victorian woman, a person of moods and periods of depression. . . . He had the capacity of investing even the simplest matter with an aura of mystery. . . ."[46] This is not praise. Madame Pandit may have had a score to settle; Krishna Menon hadn't proved reliably helpful to her at the UN. Some Indian literature in English lionizes him as a "man of the century," but clearly he was a handful.[47] I dwell on this profile because Krishna Menon was the target of one of very few completely disparaging letters from Hammarskjöld I've encountered.

The immediate circumstance was that Krishna Menon claimed to the press, in advance of any word from Hammarskjöld, that the four airmen's release was an Indian success—therefore his own—rather than a link in the chain of negotiation between Hammarskjöld and Zhou. The editors of the *Public Papers* suggest that "Menon was overanxious to bolster his own and India's prestige with the West as a non-aligned go-between with Communist China. Had he simply asserted that India's influence had also been helpful he would have met agreement in most quarters."[48] Hammarskjöld had been meeting privately with Krishna Menon from time to time to keep things as sorted out as possible. In press conferences of June 2nd and 16th, he went easy. He expressed his agreement with Krishna Menon's recent call for restraint (a theme he himself had emphasized from the first), expressed thanks for his efforts and India's concern, and voiced no criticism. On the other hand, more than a year later in a long letter to his friend Alva Myrdal, then serving as Swedish ambassador to India, he spoke his mind: "Mr. Menon dislikes me heartily. He has several reasons for that. First of all, he has never gotten anywhere in his attempts to use me in his game (on some occasions I have even had cause to cross his plans). Further, I have in all innocence happened to stand in the way of his attempts to expand his position in Washington in connection with the Chinese prisoners of war affair."[49]

The dénouement of his efforts, and Zhou's, was not far off. Meanwhile there was other UN business to see to—not least the San Francisco conference, at which his June 20th welcome address included a memorable aphorism: "The United Nations should stand for that diversity which is the condition of freedom, as much as it should stand for that unity of common purpose which is the basis of peace."[50] With a minor edit or two, this should be engraved on a wall at UN headquarters. I have plans for quite a few walls.

Something altogether good

For his fiftieth birthday on July 29th, Hammarskjöld found his way after meetings in Geneva to the south Swedish coast where his friends Bo and Greta Beskow had purchased for him a small house near their own summer home—precursor to the larger farmhouse which is now a public museum and retreat for members of the Swedish Academy. Not nearby but scarcely out of reach, the Chinese embassy in Stockholm was aware of his week-long holiday and, according to Urquhart, had inquired as to what Mr. Hammarskjöld might like as a gift for his birthday. The political climate had warmed a little more: the United States agreed on July 25th to upgrade its bilateral meetings at Geneva with the People's Republic of China from the consular to the ambassadorial level. The symbolism was meaningful. And so Hammarskjöld, with no particular expectations, had a holiday week to look forward to. His brother Bo and his wife showed up a day or two before the actual birthday. "That day I will always remember as one of the lightest and warmest I have been allowed to experience," Dag wrote to Bo a few weeks later. "It was so good to feel how strongly we belong together— and what fun we can have (like 23 years ago!)."[51] On the very day of his birthday, Friday, July 29th, determined to avoid even well-meaning journalists, he and the Beskows with the ever-loyal Bill Ranallo betook themselves to the Baltic Sea. "I went cod fishing," Hammarskjöld later told the UN press corps, "and I did not catch a single cod, so even the cod kept out of the picture, which was quite appropriate and in line with my intentions."[52] Perhaps early that morning he had recorded in his journal a dry summons from Thomas à Kempis: "Why do you seek rest? You were only created to labor."[53]

Sunday was apparently a spectacular day. Sture Petrén was unable to get away. "We missed you," Hammarskjöld wrote to him later with zest and the instincts of a poet of the natural scene. "Sunday was sunny, irresponsible and in all a real vacation day. . . . And the wind blew mildly, smelling of grain from Vemmenhög."[54]

On Monday at his rural retreat, Hammarskjöld heard the news: China was releasing the eleven airmen. Zhou Enlai had sent a message intended to reach him before the public announcement, but he first heard from other sources. A second message from Zhou, relayed by the Swedish embassy in Peking, caught up with him the next day in Geneva, to which he had flown without delay when the news broke. Reporting Zhou's words, it read that "this release takes place in order to maintain friendship with Hammarskjöld and has no connection with the UN resolution. Zhou Enlai expresses the hope that Hammarskjöld will take note of this point. . . . The Chinese government hopes to continue the contact established with Hammarskjöld. . . . Zhou Enlai congratulates Hammarskjöld on his 50th birthday."[55] This was the birthday gift Hammarskjöld had had in mind—his ally, the National Library director Uno Willers, had said as much when asked by the Chinese ambassador in Stockholm. The *New York Times* ran a headline article on August 2nd which attributed the airmen's release to the improving climate between the United States and China, and neglected to mention Hammarskjöld: "Peiping Frees 11 American Fliers as U.S.-Red China Parley Starts; Dulles Credits Policy of Patience." Difficult not to recall how impatient Dulles had been immediately after Hammarskjöld's return from Peking. Urquhart writes that at this point it suited Hammarskjöld to keep the UN and himself out of the picture insofar as possible; he was pleased to see improved relations between China and the United States and thought best to leave space around that. But he received praise from many quarters. His reputation among world leaders, good and reasonable before, abruptly soared past good and reasonable. "He . . . finally got those people out," Urquhart commented in the course of the UN oral history project. "It was then that Dulles suddenly realized . . . that Hammarskjöld got results. I must say—greatly to everybody's credit—they then realized they were dealing with a major international figure of a very unusual kind. . . . That was his great breakthrough with the

United States. And the British, who had been somewhat critical of him, also realized he was someone to reckon with."[56]

Not every point in Zhou's message had delighted Hammarskjöld. In a note to Andrew Cordier he weighed how best to reply: "I must keep the ball in the air, and for that reason I must emphasize my wish for continued contacts. At the same time, I feel that I must rub in that Zhou Enlai cannot make a distinction between Mr. Hammarskjöld and the Secretary-General. Finally, it must all be dressed in such terms as to maintain the friendly atmosphere on which Zhou Enlai himself now puts such heavy stress. . . . I have this time had to indulge in some 'double-talk' as the letter has an appearance which is much more positive than its rather restrained substance when analyzed."[57] The "Peking formula," separating Hammarskjöld from the General Assembly resolution, could not be perpetuated. Hammarskjöld's circumspection was soon more than matched by Zhou's.

In the weeks following the airmen's release, there was a little joy to be had, and a little fun. At a press conference in New York, one of the journalists carried provocation to a high point by referring to other diplomats seeking credit for the good outcome as "competing kidnappers who are trying to take credit away from the United Nations." Hammarskjöld hit the roof. "I object very strongly to the language in various details, if you will excuse my saying so." The journalist backed off a little, Hammarskjöld too, and he finally expressed with considerable grace how he felt about things. "Many things have happened during my time here as Secretary-General for which I have great reason to be very grateful. However, with the present perspective, I would say that no event or anything which I have been permitted to do ranks higher on that list of causes for gratitude than my trip to Peking."[58] This we can leave as his public valediction on the entire episode, December 1954 through early August 1955, but in his privacy there was more.

To friends with whom he corresponded, he bore witness to his joy and relief, writing at times with the healthy self-satisfaction of a master diplomatic craftsman, at other times as a man of prayer who refers all good to the Lord. His letter to Sten Selander is by and large of the first kind, though listen for verbs in the passive voice implying the mystery of providence:

> I am sure you understand how happy I am for my released prisoners. It is so seldom you get to feel you have achieved something. At the same time the rather mad Peking trip now appears as something *altogether* good—actually as the thing I am most grateful for having been allowed to do. It has been

a little like being allowed to make poetry in action—all the way through it has depended on *my* belief in the possibility, *my* assessment of the outcome—and now the whole thing has been able to be rounded off just as I had dreamt. A lot may happen that is unpleasant (and much that is good) but what has happened is a completed chain of actions in balance.[59]

Writing to his revered early mentor in the Swedish government, Ernst Wigforss, he takes a similar view. With both Selander and Wigforss there was a certain vision of how actions can be shaped by thoughtful intention—that vision with Selander was "poetry in action," while with Wigforss, less poetically, it had to do with closeness of match between concept and result. "You understand what joy it gave me to get the prisoners out," he wrote to Wigforss. "The stakes were at times very high, always rooted in a perhaps naïve conviction about the way I was here blessed, as you once wrote, with the possibility of living out a personal idea and plan in political action. And whatever the comments will be in the end, I believe in the positive effects of what has happened."[60] Late in his life, and many battles later, Hammarskjöld would all but disavow the notion of any possibility of poetry in action. In a letter to which we'll return, he wrote, "It is a beautiful concept and there may be some little element of truth in it, but basically it is an illusion."[61]

In still another letter from these weeks, Hammarskjöld expressed the feelings of a man of prayer. He borrowed lines from a poem by Bertil Ekman: "Today," he wrote, remembering Ekman's lines, "we accomplished something, God and I. That is to say, it was God who built while I stood below with the paint pot, shouting."[62] It may seem as if these two personae— the master craftsman and the man of prayer—are at peace with one another, but it wasn't quite so. Their relations needed care and thought. In *Markings* Hammarskjöld recorded a sequence of entries, the first dated the very day when the airmen were released, which reflect inner turmoil as he negotiated now with himself and, as he put it in the first page of *Markings*, with God.

> "God spake. . . . "
>
> And, a few verses earlier: "As for the children of men, they are but vanity. The children of men are deceitful upon the weights. Give not yourselves unto vanity."

He couldn't be more consistent: he is reverting here to Psalm 62 and to the very lines he recorded in his journal before setting out for Peking. Here he adds verses 9 and 10, difficult to interpret in some other way than as an admonition to himself, especially in light of the next entry:

> "Not unto us, O Lord, not unto us but unto thy name give the praise—"
> A troubled spirit? Isn't the cause obvious? As soon as, furtively, you
> sought honor for yourself, you could no longer transform your weakness
> into strength. So you were "led into temptation," and lost that certainty
> of faith which makes saying Yes to fate a self-evident necessity, for such
> certainty presupposes that it is not grounded in any sort of a lie.[63]

He begins here with the opening verse of Psalm 115, a fierce indictment
of the idols men worship: "they have ears, and hear not. . . . They that
make them are like unto them." Hammarskjöld's political willingness to
distance himself and the UN from the praise that followed the airmen's
release finds its internal match here: it was good and more than good
that things worked out so well; there was no good reason to linger. As we
heard Hammarskjöld say toward the beginning of the venture: "If I have
done what I hope I have done, that is part of what I should do."

The question of relations between the master craftsman and the man
of prayer remained open for years to come. By mid-1956, with another
outstanding diplomatic achievement in progress, he had a new way of
looking at it:

> To rejoice at a success is not the same as taking credit for it. To deny
> oneself the first is to become a hypocrite and a denier of life; to permit
> oneself the second is a childish indulgence which will prevent one from
> ever growing up.[64]

It wasn't long before Zhou Enlai and the Chinese regime he served took
their distance from Hammarskjöld. The immediate cause was Hammarskjöld's brief report to the General Assembly on the Peking negotiation
and its outcome. From the Chinese perspective it reengaged the notion
that Hammarskjöld had been acting under the UN resolution, which the
Chinese had disavowed from start to finish. Though the two diplomats
would exchange communications with one another at long intervals, the
rapport they had developed gradually dissipated. Each was the servant
of a master—Hammarskjöld of the UN, Zhou of the People's Republic.
Their places in the scheme of things prevailed, like two planets briefly
conjunct in the astrologic skies, soon revolving on.

11

Causal Chains

For all its drama, the Peking negotiation was an elegant chamber composition marred only by occasional fits of coughing in the audience. The Middle East in 1956–57 wants some other description: always tumultuous and periodically violent, it drew into complex scenarios five regional states (Israel, Egypt, Jordan, Syria, Lebanon), two superpowers (the United States, the Soviet Union), and two European powers (Britain and France)—plus the UN. The region was churning with anger and mistrust, conspiracy and threat, outside pressures and a partially concealed but grim arms race. Both armies and small bands—the latter ranging from trained commandos to villagers and wandering shepherds—were poised to cross borders. To all of which Hammarskjöld said, in effect, what he said in May 1955 at a press conference exploring the chances of nuclear disarmament: "There have been no precedents or experiences which entitle us not to try again."[1] In the canon of Hammarskjöld statements, this is one of the most memorable; it too should be engraved on the walls of public buildings where serious matters are decided.

The months preceding Hammarskjöld's consuming engagement with the Middle East brought a sequence of successes. We have already noticed the June 1955 gathering in San Francisco to commemorate the 10th anniversary of the UN. A well-publicized event, earning Hammarskjöld his first *Time* magazine cover, that occasion also gave him what we have interpreted as a difficult personal passage when he measured the magnitude of the secretary-general's task against the reality of international affairs. The month of August saw a significant gathering at Geneva, the International Conference on the Peaceful Uses of Atomic Energy. Opening that event, Hammarskjöld found a way to drop down from expected generalities to evoke what he perceived as the anguish and obscure guilt felt by millions worldwide—and the breath of hope now experienced. His central role in international affairs brought essentials into sharp focus, and he knew how to state them without diminishing the formality of public speech. "The exploitation of nuclear energy for social and economic ends," he said, "will be a considerable relief from the oppressive thought that, in unlocking the atom, we had done no more than unlock the most sinister Pandora's Box in nature. . . . We all should render our thanks to the scientists who, by moving in this direction, will expiate on behalf of all of us that feeling of guilt which has so universally been felt, that man in his folly should have thought of no better use of a great discovery than to manufacture with its help the deadliest instruments of annihilation."[2] Urquhart has written that 1,400 scientists attended the two-week conference, masses of papers were read, and fundamental information was shared. In his eyewitness view the conference built "a new bridge . . . between East and West during . . . the most constructive and promising year for international peace since the beginning of World War II."[3] That the UN prepared and hosted the event was a sign of its growing maturity.

Another sign, positive in itself and promising, was the admission during the fall 1955 session of the General Assembly of sixteen new member nations ranging from Albania and Austria at the near end of the alphabet to Spain and Sri Lanka further on. On principle and for practical reasons, Hammarskjöld favored universal membership insofar as politics would permit. We have heard him argue that "the idea of the United Nations as a club to which only the like-minded will be admitted, in which membership is a privilege and expulsion is the retribution for wrong-doing, is totally unrealistic and self-defeating." Every new admission—Cambodia, Laos, Jordan, Nepal, Hungary, and others—introduced previously unheard perspectives and personalities and tied the UN more closely to the problems that each nation would face.

United Nations Day, October 24th, found Hammarskjöld convening the musicians of many nations to offer a festive concert at UN headquarters and by radio to a large public. The performers' names and their program can't help but impress: Leonard Bernstein conducting the Philadelphia Orchestra and the Russian virtuoso Emil Gilels in a performance of Tchaikovsky's first piano concerto; Sir William Walton leading the orchestra in one of his own compositions; a New York chorus performing sections of Beethoven's *Missa Solemnis*. In this annual setting, Hammarskjöld never failed to evoke the UN's ideals and the world's realities. This time he referred to unnamed spiritual and political leaders—leaving his listeners free to recall their own cultural traditions—from whom the UN could draw inspiration.

> What are ten years on the long road of mankind from the life under the law of the jungle to the full translation into action of the ideals of its greatest minds through the ages? In general terms, it may be true that man in the

Causal Chains   239

development of his spiritual and ethical maturity lags far behind his own technical achievements. In general terms, this may be true—but it is not true of those few who in their personal lives and as leaders have shown how man truly can live at peace with man. Although we are only at the beginning of our efforts to master the world which is now ours, we have seen in the life and teachings of those men what should be the road to mastery.[4]

Here, as so often, he emphasized the capacity of the individual to influence events and the permanent value of ideas and examples that float toward us from the past. As well, he retained the idea of mastery, though we have heard him debate it with himself. Not harsh, iron-fisted mastery; courageous and focused nonetheless.

In mid-November, as the year was drawing to a close with the General Assembly in session, Hammarskjöld could be lighthearted. "I owe you a letter long since," he wrote to the Belfrages. "But you cannot imagine how hectic things have been here—and are. We have many large balls in the air, you had better maneuver not to get one on your head!"[5] That was one way of saying it. There was another. In his year-end message for 1955, broadcast by UN Radio, he warned that the dream of the United Nations could become a harmful illusion if it was not well tended.

Mankind united in peaceful competition, free from fear and free from want, a mankind where man has truly come into his own—this great dream is exacting. It may demand great sacrifices. But it deserves the deepest loyalty. . . . Short of our unreserved devotion it will remain a dream, lacking substance. If this is not recognized, it may even blind us to reality—and become a danger, though it should be a source of strength.[6]

"This great dream is exacting" echoes beyond its place and time—New York, 1955—as the call to arms of a man of peace.

At a press conference earlier that day, December 22nd, Hammarskjöld was discussing some of the nonpolitical branches of the UN's work. Much of it, he thought, wasn't adequately appreciated by the public. "There is progress," he said, "but it is very slow." Then he made a remark that casts light forward onto the strenuous, often monumentally frustrating experiences that lay ahead for him in the Middle East: "You will certainly hear me preach very many more sermons before I have converted those I want to convert, if I ever do it. I am quite sure that if I do not convert them, events will."[7] This last is the hard epigraph for more than he knew at the time.

A long day's journey

We can give only limited attention in this book to Hammarskjöld's cultural interests. I hope that much nonetheless becomes apparent through seepage. But we shouldn't take leave of the fortunate year 1955 without acknowledging a personal exercise in convening power. In the course of the year Hammarskjöld had heard from a Swedish friend, Karl Ragnar Gierow, director of Dramaten, the Royal Dramatic Theater in Stockholm, that an unpublished play by the American playwright and Nobel laureate Eugene O'Neill might be shaken loose from a closed archive and given its first production. Why not in Stockholm, where O'Neill was at the time more appreciated than in the United States? Born within a year of one another, Gierow and Hammarskjöld belonged to the same circle in Stockholm, an informal grouping that called itself "the Ten" and functioned something like a sous-Academy, an ad hoc, deliciously intelligent circle meeting over dinner from time to time and interested in one another's activities. Hammarskjöld may not have attended a single such gathering since leaving Stockholm; he was nostalgic on the subject. Somehow he put Gierow in touch with the playwright's widow, Carlotta Monterey; correspondence ensued, and Gierow concluded by late summer that a personal meeting in New York might help. Could Hammarskjöld lend a hand?

Hammarskjöld replied by telegram: "Please reserve evening 15th for small dinner with Mrs. O'Neill. Happy if you would reserve also Friday evening for dinner with other guests. Are there any special people you would like me to invite? Personally I have in mind among others Helen Hayes, Katherine Cornell, and W. H. Auden."[8] This telegram would disclose shameless celebrity collecting, were it not part of a concerted campaign to bring an O'Neill masterpiece, *Long Day's Journey Into Night*, to the stage—and were this not some of the company Hammarskjöld kept when time permitted. Later in the year, when Gierow was again in town to see Mrs. O'Neill, Hammarskjöld even produced Greta Garbo as a dinner companion.

Upon returning to Sweden after that "evening 15th," Gierow sent a note to Hammarskjöld that reflects what must have been the ease and good humor of the Ten: "In what way should Dramaten and I thank you for this fine help? To appoint you as honorary actor is of course, in view of your present position, not such a bad idea, but after all the other honorary appointments that are heaped on you, the glory of this one might fade a bit. The title world's greatest theater agent isn't either of a kind you would accept without hesitation, not even *honoris causa*. . . . I think it will please you when I tell you that a most charming letter from Mrs. O'Neill puts the play at our disposal."[9]

Long Day's Journey successfully premiered in Stockholm on February 2nd, 1956, and went on to a prize-winning New York production in the fall. On opening night in Stockholm, Gierow had a thought for his friend, to whom he wrote a brief note: "Not that I have a clue as to when and where this letter will reach you, but from our friend Per Lind I have learned that your itinerary does not allow for a detour to the O'Neill opening night, let alone to Sweden while the piece is playing here. That is, indeed, unfortunate. World politics has started making itself important in a way that appears ever more inconsistent with decency and good manners."[10] Although Hammarskjöld never saw the Stockholm production and didn't think too highly of the New York production, his cooperative effort with Gierow renewed interest in O'Neill, now widely considered the greatest American playwright.

Cultural enterprises—as a patron and instigator of good things, as author and translator, as a congenial host for writers, artists, and performers, and as a member of the Swedish Academy charged with awarding the annual Nobel Prize in literature—represented for Hammarskjöld a necessary rest. To the poet Erik Lindegren in mid-1956, he wrote as much; at the time Lindegren was translating some of the poetry of Saint-John Perse from French into Swedish and using Hammarskjöld as his first reader. "Warm thanks for your three letters," Hammarskjöld wrote. "You don't know the joy you have given me with . . . the new translations, first, of course, for what they give but also because no spiritual exercise better fits my present existence than close reading of these poems. Intellectually it's a considerably more suitable activity than I've devoted myself to lately. It is refreshingly free from cheap effects and clearly activates other brain cells than the ones I use at work. . . ."[11] Hammarskjöld appended pages of detailed comments on the draft translations. He was resting.

Resting and regaining perspective. Friendships, meetings, and correspondence with writers and artists gave him a reliable alternative world. A letter of early January 1956 to Sten Selander, the multitalented writer, professor of botany, and Academician with whom he so enjoyed exchanging views until Selander's untimely death in mid-1957, makes all this very clear.

Thanks for your long letter of the 29th—as always more welcome than you can imagine. Your letters are one of the bridges to a familiar living world, where I need human roots so as not to drift off into a Sargasso Sea of internationalism. God knows I see more of "the world" and man—and unruly human behavior in "striped pants"—than maybe anyone else, but as an experience this has substance and perspective only if you manage to keep a solid basis in human contacts, which enable you to measure depth and width.[12]

I remember an old woman

In typically understated manner, Hammarskjöld shared at a December 1955 press conference his plan for a far-ranging trip. "For the Secretary-General it is rather natural, first of all, to get to know this operation, to get to the point where he really feels identified with what is going on in this house and in this Organization generally. Then is the time . . . when visits to Member countries may prove to be of the greatest use. I believe that I have now reached a stage, which is somewhat mid-term, where it is natural and useful for me to do my utmost to cover the greatest number of Member countries."[13] He left for the Eastern Mediterranean, the Middle East, and Asia-Pacific on January 15th and returned to New York nearly six weeks later. Greece, Turkey, Egypt, Israel, Jordan, Lebanon, Syria, Iran, Pakistan, followed by India, Burma, Thailand, Indonesia, Australia, and New Zealand. Privately, he expected his travels to be "rewarding but hardly pleasant." He sent a cranky note to Selander on the eve of departure: "I am writing partly because this trip will cause an unusually long break in our correspondence, partly because I get angry when I think how 'fun' it would have been to have you as a companion on a trip like this: you know how it enriches experience, especially of human beings, when it can be discussed at the time. I have the best companions, that's true—but, alas, on another wave length as soon as it's not about politics."[14] In point of fact, he was getting this wrong: among his companions was George Ivan Smith, a senior UN communications director, Australian, with whom he would enjoy a high level of professional trust and long friendship encompassing literature and much else.

Though the journey was what he would later call a "natural and modest move" on his part, its impact in the countries he visited was greater than he expected, and greater than expected for him personally. Where external impact was concerned, among other things he hoped that the political leaders he had met and the general public in countries visited might now reconsider a view he had encountered, to the effect that the United Nations is just a big machinery, a political, diplomatic machinery in New York, where we . . . are very far from the currents and the deep emotions and the real problems of the . . . world. There is a feeling that there is some kind of inner temple in New York to which some have easier access than others. . . . To the extent that this trip of mine could serve to drive home the fact that there is no such inner temple, but that, if we talk about this as a secular church, it expands all around the world, with equal rights for all and equal interest in all, it would in fact have been sufficiently justified.[15]

Hammarskjöld met David Ben-Gurion, prime minister of Israel, and Gamal Abdel Nasser, president of Egypt, both for the first time. They were, in Urquhart's phrase, the "two premiers who mattered" in the region.[16] A legend in his own time and now, David Ben-Gurion (1886–1973) was an early leader toward the establishment of the State of Israel and the country's first prime minister. Something like a biblical prophet and very like a warrior-king, he was a secular Jew of wide culture and philosophical interests—certain in that regard to attract Hammarskjöld's interest. A practical visionary, he recognized his mission and accomplished it. While the phrase "the eleventh commandment" has had varied uses, for Ben-Gurion and his generation it had just one, rooted in the Holocaust. To paraphrase a later Israeli politician: "By our side fight the six million, who whisper in our ear: do not get murdered—the commandment that was omitted at Mount Sinai."[17]

Gamal Abdel Nasser (1918–70) was no less central in the creation of an authentically sovereign, modernizing state in the region. Coleader of a military coup in 1952 that ended a corrupt monarchy and accelerated the process of freeing Egypt from decades of British domination and centuries of Ottoman domination, he too was a legend in his own time and now. His bright energy and vision gave new hope to his vast nation and to many Arab states under the banner of Pan-Arabism. Demonized by some in the West, he comes across in his short book predating the Suez Crisis, *The Philosophy of the Revolution*, as neither demon nor angel but an interesting human being with a folkloric, appealing voice.[18] Blending the history of his country with autobiography and aspiration, the book is more like an extended conversation than an Arab *Mein Kampf*, as some in the West described it. Together with Nehru and others, Nasser helped to craft a policy of nonalignment in the Cold War that changed world politics and the dynamics of debate and decision in the UN General Assembly. Nasser's biographer and confidant, the journalist Mohamed Heikal, has written that Hammarskjöld and Nasser, "the intellectual Swede and the Arab man of action, had little in common.

But they liked and trusted each other. And the one factor that they did have in common was big enough to overshadow most of their differences. They both put their faith in the United Nations."[19]

Hammarskjöld was shy of the press as he traveled in the Middle East, but in the Asia-Pacific region he made a sort of linked garland of press conferences as he moved from one capital to the next. Upon his return, the UN press corps naturally asked for his views of Ben-Gurion and Nasser. Both sides of that exchange are enlightening, the question indicating where intelligent public opinion stood at the time, Hammarskjöld's response giving us his first impressions of political leaders with whom he would soon be working closely.

> *Question:* Now that you have personally met Premier Nasser of Egypt and Ben-Gurion of Israel, I wonder whether your discussions with them . . . gave you an opportunity of seeing whether these two men, who hold the peace of the Middle East in their hands . . . , could ever possibly get together in a discussion. Do you see that possibility?
>
> *The Secretary-General:* Both have very strong personalities. Both are men with very great political experience, that is to say, political maturity. I guess that it is rather naive for me or for anybody to say that this can never be done or that that can be done. They are masters of their own procedure and their own life, and I have never seen difficulties that prevented leading politicians of great maturity and strong personalities from getting together when they felt it made sense.[20]

These are draft views; Hammarskjöld's familiarity with them both, as political leaders and as individuals, would increase.

In New Delhi, in early February, Hammarskjöld added to the swarm of ideas he wished the public to recognize as central to the UN's mission. He offered there "a speech without text," he apologized, "perhaps a rather rambling speech, from notes . . . made on the plane coming here."[21] Published later as a pamphlet, it was one of his best, providing a fresh overview of the UN at work and exploring at some length the issue of international aid. While there is much of interest, we should take time only to look at his discussion of aid, which he dared to couch initially in terms of the Christian notion of charity.

> There is in one of the Christian texts a statement which I think reflects ideas common to all philosophies and all great religions. I refer to the famous words of Saint Paul about the need for faith, hope, and charity

. . . . I think that it is proper to say that to the man deeply concerned about peace, about world affairs, in simple human terms the United Nations stands as a symbol of faith. It is also an instrument for action inspired by hope, and in many corners of the world it stands as a framework for acts of charity. Now I want to be very clear from the very beginning so that nobody, when I use the word "charity," misunderstands it. I mean it in the original sense as something a brother does for a brother, not as a handing-out operation with the benevolence of the "haves" in relation to the "have-nots" . . . I would refer here to another precept, which tells us that what you do to help your neighbor, you should do privately and not in the open. There is something which is very sound in this advice also in the field of international sharing, international cooperation, because I think that it is not in keeping with the very spirit of this sharing if the country which gives wants to put it on its flag that it is the donor, or if the country which receives has to be constantly reminded of the fact that it receives. It is not a gift from one to the other; it is a sharing, a sharing in the name of solidarity which is a "must" in our world and not something of our free choice.

For that reason, the multilateral forms of financial, economic, and social cooperation are better for both parties and will in the long run undoubtedly give the better results. I hope that this will be increasingly recognized.[22]

Behind what Hammarskjöld is saying here may lie what proved to be the deep learning of his journey, still incomplete at the time he spoke in Delhi. As he traveled, he was seeing something he had known of, even spoken of with eloquence and feeling, but had never directly witnessed on the scale of the world. He was seeing the misery of humankind and the spark of life in hard conditions. Though he met with political leaders in polished surroundings supplied with every comfort, his eyes took in more, and field trips—touristic and professional—showed him more. That this was so became evident in his opening remarks at the first New York press conference after his return, prompted not by a question but by his own sense of things. The journalist listening with greatest understanding was Peter Freuchen (b. 1886), a Dane well known to Hammarskjöld and only a part-time journalist. Freuchen was a friend and champion of the Inuit peoples, a hero of early exploration in the Arctic and Greenland who had lost a leg to frostbite decades earlier. A widely read author, an adviser and screenwriter for Hollywood films set in the far north, and married at one time to an Inuit woman, Freuchen had lived half his life among Eskimos. He knew what it is to have scant possessions and security, though he was now living in some comfort in Connecticut. To the sorrow of many, including the UN press corps, he was to die a year later, in 1957.

It seems providential that he was on hand at the press conference to draw Hammarskjöld into saying something more of his impressions of common people. Their exchange occurred at the end of the hour. In his opening remarks, Hammarskjöld offered a tour d'horizon in which the objectivity of a proper secretary-general quickly ceded to warmth.

> I should like to say something first of all that has no news value but that is of considerable importance to me and to my own reactions. First of all, this trip was a very great emotional experience. It was an emotional experience because it brought me in contact with people in very many Member countries in a way which added considerably to my understanding of the human elements in the problems which we are handling here. I remember very many personalities and very many situations. I remember the enthusiasm, the pure enthusiasm, of the young people in the collectives in Israel. I remember an old woman quite alone in a refugee camp in Beirut, scared of people, tired. I remember the young workers in an Indian village at the end of a long day breaking out in a dance with a zest of life going far beyond anything I have ever seen. I remember the old women in the peace pagoda at Rangoon, praying for peace with flowers in their hands—poor, poor people who did not know much about the ways of this world, but knew that short of peace there was no future for them.[23]

He went on to explain that his contacts with staff of the United Nations Relief and Works Agency (UNRWA) in refugee camps had been important to him. And went on to wrestle audibly with two internal impulses: the rationality of a senior diplomat and the feelings of a person who had been deeply touched.

> The experience was always one and the same: the enormity of the task which all responsible governments in the world have before them, the enormity of the plight of those people who have been thrown around in the world owing to political circumstances over which they have had no control. . . . We in the United Nations are doing what we can, with somewhat modest means . . . to assist the governments in what they are doing. . . . I do feel strongly that . . . it is an imperative need to live up to the economic needs of the vast majority of mankind. I say this with

a cold mind and thinking only of the political problem. There is no sentimentality, no emotionalism at all in these comments. . . . For those people out in those countries . . . , the United Nations is a symbol; the United Nations is, so to speak, the guarantee that there is sense in the world and that there is equity in the world. . . . How great our moral responsibility is, and how endless the demands . . . for devotion and for the giving out of all we possibly can.[24]

It was to this that Peter Freuchen returned at the end of the press conference. Though he seems not to have been fully at ease in English, his language is worth recording here:

Mr. Freuchen: I was very touched with your speech in the beginning. You said that there would be absolutely no sentimentality in your comments. We know that the statesmen have had a big failure because everything is not at present as it should be. You said, too, that you had talked to the little man in the street, and you had grown a tiny bit wiser. Is that really possible? At the same time, why not be sentimental and talk in a sentimental way to the world? We know, as you said, that they are starving in some places. . . . Is it not a way out to talk to people in a more sentimental way and to keep away from politics?

The Secretary-General: Mr. Freuchen, I talked to you in an emotional way. I willingly recognize that it was emotional because, as I said, this was also a very great emotional experience. But I hate the "sob-sister" approach, so to say. It is not a question of being kind to anybody; it is a question of sheer wisdom and strong human feeling.

As to the first point, my chances to talk to the man in the street are very slight. But there are a thousand and one ways in which you can grasp the identity of a person and see a little under what circumstances he lives and how he reacts to you and to problems. Perhaps that does not make me wiser, but it certainly has sharpened my senses in some respects. What made me wiser was the total experience.[25]

It's not often that we can correlate an undated entry in *Markings* with Hammarskjöld's public life. At some point in the late summer or fall of 1955, he wrote out a thought grounded in Jesus's parable of the talents in Matthew 25. It reads like preparation for these perceptions. The entry opens with a beautiful line from a poem by Hjalmar Gullberg, a fellow Academician whom he held in high regard. He might have been reading Gullberg when the following occurred to him:

"Those marked by suffering, those who have beheld—" You can, if you choose, enter into their consciousness and learn—without having gone through their hard school—to see and hear like one who "hath not" and from whom "shall be taken away even that which they hath."[26]

Causal chains

Hammarskjöld began thinking about chains of cause and effect soon after the airmen were freed. We have heard him describe the Peking negotiation and its slow consequences as "a completed chain of actions in balance." When the Security Council dispatched him to the Middle East in early April 1956 to work with the region's leaders on restoring adherence to armistice agreements, a pattern of raid and reprisal was getting seriously out of hand and the underlying politics of the region were sour. The concept of causal chains must have steadily enriched in his mind as he shuttled for a month from capital to capital. It became something like a master metaphor. The idea is obvious—what human affairs escape cause and effect?—but his version was vivid and serviceable. Returning to New York on May 6th, he kept an appointment some days later to give a talk in Williamsburg, Virginia, and there the concept reappeared, again in a positive light. That would change.

He was speaking of the Virginia Declaration of Rights, signed into law on June 12th, 1776, which keenly interested him as the first constitutional statement of its kind and precursor of the Universal Declaration of Human Rights adopted by the United Nations in 1948. "At one end of the chain," he said, "we have a declaration by a group of far-sighted men, framing the life of a new small community. At the other end of the chain we have a statement by the first international organization that can claim to speak for the world."[27] At the time he gave this talk, he was still thinking about his recent experience in the Middle East and coded into its closing paragraphs a new insight. He explained in a letter to Leif Belfrage:

Assignment Middle East was more fantastic than you would have guessed. An enormous experience and an enormous effort. Our Lord was very gracious and what could have been a disaster in more than one sense now seems—from within—a miracle. And the miracle continues! You feel strangely "taken care of" when you certainly try to give everything but miss so much—and see even omissions turn in your favor. . . .

The literary associations were numerous. Sometimes it was as if you were a spectator [at a performance of] *Oedipus*. You saw them caught in the causal chain, making the wrong choice and again making the wrong choice. Maybe you could say that what we succeeded in doing was breaking the causality by rushing up on stage and forcing them to *see* for themselves—for a moment! And then? My real comment on the situation you won't find in the official report but in the last pages—and especially in the last paragraph—of the attached speech.[28]

He enclosed a copy of the Williamsburg speech, which concluded with these words:

We all know how, when moved by fear, people may act against what others see as their own best interest. We know how, when people are afraid, they may act even against their own fundamental will. We have seen how, when influenced by such actions, the course of events may take on aspects of inexorable fatality up to the point where, out of sheer weariness, no resistance to the gravitation into open conflict any longer seems possible. This is a constantly repeated tragedy.

Why is war and fear of war in the headlines of every daily paper, if not because man fears man and nation, nation? . . . Can there be a greater challenge for us to work for such a recognition of the dignity of man as would eliminate the fear which is eating our world like a cancer? . . .

If, at long last, the recognition of human dignity means to give others freedom from fear, then that recognition cannot be simply a question of passive acceptance. It is a question of the positive action that must be taken in order to kill fear.

This is not a question of abstract ethical principles. I state conclusions from some very concrete recent experiences. It is when we all play safe that we create a world of the utmost insecurity. It is when we all play safe that fatality will lead us to our doom. It is "in the dark shade of courage" alone, that the spell can be broken.[29]

These lines are remarkable. Moved by his intense experience in the Middle East, Hammarskjöld turns most unusually to extreme images— "eating our world like a cancer," "to kill fear"—and a preacher's wave of repetitions. As if recalling Greek tragedy, he evokes the descent of fate: "Out of sheer weariness, no resistance to the gravitation into open conflict any longer seems possible." Uncharacteristically—he must have been writing or revising at top speed—he made a minor literary error: the beautiful phrase about courage from Ezra Pound's book-length poem, *The Cantos*, is slightly misquoted.[30] However, he makes it do for him what he wishes; it enhances the sense of unsmiling courage in the face of grave difficulty. His striking thought about playing safe takes up words spontaneously said by him not long before to both Ben-Gurion and Nasser. Playing safe in the Middle East meant persisting in familiar patterns of aggression and refusing to risk unilateral peacemaking measures that invite matching actions from the other side.

Reporting a few days earlier to the Security Council on his efforts in the Middle East, Hammarskjöld had relied on the metaphor of causal chains: "If we have previously experienced chain reactions leading to a continuous deterioration of the situation, we may now have the possibility of starting a chain of reactions in the opposite direction."[31] Privately he shared with friends and his brother Bo a more vivid sense of things. To a friend he spoke of being "absorbed in my wildest attempt ever to break one of these chains of causes forged by fear and leading to destruction."[32] To his brother he wrote at some length.

> "Assignment Middle East" was both much more and much less than is evident in public discussion. Much more, because this can be the start of a peaceful revolution. Much less, because we only managed to break one fatal causal chain without being able to *decide* the direction of this new development—whatever little we could do to influence it.
>
> As a personal experience it was incredible: the individual still can play a decisive role—if he can act without reservations (separate or private). But you wear out your nerves! And I sleep like a puppy. . . . Let's hope for the best. But now I am "united in marriage" to the Palestine issue and one must take the consequences "to the bitter end."[33]

There is a further thought about causal chains from a considerably later letter (April 1958) to a fellow member of the Swedish Academy. "You can feel the threat against the future stronger and stronger," he wrote then, "but paradoxically enough parallel to that is growing an irrational conviction that we shall be able to break through the causal chain of fear, clumsiness, self-assertion and plain common stupidity."[34] Now we can populate the metaphor with values: fear, clumsiness, egotism, stupidity, repetitively bad choices, the need for national leaders to see for themselves in moments of dispassionate awareness and for interventions by helpful mediators, as if there is a "spell" (this is another of his recurrent metaphors) which can only be broken through cooperative effort. The idea, somewhat desperately stated, that leaders must *see* for themselves" evokes Hammarskjöld's conviction that understanding is a work in progress. Abrupt changes in perspective are not just possible but needed, and political leaders must not permit themselves to be wholly bound by habitual frames of reference. "It should not be overlooked," he said in May 1956, "that even with the best of men half-hearted and timid measures will lead nowhere. The dynamic forces of history will overtake us unless we are willing to think in categories on a level with the problem."[35]

One last metaphor: redirecting a river's flow. He produced it at a press conference in summer 1956: "We are in the middle of a run where we do something which is rather unusual—or rather we *try* to do something which is rather unusual in diplomatic and political history—and that is to change the direction of a stream. If in such a situation you manage to keep your stand and, so to say, consolidate it, I wouldn't exactly call it progress but I am not unhappy to be able to know that that much is a fact."[36]

On August 17th, Hammarskjöld issued a public statement from UN headquarters in response to four bloody incidents along the armistice demarcation line between Israel and Egypt. In the first incidents, Israeli lives had been lost; in the second, Egyptian. "Whatever the sequence of cause and effect," he wrote,

> and whatever the arguments which might be brought out as a reason for acts of violence, the one who resorts to such acts, whether starting or prolonging a chain of disturbances, takes on himself a very great responsibility for the final development in the area. The difference in the degree of responsibility borne by those found to have initiated such a chain of disturbances and by the other party does not remove the grave responsibility of the latter for a resort to acts of violence in contravention of the rules of the Charter. This, apart from all legal considerations, is the uncontradictable thought behind the repeated condemnation by the United Nations of acts of violence, understood to have been in retaliation, and the view that such acts cannot be considered as acts of self-defense in the sense of the UN Charter.[37]

Article 51 of the Charter affirms "the inherent right of individual or collective self-defense if an armed attack occurs against a Member of the United Nations, until the Security Council has taken measures necessary to maintain international peace and security." However, reprisals were disallowed on the borders governed by armistice agreements since Israel's War of Independence in 1948, and monitored since 1949 by the United Nations Truce Supervision Organization (UNTSO), an unarmed force charged with observation and reporting. The expected recourse was to UNTSO, whose chief of staff was the highly respected Canadian general E. L. M. Burns, and to the Security Council, which took a close interest in maintenance of the general cease-fire it had brought about through the mediation of Count Bernadotte and his successor, Ralph Bunche.

In a stinging letter to Ben-Gurion in late September 1956, Hammarskjöld returned to this topic. Retaliation, disproportionate if Ben-Gurion saw fit for political reasons, was a policy by which the prime minister counted on persuading Israel's neighbors of his country's implacable firmness.

> As you well know, it is the Security Council that has repeatedly publicly condemned acts of retaliation. That I share their view is irrelevant in view of the fact that it would all the same be my duty publicly to maintain that stand. . . .
>
> The situation is quite clear. You are convinced that a threat of retaliation has a deterrent effect. I am convinced that it is more of an incitement to individual members of the Arab forces than even what has been said by their own Governments. You are convinced that acts of retaliation will stop further incidents. I am convinced that they will lead to further incidents as they give both the immediate reason for counteraction from the other side and a legal justification which, if applicable to you, must be equally applicable to the others. You believe that this way of creating respect for Israel will pave the way for sound coexistence with the Arab peoples. I believe that the policy may postpone indefinitely the time for such coexistence.
>
> However, I think the discussion of this question can be considered as closed since you, in spite of previous discouraging experiences, have taken the responsibility for large-scale tests of the correctness of your belief.[38]

His cool, dry tone notwithstanding, Hammarskjöld had a strong sense of fellowship with Ben-Gurion. Nearly the same can be said of his relations with Nasser, who was temperamentally unlike Hammarskjöld but dedicated and interesting in ways that Hammarskjöld recognized. Toward the end of his life, Hammarskjöld is reported to have sent Nasser a characteristic note: "I appreciate that you never deceived me, and that you were sincere in everything you undertook."[39] A third participant of importance was Nasser's foreign minister, Mahmoud Fawzi, on whom Hammarskjöld had come to rely both in Egypt and at the UN for cool, dry thinking and the friendship of a comrade-at-arms.

A little of this and a little of that, added together

It was with these charmingly evasive words, among others more precise, that Hammarskjöld left for his second round of meetings in the Middle East. At a press conference in New York on the eve of his April 6th departure, he had been asked, "I wonder if you could give us a statement on what you consider . . . the overriding general difficulty, the greatest difficulty you face . . . ?" He responded, "It is extremely difficult to reply to that question. You know, it is a little of this and a little of that, and added together it creates a situation of some delicacy."[40] The situation of some delicacy was an increase in bloody raids and reprisals at flashpoints along the Israeli-Egyptian armistice demarcation lines, periodic violence along the Israeli-Syrian border and the Jordanian border, tension nearly always and everywhere, an intensified regional arms race, all pointing toward a possible renewal of war between Israel and its neighbors into which the major powers might be drawn. The Security Council considered the situation a threat to international peace and security. Hammarskjöld responded promptly to its April 4th resolution calling on him to meet with the region's leaders and take steps with them to restore adherence to the armistice agreements in place since the end of Israel's War of Independence. The Council's mandate was limited in scope; there was hope of success within its bounds. It also gave him the opportunity to continue building relationships in a region where war was thinkable.

He would have wanted, as for Peking, to talk the issues through in advance with his friend and former colleague, Sture Petrén. In late March, as the Security Council debated with little acrimony the best approach, he had written to Petrén.

These last days I have had special reason to think of you. In the Palestine affair I happen to face a decision that largely parallels the Peking business, where you came in as the first one in the personal picture. This time, too, I've come to the conclusion that I ought to put in play the job and myself . . . , unfortunately now with great risk of losing even with an ace on the table (with *higher* cards the chance to win anything would be *quite* non-existent). It would have been good to discuss this with you—as we did last time. . . .

From the latest trip there is much to tell. . . . It was tremendously rewarding and changed my perspectives to a great degree. I came home with two unexpected favorite countries—Burma and New Zealand—and an entirely new view of Buddhism as a life- and atmosphere-creating factor. The difficulty to "accomplish" something seems greater than ever after this deep-sea dive—but also the reasons to stake everything in the effort.

You would enjoy all the conflicts, undercurrents, and speculations that play a role in a case like this. At least as juicy as autumn '54! And with Krishna somewhere in the background—I think—awaiting the moment to "step forward." Oh, humanity, you certainly do deserve better.[41]

It is difficult to interpret what he meant by "higher cards"—perhaps Western heads of state with a stake in the Middle East. Krishna is Hammarskjöld's reliable bête noire, V. K. Krishna Menon.

Hammarskjöld was entering a world where instability was the norm. One of his earliest biographers remembered someone suggesting that "Hammarskjöld's motto ought to have been *Per ambigua ad astra*"— through ambiguity to the stars.[42] Wise ambiguity would soon be needed in the Middle East, but for the moment he was counting on a subset of ambiguity: the provisional. At his parting press conference, April 5th, he was interesting on this topic, tied to his conviction that the passage of time can have a certain magic:

There are quite a few situations where we must live and learn to live with provisional arrangements, because there is no solution to the long-range problem which we can find overnight. We must simply grow into the solution. In the meanwhile the very best thing you can do is to consolidate and keep clean the lines within the framework of the provisional solution. I think that for the time being if we can get compliance with the armistice agreements in their integrity, we should be quite happy and not too impatient.[43]

The situation in Palestine was as complex then as it is now. Nothing matches the book published by General Burns in 1962 for its meticulously detailed picture of conditions "on the ground" in Hammarskjöld's years. He and his colleagues within UNTSO, the truce supervision commission charged with observing and reporting how the armistice agreements were holding up, dealt daily with border incidents and governments. Trusted by Hammarskjöld and entrusted by him with still greater responsibility as time went on, Burns had impressive scope of mind; he could closely analyze a border incident but also vividly characterize the larger picture. "The complexity of the Middle East problem," Burns wrote, "and the Palestine problem within it . . . is like a large ball of string. Several loose ends protrude, but when one begins to draw out any particular little bit of string, one finds it is inextricably tangled up with the other pieces in the ball. It constitutes a Gordian knot, and so far no Alexander bold enough to cut it has come along."[44] This is his filiform version of causal chains.

On the day of Hammarskjöld's departing press conference, a pair of incidents occurred in the Gaza Strip, controlled at the time by Egypt, which typified and took to a further extreme the border violence that brought Hammarskjöld to the region. On April 4th Egyptian troops had killed three Israeli soldiers on Israeli territory at the demarcation line—the Israelis had a policy at the time of patrolling provocatively close to the line. Burns writes that incidents of this kind almost invariably gave rise to further and larger violence. The following day, in an exchange of mortar and artillery fire, the Egyptians targeted some Israeli settlements and caused casualties. Retaliating at once, the Israeli forces shelled the center of Gaza City, which was crowded with civilians. The Israelis later explained that their rounds had gone astray from intended military targets: 56 Arabs were killed and 103 wounded, women and children among them. An American UNTSO officer had spent the day persuading the combatants to cease fire; he prevailed only that evening, after a day's warfare. Smaller-scale combat continued in the days that followed, with one altogether miserable incident—the murder of Israeli school children by Egyptian fedayeen, irregular forces partially controlled from Cairo but often acting on their own. The Israelis captured and killed some of the marauders; others returned to Egypt where the newspapers hailed them as "heroes . . . back from the battlefield."[45] Toward the beginning of these incidents, General Burns had sent a message to Ben-Gurion asking him to ensure that Israeli patrols come no closer than five hundred meters to the demarcation line. Ben-Gurion agreed "as a special gesture in view of the Secretary-General's forthcoming visit, and subject to Mr. Hammarskjöld's obtaining a promise from Premier Nasser to give a binding order to his troops not to fire on Israelis in Israeli territory."[46] Hammarskjöld's influence, blending something of his own dignity and that of the UN, was drawing near.

Gaza was not the only tormented border. Burns recorded that "by August 1955 the number of unsettled complaints on the Jordan-Israel . . . docket stood at 2150."[47] The demarcation line with Syria was similarly unstable. Burns provided a partial list of violent incidents at the Jordan-Israel demarcation line in May and June 1956, immediately after Hammarskjöld's month in the region: "On June 5 two Israelis were wounded during an exchange of fire which followed the uprooting of trees on the Jordanian side of the demarcation line by an Israeli tractor. On June 24 two Israeli policemen were killed. . . ."[48] The inventory of incidents is longer. The demarcation lines were notional, often the proverbial line in the sand; the killings were not.

In approaching Nasser, Ben-Gurion, young King Hussein of Jordan, and other regional leaders in this first exercise of shuttle diplomacy, Hammarskjöld had a Nobel Prize–winning set of armistice documents to work with; you'll recall that they were negotiated by Ralph Bunche in succession to his assassinated superior, Count Bernadotte, and for his accomplishment Bunche received the Nobel Prize for peace in 1950. The four armistice agreements skillfully foresaw many difficulties, among other things by making a sharp distinction between immediate self-defense (an inherent right) and calculated reprisal (prohibited). Hammarskjold took a legalistic view as to which is which in a given circumstance: "Whether a certain action is justified as self-defense or not is something which under United Nations legislation can only be decided by the Security Council. I may have my views on the concrete cases, but . . . they would just be my private views. . . . They may be of interest but not of significance."[49]

To follow Hammarskjöld at work, we cannot do better than read General Burns's eyewitness account:

> For the next month Mr. Hammarskjöld devoted himself with the most untiring energy to the mission with which the Security Council had entrusted him. He flew from Cairo to Jerusalem, from there to Amman and Damascus and Beirut, then retraced his itinerary. At each capital he had exhaustive discussions with the heads of state and the foreign ministers; sometimes the military heads took part. I accompanied him throughout, with some of my advisers. . . . But the great burden of this negotiation was undertaken by Mr. Hammarskjöld himself. Throughout this grueling program his stamina was astonishing; he never seemed weary, nor did his perceptions flag. His name had become synonymous with diplomatic skill, and he deployed his great resources throughout the four

weeks of his mission. At the beginning of it he found a situation in which all-out war seemed possible within hours; at the end, though he had not accomplished all that he had hoped for, he had secured engagements from all the countries which, had they been kept, would have ensured stability under the general framework of the armistice agreements.[50]

Moving rapidly from capital to capital, he secured agreements as he went and immediately publicized them through the media in order to hold his negotiating partners publicly to their commitments. Hammarskjöld's biographers have uniformly noticed that, normally publicity shy, he was now using the media as an integral part of his strategy. He was also using an approach he may have discovered just in these weeks, though he mentioned it to his working team as if it were a diplomatic proverb of long standing: "An essential rule in such negotiations is never to stay in one place for a moment longer than . . . necessary."[51] Because he was on the spot—on many spots—and accompanied by General Burns, issues were referred to him with which the general would normally have dealt on his own. Urquhart's account of day-to-day negotiations includes, for example, a "scuffle between Israeli and Syrian fishermen on Lake Tiberias," during which the Israelis had to leave their nets behind in a rush. Hammarskjöld negotiated a set of agreements governing the lake, one site and issue among many.[52] A little of this and a little of that, added together, as he had predicted.

General Burns must have been Hammarskjöld's first mentor where military affairs are concerned. Just a few months earlier, during his relatively short visit to the Middle East, Hammarskjöld had deferred to Burns in a note to the British foreign secretary, Selwyn Lloyd. The topic was Burns's assessment of the regional situation at the time: "It is obviously not for me," he wrote, "to add anything to these observations on the military aspect of the question raised, but I may say that I find the General's presentation convincing."[53] Hammarskjöld had no military background, yet he was increasingly involved in military affairs. On behalf of the Security Council he was already commander-in-chief of UNTSO, the unarmed military team serving under General Burns, and he would soon be commander-in-chief of a much larger armed force. Typically he had a skilled team of administrators and military officers directing, but the ultimate responsibility was his, and Security Council resolutions generally and deliberately left much to his judgment. The role seems out of character.

When I had the opportunity to raise this issue with Brian Urquhart, he replied that Hammarskjöld was "a very unmilitary man" but an unbelievably quick study. He had witnessed that many times over. When Hammarskjöld began meeting with his nuclear energy advisory board, the Nobel laureate I. I. Rabi asked Urquhart, "What sort of guy is this Dag Hammarskjöld? He seems able to talk to us almost in our own language." Urquhart remembers replying, "Well, when Hammarskjöld decides to master something, he masters it." Urquhart saw this also in connection with marine insurance, a rude topic if ever there was one. To Urquhart's permanent amazement, Hammarskjöld not only mastered its intricacies but worked out a solution to a major insurance-related problem at the Suez Canal in early 1957.[54] Hammarskjöld's military education had begun. His specialty would be peacekeeping. By the time of the Congo Crisis some years later, he had long since learned the trade. General I. J. Rikhye, his valued military adviser in those years, said as much: "Of all the political leaders . . . I know, he stands out as the one who was really a soldier's political leader. . . . He had a family tradition of civil service, politics and the military were integral to his background. Therefore he had no hang-ups. A lot of people in the UN have terrible hang-ups about working with the military. He had no such hang-ups. . . . When he went to the field he was able to get the best from his senior military commanders."[55]

There was a little fun to be had, and much insight, in the course of this demanding month-long Middle Eastern exercise. Noting Hammarskjöld's emphasis in press conferences on the need for flexibility in response to fluid, changing circumstances, an Egyptian newspaper dubbed him Mr. Flexible and referred to his communications director, George Ivan Smith, as Mr. Fluid. They happily adopted the nicknames in some of their private communications with each other, sometimes adding appropriate military ranks: General Flexible and Corporal Fluid.[56] Hammarskjöld must also have had a serious kind of fun on April 14th, though he surely didn't let on, when he stage-managed a little demonstration on the often violent demarcation line between Egyptian Gaza and Israeli territory just beyond. He arranged for a convoy of white-painted UNTSO jeeps to drive him along the Egyptian side of the line to a UN checkpoint at Kilometer 95, where he took leave of his Egyptian escort and, a hundred meters on, was met by an Israeli military escort and members of UNTSO.[57] It was a parable.

Curious, this feeling of fate

At this time of intense concentration, circular travel, and ceaseless nego-tiation, was Hammarskjöld pressed flat against daily demands or was he able to sustain his inner life and spirited attitude? There is a little nexus of days, April 20th to 22nd, when we can know something about that. On the first of those days he offered an apt and creative summary of the state of affairs. "This particular job," he said, "is a little bit like building an arch. I feel that I have now added a second stone to the first one, and that it is just as good as the first one. However, you know that in build-ing an arch the construction is not stable until all the stones have been fitted in."[58] The elements of the arch were separate agreements with each regional leader, piecework gradually summing to the needed whole. He would have discovered his simile in the ancient architecture all around. Given the sparkle of his comment, we can be sure that Hammarskjöld was at ease in his mission, however great the strain at times.

For his own quite private purposes, there was something more. At the outset of the mission, while in Rome before flying on to the Middle East, he was thinking about a passage in Meister Eckhart. He transcribed it into his journal: "There is a contingent and non-essential will: and there is, providential and creative, an habitual will. God has never given Himself, and never will, to a will alien to His own: where He finds His will, He gives Himself."[59] In the remote but exact idiom of another era, Hammar-skjöld was again looking into the link between two wills—one's own and another that surpasses. "Not I, but God in me": this remained his prayer and need. Toward the end of May, after his return from the Middle East, Hammarskjöld sent a retrospective note to George Ivan Smith. "Curious, this feeling of fate which we had so strongly when in the region," he wrote, "and from which even now I cannot get away—fate requiring the sacrifice of unreserved engagement, but somehow bowing to such engagement."[60]

With Eckhart's thoughts about will in mind, we can return to those three days in April. A brief entry in *Markings* makes clear how Hammar-skjöld worked to temper his will so that a "providential and creative" will might somehow influence the course of events. He was practicing what he called stillness. No doubt as a reminder to himself, he wrote:

> Understand—through the stillness,
> act—out of the stillness,
> prevail—in the stillness.

"In order for the eye to perceive color, it must divest itself of all colors."[61]

The passage quoted here from Eckhart (the fourth line) speaks to the receptiveness, free of self-will, that can welcome an influence not of one's own making. That this passage in Hammarskjöld's edition of Eckhart falls only a few pages on from the lines about God's gift of Himself suggests that Hammarskjöld had just a little time during this month of shuttle diplomacy to touch back into the realm where he met and thought alongside Eckhart. He wasn't reading much, but reading well.

The full passage in Eckhart where these few words appear has an almost monstrous beauty and assertiveness. Eckhart was no taker of tentative positions, as his clerical peers recognized when they called him before the Inquisition in 1326 to answer charges of heresy. (He came to no harm.) "If my eye is to perceive color," Eckhart wrote, "it must be free of all colors. If I see the color blue or white, then the seeing of my eye, which perceives the color, is exactly the same as what it sees, as what is seen by the eye. The eye with which I see God is exactly the same eye with which God sees me. My eye and God's eye are one eye, one seeing, one knowledge, and one love."[62] We can't know what Hammarskjöld made of the full passage, but the very next entry in *Markings* has something of the breadth and direction of Eckhart's thought. It is a prayerful poem.

> To love life and men as God loves them—for the sake
> of their infinite possibilities,
> to wait like Him,
> to judge like Him
> without passing judgment,
> to obey the order when it is given
> and never look back—
> then He can use you—then, *perhaps*, He will use you.
> And if he doesn't use you—what matter. In His hand, every moment
> has its meaning, has greatness and glory, peace and coherence.[63]

The entry enriches our understanding of what he meant by stillness; it must be these things and more—a capacity to wait, enough distance to see, the wisdom not to condemn, the courage to engage without anxiety or presumption. Presumption is not a still thing.

I don't suppose we'll fully understand Dag Hammarskjöld, no matter how closely we look. He'll walk away free in the end. That is surely for the best. These thoughts come to mind in response to two further entries in *Markings*, one certainly written in the Middle East, the other likely written there. They follow one another, as if they belong together. Better to start with the second, an austere poetic reflection on the entire month's experience of negotiation.

> On the field where Ormuzd has challenged Ahriman to battle, he who chases away the dogs is wasting his time.[64]

This vivid image applies to the Middle East and to all efforts to set difficult things right. Hammarskjöld may have chased a dog or two before noticing the waste of time. Reading this entry, which evokes a divine battle between good and evil, we do well to remember that he consistently located motivation and decision in individuals, not nations. He looked specifically at this issue in a letter to Bo Beskow in early June, not long before something broke again:

> Anytime something can break again. We live in rather a foolish world, and it doesn't get any wiser through the ruth- (not to say shame-) less propaganda from a well-known direction to which it is subject. If people would only remember Fröding's simple words "that nobody is evil and nobody is good," they would be able to become immune to this simple propagandistic picture of villains and saintly martyrs, watched by indifferent people who for unknown reasons want to be on good terms with the villains. In the long run this simplification is so tiresome that maybe we could return to realism. It is hard to keep up the notion that anybody who finds *anything* good to say about Nasser, or *anything* to object to in Ben-Gurion is an anti-Semite—and thus a crypto-Nazi. Well, let us hope for a spiritual healing. And let us stay healthy ourselves![65]

The second entry in *Markings* that records private reflections in the Middle East is, in form, a commentary on familiar passages in the Gospel of John, but almost certainly inspired by direct experience. He must have been standing on a height of land in Israel or Jordan, overlooking a wide landscape. The entry is printed here as Hammarskjöld wrote it, without quotation marks, to retain the continuity he must have felt between the abstract beauty of the lines from John and the experiential flash of sensation, symbol, and understanding he records.

> The wind bloweth where it listeth—
> so is everyone that is born of the spirit.

> And the light shineth in darkness,
> and the darkness comprehended it not.

Like wind— In it, with it, of it. Of it just like a sail, so light and strong that, even though bound to the earth, it gathers all the power of the wind without hampering its course.

Like light— In light, lit through by light, transformed into light. Like the lens which disappears in the light it focuses to new strength.

Like wind. Like light.

Just this—on these expanses, these heights.[66]

The words are large; they take in a very great deal. But they lead on to "just this," irreducibly simple experience. Now in poetic rather than theological terms, he is thinking again about two wills and their relation. The sail belongs to the Earth, but it is capable of gathering "all the power of the wind"; the lens is a real object of this Earth, like ourselves, but it "disappears in the light."

It wasn't lost on Hammarskjöld that he was in the Holy Land, where Judaism and Christianity were born and where Jesus lived out his ministry and Passion. George Ivan Smith could recall "a long walk with him at Jerusalem. We were going up and down inside the [UN] compound because diplomatically he could not easily go into Israel or Jordan. On one side there was the clear sight of Jerusalem and on the other side the hills of Moab and of the village where Lazarus was raised from the dead. It was probably under the impact of the surroundings that he revealed to me for the first time the intense strength of his Christianity."[67] We can measure something of that impact through this most intense of entries in *Markings*, recording a moment when the wind and light of the Holy Land entered him.

A worrisome mentality

When Hammarskjöld returned from the Middle East on May 6th, a sweet letter awaited him. It was from Lincoln Kirstein, cofounder with George Balanchine of the School of American Ballet and New York City Ballet, an exceedingly bright man whose company Hammarskjöld enjoyed. Kirstein's refined fan letter, surely a pleasant surprise, conveys the public appreciation that had gathered behind Hammarskjöld. "As the hopes of the world have been following you," Kirstein wrote, "I just wanted to tell you that my wife and I have been praying for your success. We feel your deep patience and cheerful imagination make our chances for living day to day possible. How many millions there must be like us!"[68]

On May 9th Hammarskjöld made a detailed report to the Security Council about the results of his mission. He concluded with caution: "It is still too early to say what has been achieved in substance, but the efforts made, in my view, were necessary as an initial step. What has been done may open the door to new fruitful developments. . . . The final settlement is probably still far off, but even partial solutions to the harassing problems of the region would be a contribution."[69] He had successfully reinstated the cease-fire along all borders—but for how long? He had convincingly demonstrated to all of the region's leaders, as he said later in the month, that "they can always count on the sympathetic and impartial assistance of the Secretary-General, within the framework set by what they consider possible and desirable in their efforts to make further progress."[70] Sending a copy of the report to Östen Undén, the Swedish foreign minister and a wise friend, he included a private account of personalities and the overall situation in the Middle East. Though the following extract from his letter is somewhat long, it could not be more worthwhile. Among other things it gives Hammarskjöld's candid assessments of Ben-Gurion and Nasser.

> The real situation in the Middle East is very different from what the world has been led to believe. In some respects it is better, because there is undoubtedly a very real will to peace to be found at key points, irrespective of the side, but there is also a mentality which shocks me and makes me most worried. My greatest reason for concern is the Israeli attitude which, on the inside, is one of the harshest intransigence but, as presented by the Israeli propaganda, one of a nation wishing only to live at peace with its neighbors, although continuously harassed by them. (I have experienced this contrast practically daily and in the most striking forms; for example, screams to the world about the danger created by this and that intrusion of civilians over the demarcation lines, only too understandable in light of the prevailing circumstances, and at the same time a flat refusal to accept observer arrangements in order to forestall such transgressions.)
>
> If you read the report carefully, I think you will find that the balance between the stands of the two sides does not correspond to the general ideas you find in the world press. And yet I have, in order not to make this document a speech for the prosecution—and in that way create further difficulties—played down the inconsistencies and the some-

times incomprehensibly negative reactions on the Israeli side which rendered this effort, as all similar efforts, exceedingly difficult.

The only man in the Middle East on whom efforts toward solutions can safely build at present is Dr. Fawzi of Egypt. His sincerity, seriousness and competence as well as his international perspective make him a real asset. . . .

I know by now both Nasser and Ben-Gurion very well. Their two tempers are such that a clash between them represents a constant risk factor. In spite of all noises and all actions which seem to indicate the opposite, I am personally convinced that neither of them has any plan to attack the other one; that, in fact, each wishes to avoid a war. The trouble lies on a different level. Each has the deepest suspicion of the other one, but their ways of protecting their security represent opposite extremes. Nasser has a very great patience, but a lot of the guerilla mentality which makes him assert himself, so to say, under the table and in irregular forms. Ben-Gurion, on the other hand, is extremely impatient and believes it to be the height of morality to respond to the policy of the other one by blunt, open strokes, not understanding the complete futility of such retaliation and its exceedingly dangerous psychological consequences. Both have pushed self-righteousness to the extreme point of honestly believing that they always are right. In the case of Ben-Gurion it goes even one step further than in the case of Nasser, as he—in perfectly good faith—is blowing up every single incident, whatever its origin, as a sign of the treachery of the other side, while never admitting publicly even fully evidenced transgressions and incursions. . . .

I do not blame any of them but I have to note that these are their attitudes and to note also in what risks they involve the two countries and all of us. . . . As I said to both Ben-Gurion and Nasser, when "everybody is playing safe in the way you do, the result is a state of utmost insecurity." . . .

My views explain why I consider that it would be most unwise to take sides and to get committed to any of the two parties in the present conflict. . . . I hope one day to be able to give you the inside story which has elements of the "Thousand and One Nights," of the "Merchant of Venice," and of "Oedipus Rex."[71]

And yet . . . This braking phrase, "and yet," is proving so necessary as we explore Hammarskjöld's experience in the Middle East. Despite his disapproval of key elements of Ben-Gurion's policies and attitudes, Hammarskjöld admired the old warrior and felt they had a special affinity. He wrote as much to Per Lind soon after his return: "The greatest individual experience certainly was to be able to get to know Ben-Gurion thoroughly, whom I have learned to like very much notwithstanding the fact we are disagreed on much and have very violent exchanges of views."[72] On his side, Ben-Gurion also was intrigued. "After their first meeting," Urquhart has written, "Ben-Gurion, who . . . had already found that Hammarskjöld's detailed knowledge of Middle Eastern problems was as formidable as his skill in negotiation, jokingly asked, 'And where did they find *you?*'"[73]

Hammarskjöld's correspondence with Ben-Gurion reveals the strength of his wish to call him back to objective values, calmer views, which underneath it all he was quite sure they shared. He also felt that they needed to meet directly for the magic of political agreement and personal communion to have its best chance of occurring—to sit down in government offices or at Ben-Gurion's home at Sde Boker, a kibbutz in the Negev desert, where he and his wife Paula lived simply. "One of the most positive elements in my previous efforts to help towards bettering the situation in the Middle East," Hammarskjöld wrote to Ben-Gurion in late June,

> was the strong feeling I got that back of all problems and difficulties and—sometimes—even marked differences of views, there was between us, on a much deeper level, a meeting of minds where you understood what I was trying to do and where I could see eye to eye with you concerning your basic aims and fears. It is unavoidable that this common denominator be overshadowed by current events and worn thin by time if it is not maintained. That can be done only by personal contact. Whatever the excellence of the intermediaries, neither they nor any exchange of messages can maintain fully vital the basis on which I hope to continue my cooperation with you for peace.[74]

Later in the year, when their discussions had taken a difficult turn, Hammarskjöld sent Ben-Gurion another message referring to their meeting of minds.

> We have had to conduct [our] exchange of letters under the principles proper to our different positions. As things have turned out, we may on that level have seemed to drift apart. Given the events and situations to which we have had to react, that may have been difficult to

avoid. I don't think that either of us would have respected the other one for compromises or evasions accepted only in order to smooth out differences. For me, however, the understanding established in our direct contacts has always remained a kind of "ultimate reality."[75]

The letter carries the date October 3rd. The "ultimate reality" was the kinship that bound the two men, warriors each in his way, philosophical seekers each in his way, equally relieved to leave the city behind for a plain meal in a desert oasis. And yet . . . Ben-Gurion in October had neglected to mention that within weeks—the details weren't quite settled—Israel might launch a land, air, and sea war against Nasser's Egypt, to be followed by a French attack, or possibly an Anglo-French attack by sea and air to occupy the Suez Canal and unseat Nasser. France and Britain had also omitted mention of these possibilities, elaborated even as Hammarskjöld was doing his all to help the adversaries achieve a peaceful settlement of their differences.

Illustrations

Fig. 1 Dag Hammarskjöld trekking in the Swedish far north.
(photo: Gösta Lundquist, in the collection of Nordiska Museet)

Fig. 2 Hjalmar Hammarskjöld, Dag's father.   *(photo: private collection)*

Fig. 3 Agnes Hammarskjöld with her son Dag.   *(photo: private collection)*

Fig. 4 The Hammarskjöld sons (from left to right): Bo, Dag, Åke, Sten.
(photo: Swedish National Library)

Fig. 5 Axel Hägerström,
professor of philosophy
at Uppsala University.
(photo: private collection)

Fig. 6 Archbishop Nathan Söderblom,
early mentor and family friend.
(photo: private collection)

Fig. 7 Greta Beskow in
Hammarskjöld's
photograph at his home
in Brewster, New York.
(photo:
Dag Hammarskjöld,
in the collection of the
Swedish National
Library)

Fig. 8 Dag Hammarskjöld, secretary-general elect, and Trygvie Lie, outgoing secretary-general, at Idlewild Airport, New York, April 9, 1953.

(photo: Lisa Larsen/Time & Life Images/Getty Images)

Fig. 9 The oath of office, April 10, 1953.   *(UN Photo/AK)*

Fig. 10 Andrew W. Cordier, executive assistant to the secretary-general, standing to count votes in the General Assembly, October 14, 1958.   *(UN Photo/YES)*

Fig. 11 Dag Hammarskjöld with Ralph J. Bunche, Nobel laureate, under-secretary for special political affairs, October 13, 1955.   *(UN Photo/MB)*

Fig. 12 Dag Hammarskjöld and Zhou Enlai, Beijing, January 10, 1955. Hammarskjöld's security guard, Bill Ranallo, stands between and behind them.
(UN Photo)

Fig. 13 The Room of Quiet, United Nations Headquarters. Designed in part by Dag Hammarskjöld, with a fresco by Bo Beskow.

(UN Photo)

Fig. 14 Dag Hammarskjöld and Martin Buber, Jerusalem, January 2, 1959.

(UN Photo/FS/gf)

Fig. 15 Patrice Lumumba, prime minister of the newly independent Republic of the Congo, late July 1960, at a meeting of the United Nations Security Council.
(photo: Bob Gomel/Time & Life Images/Getty Images)

Fig. 16 Dag Hammarskjöld and Patrice Lumumba at United Nations
Headquarters, July 24, 1960.   *(UN Photo)*

Fig. 17 Hammarskjöld in Katanga, August 14, 1960. *(UN Photo/HP)*

Fig. 18 Unveiling of the sculpture *Single Form* by Barbara Hepworth, in memory of Dag Hammarskjöld. United Nations Headquarters, June 11, 1964.

(UN Photo/Yutaka Nagata)

Fig. 19 Ben Shahn, *Portrait of Dag Hammarskjöld*, 1962.
(photo: Swedish National Museum)

12

Unrighteous Shooting Wars

The British Empire was, among many other things, cozy. At its height before World War I, and even in the less tranquil interwar period, there was almost always a recognizable scene no matter how distant from the British Isles: travelers could find high tea; civil servants and the military posted abroad lived in communities along familiar lines; business people and high government officials found their own kind in exclusive clubs from Rangoon and Bombay to Cairo and Nairobi; native servants were ever at hand to bring more tea, and they vanished at night. Rebellions and expeditions occurred from time to time—young Winston Churchill reported avidly on several for home newspapers—but there was a settled order with the scent of forever. The Other posed no threat. The freedom movement in India was a notable exception, but its leaders were anglicized; the Indian Other spoke English beautifully. One of them, Rabindranath Tagore, won the 1913 Nobel Prize in Literature.

For those who had lived this imperial idyll, the rapid dissolution of the empire after World War II, especially India's independence in 1947, engendered complex emotions: ineradicable nostalgia, the determination to keep and defend what could be kept and defended, anger and humiliation over losses of prestige and influence, realistic acceptance that Britain could no longer afford an empire or expect world opinion to endorse colonialism. "Direct British rule is disappearing," wrote the exemplary British general who commanded Jordan's Arab Legion. "History will record that we sailed the seas, that we conquered, that we ruled. But will she remember also that we loved . . . ?"[1] Loved or unloved, the Other emerged into daylight, acquired political power, and did everything possible—sometimes with wisdom and diplomacy, sometimes through terror and violence—to hurry Britain home. Among those Others, none was less welcome to Anthony Eden, British prime minister in 1955–57, than Gamal Abdel Nasser. In the months before Eden turned loose an army against Egypt, he is reported to have said, "What's all this nonsense about isolating Nasser or 'neutralizing' him . . . ? I want him destroyed. . . . I want him removed. . . . And I don't give a damn if there's anarchy and chaos in Egypt."[2] At much the same moment, president Dwight Eisenhower expressed a detached perspective. "Nasser embodies," he said, "the emotional demands of the people of the era for independence and for 'slapping the white man down.'"[3] The distance between their views would matter.

There were two wars in the fall of 1956. One of them—the Suez Crisis—has attracted retellings and reexaminations to this day. From its shelf in history it radiates an essential warning wrapped in a fascinating story. Many leading participants in the event later wrote about it to shed light or to lie. Like a diagram that induces optical illusions, its key incidents come in many versions. It has all the features of tragedy: in Eden a flawed protagonist with the power to enact his dream and his fall; in France, Britain, and Israel, nations aggressively conspiring; and, without any doubt, terror and pity—terror that major Western powers could be so coldly unwise, pity for all concerned, both warriors and victims. Israel gained a little, thanks to Ben-Gurion's furious obstinacy. Nasser gained a great deal; he became a hero across the Arab world and beyond. France didn't solve its problem, which wasn't Egypt at all, it was Algeria. Britain disgraced itself. And the United Nations, with crucial leadership from the United States and Canada and the support of nearly the entire General Assembly, coaxed all parties back on the rails.

The other war, the brutal Soviet suppression of a democratic revolution in Hungary that had proved itself capable of organizing a responsible government in a matter of days, was sealed off from Western influence and nearly worldwide protest. There was little to be done to aid the "freedom fighters." The United Nations had no leverage, only indignation; Hammarskjöld searched for a way in and found none. The United States was unwilling to treat the issue as a cause for war with the Soviet Union. Britain and France had for the moment shredded their standing in world affairs and supplied the Soviet Union with an incredibly awkward parallel at Suez to its violence in Hungary. The only relief that could be offered was to receive the huge number of Hungarian refugees fleeing their country—some two hundred thousand—and this was done. Two wars, then—one within reach of Western influence and the United Nations, the other beyond reach. In light of the severely limited scope of action available to Hammarskjöld where Hungary was concerned, this chapter looks only at the Suez Crisis. Bernhard Erling, in his commentary on *Markings*, may be right that Hammarskjöld was thinking of Hungary in early December 1956—and if this isn't right, it should be—when he added these few words to his journal:

The question answered itself:

"I believe that we should die with decency so that at least decency will survive."[4]

Had he been speaking with a Hungarian refugee?

Hammarskjöld's negotiations in the Middle East in the spring of 1956 will seem in retrospect like a small light shared, welcomed, and doused. And yet there was a gain: he now knew the key figures in the region quite well, and they trusted him. He in turn had come to trust General Burns.

The Suez Canal has not been news in a long time. For most of us it is simply *there*, unremarkably providing a link between the Eastern Mediterranean and the Red Sea that spares shipping the long voyage around Africa's Cape of Good Hope. In 2010, nearly nineteen thousand passages were registered. The canal was one of the wonders of nineteenth-century entrepreneurship and engineering, a feat worthy of Jules Verne's imagination and admired by his savant hero, Captain Nemo. Under the direction of a former French consul to Egypt, Ferdinand de Lesseps, with financing initially from French private interests and Egypt, construction began in 1858 and the canal opened to maritime traffic in 1869. Today somewhat longer and deeper, it was initially 102 miles long and 26 feet deep, wide enough for one-way traffic with berthing areas for traffic in the other direction. Smooth water without locks from one end to the other, it was Europe's lifeline: much of the oil from the Middle East traveled through it. It was Britain's highway to and from its Asian empire. Any threat to it was a large threat. Any imagined threat was a large threat.

Construction of the canal became a permanent part of the Egyptian anti-imperialist narrative owing to De Lesseps's use of forced labor and the deaths of a vast number of Egyptian canal workers: Nasser put the number at 120,000 in a historic speech.[5] In 1875 the British government under Benjamin Disraeli purchased the Egyptian interest in the canal from a cash-hungry regime and amassed a 44 percent minority share, the rest remaining in French hands. Soon after, in 1882, Disraeli's successor, William Gladstone, intervened in an Egyptian political controversy by dispatching an army of occupation that seized control of the canal and, settling into permanence, ensured Britain's domination of Egyptian politics until the mid-twentieth century. Overall management of the canal was legally defined in 1888 by the Convention of Constantinople, championed particularly by France as a curb to British ambition and signed by numerous maritime powers in order to internationalize insofar as possible the canal's status and operations. In that period Egypt was doubly distanced from sovereignty by an imposed, longstanding Ottoman monarchy functioning as a puppet government under British control. Even this brief history of the Suez Canal is enough to reveal sufferings, humiliations, and exclusions that could not but weigh on the first independent political leader in modern Egyptian history.

After his return from the Middle East, Hammarskjöld remained in touch with the region's leaders and their UN delegations on what he described as nearly a daily basis. For several months he expressed moderate optimism. "This is an operation in which . . . if you have made progress in the initial stage and managed to maintain it, you should be quite satisfied. My dream is, so to speak, to see the legal cease-fire converted into a state of mind. I firmly hope that that process is going on. . . ."[6] He dismissed fears that something would just have to go wrong. "The favorite game of this age," he remarked in late June, is "to fear big ghosts and all sorts of risks, and for that reason [shy] away from what we should do. . . . I do not believe that world peace is threatened. . . . That does not mean, of course, that we may not have a mess."[7] A few weeks later, he admitted that he had "no ready-made plan for solving anything in the region. I do not think that anybody, in fact, has one. That does not mean that I do not have certain ideas about the direction in which things should go. I feel, however, that such ideas should first of all be aired and tried out with the governments in the region."[8] On a brief mid-July trip to Israel, Egypt, and Jordan, he must have done just that but described the trip, attractively, as "a check-up visit, without any agenda, without any specific questions to negotiate, in order so to say to deepen the groove in which we are playing this melody."[9]

The melody would change. In the months and year preceding, Hammarskjöld had of course been aware that forces within and affecting the region could explode at any time on a scale far beyond border violence. In his own phrase, there prevailed "a state of utmost insecurity." Eden, although sympathetic to Arab interests through much of his career, had turned against Nasser, whom he regarded as working to eliminate British influence not only in Egypt but across the Middle East. Britain and France had long held sway. It was no longer so. The decisive event for Eden was not large but had large symbolism: on March 1st, 1956, young King Hussein of Jordan summarily dismissed a British general known as Glubb Pasha, who had loyally and very ably served the pro-British regime since 1939 as head of its armed forces, the respected Arab Legion. Glubb Pasha (1897–1986) with his improbable name—he was Lieutenant-General John Bagot Glubb—was among the surviving relics of the empire that was. Although it has long since been clear that Hussein dismissed the general in order to declare his own authority and better align with the region's Arab nationalism, Glubb himself thought their age difference was the main factor, and Eden was convinced that Nasser's growing influence in Jordan was the cause.[10]

Eden was not well, though few were aware of his chronic medical problems. Botched surgery in 1953 had left him subject to periodic, painful infection and high fever, and some of the medicines he took had greater psychological side effects than were recognized at the time. We can come surprisingly close to Eden in the early months of the Suez Crisis thanks to a remarkable eyewitness, Anthony Nutting, who served Eden loyally at the time from his senior post in the Foreign Office, although he was increasingly appalled by the prime minister's impulsive judgment and furious temper, wholly out of character. He resigned when Eden made the inalterable decision to lead his country into what Nutting later described as "a sordid conspiracy . . . morally wrong and politically insane."[11]

There were other factors, grave ones. Like Britain, France was losing empire. In March 1956, both Tunisia and Morocco shed their French colonial status and acquired independence after considerable turmoil and violence. France drew the line at Algeria, so important to its identity that Algeria had been designated an integral part of the nation rather than an overseas colony. The ultimately successful Algerian struggle for independence, launched in November 1954 and savage on both sides, was supported from afar by Nasser's strident Radio Cairo. The French assumed that Egypt was providing the Algerian rebels not only moral support but also arms, military training, and funds. It was apparently not so on a major scale, but the assumption was enough to make Nasser as much the enemy of France as he was the enemy of Britain. For the French, he became "the dictator of the Nile."[12] For Eden, he was another Mussolini, even another Hitler who must not be appeased.

Egypt's far from secret contract in late 1955 to purchase massive quantities of arms from Czechoslovakia—an agreement approved by the Soviet Union and initially brokered by Zhou Enlai, with whom Nasser had a good understanding—signaled a new challenge to Israel's security.

Needing arms and a reliable great-power ally, Israel found both in France, whose prime minister, Guy Mollet, and minister of foreign affairs, Christian Pineau, were well aware of Israel's potential to help cut Nasser down to size. Nasser's arms purchase prompted Israel to consider a preemptive war to eliminate certain problems—Egypt's blockade of Israeli shipping through the Gulf of Aqaba, the threat of *fedayeen* border raids—before the Egyptian military had fully trained in the use of its new weapons, which were to include bombers capable of reaching Israeli cities.

As if these tensions weren't enough, there were others just as unsettling. Soon after taking power in 1952, Nasser and his fellow officers set their sights on constructing a dam on the Nile to control seasonal flooding and open up vast new lands to irrigation and agriculture. "Tomorrow," he promised, "the gigantic High Dam, more magnificent and seventeen times greater than the Pyramids, will provide a higher standard of living for all Egyptians."[13] Relations with the United States were good in 1954 when Nasser consolidated his power. Though with Britain there were sharp difficulties, there was also a search on both sides toward a sensible future relation. Despite appearances to the contrary, Nasser had no wish to join a bloc, either Soviet or Western; he preferred to do business with all from a position of nonaligned independence. To finance the dam, he turned first to the United States, the World Bank, and Britain, and with some stops and starts the financing advanced. The Eisenhower Administration calculated that much good could come from generosity, not only toward Egypt but in the region as a whole. However, the Czech arms purchase, implying that Nasser might after all side with the Soviet bloc, had a cooling effect, as did Egypt's recognition in May 1956 of the People's Republic of China. (US recognition would come only many political generations later, in 1979.) On July 19th, the United States abruptly informed Egypt on a rather flimsy pretext that it would be unable to participate in financing the Aswan High Dam, and the other sources of funding promptly withdrew. When Nasser first heard of the United States' withdrawal, he said, "It is an attack on the regime and an invitation to the people of Egypt to bring it down."[14] Some years later, in 1960, in an otherwise cordial meeting with Eisenhower at the UN General Assembly, he made clear that the withdrawal of funding and public questioning of Egypt's economic solvency had been an affront to his nation's dignity.[15] "Dignity" had been his watchword over the years; it was among the sustaining ideals of postcolonial leadership.

The Aswan High Dam was eventually funded by the Soviet Union in 1958 and completed in 1970. Designed by a consortium of Soviet and Egyptian engineers, it was built by a vast number of Egyptian workers using Soviet machinery. Upstream from the dam is an enormous reservoir, Lake Nasser. Over the years, the results have been good (flood control, irrigation, hydroelectric power) and not good at all (reduced downstream soil fertility, making industrial fertilizers necessary; incursion of the saline waters of the Mediterranean).

The slow pace of the funding negotiations had raised doubts in Nasser's mind. When the bad news reached him, there was already the germ of an alternative plan in place.[16] A week later, on July 26th, he delivered a long speech to a crowd in Alexandria. It radically redefined the situation.

> I tell you today, dear citizens, that in building the High Dam we will build a fortress of honor and glory, and we demolish humiliation. We declare that all Egypt is one front, united, one inseparable national entity. All Egypt will struggle to the last drop of our blood to build the country. . . . We will build a strong Egypt, and that is why today I have signed the government's declaration on the nationalization of the Canal Company. . . . We will go forward to destroy once and for all the vestiges of occupation and exploitation. After one hundred years, each of us has recovered our rights, and today we build by demolishing a state that existed within our state; the Suez Canal [is now] for Egypt, not for exploitation. We will watch over the rights of all. The nationalization of the Suez Canal is an accomplished fact. . . . Now it is Egyptians like you who will direct the Canal Company . . . , who will guide navigation in the canal—which is Egyptian territory.[17]

It was a completely unexpected move and, at least in the analysis of legal scholars advising the Eisenhower administration, a legitimate move. Nasser clarified later that shareholders of the company would be compensated fully and fairly and that Egypt would operate the canal in the proper manner, serving the shipping of all nations equally—with the exception of Israel, whose shipping had long been refused on the grounds that Egypt remained in a state of war with Israel. (Hammarskjöld would later negotiate this issue.) Nasser calculated that the nationalized canal would generate funds to build the Aswan High Dam and, as his speech stridently stated, the buyout of foreign interests would remove the last vestige of the imperialist past.

Nasser had now given Eden the legitimizing pretext for war that had so far been missing: the Canal Company must be returned to international ownership and management; Nasser must be removed from power because, no matter what he said, his word could not be trusted. He had placed his unreliable hand on what Eden described as "the windpipe" of Great Britain and Western Europe. The French had the same attitude. And Eisenhower did not. From the very first, as messages began crisscrossing the English Channel and the Atlantic, the war party in England and France encountered caution in Washington. The insistence of Eisenhower and his secretary of state, John Foster Dulles, on persuading Egypt to place a restructured international authority over the canal led to a round of high-level meetings through the summer among Suez Canal users. The United States' strategy was essentially to stall for time while tempers cooled in Europe and Nasser could be persuaded to accept arrangements that respected Egyptian sovereignty while taking into account the concerns of other nations. The United Nations as such was not a participant, although very senior diplomats and government officials, long familiar at the UN, represented their countries' interests at the summer talks. While Hammarskjöld was no doubt well informed, publicly he restricted his scope to the assignment he was still carrying: to safeguard and extend calm on all Israeli-Arab borders. A week after the canal was nationalized, he remarked at a press conference that "my advice has not been considered that interesting on this question [of the Suez Canal]. I have been informed about certain aspects by the Permanent Representative of Egypt. That is all."[18] He could not have been more low-key.

Hammarskjöld's birthday, aet. 51, fell just three days after Nasser's July 26th nationalization speech. A dated entry in *Markings* for his birthday and the two weeks following returns to a notion that had been developing in his mind for some time: the medical or therapeutic role of the secretary-general. At a press conference in March, he had likened the activities of the UN in the Middle East to those of a nurse: "It is very much like the constant attendance of a good nurse, which may be just as important as the operation itself. Surgeons' operations are news, the work of nurses is not."[19] Now, on his birthday or soon after, when the pace of events had dramatically quickened, he had graduated from nursing to medical intervention—and a good deal more. Citing one of his earliest literary heroes, the seventeenth-century physician and master of prose Sir Thomas Browne, he recorded that it is not enough to cure the body when the soul—the "state of mind," as we have heard Hammarskjöld put it—is distressed.

"I cannot go to cure the body of my patient, but I forget my profession, and call unto God for his soul."

"We carry with us the wonders we seek without us."

Sayings resonant with significance—to one who is seeking the Kingdom of God, they contain the truth about *all* work.[20]

The first brief passage from Dr. Browne's *Religio Medici* tells us something we might otherwise overlook: Hammarskjöld brought to Middle Eastern negotiations a dual attitude. Outwardly he was a diplomat at work, inwardly that and more. Whatever it means to forget one's profession and call unto God for a soul, his internal attitude was something like that, unrevealed but no doubt felt. As we'll see, the medical metaphor lingered: a month later he assigned himself the role of midwife. And after all was done and peace reestablished, he commented, "While all the wounds remain, they are no longer infected."[21]

Nasser rejected the proposed solutions from the round of summer meetings and insisted that Egypt could not only manage the canal in a perfectly satisfactory manner but was already doing so. As Eisenhower noticed, the statistics bore him out; canal traffic had actually increased since nationalization. Meanwhile British and French military forces were massing within reach of Egypt; this was evident. Entirely unevident, secret meetings between the French and Israelis would soon assemble a war strategy that included covert deliveries of advanced aircraft and other armaments to Israel. In parallel, the French and British were holding secret talks. The completed plan had not yet taken shape. The Tripartite Declaration of 1950, by which the United States, Great Britain, and France had bound themselves to act together against any aggressor in the Middle East and to maintain a balance of arms between the Arab states and Israel, had become a dead letter—except for the Americans. Eisenhower often referred to it; to his mind, adherence was a matter of honor and common sense. He and his administration had no knowledge of the war planning, although US spy planes at high altitude kept track of the massing of military forces, the British around the islands of Cyprus and Malta, the French at Algiers. Eisenhower was also aware that advanced French aircraft on Israeli airfields were, as he put it, "multiplying like rabbits."

In mid-September Hammarskjöld shared with Bo Beskow a vivid overview:

You are forced to learn patience not only with Nasser and Ben-Gurion but also with Pineau, Eden and, and— It is on long and winding roads that we have to walk all the way up to the visible (yet not very appealing) destination.

We have now come very close to the breaking-point of the Asian renaissance. And Europe seems in this situation to be lacking both policy and ability to unite around a policy. The only dividend to "the white man" in this bankruptcy seems to be going to Moscow, which definitely has no reason for complaint.

The UN's role in the latest development is much more important than readers of newspapers could imagine: it is at present for natural reasons altogether behind curtains. However, I sometimes feel like a policeman at the window-sill trying to convince a would-be suicide not to jump, an honorable but rather "frustrating" task: if he jumps, so much the worse—if he doesn't jump, who then could tell if the attempt at persuasion had meant something or he would have reconsidered in any case?[22]

It is now early October. Hammarskjöld has written into the introduction to his annual report, released on October 4th, a wide perspective on nationalism that readers could easily decode as his view of the Suez situation.

Nationalism can be a constructive element, raising the dignity and stature of people and mobilizing their best moral resources. But, in a period of severe emotional strains, it may also find expressions which are in fact hostile to the steady growth of the very national life it aims to serve. The United Nations may help in avoiding such a self-defeating development.

Within the community of nations, so great a change in the political relationships must arouse deep emotions on all sides. Positions long vital to great nations are involved. And on the other side the intensity of aspirations for equal status creates pressures for extreme action. I am convinced that in this situation the United Nations could be a source of greater assistance to governments than it has so far been. . . . We should, I believe, seek a development which would give greater emphasis to the United Nations as an instrument for negotiation of settlements, as distinct from the mere debate of issues.[23]

As it happens, the issue of Suez reached the Security Council on the following day, October 5th, at the request of Britain and France. The United States didn't trust their motives: if and when it foundered, the Council debate might serve by unstated design to reinforce the war party's pretext for taking the Suez Canal Zone by force. But for better or worse, the UN now had its opportunity. Meanwhile, secret war planning continued in London, Paris, and Tel Aviv.

After a few days of discussion the Council asked senior officials of Britain, France, and Egypt to meet privately with Hammarskjöld to develop, if possible, a proposal for review. There were six such meetings, October 9th through 12th, attended by Fawzi for Egypt, the French foreign minister Christian Pineau, and Eden's foreign secretary, Selwyn Lloyd. While Pineau is said to have gone into the meetings with the adamant though undisclosed attitude that only war could solve the problem, Lloyd may have been more open to a negotiated settlement, and Fawzi—whom Hammarskjöld admired and trusted—brought a surprisingly conciliatory attitude. He made clear that Egypt was willing not to cede sovereignty and ownership but to make certain compromises that would decisively reassure the Western Europeans. There emerged from the meetings Six Principles, worded with simplicity and directness in a Security Council resolution unanimously adopted on October 13th.[24] The principles included "free and open transit through the Canal without discrimination, overt or covert"; respect for the sovereignty of Egypt; insulation of Canal operations from the politics of any country; tolls and charges to be decided by agreement between Egypt and canal users; allocation of a fair proportion of dues to development; and, finally, dispute resolution through arbitration.

There was a sense of relief in some quarters—and clenching toward war in others. To Beskow on October 20th Hammarskjöld wrote a marvelous letter, in part jubilant, in part gravely concerned:

> Suez was my third child. The parents arrived in a state of great bewilderment and some fury. God knows how this will end—but the brat cries less now and perhaps, with good assistance, I can teach it to walk. . . .
>
> The other day I gave Dr. Fawzi the following description of the situation:
>
> "Tragicomedy in three acts:
>
> Act 1. The Secretary-General is chaperone (a stage passed by now).
>
> Act 2. The S-G has shown some talent to appear on the stage as an (alas, so moral) procuress. (This scene is still to be written.)
>
> Act 3. The S-G is allowed—with good luck—to try his talents as a midwife." . . .

Palestine is a complete mess. In the shade of Suez and the American [presidential] election the Israelis have seen the chance to arrange
things in their favor—as they believe. But I am afraid they will have to
pay one day. With the sympathy I have for them *on one level*, it hurts me
to see them, on another level, behave in a way that I have to condemn
officially. Not because of what this means in the way of trouble for me,
but because of the split in Israel that it shows and which may once more
cause them unhappiness.[25]

Hammarskjöld's lighthearted account of the Suez negotiations was be-
lied by events of which he could have no knowledge at the time. On
October 15th, Selwyn Lloyd was unexpectedly called back to London
by Eden, where he joined secret talks in London and Paris with their
French counterparts and French military leaders. At this point the draft
plan of action came into focus; it was to build on the "Israeli pretext."
On October 21st, a French military aircraft ferried Ben-Gurion with
his top military associates—among them the famed Moshe Dayan—to
a meeting with the French outside of Paris. Ben-Gurion, whose unruly
white hair made him as unmistakable as Albert Einstein, was somehow
persuaded when his party landed in France to wear a hat as a disguise.
Soon restored to fighting form, he was not initially taken with the role
assigned to Israel. Its army was to launch a campaign against Egypt in
the Sinai and press on toward the Suez Canal while meeting its own
objectives along the way, primarily occupying the Gaza Strip and gaining control of enough territory in the Gulf of Aqaba to overturn Egypt's
blockade of Israeli shipping (the gulf provides an outlet to the Red Sea).
The Egyptian armed forces would naturally answer the Israeli aggression, and the war would be on. However, *dei ex occidente*, the British and
French would then issue an ultimatum demanding that the belligerents
cease fire and retreat to lines ten miles east and west of the Suez Canal
and that Egypt permit a temporary occupation of the Canal Zone by
British and French forces. Were either combatant to refuse—the Egyptians could be relied on to refuse, the Israelis would cooperate—a Franco-British force would invade, separate the combatants, and seize the
Canal Zone to protect and operate it. All of which would demonstrate
that Nasser was an ineffective leader, who would then be cashiered by
his own people. That was the idea.

Ben-Gurion questioned the need for Israel to appear to be the primary aggressor. As well, who was to say that the Soviet Union wouldn't

defend Egypt against a Franco-British attack—from the air, or by means of "volunteers" on the model of Chinese forces dispatched to the Korean War a few years earlier. (From the first, as Eisenhower weighed Eden's attitudes, he had worried about this possibility. World War III—ignited by Eden's imperial longing and Mollet's awkward problem in Algeria?) And then, Israel needed an ironclad guarantee that its allies' air forces would eliminate the Egyptian air force before the new bombers could harm Israeli cities. Ben-Gurion also insisted on the participation of British arms, a matter left open to that point.

Selwyn Lloyd soon appeared at the conference. Lloyd admitted to the company that the talks in Hammarskjöld's office just days earlier, and the Security Council's acceptance of the Six Principles as a basis for negotiation, promised a sensible solution to the Suez issue. But for Britain, as for France, a further goal remained: regime change. Nasser must go, invasion was the means. As the meeting wore on, there was considerable difficulty, especially between Lloyd and Ben-Gurion, both of whom could remember earlier, hard days between Britain and the nascent State of Israel. However, all were able to agree to a strategy put forward by Moshe Dayan involving an initial Israeli parachute drop near the canal and troop movements into the Sinai, followed by the Franco-British ultimatum, efficient destruction from the air of the Egyptian air force on the ground, and invasion by air and sea. Ben-Gurion wrote in his diary: "I have weighed up the situation and if effective air measures are taken to protect us during the first day or two until the French and British bomb the Egyptian airfields, I think the operation essential. This is a unique opportunity [in that] two powers . . . will try to eliminate Nasser and we will not face him alone as he grows stronger."[26]

It was now October 24th. The Israeli incursion was to occur on the 29th, followed a day later by the Franco-British appeals to the Israeli and Egyptian governments. The Franco-British assault would begin on the 31st, and a short war was scheduled. As it happens, October 24th is UN Day, the anniversary of the entry into force in 1945 of the UN Charter. It's a gala day, a party. Hammarskjöld again delighted in bringing the best of music to New York headquarters and by radio worldwide. This year, prefacing a performance of the magnificent choral movement of Beethoven's Ninth Symphony, he offered a brief commentary: "The faith to which Beethoven wished to give expression in his Ninth Symphony . . . was the dream of a poet. To translate this dream into action, and thus to give mankind the security it can achieve only through cooperation and the strength it can win only through fusion, is the task of realists."[27] In a further irony, earlier in the day Hammarskjöld had written a closely reasoned, tranquil letter to the Egyptian foreign minister, Dr. Fawzi, to share with him his understanding of the practical implications of the Six Principles established by the private talks in his office. The most telling lines were these: "In my understanding, . . . the *principle* of organized cooperation between an Egyptian authority and the users [should not] give rise to any differences of views, while, on the other hand, it obviously represents a field where the arrangements to be made call for careful exploration. . . . The cooperation requires . . . an organ on the Egyptian side (the authority in charge of the operation of the Canal), and a representation of the users, recognized by the Canal authority (and the Egyptian government) and entitled to speak for the users."[28] Fawzi replied when the war was already under way, on November 2nd, saying that he agreed with nearly every point in Hammarskjöld's letter. Their exchange of letters, a seemingly inaudible, ill-timed counterpoint to the violence now focused on Egypt, would in the end have staying power. What they wrote was the basis for what would be, after the war.

The Israeli attack was brilliantly successful. Within a short time Israeli troops were twenty miles from the canal and gaining on their other war objectives. Eisenhower was furious: "Foster," he said to his secretary of state, "you tell 'em, God-damn-it, that we're going to apply sanctions, we're going to the United Nations, we're going to do everything [to] stop this thing."[29] The US ambassador to the United Nations, Henry Cabot Lodge Jr., requested a meeting of the Security Council on the morning of October 30th, which as it met received news of the Franco-British ultimatum to Israel and Egypt. Two resolutions calling for an immediate cease-fire and noninterference by outside powers were vetoed by Britain and France—their first use of the veto since the founding of the UN. At that point the intended pattern of events became reasonably evident; it had been naïve to think that the "Israeli pretext" would take anyone in. The following day, Hammarskjöld opened the Security Council session by stating that had a meeting not already been called by the United States, he himself would have done so. In measured but unrelenting language he made clear where he stood and what stars he guided by, and obliquely offered to resign if his stance was unacceptable. That cannot have been easy.

The principles of the Charter are, by far, greater than the Organization in which they are embodied, and the aims which they are to safeguard are holier than the policies of any single nation or people. As a servant of the Organization, the Secretary-General has the duty to maintain his usefulness by avoiding public stands on conflicts between Member Nations unless and until such an action might help to resolve the conflict. However, the discretion and impartiality thus imposed on the Secretary-General by the character of his immediate task may not degenerate into a policy of expediency. He must also be a servant of the principles of the Charter, and its aims must ultimately determine what for him is right and wrong. For that he must stand. A Secretary-General cannot serve on any other assumption than that—within the necessary limits of human frailty and honest differences of opinion—all Member Nations honor their pledge to observe all articles of the Charter. . . . The bearing of what I have just said must be obvious to all without any elaboration from my side. Were the Members to consider that another view of the duties of the Secretary-General than the one here stated would better serve the interests of the Organization, it is their obvious right to act accordingly.[30]

The Council members heard Hammarskjöld's implicit offer to resign and took much time, despite the urgency of the matter before them, to express their confidence in him—the British and French no less firmly than all the others. A day later he described the developing Suez Crisis as "two permanent Council members engaged in an unrighteous shooting war against another member state." Urquhart said of this moment, "Hammarskjöld was disgusted. He just thought that European Powers didn't behave like that, and I think it was a very big disillusionment for him."[31] At some point during the Council sessions, Hammarskjöld passed a note to Lodge: "This is one of the darkest days in postwar times. Thank God you have played the way you have. This will win you many friends."[32]

With the Security Council paralyzed by French and British intransigence, a simple majority vote in the Council transferred the issue to an emergency session of the General Assembly, which began marathon meetings on November 1st; they lasted well into early morning hours. On the previous day, the Franco-British aerial bombardment of Egyptian military airfields had begun. The General Assembly met as that was proceeding. Leaflets dropped over Cairo warning the civilian population to keep its distance from military targets also called on the Egyptians to rid themselves of Nasser. This wasn't just about Suez.

If Britain and France had been relying on the United States to support or tolerate their action—there is evidence this was so—then they
were disappointed. The United States and Canada led the response at
the UN and, through independent measures that would have a decisive
impact on the course of events, the United States set out to knock at
British vulnerabilities to which Eden and his cabinet hadn't given due
thought. Eisenhower was angry. He and his nation had been "double-
crossed," as he put it, by their closest allies.[33] They had ignored good
counsel through the summer and fall and hidden their war plan. "We
cannot and will not condone armed aggression," Eisenhower said on November 1st, "no matter who the attacker, and no matter who the victim.
We cannot—in the world any more than in our own nation—subscribe
to one law for the weak, another law for the strong; one law for those
opposing us, another for those allied with us. There can be only one law
or there will be no peace."[34] And yet there was as much sorrow as anger
in the American attitude. Eisenhower and Dulles would now push hard
to stop the war—and push to provide Britain and France with a face-
saving exit from their folly. These were friends in the cold world of the
Cold War, though at the moment the meaning of that friendship was in
doubt. Israel was also in the dock, but at this point a lesser concern than
its Great Power allies.

In the small hours of November 2nd, the General Assembly adopted
a resolution by an unprecedented majority of 64 to 5, with 6 abstentions,
which essentially restated the defeated Security Council resolution calling for cease-fire, withdrawal, restoration of Suez Canal traffic, and the
absence of interference by other nations. (There is no right of veto in
the General Assembly.) As well, it called on the secretary-general to
observe, report, and take further actions as appropriate. That morning
Hammarskjöld issued as a press release words a good deal larger than
anyone could have anticipated. He may have read the release to the
press corps; it has that feel. The initial topic was ideas brought by the
General Assembly for "a fresh, positive approach to the Middle East."
But his tone changed within a sentence or two. Abruptly he offered a
credo, an "I believe" impelled by just anger. He had scarcely ever spoken
in public with such intensity of feeling, apart from his exchange with
Peter Freuchen about the sorrows and joys of ordinary people. His words
were white-hot. There was no wit now, no diplomatic finesse, no joy in
grasping the pattern of events and nudging them forward. He must have

felt the time had come to offer the media a framework of conviction for their reporting. And to avoid what he once called "death by moral strangulation," he chose to speak freely.

> In considering those proposals, we must have a clear view of the conditions under which they may prove useful. I do not believe that propaganda is the way to friendship. I do not believe that it is by invoking the letter while forgetting the spirit of the law that you build a future of peace. I do not believe that acts of violence, whatever the reason, lead to cooperation. I do not believe that victories, bought at the price of violations of treaty obligations, create confidence among neighbors. But I do believe that respect for decisions of the United Nations earns those concerned the support from the world community which every nation needs.[35]

To Eden's dismay if not Mollet's, support from the world community with very few exceptions was not to be had. In his book published twenty years later, *1956, Suez*, Mollet's foreign minister, Christian Pineau, refers time and again to French sangfroid throughout the crisis and notes with a pang of regret that Eden lacked a robust supply. While the French "seemed prepared to ride out world opinion," in Lester Pearson's view—we'll soon catch up with this key figure—"in London there was surprise and shock at the violence of the reaction against what they had done."[36]

The assault on Egypt continued as if it had its own mind. The Anglo-French armada of warships and troops dispatched from Cyprus was at sea on November 3rd. On the 4th, both the Israeli and Egyptian governments accepted a cease-fire, but the armada continued churning forward as if that had not occurred. Anglo-French parachute drops at the northernmost terminus of the canal began early on the 5th, with a shoreline bombardment and troop landings on the 6th. The plan was to occupy key points along the entire length of the canal as far as the city of Suez, the southern terminus and gateway to the Red Sea.

Despite this glorious World War II–like activity—amphibious landings, paratroops raining down, bombing sorties, desert warfare—the war plan had failed to foresee two countermeasures efficiently taken by Egypt and its Syrian ally. As soon as they had grasped the scope of the assault against them, the Egyptians sunk "blockships"—old vessels loaded mostly with cement—at key points in the Suez Canal. The British and French had come to safeguard the canal. It was now an impassable marine graveyard.

And they had come to safeguard the oil supply—but Syrian army engineers sabotaged the pumping stations of a British pipeline carrying oil from Iraq to port in Lebanon, and Egypt's allies elsewhere declared an oil embargo. Britain would soon be starved for oil unless the United States proved willing to step in with its own resources and shipping. "Those who began this operation," Eisenhower said to a US petroleum expert, "should be left to work out their own oil problem—to boil . . . in their own oil."[37] He didn't sustain that vehemence in the longer run, but he was well aware that the United States had powerful leverage apart from the UN, and he used it.

A second issue had been overlooked or underestimated by Eden and his advisers: the stability of the British pound. As soon as war broke out, there had been a run on the currency. British reserves, already in poor shape, were rapidly depleting—and the United States used its influence to ensure that the process continued unchecked. Britain's chancellor of the exchequer, Harold Macmillan, may have mistakenly exaggerated the problem when he raised it with Eden, but Eden accepted his doomsday view. Though the French were reasonably satisfied with the course of events since October 29th, the British were abruptly faced with discouraging adversities. The Israelis had fulfilled their part of the bargain, and they had their prizes—control of the Gulf of Aqaba and the Gaza Strip. They would be slow to part with them.

Every hour eye to eye

We last saw Hammarskjöld on the morning of November 2nd, when he insisted that the press corps look past the superficial excitement of gunboat diplomacy to understand that the assault on Egypt violated the UN Charter and common sense. He was now living nearly without sleep and would do so for days to come. This capacity in times of crisis became part of his legend in his lifetime. Even Eisenhower, who knew more than a little about duty, was impressed: "The man's abilities have not only been proven, but a physical stamina that is almost remarkable, almost unique in the world, has also been demonstrated by a man who night after night has gone with one or two hours' sleep, working all day and, I must say, working intelligently and devotedly."[38] This from a press conference. Hammarskjöld caught wind of the remark and sent the president a demurral that no one could seriously believe. "I assure you," he wrote, "that there is nothing particularly unusual about the energy that I have devoted to my task, except that I have had a deep sense of the great importance of timing, lest the catastrophe, already serious, should degenerate into something even worse."[39]

Brian Urquhart provides a vivid participant's description of the UN in times of crisis. "The days and nights are filled with endless contacts, meetings, maneuvers, arrangements, drafting of cables, speeches, telephone calls, interviews with ambassadors, dealings with the press and making formal reports to the Security Council or the General Assembly. In all this hubbub the Secretary-General must keep a clear head and a balanced picture of the situation. He must preserve an imaginative, constructive, and forward-looking approach to a constantly shifting series of problems and a kaleidoscopic panorama of changing national policies. Hammarskjöld, by his capacity for concentration and thinking ahead, was a master at this game."[40]

I don't know how Hammarskjöld found just the lines he needed in the Book of Psalms, but a short series of entries dated to these very days, November 1st through 7th, begins with stunning words from Psalms 4 and 37. When did he have time to open Psalms, and open his journal? Reading the first entry now, one can't help but pass as if cinematically from the boisterous visible scene described by Urquhart to the invisible "room of quiet" somewhere in him. He used no quotation marks, as if nothing distanced these words from his person.

> I will lay me down in peace, and take my rest: for it is thou, Lord, only, that makest me dwell in safety.
> Hold thee still in the Lord . . . fret not thyself, else shalt thou be moved to evil.[41]

There is magic here, a return to ancient attitudes. This was often Hammarskjöld's way. The psalmist calls to him, and through the psalmist he calls to himself, to remember the faith and quietness of mind with which he wished to approach all difficulties, including the one now before him. Something of this lay behind his excellence in times of crisis. Strange that in a week when he was taking little rest in the ordinary sense and dealing "every hour, eye to eye" with people in crisis he should write out these beautiful lines about rest and stillness and the danger of a fretful mind. That he did so was richly in character.

There is a second entry just following that we should consider. Taking the form of a compressed poem, it conveys the values and awarenesses by which he wished to be guided. We are still in the room of quiet. The passages from Psalms concern an attitude privately embraced; this concerns a quality of mind and heart that extends outward from that attitude to engage with people and events.

> Every hour
> Eye to eye
> With this love
> Which sees all
> But looks on
> With patience;
> Which is justice,
>   but does not condemn
> If our glance
> Mirrors its ownIn humility.[42]

It is one of Hammarskjöld's more difficult poems. Its compression mirrors the tensions of this moment in his life and the life of the UN community. But as so often he is pointing toward a "third party" to the transactions we humans engage in—an all-seeing, patient, undeceivable love that insists on intimacy ("every hour / eye to eye") and offers understanding.

Some months later, at a time when he was rather fed up with Ben-Gurion but reaching out to him, Hammarskjold restated this theme in terms of two levels of duty. There is again the immediate concern and something more, of greater authority. "I fear that in our never-abandoned efforts," he wrote,

> to get nearer to the target we have in common—in your case peace for Israel, in my case perhaps just simply peace—we may have reached a dead point. . . . Such a situation requires some boldness. Indeed, it seems to me to be a situation where we must individually try to transcend our immediate duty in order to fulfill the higher duty of creative action. You know that my personal confidence in your ability in this respect has never flagged.[43]

In the unfolding of the Suez Crisis, in the very early days of November 1956, the duty of creative action lay just ahead.

We saved you from success

Lester B. Pearson (1897–1972) is the person for whom Toronto Pearson International Airport is named. He was a gifted one. His three-volume memoirs reflect a remarkable, bluff character—clear headed, realistic, forward looking, optimistic without dreaminess.[44] He was a North American, the kind of person the continent can breed when the soil is just right. Hammarskjöld liked and trusted him. As president of the General Assembly when Hammarskjöld became secretary-general, he had been among the first to welcome him. The ease with which the two men conferred and uncovered a course of action in the early days of the Suez Crisis reflected the mutual respect they had gained for one another in the intervening years. At the time, "Mike" Pearson—everyone called him that—was Canadian secretary of state for external affairs (or foreign minister) and chief of delegation at the UN. In the mid-1960s he would go on to serve his country as a notable, outspoken prime minister.

November 2nd was a day of transitions. The General Assembly in near unanimity called for a cease-fire, Hammarskjöld gave the media a moving lesson in geopolitical morality, and Mike Pearson proposed in the General Assembly a promising new idea. Pearson writes: "We had learned in advance of Eden's intention to state in the British House of Commons that 'police action there must be to separate the belligerents. . . . If the UN were then willing to take over the physical task of maintaining peace, no one would be better pleased than we.' It was not much, but it was something."[45] On the basis of that something, and after hallway conversations with members of other delegations to measure likely support, Pearson floated the idea of creating a United Nations Emergency Force "to move in and police the cease-fire" as a prelude to achieving a political settlement.[46]

Hammarskjöld was initially skeptical. Pearson had vivid memories of the November 3rd session of the General Assembly, which lasted half the night: "Hammarskjöld still seemed pessimistic and worried. I can still picture my talking to the Secretary-General. He did not think that we could get this going quickly enough to prevent the British and French from being condemned as aggressors. When he came to see me again at my desk in the Assembly two or three hours later, he said he had changed his mind. He now felt this was our only hope and thought there was a good chance of it succeeding."[47] And he set to work with Pearson and a small circle of senior diplomats to flesh it out, assisted by Bunche and Cordier. After a searching debate in that November 3rd session, the Assembly passed two cease-fire resolutions, one of which called on the secretary-general "to submit . . . within forty-eight hours a plan for the setting up, with the consent of the nations concerned, of an emergency international United Nations force to secure and supervise the cessation of hostilities."[48] The four nations at war were among nineteen that abstained in the vote, but not one member nation opposed.

Ideas were explored and specified by Hammarskjöld and his advisory team, followed by debate and vote in the General Assembly. The first result of this process was to call on E. L. M. Burns, the Canadian general responsible for the UN Truce Supervision Organization, whom Hammarskjöld held in high regard, to take command of the nascent UN Emergency Force (UNEF) and recruit officers among his current staff and farther afield. Meanwhile Hammarskjöld with his advisors worked toward their forty-eight-hour deadline of setting out a plan for UNEF. There was no difficulty at all in recruiting military units from member nations; on the contrary, some diplomats were offended that troops from their countries were left out. Unmistakably, and in full sight of the global public, the UN General Assembly was now earning its keep—for the moment it was no longer a "static conference machinery" (the phrase is Hammarskjöld's) but a dynamic, energized company of peacemakers. There were, of course, dissonant voices and episodes: the Soviet Union and China threatened to send "volunteers" to fight alongside Egypt (but didn't); the Soviet Union proposed a joint campaign with the United States to shut down the war (Eisenhower, appalled, refused); and some nations didn't understand why the United States wouldn't deploy the vast US Sixth Fleet, already stationed in the Eastern Mediterranean, to block the Anglo-French armada.

Urquhart writes that "just before lunch on November 5, Hammarskjöld started writing his main report on the establishment of the United Nations Emergency Force. . . . This document both laid the foundations for an entirely new kind of international activity and set out principles and ideas that were to become the basis for future UN peacekeeping operations. By lunchtime, he had dictated three pages, which he read during the meal to Pearson and Cordier, and during the afternoon he dictated the remainder in bits and pieces between other commitments."[49] Urquhart was entering a closer collaboration with Hammarskjöld. He remained a senior member of under-secretary Ralph Bunche's staff, but as he said of himself, "With six years of service in the British army in World War II, I was the only person on the thirty-eighth floor with firsthand military experience."[50] He would soon put that experience to work. Urquhart's admiration for Hammarskjöld's strategic clarity and personal stamina through this period is one of the emotional realities of the scene, viewed from our current perspective many years later. Urquhart was able at the time to appreciate both the precision of what Hammarskjöld was doing and the unusual mind shaping that precision—and the spectacle, if we can call it that, was not just intellectually satisfying, it was moving. His oral history of Hammarskjöld at work on the UNEF plan records his admiration and carries us a step further:

> Hammarskjöld always had a great sense of establishing legal precedents in everything he did, no matter how much of an emergency it was. He was always looking at what it would mean in historical terms and what it would mean for the future, which is one of the reasons that he was such a remarkable person. He always found time to do this, and he was determined that this agreement should in some way be an advance on previous things of its kind and a model for the future. . . . I think that people always overestimate the practical side of this and always underestimate the enormous political problems that underlie the concept of using troops for this purpose. This is where Hammarskjöld showed an extraordinary perceptiveness and capacity for really thinking while he was working 24 hours a day. It was one of his great and remarkable qualities. He never stopped thinking about what it really meant in terms of sovereignty, international law, the use of various organs of the United Nations. [51]

Hammarskjöld submitted his report to the General Assembly on November 6th, and debate continued through the following day. On the 7th, he took the podium twice, initially to convey in plain language his sense of urgency: "I only wish to express my earnest hope that a decision in line with my proposals will be taken promptly so as to permit us to get going. There should not be left in the minds of people any uncertainty about the determination of the United Nations."[52] Later he responded to various issues that had come up, remarking among other things that "there is no intent in the establishment of the force to influence the military balance in the present conflict, and thereby the political balance affecting efforts to settle the conflict."[53] This is, I believe, his first formulation of an issue that would become heatedly difficult in the Congo Crisis of 1960–61. In due course, two related resolutions calling UNEF into existence were accepted by a vast majority with the usual small number of abstentions. Only Israel cast a negative vote against the second resolution, which called on it to return to the armistice lines established in 1949, but a rapid exchange of views between Hammarskjöld and the Israeli foreign minister, Golda Meir, brought the clarification that Israel would withdraw if certain conditions were met. That was enough for the time being. UNEF would be directed on behalf of the General Assembly by the secretary-general and an advisory committee, and commanded in the field by General Burns. With no military experience but an incalculably large grasp of politics, law, history, and human nature, Hammarskjöld had become something very like a commander in chief.

There were always two sides, mutually nourishing: one visible, the other invisibly alive. Visibly, Hammarskjöld was more relaxed and spirited when UNEF won its way in the Assembly. "Now, corporal," he said to Ralph Bunche, "go and get me a force!" It was Bunche's task, therefore Urquhart's with him, to assemble, organize, and in all ways ensure that the peacekeeping force arrived promptly in Egypt, where General Burns was also getting organized. Urquhart adds that "Hammarskjöld addressed Bunche as 'corporal' on the ground that with so many generals around it was a more distinguished appellation."[54] That was fun, and it speaks to the resilience of the team now charged with creating a small, special-purpose army. Privately, Hammarskjöld was touched by the logic and clarity that were beginning to emerge. At some point during these days, perhaps after the General Assembly approved the UNEF plan, he found himself recalling the ancient notions of the Fates weaving destiny and of hidden providence. The lines are from his journal:

> Imperceptibly our fingers are guided so that a pattern forms as the threads are woven into the fabric.[55]

Later in the month, when he was negotiating with Nasser practical details governing UNEF's presence on Egyptian soil, the metaphor again came to mind in a line that reads like a fragment from a modern psalm:

> Somebody placed the shuttle in your hand: somebody who had already arranged the threads.[56]

To be entirely and willingly responsible offered him the intuition of another hand at work, taking its share of responsibility.

In the afternoon of November 6th, Anthony Eden had gotten in touch with his French counterpart, Guy Mollet. Mollet's foreign minister recalled that moment in his book: "Anthony Eden was on the line. I hear the broken voice of a man who had reached the limit of his resources and was ready to collapse. 'It's not possible any longer,' he said in substance. 'We must stop. The pound is even lower and we're running the risk of a panic. What's more, I've just had a telephone call from Eisenhower.

He gives me 12 hours to order a cease-fire. . . . I've already accepted
. . . . You accept, don't you?'"[57] At midnight, in Egypt, the Anglo-French
cease-fire took effect. The invasion force had advanced twenty-three
miles along the Suez Canal, and there it stopped. The nine-day shooting war was over. On November 23rd, his health and nerves in serious
jeopardy, Eden left England for a three-week rest in Jamaica. On January
9th, 1957, he would resign the office of prime minister on grounds of ill
health. He had been the best of men in peace and war until illness and
the obsolete dream of empire possessed him.

It wasn't until December 22nd that the invading force fully withdrew. Successively abandoning positions as UNEF forces took their
places, and helping UNEF in a remarkably cooperative spirit, its units
awaited their turn to board ship and go home. General Burns arranged
for the purchase of masses of Anglo-French supplies. Hammarskjöld
read the political situation and decided to exclude the French and British from UNEF service and from helping to clear obstacles from the
Suez Canal—the latter a decision that struck them as irrational because
they had salvage vessels on hand and considered that no one knew better than they how to go about it. The pragmatic solution eventually adopted was to use their vessels and personnel for a few weeks to complete
projects already begun, and in that interval to put the vessels, flying the
UN flag, under UN command. They departed by the end of January. A
larger fleet of salvage vessels hired primarily from Dutch and Danish
companies, with an impressive total of seven countries participating,
looked after the rest.

All eyewitnesses to the period emphasize that UNEF was a leap into the
unknown. Urquhart put it best: "The United Nations Emergency Force
. . . would be the first of its kind in history. There was no previous experience on which to draw, all arrangements had to be improvised, commitments would be required for which there were no precedents."[58] Bunche
and Urquhart were improvising on all fronts at UN headquarters and soon
after at a staging airfield near Naples, from which UNEF contingents flew
to Egypt. Burns was in constant touch with Hammarskjöld on everything
from grand strategy to details. Urquhart tells a sweet story: UNEF troops
were to be easily distinguishable from other troops by their UN-blue helmets or berets—but no one had blue helmets or berets. He decided that
the best solution was to dunk US army helmets in blue paint. And that
is how the troops went forth. On his side, Burns needed everything and

initially had nothing. The first UNEF troops to reach Egypt, Norwegians and Danes arriving on November 15th–16th, were led by regular army officers but they were largely national service conscripts with little training. On the other hand, Burns felt that all the troops initially seconded to UNEF—Norwegian, Danish, Swedish, Finnish, Indian, Colombian, with air and logistical support from Canada—were good and willing. At its height, the Force would number some six thousand. Years later, with imperturbable pluck, Urquhart explained something well worth hearing:

> The great thing about UN [peacekeeping forces] is that they very specifically don't have to fight. If they are going to fight they aren't any good, anyway. So all you have to do is put people in a transport aircraft and get them somewhere, and being there is three-quarters of the job. There are lots of other things they can do, but actually their presence is the initial point. . . . We could put a completely assorted bunch of troops into C-110s, the most sick-making aircraft in the world without any exception, and fly them airsick as dogs into Abu Sueir on the Canal, and their actual arrival, even if in a somewhat moth-eaten condition, was already half the game politically and practically, because they provided a cushion between the British and French on the one side and the Egyptians on the other. They provided a physical buffer on the ground, a symbol, and you could say to the British and French: "OK, we're now arriving. We're taking over. There is no need for you; forget it. And furthermore it's going to be safe for you to leave. You're not going be shot at when you're leaving."[59]

The motto "Let Dag do it," ever since associated with his name, may have been pronounced in near facsimile for the first time at a November 12th press conference. A journalist said, "[The Great Powers] are throwing everything on your lap. They are saying: 'Let George do it. Let Mr. Dag Hammarskjöld handle it.' . . . An American political pundit has said . . . : 'Fortunately, the management of the undertaking is in the hands of Mr. Dag Hammarskjöld, as competent, as cool, as astute, and as objective a diplomat as we have seen for many a long day.' But to me it seems that they are sort of making you, if there is a failure, a scapegoat for this whole thing."[60] Hammarskjöld responded gracefully, saying that "if it would in any way help the United Nations for me to be a scapegoat, I would be quite happy to be one," but the journalist's point wasn't lost on him. A little later, when the Suez Crisis had moved on but was far from resolved, he returned to the issue in letters we'll shortly read.

Hammarskjöld flew to the staging airfield near Naples on November 14th, where he conferred with General Burns, and flew on to Egypt with the first UNEF troops on November 16th. It was very much part of his vision to witness the birth of the new peacekeeping force and to underscore its importance to the world in the most direct way—by showing up. With Nasser and Fawzi, who were sensitive to the least suggestion of infringement of Egyptian sovereignty, he had a crucial diplomatic agenda: to reach agreements about the presence and composition of UNEF, the clearing of the canal, and whether Egypt had the right at any time to insist that UNEF withdraw. This last was interesting. Hammarskjöld took a risk by sending troops in before this—and other matters—had been worked out. "There was an element of gambling involved," he later wrote. "I had a feeling that it . . . was a must to get the troops in and that I would be in a position to find a formula, saving the face of Egypt while protecting the UN stand, once I could discuss the matter personally with President Nasser."[61] With Nasser and Fawzi, Hammarskjöld acknowledged that Egypt had the right at any time to order the departure of UNEF—but by voting for the General Assembly resolution that created the force and defined its mission, Egypt had effectively agreed to allow UNEF to complete that mission. Were there a disagreement about completion, the issue would have to be brought to the United Nations for mediation. It was tightly reasoned. This may have been what Hammarskjöld (or Pearson—the comment wanders between them in the literature) had in mind when he told the advisory committee upon his return to New York that the arrangements were "becoming almost metaphysical in their subtlety. I have no complaint about that because if, from the beginning of this operation, we had attempted to be specific, we would not have had an operation at all."[62] In any event, Nasser and Fawzi reluctantly accepted Hammarskjöld's understanding—Hammarskjöld had gone so far as to threaten to withdraw the troops at once, absent their approval—and further agreed with him that the UN should reserve to itself the task of clearing the canal.[63] With metaphysical subtlety at the top level and the right boots on the ground, the operation was making its way.

He had little time for his journal, but there are nonetheless a few entries from this period when he was negotiating in Cairo. Among the most telling, an extremely compact guide to the ways of the world:

> From injustice—never justice.
> From justice—never injustice.[64]

He was turning in a bravura performance. An editorial in the *New York Times*, November 20th, captured the perspective of many:

> Mr. Hammarskjöld got back from Egypt yesterday morning. . . . He may have slept a little on the way home, but many of his associates believe that he actually sat up writing his notes. . . . He proceeded with scant delay to UN headquarters. . . . He had appointments there with spokesmen on both sides of the cold war barrier. He could talk to those spokesmen on equal terms. Much of his power and effectiveness lies in the fact that he is trusted everywhere. . . . We can thank our luck, and UN's luck, that at this moment—and at some other critical moments—Mr. Hammarskjöld was available.[65]

Despite these warmest of words, Hammarskjöld wasn't persuaded that the *Times* fully understood. "Some day soon," he wrote to Arthur H. Sulzberger, its publisher and president,

> we should have a talk. . . . I guess that basically the *New York Times* is inspired by the feeling that, once it was started, it would have been good if the British-French-Israeli action had succeeded. I hold that such an outcome would have been a major catastrophe in which the death of the United Nations indeed might have been one of the less significant elements. It may well be that the United Nations' effort will ultimately fail and, if so, S.O.S. But against the risk we are running stands that certainty of what we have avoided.[66]

Like Eisenhower, Hammarskjöld believed that an Anglo-French occupation and overthrow of Nasser could have been the opening salvo in a nuclear world war.

Toward the end of November, he had time for correspondence. Writing to Max Ascoli, a New York–based journalist and academic whom he respected, he formulated a most Hammarskjöld-like, original view of what he had done and why—and returned to the notion of the secretary-general as scapegoat.

> In the vacuum which suddenly developed in the Suez crisis, I had, for what it was worth, to throw in everything I had to try to tide over; it was one of those irrational and extremely dangerous situations in which only something as irrational on a different level could break the spell. But it is an entirely different thing, every time the big powers run into a deadlock, to place the problem in the Secretary-General's hands with the somewhat

naïve expectation that he can continue to turn up with something. It is a matter of course that a continued use of the office of the Secretary-General in that way sooner or later leads to a point where he must break his neck, politically. If, as in the Suez situation, the very facts, as established by the policy of the various big powers, force the Secretary-General into a key role, I am perfectly willing to risk being a political casualty if there is an outside chance of achieving positive results. But if the Secretary-General is forced into a similar role through sheer escapism from those who should carry the responsibility, there is place for a solid warning. Politically, the Secretary-General should be, and is, most expendable, but he should not be expended just because somebody does not want to produce his own money.[67]

He is almost certainly referring here to the Hungarian crisis: he knew, and everyone knew, that the secretary-general could do nothing or next to nothing to dissuade the Soviet Union from crushing the Hungarian popular uprising of late October/early November, but he had been asked to give it a try. "Irrational on a different level"—what an extraordinary view of UNEF, perhaps not even fair to it. But this is how he saw things at the time, and the concept of a peacekeeping force, springing up from one day to the next, deployed just two weeks later, had something of the irrational in it: threads in a prearranged pattern.

In the second week of December, with UNEF on the ground in Egypt reaching a substantial number—some 3,500—Hammarskjöld felt that it was time to give the troops a strong definition of their mission. Ralph Bunche wrote a radio address for him, which he must have fully endorsed. It comes as a surprise in the tumultuous Suez Crisis to hear again this quiet, focused voice as it frames the soldiers' circumstances. "As members of the United Nations Emergency Force," he said,

> you are taking part in an experience that is new in history. You are soldiers of peace in the first international force of its kind. You have come from distant homelands, not to fight a war but to serve peace and justice and order under the authority of the United Nations.
>
> Thus the opportunity for service which is yours is not to be measured by your numbers or your armor. You are the front line of a moral force which extends around the world, and you have behind you the support of millions everywhere.[68]

This wasn't all he had to say in December; some things could be said in confidence only. To Uno Willers, the director of the Swedish National

Library who had been such a help during the Beijing negotiation, he wrote on December 19th that he was living through "a time when the strongest experience for me . . . has been the moral shock caused by the mixture of bungled work and dishonesty in men the people have elected as leaders."[69] On the same day he wrote to his fellow Academician, Sten Selander: "We live in an evil, busy time and it's hard to find an opportunity for exercises of the mind and spirit, the defense of which is what all efforts to suppress barbarism are about. I would like to tell you about my experiences this autumn, which, alas, have shown more of human misery than of human greatness."[70] This was written in early winter. Even by spring 1957, that tone persisted: "As you can well understand," he wrote to the poet Hjalmar Gullberg, "I have had a very eventful winter, filled with conflicting experiences. The signs of unselfishness, faithfulness, and certainty of belief that I have seen are needed to counterbalance stunning expressions of irresponsibility, superficiality, and vulgarity. International politics is not a beautiful game—even if one can see a good deal in it that is beautiful."[71] And he added to the letter a few wistful lines, slightly misremembered, from a Gullberg poem that had lately come often to mind:

Hem vill jag gå ifrån stridiga	I want to go home from clashing
viljor och spelet om makt	wills and power games

The canal clearance operation, with thirty-two vessels manned by nearly five hundred seamen, including forty-five divers, was directed by an American, lieutenant-general Raymond A. Wheeler, a veteran of the Burmese theater in World War II who was both a former Panama Canal engineer and the recipient, for his wartime service in a British command, of an honorary knighthood. Hammarskjöld had full confidence in him and was thoroughly offended—here begins a legend that must be told—when a British lord denigrated him as "an old Middle Western grocer" who couldn't possibly be up to the task. In the oral history setting that so suited him, Urquhart recalled that "Hammarskjöld flew into a wonderfully well-contrived rage about this and said, 'Well, perhaps we'd better have this out in the open. If anybody knows General Wheeler's credentials, General Wheeler doesn't at all mind being called an old Middle Western grocer. In the United States apparently this is a term of affection and endearment. But the plain fact of the matter is that these are his credentials, and maybe it would be good if the British Government would stop making silly remarks to cover its own mistakes.' And there was quite a considerable row."[72]

The clearance operation strikes one, at this distance, as cheerful. No one was shooting at anybody else, the Egyptian government was pleased to host an effort very much in its interest, and the huge challenge was overcome ahead of schedule. The UN salvage team had something to prove to the British and French, who had asserted their stunning competence in salvage operations and had badly wanted the assignment as a token of their continuing role in Egypt. There was bravado in doing something so difficult so well. *Time* reported in the style of a minutely detailed thriller: "A Dutch diver named Flip Gwoud suited up aboard a Danish launch. . . . Then he slid over the side to mark [a] sunken wreck. . . . Minutes later the Danish tug *Protector* chugged past to start work on a wrecked dredger."[73] A good time was had by all, not least by Hammarskjöld who enjoyed some hours observing and photographing on the water. It was a rest.

Not cheerful were the months of negotiation needed to obtain Israeli compliance with the terms of the General Assembly resolution calling for withdrawal to the 1949 armistice lines. The Israeli Defense Force withdrew in stages, but Ben-Gurion and his colleagues played their cards well, and slowly, to ensure that at very least the blockade of Israeli shipping through the Gulf of Aqaba would be permanently eliminated, even if Israel was pressured into withdrawing from the Gaza Strip. On February 20th, Eisenhower reserved television time to state his views to the American people. "Israel insists on firm guarantees," he said, "as a condition to withdrawing its forces of invasion. . . . Should a nation which attacks and occupies foreign territory in the face of United Nations disapproval be allowed to impose conditions on its withdrawal? . . . If the United Nations once admits that international disputes can be settled by using force, then we will have destroyed the very foundation of the organization, and our best hope for establishing a real world order."[74] Bowing to pressure from many sources, the Israelis withdrew by March 16th behind the armistice lines they had crossed in force on October 29th. One of Ben-Gurion's biographers, who had unfettered access to the Old Man, as he was called, and to his papers, drew up the debits and credits of Israel's participation as follows: "The Sinai Campaign brought Israel rich dividends, first and foremost ten years of peace. One after another her borders fell silent. The *fedayeen* did not return to Gaza. . . . Ben-Gurion's vision of the future of [the Gulf of Aqaba] was also largely realized. Its port became the southern gateway to Israel, freedom of navigation was guaranteed. . . ."[75] And on from there: the list of gains is long and credible.

We should read two letters. Hammarskjold wrote the first on January 5th in the new year, 1957, to his brother Bo. He reported that he had of necessity worked on both Christmas Eve and Christmas Day—but now he had a moment.

> The most troublesome issue I had to deal with was probably clearing the canal—this owing to the absolutely incredible methods of negotiation from the English (*not* the Egyptian) side. You sometimes feel ashamed of "your people." On the other hand, the English are, you know, not least according to Swedish experience, traditionally more ruthless than others when hard pressed. . . .
>
> Even apart from work it has been a strange Christmas, balancing on the edge of disaster. Another couple of adventures like the Franco-British or the Russian and it won't just be the UN that will have to close down. Confronted with all their criticism, my standard phrase to the English now is: "You should be grateful; we saved you from success."
>
> So far, everything on my front has, however, gone amazingly well. One "impossibility" after the other has been tried—and shown to be possible. The price, for me, apart from other things, is continuous personal risk taking. *Somebody* must be the scapegoat if things go bad, and the Secretary-General is of course the most natural choice unless he is willing to go into hiding.[76]

A second letter, to his former aide Per Lind, vividly depicts the atmosphere prevailing after the most severe difficulties had been overcome but the crisis was not quite over. It dates to mid-March.

> It is a pity that you are not around. It would have been refreshing to have you in the 24-hour working team which has been running this show now for five months, I can well say, without any interruption whatsoever. As you know, the team spirit is fine and for that reason, in spite of the incredible pressure and the unreasonable responsibilities, we have on the whole had quite a good time and on the human level quite some fun. The solidarity is admirable and the spirit anything but weak, but I would dress up reality if I did not tell you that I think all of us by now are quite tired and that it therefore becomes increasingly difficult every morning to activate

the energy for new initiatives and new decisions rendered necessary by the sometimes maddening difficulties which arise every day.

Yesterday was a typical day. Somehow everything seemed to go wrong all through, and even stout Andy, when we finally left the office, characterized the day as nightmarish. In spite of that, when Andy, George Ivan Smith, and I had dinner together at my place (dinner prepared for Mike Pearson who did not turn up), we had one of the most irresponsibly jolly evenings I remember in a very long time.

To analyze what is happening would take me too long. The smoke and fog are enormous and the tools of propaganda and smear worse than I have seen since the high days of Hitler. It is difficult, in that situation, to hear the low voice of reason or see the clear little light of decency, but, of course, both endure and both remain perfectly safe guides. Personally I still feel as I have done from 30 October onward that no one in my job can run this properly, short of a miracle, without breaking his neck politically. So far it has not happened, but that is, by God, no guarantee for the future. However, so what!

In a curious instinctive way I feel that we are on the right road and that finally we will get through. I have absolutely nothing which I can invoke in favor of such optimism, but, all the same, I think it is closer to reality than all the Cassandra cries. . . .

On Monday I leave for Cairo. . . . I do not believe in the possibility of any satisfactory result, but follow simply the rule that nothing must be left undone or untried. It is a little bit wearisome to be the eternal scapegoat for impossibilities created by others, but that matters, of course, less than nothing as long as it is part of the slow building up of what we are striving for.[77]

On the same day Hammarskjöld also put a note in the mail to Bo Beskow to express his weariness but adding an original reflection about the fixity of Western attitudes toward the lands of the Bible:

The next few days I have to go on a new round with the boys from the Nile. It is funny to go to a negotiation when I know beforehand that half the world will say afterwards that it failed. But yet it makes sense going, in view of the fact that short of such an effort, the situation would be more unsatisfactory than it need be.

This is a fight which started some three thousand years ago and found magnificent literary expressions even in some of those Psalms which our dear clergy has recited for hundreds of years—thus unwit-

tingly building up a clear-cut view in our simple souls of . . . the relations
between all those fighting tribes. . . .[78]

There was reason for pride among the members of the "24-hour working
team." Several years after he had played a central role in the development of
UNEF, Ralph Bunche returned from an inspection trip and commented to
the advisory committee, "Since my last visit two years ago, UNEF has become an institution." He considered it his finest achievement, outstripping
even the Israeli-Arab armistice negotiations for which he had been awarded
the Nobel Prize.[79] Mike Pearson, acknowledged as the originator of the idea
of a peacekeeping force, for which UNEF became the permanent model,
received the Nobel Peace Prize in 1957. In his Nobel Lecture, he said in part:

> The birth of [UNEF] was sudden and it was surgical. The arrangements for
> the reception of the infant were rudimentary, and the midwives . . . had no
> precedents or experience to guide them. Nevertheless, UNEF, the first genu-
> inely international police force of its kind, came into being and into action.
>
> It was organized with great speed and efficiency even though its func-
> tions were limited and its authority unclear. And the credit for that must go
> first of all to the Secretary-General of the United Nations and his assistants.
>
> Composed of the men of nine United Nations countries from four
> continents, UNEF moved with high morale and higher purpose be-
> tween national military forces in conflict. . . . I do not exaggerate the
> significance of what has been done. There is no peace in the area. There
> is no unanimity at the United Nations about the functions and future
> of this force. . . . But it may have prevented a brush fire becoming an all-
> consuming blaze at the Suez last year.[80]

Pearson could not have foreseen at the time the growing need in later
decades for UN peacekeeping forces. In June 2011, 115 member nations
were contributing some one hundred thousand soldiers, police, and military experts to worldwide peacekeeping initiatives.[81]

In an inventory of justly proud midwives who brought UNEF to
birth, Hammarskjöld must of course be included, but his correspondence and public talks in roughly the second half of 1957 reflect a little
pride, a little weariness, and a great deal of wariness. In early April, to his
friend Sten Selander, he was altogether candid:

> The Cairo trip was no greater pleasure than usual. Negotiations of this
> kind are in more ways than one a very grim experience. I read with
> amused irony the French and Israeli press with their thoughts of my

appreciation of Nasser. If they had any idea – ! I see that now Tingsten, with scarcely curbed joy, has picked up the theme. There is certainly very little reason for happiness in this world.

My most serious objection to the present work style and stubborn load of more and more "problems" is that all normal human relations with friends at home and friends over here are falling into decay through enforced neglect.

That ought to be remedied, however, if and when insisting on a minimum of consequence and fairness has made me unpopular enough to make reelection impossible. If that happens, which is more than a theoretical but not yet a practical possibility, I must say that . . . it would be a humanly welcome change. . . . But why theorize about the future? The situation is indeed such that we all will have to take every day as it comes.[82]

"How nice it would be to forget the Middle East for a couple of weeks!" Hammarskjöld wrote to his brother Bo some weeks later.[83]

At a press conference in early June, asked whether anything good was going on in the Middle East, he gave an interesting answer: "There are fundamental changes . . . , and I for one believe that those changes are for the better. . . . A continuous development . . . has been going on . . . behind the smoke screen of continued difficulties; and one day, if we manage to lift the smoke screen, I think we may have the pleasant surprise of seeing some solid progress. It is rather intangible, you know, as regards these matters, because progress necessarily is up to 50 percent psychological. For that reason it is difficult to put your finger on it and describe it."[84]

Speaking at a UN Correspondents Association luncheon a few weeks later—he was again taking time for this kind of civilized activity—he returned to the medical metaphor that had first occurred to him more than a year ago.

The present period is . . . in a certain sense the lull after the sound and the fury. It is, for that reason, a period of convalescence, when it is not a very good idea to stir things up, to make too much noise about lingering symptoms of the illness. It is a period when the temperature should be kept as low as possible, but when, on the other hand, it is all right to have as much fresh air as possible around the bed. From my point of view, that means that I have to—not exactly lie low—but exert more than ever whatever efforts I can make in the direction of keeping alive a sense of perspective; of keeping alive the feeling that, although we

have certainly passed through an illness—a bad one—there are strong
and solid chances that the patient will convalesce and get out of bed,
provided that we respect some very simple laws of nature.[85]

By mid-November 1957, when the General Assembly was in session, the
medical metaphor had marched on to become a witty view of the state of
mind of participating delegates. Hammarskjöld was again bringing Per
Lind up to date:

> You are quite right in your feeling that this session of the General Assem-
> bly is of a completely new type. . . . Everyone behaves as if he had a major
> headache and for that reason is rather afraid that anybody else will make
> too much noise. We have had enough reasons for big noises but on each
> occasion people have started busily to play the stories down . . . .
>
> On the whole, the UN gave the impression of a body where all sorts
> of minor corpuscles, after a self-inflicted wound, rushed to the place
> carrying away bugs and bringing neutralizing enzymes. I have never seen
> the self-healing processes, which are possible in the UN, so strongly dis-
> played. This does not mean that we have seen the end of the story.[86]

This is fun. Hammarskjöld was in good form. Of course he was pleased
with the outcome in Egypt, and of course he knew that lasting peace had
not come to the Middle East. Looking back several years later, he would
say of the UN, "I do not know the exact capacity of this machine. It did
take the very steep hill of Suez; it may take other and even steeper hills."[87]

In his undisclosed inner world, the master diplomatic craftsman
and the devoted man of prayer continued their conversation. Between
Christmas 1956 and New Year's Day—despite what he had written to
his brother—he seems to have had good time to think things through,
to uncover the bones of the experience. On Christmas Eve he recorded
a passage from Meister Eckhart that boldly restates his ideal of selfless
service: "If, without any side glances, we have only God in view, it is He,
indeed, who does what we do. . . . Such a man does not seek rest, for he
is not troubled by any unrest. . . ." And he closed the year with an entry
that discovers in his experience of the Suez Crisis an impulse, warm and
austere, toward the future:

> Gratitude and readiness. You got all for nothing. Do not hesitate, when
> it is asked, to give your all, which in fact is nothing, for all.[88]

13

Into All Corners of the Earth

I t could be said in low language—for example, by Hammarskjöld's colleague George Ivan Smith: "I think the concept of 'Leave it to Dag' was the farthest [thing] from his own mind. It was a political imperative . . . put upon him by people who didn't know what the hell else to do."[1] And it could be said in high language—by U Thant, his distinguished successor as secretary-general: "It became a common practice, when any difficult situation came along, for the major organs to say in so many words, 'Leave it to Dag.'"[2] However said, it had become true. After Peking and Suez, Hammarskjöld was trusted and admired by nearly all. The French and British whom he and the North American democracies had saved from success might snipe at him in a residual sort of way. Some Israelis believed he was too good to Nasser. In Sweden the widely read Tingsten railed on. But Hammarskjöld now had the reputation of a diplomatic miracle worker and a man of startling goodness. His influence—or hope for his calming, reasonable influence—reached nearly "into all corners of the earth." The phrase is from a mid-1958 talk he gave in London to members of both Houses of Parliament, specifically from a passage easily missed that begins with a pleasantly expressed cliché and ends with a statement of moving simplicity. "The United Nations is not a new idea," he said on that occasion. "It is here because of centuries of past struggle. It is the logical and natural development from lines of thought and aspiration going far back into all corners of the earth since a few men first began to think about the decency and dignity of other men."[3]

By spring 1957, he was beginning to ponder his possible reelection in September to a second five-year term as secretary-general. He wrote to his old boss in the Swedish foreign ministry that he could accept another term only if the vote were unanimous. "I'm convinced that this standpoint," he wrote, "is not only personally and morally correct but also the only one that is politically defensible. Given what the tasks of the Secretary-General have turned out to be, in an emergency situation he cannot fulfill his office without the freedom he owns through a unanimous election."[4] All was well: on September 26th the Security Council made a unanimous recommendation to reappoint, and the General Assembly followed suit, its vote also unanimous. The day came as close to a "love-in" as the UN can produce. The president of the General Assembly, a New Zealander, praised Hammarskjöld as "surely our supreme international civil servant."[5] The foreign minister of Denmark must have spoken for many when he said: "Dealing always with the most difficult and controversial matters, and often walking untrodden paths and hoping against hope, Mr. Dag Hammarskjöld has succeeded in finding solutions where none seemed to be in sight. But even more, in so doing he has won our admiration and respect and, I might almost say, a universal confidence very rarely enjoyed by any man and certainly unique in the field of politics."[6] Speaking cordially for India but adding a dash of personal salt to the general sugar, V. K. Krishna Menon remarked, "I have some things in common with the Secretary-General. I do not always understand him, and he does not always understand me. But both of us go back afterwards and try to understand each other."[7]

Some years later, Urquhart found what he describes as "a slip of paper attached to Hammarskjöld's copy of his acceptance speech on which, while on the podium after making the speech, he had written in pencil":

Hallowed be Thy name
Thy Kingdom come
Thy will be done
26 September 57
5:40[8]

This while the laudatory speeches were nearing conclusion. It was not a countercurrent, as if something had to be denied; it was the other current, flowing just alongside.

His acceptance speech was not part of the love-in. Of course he expressed gratitude and warmly acknowledged both delegations and Secretariat colleagues, but his thinking about the task ahead displayed dry truthfulness. He spoke a little of himself and the challenges of his role, and a little about the Charter as a steady guide. He returned to his experience of mountaineering, which he seemed never to lose from sight. He introduced a provocative metaphor, intriguing to visualize, for the complex pattern of multilateral diplomacy. And then delivered what were to be the fateful words of the occasion, pointing to a larger freedom he would need in future to serve effectively—words recalling those written privately to Ben-Gurion a few months earlier about situations "where we must individually try to transcend our immediate duty in order to fulfill the higher duty of creative action."

> Whether my service has met the needs of this difficult period in the life of the Organization and, indeed, the world, is for others to decide. . . . Your decision is in these respects an encouragement for the future and a highly valued expression of confidence.
>
> Nobody, I think, can accept the position of Secretary-General of the United Nations, knowing what it means, except from a sense of duty. Nobody, however, can serve in that capacity without a sense of gratitude for a task, as deeply rewarding as it is exacting, as perennially inspiring as, sometimes, it may seem discouraging. . . .
>
> We cannot doubt that the main direction of the work of the United Nations, as determined by the purposes and principles of the Charter, indicates the path which the world must follow. . . . Service of the United Nations guided by those principles is profoundly meaningful—whether it bears immediate fruit or not. If it paves one more inch of the road ahead, one is more than rewarded by what is achieved. This is true whatever setbacks may follow: if a mountain wall is once climbed, later failures do not undo the fact that it has been shown that it *can* be climbed. In this sense, every step forward in the pioneer effort of this Organization inevitably widens the scope for the fight for peace. . . .
>
> In the multidimensional world of diplomacy, the Euclidean definition of the straight line as the shortest way between two points may not always hold true. For the Secretary-General, however, it is the only possible one. This line, as traced by principles which are the law for him, might at times cross other lines in the intricate pattern of international political action. He must then be able to feel secure that, whatever the difficulties, they will not impair the trust of Member governments in his Office.
>
> I do not believe that the Secretary-General should be asked to act, by the Member states, if no guidance for his action is to be found either in the Charter or in the decisions of the main organs of the United Nations; within the limits thus set, however, I believe it to be his duty to use his office and . . . the machinery of the Organization to its utmost capacity and to the full extent permitted at each stage by practical circumstances.
>
> On the other hand, I believe that it is in keeping with the philosophy of the Charter that the Secretary-General should be expected to act also without such guidance, should this appear to him necessary in or-

der to help in filling any vacuum that may appear in the systems which the Charter and traditional diplomacy provide for the safeguarding of peace and security. . . .

Future generations may come to say of us that we never achieved what we set out to do. May they never be entitled to say that we failed because we lacked faith or permitted narrow self-interest to distort our efforts.[9]

There are two provocatively mixed messages here: the member states must be careful not to ask of the secretary-general actions exceeding the framework of the Charter and should fill out their resolutions with practical guidance—but the philosophy of the Charter calls on the secretary-general to fill any vacuum according to his judgment of what is needed, always in keeping with the Charter. It is not a promise of rebellions to come; it does state his understanding, after years of experience, of the expanding political role of his office, and suggests that he would, if necessary, risk his tenure in office for the sake of peace and security. This is almost certainly a lesson from Suez, when he could not stand by in a neutral uniform and permit the aggressors to set the agenda. As so often, he concluded his talk by recalling the need for faith. A few years later he restated in an interesting way that in remarks of this kind he did not have in mind religious faith only. "We must accept the risks," he said then of a difficulty that lay ahead. "We can accept them as an act of faith or an act of conviction, but we should do so."[10]

Some time after 5:40 p.m. (the moment meticulously noted on that slip of paper), and no doubt after a congenial dinner with colleagues, Hammarskjöld found his way to the privacy of his journal. An entry, again meticulously dated, travels from a passage in Meister Eckhart to a new promise to his Lord:

"The best and most wonderful thing that can happen to you in this life, is that you should be silent and let God work and speak."

Long ago, you gripped me, Slinger. Now into your storm. Now toward your target.[11]

The lines from Eckhart recall the Lord's Prayer: Thy will be done. He had discovered in Eckhart's teachings and in his own life that those words are not necessarily empty, that a certain willingness and responsiveness allow something other to enter the scene and, however obscurely, provide direction. A few months earlier he had written in *Markings*, "Forward! Thy orders are given in secret. May I always hear them—and obey."[12] Orders given in secret perhaps even from oneself, though they still must be heard: this is one of the many paradoxes at the inner frontier between robust self-directed living and obedience to "someone or something," as he would put it near the end of his life. Hammarskjöld's own words—"Long ago, you gripped me"—have enough subsurface literary associations to make a scholar happy (see note 11), but the gist of what he writes is clear: though he has long been held, and held hard, in the hands of God, he intuits that in the years ahead he must advance—need one add, courageously—into a storm of God's making toward a target of God's choice. This is biblical language echoing the impassioned Prophets rather than the Gospel narrators. "You will be visited by the Lord of hosts . . . with whirlwind and tempest," promises Isaiah (29:6). In the evening after his public reelection, Hammarskjöld privately and fiercely rededicated himself. It must have been quiet in his New York apartment. Perhaps in that quiet he could see ahead—no details, of course, but the certainty of storms.

A few weeks later he sent off a note to his fellow Academician, Pär Lagerkvist, the novelist much his senior with whom he felt free to explore the fine points of experience. In a few pages we'll listen in on their exchange about responsibility and power. For now, Hammarskjöld simply wanted to register his attitude toward reelection.

> No matter how tired, honestly speaking, I often am from this constant responsibility, these constant demands for initiative, these endless conflicts—and no matter how frightening the prospect of another five years may seem—I had no right in this situation to provoke difficulties which all the governments were unanimous in trying to avoid. Even less could I fail to accept such a responsibility out of mere "homesickness," no matter how strong in this strange and rootless environment.[13]

Something of the mood here—a little blue, quite weary—would come over him at times. In a letter written in the late winter of the coming year, 1958, he expressed that mood with a poet's vision and a secretary-general's doubts. He was writing to another of his friends in the Swedish Academy; they were his indispensable friends, hidden in the distance, responsive to the least shift of thought or feeling in words on the page.

> Last Sunday I escaped the city. The thrushes have just arrived but have not yet been broken up by the stream of migratory birds, so I saw them in hundreds. Going back in the twilight, a flight of starlings swept north over the Hudson: wave after wave like whirling ash in the strong wind. What is time-

less, forever repeated—will we sometime put an end to this also, in our immense inability to solve the problems of human coexistence?[14]

The Room of Quiet

The Room of Quiet is a nonsectarian space for meditation and prayer on
the ground floor of the Secretariat building (fig. 13). It is beautiful, and
so closely associated with Hammarskjöld that one could easily think it
his initiative from start to finish. In fact it has a charming pre-Hammar-
skjöld history. By the time he reopened it for public use in December
1957 after extensive renovation, it had indeed become his project in collaboration with the building's distinguished chief architect, Wallace K.
Harrison, and Hammarskjöld's friend, the painter Bo Beskow. It remains
to this day a small space where his large view of the relations between
inner life and the world's work is preserved. I doubt that he would have
initiated this project; as we know, he was a very private man in some
respects, unlikely to insist on something of this kind. But he didn't have
to initiate it: the Reverend Weyman G. Huckabee had taken care of that
years earlier. Hammarskjöld had only to recognize that the sincerity and
persistence of Huckabee and his companions in the Laymen's Movement
represented not just American folklore at his doorstep but an almost
uncannily able group of people who deserved a warm reception.

The legend of the Room of Quiet—originally termed the Meditation
Room—begins in the heroic period when the UN had no permanent
home. Reverend Huckabee turned up in Paris for the 1947 or 1948 meeting of the General Assembly at the Palais de Chaillot, and with the support of influential friends proposed setting apart a space for prayer and
meditation. He also thought it would be good to open and close Assembly
sessions with a minute of silence. He made a little headway, not least because he found an unexpected ally in Sir Muhammad Zafarullah Khan,
Pakistan's first foreign minister and head of delegation, a devout Muslim
who had been known to seek refuge in telephone booths for his daily
prayers.[15] Some space was set aside, the details unclear. A few years later in
the temporary UN quarters at Lake Success (New York), Huckabee and
his group, now renamed the Friends of the Meditation Room, had scarcely
better luck. Huckabee recalled that "they struggled, and sometimes they
were given a tiny corner, and sometimes they were not given anything at
all. They prayed." However, as the new UN buildings reached completion,
their luck turned. Somehow they got onto Trygvie Lie's calendar, and their

interfaith membership appeared in his office just as he was complaining that "There's some strange group trying to get some kind of meditation center going here, and I don't know much about it and I don't know what I feel about it." Huckabee introduced himself as the leader of that strange group and made their case—to which Lie surprisingly responded, "Well, if that's what you people want, we'll see that you have it." A somewhat awkward, V-shaped space for which there was no planned use on the ground floor of the Secretariat building was allocated and soon furnished with featureless curtains, a "large tropical tree trunk from Africa with a bowl of flowers or greenery on top," and semicircular rows of chairs. It was plain; it felt like the space under stairs in homes. But it was a sketch of the idea.

Soon after Hammarskjöld took office, the Friends made contact with him and demonstrated the sincerity of their wish to improve the Meditation Room by making a donation for that purpose. They could not have known he was a religious man—even his superb early credo commissioned by Edward R. Murrow lay several months ahead. But he had already discovered the Meditation Room and had thought about it. He received them well. In response to their donation, he made brief remarks that found their way into the UN archive:

> The gift that I have just received on behalf of the UN is highly significant. I welcome it warmly and I wish to express our deep gratitude . . .
>
> Our Meditation Room is modest. It is not the center of the house in a physical sense, but it should be the center in the spiritual sense. I do not believe in the possibility of such cooperation as we are engaged in without the deep inspiration of faith in ideals which we all share. "Ideals" in itself is a general word. What I mean here are the ideals established by our deepest faith and highest longings. . . .
>
> What is achieved on our long road toward a better world is achieved in cooperation between all men of good will truly dedicated as participants in a joint worldwide effort. The Meditation Room should be a place where they can all meet. . . .[16]

Some years passed, the Friends made further donations, funds were somehow found for a major renovation, and one of the best architectural minds of the era was brought to bear. As the project advanced, Hammarskjöld influenced virtually every element of design and execution. Though small in scale, it was bold in other respects. A footing into bedrock had to be added through several lower floors to support the massive iron-ore altar that darkly dominates the space, and the overall aesthetic had moved on from Salvation Army to taut Modernism. In April 1957, Hammarskjöld sent a note to Reverend Huckabee in advance of a meeting with the Friends scheduled for a few days later. "It has, of course," he wrote, "been most difficult to design a room which would meet everybody's wishes, but as I hope to explain to your group on April 24th, we have tried to design it in such a way as to provide a room of such dignity and simplicity as would cause increasing numbers of people in due course to cherish it and to regard it with the solemnity and seriousness which such a room should obviously command."[17] On the 24th at his meeting with the Friends, a pre-inauguration of the renovated space, Hammarskjöld made some carefully written remarks which served as a first draft of the text available to this day at the entrance to the Room of Quiet. At that time the ensemble was not quite finished; in August through November 1957, Bo Beskow, accompanied by his wife Greta, relocated from Sweden to New York and to Hammarskjöld's apartment to execute the fresco painting visible in figure 13.

Like the Murrow credo of four years earlier, the text establishing the intended atmosphere and purpose of the Room of Quiet is a perfectly transparent statement of Hammarskjöld's values, but not only his. They are values respected worldwide, lofty values reaching past us but for that very reason inspiring. What he wrote draws on his familiarity with the Bible and Meister Eckhart, with the Taoist classics, and with the expressive language of modern art.[18] Hammarskjöld spoke here in the language of *Markings* and as the undeclared poet who observed starlings wheeling like ash over the Hudson. Only twice in his UN years did he thoroughly break his unstated rule of sharing little of his inner life with the public: for the Murrow talk, and for this.

A ROOM OF QUIET

The United Nations Meditation Room

This is a room devoted to peace
and those who are giving their
lives for peace. It is a room of quiet
where only thoughts should speak.

We all have within us a center of stillness surrounded by silence.

This house, dedicated to work and debate in the service of peace, should have one room dedicated to silence in the outward sense and stillness in the inner sense.

It has been the aim to create in this small room a place where the doors may be open to the infinite lands of thought and prayer.

People of many faiths will meet here, and for that reason none of the symbols to which we are accustomed in our meditation could be used.

However, there are simple things which speak to us all with the same language. We have sought for such things and we believe that we have found them in the shaft of light striking the shimmering surface of solid rock.

So, in the middle of the room we see a symbol of how, daily, the light of the skies gives life to the earth on which we stand, a symbol to many of us of how the light of the spirit gives life to matter.

But the stone in the middle of the room has more to tell us. We may see it as an altar, empty not because there is no God, not because it is an altar to an unknown god, but because it is dedicated to the God whom man worships under many names and in many forms.

The stone in the middle of the room reminds us also of the firm and permanent in a world of movement and change. The block of iron ore has the weight and solidity of the everlasting. It is a reminder of that cornerstone of endurance and faith on which all human endeavor must be based.

The material of the stone leads our thoughts to the necessity for choice between destruction and construction, between war and peace. Of iron man has forged his swords, of iron he has also made his plough-shares. Of iron he has constructed tanks, but of iron he has likewise built homes for man. The block of iron ore is part of the wealth we have inherited on this earth of ours. How are we to use it?

The shaft of light strikes the stone in a room of utter simplicity. There are no other symbols, there is nothing to distract our attention or to break in on the stillness within ourselves. When our eyes travel from these symbols to the front wall, they meet a simple pattern opening up the room to the harmony, freedom, and balance of space.

There is an ancient saying that the sense of a vessel is not in its shell but in the void. So it is with this room. It is for those who come here to fill the void with what they find in their center of stillness.[19]

And he signed it: this was, and remains, his personal message to those who have anything to do with the UN.

Striking here is the encounter between Hammarskjöld, surely one of the most sophisticated and religiously knowing men of his time, and the good-hearted Friends of the Meditation Room. They were ambassadors from grassroots America—but haven't we heard him say, "I take pride in belonging to the family of grasses, and I remain quite green." He wasn't put off by them; they weren't put off by him. Not at the center of the Secretariat building, their shared creation is just a little to the side, like the heart. Reverend Huckabee went on to become the director of Wainwright House, to this day a respected cultural and spiritual center north of New York City. Witnesses to the Hammarskjöld years report that, among other occasions, the secretary-general would spend time in the Room of Quiet before traveling and after his return. I do not know whether thoughts and prayers linger in such spaces. Some say they do.

Linnaeus

Bo Beskow, artist in residence in autumn 1957, would have been aware of Hammarskjöld's comings and goings during the twelfth session of the General Assembly, meeting from mid-September to mid-December—and aware of his unedited views. For this reason, his arch comment on the drafting of an address Hammarskjöld was to give at the Swedish Academy on December 20th must reflect both some of the facts and much of Hammarskjöld's eternal difficulty with ambassador Krishna Menon. "Most of the draft," reports Beskow, "was written in the General Assembly, during a marathon speech by a certain Indian delegate, who put everybody else to sleep and then fainted, keeping up his faint until all the photographers and he were satisfied. The whole show was obviously for the home market."[20] It is plainly inconceivable that Hammarskjöld wrote his brilliant piece, "The Linnaeus Tradition and Our Time," entirely during an endless speech in the General Assembly, but there is no reason to doubt that he improved the time by adding to it. He would have needed the complicity of the president of the Assembly, immediately to his left. Perhaps the president also had a project.

It was Hammarskjöld's turn, in a traditional rotation, to serve as the Academy's *direktör* and offer an address on a topic of his choice. He took advantage of the nationwide celebration of the 250th anniversary of the birth of Carl Linnaeus, the eighteenth-century creator of modern plant and animal taxonomy, a fearless explorer and scientific genius, to evoke key themes in Linnaeus's life and in the life of modern nations. In tone the address is remorselessly, joyfully literary. Many pages ago we heard him remark that the mind of someone who reads only UN reports would be a little odd.

He might have said the same of someone who writes only UN reports. His Linnaeus talk broke those bonds. For a moment he set aside post-Suez negotiations and all such to explore among friends an extraordinary eighteenth-century sensibility. For a moment he became Swedish again. But he never ceased being secretary-general. His closing thoughts are an early sign of a theme that would preoccupy him to the end: the relations between the West and the newly independent nations of Asia and Africa understood not only as political entities but as the homelands of rich cultures.

In chapter 2 we paused over Hammarskjöld's early and lifelong affinity with Linnaeus. As late as 1956 in Cairo, soon after the cease-fire, he almost certainly had Linnaeus in mind as he wrote out what he called his "devise," his personal motto: "Numen *semper* adest" (the divine *always* enters in; see pp. 30–31). Linnaeus's motto was much like it. We know that Hammarskjöld hung in his New York apartment a reproduction of the famous portrait of young Linnaeus in rustic Sami clothing with a rakishly tilted, red felt hat and Sami mittens and tools dangling from his belt—an amazing, willful depiction in an era when gentlemen wore wigs, like J. S. Bach. It was this Linnaeus, the traveler and explorer, close observer and poet of the everyday, on whom Hammarskjöld chose to dwell in his talk; this Linnaeus who possessed what Hammarskjöld called a "drastic imagination"[21] and almost inconceivably penetrating insights into structure and process. Those gifts would naturally appeal to him—such things can be useful in international affairs.

In his careful and, I think, joyously written text, Hammarskjöld must have proved to himself that he could still think elegantly and at length about something other than UN affairs. Just two of its concerns need attention here. The first is simple and unsurprising: at times, when he wrote about Linnaeus, he could as well have been writing of himself. Linnaeus was a mirror and guarantor that he was on something like the right track. "Freshness and precision, enthusiasm without lyricism, an instinctive eye for meaning and causality"—these are values Hammarskjöld picked out for admiration in Linnaeus's writings.[22] In cast of mind and style on the page, Hammarskjöld was quite like this also. The same is true of their shared reverence for Nature and for the presence within it of something more: "Deep down, it was a world full of meaning.... [His] lines reverberate with the happy humility before the mystery which from the outset gave his accounts their paean note. Life, to Linnaeus, became a *mysterium tremendum*. It remained, till the end, a *mysterium numinosum*."[23] This, too, was like Hammarskjöld. He even found in Linnaeus a vivid reflection of his own galling fault (a certain arrogance, he struggled with it) and one of its cures (a sense of humor): "Linnaeus' humility as an observer and a researcher did not exclude a strong self-confidence. In a less generous general setting his reactions sometimes would have had a petty ring. Until dignity became a burden and melancholy caught up with him, he was saved by his lively eye for those amusing features which are rarely lacking in even the most somber situation. . . ."[24]

Going on to ask whether Linnaeus continued to be read by the Swedish general public, Hammarskjöld explored what he perceived as a break in cultural concerns that separated his contemporaries from the classics—and then moved into the terrain where his newest thoughts lay. His theme was globalization and the need for Europe to welcome new nations and cultures. He was beginning to think through the European colonial past and ask for a resilient new postcolonial attitude. It's not difficult to match his expression "sterile self-assertion" to recent events. The Linnaeus talk became a meditation on Suez.

> This generation has seen Europe lose much of the powerful position it occupied for centuries, and a wave of nationalism has swept the continents. The revolutionary events we witness have led many into a defeatism which, although unspoken, is revealed by its inseparable companions: fatigue, bitterness, and sterile self-assertion. . . . Only those who do not want to see can deny that we are moving these days in the direction of a new community of nations. . . . The democracy of human rights, with equality for nations irrespective of race and history, which has come nearer with the rebirth of Asia and Africa . . . , may open the door for new spiritual contacts, impulses, and problems. To give it a reality, much must be jeopardized and perhaps sacrificed, but this is the price of an evolution, the main direction of which we can agree with. . . .
>
> Europe is certainly able . . . to keep a place worthy of its traditions. What has been lost in power can be made up by leadership. One condition is that Europe understand how to develop and maintain the values which are the foundation of her spiritual greatness. In this, every nation has a role to play.[25]

"What has been lost in power can be made up by leadership." This is a new thought, one that will stay with him and develop. He is looking with deepest interest toward Asia and Africa. While many issues and emergencies will need his participation in the years explored by this chapter and the next—the years between the Suez Crisis of 1956–57 and the

Congo Crisis beginning in June 1960—it was, I believe, the problems and promise of the new nations of Asia and Africa that renewed his sense of mission and his verve, and fully justified his acceptance of a second term. Those nations were distant, of course; he would travel to many of them in the years between Suez and the Congo. But they were also becoming UN member nations, and their delegations were at hand. The balance of power was shifting in utterly interesting and significant ways in the General Assembly, where all nations have equal voice and one vote.

In that melancholy late winter letter where he spoke of starlings whirling over the Hudson River, written a few months after the Linnaeus talk, he assembled an overview of the recent past and what might well come next.

> While the sun outside the windows does its best to create a spring feeling, it sheds a mixed light in the world where my professional responsibility lies. If the Suez crisis could be labeled the overture of a drama we must endure before we get a new balance between Western Europe and the "colored" peoples, I think we are now in the first act.... Whether this drama is able to develop to a point of purification and balance will depend to a great extent on what we can do within the UN and with the UN as a framework....
>
> The development I have in mind is overshadowed by the verbose tirades now characterizing "the Cold War" but, as a matter of fact, this is what gives the Cold War its spooky dynamics. I do not believe that Russia and America with open eyes would take the step into armed conflict, but if we do not manage Asia-Africa . . . , this more fundamental conflict can force the Big Powers over the border so far drawn by reason around their operations.
>
> All the thousand and one details that I am supposed to do my—tiny—best to disentangle from one day to the next are subordinate to the perspective I mentioned. . . . In comparison . . . , the disarmament issue seems almost an academic exercise, due to the fact that the Great Ones, incapable of dealing straightforwardly with the point at issue, now devote all their interest to procedural matters!
>
> I would like to tell you how the various issues are reflected in day-to-day work, with its impressive harvest of experience of the clash of interest between common, decent good will and stupidity in individuals who are swayed by considerations of personal or "national" prestige in a world where the share price of a politician on the exchange of public opinion rises and falls with the impression he makes every day via headlines and television quiz programs.[26]

To finish out the year, Hammarskjöld flew from Stockholm to the Middle East, to spend Christmas with the UNEF troops in Gaza and meet with the Egyptian leadership. As this is Hammarskjöld, we can expect some sign from him that he had passed from wintry Sweden to a coastal outpost of the Holy Land at Christmastide. Two entries conclude the year in his journal. The first, written in Sweden on the eve of departure, probably refers to Tingsten's predictably sour editorial about the Linnaeus talk in *Dagens Nyheter*, his newspaper:

> The madman shouted in the market place. No one stopped or answered him. Thus it was confirmed that his thesis was incontrovertible.[27]

In the style of a Kafka parable, this is nearly all Hammarskjöld would say in response, and it was said privately to settle his own mind. True, he also protested privately to a few Swedish friends about what he called Tingsten's scribblings: "All the noise *Dagens Nyheter* caused . . . seems to me a bit comical, unfounded as it was, but the hostility in tone nevertheless made me a little sad."[28]

On Christmas Eve in Gaza, facing the Mediterranean from an ancient shore, he wrote quite differently:

> In Thy wind—in Thy light—
> How insignificant is everything else, how small are we—and how happy in that which alone is great.[29]

Responsibility and power

I don't know whether Pär Lagerkvist (1891–1974), the 1951 Nobel laureate in Literature, is still read. For my generation, which began seriously reading in the 1950s, his short novels—*The Sybil*, *The Dwarf*, *Barabbas*—offered an unforgettable experience of narrative clarity and moral acuity. Like his fellow Nobel laureates, Hermann Hesse and Albert Camus, he taught a sound—spare, focused, understated—and a way of looking at the world that struck me as both stoic and vulnerable. That attitude would do. A member of the Swedish Academy since 1940, Lagerkvist was on hand to greet Hammarskjöld when he joined in 1954. Hammarskjöld's correspondence with some of his fellow Academicians was incomparably rich; he was able to speak his mind with them and reveal something of his feelings in utmost confidence that he would be understood and that his words would go no farther. With Lagerkvist in January and August 1958, he took up the topics of responsibility and power. The pair of Hammarskjöld letters asks to be read nearly in full. There is little here to abridge if we are to understand the remarkable probe of motives and attitudes ignited by Lagerkvist.

Dear Pär

Your letter was a message from your world, and so good to receive. Thanks!

What you say about my present task reflects the problem with all the insight I know I can count on from you: I am, as you say, enviable. But I would like to specify the balance in my own words.

The unique, totally undeserved gift I have been given is the opportunity to engage in a decisive way in one of the greatest experiments of mankind and of this era. It is incredible to know that everything you can do, insofar as possible, to bring this experiment to maturity, even if it should fail, contributes to laying the foundation of something that has to succeed in the end.

When I say "everything," I mean things big and small: where quality is concerned, nothing in this work is meaningless, not even the most insignificant details, since the fate of the experiment and the success of this offensive into unknown territory are decided by the strength at the weakest point in the total effort. The satisfaction this gives at every moment, and facing every difficulty, of course means that only in moments of physical weariness do you shrink away in disbelief from the blows received, the stings, which are also part of day-to-day experience. They would be evil only if you let yourself be affected by them, by creating bitterness or affecting the direction of action itself. You can be quite relaxed: there is no risk that I'll lose perspective.

I regard it as naiveté if people believe that you can keep a position like this out of vanity or motives of that kind. In light of what I've said, you see that I am happy for every moment I have this task and am given these possibilities, but also that it would be treason to have this feeling of happiness if I weren't ready to give up the position at the very moment I felt that would be the right thing for the sake of the overall undertaking. It would also be treason if I permitted the wish to continue in any way to influence how I carry out my task. Here the circle joins: those who question my motives and at the same time amuse themselves by taking pot-shots at what is being achieved are tempters in the sense that if I were affected by their pot-shots they would be right to cast suspicion on me.

It is not easy to analyze these questions in a letter, but I think your point of departure is such that you'll have no difficulties understanding what I'm trying to say.

One of the great sacrifices is exile from the environment by which you have been molded. In this work, of necessity, one is very lonely and for that reason has an increased, childish need for still "feeling at home" somewhere. Even that carries little weight in light of what the task gives; one simply has to learn that part of the price of this effort is isolation, compensated by the feeling of a deeper and wider solidarity with the many people, known and unknown, who have fully accepted the same demands. For that reason, letters like yours carry such weight with their messages both "from home" and from other participants in the Journey to the East.[30]

It is an exercise in "conscious self-scrutiny"; the term, you'll recall, is his. He describes what he writes as an analysis, but it is just as much a synthesis, drawing together fragments of perception into a well-seen whole. Awareness is spectacular when it functions in this way, detached enough to take in what occurs, attentive enough to catch every detail, concerned enough to come close. His word "treason" is striking: it gives weight and drama to his conviction that he must remain free inside. His concluding reference to the Journey to the East shows how much he cared for Hermann Hesse's classic novella of that title, which begins, "It was my destiny to join in a great experience. Having had the good luck to belong to the League, I was permitted to be a participant in a unique journey." Hammarskjöld could have written identical words about his participation in the United Nations. He had in mind to translate Hesse's novel into Swedish but never found time.

Although written more than a half year later, Hammarskjöld's second letter on power and responsibility reads as part of the same conversation. The second half of the letter, concerning Nobel Prize candidates, may seem to wander into lesser terrain, but where he writes of triumph and tragedy he is already thinking along lines that would surface again, and powerfully, in the last months of his life.

Dear Pär

Your very welcome letter came as an encouraging greeting from a wiser, warmer, and lighter world than the one in which I live. Just the address Rönnäng [a village on the North Sea island of Tjörn] is to me so rich in associations of a free horizon and "real" people that it feels like a fresh breeze.

What you say about the importance of my attitude to work I think hits the target. It is easier to accept influence, responsibility and "power" if you feel personally free and prepared to retire at any time. Honesty demands, however, that I add one thing. In the drama itself lies a temptation: you can fall in love with the stimulation of responsibility and influence to the degree that at a superficial level you are tempted, after all, to cling to a position which, from a more elevated perspective, you regard as a possibility as long as you are totally free in relation to it. The risk of such a poisoning is of course something quite different from the joy in the task I once wrote to you about, did I not? It is destructive and falsifies both the way you look at others and your own judgment at work.

I do not quite agree with you that what is happening in the Academy sinks into insignificance compared to what we experience here. The relevant common denominator lies on a purely human plane, and there the scale of values is different. Sten Selander once wrote that he envied my being allowed to "create literature" in action. My envy goes in the opposite direction. Common to both ways of life is the possibility of a creative contact between the individual and the context of reality in which he is placed.

Reflections in this direction have new reality for me while reading *Dr. Zhivago*—as, by the way, earlier while reading Perse's *Amers*. What a harrowing book *Zhivago* is on the different levels you can read it! Common to Pasternak and Perse—as far as I can see, the two greatest of the "unawarded"—is the mature reconciliation with life for which they have fought, a reconciliation where the distinction between triumph and tragedy is totally obliterated in a victorious and affirmative humanity. A critic has no difficulty in finding weaknesses in both of them—as far as *Zhivago* is concerned, even grave weaknesses at times—but what do they matter in relation to the whole? ...

You might guess how much I would like to come to Sweden and how warmly I then would hope to get a chance to talk with you in peace and quiet. Now the Middle East has smashed all plans....[31]

The analysis of power and temptation, and the heartening reference to "joy in the task," speak for themselves: this is Hammarskjöld thinking aloud on the basis of his own reconciliation with life. But he goes further, into crushingly difficult terrain where he joins other thinkers and writers formed by their experience of total war, massive dislocation, and resistance to nihilism. I'm thinking particularly of Lagerkvist himself and of Hesse, Camus, and Miłosz, while Hammarskjöld is thinking of Pasternak and

Perse. On that terrain, where he has taken risks as secretary-general and will of necessity take more, Hammarskjöld has glimpsed the possibility of "a reconciliation where the distinction between triumph and tragedy is totally obliterated in a victorious and affirmative humanity." Catching echoes from so much in Western literature and experience, from the conversation on Socrates's last day to Nicholas of Cusa's "coincidence of opposites," this is not a small thought. It values effort above outcome and foresees deep solace at the moment when all appears lost.

A positive and overriding discipline

The year 1958 began with a certain ease for Hammarskjöld. He resumed regular press conferences—and resumed the pleasing game of cat and mouse with journalists who pressed him for more information than he could wisely provide. For example, in this delicious exchange with Joseph Lash, later to be one of his first and best biographers, concerning the possibilities for peace in the Middle East:

The Secretary-General: I have my dreams.

Mr. Lash: You have dreams?

The Secretary-General: Yes, not plans.

Mr. Lash: Would you care to share them with us?

The Secretary-General: I very rarely share my dreams with anybody.[32]

And that was the end of the press conference. This wasn't news, but it was fun, Garbo-like. One can imagine his words in her smoky voice.

The earlier pages of this chapter make clear that his reelection to a second term beginning in April had prompted him to renew and in part redirect his thought. He was looking at many things freshly, foreseeing trouble or challenges to come, making time for public talks. A second swarm of ideas emerged, as multiple and rich as the first. Expressed in a letter to Eyvind Johnson, his prevailing attitude was taut and lively. In that particular letter of late January 1958, he characterized his experience in a most original way and measured the atmosphere in Sweden, recently visited, in terms that shed light on settled, well-off societies.

> I live in a very obvious way right in the middle of the stream and I am forced to adjust my nerves so that they react as exactly and quickly as possible to the many evil and few good things that every day push us forward on the threatened road of mankind.

Living like that, torn away from the shores, one looks for landmarks and points of support. Of course, one first returns to oneself, in an inner sense. But one tries also to connect with one's own environment, happy to encounter something that is on the whole so "decent," so balanced. At the same time, it's worrisome that this decency is a reflection of self-sufficiency, that all these balanced people lack humility and protect themselves by not taking far greater responsibility. They believe themselves to participate because they are judges, but they lack the participation based on a sense of responsibility and an awareness that they too are in the prisoner's dock. . . .

Forgive me these effusions. Time only allows me to dictate a letter, to which I would liked to have given more thought. What you get is thus only a rather childish attempt to crystallize reactions that I constantly need to understand myself and throw more light on.[33]

Nowhere did he say so clearly that correspondence with trusted others was an extension of his unceasing concern to think things through, discern patterns, find words. Neither a wholly intimate journal entry nor a public statement, correspondence occupied middle ground where friendship has its place. His remark here about judges and defendants speaks to another sort of "poisoning," to recall a word in his correspondence with Lagerkvist.

The diplomatic agenda between the start of the year and the beginning of the second term was moderate in comparison to Suez and its aftermath. In cooperation with the Security Council he played a role, not for the last time, in calming relations between France, the former colonial power, and Tunisia, the former colony in which France insisted on maintaining military bases until certain treaty arrangements had been settled. Reacting to the French bombing of a village near the Tunisian border with Algeria—a reprisal for pro-Algerian military activity centered there—the Tunisian government applied pressure by refusing to allow food and other supplies into French installations. The immediate issue was worked through with the help of mediation by the United States and Britain; the longer-term issues of French bases in Tunisia and Algerian independence remained. Meanwhile, among the Great Powers disarmament talks were going on and on in a cloud of propaganda from all sides. The issue had become even more urgent since the Soviet Union in October 1957 had successfully launched Sputnik, the first satellite in Earth orbit; the implications were obvious for the future of surveillance and warfare. At the end of March, the Soviet Union unilaterally suspended its nuclear arms testing, an initiative welcomed by Hammarskjöld and met with suspicion by the United States. A month later, the United States proposed an Arctic international inspection zone to prevent surprise attacks, an initiative welcomed by Hammarskjöld and met with suspicion by the Soviets. Acutely aware of the complete lack of trust between the nuclear powers, and of the complete lack of trust between neighbors in the Middle East and elsewhere, Hammarskjöld recognized a theme he felt obliged to bring to public attention. The rather grand occasion for doing so was a lecture at Cambridge University in early June under the title "The Walls of Distrust"; he was to receive an honorary doctorate. As he approached that gathering, he went out of his way to spend time in conversation with a like-minded thinker whom he had recently discovered, the Israeli religious philosopher and social thinker Martin Buber, who quickly became a personal friend. Their dialogue, conducted in part through correspondence, has attracted admiring attention.[34] Hammarskjöld belonged with Buber, and Buber with Hammarskjöld. Sitting together in Buber's home in suburban Jerusalem, they lean toward one another with brimming goodwill (fig. 14).

Apart from Tunisia and disarmament, the early months of 1958 took Hammarskjöld to Moscow for high-level, unpublicized conversations; London, where he addressed members of both Houses of Parliament; and briefly Geneva to meet with Fawzi about Egyptian and Middle Eastern affairs. He was following an agenda he had stated with new clarity in a talk at Ohio University in early February: "We cannot afford to reckon peace as merely the absence of war. We have to make of it a positive and overriding discipline of international life."[35] Steely and clear-sighted, these are again words to be engraved on walls in nations' capitals.

As the General Assembly was not in session at the beginning of Hammarskjöld's second term, April 9th, the calendar was open for recognition events less stately, more welcome. The press corps timed a luncheon for him perfectly on that very day, and the Secretariat staff recruited him with little notice the next day to a gathering in the General Assembly hall, which they had to themselves. Hammarskjöld's thought, and surely his heart, soared in response to both gatherings. With the journalists whom he had come to know so well, he found himself speaking freely in a spirit of exploration; an entire worldview resounded in his remarks. He confronted his own steady optimism, his faith.

> The slow, slow growth which goes beyond not only our time but really beyond the span of generations . . . seems to us too slow because it

cannot be put down in figures and letters and dots and points. There is just no way of saying how far we have got. You have to have it in your fingertips; you have to have the feeling and even what you have in that way is insufficient for you to say, "We have made progress." Finally, you fall back on that most elusive of things, your confidence in the fact that progress has been made, that we are moving in the right direction, although you cannot prove it, perhaps not even to yourself. . . .

Very often I ask myself in line with your own questions: "But really, have you got a solid basis for what you say when you voice this so-called optimism?" And somehow the whole system replies, "Yes, you have," and yet I cannot spell it out. . . .

I cannot belong to or join those who believe in our movement toward catastrophe. I believe in growth, a growth to which we have a responsibility to add our few fractions of an inch.

It is not the facile faith of generations before us, who thought that everything was arranged for the best in the best of worlds or that physical and psychological development necessarily worked out toward something they called progress. It is in a sense a much harder belief— the belief and the faith that the future will be all right because there will always be enough people to fight for a decent future. . . .

It is in a sense a switch from the atmosphere of pre-1914 to what I believe is the atmosphere of our generation . . . —a switch from the, so to say, mechanical optimism of previous generations to what I might call the fighting optimism of this present generation. We have learned it the hard way, and we will certainly have to learn it again and again and again.[36]

"Somehow the whole system replies." What a striking expression, implying something we haven't detected earlier in Hammarskjöld's vision of things: a perception of worlds upon worlds or worlds within worlds. It would encompass the UN in all its complexity, sovereign governments, political leaders, public opinion, cultural and religious influences, and who knows what more, all of which can somehow speak with one voice to a very good listener. We as listeners will also detect here Hammarskjöld's unstudied humility, which allowed him, a global leader of consequence, to say "you have to have it in your fingertips . . . , you cannot prove it." When he felt free to be plainspoken, the sensitivity behind the remarkable intellect shines through. Always he felt the grind between generations—between his father's generation formed in the nineteenth century, his mentor Wigforss's generation of social planners, and his own generation that had known two total wars and understood that a third must not be permitted. "The future will be all right": this is the simplest and best reassurance from a man of few illusions.

On the following day, the chairman of the Secretariat staff committee paid Hammarskjöld a number of thoughtful compliments. "You have created a new style in contemporary diplomacy which you carry out with imagination and with verve. You have provided a quiet center and a calm course."[37] Hammarskjöld again felt invited to speak with simplicity and feeling. In a venue accustomed to close calculations of political risk and advantage, he spoke spontaneously—first of himself and then of the bond among those present, the men and women of the Secretariat. In what he said of himself there is heartfelt truth, not of a kind to engrave on a nation's walls; it is more intimate than that.

> I was standing here in this very place five years ago this very day, and in fact this very hour. I was facing a rather unknown kind of journey. I knew only one thing and that is that nobody can do more than is in his power, and I had only one intention and that was to do that much. I had only one simple rule, which may sound terribly selfish, but that rule is a fairly valid rule. I felt that this kind of job . . . carries with it very considerable risks. There is very much you can lose on them. But I knew . . . that there is one thing . . . nobody ever needs to lose, and that is his self-respect. And if I had any promise which I had in mind and which I gave to myself five years ago, it was just this one: whatever happens, stick to your guns, so that you can feel satisfaction with what you have done, whatever the outcome.[38]

Although his listeners could not have known it, comments he made a little later on the quality of community in the Secretariat all but erased the boundary between the religious perspective of *Markings* and the directness typical of Hammarskjöld's public statements. His thinking began with a nicely reasoned distinction between teamwork and belonging, but—perhaps to his own surprise—developed into heartfelt words touched with longing.

> Teamwork may easily mean simply that people work for the same purpose, that we are . . . formally tied together by the very fact that we are on the same payroll, that we are under the same rules, and so forth. From my point of view, that is not enough. We are not what we should be, we have not reached the full strength of our possible contribution, until we have

managed to develop within ourselves, and in our relations with others, the sense of belonging. We are no Vatican, we are no republic, we are not outside the world—we are very much in the world. But, even within the world, there can be this . . . sense of belonging, this deeper sense of unity. I hope that we are on our road to that sense. I feel that we have moved in that direction and, to the extent that it depends upon me, I can give you one assurance: whatever I can do for that purpose, I will do.[39]

This was the consecration of the second term.

We can't know at what time of day Hammarskjöld typically opened his journal, but there is a dated entry for April 10th, probably meditated and written that evening after the richly felt events of the day. Its importance has not been missed by authors and readers; it reads like a new credo, as if in these two days of vivid experiences and warm personal acknowledgments he found an impulse to look anew at the fundamentals of his map of life. He began where he often began, with the definition of faith in St. John of the Cross, the Spanish mystic and teacher, and moved on to situate himself between an inmost mystery—the Other—and the life of action and responsibility to which he also belonged. From this naturally emerged a charge to himself, an acknowledgment of duty.

> In that faith which is "God's union with the soul,"
> you are *one* in God
> and God wholly in you,
> just as, for you, He is wholly in all you meet.
> With this faith, in prayer you descend into yourself to
> meet the Other
> in the obedience and light of this union;
> see that all stand, like yourself, alone before God,
>   that each act is a continuing act of creation—conscious, because
> you are a human being with human responsibilities, but governed, nevertheless, by the power beyond consciousness which created man.
>   You are free from things but encounter them in an experience which has the liberating purity and penetrating clarity of revelation.
>   In that faith which is "God's union with the soul," therefore *everything* has meaning.
>   *So* live, then, and so use what has been put into your hand . . . [40]

This, too, is a consecration. Hammarskjöld asserts and acknowledges a sacred world, and does so with spiritual courage by daring to see himself, all others, and all elements of God's creation as immersed in a constant revelation. The insight is an invitation to live. Revelation resides in the encounter. The "positive and overriding discipline" of which we heard him speak where world affairs are concerned finds its internal parallel in this stunning summary.

Stepping back from the entry, we should notice a concept new to *Markings*: the Other. It appears only here and in the very next entry. The translation is good, from Sw. *den Andre*. Hammarskjöld would have had the word and concept from his familiarity with Kierkegaard's thought and his early reading in Rudolf Otto's *The Idea of the Holy*, which speaks of the encounter with the "Wholly Other" as an aspect of mystical experience. Should we intuit that he has moved on in his life of meditative prayer from a more marginal experience "at the frontier of the Unheard-of"—language earlier in *Markings*—to a more direct, unshielded experience of the mystery of being? That seems right. We don't need utter clarity here; even Otto closed his discussion of the Wholly Other by writing that we can "*feel* its special character . . . without being able to give it clear conceptual expression."[41] In the classic Sufi fable *The Conference of the Birds*, the Wholly Other at last reached by a ragtag company of birds reveals itself as deeply akin to themselves, Other in its majesty and unfathomable mystery, yet birdlike, flesh of their flesh, feather of their feather.[42] Wherever one looks in religious literature or experience, this is the mystery of transcendence and immanence, of the Wholly Other and its trace in us and in all things. Hammarskjöld didn't solve it, as if it were a riddle that would yield; he experienced it. "You have to have it in your fingertips; you have to have the feeling."

The impromptu ceremony of these days concluded with a *New York Times* article on April 13th for which Hammarskjöld must have given an interview; one hears him in it.

"The worldwide prestige enjoyed by Dag Hammarskjöld," it begins, " . . . is one of the extraordinary phenomena of our age. For a decade the United Nations has been the principal battlefield of the 'cold war,' and yet he continues to enjoy the confidence and respect of both sides—and the neutralists as well. . . . As he sees it, if the Soviet Union and the United States are trying to build a house and can't agree on the roof, this is all the more reason why they should work together on the basement if they can."[43]

The walls of distrust

Work on the basement became messy and mean-spirited soon after the wave of well-wishing. The Security Council debate on two proposals, Soviet and American, was a harsh exercise in distrust, the proposals calling respectively for the cessation of flights over the Arctic by US military aircraft and for the establishment of an Arctic early warning system to deter surprise attacks by either party. Hammarskjöld had long since come to grips with intense distrust, notably in the Middle East. We have read his white-hot letter to Ben-Gurion, written at the end of July 1956 to express with some desperation his own attitude. "Please do not believe," he had written, "that I permit myself to be taken in by *anybody*, but realize, on the other hand, that I cannot work on the general assumption of people trying to double-cross me even when this runs counter to their own interest. Being afraid of being fooled to that extent, I would fool myself. I could then just as well stop all efforts."[44] But his individual practice was far ahead of the practice of nations pursuing Cold War strategies in the Security Council. He was aware of a regrettable and potentially dangerous duality in the attitudes of leaders and did what he could to overcome it—but, as he told a group of American state governors, "the game goes on."

> It is one of the surprising experiences of one in the position of the Secretary-General of the United Nations to find in talks with leaders of many nations, both political leaders and leaders in spiritual life, that the view expressed, the hopes nourished and the trust reflected, in the direction of reconciliation, go far beyond what is usually heard in public. What is it that makes it so difficult to bring this basic attitude more effectively to bear upon the determination of policies? The reasons are well known to us all. It might not be understood by the constituency, or it might be abused by competing groups, or it might be misinterpreted as a sign of weakness by the other party. And so the game goes on—toward an unforeseeable conclusion.[45]

The ill-fated Security Council debate coincided in time with his first contact with Martin Buber, whose newly published book of essays and talks, *Pointing the Way*, he had just read with a sense of powerful kinship.[46] As Buber happened to be in Princeton when Hammarskjöld first wrote to him, they were able to meet at the UN for two uninterrupted hours on May 1st, just two days after Hammarskjöld had most unusually requested the floor in the Security Council to state his view of the impasse that had been reached and, more broadly, of the crisis of trust as he perceived it. Hammarskjöld's thought and Buber's on the damage done by distrust now run parallel.

A week before his intervention in the Security Council and that first meeting with Buber, he was uneasy. "We have had a troubled and unsteady spring," he wrote to Eyvind Johnson.

> The flight of starlings I told you about must have been too early. Not only in the external sense. You can feel the threat against the future stronger and stronger, but paradoxically enough parallel to that is growing an irrational conviction that we shall be able to break through the causal chain of fear, clumsiness, self-assertion and plain common stupidity. Have you read Martin Buber? The old Hasidic mystic has in his old age given some of the purest and most touching expressions of "conversion," in which he as one of the old prophets sees the only rescue. "The only reply to distrust is candor." "We must create the simple trust which alone makes human speech possible in a world where we have forgotten how to talk to each other." I don't have the text in front of me and consequently don't quote word for word, but I believe that I've rendered his words correctly enough for you to see at what level he encounters the key issues of our generation. As a practitioner in the hazardous field of international politics I can only confirm how right he is: behind the development lies a disease, which has struck at some of the simplest but also most vital elements in ordinary human coexistence.[47]

It would have been with thoughts of this kind that he decided to speak in the Security Council. He was diffident—"It is most unusual, as you know, for the Secretary-General to intervene in a debate of the Security Council"—but also sure of his ground. "The Secretary-General has not only the right but the duty to intervene when he feels that he should do so in support of the purposes of the Organization and . . . the Charter." He reminded the Council that he had welcomed the Soviet decision to suspend nuclear testing and took the floor today to express support for the United States' proposal on inspection because it might end the disarmament stalemate. Knowing the need to be impartial and even-handed in everything he said, he advanced with utmost care a broader analysis. Governments had thus far been too ambitious and should be satisfied with "just making a dent in this intricate and vital problem from which a rift could develop, opening up the possibilities of a true exchange of views." He also observed a tendency of governments to wait for others to make the first move. And then he expressed the perspective he now knew he shared with Martin Buber: "Still another reason, and of course the basic one, is the crisis of trust from which all mankind is suffering at the present juncture and which is reflected in an unwillingness to take any moves in a positive direction at their face value and a tendency to hold back a positive response because of a fear of being misled. . . . Good faith . . . is, of course, not the same as to let down one's guard." Small positive moves, he suggested, "could, if followed through, provide a first frail basis for the development of some kind of trust." He concluded disarmingly with words of trust: "I trust that my intervention will not be misinterpreted as a taking of sides, but merely as an expression of profound feelings which are current all over the world and . . . have a right to be heard here. . . ." To which he joined a modest hope and crisp assessment: "I hope that each one of the governments represented around this table will try out the line of trust as a way out of the disintegration and decline under which we now all suffer."[48] It was a bravura performance: soft-spoken, impartial, a breath of reason and decency.

Hammarskjöld knew that he had taken a risk by intervening but thought it a necessary one. He must have been reasonably pleased with his contribution. To Beskow, no doubt later in the day, he wrote in a light vein with an especially witty, almost surreal swipe at an unnamed adversary, surely Mr. Tingsten, the Swedish editorial eminence:

> Here everything is as usual. The wheels keep turning very fast, but the engine lasts, its vitality defying all the eager claims that it never was anything and anyway now is moribund. It pleases me to see that our loudest critic now pronounces his death sentence in the name of world federalism: it is about the same as declaring dentists useless because they cannot supply us with eternal life. But, as you know, the streams of emotion in this case are simple, deep, and utterly personal, so every hope of logic in his external reactions is out of the question.[49]

He also took time to write to George Ivan Smith, the UN communications director whom he often included in professional travel. He had shared with him Buber's book. "I am happy that Buber struck a chord in your UN soul as it did in mine. What a truly remarkable fellow and what an influence he might have on his own people if they really listened. . . . If we could make him understand our philosophy on Israel it might be of value beyond the human and personal sphere."[50] Buber represented for

Hammarskjöld a welcome alternative to Ben-Gurion, whom he admired for what he was and what he had accomplished—but with a grain of reserve. In an assessment of the two men shared privately with the Nobel Prize Committee, he wrote: "If Ben-Gurion and his predecessors have taken up the legacy of militant nationalism which characterized historic Israel, Buber can be said to have given new life to essential features of the prophetic tradition. One might venture to predict that this time as well the voice of the prophet will be shown to penetrate further into the future than the voice of the military leader."[51] Relations between Buber and Ben-Gurion were strained. With his vision of peaceful coexistence between Jews and Arabs, Buber was marginal in Israeli politics although respected, even loved by readers of many faiths worldwide.

On the following day in the Security Council, the Soviet ambassador made clear that his government was displeased. "The addition of Mr. Hammarskjöld's voice to the chorus of representatives of NATO countries and their allies glorifying the United States propaganda maneuver did not alter the character of that maneuver or make it any more attractive; nor did the Secretary-General's statement contribute towards strengthening his own authority. Indeed, quite the contrary."[52] This was a sorry misrepresentation. Hammarskjöld had spoken with "the low voice of reason" and offered "the clear little light of decency"—these are his own words from the months of Suez—but even the UN press corps, let alone an angry Soviet ambassador, questioned his intervention. The journalists sensed something new here; they probed in a friendly way for what it was. In keeping with the Charter's definition of the secretary-general's scope, he had promised to take more independent initiatives than in the past. Without calling attention to it, he had begun to keep that promise. As matters developed, the seemingly fruitless debate in the Security Council led on in mid-May to just the sort of "dent" that Hammarskjöld thought possible: a decision to explore jointly the technical aspects of nuclear detection devices that might someday be stationed in the Arctic.

On Saturday, May 3rd, doubtless a day of rest, Hammarskjöld sent off a volley of letters to Sweden that recorded his personal perspective on recent events. To Beskow he referred in passing to a new difficulty in the Middle East but focused on the Security Council. "You are quite right," he wrote,

> that the last few weeks have been rather tense. First there was the "parade" in Jerusalem and then we got the new and very venomous conflict

between the USA and the USSR. I had to play fairly high stakes in both cases with a reasonable degree of short-term success and some hope for the future. I have sent you the texts concerning the Arctic story and I think that they will tell you, better than I could sum up in a letter, how I look at the present situation. It is obvious that this seems to me to be one which fully warranted the risk-taking involved in the operation last Tuesday [in the Security Council]: the Russians may make big noises but there is no misunderstanding in their mind as to why I did it, and that is really all that matters for the continued work here.[53]

And so—how otherwise could we have known?—Hammarskjöld wasn't upset by the Russian attitude, which he charged up to "the game goes on." The parade celebrating the tenth anniversary of the State of Israel included a display of heavy armaments in Jerusalem. The military emphasis had prompted protests from Jordan and other countries, including the United States.

To his brother Bo he wrote much the same as to Beskow but more openly shared his anxiety:

Maybe I can dare to say: "victory on points." Neither Israel's nor the Soviets' expressions of discontent should be taken seriously. They were unavoidable "for public consumption," and behind them both are hidden understanding and respect.

Otherwise everything is fine. Knock on wood. . . . But the world is in a fix. I am beginning now to be really worried. The American flights are a nastily ingenious form of the war of nerves—no matter how reasonable their motivation may be. And when will the Russians answer? Instinctively I have the feeling that we have now cocked the rifle. Let's hope I'm wrong.[54]

With another correspondent, the poet and translator Erik Lindegren, he returned that day to the theme of distrust and the need for honest dialogue, now enriched in his mind by his contact with Martin Buber. "Things are not going so well," he wrote,

and I think the time has come for the so-called intellectuals to make their voice heard with greater urgency. I saw the other day old Martin Buber—he really is a great man—who said that he felt we have reached a stage where individual life has been completely gobbled up by political life. . . . I think he is basically right, and that is one reason why poets should add a new dimension to their task as guardians of straightforward human communication in which respect for the word is still maintained.[55]

He himself took up that challenge in the talk he gave at Cambridge University in early June, the occasion at which he received an honorary degree. He must have decided to offer in that elite public forum a fuller version of the thoughts that some weeks earlier had received a mixed reception in the Security Council. Not defiantly, but deliberately, he went over the heads of the Security Council membership to enlist public understanding through a talk that would find its way into the media. He spoke not of international policy but of human attitudes. One further decision is easily detected: he permitted himself to speak with the flair and nuance of a man of letters.

After graceful introductory words about his student year in Cambridge and the university's importance "as a fact and as a symbol," Hammarskjöld turned toward more musical language, addressing ear and feeling as much as mind. The rhythms tend to be terse, sentence endings abrupt in the early paragraphs. Repetitions of key words confer an initial chant-like quality. I do not believe that any of this is contrived for dramatic effect. He didn't much like drama or effects. He had thoughts to share and a compelling sense of urgency; the rest followed. In the Security Council he had spoken of the "nightmare" facing the peoples of the world in the nuclear age. Here he very nearly pleads with his audience to face that nightmare, understand it, and participate in dispelling it.

> We meet in a time of peace which is no peace, in a time of technical achievement which threatens its own masters with destruction.
>
> We meet in a time when the ideas evoked in our minds by the term "humanity" have switched to a turbulent political reality from the hopeful dreams of our predecessors.
>
> The widening of our political horizons to embrace in a new sense the whole of the world, should have meant an approach to the ideal sung in Schiller's "Ode to Joy," but it has, paradoxically, led to new conflicts and to new difficulties to establish even simple human contact and communication.
>
> Korea, China, Indonesia, Kashmir, Palestine, Hungary, North Africa. There are fires all around the horizon, and they are not fires announcing peace. More perturbing than all these smoldering or barely controlled conflicts are the main underlying tendencies, which we all know only too well and which preoccupy our minds and darken our hopes.[56]

It is touching that Schiller's "Ode to Joy," the text of the choral movement of Beethoven's Ninth Symphony, came to Hammarskjöld's mind. By arranging for performances of the symphony at nearly every UN Day celebration, he had defined that work as the musical transcription of the struggles and ideals of the United Nations. He went on to make three linked points about the slow development of the UN, about maturity, and about a theme we have previously noticed: the substitution of true leadership for arrogant power. What he says of maturity could also be written on nations' walls, but we may have exceeded our due in that regard.

> We may well rejoice in having taken the first steps toward the establishment of an international democracy of peoples, bringing all nations— irrespective of history, size, or wealth—together on an equal basis as partners in the vast venture of creating a true world community. But we have taken only the first steps, and they have often proved painful. There is a maturity of mind required of those who give up rights. There is a maturity of mind required of those who acquire new rights. Let us hope that, to an increasing extent, the necessary spiritual qualities will be shown on all sides.
>
> Today we are in the middle of this development and, naturally, we tend to judge it from the viewpoint of our own past and our own immediate interests. This may explain why many now show reactions which seem to reflect a kind of despair of Western civilization. But, where is the reason for such defeatism? Is it not possible to establish and maintain a spiritual leadership, whatever the changes in other respects?

He was thinking again of the process of decolonization and of learning to share the world and power with newly independent nations emerging in Asia and Africa. He wanted no more Suez-like crises. He warned, as well, against permitting the Cold War with its power blocs and righteous propaganda to blind his listeners to the fact that

> the dividing line goes within ourselves, within our own peoples, and also within other nations. It does not coincide with any political or geographical boundaries. The ultimate fight is one between the human and the subhuman. We are on dangerous ground if we believe that any individual, any nation, or any ideology has a monopoly on rightness, liberty, and human dignity.
>
> When we fully recognize this and translate our insight into words and action, we may also be able to reestablish full human contact and

communications across geographical and political boundaries, and to get out of a public debate which often seems to be inspired more by a wish to impress than by a will to understand and to be understood.

Soon he found his way to a passage in Buber's book offering brilliant insights into the decay of dialogue and growth of distrust. He chose simply to quote the passage at length as an expression that could not be improved upon. Drawing toward his conclusion, he issued his call to the individual:

> All of us, in whatever field of intellectual activity we work, influence to some degree the spiritual trend of our time. All of us may contribute to the breakdown of the walls of distrust and toward checking fatal tendencies in the direction of stale conformism and propaganda. How can this be done better or more effectively than by simple faithfulness to the independence of the spirit and to the right of the free man to free thinking and free expression of his thoughts.

He was not Buber; he was a fieldworker who did some of his most original thinking in the diplomatic scenes to which his position dispatched him. Returning from the Middle East some six months after giving this speech, he put a note in the mail to Sir Dennis Robertson, a distinguished Cambridge economist whom he might have first met in the course of postwar monetary negotiations. He began with reflections about "the odd ways in which we men run our business," and continued: "My last trip repeated the experience of the importance of friendly but critical common sense in keeping some of our friends away from mischief; the pathetic thing is that it should be so easy to nip some conflicts in the bud provided you manage to say the simplest things in a way that registers."[57] This is a fieldworker's report on dismantling walls of distrust in one corner of the Earth.

14

Face the Cold Winds

"I think the United Nations should face the cold winds of the day," he said to the UN press corps at one of their luncheons.[1] When Hammarskjöld returned to New York from Cambridge, cold winds were blowing. The situation suddenly facing him seemed like a Suez Crisis in the making with Middle Eastern nations in conflict and jeopardy, soon a murderous coup, abrupt Western military interventions, Soviet threats, a deadlocked Security Council, and an emergency session of the General Assembly. But the Lebanon-Jordan crisis was short lived; by late autumn it had passed. A resourceful exercise in diplomacy in the General Assembly by many, by Hammarskjöld, and among the Arab member nations generated solutions that all could accept with a certain pride of workmanship. One lasting outcome was elegant: a new, modest, but effective UN presence in the region, and on that model soon in other regions of the world. Hammarskjöld worked tirelessly toward this happy dénouement. If we take time to follow this story in some detail, it is not so much for the sake of its baroque plotline as it is to know the context in which Hammarskjöld devised a new peacekeeping strategy. The situation was dangerous, although from his perspective as a veteran of conflicts in the Middle East, it was also familiar and grimly amusing: "As you can imagine," he wrote to Lindegren in midsummer, "I'm living altogether in an ongoing robbers' drama, with strong elements of Gilbert and Sullivan but also of Grand Guignol: this sounds entertaining, and it *would have been* entertaining were it not for the risk that it all end with Götterdämmerung."[2] Grand Guignol was a Parisian theater, shuttered in the early 1960s but famous in its time for elaborately bloody melodramas, precursors of the horror film.

The Lebanon-Jordan crisis also, and more mildly, resembled a hand-held board game popular in Hammarskjöld's era in which one space in a grid was open, all others occupied by sliding squares numbered from one to thirty or so in random order. The goal was to slide squares in all directions around the open space to put the numbers in order. It took patience and flanking maneuvers to succeed, and you had to keep an eye on the whole board to move strays to their proper places. Something like this happened in the Middle East: there was little room for maneuver, but enough. The crucial difference between the crisis and the game is that each square was a nation, political leader or faction, or outside force such as the United Nations, and some had no idea they were allocated just one square.

In earlier years Lebanon had enough tranquility, and has always been beautiful enough, to project in other parts of the world a dream of many races and religions living in harmony in a pleasant place beside the sea. Khalil Gibran, the Lebanese-American poet, would write of "temples roofed with dreams" in his native land. That dream of quiet polity was shaken in 1958 by a domestic conflict between Camille Chamoun, a Christian president seeking a constitutional change to permit him to stand for reelection, and an increasingly militant, predominantly Muslim opposition encouraged by Nasser's Pan-Arabism and alleged to be supplied with arms by neighboring Syria. Since February of that year, Syria had formed a new combined nation with Egypt, the United Arab Republic (UAR), which gave political form to Nasser's growing influence to the north. As the president of a UN member nation, Chamoun filed a complaint with the Security Council on May 22nd, claiming UAR interference in Lebanon's domestic affairs and a threat to peace in the region. The Council took up the topic on June 6th, with Hammarskjöld deeply engaged both at the conference table and privately with delegations. A resolution adopted on June 11th instructed the secretary-general, as he wished, "to dispatch urgently an observation group" to Lebanon with the mission of verifying along the Lebanese-Syrian border whether arms, personnel, or other supplies were being clandestinely slipped into Lebanon to strengthen the opposition National Front, which controlled much of the border territory.[3] The group was to document incursions, report to the UN, and thereby alert world public opinion. As his chief of staff, Andrew Cordier, was already on the way to the Middle East, Hammarskjöld managed to set in motion at once what was soon called the United Nations Observation Group in Lebanon (UNOGIL). He and Cordier borrowed instant staff from the UN Truce Supervision Organization headquartered at Jerusalem, and within a few days three senior figures, including the Indian diplomat Rajeshwar Dayal, had agreed to lead and develop the new organization. Hammarskjöld insisted from the beginning that the Security Council resolution stipulated an observer group, not an armed peacekeeping force on the pattern of UNEF, though he was pressured from several sides and at some length to consider that option. He was determined to match the remedy to the illness, which was serious but not overwhelming.

Lebanon was the target of a racket of anti-Chamoun propaganda from UAR radio stations. Questioned about propaganda at a press conference the day after the June 11th resolution, Hammarskjöld broadened the topic: "[It is] simply something that I would like to see disappear from this world—not only in this case, in this or that specific direction, but generally."[4] In a new exercise of shuttle diplomacy, he went out to the Middle East on June 19th to confer with the leaders of the nascent UNOGIL as well as Chamoun, Nasser, and other regional leaders. Nasser pacifically agreed to do what he could to stop any flow of arms and personnel across the Syrian border and to moderate the propaganda war. Chamoun remained nervous, his diplomats calling for a UNEF-like force to close the border with Syria while he made clear to Eisenhower that, failing all else, an armed intervention by US troops would be welcome. He had not concluded that he himself should go. The situation remained quite grim, scarcely lifted by its few Gilbert and Sullivan moments—such as a large cake served by Chamoun at a banquet for Hammarskjöld with a message on top: "United Nations Save Lebanon." Hammarskjöld drily commented, "Only the Lebanese can save Lebanon."[5] And then, the diligent observation team determined that the nocturnal traffic of cross-border trucks from Syria wasn't arms shipments but groceries, customarily transported in the cool of night to morning markets.

Everything changed on July 14th, so rapidly that one has the impression the gun was already cocked, as Hammarskjöld wrote to his brother in early May—though that was another gun. There was a bloody coup that day against the Iraqi government, one of few reliable Western allies in the region. King, crown prince, and prime minister were murdered by a coterie of army officers; a republic was proclaimed; and new policies were immediately announced, among them withdrawal from the Arab Union with Jordan—another reliable Western ally—and a policy of nonalignment in international affairs. The United States and Britain, Lebanon and Jordan all perceived the coup as a highly threatening, Nasser-inspired, Soviet-influenced venture likely to topple neighboring regimes and reduce Western influence. At Chamoun's urgent request, President Eisenhower ordered a Marine landing in Lebanon the next day and dispatched the Sixth Fleet to the region. Jordan made a parallel request to its ally, Great Britain, which sent troops soon after to deter a perceived plot to overthrow the Jordanian government. What had been a reasonably manageable political drama had suddenly acquired a volatile Suez-like character, this time with the participation of the United States.

In the Security Council, US Ambassador Lodge made the case that his country had dispatched troops to protect the lawful government and deter what it called "indirect aggression" on the part of unnamed powers—of course the Soviet Union, presumed to be pulling strings behind the scene. In the debate that followed, Hammarskjöld stubbornly hewed to his path by distributing frequent reports from the field about the activities of UNOGIL and recommending expansion of its personnel and equipment, while Lodge was urging the Council to authorize a UNEF-like force as an outgrowth of the observer group. Serving its rotation in the Council as a nonpermanent member, Sweden argued for suspending UNOGIL in light of the presence of foreign troops in Lebanon; that cannot have pleased Hammarskjöld. The Soviet ambassador furiously called for the immediate withdrawal of US and British troops. Various resolutions were introduced for debate, the most impressive clearly intended to solve the problem and reconcile adversaries rather than score propaganda points. On July 22nd, after the Security Council failed to pass a resolution of any kind, Hammarskjöld took the floor to state that, in keeping with the June 11th resolution, he would continue to develop UNOGIL "so as to help to prevent a further deterioration . . . and to assist in finding a road away from the dangerous point at which we now find ourselves." He reminded the Council of what he had said some months ago about the need for the secretary-general to fill any vacuum that may appear in the systems provided by the Charter and traditional diplomacy, and promised to keep its members fully informed of his intentions and actions. And he again obliquely offered to resign: "Were you to disapprove of the way these intentions were to be translated into practical steps, I would, of course, accept the consequences of your judgment."[6] As he had written to Pär Lagerkvist in January, "it would be treason . . . if I weren't ready to give up the position."

Three strands wrapped around each other at this time: Eisenhower sent an able emissary to hold discussions in Lebanon, Nasser sought counsel from Khrushchev in Moscow, and Khrushchev fired off alarming letters to a number of heads of state—"the world is standing on the brink of catastrophe"—while simultaneously calling for a summit conference to resolve this and other issues.[7] You would think that rough outweighed smooth here, but in point of fact the situation began changing for the better. The American emissary, Robert Murphy, managed to persuade Chamoun to stand down from office in due course and encouraged General Fuad Chehab, the long-term commander of the Lebanese armed forces and a Christian trusted by all factions, to stand for election. That in itself was a formidable victory. Some months later, an Egyptian diplomat remarked that it would have been enough to send in Murphy without the troops. But a general solution lay quite far ahead. The summit idea soon vanished in a cross-fire of disagreement among heads of state. On August 7th the Security Council called for an emergency session of the General Assembly, which convened the following day. Meanwhile it was becoming clear that the new regime in Iraq was not in the Soviet camp. They had meant what they said: they were nationalists, neutral in foreign policy, independent, finding their allies as Nasser did among the countries that participated in the 1955 Bandung conference.

A week earlier, Hammarskjöld had sent a note to his brother Bo: "1,000 Marines on the shores of Beirut," he wrote, "with nothing to do but drink Coca-Cola. The Russians are served their diplomatic successes on a platter. Today the 'summit' is 'on again'! Let's see how things are tomorrow! And if it's happening—let's see how we'll fare in it! Khrushchev against Eisenhower is not a sporting match."[8] On the very day he wrote, General Chehab was elected by the Lebanese Chamber of Deputies to succeed Chamoun in September, and US troops in Lebanon were reaching their maximum of fourteen thousand, presumably all drinking Coca-Cola as there was nothing else to do. Hammarskjöld insisted that there be no interaction or cooperation between UNOGIL and US forces; he wanted no confusion.

The General Assembly session was episodic. After Hammarskjöld made an opening statement on August 8th, the subsequent debate led to an adjournment until August 13th, when President Eisenhower visited the Assembly to give a thorough account of the situation as he saw it. In the intervening days, a great deal of hallway diplomacy occurred, with Hammarskjöld doing his best to thin walls of distrust. In his opening statement, Hammarskjöld had anticipated changes in the Lebanon-Jordan situation that might call for a changed UN approach. "Recent experiences," he said, "may be taken as indicating that some form of United Nations representation in the country might be a desirable expression of the continued concern of the Organization for the independence and integrity of Lebanon. If that proves to be the case, forms should be sought by which such representation would adequately serve the purposes of the Organization in the region."[9] In dry language, this is an early reference to a new thought: Wouldn't it make sense to position a UN representative—a "UN presence"—in that part of the Middle East, modest in size, discreet in diplomatic style, a voice of reason, with a direct line to the secretary-general?

Before further exploring this idea, we should listen to Eisenhower and the speakers immediately after. Their words captured the atmosphere of that moment. "The lawful and freely elected Government of Lebanon," Eisenhower began, "feeling itself endangered by civil strife fomented from without, sent the United States a desperate call for instant help. We responded to that call. On the basis of that response an effort has been made to create a war hysteria. The impression is sought to be created that if small nations are assisted in their desire to survive, that endangers the peace. That is truly an 'upside down' portrayal. If it is made an international crime to help a small nation maintain its independence, then indeed the possibilities of conquest are unlimited." He defended British aid to Jordan and argued for the creation of a standby UN force ready at a moment's notice to intervene (an idea which to this day hasn't found enough support). The key phrases throughout his address were "fomenting from without" and "indirect aggression."[10] Though he spoke as a Cold Warrior addressing the Soviet Union without mentioning it by name, he also took care to project a decent and sensible vision of peace, arms control, and cooperation, and offered his assurance that US troops would be withdrawn as soon as the Lebanese government so requested.

Responding at once, the Soviet minister of foreign affairs Andrei Gromyko heatedly described the US and British interventions as "an armed invasion of the Near East, designed to consolidate their domination of the region, to retain control over its natural wealth and to reimpose the colonial system upon the peoples of the Arab countries, who for centuries have languished under foreign oppression." He warned that US and British policies could "push mankind into the abyss of a new war with all its grievous consequences." Next to speak was Mahmoud Fawzi, foreign minister of the recently formed UAR and, as we know, a trusted friend of Hammarskjöld's. He perceived his role as general pacifier, speaking with the authority of a regional leader well known to all delegations. He began by providing reassurances about the competence and peaceful intentions of the new Iraqi government, which he expected to "copiously contribute to the work of this Organization," and went on to describe the excellence of Suez Canal operations and colorfully chide Egypt's former adversaries. "The prophets of gloom and the monsters of war who took nationalization as a pretext for their miserable adventure in 1956 should be hiding their faces, and the steady and the fair can rejoice." This was the UN; people sometimes spoke in keeping with their regions' norms of rhetoric. Naturally, he called for prompt withdrawal of the US and British forces, but he concluded—again lyrically—with words of reserved praise for Eisenhower that the president would be unlikely to hear in any other forum: "A hand was raised before us today over the heads of many people. It occasionally marked and punctuated words of blessing and, in its own way, offered good cheer. We have not been able yet to ponder and appraise the real portent of those words."

In the days that followed, Western and Soviet draft resolutions both stalled despite what has been described as a reasonably calm, consensus-seeking atmosphere.[11] Fawzi again found his way to the middle by proposing that the ten Arab member states meet separately to draw up a proposal—this very much in keeping with what Hammarskjöld hoped. On August 21st the resulting proposal was accepted by that rarest of things, a unanimous vote. It called on the secretary-general to take such steps in cooperation with the governments of Lebanon and Jordan "as would adequately help in upholding the purposes and principles of the Charter . . . in the present circumstances, and thereby facilitate the early withdrawal of the foreign troops from the two countries." It neither condemned nor condoned what had occurred.

Hammarskjöld was delighted with the Arab states' cohesion and ability to settle matters in the Assembly. Meeting the press on the day after their successful resolution, he said that "yesterday was one of those days in the life of this Organization when it showed its invaluable contribution to present politics in the international field and to present diplomacy. The result, I think, is one which must be hailed by everybody . . . . For those who like to sharpen their wits on the weaknesses of the Organization, it is . . . a day they should remember before starting all over again."[12] Questioned about the notion of a UN presence—the term had begun to circulate—he replied that it is "practically anything from one man up to quite a few. The decisive factor is what . . . terms of reference we give either to one man or to many. . . . For that reason I really feel it extremely difficult to define. I can define roughly the limits and I have tried to do so. I cannot define in concrete and substantive terms what it means. That would be in fact to limit the flexibility in a way which I think is very unwise."[13] This is long. One of Hammarskjöld's early biographers remembered a much shorter version: "About this time," Kelen writes, "Hammarskjöld enriched the diplomatic vocabulary with the term 'UN presence.' Asked to define it, he replied, 'There is a UN presence whenever the UN is present.'"[14]

George Ivan Smith had his own colorful version of the origin of the term. Traveling with Hammarskjöld in the weeks following the Arab states' successful resolution, he was drawn into a conversation about UN options for continuing to help without being heavy-handed. They were in Amman, capital of Jordan. "[Hammarskjöld] discussed the problem," he recalled, "as we paced up and down on the flat roof of [a] crummy hotel. It is a nice touch of history, because while he was searching for some kind of diplomatic method, we could see over the road the ruins of an old Greek theater and chickens were jumping up and down on the stone balconies. So he said, 'You see, if we bring military people in, the surrounding Arab states will take that to mean that they were in fact regarded as a threat to Jordan. But something has to be done.' (A long pause). 'Perhaps just a chap kicking around here . . . ' Later that day at my press conference, I interpreted that as 'U.N. presence.' The 'chap' was to be Piero Spinelli, head of the UN's Geneva office, who conducted a mission in Jordan and thus established the basis for what today is firmly established as a system of personal and special representatives of the Secretary-General."[15]

In the course of that fall, as the trusted and able Spinelli developed his role as United Nations Special Representative in Amman with regional responsibilities, the cold winds of the Lebanon-Jordan crisis abated further. Despite renewed propaganda and ugly incidents, there was an underlying will to peace and nothing said or done was enough to undo it. No longer needed, UNOGIL was withdrawn after the British troops had made their own withdrawal, completed in early December. Urquhart writes very warmly of what he calls "a new experiment in preventive diplomacy,"[16] and Hammarskjöld's innovation remains an important tool. There are today some seventy special representatives of the secretary-general on assignment worldwide. The region remained explosive; there was intense and prolonged violence to come. But it hadn't exploded this time.

On November 6th, Ambassador Lodge informed the UN by letter that US troops had been withdrawn at the end of October, and he added a note of thanks to Hammarskjöld: "The United States wishes to express its appreciation for the untiring efforts of the Secretary-General which have contributed to the establishment of conditions making possible the withdrawal of United States forces."[17] In the oral history to which we frequently turn, Urquhart comments on the reality behind this formal expression of thanks: "In Lebanon [Hammarskjöld] did a remarkable job of solving what was in fact an extremely hairy problem. After all, there was a civil war in which the United States had suddenly landed 14,000 Marines. He has never received credit for it because nobody wanted to admit it was a mistake, but the fact of the matter is that it was Hammarskjöld who provided the basis upon which Eisenhower was able to withdraw the Marines with honor . . . , and he did it in a fantastic personal negotiation with the Lebanese, with Nasser, with the Syrians, the Americans, the British, everybody. That was high-level personal diplomacy, and he could do that."[18]

Letters from that summer and fall reflect Hammarskjöld's private thoughts about this public sequence. A few days after the Arab states' resolution, he took a moment to put a note in the mail to Bo Beskow, who had written about summer doings at Rytterskulle, his seaside home near Hammarskjöld's farmhouse in southern Sweden (then undergoing renovations for his future use). The topic was Maria, Bo and Greta's young daughter, Hammarskjöld's goddaughter. "While Maria is discovering the world," he wrote, "we're doing our best here to keep it in a state such that her discoveries will still matter when she's fully grown. In all the noise, it's good to know that something so genuine remains as life around Rytterskulle."[19] A month later he gave another Swedish friend his impressions. He sounded weary. "After my very 'hot' negotiations in the Orient," he wrote, "I have now been home for a fortnight. In the battlefield it seems rather neat and tidy, but the landmines are densely placed all around. Here in so-called headquarters I am buried in report writing, administrative presence at debates, and conversations with a number of foreign ministers who eloquently illustrate the truism about small wisdom, etc. In this situation now and then I take a pause for breath, best filled by rereading one page or another from Pasternak."[20] His remark was fair enough about being buried in report writing: an extensive report to the General Assembly on the Lebanon-Jordan affair is dated September 29th, and a nearly book-length summary of "lessons learned" in the UNEF operation reached delegations on October 9th.[21] The report was intended both to document UNEF as a model for future use and to demonstrate the need to adjust peacekeeping operations to the circumstances of time and place.

Early in October, when it was clear that the foreign troops would soon go home and the typically uneasy peace, or half- or quarter-peace, of the Middle East would again prevail, Hammarskjöld wrote to his friend Eyvind Johnson a letter that reads like his final private word on the matter:

It is only now that I feel I am reasonably well on the upper side of the turmoil into which your letter dropped with its note of poise and warmth. And now there are new, dark thunderheads on the horizon . . .

You may well guess that the events of the last three months have given me ample reason to reflect on how responsibilities are carried—or not carried—by those who are called upon by their fellow men to lead. At least in politics I know what may justly be called the sin against the Holy Ghost: to invert the words of the High Priest and to say of oneself that it is better that the people suffer for one man than that one man perish. You would not believe me, but it is true of more than one of the political leaders, hailed by their peoples, that they basically act and speak guided by this perverted concept.

However, I am sure that digging into the times of Charlemagne you have them before you, those overlords who believe that history is made for their sake [at the time, Johnson was writing a novel set at the court of Charlemagne]. Thus what I can tell you is only what you know already: we have not changed since the Middle Ages, in spite of the somewhat more fanciful political suits we wear and the somewhat more high-sounding phrases we use.

As a counterpart to this type of experience it is invigorating to read Pasternak, that lonely man, who, in an atmosphere of the highest pressure, manages to rise above cruelty and, indeed, above all petty conflicts, crystallizing a mature reaction to the making of history and the fate of individuals in the grip of history. . . . *Dr. Zhivago* and *Amers* [by Saint-John Perse] both are works, happening to reach us in one and the same year, in which the highest maturity and depth of perception are reflected so as to make them spiritual monuments which, I am sure, will stand up and be understood also in a distant future.[22]

Hammarskjöld's long perspective, evident in these closing words, often gave him steadiness and solace as he dealt with the day's and month's dramas. At the beginning of his second term, we heard him speak of "the slow, slow growth which goes beyond not only our time but really beyond the span of generations."

The clarity of autumn

Hammarskjöld to Johnson was a Sabbath letter; he would have been at his weekend home in Brewster. On the following day, and in the week following, he wrote the first of what would prove to be many brief poems in later pages of *Markings*. He must have gone hiking in the woods around his home, as always with his security guard, Bill Ranallo, perhaps with others also, and later recorded his impressions.

> Silence breaks through
> The mind's armor,
> Leaving it naked before
> The clarity of autumn.[23]

To be conscious remained a high adventure: to be capable of seeing, feeling, knowing with enough sensitivity to perceive and interpret the broad structure and nuances of all things encountered—a political drama, the clarity of autumn.

"Pasternak, that lonely man," he had written. He could have been speaking of himself. There are few entries in *Markings* in the difficult period just past. On his birthday, July 29th, a day when he often penetrated more deeply the world of spirit to which he also belonged, he had recorded only a desolate short note:

> Didst Thou give me this inescapable loneliness so that it would be easier for me to give Thee all?[24]

But his sense of affliction had its boundary. In those summer months he also recorded one of the most beautiful entries to be found anywhere in his journal, from a moment of revelation that came of itself:

> You wake from dreams of doom and—for a moment—you *know*: beyond all the noise and gestures, the only real thing, love's calm unwavering flame in the half light of an early dawn.[25]

We can easily lose—as he sometimes must have lost—contact with this Hammarskjöld, the poet and man of prayer who knew the permanent value of fleeting insight. The long exercise in the Middle East, the endless travel, the innumerable encounters and negotiations took their toll on him. A stunning prayer from that summer or fall, just eight words, creates a hierarchy of ownership that leaves nearly everything unsaid yet speaks volumes about his sense of duty.

> Lord—Thine the day,
> And I the day's.[26]

Two weeks after his summarizing note to Johnson about the recent crisis, he had what must have been a splendid night out at a concert in the company of Mr. and Mrs. David Rockefeller—there was time again for such good things—but he remained subject to weariness.

> Too tired for company,
> You seek a solitude
> You are too tired to fill.[27]

The fall social calendar was nonetheless elegant. Lincoln Kirstein, the co-founder of New York City Ballet who offered him such encouragement, sent a note not only inviting him to a performance but thanking him for something more: "I should like to report to you that the project so graciously instituted by yourself at lunch last month has come to a most happy fruition. Birgit Cullberg has completed her ballet on the tragedy of "Medea" for the New York City Ballet and all of us who have seen the rehearsals feel it will be a very great artistic success. . . . As parent of this happy event, would you and Madame Rössel give us the pleasure of dining with us before the opening?"[28] Agda Rössel was the recently appointed permanent representative of Sweden to the United Nations; Kirstein may have known that Hammarskjöld enjoyed her company, but it was fitting in any case to extend an invitation to her because Cullberg was a leading Swedish choreographer, later the director of her own well-received ballet company. Hammarskjöld and Kirstein helped one another; for example, in the spring of 1959 Hammarskjöld arranged an introduction to the Japanese royal palace when Kirstein was about to bring the imperial household ballet and musicians to New York (and, naturally, to the UN for a performance). Kirstein reported that "a great deal of the complexity of the negotiations was eased by your kind words to Mr. Matsudaira [head of the Japanese delegation]. I was received in the Palace as if I had the highest credentials."[29] Kirstein's way of helping Hammarskjöld was more intangible: a man of arts and letters, a practical institution builder, he was extraordinarily intelligent and a resourceful conversation partner. Beyond that, his few letters to Hammarskjöld show that he had a good heart, an innocent wish that good prevail.

At the end of the year, which finished out diplomatically without great stress, Hammarskjöld had to face the loss of his friend and colleague, Ahmed Bokhári, under-secretary for public information, with whom he had traveled to China and worked closely over the years. Speaking at a service for him at Pakistan House, he described this scholar and diplomat in terms easily applied to himself: "He was a shy and reticent man. His words were carefully chosen as a precise and truthful expression of his deepest feelings." Hammarskjöld admired his breadth of culture, rooted in his native land and Islamic faith but open to the world and deeply versed in world literature. He perceived in him a living sign that what Bokhári had once called for—"a new comradeship, a universal fellowship, a world communion"—might, after all, and after who knows what trials, prove slightly possible.[30] If Hammarskjöld had an impossible dream, it was not world government, as some have baselessly claimed. He knew only too well the durability and self-protectiveness of sovereign nations. It was the dream he shared with Bokhári of an emerging global culture suspended from the "great traditions" (neither he nor Bokhári could have anticipated today's microchip-based technologies around which a pragmatic global culture has developed). In Hammarskjöld's mourning note to the delegations and Secretariat staff about Bokhári's passing, he voiced that dream: "[Ahmed Bokhári] reflected in his personality the possibility of a synthesis of great traditions on which it is the task of our generation to build one world. He also knew in a deep personal sense the difficulties and tensions which must accompany such a process." He returned to this theme in June 1959, in a brilliant talk on Africa and Asia which we'll soon encounter.

Hammarskjöld went out in mid-December to the Middle East in time to spend Christmas with the UNEF forces in Egypt and meet his negotiating partners in Egypt and Israel. There were, as always, provocative issues—uppermost at the time was a bitterly contested dispute over Israeli cargoes passing through the Suez Canal. While in the region he took a close look at the very substantial UN aid program for Palestinian refugees, about which he had committed to make recommendations at the next session of the General Assembly. In an exercise of what he called "out-of-the-way tourism with a strong personal accent," he took time to meet with Martin Buber in Jerusalem.[31] He went on to Addis Ababa to give a year-end talk at the first meeting of the new Economic Commission for Africa and, after a brief tour of countries in the region, returned to New York on January 9th. At Addis he expressed hope for Africa: "One day we may look back to the establishment of the Commission as marking the moment when Africa began to assume its full role in the world community."³²

Choppy waves and undercurrents

At a press conference in mid-January 1959, Hammarskjöld commented on the Middle East in terms widely relevant: "I have enough confidence," he said, "in the basic common sense of human beings and the basic good will of human beings to count that also as a factor in politics."³³ Through the year ahead, some international issues in the UN's care confirmed his optimism, others though grave were held at a distance from the UN—especially a Soviet-ignited controversy among the four occupying powers over the status of Berlin—and some later in the year were not reassuring about goodwill or common sense.

There was an encouraging sequence at the turn of the year. Hammarskjöld had nearly always traveled to trouble spots, but his new method of outreach through Special Representatives grandly met a test. The situation was a border dispute between Cambodia and Thailand. Both governments had preferred to ask Hammarskjöld for a mediator rather than set in motion the machinery of the Security Council. Within a short period of three weeks, a recently retired Swedish ambassador dispatched by Hammarskjöld had helped the governments resolve their dispute. "Without in any way making this a precedent," he commented at a press conference in early February, "I responded to the [governments'] invitations and a representative was sent there, with the acquiescence of . . . the Security Council. You can see how much more effective and smooth-working such a technique is than the regular one, which involves all the meetings and debates, and so on. . . . I believe that in the future we shall have further cases. . . . All this builds up a sum total of experience which one day, I feel, may usefully be codified."³⁴ In other words, become a precedent. He was again making good on his commitment to fill gaps in the system in ways fully in accord with the Charter. The UN and his office remained works in progress.

In late winter Hammarskjöld began a four-week trip that took him from Pakistan, India, and Nepal to the nations of Southeast Asia and the Soviet Union. It seems as if there was either fire or folklore whenever Nikita Khrushchev entered the picture. In this instance, as a break from talks in Moscow Hammarskjöld flew with Khrushchev to spend twenty-four hours at his villa in Sochi on the Black Sea. There was fire: over dinner Hammarskjöld proposed an arch and wonderful toast, "to honest sinners now on record," which Khrushchev and his companions refused to drink. He found a substitute, not as interesting. On the following day there was folklore: he and Khrushchev shipped out on their own in a rowboat. This fascinated the press and the world—two such unlike men, not an Owl and a Pussy-Cat but equally mismatched, confined to a minimal bark on a distant sea. Urquhart recounts that Hammarskjöld later thanked his host by letter: "Although the boat trip was a bit on the silent side, not because of a lack of will but because there was no place for an interpreter, I shall always remember it with great pleasure. I have carefully noted that next time you will leave it to me to row you. A third time we may perhaps arrive at rowing with four oars."[35] His graceful irony about someday rowing together marked the beginning of a sporadic, teasing joust between the two men—heavy with meaning, light in tone—in which the rowboat was prominent. Home again, at an April 16th press conference Hammarskjöld was closely questioned about this matter, the journalists for once feeling free to exercise their own sense of irony where the dignified secretary-general was concerned. One of Hammarskjöld's favorites, Kay Rainey Gray, put it this way: "We read in the *New York Times* this morning of a venture which reportedly concerned only you, a rowboat, and Mr. Khrushchev. If you can confirm this, could you tell us what language you had in common, or was it a mutual love of the sea?" Hammarskjöld responded in kind: "It was a very pleasant trip. We were certainly united in our love of the sea. The language was the language of the sea. That is to say, you can point out directions; and for the rest, faces can express the pleasure which one takes in the trip."[36]

Hammarskjöld must still have had the Black Sea in his mind's eye when, very few days after his return from the Soviet Union, he traveled to Mexico City to speak at a UN meeting. In his press conference there he drew on those impressions to convey the state of international politics:

We have a kind of accelerated rhythm in which world danger comes and world danger goes and keeps us all wide awake at the breakfast table. In fact, the trends, the undercurrents are slower and stronger. What we see in those press reactions seems to me to be only the somewhat choppy short waves at the surface, and the real trend is the deeper swell in the sea. If you come to that deeper swell, I must say that I think . . . this generation is less in world danger than previous generations, and that is because I think this is the first generation in which the full impact of war on human life and the development of human society has been realized down to the bottom of the heart.

For some reason—perhaps the sunny climate, perhaps simply that he was no longer in wary conversation with Khrushchev—he was especially brilliant in Mexico. He enlarged in the press conference on the theme of danger and the response of the community of nations:

> I do not believe that we have had in recent history a more serious chance to solve international conflicts by negotiation than we have now. This is partly a reflection of what I said about the deeply felt danger of war, but it is also partly a reflection of the fact that one sees the enormous risk that, short of conflicts, may become unmanageable. . . . The greater chance for negotiation has been, so to speak, bought at the price of the greater risk which has created this new kind of awareness. That is to say, on the one side we have today greater dangers, perhaps, than we have had before because of the sharpness of conflict and the scope of conflict. On the other hand, this very danger has activated a will to negotiation which goes beyond previous experience. Permit me to be a bit optimistic and to say that I think that the will to negotiation is strong enough and the wisdom back of it is great enough for us to overcome the risk. Let us hope, therefore, that we have not bought our new wisdom too dearly.[37]

His formal talk at the conference was just as fresh, though it concerned the classic topics of the UN as a new diplomatic tool and the scope of his own office. "Working together, the representatives . . . get to know each other, . . . find common human denominators, get to appreciate the integrity of the one who may be his opposite number." He added a few words about his experience as an international civil servant that should be put in the balance against the longing to return to Sweden and to his circle of friends there, which we have encountered in private correspondence.

> The Secretary-General is, in his reactions, cut off from his allegiance to any one country—I think, of course, in the first instance of his native country. Again, it is natural to ask how this is possible without a draining of the spirit which might seem to be an unavoidable result of such a denationalization. The reply is simply that to the extent that he . . . can eliminate all such allegiances and fall back on himself, he will find a new home country which is everywhere in the sense that he will find open doors wherever he goes.[38]

One could easily pass over his reference to falling back on oneself, but in his lexicon these words or words much like them pointed to a fundamental act, a return that is clear on one level, paradoxical on another. At the level of daily experience—for example, when he spoke with journalists about "falling back on that most elusive of things, confidence"—he must have meant that one may have anxious concerns of many kinds but there is another knowledge deeper down, more native to one's understanding and intuitively satisfactory. At the level of religious life, the concept of falling had another, not entirely unrelated meaning. The entry in *Markings* is from Christmas Eve, 1955:

> God desires our independence—which we attain when, ceasing to strive for it ourselves, we "fall" back into God.[39]

Without extending this discussion, we can take it that Hammarskjöld understood something excellent about falling and falling back. When he fell just right, he recovered independence of mind and heart, knew himself to be in God's hands, and saw open doors wherever he went. This is an acrobatic feat worthy of further study.

A world of different thoughts and emotions

Time permitting, Hammarskjöld prepared by thought and travel for what he surmised to lie ahead. This was never truer than for Africa. At the beginning of 1958, he was already thinking about the future role of the UN in emerging nations "where an independent administrative tradition is lacking. A country without a trained civil service finds itself at a grave disadvantage. . . . Many new countries lack a social structure which permits a corps of administrators to be rapidly recruited. . . . I have suggested developing a United Nations international administrative service."[40] This was forward looking and necessary; administrators on loan from the UN and member nations to newly independent countries would prove their value.

Eight countries on the continent of Africa, founders and more recently admitted, were member nations at the time Ghana was admitted in 1957. In the fall 1960 session of the General Assembly, three days before Khrushchev added his weight to what would prove to be a ferocious year-long attack on Hammarskjöld, the Assembly pacifically admitted twelve new African countries as member nations, the great majority sub-Saharan, with three others admitted soon after. Hammarskjöld was fully prepared to welcome them. Earlier in the year, he had remarked at a press conference that "I do not believe that the small nations have less . . . understanding of central political problems of concern to the whole world than those who are more closely related to them and who

traditionally wield greater power in the international councils. For
that reason, I cannot—and this is not only the official stand taken by
the Secretary-General, it is a matter of personal conviction—share the
view of those who regard the possible influence of smaller powers as a
danger—I would add, in any context."[41]

In Hammarskjöld's thinking, Africa was "the great new continent."[42]
On May 4th at the University of Lund in southern Sweden, he gave a
talk under the title "Asia, Africa, and the West" that offered his vision
of the new situation.[43] What he said was both brilliant and warm; he
was unmistakably communicating the outcome of long private reflection
and of dialogue with political leaders and men and women of goodwill
in both regions. Expressing sensible attitudes toward what was to come,
he spoke as a participant in cultural change, rather than as a diplomat.
Trade, aid, alliances and animosities—all of that would enter the picture
in due course, but it wasn't the topic here. He was interested in identities.
He had no program other than to look at the mind of the West, the mind
of the newly independent or soon to be independent peoples of Asia and
Africa, and their relations in the past and now. Years ago, you may recall,
he told an American university audience that "I have always considered
myself, and still have the ambition . . . to be primarily a university man."[44]
Now he was a professor of the world.

He began with an intimate story that clearly pleased him. "In one of
the capitals of the Orient," he said, "one of the smallest and least accessible
ones—I had a conversation recently which happened to turn on questions
of religion. This happens often in that part of the world." He was already at
ease. We can be sure he initiated the conversation—how unlikely that it just
"happened." I suspect that he also welcomed small and inaccessible; at last
he could have a little peace. The upshot was that his conversation partner
proved to know a great deal more about Western and even Scandinavian culture than most Western people would know of his culture. This observation
led Hammarskjöld to think about European attitudes, particularly attitudes
toward the Other, the peoples and cultures of Asia and Africa.

> In today's perspective, the Europe of the early nineteenth century ap-
> pears as a tightly closed cultural world, highly developed but essentially
> regional in character. Goethe's "universality" was combined with a firm
> conviction of the supremacy of the European man of culture, a suprem-
> acy which erected invisible walls around his spiritual life in relation to
> other parts of the world.

As time went on and the military and political influence of Europe was extended further and further in Asia and Africa, this conviction of supremacy found increasingly concrete—and increasingly simple—expressions. In many cases, it came to be represented by persons whose only superiority over those they had to deal with lay in the power they had back of them. Nobody should minimize the admirable achievements frequently attained by the colonizers of the nineteenth century. But nobody should forget that colonization reflected a basic approach which may have been well founded in certain limited respects, but which often mirrored false claims, particularly when it touched on spiritual development. Applied generally, it was untenable.

Europe remained closed minded, he continued. Scholars explored the cultures of colonial peoples, but their findings had little or no impact on mainstream culture. "Such integration is difficult in any case," he said. Behind the invisible walls of European life,

it was . . . almost impossible. To make it a reality required an intellectual humility and an open-minded set of values, which came about only when European man was shaken in his self-confidence and saw the walls around his closed world crumble before the pressure of new forces which Europe itself in large part had called into being.

To a Westerner of a later generation who is facing today's Asia and Africa, it is a useful exercise to go back to the works about these areas written by distinguished Europeans whose mental attitude was shaped in the main before the First World War. What strikes one in the first place, perhaps, is how much they did *not* see and did *not* hear, and how even their most positive attempts at entering into a world of different thoughts and emotions were colored by an unthinking, self-assured superiority. . . .

The First World War brought the world across the Atlantic into the picture in earnest. The Second World War opened the door for Asia and Africa. Between the wars, Europe passed through a period in which old forms and norms were dissolved. . . . The whole closed European cultural circle was broken up in a reappraisal of all values.

That had been his own moment—you may recall that some years before reaching the UN he had written to his mentor, Ernst Wigforss, that his generation experienced the disorder of ideas and values, as if it lived in a "bombed-out city, in which the inhabitants are happy to be able to join shattered ruins into a temporary shelter." This wasn't colorful language; it was a description of much of Europe at the time.

Yet there was hope. From the breakdown of European culture there had emerged "the beginning of a new synthesis on a universal basis." This is the theme we noticed in his mournful praise of his late colleague, Ahmed Bokhári.

> Depending on temperament and background, reactions to this evolution may vary. One may reach back for the imagined calm of the closed world. One may find one's spiritual home in the very disintegration and its drama. Or one may reach ahead toward the glimpse of the synthesis, inspired by the dream of a new culture in which there is achieved, on a level encompassing the whole world, what once seemed to have become a regional reality in Europe.
>
> He who chooses the latter course will be disappointed, if he believes the task to be easy or the goal close. But he can count on the richest satisfaction in meeting different spiritual traditions and their representatives, if he approaches them on an equal footing and with a common future goal in mind.

Here he introduced an urgently needed thought. Is the cultural synthesis he foresees destined to be homogeneous? Will the specificity of cultures disappear as people from many parts of the world move toward common ground? He didn't think so. Those who are capable of meeting others "on an equal footing and with a common future goal" will

> find rich satisfaction in the progress [they] will note in the direction of a human community which, while retaining the special character of individuals and groups, has made use of what the various branches of the family of man have attained along different paths over thousands of years.

He was looking toward a possibility that scarcely existed in his era—a global multiculture, a unity that preserves diversity. This is the language he used a half year later when he returned to this topic with a university group in Somalia. He pointed then to two necessities:

> to create an international world, a world of universality and unity, and on the other hand to save not only . . . the personality of Africa, but the personality of each country, each group, in this wonderfully rich continent. I think it is possible. . . . I think that you will see that what is needed is unity with diversity, diversity respected within the framework

of an even deeper respect for unity. You *can* create, and I know you *will* create, the African personality as part of the picture of mankind today. But I know that, in doing so, you will preserve all the richness you have inherited; each group, each people within this continent.[45]

Perhaps we now know enough of Hammarskjöld's thought as he prepared himself, and all who could hear him, for the journey signaled by decolonization and the emergence of new sovereign nations in Africa and Asia. There is much more in his superb talk at the University of Lund. He spoke in vivid terms about the encounter between what he called "opulence"—the wealth of the West—and material poverty in nations whose peoples are "more conscious than we are of how true it is . . . that man lives not by bread alone." And he raised again the distinction, which he thought crucial, between leadership and coercive power. He drove that point home in a most Hammarskjöld-like way:

> Leadership—the word I have used to designate what may come instead of superior power—is a dangerous word if one does not keep in mind that the most influential leaders in the European cultural evolution were askers of questions like Socrates or the carpenter's son from Nazareth.

That life be conducted with decency

We are on the bridge now to Africa. To the exclusion of much but not all else, the Congo Crisis occupied the last fifteen months of Hammarskjöld's life and work. However, the bridge is crowded at this near end. The plight of Laos from early 1959 forward was a great concern. Not that it matters to the diplomatic narrative, but Laos was a country he had come to love in a region he had come to love. It was after his visit to the region in mid-1958 that he had written to Beskow, "how much more mature and fine the Asiatic art of living is compared to ours." Urquhart devoted an entire chapter to narrating the endless complexities, threats, and episodic violence experienced by that country caught in a civil war and in the Cold War, subject to covert pressures from all sides. Hammarskjöld used every resource he could marshal to establish Laos as a neutral, nonaligned country free to focus undisturbed on its economic and social development. For his aims and some of his methods—in part uncharacteristically clumsy because others, including the government of Laos, were clumsy—he was criticized by both the United States and the Soviets. To their displeasure, he projected himself personally into the

picture by going to Laos in November 1959, under his Charter obligations, to establish a better understanding of the situation. From the defeat of the French at Dien Bien Phu in 1954 to the confusion in Laos in
1959–60, the signs were already pointing toward the Vietnam War and
its destructive impact throughout the region.

Hammarskjöld told his brother what he could, in brief, in a letter of
late September 1959:

> Laos . . . is a strange story, to a great extent recalling Lebanon and Jor-
> dan, i.e., it is full of the romanticism of political robbers, with the East
> and West competing cloak and dagger style. The population itself, its
> government included, seems primarily confused and reacts irrationally
> and in sudden bursts. Their initiative in the UN was incredibly ill-
> staged and caused me great difficulties. I am satisfied with the outcome
> in the first round even if the boxing was far from clean.[46]

With a bow toward Brian Urquhart's chapter on Laos and the close treatment of the topic in Hammarskjöld's *Public Papers*, we should move on.
There is little to be gained here from engaging with the details of that
unfortunate, scrappy crisis. Urquhart's own valediction reads, "his good
intentions and his ingenuity were not high enough cards to play in a
competition for influence between superpowers."[47]

He had no better luck with another initiative, this one concerning aid
and planning on behalf of the Palestinian refugees. The United Nations
Relief and Works Agency (UNRWA) provides to this day a comprehensive aid program to that refugee community, now numbering some five
million—in Hammarskjöld's era, some one million. At the end of June
1960, UNRWA's mandate was scheduled to expire; Hammarskjöld had
been asked by the General Assembly to recommend helpful or necessary
changes. He did so in an extensive report delivered in mid-June 1959,
which drew on the skills in economic analysis he had exercised years ago
in the Swedish government.[48] It must have pleased him to bring those
skills back in service to the UN and in relation to a massive humanitarian problem that we know had touched not just his mind but his heart.
As always, he was careful to set limits. Not intended to solve the refugee
problem in its totality, the report focused on a single theme: UNRWA's
work toward reintegrating the refugee population into the economic life
of the region. He did write, however, that "development along the lines
. . . discussed might facilitate steps toward a resolution . . . with justice

and equity for all concerned." This was probably the first annoying line in the report; there would prove to be others.

Although the Arab states had initially expressed interest, after the report was published they rejected its emphasis on economic reintegration because it appeared that the price of accepting Hammarskjöld's approach would be to accept large-scale refugee resettlement in Arab lands rather than large-scale repatriation to Israel, from which the original refugees had fled or been driven in 1948 during the war known to Israelis as the War of Independence and to Arabs as the Catastrophe. Hammarskjöld defended the report. Responding in late July to a journalist who advanced the idea that the report "makes the Arab refugee problem look like part of the economic problem of the Middle East rather than a political problem," he said that it did nothing of the kind. "I think the general economic aspects have been somewhat neglected, and I have given them a place more in focus; it is to correct a lack of balance. . . . I do not think that I have in any way blurred, as you said, the political or legal issues involved, . . . so people can just forget about that fear and suspicion."[49] He sounds peeved; he must already have had his fill of criticism. He defended the report again in his introduction to the fourteenth Annual Report, published in late August—but in the autumn let it go and recommended continuation of UNRWA without reference to the report. "I have no reason," he said in a key committee meeting, "to explain here my own reactions to various arguments . . . or even to try to correct the misunderstandings which—frankly, somewhat to my surprise—have been apparent."[50]

Two rounds, two defeats: Laos, "that hopelessly entangled and mishandled affair,"[51] as he described it to a friend, was not working out well, and Hammarskjöld's remarkable perspective on the Palestinian refugee question found no takers. There was a third defeat. He stood apart from it; others carried the concern. He knew from the beginning that defeat lay ahead, but he witnessed from beginning to end. The debate bore his stamp, though he took no public role in it.

The question of Tibet seems to have been first publicly raised with Hammarskjöld at a press conference in April 1959. The journalist's question: "I should like to ask you . . . whether you could tell us something about the United Nations and Tibet, in view of the present difficulty there." Hammarskjöld initially let the question go and responded to an unrelated issue also raised by the journalist—who came back insistently. "Could you answer my first question about Tibet?" To which he responded as he sometimes did when an issue wasn't on the UN agenda: "I know just as much about Tibet as you do, from the newspapers." A look at the *New York Times* for March 20th and thereafter yields headlines such as "Tibetans Battle Chinese in Lhasa: Populace Joins Rebel Group in Resisting Red Attempt to Seize Dalai Lama." Later in the press conference another journalist reverted to the issue yet again, saying that when UN member nations use force, they have to "bear the full brunt of world public opinion in this House. Now where do you focus the weight of world public opinion where a country not represented in the United Nations uses troops, such as in Tibet?" At that point, Hammarskjöld obviously felt constrained to respond properly. He described the two stumbling blocks that would impede any UN debate about Tibet: "I think that a member nation can discuss such an issue within the United Nations," he said. "In that sense the United Nations can be the focus of world opinion.... But you should remember that there are two complications in the matter. The discussion would refer to a non-member nation .... And secondly it refers to a relationship within that country which under international law, constitutional law, is such a complex one that I think . . . the famous Article 2.7 might be invoked by some parties."[52] He was referring to Chapter 1, Article 2.7 of the Charter: "Nothing contained in the present Charter shall authorize the United Nations to intervene in matters which are essentially within the domestic jurisdiction of any state or shall require the Members to submit such matters to settlement under the present Charter."

The press corps was responding in April to news of the revolt that had begun in Lhasa on March 10th, pitting Tibetan patriots against the Chinese army of occupation and regional government. The reported violence and destruction was terrible. While there had been armed resistance for years in eastern Tibet, this culminating incident had begun when Chinese officials appeared to be laying a trap for the Dalai Lama, the spiritual and political leader of Tibet, by insisting that he come unprotected and without customary ceremony to a festival. Thousands of Tibetans rallied to protect him and violence broke out. The hard-fought revolt that spread throughout the country led to tens of thousands of deaths and casualties. With the agreement and urging of his government, the Dalai Lama secretly left Lhasa on March 17th and crossed into India on the 31st; the difficulty and dangers of his mountain journey have become legend. "We must have been a pitiful sight," the Dalai Lama later wrote, "to the handful of Indian guards that met us at the border—eighty travelers, physically exhausted and mentally wretched from our ordeal."[53] In North India he and soon some twelve thousand refugees—the first wave of many— were permitted to establish a government in exile and community. This was a critical turning point in events that had begun nearly a decade earlier, in November 1950, when Chinese communist troops invaded eastern Tibet and instituted an increasingly harsh and encompassing occupation. At that time the Kashag, or cabinet, of the Tibetan government had written to the United Nations an eloquent appeal for help based on the hope, however remote, that the United Nations police action then under way against North Korean aggression modeled a similar force that could come to the aid of Tibet.[54] As again in 1959, the appeal was taken up by a small member nation, El Salvador, and submitted to the General Committee of the General Assembly, which was responsible for debating and voting on issues proposed for inclusion in plenary sessions of the Assembly.

The debate that ensued in the General Committee rehearsed nearly all of the arguments that would be brought to bear in Hammarskjöld's time. There were impassioned pleas for justice for a small, overwhelmed, and uniquely dignified nation. There were impassioned assertions that Tibet was a legitimate province of China, therefore wholly removed from UN concern by Article 2.7—and furthermore the Chinese were engaged in a civilizing mission to democratize centuries of serf-like oppression of the common people by the monasteries and land-owning nobles, and still further, the People's Republic of China, not a member nation, wasn't present to defend itself. Finally, there were various shades of temporizing that acknowledged the humanitarian concern but saw fit for one reason or another to do nothing. Some member nations couldn't dare to upset China; others with their own colonial problems had no wish to open the door to UN debate at some later time. The Indian ambassador, whose country would later prove crucial to the rescue of Tibetan culture, expressed his government's certainty that "the Tibetan question could still be settled by peaceful means. . . . His delegation considered that the best way of obtaining that objective was to abandon, for the time being, the idea of including that question in the agenda of the General Assembly."[55] On December 8th, 1950, El Salvador passed to all delegations through the secretary-general a deeply saddened note from the Kashag. "We have

heard with grave concern and dismay of the United Nations decision setting aside the discussion of our appeal. . . . The agony and despair which
prompted us to seek . . . assistance . . . will be better appreciated by those
nations whose liberty is always at the mercy of being jeopardized by the
aggressive designs of their more powerful neighbors."[56]

Nearly ten years passed, immensely difficult years for Tibet ending with
the exile of the Dalai Lama and his government. On September 9th, 1959,
Hammarskjöld received a long cable written by the Dalai Lama from New
Delhi. "Your Excellency," he began, "It is with the deepest regret that I
am informing you that the act of aggression by Chinese forces has not
terminated. On the contrary, the area of aggression has been substantially
extended with the result that practically the whole of Tibet is under the
occupation of the Chinese forces. I and my Government have made several appeals for peaceful and friendly settlement but so far these appeals
have been completely ignored. In these circumstances and in view of the
inhuman treatment and crimes against humanity and religion to which
the people of Tibet are being subjected, I solicit the immediate intervention of the United Nations."[57] The cable goes on to detail the legal basis
for recognizing Tibet's independence from China and the oppression of
the Tibetan people. "The sufferings which my people are undergoing are
beyond description and it is imperatively necessary that this wanton and
ruthless murder of my people should be immediately brought to an end. It
is in these circumstances that I appeal to you."

There is no need to follow closely the next few weeks of discreet
diplomacy setting the stage for open debate, but the result is clear: on
September 29th two small member nations, Ireland and the Federation
of Malaya, proposed the "Question of Tibet" for inclusion on the agenda
of the General Assembly.[58] "After study of the material available," their
ambassadors wrote, "the conclusion is inescapable that there exists *prima
facie* evidence of an attempt to destroy the traditional way of life of the
Tibetan people and the religious and cultural autonomy long recognized
to belong to them."[59] The topic was sent to the General Committee, where
it had died a decade earlier, and the debate was on—with previous points
of view duly marshaled plus a very few new ideas, all delivered with greater
vehemence by opponents of inclusion and greater eloquence from Tibet's
friends. The Malayan ambassador, Ismail Kamil, and Ireland's Frank Aiken
were genuinely heroic in their insistence on inclusion and in the felt words
and clarity of mind they brought to bear in the course of bitter debates.

"The moral conscience of mankind . . . represents a force which must be reckoned with even though it is an intangible force," Aiken said. "If the Assembly demonstrates that it is prepared to condemn wholesale violations of human rights, wherever they are perpetrated, it will be maintaining intact that invisible but effective barrier against further acts of oppression which is constituted by a vigilant world opinion."[60]

Distant Tibet, the world's most isolated and perhaps least known country in that era, became an object of severe Cold War contention. One could safely say anything at all; the facts were far away. Speaking for the Soviet Union, Vasily Kuznetsov launched arguments that were to be heard again and again. "We are dealing with a question which the United States is pushing with all means at its disposal in order to worsen the atmosphere which had appeared to be improving. . . . An attempt is being made to utilize the United Nations in order to intensify the cold war. A non-existent Tibetan question has been fabricated in order to worsen the international situation and the atmosphere in the Assembly." The other arguments were soon set in place: Tibet was and is part of China, therefore under Article 2.7 protection, and anyway "there is a touching solicitude for a small band of feudal lords and abbots who have violated the rights of the Tibetan people. . . . Never has there been such a state of rightlessness and oppression as in feudal and servile Tibet. . . . Before the eyes of mankind, some delegations are engaged in a hypocritical farce."[61]

The debate in the General Committee reached epic proportions—over Tibet, where no one had ever been. It was as if the soul of the world had slipped into UN headquarters alongside this issue and now stood trial. Some delegates must have recalled the inability of the UN to defend Hungary against Soviet invasion. Older delegates would have recalled the appeal of Emperor Haile Selassie of Ethiopia in 1936 to the League of Nations: Who could forget that diminutive man of large dignity, pleading in vain for the League to act against Mussolini's vile attack on his ancient country? On behalf of another remote and ancient nation, the battle was now fiercely engaged. With obviously genuine feeling, ambassadors argued their values and those of the common Charter; they reasoned with utmost attention; the West and the Soviet bloc, Asia and the South all found their voices, humane or derisive, freely thoughtful or sourly doctrinaire. It was astonishing—over Tibet, where no one had ever been.

In the absence at that time of the "Responsibility to Protect" doctrine developed by the UN in recent years, delegates who cared for the sufferings of Tibet provided spontaneous first drafts through their words of advocacy; they felt the doctrine in their bones, although a half-century would pass before it became a UN norm and a basis for action.

A vote on inclusion was taken on October 12th: 43 in favor, 11 opposed, 25 abstentions. That put Tibet on the agenda. In the follow-up discussion which is customary in the General Committee, Frank Aiken of Ireland once again spoke with distinction and moral force: "Our mind revolts against any idea that, by reason of legalistic claims which were never freely accepted by the Tibetan people, we should treat Tibet . . . as an internal Chinese question which we have no right even to discuss . . . . I cannot conceive how any nation which has undergone foreign rule, whether for long or short periods, can regard the past period of Chinese imperial hegemony over Tibet as depriving Tibet of a claim on our attention now."[62] He was speaking for Tibet as an Irishman who had fought his country's war of independence against the British.

The topic was taken up by the General Assembly in its sessions of October 20th–21st, during which Aiken spoke from his acute recognition that a trial of the UN itself was under way. "The question of Tibet is a test case, a challenge to this Assembly. If, despite our Charter, a powerful country may force its will, with impunity and without protest, upon a distinctive people one-hundredth part of its size, by what principle could it be denied the right to impose its will by force upon a nation one-tenth or one-half its size? . . . This Organization represents the experience of our evolving world order. It cannot escape its responsibilities. . . . I have little doubt that the vast majority of the ordinary citizens in every country represented in this Assembly would not wish that what has been done in Tibet should be done to themselves or to their own children."[63] His were nearly the last words spoken before a vote was taken on a resolution submitted by his own delegation and the Federation of Malaya: 45 in favor, 9 opposed (the entire Soviet bloc), 26 abstentions—adequate to pass the resolution. Its core language referred to the traditional autonomy of the Tibetan people and "call[ed] for respect for the fundamental human rights of the Tibetan people and for their distinctive cultural and religious life."[64] There was no mention of China; it wasn't needed. The resolution would have no practical impact whatever on the Tibetans' sufferings, but the long debate had stirred and informed public opinion. Tibet would not be forgotten.

Where was Hammarskjöld? Witnessing from his high seat in the General Assembly and doubtless active behind the scene, he never spoke publicly. He had known from the beginning that the UN would be unable to act, apart perhaps from providing assistance to refugees. According to a Tibetan historian, well before the debate he had privately made clear to the British Foreign Office that he wished to "create the impression that some thought was being given to Tibet at the UN" and to reassure the public—Tibet was much in the news—that the UN was not "in a state of innocence" where Tibet was concerned.[65] This sounds calculated, and of course it is. But in practice he set the drama in motion by distributing the Dalai Lama's communication, and surely he had something to do with the readiness of Ireland and the Federation of Malaya to champion Tibet.

Earlier in the year, he had written a few lines in his journal that come to mind:

> Conscious of the reality of evil and the tragedy of individual lives, and conscious, too, of the demand that life be conducted with dignity.[66]

The fit is perfect with the debate on the Question of Tibet, its scale and occasional grandeur, and its powerlessness to change fate.

The Dalai Lama reverted twice more to Hammarskjöld and through him to the UN, in 1960 and 1961, and twice more the General Assembly essentially reenacted the debates of 1950 and 1959. Nikita Khrushchev was in New York in October 1960 to bring a series of strident messages to the General Assembly. While he took little notice of the Question of Tibet, he did take a passing swipe at it in an Assembly speech on disarmament. "Why should you raise the Tibetan question?" he asked. "But . . . do raise it, if you need to. While moving about in New York, I see always Americans chewing gum—this is their habit. Now instead of gum you want to give the Assembly delegates a piece of cotton for them to sit and chew on. Those who have an itch for this may do it, but we are not going to."[67] There were finer voices than this one. Frank Aiken again voiced the moral center. "My delegation is not concerned with the rights of white men, or brown men, or black men: we are concerned with the rights of men. Those rights are universal and immutable. . . . Looking around this Assembly, and looking at my own delegation, I think how many benches would be empty

here in this hall if it had always been agreed that when a small nation
. . . fell into the grip of a major Power, no one could ever raise the case
here; that once they were a subject nation, they must always remain a
subject nation."[68]

On December 20th, 1961—Hammarskjöld was no longer there—the
General Assembly adopted a resolution by a majority of fifty-six votes to
"solemnly renew its call for the cessation of practices which deprive the
Tibetan people of their fundamental human rights and freedoms including their right to self-determination."[69] There the matter lay, unresolved.
If there was a victory here, it was of Hammarskjöld's kind. In one of his
letters to Pär Lagerkvist he wrote of rare occasions when "the distinction
between triumph and tragedy is totally obliterated in a victorious and affirmative humanity." Certain nations and their diplomats—preeminently Ireland and the Federation of Malaya—had demonstrated persevering
humanity, all the while knowing that little or nothing could be achieved.
Unforgettable. The Dalai Lama's publication of the transcript of UN
proceedings on the Question of Tibet 1950–61, including every kind
and unkind word—the Soviet ambassador once referred to "this Tibetan
vaudeville"—was itself an unforgettable act. What other national leader
would have done that?

A very peculiar set of problems

Recognizing that he needed greater knowledge of Africa and familiarity
with its leaders, Hammarskjöld undertook an extended tour of twenty-
four countries, leaving New York on December 22nd and returning at
the end of January. Senegal, Liberia, Ghana, what was then still the Belgian Congo and its neighbor across the river, the French Congo, and
many other countries on the massive continent, finishing up along the
northern tier of Muslim nations. Before his departure he joined the UN
press corps for lunch and conversation. They were, of course, interested
to sound him out on the impending trip. "Africa is, as you know," he said
in reply to their questions,

> the great new continent coming to the United Nations. It has started al-
> ready. It will be much more so one year from now, not to speak about two
> years from now. It will be a most important group with a very peculiar set
> of problems. I have wanted first of all . . . to get at least the personal con-
> tacts necessary for the right kind of discussions and exchanges. . . .

> We all live in a mildly irrational world where the symbol may be more important than . . . words. . . . That I cut this time off from the work here and feel that this is a case for personal contact is interpreted by our African friends as a demonstration of the very live, very active interest we take in the African development. . . . It is awfully pretentious and preposterous to regard oneself as a symbol—I do not, frankly—but I must note that the fact that one demonstrates an interest in tangible and unmistakable terms is of significance for the harmonious development, and under such circumstances I feel that I have to shoulder that special responsibility.[70]

He tended to wrestle with the question of his symbolic role. Here he obliquely accepted it: somewhere in all those uncomfortable words is a microscopic acknowledgment that he was, after all, the living symbol of the United Nations. However, in a conversation with Rajeshwar Dayal and his wife Susheela in spring 1961, he became positively childish when she pursued the matter past his comfort zone. Madame Dayal was enormously fond and respectful of Hammarskjöld and seems to have treated him with something like the insouciant intimacy of a sister. She reports that they had been speaking of the men and women of the UN who served him so loyally. "Dag said that his presence, his person, should not matter to them. It was the impersonal, the idea of the UN that was important, and it was into this that their idealism and their loyalty should be transcended. But, I replied, I had seen what his presence did to people; how it illuminated and inspired their spirit. It was not just the concept of a United Nations that they loved, it was him, the embodiment of that concept. I asked him, 'Can you think of an abstract thing?' He was quiet for a moment, and then he replied, 'Of course not. People need a symbol, that is right.' He added with grave honesty, 'But if they must have one, then it should not be a person. Let them take the UN building as their concrete symbol, not me!'"[71]

And so, with grave honesty, he entered Africa. It was a whirlwind journey, but he had just enough time to connect, to understand more, and to map for future purposes the men and women of authority and influence across much of the continent. Along the way, he shared his thoughts in meetings and press conferences, nowhere more notably than in Tangier toward the end of the trip. He was in a position then to summarize what he had been learning.

> The emergence of Africa on the world scene, more than any other single phenomenon, has forced us to reappraise and rethink the nature of re-

lationships among peoples at different stages of development, and the conditions of a new synthesis making room for an accelerated growth and development of Africa.

So far, so good. But he couldn't help but dwell on the most important deficiency he had encountered:

> In Africa, the scarcity of skills and the magnitude of the adjustments to be made create problems which no one should underestimate. To forge modern states with the imperfect tools at hand is not an easy task. That these ventures should succeed is of the greatest importance, not only to the peoples of Africa but to the world as a whole.[72]

He had a clear vision of the leadership and management challenges that lay ahead and, more surprisingly, of the subjective experience of independence after generations of colonial submission.

> However peaceful and orderly the transition, independence still represents a kind of shock impact, in that it confronts countries with an entirely new set of conditions. Newly independent countries . . . will have to decide on difficult problems of monetary and currency systems. . . . They will . . . have to move toward a certain model of social organization, to define the role and magnitude of the public sector . . . . These are momentous decisions, and not always reversible once they have been made. What is more, they may have to be made at a time when a country may lack a precise notion of its own identity . . . and when it has not been able to get a clear picture of its own resources and needs.[73]

Still, he was heartened. Landing in New York after his exhausting journey, he spoke to the press with confidence: "One most encouraging fact is that over a wide range of countries you find . . . African leaders of the highest seriousness, devotion, and intelligence."[74] That is the formula: seriousness, devotion, and intelligence. A few days later, he would return to this theme. "There are extremely able people all around the continent . . . , but they are few," and he went on to describe presciently the situation which the UN would encounter in the Congo when that vast country, the size of Western Europe, would soon achieve independence. He was also modeling in advance the attitude of seriousness, devotion, and intelligence that would be required of UN personnel and all others coming to the aid of new African governments.

The period of growth, of education, and of political formation in Africa has been a very short one . . . and in such a short period, and with efforts on a fairly limited scale in most cases, it is quite natural that there has not emerged the kind of social grouping, the kind of social classes, from which you can recruit a broad administration and a broad political leadership. The countries will have to live with few people, and quality will have to make up for numbers and quantity. But there is a limit to what any man can do, and for that reason, if we are not to overburden these people, if we are not to put them before an impossible task, they must get assistance in human terms, they must get people, experts, technicians, and—why not?—officials to the extent that they want, temporarily and transitionally, to employ foreigners. . . .

People and money and education do not mean a thing unless they are given and provided in the right spirit. By the right spirit, by . . . moral support, I mean . . . attitudes . . . which reflect an understanding of the problems facing those countries, a sympathetic understanding, neither a feeling of false superiority, nor a feeling of sterile pessimism, nor a feeling of facile optimism. What is needed is realism and understanding.[75]

In the first months of 1960, the affairs of the world marched on with Hammarskjöld alongside, a little freer than usual. He found time to give a talk in Stockholm in late February to the Swedish Tourist Association, of which he remained an officer. Though he was no longer able to wander the mountains, he still felt their pull. He spoke as a Swede, grateful for the native landscape and the rich poetry it had evoked over the years. But Africa remained on his mind. He made time in his talk to explore what he called "the new nationalism" as a parallel to nineteenth-century Scandinavian experience. There could be distortions, of course ("a nationalism seeking self-glorification at the expense of others"), but in many African countries he reported that he had encountered young men and women in whom "there has been an awakening to a living sense of heritage and resources, and to a healthy pride in the awareness of one's individuality . . . . That which is one's very own is experienced not as something provincial on the outskirts of the world, but as an essential part of the resources humanity as a whole has to manage. Such a national feeling can be harmoniously merged with a feeling of international responsibility. . . . It can appear in the 1960s south of the Sahara as well as in the 1880s and 1890s in Scandinavia."[76] He was thinking even in that rather cozy Swedish setting of the world at large and its needs. "A young nation which is a mature nation knows itself without overbearing or self-infatuation, but it also feels its strength in being faithful to its heritage and its individuality."[77] It was a prescription for a good beginning.

On May 1st a US high-altitude spy plane, a U-2, was shot out of the sky over Soviet territory by surface-to-air missiles, its pilot captured, its aerial photography disclosed. A four-power summit meeting in Paris (Eisenhower, Khrushchev, Macmillan, de Gaulle) went ahead midmonth but collapsed as soon as Khrushchev and Eisenhower confronted one another over the incident. The Cold War became colder. On the very day of the U-2 incident, Hammarskjöld was scheduled to give a talk at the University of Chicago. Certain lines in that talk, reflecting his dry heroism and steady faith, are among those frequently cited by people who cite Hammarskjöld. "Working at the edge of the development of human society," he said, "is to work on the brink of the unknown. Much of what is done will one day prove to have been of little avail. That is no excuse for the failure to act in accordance with our best understanding, in recognition of its limits but with faith in the ultimate result of the creative evolution in which it is our privilege to cooperate."[78] Later, when a journalist questioned him about the talk, he related the expression "creative evolution" to the ideas of Henri Bergson, the French philosopher whose influence on him we have already encountered.

He had pleasures in these months. Since the summer of 1959, he had been experimenting with haiku poetry, the compact Japanese form—just seventeen syllables—which was beginning to find worldwide practitioners. He kept nearby a recently published guide to haiku style that was inspiring many in the West to try their hand.[79] His journal was now filled with examples. It was the perfect form for a very busy man, and through it he had spontaneously begun to explore his past as far back as childhood in Uppsala. He was also collaborating with Karl Ragnar Gierow, director of Dramaten, the Swedish Royal Theater, on a Swedish translation of the modernist verse drama *Antiphon* by Djuna Barnes, an arch-bohemian American author whose company he enjoyed. The verbal complexities of her play offered a perfect counterpoint to his working life. He had also successfully championed his admired friend Saint-John Perse for the 1960 Nobel Prize in Literature, awarded that October, and was soon to publish a Swedish-French edition of his own translation of Perse's long poem *Chronique*.[80] Interviewed during the fall 1960 session of the General Assembly by a French journalist—the French temporarily found him interesting, although de Gaulle could scarcely bring himself to acknowledge the existence of the UN—he spoke for an hour about poetry, translation, and their place in his own life and the lives of several French diplomats of his era. At the end of the interview he commented, "You see, apart from the past two or three months, I have always managed to devote one or two hours each day to what I call serious matters, and I intend to continue doing so." The journalist was listening: "Serious matters, sir?" Hammarskjöld continued, "Yes, serious matters that count in a man's personal life, in any case in mine. I read, and translation is a kind of reading. A poet hasn't only absolute value, he also has value relative to others. How could I fully appreciate Saint-John Perse if I didn't also know Aragon, Supervielle, or Henri Michaux?"[81] And so, in the course of what we'll soon encounter as the most tempestuous session of the General Assembly in his UN years, Hammarskjöld found time to enjoy and share his undisclosed identity as very nearly a French intellectual, a poet among poets. In all respects it must have been restful—restful to think about such things, restful to converse about them.

Some pages ago we located Hammarskjöld at the near end of a bridge to Africa. Through his long journey in early 1960, he crossed over. On June 30th, when the Congo became an independent nation, he sent a message to its leaders and people through Ralph Bunche, who had traveled to the Congo as his representative at the independence ceremonies. What he said reflects his thought and experience of the new Africa, his hope, and his whispered concern that all would go well. "It is a fact that must be reckoned with," he wrote,

> that political evolution in your country has been distinguished by an exceptionally rapid pace in quite recent times. The broad principles of government for the future independent state were enunciated at the Round-Table Conference in Brussels which took place as recently as the beginning of this year, providing only the provisional framework of the Congo's future political institutions. I trust that I may find sympathetic ears in expressing the friendly hope that the elected leaders and representatives of all the regions of your vast and diverse nation will be of a mind to cooperate purposefully in the completion of the structure of solid and stable national government, toward ensuring good order and progress in the Congo society, with just regard for the rights and interests of all segments of the population.[82]

At a press conference later in the day, he expressed again his dry heroism and steady faith; they would be needed. We have heard some of these words before. Their context is the birth of the independent Congo. "The leaders who have emerged in various African countries have shown the instinctive political sense of a good politician and a sense of responsibility which is based also on national pride. In these circumstances we must accept the risks; we can accept them as an act of faith or an act of conviction, but we should do so."[83]

It's best to be careful with symbols. Depending on one's cast of mind, they infuse experience or have no role whatever in the stern factuality of experience. Here we might dare recognize a symbol, a lively one. When Hammarskjöld visited Somalia in the course of January 1960 and gave a notable talk there, someone in authority thought to offer him a special gift: a pet monkey. He named it Greenback and took it home. Thereafter the apartment at Seventy-Third Street housed Mr. Hammarskjöld, the household staff, frequent dignified guests, and a monkey. Ralph Bunche could recall Hammarskjöld's "poignant affection for Greenback, the little pet who was a monkey in every sense, wildly playful, an irrepressible show-off, a born 'ham' whenever visitors were present."[84] Greenback had a long rope, serving him as a jungle vine, tied somewhere toward the top of a staircase. He must have had a good time with it. Hammarskjöld photographed him, looking as poised as can be on a windowsill of his apartment. Greenback had other friends, among them Toddy Ranallo, the wife of Hammarskjöld's security guard, who once in a letter inquired after his well being. It sounds as if Greenback sometimes boarded with the Ranallo family when the secretary-general was away: "How is 'Greenback' doing? I confess to missing him somewhat. He was a pretty good fellow and can visit any time."[85] At the far end of the bridge to Africa, Hammarskjöld had acquired a companion.

15

Like Fighting an Avalanche

"Blood, grime, sweat, earth," Hammarskjöld wrote in his journal years ago, in 1954, "where are these in your world of will? Everywhere—the ground from which the flame ascends straight upwards."[1] His faith in ascending transformation met its harshest test in the Congo Crisis of 1960–61.

A long arc links the late nineteenth-century Scramble for Africa by European nations greedy for colonies to Hammarskjöld's moment when colonial power receded from the continent. The scramble had been solemnized in 1884–85 by the Berlin Conference, which laid ground rules for cooperation and agreed on the territorial claims of five nations and one individual, King Léopold II of Belgium.[2] Léopold had resourcefully hired the famed explorer of the Congo Basin, Henry Morton Stanley, to make treaties far and wide in the Congo with many hundreds of local chiefs—treaties the chiefs did not begin to understand—and to create what came to be known as the Congo Free State. It was a possession not of the Belgian nation but of Léopold himself through a seemingly benign organization he controlled, the International Association of the Congo. Among its stated goals were to eliminate the slave trade, bring the Christian faith and other benefits to the region, and ensure free trade. Its actual goal was to enrich Léopold personally, initially through the ivory trade and soon the trade in rubber, which overnight became a major commodity in the industrial world for the manufacture of tires and other products. But the term "trade" is a misnomer: through his armed and typically brutal agents, Léopold established the nearest thing imaginable to a slave labor colony, which disrupted and destroyed the traditional order of life in the Congo and subjected village Congolese to terror and mutilation, murder, exhaustion, and famine. The population declined under Léopold's regime from an estimated twenty-five million to fifteen million. What he had set in motion from afar—he never visited the Congo—went largely unnoticed until 1890, when there occurred the first of an accelerating series of informed protests. The author of this groundbreaking document was an African American, George Washington Williams—a Civil War veteran, ordained minister, and writer who, though he had met and been charmed by Léopold, felt conscience bound to send him a harsh indictment of the regime in the Congo Free State after traveling there for some months. His open letter, soon published as a pamphlet, found its way into major newspapers in Europe and the United States.

Slightly more than a decade later, he was followed by a remarkable crusading journalist and author, the Anglo-French E. D. Morel, and by a man of great gifts and ultimately tragic fate, the Irish patriot Roger Casement, then serving as British consul to the Congo Free State. Casement was the author of an investigative report published by the British government in 1904.[3] His narrative had the cool formality of a proper government report, but its content—as he well knew—recorded the inexcusable treatment of Congolese villagers, men, women, and children, by the militarized agents of Léopold. Mark Twain, Joseph Conrad, and Arthur Conan Doyle also joined the assault on what Morel had called "a secret society of murderers" headed by a king.[4] The American's contribution was an odd piece, not his best, entitled *King Leopold's Soliloquy: A Defense of His Congo Rule*, published as a pamphlet in 1905.[5] By 1907, it had appeared in a new edition with Morel's introduction. One of the vivid moments in Mark Twain's indictment has Léopold railing against the camera, the "kodak": "The kodak has been a sore calamity to us. The most powerful enemy that has confronted us. . . . I was looked up to as the benefactor of a down-trodden and friendless people. Then all of a sudden came the crash! That is to say, the incorruptible Kodak. . . . The only witness I have encountered in my long experience that I couldn't bribe." It was photographs of maimed children, chained village women, and much more that drove home to European and American public opinion the truth of written accounts.

Like many others of his generation, Hammarskjöld would first have thought about the Congo thanks to Joseph Conrad's novella *Heart of Darkness*, serialized in 1899, published as a book in 1902, recognized as a masterpiece by young Dag's time. Drawing on Conrad's experience as a riverboat captain on the Congo, it tells the story of a journey toward the jungle station of Mr. Kurtz, who embodied the cruelty and strange sophistication of Belgian commercial agents collecting rubber and ivory from coerced villagers whose lives and deaths they controlled. "We called at . . . places with farcical names," says Conrad's narrator of the first stage of his journey, "where the merry dance of death and trade goes on in a still and earthy atmosphere as of an overheated catacomb. . . . It was like a pilgrimage amongst hints for nightmares."[6] Many readers know where the journey ends—with the dying Mr. Kurtz, making a last review of his life, crying out "The horror! The horror!" As I mentioned in an earlier page, Hammarskjöld kept an etched portrait of Conrad in his New York apartment; he may have had it for long years in Sweden.[7] A presiding spirit in his life, Conrad pointed toward a passion for observation and deep humanism without illusions. As Hammarskjöld entered the drama of the Congo in July 1960, and called on the resources of the member nations to rescue a suddenly unstable beginning there, he would surely have looked at the portrait of Conrad to acknowledge that his own journey into the heart of darkness—but could there be light?—had begun.

In 1908, Belgium responded to the unbearable criticism of Léopold's Free State by insisting on the transfer of control to the nation. From that time forward to 1960, the Belgian Congo developed much along the lines of other European colonies in Africa, with one pervasive policy exception that set it apart. Industry, primarily large-scale mining of copper, cobalt, uranium, diamonds, and other minerals, advanced under the control of holding companies managed by Belgian executives and engineers on behalf of Belgian and other European and American investors. Medical facilities and missionary-led primary and secondary schooling reached across the country; the near elimination of epidemic sleeping sickness was a fine achievement. River and rail became peaceful highways for goods and people. An indigenous middle class took shape in increasingly attractive, growing cities. This was all to the good and seemed to sum to a reasonably model colony that had lived down Léopold's disgraceful heritage.

But the Belgians did little, and late, to prepare the Congolese for independence by developing civil society and providing opportunities for higher education, senior management roles, and political experience. This was the crucial difference from many other African colonies; the Congolese were excluded from all but subordinate positions in government, business, and the military. The contrast was considerable with the French and British West African colonies that became independent Guinea and Ghana. While there was no "gold standard" among the European colonies, it was nonetheless true that the first Guinean president, Ahmed Sékou Touré, had gained long and rough political experience in the anticolonial movement, as did the first president of Ghana, Kwame Nkrumah, who as a young man earned several higher degrees in American universities. By one count, in the years prior to independence there were some five thousand African students from the French colonies attending French universities. In 1958, speaking from Brazzaville in the French Congo, just across the wide river from Léopoldville, president Charles de Gaulle offered independence, with or without a close link to France, to all French colonies in sub-Saharan Africa. The emerging Congolese political elite were listening; this was an extraordinary change of policy. Belgium had no parallel intention. It expected to remain in the Congo for several more decades, and Belgian nationals counted on remaining comfortably at the helm of all major enterprises and in senior roles in the government of an independent Congo. At independence in June 1960, there was not a single Congolese army officer, and the number of university-educated professionals in the population of some fourteen million could be counted on two hands. There was no Congolese doctor, just one lawyer—and so it went. The University of Lovanium, located in a suburb of Léopoldville, had opened only in 1954. Tens of thousands of Belgians ran everything, lived separately in their own neighborhoods, frequented their own clubs and restaurants, and typically regarded the Congolese as inferiors, although of course there were those who lived and worked among Africans wholeheartedly and without racist sentiment. Black residents of Léopoldville liked to cross the river to the French Congolese capital of Brazzaville, where they were free to sit in the same bars as whites and drink the same wine.[8] A mirror of common Belgian attitudes is naïvely available in the comic strip *Tintin au Congo*, published in 1930 by Hergé for Belgian (and French) children of all ages.[9] The Congolese are uniformly caricatured; somewhat hapless and ridiculous, not one speaks proper French. Despite any and all obstacles, a class of younger Congolese, called *évolués*, had taken advantage of the limited educational opportunities on offer and acquired enough tools of inquiry to complete their educations on their own; in part self-made men and women, they were aware of the rapid movement toward independence in much of Africa and determined to shape the politics of a new era in their country.

The Congo had lurched toward independence since 1958. In the spring of that year, in his Cambridge talk on walls of distrust, Hammarskjöld had offered an austere blessing over the process of decolonization in Asia and Africa, which was gaining momentum. "There is a maturity of mind," he said, "required of those who give up rights. There is a maturity of mind required of those who acquire new rights. Let us hope that, to an increasing extent, the necessary spiritual qualities will be shown on all sides."[10] That was his wish. He was also preparing. His Swedish countryman, Sture Linnér, recalled that Hammarskjöld had approached him with a request during his long tour of Africa. They had known and liked each other in Uppsala as young men and came across one another again in Liberia, where Linnér (despite his doctorate in ancient Greek literature) was an executive in an American-Swedish-Liberian mining company of which Hammarskjöld's brother, Bo, was chief executive. Hammarskjöld said, "I would like very much for you to be prepared to go to the Congo in about a year's time because I foresee great trouble there. . . . It's more a hunch than anything else. But somehow I am convinced there will be. I would like you to come because you don't know the rules and regulations, and I would not like you to become acquainted with them because I need someone I trust who speaks the same language, in more than the literal sense, and who understands toward where I would be driving and who would not feel hampered by the usual civil servant caution, looking things up in the textbook all the time, but would go ahead and create rules, breaking the old ones in the process if necessary."[11] This fair warning converted into fact some months later when Bo joined forces with Dag to persuade Linnér of his higher duty. "I was asked by . . . Hammarskjöld," Linnér continued, "to go down to the Congo together with Ralph Bunche to represent the Secretary-General at the festivities in connection with the independence of the Congo in June, 1960. . . . With a glint in his eye the Secretary-General then said that this would take a week or two or maybe a year or possibly two. 'So do your packing accordingly,' which I did. And it turned out that the latter time frame was the one. . . . It was decided that I should stay on when the crisis broke out. I became Chief of Civilian Operations."

Years later to sit with Sture Linnér in Stockholm, in the lovely home he kept there, was a privilege that many of us interested in the Hammarskjöld legacy have shared. In his early nineties, he still spoke of the Congo with such vividness and warmth that one sensed, magically, a widening circle that flowed out to the past and restored both its immediacy and its pain.

On June 29th, King Baudouin I, accompanied by his prime minister, foreign minister Pierre Wigny, and other Belgian officials, flew in to participate in the independence ceremonies. There were speeches to give, festive occasions to share in, and papers to sign, including a treaty of friendship between the two countries. Earlier in the year a constitution had been written, the Loi Fondamentale, to structure a parliamentary government with a president, prime minister and cabinet, upper and lower houses, and provincial presidents. On hand to greet the king and his entourage were the newly elected president Joseph Kasavubu, the prime minister Patrice Lumumba (who not many months earlier had been jailed by the Belgians for inciting political unrest), and other officials including Moïse Tshombe, soon to be president of the wealthy province of Katanga in the southeast, where many of the mining interests were concentrated. Ralph Bunche and Sture Linnér were in attendance. Young and handsome in a brilliant white military uniform, the king was entering Léopoldville in an open car at a ceremonial pace when an unpleasant thing happened: a Congolese man reached in, stole his sword, and tried to make off with it. He was quickly stopped; no harm done. But it was unsettling. The vast artificial distance between the white colonists and the Congolese population had been breached by an act of petty violence that was, in equal measures, symbolic and bizarre.

June 30th, 1960, was an overwhelmingly festive day in Léopoldville and across the country, which we should remember is the size of Western Europe. The sound in the streets was a buoyant new tune. Everywhere they were singing "*Indépendance cha-cha to zuwi ye!*": roughly, "We've claimed our independence, cha-cha."[12] The king's speech that day—about which, to his thorough irritation, Patrice Lumumba knew nothing in advance—reflected another reading of history. It should have been anodyne, graceful: adieu to the old, welcome to the new. Instead Baudouin praised to the skies his grandfather, Léopold II, and in the manner of Shakespeare's Polonius laid on well-intended advice to the country and its new leaders. "The independence of the Congo is the conclusion of a work conceived by the genius of King Léopold II, which he undertook with tenacious courage, and which Belgium has continued perseveringly. . . . Léopold II . . . did not come in the guise of a conqueror, but of a civilizer."[13] And so on. Kasavubu as president responded pacifically. Reading a speech said to have been prepared for him by Belgian advisers, he was anodyne and graceful.[14] Then it was Lumumba's turn. He too had not shared his speech in advance with the king's party. In point of fact, he was not on the published agenda but had quietly arranged otherwise. What he said has never been forgotten. It was a shout of just anger, a joyous, strained cry of independence. Through him the mind and heart of the Congo turned with bitter honesty toward the former colonial power. His message was intensely impolitic and altogether true. Transmitted around the world, it frightened the Western powers with which the Congo would need good relations and put Belgium on notice that its scarcely concealed strategy of legal change without fundamental change was unlikely to work out well. Transmitted by radio across the Congo, every word elicited a passionate response: "People glued to the radio in the villages . . . cheered and clapped," and sang and danced "Indépendance, cha-cha" in the streets.[15]

Baudouin had said that Belgium was generously granting independence to the Congo. Lumumba disagreed.

> Though the independence of the Congo is today being proclaimed . . . , no Congolese worthy of the name can ever forget that we fought to win it, a fight waged each and every day, a passionate and idealistic fight. . . . We are proud of this struggle . . . down to our very heart of hearts, for it was a noble and just struggle, an indispensable struggle if we were to put an end to the humiliating slavery that had been forced upon us.
>
> The wounds that are the evidence of the fate we endured for 80 years under a colonialist regime are still too fresh and painful for us to be able to erase them from our memory. Back-breaking work has been exacted from us, in return for wages that did not allow us to satisfy our hunger. . . .
>
> We have been the victims of ironic taunts, of insults, of blows that we were forced to endure morning, noon and night because we were blacks. Who can forget that a black was addressed in the familiar form, not because he was a friend, certainly, but because the polite form of address was to be used only for whites? . . .
>
> Who can forget . . . the volleys of rifle fire in which so many of our brothers perished, the cells into which the authorities threw those who no longer were willing to submit to a rule where justice meant oppression and exploitation?
>
> We have grievously suffered all this, my brothers. . . .
>
> The Republic of the Congo has been proclaimed and our country is now in the hands of its own children.
>
> We are going to begin another struggle together, my brothers, my sisters, a sublime struggle that will bring our country peace, prosperity, and grandeur. . . .
>
> I ask all of you to forget the tribal quarrels that are draining our strength and threaten to earn us the contempt of those in other countries. . . .
>
> This is what I wanted to say to you in the name of the government on this magnificent day of our complete and sovereign independence.
>
> Long live the independent and sovereign Congo![16]

Lumumba's honest reference to tribal quarrels acknowledged that all was not well in the new world that he and his colleagues would now set out to construct. After bearing up during the speech, Baudouin wanted nothing better than to leave the Congo at once, but he was prevailed upon to stay the planned course, as Lumumba was prevailed upon to offer a gracious toast at dinner expressing gratitude to Belgium for its legitimate contributions to the Congo.

Three leaders at independence, and one in the wings

"I am self-taught and I have never stopped learning," wrote Patrice Lumumba (1925–61) to a Belgian publisher in 1957 (fig. 15).[17] This has the ring of the man. Born in the central Kasai Province of the Congo, educated in missionary schools and in a specialized course for postal workers, he became a postal clerk, served a short jail sentence for dicey financial dealings on the job, and later became a notably successful beer sales representative, all the while finding his way into nationalist politics. A founder and soon leader of a major political party, the Mouvement National Congolais (MNC), he reached the top of Congolese politics with a small cohort of other *évolués*, some of whom were his loyal allies, others open or undeclared enemies in a political environment in which enmity could have far-reaching consequences.[18] There are many, many descriptions of him. Few who met and worked with Lumumba could resist the impulse to describe him, as if one had to record something solid about this mercurial man. "In July and August of 1960," Ralph Bunche said some years after that date, "I was seeing Patrice Lumumba almost daily. He was an electric figure; his passionate oratory could entrance an audience and, as it sometimes appeared, even himself; he was indefatigable; he was quickly perceptive and shrewd; also he was deeply suspicious of almost everyone and everything. He may have been subject to leftist influence, but I did not regard him as anyone's stooge and felt that he was not greatly concerned with ideology. Mr. Lumumba, it must be said, was one of the few Congolese who seemed to grasp the vital necessity of national unity in a new nation, and he strove against all the divisive forces of tribalism and special interest to promote his unity. Unfortunately, however, he and most of his colleagues in his Cabinet had little knowledge of and apparently no deep interest in government and administration as distinct from crude politics and political maneuver."[19] This temperate retrospection skips over the dreadful difficulty Bunche had with Lumumba in summer 1960, when he wrote to his wife in sorrow about "the insane fulminations of one reckless man."[20] That man was Lumumba.

Rajeshwar Dayal, the third UN representative in quick succession to oversee Congo operations, made his own word portrait: "Lumumba . . .

was tall and slim, with earnest bespectacled eyes and a small beard. Quick and intelligent, he appeared to be driven by an almost desperate courage. In his impatience to get things done, he seemed possessed by some inner force which made him tense, like a coiled spring. Yet he could be charming and likable. . . . But a man fired with such dynamism and feverish energy stood in danger of becoming the victim of his own restless nature."[21]

As we have heard Lumumba pointedly address himself to his Congolese brothers *and sisters*, we should collect the impressions of a woman who stood near him, Andrée Blouin. She is routinely maligned in much of the literature about the period as a disconcertingly elegant courtesan of mixed European and African parentage and as a political grey eminence whispering who knows what into the ears of her enchanted Congolese friends. That can't be right. In her autobiography, she is persuasively revealed to have been an early and forceful African feminist, a person of wide intelligence and useful experience and of impeccable loyalty to the cause of African nation building. When she first met Lumumba before independence, her quick assessment was: "He's brave and he's sincere. Above all, he is *committed*. . . . He won't disappoint Africa."[22] Many years and events later, she offered a larger view: "Sometimes goodness and simplicity are misinterpreted during the lifetime of a genius and are recognized only after his death. I think Patrice was such a genius. Perhaps he was not meant to go the whole way in his work, but only to be the apostle who opens the path. . . . Everyone knew that there was no one equal to this great African."[23]

Another person loyal to Lumumba whose views can be trusted was Thomas Kanza, the first lay Congolese graduate of a Belgian university (Congolese priests did prepare in Belgium) and Lumumba's head of delegation to the UN. Hammarskjöld took him under his wing as a promising and thoughtful advocate for the Congo. Kanza's book on the Congo Crisis speaks wisely, without ideological baggage, from within the Congolese community of thought and experience. More consistently than any other account of the period, his book allows one to feel the meaning of people and events. "People who were with [Lumumba] a great deal," Kanza has written, "found him the personification of dynamism, watchfulness, and insight. His look was so penetrating that it could be an almost tangible reproach to some; whereas to others it expressed a real sense of understanding. . . . Lumumba was a very special kind of man: he achieved success through the strengths of his nature, but could not hold on to it because of the weaknesses. . . . Could he have acted in any different way? God alone knows."[24] We have heard enough warnings in these vivid character sketches to know that great difficulties lie ahead.

Joseph Kasavubu (1910–69) was a wholly different kind. President from independence until a coup d'état in 1965, he rose to high office in an alliance of necessity with Lumumba and became his enemy. Educated in missionary schools and originally destined for the ministry, for a while he was a school teacher and, like Lumumba, entered nationalist politics, in his case from a base in a large tribal party, Alliance des Bakongo (ABAKO), which served the interests of his own Bakongo people, dominant in Léopoldville and its region and across the river in the French Congo, where Lumumba had few friends and Kasavubu had many. Descriptions of Kasavubu that diligently seek the essence of the man—there are nowhere near as many as for Lumumba—often end in criticism or even derision. He seems one who marshaled clarity of direction and firmness in the struggle for independence but later slowly lost his way. Carl von Horn, the Swedish major general swept out of UN duties in the Middle East to be the first commander of UN peacekeeping forces in the Congo, had nothing terribly complimentary to say of him: he was "'King Kasa' to his supporters, a portly, plump-cheeked figure, inordinately conscious of status and occasion."[25] Dayal described him as "devious and slow-moving"—this last trait inspiring Hammarskjöld to say unkindly that he was "like a water buffalo," and Kanza compared him to a crocodile "sleeping open-eyed beside the river."[26] At least the analogies reflected local wildlife. Dayal added that "if Kasavubu claimed to be the father of the nation, Lumumba regarded himself as the messiah of his people."[27] Their temperaments could hardly have been more unlike. The role of president in the new republic was designed by the Loi Fondamentale to parallel the Belgian king's role, responsible but only distantly involved in the day-to-day. However, as things worked out, Kasavubu was involved in nearly everything and needed to be, though he came to resent that Lumumba increasingly acted without him.

From this early moment there is a further prominent political leader to meet: Moïse Tshombe (1919–69). His press and reputation in the West during his years as president of the secessionist province of Katanga were much more favorable then than now. Born to a prosperous business family, he was educated in the missionary system, became an accountant, and cofounded the Confédération des Associations Tribales du Katanga (CONAKAT), a party focused on the interests of Katanga. Pro-Western and anti-Communist, with Belgian support he set in motion political and economic events that turned what might have been no more than a long moment of chaos in the first weeks of independence into years of frustrating stalemate and periodic bloodshed. Three months after Hammarskjöld died on his way to a meeting with him, he had his *Time* magazine cover—a privilege never extended to Lumumba. "He was the solemn black defender of white capitalism in middle Africa, a rarity," *Time* wrote in its cover story for December 22, 1961. "Urbane and charming . . . , volatile and unpredictable . . . , Tshombe had his friends in the U.S. Congress."[28] *Time* was writing in the past tense, as if Tshombe were finished politically; that was far from so. Urquhart's eyewitness view cuts to essentials: "Tshombe was a charismatic but fundamentally weak figure who was constantly being manipulated by other people for their own ends. . . . His public relations firm in Geneva did a wonderful job of presenting him to the world as a civilized, popular, successful, anti-Communist, pro-European African leader. He was nothing of the kind."[29] Conor Cruise O'Brien, a writer and diplomat who had a fateful tour of duty in Katanga, wrote of Tshombe that "neither statements of fact nor written engagements could be relied on; no contradiction, no detected lie caused Mr. Tshombe the slightest embarrassment. If caught out in some piece of duplicity—on political prisoners, refugees, mercenaries, or anything else—he would show absent-mindedness, tinged, I sometimes imagined, with a paternal compassion for the naiveté of anyone who supposed he would tell the truth. . . ."[30]

Joseph-Désiré Mobutu (1930–97) was scarcely visible before independence but quickly found his place, and then another and another. Born in humble circumstances, his father the cook for a Belgian judge, he showed promise and was guided by the judge's wife into a Christian Brothers boarding school. A bit of mischief there landed him in the army, but he continued his education independently—again, a self-made man—and in 1956 became a journalist writing for a Léopoldville daily. Placing his hope in Lumumba and the MNC, Mobutu earned Lumumba's confidence and soon became his personal aide and, for a few weeks, a deputy minister. In the crisis that engulfed the army after independence, Lumumba turned to Mobutu to take things in hand by appointing him chief of staff, second in command of the newly renamed Armée Nationale Congolaise (ANC), whose Belgian officers had been summarily fired. In the weeks that followed, Mobutu became a secret protégé of the enormously able CIA station chief in Léopoldville, Larry Devlin, who guided him, and financed him, toward events in September that crippled Lumumba's political career and placed Mobutu alongside Kasavubu at the center of power. Devlin deftly described Mobutu at this early stage of their working relation: "He was in full military dress, tall, rail-thin, and very, very young. He almost looked like a high school kid all decked out in an ROTC uniform."[31] But Mobutu had ideas and ambition. In later years, as many readers will recall, he would become Mobutu Sese Seko, president of the Democratic Republic of the Congo (or Zaire) for thirty-two years, a reliable ally of the United States and a thieving dictator.

We now have our four. Of course there were others; we shall meet a number of them.

A kind of Congo-inferno

Bunche's comment about the absence of interest in government and administration, and everyone's implication that Lumumba was brilliant but impulsive, presage the catastrophe that fell on the Congo only days after independence. Bunche's view wasn't entirely just: there was interest in governing well, but scant experience and overwhelming conditions. The new Congolese administration had only weeks in office before independence. It would have needed not weeks but months to analyze in advance the stresses that could be expected in key sectors of society and envision wise strategies. Instead, as Kanza has written, the Belgians did next to nothing until the last moment to share power or invite future ministers to shadow them and, to Kanza's shame, Lumumba's cabinet frittered away its early meetings. "All of us were happy, or at least cheerful and satisfied, at being ministers. It was play-acting; some of it pure comedy, some nearer to tragedy. We were ministers; we, the colonized, now had titles and dignity; but we had no power at all over any of the instruments we needed to carry out the functions expected of us. We argued about offices . . . and how they should be shared among us. . . . In short, we talked endlessly, laughed ourselves silly, and concluded by generally agreeing that the Belgian colonizers were to blame for all our troubles."[32] Imagine being given abruptly, without preparation, the sovereign responsibility for a country the size of Western Europe with numerous tribes, some locked in hereditary enmities; with a history of rigid racial division and resentment; with vast disparities between village and city; with webs of pitiless intrigue and ambition crisscrossing the land before you even begin to take hold. One might stumble. The situation resembled an unwritten novel by Kafka.

The trouble began locally on July 3rd with intertribal violence in a quarter of Léopoldville and became nationwide on the 5th and days following. The events of July 5th were ignited by thick-headed comments from the Belgian commander of the Armée Nationale Congolaise, who should have known better, and by a grave oversight of Lumumba's, who should have known better. In the first days of independence, Lumumba had raised the salaries of all government workers but did nothing for the army, which served both as a national police force and as a defense against foreign aggression. His own cabinet—twenty-three ministers, ten secretaries of state, four ministers of state, to reflect the tribal diversity of the country—took to their new chauffeured cars and swanned around Léopoldville. (Lumumba had to order the cars back to the garage at the end of the work day.) Meanwhile general Emile Janssens gave a lecture to the Léopoldville garrison during which he famously wrote on the blackboard "After independence = Before independence." I doubt that Glubb Pasha, the British head of Jordan's Arab Legion, would have done that. Whatever message about discipline Janssens meant to convey, his men heard that their lives and opportunities would remain as pinched as ever—that there would be no increases in pay and grade, that Belgians would continue to officer the army, and Congolese as in the past would be sergeants at best in their own country.[33] The garrison mutinied. They roughed up their Belgian officers and roamed Léopoldville in bands, looking for white people, looking for trouble. Ralph Bunche wasn't immune: on July 8th Congolese soldiers invaded his hotel room and forced him at gunpoint to join other hotel guests in the lobby. He thought best to cooperate until they abruptly left.[34]

The mutiny quickly spread to other garrisons across the country, and soon there were reports of rape and every kind of violence against whites. Lumumba went out to the Léopoldville garrison—he never lacked the courage to confront—where he promised to fire all Belgian officers and instantly raise all ranks to the next rank and pay grade. But the damage was done. The news of chaos, personal danger, and rape spread through the Belgian and expatriate communities, and they fled by the thousands—by car across borders to neighboring countries, by air to Belgium and elsewhere, by ferry and private launch across the river to the safety of Congo (Brazzaville), where the flamboyant Abbé Fulbert Youlou would soon be head of state of his newly independent country. Lumumba and

Kasavubu together flew to city after city in their new nation to calm the army and calm nerves—this was their finest and bravest moment of cooperation—but they were unable to stop the mutinies for long or end the torrential flow of Europeans out of the country. With them left virtually all of the professional expertise that had kept the Belgian Congo functioning, the doctors, engineers, judges, teachers, bankers, and plant managers, the air traffic controllers, the government administrators so needed to make a sound transition—gone. The exception was Katanga Province, where events began in the same way but took a different course.

There was a further insult of enormous consequence. After several Europeans were killed by mutinous soldiers on July 9th in the cities of Luluabourg and Elisabethville (the administrative center of Katanga Province, now Lubumbashi), Belgium deployed masses of its own troops to safeguard European life and property from military bases it had retained by agreement with the new government and sent paratroops from home to reinforce them. The central government had not been consulted, and Moïse Tshombe in Katanga had asked for troops; they were wanted there. It was as if the celebrations of June 30th had been annulled, the country swatted back to colonial status. Lumumba spoke to the Congolese people via radio, a crucially important communication link: "We have demanded independence so that peace and order may reign in the Congo. We want to build our country, not tear it to pieces. . . . We need the cooperation of Europeans in order to do so. We cannot tolerate their being the object of violence or harassment. . . . [But] the Congolese government will not tolerate the sending of Belgian troops to the Congo without our consent . . . . Belgium bears a grave responsibility."[35]

On July 11th, Tshombe and his Belgian advisers exploited the chaos to declare the secession of Katanga from the Republic of the Congo. It was to be henceforth an independent state, closely allied with Belgium and under the protection of the Belgian military. This action was certainly long prepared, but it might well have taken a more pacific form if the rest of the Congo had not disintegrated. Katangese leaders in government and business had been thinking for some time that a federal structure in the new Congo would better serve their aim of protecting Katanga's exceptional wealth. But under the circumstances, secession would do. It was a heavy blow to the central government. It struck at the vision of a unified nation, rising above tribal and regional differences to become a single people, a model for all of Africa. It was a shameless violation of the

Loi Fondamentale under which the nation had achieved independence. And far from least, it threatened to impoverish the rest of the Congo by removing from the national economy some 50 percent of its expected annual revenues and 75 percent of its foreign exchange reserves, generated by the mining operations of the Union Minière du Haut Katanga. Not easily reversed, this political maneuver with endless consequences was to weigh on Lumumba and Hammarskjöld to the ends of their lives.

On July 12th, the day after Katanga's declaration, Hammarskjöld received the first of several cables from Kasavubu and Lumumba requesting "urgent dispatch by the United Nations of military assistance . . . to protect the national territory of the Congo against the present external aggression which is a threat to international peace." The cable also accused the Belgian government of "colonialist machinations" in Katanga "with a view to maintaining a hold on our country."[36] One of Hammarskjöld's early biographers recorded his reaction. He was in Geneva for a meeting. Leaving at once for New York, he had already understood that the UN would need to respond. "I must do this," he said. "God knows where it will lead this Organization and where it will lead me."[37] He chose to "do this" by invoking Article 99 of the Charter for the first time in UN history. You may recall that it reads, "The Secretary-General may bring to the attention of the Security Council any matter which in his opinion may threaten the maintenance of international peace and security." In earlier pages we have heard Hammarskjöld explore the idea behind the words. He tended to minimize. For example, in Djakarta in 1956, he said that "[Article 99] is . . . somewhat violent and dramatic . . . . It is a kind of political H-bomb, and for that reason it has more importance in principle than it can possibly have in practice. However, it does mean the Secretary-General is recognized as having rather far-reaching political responsibilities."[38] At the outset of the Congo Crisis, he preferred to maximize. F. T. Liu, who worked with Bunche and Hammarskjöld in the Congo, sheds light: "I believe that the Security Council could convene without Article 99, but I think . . . Hammarskjöld wanted to stress the importance of this problem. . . . 1960 was . . . the year that the decolonization process started in full force, and he felt that what happened to the Congo would be extremely important—because of the timing, because the Congo had a unique strategic position, and because the Congo had very great natural resources. Therefore he wanted to do something to settle the problem."[39]

Summoned by the secretary-general, the Security Council met for the first time on the question of the Congo on July 13th. Hammarskjöld had been cautious: he had queried the African member states, which agreed that prompt UN intervention was needed, and had checked with the Council delegates to ensure that they found the use of Article 99 sensible under the circumstances.[40] His exercise of that right pointed with the nonchalance of fate, which sometimes makes signs no one understands, toward a future balance of responsibility against which he had to struggle. His masters in the Security Council and General Assembly tended to pass resolutions that left far more to his executive judgment than he wished. In a few months' time we'll hear him remind the General Assembly, "This is *your* operation, gentlemen."

In his opening statement on July 13th, recommending action, Hammarskjöld recalled the principles governing previous peacekeeping exercises and placed them at the center of whatever was to come. "It follows," he said, "that the United Nations Force would not be authorized to action beyond self-defense. It follows further that they may not take any action which would make them a party to internal conflicts in the country. Finally, the selection of personnel should be such as to avoid complications because of the nationalities used. . . . May I add that in fact it would be my intention to get, in the first place, assistance from African nations."[41] All of this will seem obvious and necessary, but much of the drama surrounding the UN presence in the Congo would turn on adherence to these policies through desperate circumstances in which nearly all parties to the events had a better idea, and noninterference in internal political conflicts was instantly interpreted as favoring one side or the other. The Council achieved consensus once attitudes toward Belgium's troop deployment had been worked through. By that time Belgian forces had occupied Léopoldville's main airport and city center and were patrolling key sites across the country. Their intervention was not a light touch, it was formidable, and on the whole welcome to Western members of the Council: how could they condone an uncontained army run wild? Reinforcing from Moscow the Soviet view, Khrushchev "asserted at a news conference," according to the *New York Times*, "that Congolese soldiers were 'perfectly right' in mutinying against their officers . . . Belgian officers are . . . colonialists."[42] And for good measure he added that the United States and its allies were behind this effort to return the Congo to colonial status. He was speaking from afar, but only for the moment: in September he would participate directly in the General Assembly. From the very first, the Congo Crisis invited Cold War attitudes and intrigue, although in the Security Council practical agreements remained possible through the summer. One of Hammarskjöld's aims from the first was "to keep the Cold War in its sharper forms out of Africa,"[43] where the departure of the colonial powers could easily give rise to a reformatted Scramble for Africa.

The successful resolution of July 14th, passed in the early hours of morning, called upon Belgium to withdraw its troops and authorized the secretary-general "to take the necessary steps, in consultation with the Government of the Republic of the Congo, to provide the Government with such military assistance as may be necessary until, through the efforts of the Congolese Government with the technical assistance of the United Nations, the national security forces may be able, in the opinion of the Government, to meet fully their tasks."[44] There was no mention of territorial integrity (i.e., Katanga), no condemnation of any party, and no timetable, but it was a start. Closing the session, the president of the Security Council remarked that "the secretary-general has once again been entrusted with a mission, one which is of the greatest importance to the maintenance of peace."[45]

Hammarskjöld at once regrouped with senior staff in his office—it was still the middle of the night—to set in motion a peacekeeping force and program of technical assistance, the latter referring to the need to fill gaps left by the departure in recent days of some twenty-five thousand Belgian civilians and to train Congolese replacements. With Ralph Bunche and Sture Linnér already on the spot in Léopoldville, Major General von Horn quickly called to the scene from the Middle East, firm willingness on the part of African and middle-power governments to supply troops, and air transport offered by the United States and USSR, a strong response was possible at once. High-level UN leaders rallied: General Wheeler, whom we know from his Suez service, arrived to oversee improvements at Matadi, the river port crucial to the UN supply line over the Atlantic, and a senior UN figure arrived to oversee restoration of food distribution across the country—even that had faltered. On July 18th, there were already 3,500 troops in the Congo, seconded to the UN by Morocco, Tunisia, Ghana, and Ethiopia, with additions expected from Guinea, Mali, Sweden, and others. By month's end there would be 11,000. ONUC was born: l'Organisation des Nations Unies au Congo.

Not that the UN was familiar to many in the Congo. Urquhart tells the classic story of a district administrator who questioned Bunche: "L'ONU, c'est quelle tribu?"—the UN, what tribe is that?[46]

The response of member nations and the Secretariat was magnificent, the strategy governing their efforts straightforward. Urquhart, who joined Bunche in the Congo within days after the Council resolution, provides a clear summary:

> ONUC's initial function in the Congo was threefold: to remove the threat to international peace and security by effecting the withdrawal of Belgian troops from the entire territory of the Congo; to assist the government in restoring and maintaining law and order, a task that included . . . training and reorganizing . . . the Armée Nationale Congolaise (ANC); and to assure the continuation of essential services, to restore and organize the administrative machinery of government, and to train the Congolese to run that machinery.[47]

Further, the Congo Advisory Group, composed of delegates whose countries were contributing troops to ONUC, was soon meeting with Hammarskjöld, and a second group of senior Secretariat colleagues convened informally as the so-called Congo Club. It would meet at great length, day or night, as circumstances dictated. Rajeshwar Dayal had vivid memories of its meetings, which he attended when at headquarters.

> The "Congo Club" appeared to be in continuous session, luncheons and dinners being generously provided by the Secretary-General. Late every evening, when the lights in the building had been turned off and the last of the delegates had departed, Hammarskjöld's suite would come to renewed life. The faithful would reassemble after a long and tiring day when there would be a review of the fast-changing panorama of events in the Congo and in the conference rooms. Messages and instructions would be discussed and dispatched and the following day's strategies planned. On days of exceptional crisis the team would remain together until well past midnight, and Hammarskjöld himself would remain at his desk on the 38th floor.[48]

By the time the Security Council reconvened on July 20th after reading Hammarskjöld's first progress report, the clear initial strategy had encountered mixed circumstances. As UNOC peacekeeping forces deployed, the Belgian troops were gradually returning to their bases (except in Katanga where they settled in), but their presence enraged Lumumba and his colleagues, and the secession of Katanga justifiably obsessed them. Bunche's relations with Lumumba were beginning to fray. He was the representative of an orderly agenda, vast in its compassion and ambition for the Congo but intolerably limited from Lumumba's perspective. Lumumba wanted the troops to do his bidding, and he read the first Security Council resolution and those that followed in that light. He wanted to break Katanga. If the UN wouldn't help him by force of arms, he made clear that he wouldn't hesitate to call on the Soviet Union; he and Kasavubu were already in touch with Khrushchev, who for the moment was sympathetically noncommittal.[49]

Hammarskjöld needed a more precise resolution from the Security Council and assurance of its continuing support.

"May I say here and now," he cautioned in the July 20th session,

> that I will have . . . to ask for much, much more from Member nations, in the military field as well as in the civilian field. There should not be any hesitation, because we are at a turn of the road where our attitude will be of decisive significance, I believe, not only for the future of this Organization, but also for the future of Africa. And Africa may well, in present circumstances, mean the world. I know these are very strong words, but I hope that this Council and the Members of this Organization know that I do not use strong words unless they are supported by strong convictions.[50]

There were other strong words. Speaking for the Soviet Union, Vasily Kuznetsov argued that "it is hardly surprising that the activities of Tshombe should have caused the financial and industrial moguls to exult. Behind these attempts to dismember the Congo can easily be discerned the desire of the Western powers to reserve for themselves the economically valuable areas of the former Belgian colonies."[51] However, the Council was able to conclude. Its resolution of July 22nd, unanimously passed, commended the secretary-general's efforts to date and called upon Belgium "to implement speedily . . . the withdrawal of its troops and authorizes the secretary-general to take all necessary actions to this effect." It also requested that all states "refrain from any action which might undermine the territorial integrity and the political independence of the Republic" and invited the specialized agencies of the UN—those that could expand the civilian aid program headed by Linnér—to join the effort. The Katanga secession had been targeted, although not by name. At session's end, the Council's president again addressed Hammarskjöld directly to recognize "the magnificent work he has done as the Council's agent" and to wish him success in his impending travel to the Congo, where it was to be hoped that "his presence and influence . . . will help."[52]

Patrice Lumumba flew to New York a few days later to confer with Hammarskjöld and make contact with the American and Canadian governments. Thomas Kanza, the newly appointed chief of the Congo's UN mission, was on hand to smooth the way; he had genuinely warm relations with both men, who treated him like a protégé, a reassuring sign of the Congo's future. A photo of Hammarskjöld and Lumumba at first meeting, taken at UN headquarters before an appropriately maze-like abstract painting, shows them beaming at each other (fig. 16). I don't think it's sensible to overinterpret, but in hundreds of photographs of Hammarskjöld shaking hands with dignitaries—handshakes are part of the job—he rarely plunges the other hand into the safety and hiding of his pocket. It probably means nothing. But over three days of talks between these two men dedicated to setting things right in the Congo, distance and mutual mistrust increasingly prevailed, never to be overcome. Kanza later wrote that he and his Congolese colleagues attending the talks "felt most uneasy, for we were witnessing a real conflict of personalities, and one which could have serious results. . . . [We] made attempts to reason with Lumumba in Lingala, counseling tact and diplomacy. . . . But Lumumba remained extremely demanding and impatient, while Hammarskjöld simply noted down his suggestions."[53] Hammarskjöld wanted to believe that Lumumba would play his role wisely. After a luncheon he hosted for the Security Council membership and the African delegates, where Lumumba gave an admirably lucid overview of the situation in the Congo, Hammarskjöld commented, "Now, no one can tell me that man is irrational!"[54] On his side, Lumumba came to believe that Hammarskjöld was covertly working to further the interests of the West—of Belgium principally, and a little later he would add the French—though scarcely any Western diplomat had understood the promise and necessity of decolonization as thoroughly as Hammarskjöld. Lumumba refused to accept the slow grind of diplomacy to which the UN was committed and its insistence on noninterference in his country's political dramas. It didn't help that in a televised press conference he answered a journalist's question about what he needed from Hammarskjöld by pointing out that he was the prime minister of a vast nation, while Hammarskjöld was merely an international civil servant. It seems inconceivable that Lumumba could have so misunderstood; all that note taking may have misled him into thinking that Hammarskjöld was more secretary than general. Hammarskjöld watched television that day; their relations chilled still more. Kanza summarized the result of Lumumba's North American sojourn: nothing had occurred "to amend the reputation he had achieved in the West as an anti-colonialist extremist."[55]

Lumumba left New York for Washington and Ottawa in search of nation-to-nation aid; it was not forthcoming, both countries would continue to work exclusively through the UN. That he had a private talk with the Soviet ambassador to Canada immediately became public knowledge and added to Western mistrust. Hammarskjöld flew to Brussels—an action resented by Lumumba, who viewed it as proof of complicity—where in a day of consultations he encountered intransigent attitudes on Katanga and the withdrawal of troops from all parts of the Congo, including military bases. He was joined by Kanza for the flight from Brussels to Léopoldville. En route, they spoke at length. "All he thought of Lumumba," Kanza later recalled, "could be summed up in this phrase: 'Let him play with fire if he wants to—but he'll certainly get burnt.'"[56] On his side, Lumumba made a slow, joyful return to Léopoldville by way of a grand tour of independent African countries—Tunisia, Morocco, Guinea, Ghana, Liberia, Togo—to consult with government leaders and seek assurances that they would send troops to the Congo to help him close down the Katanga secession if the UN failed to do so. Only Guinea and Ghana, the most radical regimes, expressed willingness. Lumumba shared with Kwame Nkrumah of Ghana, who was both friend and adviser, the longing for a Pan-African future that would unite many countries in a mutually beneficial federation headquartered at the center of the continent, possibly Léopoldville. Alongside its practical agenda, Lumumba's return had in part a dreamlike character; it was a kind of vision journey, an exercise of membership, an early rehearsal of Pan-African unity. In those respects it embodied the best of what he was. It was also very probably unwise: he should have returned directly. He had left grave difficulties in the hands of his deputy prime minister, Antoine Gizenga (b. 1925), a loyal ally described by Kanza as "a splendid second-in-command."[57]

Hammarskjöld took to the Spartan life of his UN managers in the Congo. They lived and worked in a misleadingly named apartment building, Le Royal, where the elevators worked sometimes and the telephones sometimes. They met in "the snake pit," a space large enough for a conference table. They generally ate military rations—in the snake pit, where else—in preference to the menu of a Greek restaurant on the ground floor. Hammarskjöld didn't mind; the not very serious deprivations would have reminded him of camping, and the work at hand, though challenging, must have been a holiday from the abstractions of the Security Council. His agenda in the Congo was to meet with Congolese officials, to convey the patient but persistent path implied by the Security Council resolutions governing UNOC, and to arrange if possible for UN peacekeepers to replace Belgian troops in Katanga. The first few days of meetings revealed the intransigence of the Congolese, so like that of the Belgians: they insisted on the enforced departure of Belgian troops from the whole of the Congo and the rapid entry of UN peacekeepers into Katanga with guns blazing if need be.

On the evening of July 31st, Hammarskjöld was the guest of honor at a dinner party thrown by Gizenga where, to the surprise of many who had expected a few pleasant toasts, Gizenga went to a microphone to deliver a stinging speech about the UN's failure thus far to meet the most urgent needs of the Congo. "He concluded," Kanza writes, "by begging Hammarskjöld to get the Belgians out, and ended with a formal phrase of welcome."[58]

It is at this point that Hammarskjöld's voice and mind audibly reach the Congo. He had options, of course: to say nothing much in response, to fire back. Instead he spoke from the center of his understanding—of the UN's role, of the evolution of peoples and states, of the tension between free creativity and resentful memory in the life of a nation that has suffered. From this time forward, the conversation about the Congo divides into strata. On one level there were increasingly bitter disputes within the country, at United Nations headquarters, and in some of the press worldwide, filled with emotion, ill-will, deliberate misreading of facts and motives, and unrestrained self-interest—a "Congo-inferno," as Hammarskjöld described it late in the year and, he added, "a Congo-inferno where I have not a moment for myself."[59] It is true that *Markings* falls nearly silent in 1960, though there are remarkable dated entries toward the end of the year. On an altogether different level there was the steady thought of Hammarskjöld and trusted colleagues, often touched with sorrowing disbelief and ironic humor. At that level they reasoned through events and attitudes, set their course, encouraged one another, and retained, as if against great invisible odds, their calling as men of peace and common sense. This level is evident in cables exchanged between Hammarskjöld in New York and his representatives in the Congo, in statements to the Security Council and General Assembly, in correspondence. It is as if a second song had to be sung so that he and his colleagues could retain their grounding in reality and their subtlety of mind—a song of reason, often at night when one day's turmoil had subsided and the next hadn't begun. Words and insights—the right words, penetrating insights—became key resources for the circle of colleagues who, as Ralph Bunche put it in a note to his wife, were doing their best "to give first aid to a wounded rattlesnake."[60]

Words and, on rarer occasions, silence. Sture Linnér could recall an evening at Hammarskjöld's apartment in New York when he was there to report on Congolese affairs at an especially chaotic moment.

> He came and opened the door himself, no servants around. We had a simple meal while he played recordings of Bach in an adjacent room. Not a word was said during dinner. After we had finished, he said let's go to the library. And we continued listening. Toward 11 o'clock I said that it was time to say goodbye. He said I think so. And he kindly escorted me towards the door. He hadn't said anything. When we shook hands at the door, he looked at me and said, 'I want you to know that the talk we had tonight is one of the most enriching I have had in a long time.'[61]

When Gizenga had wound up his accusatory speech, Hammarskjöld responded in French, familiar to everyone. "I have found at the United Nations," he said,

> that history is important to explain attitudes, but history can enchain us, and what is important is to work for the future of peoples; and men are happiest when they have the strength and the courage to rid themselves, not of their great national memories, but of their resentments and of their unhappy memories. That gives them new strength. . . .
>
> It is for this reason that, as Secretary-General, I have a certain tendency to be anti-historic, to be as far as possible—I and my associates—creators. Creation, that is to succeed in building something new, something built on human values which exist everywhere and which can always be saved if we have the courage to do so and to rid ourselves of our bonds. . . .
>
> We desire peace in the Congo. We desire calm in the Congo. We desire independence for the Congo, and we offer to the Republic of the Congo all the assistance of which the United Nations and its affiliated agencies are capable.[62]

He was entreating the Congolese leadership to set aside their hatred of the Belgians to build something new, freely conceived on the basis of universal human values, with the temporary help of the United Nations. It was an irresistible message, scarcely heard.

The following evening Hammarskjöld returned the compliment by offering a dinner party in honor of President Kasavubu and his ministerial colleagues. In recent days he had experienced enough to know that the opening theme of his welcoming talk would perforce be the damage done by mistrust.

> Franklin D. Roosevelt, during the dark times of a great world depression, told his compatriots that they had nothing to fear but fear itself. In . . . the same sense I would like to say that in our cooperation the only thing we should mistrust is mistrust itself. . . . In a time of trouble and under conditions of complication rare in modern history, it is natural that sometimes misunderstandings develop under the pressure of intense emotions and of the difficulty of seeing clearly the play of factors of which international politics must take account. It is on these points, above all, that one must "mistrust mistrust" as something that sours relations, weakens common effort, and corrodes the very structure of society.
>
> Gentlemen, you have a great task, the task of giving the Congolese people and the Congolese nation a life in peace and unity. . . .[63]

But few in the ruling circles of the Congo were willing to take him at his word or acknowledge the effectiveness of his methods, while there and elsewhere in the world new fuel was being readied for the Congo inferno.

On August 4th, Hammarskjöld dispatched Bunche and a small UN party by air to Elisabethville, capital of Katanga, to negotiate the entry of UNOC troops as replacements for Belgian troops keeping the peace there. Their entry was a preliminary step, viewed by the Security Council as urgently necessary, toward treating the Congo as a unitary whole. Privately, Belgium had agreed neither to approve nor to oppose Bunche's mission. In Elisabethville, however, Tshombe confronted Bunche with a warning of apocalypse to come: if UNOC forces entered Katanga, Belgians would reduce the mining industry to a standstill as they fled; tribal warfare would break out; spears and poisoned darts would fly through the air; UNOC would face "a general uprising" that he, Tshombe, could not control.[64] There are picturesque photos of what Tshombe had in mind—warriors armed with weapons out of the Belgian armory and the Stone Age, menacingly posing for the photographer. Bunche assumed a degree of bluff in Tshombe's defiance, but various circumstances, including a threatening encounter at the airport with Katangese troops under the direction of Tshombe's baleful minister of the interior, Godefroid Munongo, led him to decide that it wasn't worth the risk of bringing UNOC troops in just yet. He notified Hammarskjöld, who had been standing by in Léopoldville. Hammarskjöld departed at once for New York to meet with the Security Council. Surely wise under the circumstances—Bunche had no wish and no right to gamble with lives—his decision left a wide opening for Congolese politicians and Soviet-bloc diplomats to question the competence of the UN in the Congo. Hammarskjöld's private view of the overall situation, confided to General von Horn in the course of those days in Léopoldville, was crisp: "My God! This is the craziest operation in history! God only knows where it is going to end. All I can tell you is that I had no other choice but to lay it on."[65]

In his written report of August 6th to the Security Council—such reports generally preceded and, in theory, informed the Council's deliberations—Hammarskjöld unobtrusively followed a guideline he had recorded in his journal some years earlier: "You can only hope to find a lasting solution to a conflict if you have learned to see the other objectively, but, at the same time, to experience his difficulties subjectively."[66] In this instance, he first explored Tshombe's point of view and then proposed what he regarded as an objective understanding of the situation. "The problem for those resisting the United Nations Force in Katanga," he wrote,

> may be stated in these terms: Will United Nations participation in security control in Katanga submit the province to the immediate control and authority of the central government against its wishes? They consider this seriously to jeopardize their possibility to work for other constitutional solutions than a strictly unitarian one, e.g., some kind of federal structure providing for a higher degree of provincial self-government than now foreseen. The spokesmen for this attitude reject the unitarian formula as incompatible with the interests of the whole Congo people and as imposed from outside.
>
> This is an internal political problem to which the United Nations . . . cannot be a party. Nor would the entry of the United Nations Force . . . mean any taking of sides in the conflict. . . . Nor should it be permitted to shift the weights between personalities or groups or schools of thought in a way which would prejudge the solution. . . . I believe all this can be avoided if the United Nations maintains firmly its aim and acts with clarity and tact. . . .[67]

When the Security Council began its deliberations on August 8th—as it happens, the day Lumumba returned to Léopoldville—the situation was quite fraught. The Soviet Union had communicated its resolve to "rebuff the aggressors who . . . are . . . acting with the encouragement of the colonialist Powers of NATO."[68] Nkrumah of Ghana and Sékou Touré of Guinea had conveyed their displeasure to Hammarskjöld and the Council, Nkrumah writing that "Ghana . . . and the other African states would not tolerate the construction in the center of Africa of a puppet state maintained by Belgian troops and designed to fit the needs of an international mining concern."[69] And if all this wasn't enough, on the first day of renewed deliberations in the Security Council a second region of the Congo declared independence: South Kasai, a region rich in diamond mines, formed a government at Bakwanga (now Mbuji-Mayi) under the leadership of Albert Kalonji, later and only for a time designated emperor of the new state. Just five weeks after independence, there were three governments in the Congo.

In his opening statement Hammarskjöld referred repeatedly to unspecified outside pressures on the Congo and to the impatience and distrust of the central government, all of which created "a most harmful atmosphere against . . . the United Nations." "It does not help the United Nations effort," he added,

> if it has to live under a threat of any one—or more—contributing governments taking matters in its, or their, own hands, breaking away from the United Nations Force and pursuing a unilateral policy. . . . In a state of emotion, irrational reactions are to be expected and we should have understanding and sympathy for those [in Katanga] who see themselves as being threatened. However, is it too much to expect that the people to whom I refer may lift themselves above their emotions, see present-day realities as they are and see, for that reason, in the United Nation their only valid support . . . ? The initiative now lies with the members of the Council and with the Council itself. . . . I may be able to assist with . . . concrete suggestions adjusted to the line of thinking which emerges from the debate. . . .[70]

Later in the day, he concurred with the Soviet representative's "sincere wish to help the Congolese people," which he described as his "guiding inspiration," and added with a sharp edge of irony, "I do not believe, personally, that we help the Congolese people by actions in which Africans kill

Africans, or Congolese kill Congolese, and that will remain my guiding principle for the future."[71]

With Gizenga participating in the Security Council's deliberations alongside Justin Bomboko, the Congolese foreign minister, and Pierre Wigny attending for Belgium, it was a stiff debate, but Hammarskjöld emerged on August 9th with what he needed: a stronger resolution calling upon Belgium to withdraw its troops from Katanga "under speedy modalities determined by the Secretary-General" and declaring that "the entry of the United Nations Force into the province of Katanga is necessary."[72] The language was cool, but what was now to be accomplished would need courage. A day later Hammarskjöld set out again for Léopoldville in an exercise of long-distance shuttle diplomacy. Some at least in the press appreciated his leadership. Writing on Hammarskjöld's day of departure, James Reston of the *New York Times* was characteristically eloquent: "This remarkable man is proving to be one of the great natural resources in the world today. . . . The UN is now a refuge for common sense in a satanic world."[73] Before leaving, Hammarskjöld spoke with Gizenga, Bomboko, and other Congolese delegates about the "speedy modalities" he had in mind and exchanged cables with Tshombe to secure his agreement to meet in Elisabethville on August 12th. Surprisingly, Tshombe agreed. Since Ralph Bunche had been roughly shooed out of Katanga a week earlier, attitudes had shifted, owing not least to the new Council resolution. In flight toward Léopoldville, Hammarskjöld drafted—principally for Tshombe, Lumumba, and the Council—an interpretation of a key passage in the resolution. Reassuringly from the Katangan point of view, distressingly from the central government's point of view, he reiterated that "the United Nations Force cannot be used on behalf of the central government to subdue or to force the provincial government to a specific line of action."[74] In his careful communications and preparations, there was an obvious omission. Making no effort to be in touch with Lumumba directly, he had chosen instead to inform his government through the Congolese ministers attending the Security Council debate. He also passed through Léopoldville rapidly, without making contact, so that his strategy toward Katanga would remain in his control. Lumumba noticed. Though Hammarskjöld's later reasoning about this slight was vigorous, it wasn't entirely convincing. The truth seems to have been that he didn't feel he could trust Lumumba not to interfere.

Hammarskjöld's plan for August 12th was bold and deliberately the-atrical; the world press would appreciate the fact that the UN was taking action in Katanga. He took off in a convoy of five aircraft, his own fol-lowed by four others transporting Swedish troops serving as blue-helmet-ed UN peacekeepers. When they reached the Elisabethville air space and requested landing, Tshombe instructed air traffic control to radio that while Hammarskjöld and his diplomatic entourage were welcome, the other four aircraft should turn around and go home—a distinct change of heart from a few days earlier. While the five planes circled the airport with a splendid view of the runway blocked with barrels and with troops nearby, Hammarskjöld sent his military adviser, general I. J. Rikhye, for-ward to the cockpit to make clear to ground control that he refused to land without the peacekeeping forces, and were he not permitted to land with his entire party, there would be hell to pay. Tshombe relented, the party landed. He was apparently all smiles as he greeted Hammarskjöld and had his own show in mind for the press: he paused with Hammar-skjöld directly in front of a Katangan honor guard bearing the colors of the country while a military band played the newly adopted secession-ist national anthem.[75] Urquhart could recall its refrain: "Avec vos bras et votre sang! Avec vos dents!"—With your arms and your blood! With your teeth![76] It was an extreme version of the Marseillaise. Urquhart was one of few participants in the Congo Crisis who could be counted on to record its occasionally lurid humor. General Rikhye did well also: he described their reception as "out of a Hollywood movie. . . . Bill Ranallo and I edged closer to the S-G. He seemed to have no worries as he stood at attention, with a faint smile, seeming to wonder if all this was real."[77] Did he have no worries? A classic photograph from that moment of arrival in Katanga silently argues otherwise (fig. 17). His face is a mask of worry.

There was nothing in the Charter or Secretariat regulations requir-ing the S-G, as he was called, to lead troops into harm's way. Pauline Frederick, a journalist Hammarskjöld liked and trusted, aired the issue of personal risk with him during the Suez Crisis. "He said very clearly," she later reported, "that he was quite aware of the fact that when you step out in front in a situation, you can become a target. And he was quite aware of the fact that he would someday become a target."[78] But the gamble worked; Swedish troops replaced the regular Belgian military at the Elisabethville airport and elsewhere, African and other troops soon joined them, and—dragging their feet—all Belgian troops had left Katanga a month later. Yet Tshombe also benefited: Urquhart observes that he didn't urgently need regular Belgian forces any longer, he was building up a well-armed gendarmerie led by individual Belgian and European officers, and the troops' departure allowed him to pose as taking steps to distance himself from Belgian influence.[79]

Returning to Léopoldville on the 14th, Hammarskjöld requested a session with Lumumba and the government to brief them. In place of that meeting, cancelled by Lumumba at the last minute, he received a volley of letters, necessarily answered with a volley of letters in reply. Lumumba was beside himself. Neither he nor his government had been properly consulted or included. Hammarskjöld was communicating more closely with Katanga and Belgium than with the elected government of the Congo and acting against its interests. By letter Lumumba expressed continued confidence in the Security Council while accusing Hammarskjöld of grossly misinterpreting the Council's resolutions. "The Government of the Republic of the Congo can in no way agree with your personal interpretation, which is unilateral and erroneous. . . . It is . . . clear that in its intervention in the Congo the United Nations is not to act as a neutral organization but rather that the Security Council is to place all its resources at the disposal of my Government. . . . Contrary to your personal interpretation, the United Nations Force may be used to subdue the rebel government of Katanga. . . . You are acting as though my Government . . . did not exist. The manner in which you have acted until now is only retarding the restoration of order in the Republic."[80]

The next day Hammarskjöld replied curtly, "I have received your letter of 14 August. In it I find allegations against the Secretary-General as well as objections to the Secretary-General's interpretation of the resolutions. . . . There is no reason for me to enter into a discussion here either of those unfounded and unjustified allegations or the interpretation of the Security Council's resolutions." He asked again for a direct meeting; the two men were, after all, in Léopoldville. Lumumba responded at once to reinforce his theme: "The positions you have adopted are in no sense those of the Security Council. . . ." Hammarskjöld replied still more briefly: "If the [Congolese] Council of Ministers takes no initiative which compels me to change my plan or has no other specific proposal to make, I shall go to New York this evening in order to seek clarification of the attitude of the Security Council." Lumumba fired back: "I have just this moment received your letter of today's date in reply to the one I sent you an hour ago," and extended his inventory of protests. This was not classic diplomacy; it was a *mano a mano*, unwelcome to Hammarskjöld and harmful to Lumumba's reputation. Even African friends of Lumumba's had difficulty understanding him. Habib Borguiba, president of independent Tunisia and a staunch ally who had sent troops under the UN flag to the Congo, commented disapprovingly at the time that after returning from the United States and Canada, "Mr. Lumumba shifted his rifle from one shoulder to the other and became the sworn enemy of the UN. Henceforth, nothing but words of invective and insults for Mr. Hammarskjöld fell from his lips."[81] Borguiba was implying that Lumumba's rifle had shifted from his right shoulder to his left—from cooperation with the UN to soliciting help directly from the Soviet Union and left-leaning regimes in Africa. It was at this time that Lumumba secretly requested military aid from the Soviets, who soon provided a large fleet of trucks and fifteen transport aircraft in support of the Congolese army, the ANC. This foreign aid was of no aid at all: it would soon cause terrible bloodshed and contribute to political chaos.

In the interval between Hammarskjöld's return to New York and the first day of Security Council deliberations on the 21st, there was trouble. Some ANC troops were turned loose to harass UN personnel; two ugly incidents prompted Hammarskjöld to remind the central government that United Nations assistance could not be taken for granted. When the Council convened, he chose to speak first, at length, and with an insistence that had not been heard or necessary since the early days of Suez. In part he was setting the record straight and looking to the future, in part stating the rationale for his own bold actions. "In order to carry out my mandate," he said,

> I have been forced to act with great firmness in relation to many parties. One of them has been the central government itself. I do not believe that I have ever failed in courtesy. On the other hand, I do not excuse myself for having stated clearly the principles of the Charter and for having acted independently on their basis, mindful of the dignity of the Organization—and to have done so whether it suited all those we are trying to help or not. Nor have I forgotten that the ultimate purpose of the United Nations services to the Republic of the Congo is to protect international peace and security, and that, to the extent that the difficulties facing the Republic are not of a nature to endanger international peace, they are not of our concern. . . .

Is it because the Government of the Republic has not understood this, is it because of frustration at the discovery of the limits this principle puts on the ways in which the United Nations can serve in the Congo, that we are now blamed?[82]

Recognizing that he owed the Council an explanation of his strategy for introducing UN troops into Katanga, he went on to say,

I felt that we had to try to achieve a speedy withdrawal of Belgian troops by staging a breakthrough for the United Nations Force into Katanga with token units accompanying me personally. All other lines of action seemed more uncertain and definitely slower in their effect. . . . The approach worked, and, at present, the Security Council resolution is being fully implemented in Katanga. The way in which I operated is being criticized by spokesmen of the Republic of the Congo as contrary to the aims pursued. Let me ask, what were then their aims: the speediest possible withdrawal of Belgian troops while order and security were maintained by the United Nations troops? If so, my approach proved to be adequate. Or was it something different?[83]

There is much more in Hammarskjöld's talk, shaped by hard experience days earlier in the Congo and by his knowledge that the Security Council itself had an insecure consensus. Toward the end he dared to invoke his private ideas and language—the ideas and language of *Markings*—to call on Congolese leaders and all others with their eyes on the Congo to rise above narrow concerns. He was speaking directly to Gizenga and Kanza, who were participating with other Congolese leaders in the session, and through them to Lumumba, Kasavubu, Kalonji, Tshombe; speaking to Pierre Wigny and the Belgian authorities, to Vasily Kuznetsov and his Soviet colleagues. He put his thought as a question: "Is it too much to expect," he asked,

that it will be understood that a period of utter crisis and disintegration is one in which those who work for their personal benefit are acting against the interest of the people of the country, while those who work for the interest of the people of the country will find that they themselves have profited by their self-oblivion in submission to the common cause?[84]

It was too much to expect. But the ensuing debate did bring to light the inescapable difficulty of the Council's policy of non-intervention in domestic politics. To be a forceful presence on the scene and yet have no political impact called for impeccable clarity of mind and no small luck. Hammarskjöld had both, but would his luck hold? The debate had its excesses: "A vast plot against the Congo is at present being organized by all the colonialist forces interested in keeping Africa in a state of subjection," said the Guinean ambassador. Mr. Kuznetsov for the Soviet Union expressed dismay with the whole situation while introducing an allegation against Hammarskjöld that was simply untrue. This was increasingly to be the pattern. "There is a dangerous double game in progress," he said accurately, "in which some Powers say that they condemn the aggression against the Republic of the Congo but in point of fact support and encourage it." But then he advanced a wholly inaccurate claim: "It is perplexing that some United Nations officials who have been instructed to implement the Security Council's resolutions openly act against those resolutions and participate in actions directed towards the separation of Katanga from the Republic of the Congo. How can it be explained that the United Nations Secretary-General, contrary to the clear instructions of the Security Council, . . . entered into negotiations with Tshombe, the traitor of the Congolese people, and discussed with him plans directed against the integrity of the Republic of the Congo?" Moving on, Kuznetsov offered an insight that had a grain of truth, though viewed from its left side only: "It must be said with all firmness that the position of so-called non-intervention in this conflict—when our task is that of putting an end to military aggression—actually only encourages a puppet who is sustained by foreign bayonets and who executes the will of foreign monopolies." Hammarskjöld's insistence on the peaceful means of diplomacy and civilian aid—generally undramatic, necessarily patient, largely hidden from public view—could easily be construed along these lines. But he had no mandate whatever to deploy UN forces aggressively.

Mongi Slim, the Tunisian diplomat whom Hammarskjöld considered a possible successor as secretary-general, spoke forcefully from the middle ground, and his attitudes eventually prevailed in the sense that the harshest critics for the moment retreated. African voices carried weight throughout the Congo Crisis; the so-called Great Powers could not blithely bypass them. "My delegation feels it its duty to congratulate the Secretary-General," he said,

> on the results already achieved and those about to be achieved, all of
> which have been obtained peacefully. . . . The Secretary-General has

been criticized, in particular by the Head of the Congolese Government, for the way in which he has acted in pursuit of these results. . . . Of course, any human action is open to criticism. It is quite natural to feel that such-and-such a method might have been more effective. . . . But we cannot forget, either, that it is the result which shows what any human action is worth, and the result is there to see: the United Nations forces are present in Katanga . . . and indeed everywhere else in the Congo, under a single command with headquarters at Léopoldville, the capital of the Republic. . . .

My delegation cannot share any distrust whatever with regard to the Secretary-General.[85]

The sequence of Council meetings ended without a clarifying resolution but with sufficient endorsement of Hammarskjöld's approach. He had reaffirmed, as he put it, that "it should not be concluded from the fact that we cannot lend active support to the central government that we lend any kind of support to the other party, strengthen its hand, or resist any moves from the central government."[86] As well, he reasserted the attitude he had expressed as he accepted his reelection two years earlier. Reminding the Council of the interpretation he had written in flight to the Congo a few weeks earlier and of Lumumba's vehement letters, he used the plainest possible language: "I gave an interpretation and that interpretation was challenged. I have referred the matter back to the Security Council. I have the right to expect guidance. That guidance can be given in many forms. But it should be obvious that if the Security Council says nothing I have no other choice than to follow my conviction."[87] He would be constrained to do so in many future circumstances. The Council session also ended with a strong hurrah from the American press: a *Time* cover story (August 23, 1960) featuring a luminous portrait of Hammarskjöld against a dark, storm-tossed African background. Based on Yousuf Karsh's memorable 1958 photographic portrait of Hammarskjöld, the image (both the Karsh original and this rendering) captures almost too much of his faithful attitude. It predicts *Markings* without knowing of it.

What was Hammarskjöld's private thinking about this "desperately necessary experiment in rational international politics," as he called it in a letter of early 1961?[88] There was some bitterness, and it would grow stronger over time. "We are hardened," he cabled in late September to Rajeshwar Dayal, then his representative in the Congo, "but every time you discover again that the word of Mr. Lumumba is regarded as evidence . . . because he is prime minister, while we are suspected to serve God knows what interest and therefore to color our picture, I wonder how we are able to achieve anything at all."[89] He also perceived the situation as gravely dangerous. "In this game," he again wrote to Dayal, "I hold Lumumba to be an ignorant pawn, in his utter lack of experience of the big political currents, balances and pressures. The perspective is forbidding but real, I have already said that the Congo should not be permitted to become another Korea—nor should it become a Hungary or a Munich."[90] Both remarks are close to the pain and confusion of daily events. He was also able to take in the landscape from a great height. "Time has flown away," he wrote to his fellow Academician and friend, Eyvind Johnson, in mid-September,

> and the endless two last months are, at the same time, really as if they had never existed. They have made "big news," but I wonder how many feel how big the story really is back of the headlines: the story of how a whole continent breaks into history and of the fight for its soul, staged by the Powers that be, through men as petty, as dishonest, as unintelligent—and as human—as any of those who were the protagonists in the French Revolution or the Soviet Revolution or the Nazi Revolution. It is a fourth great turn in modern history, which has, however, its specific, nearly apocalyptic character.
>
> It is a curious but perhaps logical play of destiny that the UN should be placed in the key position in this revolution. And it is an even more curious play of destiny for me to be the one forced into all those daily and hourly decisions which will determine the *sense* of the outcome—whatever the outcome.[91]

Nearly a year later, reflecting about another crisis that briefly needed him, he anchored again in his sense of inevitability: "Of course, as in the case of Suez and in the case of the Belgians in the Congo, the final outcome is given. But why, why—to repeat what I had to say on the two previous occasions—that being so, why cannot the result be reached in dignity and with the preservation of a minimum of good human relations?"[92]

He wasn't letting the Congo dim his verve, his lean into events, and he hadn't altogether lost touch with private interests. Difficult literary translation was for him the perfect rest from difficult politics, and he had one going with Karl Ragnar Gierow: a Swedish translation of Djuna Barnes's intricate verse drama *Antiphon*, scheduled for performance at Dramaten, Gierow's state theater in Stockholm. Relying on Hammarskjöld for suggestions, Gierow was leading the campaign. He sent a note to Hammarskjöld on August 2nd to recall a moment they had enjoyed during a visit in May when they had worked together on the translation at Brewster. He was speaking in poets' code, using a metaphor to hearten his friend: "I am just wondering," he wrote, "if these days you remember the thought-provoking sight we had in Brewster of the lark—wasn't it?—which with such winged elegance, such overwhelming efficiency, such weightless emphasis drove the hawk away from its hunting ground?"[93] Nearly two months later, when the Congo Crisis had intensified, he wrote again—just a cable, a friendly gesture: "Long live the lark in Brewster!"[94] To this we have Hammarskjöld's response, also in poets' code, sent that same day: "The hawk will return, but the larks warble with fresh confidence."[95]

At the very end of the year they exchanged again by cable about a tough passage in *Antiphon*. "*Duellen har sitt andrum*," Hammarskjöld offered in Swedish for Barnes's "The duel has its breathing space." And he continued, "Probably closer to her concept. I wish phrase could be used about my life."[96]

We sit on a volcano

The struggle between reason and recklessness persisted. Every movement toward political good sense met an opposite that weakened or diverted it. There was no breathing space. One event poured in after another with something resembling cruelty or malevolence. Ralph Bunche, a man of courage and rich experience as a negotiator, no longer felt he was the right person to lead the UN effort in the Congo: his relations with senior government officials had deteriorated beyond remedy; his imperfect health was suffering; he had unmet family obligations. "There is never a morning that does not begin without some new excitement," he wrote to Hammarskjöld in a tangle of negative particles reflecting his state of mind, "—bayoneted Congolese at the door, trouble at the airport, UN staff arrested, a complaint . . . coupled with a new threat from the Prime or Vice-Prime Minister, and the military boys wanting to start shooting, etc., etc."[97] The military boys were Carl von Horn and no doubt others responsible for UN military operations, with whom relations also were not good. Working alongside Bunche, Urquhart somehow remained buoyant: "Life in Léopoldville was just one emergency after another, 24

hours a day; it was fascinating," he recalled.[98] Hammarskjöld sent his chief
of staff, Andrew Cordier, to Léopoldville on an interim assignment of a
few weeks—he arrived on August 28th—and Bunche returned to UN
headquarters while arrangements were made for Rajeshwar Dayal, whom
we have already encountered, to take over the lead responsibility in the
Congo. It was Cordier's misfortune to be on duty in the Congo when one
of its most novel and damaging episodes occurred.

Hammarskjöld's introduction to the 15th Annual Report, published
at the end of August, was a model of clear reasoning about hard politics.
Over the years the introduction had become a platform from which he
could convey his perspective at a level well above the details with which
he and many dealt from day to day. It was a morally courageous exercise
in "representing the detached element in international life," though written in an evenhanded way.[99] While he covered many topics, Africa was his
focus, specifically the need to shelter the continent's new nations from
involvement in the Cold War. "In Africa," he wrote, "the beginning can
now be seen of those conflicts between ideologies and interests which
split the world. Africa is still, in comparison with other areas, a virgin
territory which many have found reason to believe can or should be won
for their aims and interests. It is in the face of all this that the United
Nations has, in the great task which it is facing in the Congo, appealed
to 'African solidarity within the framework of the United Nations.'"[100]
Later in the introduction, in effect conducting a teaching session for the
UN community, he wrote further about "keeping newly arising conflicts
outside the sphere of bloc differences. . . . Preventive diplomacy . . . is of
special significance in cases where the original conflict may be said either
to be the result of, or to imply risks for, the creation of a power vacuum
between the main blocs. . . . The ways in which a vacuum can be filled
by the United Nations . . . differ from case to case, but they have this in
common: temporarily . . . the United Nations enters the picture on the
basis of its non-commitment to any power bloc, so as to provide to the
extent possible a guarantee in relation to all parties against initiatives
from others."[101] We are in the stratum of reason, cool knowledge, the
larger pattern understood.

While he may still have been drafting his introduction, he sent a letter
to his admired friend Alexis Leger, the French diplomat and poet who
published under the name Saint-John Perse. "You must have wondered
about my life during these troubled times," Hammarskjöld wrote on Au-

gust 23rd, "when I have had to be a protagonist for reason and decency in a world disrupted by the revolution of those Africans who up to now have been suppressed and prevented from developing normally and who now . . . demand everything. I don't have to tell you how many times I would have liked to 'think aloud' with a friend like you."[102] Dayal's perspective on this "demand for everything" sheds good light: "Having had to struggle with the colonial power for their most elementary rights, [the Congolese] were inclined to overplay their hand when a little moderation would have sufficed. And they were not beyond uttering threats of one kind or another if they felt dissatisfied at the response."[103]

On the ground in the Congo, two events of vastly different character were unfolding in late August. In the open heights of statesmanship, Lumumba convened a Pan-African conference of foreign ministers at Léopoldville, August 25th–30th. In the hidden depths, he and some of his cabinet decided to put to work the Soviet gift of transport aircraft and a fleet of trucks by staging an ANC invasion of the two secessionist regions to the southeast, Katanga and South Kasai. The troops went forth and met with some success, but lacking food and other logistical support—Urquhart writes that they were flung into combat—they lived off the land and within days diverted into tribal warfare, taking sides with the Lulua against Kalonji's tribe, the Baluba, in South Kasai. The resulting pitiless massacre of unarmed villagers was qualified as genocide by Hammarskjöld when he learned of it.[104] Thomas Kanza, Lumumba's friend and best diplomat, wrote that this expedition "finally set the seal on Lumumba's political downfall."[105]

His downfall was carefully prepared in the dark, in part by his enemies in the central government, in part by networks of conspiracy in Léopoldville and across the river in Brazzaville, where Belgian diplomats had taken refuge when Lumumba's government expelled their embassy early in the crisis. This subsoil of conspiracy was so well hidden that Rajeshwar Dayal felt constrained to write his narrative of the Congo Crisis twice, once at length and brilliantly for publication in 1976, and again in his general autobiography of 1998. He had come to understand that his earlier book, like many others of that period, was "not in possession of authentic information. . . . That information has since been made available . . . under the US Freedom of Information Act. Secret cables exchanged between Washington and the US embassies in Léopoldville and elsewhere, as well as cables sent to or from CIA agents and the minutes of closed door meetings are [now] readily available. . . . ONUC was facing not only the perils of the Congolese situation, but the cloak and dagger activities of a great power. . . . Every life-saving measure, every carefully planned move to help the benighted country, was sabotaged by a deep conspiracy."[106] He was exaggerating; many UN efforts—particularly the civilian aid programs—advanced well, and the United States was far from the only meddler. An official Belgian inquest as late as 2001, prompted by a brilliant investigative book, has revealed the extent of covert Belgian interference.[107] Dayal's work with the government and its leaders was unquestionably impeded and subverted by hidden forces. His bitterness is evident. Reaching Léopoldville on September 8th, he had at once and for long months to come given his all, had literally put his own life in jeopardy and exposed his wife to a fairly nightmarish existence (she insisted on joining him in the Congo), only to discover years later that he hadn't been aware of some of the most potent forces in play. US institutions were eventually strong enough to tear back the cover, though long after the fact, and to influence future policy through the findings of the Church Committee, which in 1975–76 investigated US intelligence policies and practice.[108] It remains that the United States launched a conspiracy to eliminate Lumumba from politics and take his life, and failed to complete the second step of the mission only because others got there first; true also that in these early days the United States covertly propped up a young, inexperienced soldier-politician named Mobutu and kept the props in place for decades. The UN had, by design, no intelligence service, no spies to follow spies around town. Its people nonetheless noticed things—fat envelopes arriving on Mobutu's desk, his surprising ability to pay his ANC troops when it suited him despite the country's very evident bankruptcy. Hammarskjöld knew in general, not in detail.

We need to meet Larry Devlin, chief of the CIA station in Léopoldville, posted to the US Embassy in a benign covering role. A World War II veteran of unfailing personal courage and resourcefulness, he cannot be caricatured under any easy label. He was familiar to those in Léopoldville to whom he wished to be familiar. That excluded UN representatives; whenever possible, he avoided them. His remarkable book, *Chief of Station: Congo*, published in 2007, a year before his death, amounts to a retelling of the Congo story nearly as if the UN had no role there. He tells a Cold War story, enacted between the United States and the

Soviet Union through their agents and sympathizers in government, the media, and other key sectors. Dayal would have read Devlin's 1975 testimony before the Church Committee, which disguises him in print as Mr. Hedgman, but he was spared this book, in which the UN's policies are by and large viewed as high-minded inconveniences. "The Cold War, like it or not," wrote Devlin, "had come to a hot country and the battle lines were rapidly being drawn in the streets of Léopoldville and across this enormous, fragile country. It was my job to do something about it, and the first task was to create a network of agents and then mount clandestine operations against the Soviet Union and its allies, which were clearly setting their sights on influencing, if not controlling, Lumumba's fledgling government."[109] He was brilliant. He soon had paid agents and willing sympathizers among ministers, members of parliament, newspaper editors, labor unions, student groups. He became a personal adviser to Mobutu, whom both he and the US ambassador, Clare Timberlake, regarded as promising, and he was on good terms with Kasavubu. He could set events in motion and stop or change their courses, and did so with virtuoso skill. Was it time for a street demonstration against Lumumba? That could be arranged. A critical editorial? That could be arranged. And more still could be arranged. It is likely that the Belgians were doing as much or more through their connections to leading politicians, the anti-Lumumba press and radio, and covert operations.

Some weeks into the Congo Crisis, in conversation with Allen Dulles, director of the CIA (and brother of Eisenhower's secretary of state, John Foster Dulles), Devlin explained that the Soviets were flooding the Congo with "technicians," most of whom were intelligence agents, with the aim of gaining control of the Lumumba government, extending their influence to neighboring countries, and building "an extraordinary power base in Africa" to "outflank NATO" and, among other things, control the Congolese production of minerals critical to US arms programs. It was a potential nightmare, centered on Léopoldville, reaching the world.[110] A sound judge of character, Devlin did not demonize Lumumba. "I never believed that Lumumba was a communist," he has written. "I did believe he was politically naïve and inherently unstable. Our view in the embassy was that he did not have the leadership qualities to hold this vast, disintegrating country together and, sooner or later, the Russian bear would seize its chance and pounce."[111]

On August 26th, he received a cable from Allen Dulles.

IN HIGH QUARTERS HERE IT IS THE CLEAR-CUT
CONCLUSION THAT IF [LUMUMBA] CONTINUES TO
HOLD HIGH OFFICE THE INEVITABLE RESULT WILL AT
BEST BE CHAOS AND AT WORST PAVE THE WAY TO COM-
MUNIST TAKEOVER OF THE CONGO WITH DISASTROUS
CONSEQUENCES FOR THE PRESTIGE OF THE UN AND
FOR THE INTERESTS OF THE FREE WORLD GENERALLY.
CONSEQUENTLY WE CONCLUDE THAT HIS REMOVAL
MUST BE AN URGENT AND PRIME OBJECTIVE AND THAT
UNDER EXISTING CONDITIONS THIS SHOULD BE A
HIGH PRIORITY OF OUR COVERT ACTION.[112]

Investigating in 1975, the Church Committee was unable to ascertain beyond doubt the meaning of "high quarters" in this and still more threatening communications to come, but the phrase typically referred to President Eisenhower, and Devlin was given to understand precisely that. It is striking that Dulles had the UN in mind at a time when Hammarskjöld in all sincerity and the Security Council, despite the hypocrisy of some, were insisting on a hands-off policy.

Events that looked spontaneous weren't really. For example, an anti-Lumumba demonstration on August 25th outside the Pan-African conference, which led to a stone-throwing battle with pro-Lumumba demonstrators and police intervention to calm things down, was initially a Devlin show, set in motion by one of his most effective agents to tarnish Lumumba's reputation.[113] Meanwhile, we shouldn't forget that Soviet transports were just then carrying ANC soldiers into genocidal warfare. The Congo was pitifully vulnerable, as if a curse lay on it.

> *Congo!*
> *La cohérence des choses évanouie.*

The coherence of things up in smoke—these are words given to Hammarskjöld by the Caribbean poet and political leader Aimé Césaire in his good play of 1966, *Une Saison au Congo*.

While Hammarskjöld in New York was pressing the Belgians to keep their word on the evacuation of their troops and pressing the Soviets to explain the presence of their aircraft, trucks, and technical personnel in the Congo, Kasavubu called privately on Devlin in Léopoldville. Devlin and his network had been urging Kasavubu for some time to dismiss

Lumumba from the government. Thomas Kanza makes clear that many other voices, Congolese, Belgian, and more remote, were sending the same message.[114] "Once we heard that Kasavubu might take this action," Devlin writes, "we drafted a 'how-to' paper . . . outlining, step-by-step, the actions he should take before dismissing Lumumba and what he should do in the aftermath."[115] Andrew Cordier had also heard from Kasavubu and cautioned him about the chaotic consequences of the action he was considering.

Linnér, responsible for the UN civilian program, had had a similar experience while Bunche was still in the Congo. "Kasavubu had called me sometime before deposing Lumumba," he recalled,

> and asked me for a map of the Congo. I said, "What kind of map, how large?" He said, "It should be as large as possible because the wall behind me in my office is empty and I feel rather lost. I don't quite know where the Congo is in Africa. I don't know how the Congo looks on the map." So I brought him right away the map I had in my office. Then he said, "Let's draw up the lines for new administrative units. I'd like to add to the number of existing provinces." I said, "Wait a minute. That's not really my task to reconstruct the administrative set-up of the Congo." Then he asked, "How do you make a coup d'état? Can you give me your experience about that?" I thought he was half-joking because he had a sense of humor that came through now and then. I said, "That's easy, you avoid violence; you take over the radio station; you take away the man you want to replace, feed him well; you don't go to excesses of any kind, no physical harm of any kind. Why do you ask?" "Oh," he said, "just as a matter of interest." . . . Ralph Bunche later said to me, "You look funny." So I told him the story and he said, "Can you beat that."[116]

Devlin wasn't surprised on the evening of September 5th when Kasavubu announced to the nation by radio that he was dismissing Lumumba and six ministers from the government for betraying the people's trust and igniting civil war. He named the president of the Congolese senate, Joseph Iléo, to form a successor government. Devlin noted, with admirable self-deprecation, that Kasavubu had followed scarcely any item in the how-to paper and after delivering his announcement had gone home to bed. Linnér's improvised checklist fared no better.

Kasavubu had spoken at 8:15 that evening. Forty-five minutes later, Lumumba reached the radio station unhindered to make his own nationwide address. "In the name of th[e] government and the whole nation, I should like to make a formal refutation of what [President Kasavubu] has said. The government has had no discussion on the matter with the head of state. . . . We shall remain in power and continue the work we have been given to do. I beg that the people who have placed their trust in us remain calm."[117] A half-hour later, he went on the air again to make a devastating addition: he in turn dismissed the president. "Now he is no longer head of state. The government must take over the sovereign privileges of our republic. . . . I ask the United Nations . . . not to get involved in the differences now existing between the government and Mr. Kasavubu. . . . There is no longer a head of state in our republic, only a government by and for the people."[118]

The Congo had tripped and been pushed into a constitutional crisis. Because two ministers had cosigned Kasavubu's order dismissing Lumumba, it had some claim to constitutional legitimacy according to Hammarskjöld's legal advisers. But parliament—where Lumumba held sway—met at length, heard Lumumba speak effectively, and voted to establish a reconciliation commission and to annul both Kasavubu's dismissal of Lumumba and Lumumba's of Kasavubu.

Violence threatened: the radio could be used to send opposing factions into the streets not just of Léopoldville but far and wide, and the Léopoldville airport could be used to send ANC forces into civil war or receive troops, arms, and ammunition. Overseeing this unprecedented crisis, Andrew Cordier decided what to do without consulting Hammarskjöld, although he spoke with UN military and civilian leaders in Léopoldville. Some time earlier, Hammarskjöld had told him (calling it an "irresponsible observation") that "people on the spot might commit themselves to what the Secretary-General could not justify doing himself—taking the risk of being disowned when it no longer mattered."[119] Cordier chose that risk: using UN forces, he closed down the radio station to all comers without exception and shut the airport to all but UN traffic.

And just there Hammarskjöld's wondrous luck broke. Cordier seems not to have been forewarned or taken seriously enough that a radio station across the river in Brazzaville (where the head of state detested Lumumba) would remain at Kasavubu's service and anti-Lumumba propaganda would continue to be transmitted nationwide from Katanga, while for his part Lumumba had no further access to radio communications. Unknowingly, or so it seems, Cordier had tilted the play of forces in a domestic political conflict, despite the Security Council resolution against doing so and Hammarskjöld's repeated assurances on that score. Though Hammarskjöld would publicly defend his subordinate's action, he would be made to suffer for it at oppressive length in UN meetings soon to come, and privately he viewed the intervention as "basically regrettable."[120] For Dayal, who took over from Cordier and reopened both radio station and airport on the 12th and 13th of September, subject to their peaceful use for the public good, Cordier's actions became a lasting burden. "Throughout my tenure in the Congo," he later wrote, "the consequences of those decisions were to cast a malevolent spell over the Operation and it became a Sisyphean task to undo their damaging effects."[121]

The Security Council reconvened on September 9th. Hammarskjöld led off with a report about Congolese finances, dismal, and Congolese attitudes, prickly. He asserted that Kasavubu had some constitutional basis for his action and Lumumba had none but, given the de facto existence of two seats of government, however unstable, his instructions to the team in the field were "to avoid any action by which, directly or indirectly, openly or by implication, they would pass judgment on the stand taken by either one of the parties in the conflict."[122] About the temporary closing of the radio station and airport, he noted that the measures were taken in a situation "which it is easy to sit in New York and discuss in terms of protocol, but which it requires wisdom and courage to handle when you are at the front. Anyway, it should be clear that the steps taken cannot be discussed in terms of partisanship, colonialism, or anticolonialism."[123] We can foresee what he foresaw: he was attempting to prevent in advance an avalanche of criticism of Cordier's actions or at least set in place a reasonable perspective to which he could refer. Later in his remarks he made clear that he would no longer pass over in silence or understate the misconduct of Congolese officials. He was openly critical of the central government: it failed to honor the commitments of its ministers and accused the UN of "plotting against the government and worse" when favorable results had actually been achieved. He didn't spare the Congolese army: referring to reports from UN and International Red Cross personnel in Kasai, where the ANC had behaved barbarously, he said that "these actions obviously cannot be viewed merely as examples of internal political conflict. They involve a flagrant violation of human rights and have the characteristics of the crime of genocide since they appear to be directed toward the extermina-

tion of a specific ethnic group, the Balubas. . . . Should it be supposed
that the duty of the United Nations to observe strict neutrality in . . .
domestic conflicts and to assist the central government means that the
United Nations cannot take action in such cases?"[124] The question wasn't
rhetorical; he needed an answer from the Council. He concluded with a
forthright call to the Congolese to run their government properly—the
international community could not be asked to "foot the bill for political ineptitude and irresponsibility"—and for foreign powers to resume
channeling all assistance through the UN. "This is no longer a question
of form and legal justification," he said on this score, "but a question of
very hard realities, where the use to which the assistance is put is more
important than the heading in an export list under which it is registered,
or the status of the one to whom it is addressed."[125] This is Hammarskjöld hot, and with good reason. He spoke, no doubt, in his customarily
measured tone of voice. But he could not have been more fed up.

There was a flurry of separate messages from Kasavubu and Lumumba in the next few days, leading to a recess in Council meetings until
Kasavubu's diplomats (led by the foreign minister, Justin Bomboko) and
Lumumba's diplomats (led by Thomas Kanza) could reach New York to
participate. But which were the valid representatives of the central government? The Security Council tried and failed to resolve the question;
it would move on in a few days to the General Assembly, and a heavy-
handed solution was reached only in November. There was another
fateful arrival: the Soviet deputy foreign minister, Valerian Zorin, took
the place of the somewhat more soft-spoken Mr. Kuznetsov as head of
the Soviet delegation. Characterized by Dayal as "admittedly a difficult
man [but] not unamenable to reason," Zorin became notorious enough
in the United States by late February to earn a cover photo and story
from *Time*.[126] Looking somewhat older than his fifty-eight years, and
surrounded by three colleagues who had mastered the art of scowling,
in his *Time* portrait he has an air of decision and intelligence. Be that as
it may, he was a man with a mission: to launch an unrelenting attack on
Hammarskjöld and his leadership in the Congo.

Meanwhile, in Léopoldville, Dayal was dealing as he could with spotty
violence and contradictory decrees by Kasavubu against Lumumba and
by parliament in support of Lumumba, both of which stretched the loose
fabric of the Loi Fondamentale past the breaking point, though no one
seemed to care. A comment by Urquhart often rings in my ears: "Nobody

[in the Congo] was playing by the Queensberry or any other rules, and indeed had never heard of them. . . . There just weren't any rules—and people were scared, which . . . made it worse."[127] Queensberry rules are an Urquhart arcanum well worth bringing into the light of day. They were mid-nineteenth-century British rules for boxing matches, essentially binding even now, which included such guidelines as the following: "A man hanging on the ropes in a helpless state, with his toes off the ground, shall be considered down." Whose toes next?

In the Security Council meetings of September 14th–16th, Zorin offered a fair sample of Soviet attitudes to come at a time when his premier, Nikita Khrushchev, was steaming across the Atlantic to participate in the fall General Assembly scheduled to meet in a few days. Hammarskjöld also offered a sample of the resistance he would hereafter deploy against baseless criticism of the Congo operation, distortions of facts, and hypocrisy. But the distortions became permanent; correct one or a dozen and the next one or dozen appeared, often the same in new outfits. With Zorin's entry on the scene and soon Khrushchev's, Hammarskjöld mounted a battle for the integrity of the UN Congo operation, and for the UN itself, which he would characterize a few months later very starkly: "It is vain to argue with those for whom truth is a function of party convenience and justice is a function of party interest. But for others it may be essential that some facts are recalled and clearly and simply put on record."[128]

"What have the United Nations Secretary-General and the United Nations Command accomplished?" Zorin asked toward the beginning of a Security Council speech of marathon length. How could the assembled diplomats listen for so long? "To speak clearly and frankly, the results have been most deplorable. . . . Not only are they failing to help the Government, but they are openly striving to discredit it and are hindering it in every way in its efforts to restore order and normal conditions in the country. . . . There is very good reason to feel that the . . . Secretary-General . . . has failed to display the minimum of impartiality required of him . . . and is thus compromising the United Nations in the eyes of the world."[129]

Hammarskjöld felt constrained to respond, though one can't miss his weariness. "The members of the Council have listened to a long speech. The hour is late. It is therefore with hesitation that I use my right of reply. However, I find it difficult not to do so." Zorin had called him, he said, "the conscious tool of imperialist plans." He would rely on the peoples of Africa and Asia, for whom Zorin purported to speak, to know whether this was true or not. About the recurrent charge that he and his representatives failed to consult with the Congolese government, he told a sharp-edged anecdote: "My representative had tried for eight days to see the prime minister without result, but finally, on the night of September 5, he was summoned for four o'clock in the morning. If he was not available then, I do not blame him." He closed with a plea that would go unheeded by the Soviet bloc, though its simplicity restored for a moment the claims of reason and goodwill.

> The United Nations is engaged in a major effort to give life and substance to the independence of the Republic of the Congo. No misunderstandings, no misinformation, no misinterpretations of the actions of the United Nations Organization should be permitted to hamper an operation the importance of which, I know, is fully appreciated by all those African countries which, with great efforts of their own, support the work of the United Nations in the Congo and, indeed, seem to me to deserve better than to be told that they are misled.[130]

Hammarskjöld received eloquent, even touching support from many Council delegates; he must have been heartened. They couldn't stand to see him personally and the broader UN effort so willfully misrepresented. Serving as Council president that month, the Italian delegate paid tribute to "the tireless, patient, and courageous efforts of the Secretary-General. His report, while conceived with rigid objectivity, contains elements which indicate a grave and troublesome situation."[131] He later followed up this balanced remark with a satisfying jab at Mr. Zorin: "If, as some author has it, monotony is the worst sin of bad taste, here we have had this displayed in its fullest measure."[132] The representative of Ghana, a left-leaning nation as we know, with mixed views about the UN effort, memorably defended Hammarskjöld himself. "My president would like me to appeal to this Council to refrain from all personal attacks on Mr. Hammarskjöld. The clear vision of this man, his merited rank, his superior eloquence, his splendid qualities, his eminent services, the vast place he fills in the eyes of mankind, must embolden us to pay tribute to him."[133] But the Council could not conclude on any matter: it was unable to reach consensus about which Congolese delegation to seat and unable to pass a resolution that called for new funding and asked all member nations to refrain from providing unilateral military assistance. Over Zorin's objection, the Council endorsed a US request for an emergency special session of the General Assembly where the issues could be resolved by a two-thirds majority not subject to veto. That session convened without delay on September 17th.

Following a new pattern of truth-telling night cables to and from Dayal in Léopoldville, Hammarskjöld confidentially assessed the situation. He must still have had Djuna Barnes's play, *Antiphon*, at the back of his mind:

> Your cable this night . . . arrived as an antiphon to the somewhat un-melodious oratory of the Security Council. The Soviet delegation, obviously completely unaware of the latest developments, ran a harsh cold-war strategy of the oldest type and led the Council to a vote on the Afro-Asian resolution. . . . This was unexpected in view of Soviet sensitivity to African opinion but this round they have proven strangely unperceptive to the currents in the regional group. . . . The key melody here was pro-Lumumba. . . .
>
> I am pretty certain that . . . resolution will be carried in Special Session. . . . This . . . would give us . . . funds and it would . . . purg[e] . . . the General Assembly majority of the Soviet accusations against the Command and us all. They started with "partiality," "plotting," and "tool of imperialism" but ended after two days with retreat to "regrettable errors that should be corrected" after Zorin had heard . . . expressions of confidence from African States.
>
> The real game is on your side and I know how well you play it, truly in the UN spirit but also truly in the interest of the poor Congolese people and the rest of Africa.[134]

It was this last that was so thoroughly forgotten by many in the Congo. The senior politicians planned each other's political or actual demise as if they were guests at an anxious weekend in the country with no other concerns but one another. The needs of the Congolese people were nearly altogether overlooked, as if that could come later. In a book published some ten years after the period we're exploring, Thomas Kanza wrote that "African [leaders] devote much of their time, energy, and ability to perfecting the tactics of political combat to destroy their own opposition rather than developing and organizing the nation which is in their charge."[135] He would have learned this first in these years.

Hammarskjöld referred to "the latest developments." While the Security Council debate was under way, as usual something hazardous was occurring in the Congo. There had again been a series of very private meetings prior to very public events, this time between Colonel Mobutu and Larry Devlin and, separately, between the colonel and Hammarskjöld's representatives in the Congo. A week or so earlier, Devlin had driven to Kasavubu's presidential palace with the idea of talking with Kasavubu and his foreign minister, Justin Bomboko. To his surprise, inside the palace he encountered Mobutu flanked by soldiers with raised submachine guns. Mobutu put the soldiers at ease, sat down with Devlin, and opened an astonishing conversation. He was preparing to dismiss Kasavubu and Lumumba—to "neutralize" them, as he put it—and install what would soon be called a College of Commissioners led by Bomboko and consisting exclusively of Congolese university graduates and advanced students. This youthful group—Bomboko himself was an elder at age thirty-two—would temporarily govern and stabilize Congolese affairs as "civilian technocrats" (this was the language of the time). As Mobutu conceived it, it wasn't to be a coup d'état, at least not exactly; it would be something else and better. Putting Devlin on the spot, he wanted assurance that the United States would recognize the new government. Devlin made that promise, although acutely aware that he had no authority to do so, and later counseled with his ambassador, Clare Timberlake, to figure out next steps.

On the evening of September 14th, Mobutu called at UN headquarters in the Congo. It was by no means his first visit; he would often come over at night for a drink and talk. Dayal described him in these early days as speaking "with sadness, not unmixed with bitterness, of the state of his country. . . . Mobutu gave the impression of a Hamlet torn between opposing loyalties, unsure of himself, and full of doubts and fears."[136] On that evening he showed up to inform Dayal of his decision to "neutralize" both the president and the newly appointed prime minister, Joseph Iléo, and to take Lumumba into temporary protective custody. All this to the end of the year, not longer, as a basis for working toward reconciliation at the top of the government. Present that evening, Urquhart provides a vivid account:

> Mobutu appeared . . . in our headquarters and said he was very tired, so we put him in our bedroom. . . . He asked for a radio, so we gave him a little Philips radio, which seemed harmless enough. Then suddenly . . . the cha-cha-cha which normally played 24 hours a day on Congolese radio went off and a voice was heard taking over the country and handing it over to a Commission of Experts. It was Mobutu's voice, and he pointed at the

radio saying, "C'est moi! C'est moi!" We said, "All right, that's it, out you go. You can't declare a coup from our headquarters. That's impossible. You go out on the street with your supporters if you're going to declare a coup d'état." He didn't like that at all. He was very upset about it. He said he had thought we were friends. I said it had nothing to do with that. So we threw him out. And that added a third totally confusing element to the scene. Nobody really knew who was running Mobutu. . . . It doesn't matter who it was; it had the same confusing effect.[137]

Later that evening at a press conference, Mobutu enlarged on his program, which included suspending parliament for the moment and, on forty-eight-hours' notice, expelling the Soviet and Czech embassies from the country. It seems that he was sincerely anti-Communist then and throughout the long reign to come, but this abrupt expulsion, unwise in the larger context of the Cold War, took everyone by surprise except, no doubt, Mr. Devlin. "It was an exciting moment," Devlin recalled. "Our efforts to remove Lumumba and prevent the Soviet Union from gaining control of the Congo were at last bearing fruit."[138] Dayal was less elated. "The expulsions were a move in the Cold War," he later wrote, "in which the Congo was a mere pawn, and which was being waged through the instrumentality of the benighted and venal Congolese leaders duped into betraying their own national interests."[139] Through Kasavubu, who quickly aligned himself with Mobutu, retained the presidency and provided a veneer of legitimacy, Dayal did his best to reverse the decision but was unable to do so. Cruising at sea toward New York, Khrushchev noticed.

The UN could not accept the legitimacy of the government set in place by Mobutu's coup, but de facto meant immeasurably more than de jure in the Congo. Dayal and his colleagues had to engage with Mobutu and as before with Kasavubu, now uneasily Mobutu's man, while encouraging a return to constitutional legitimacy through reconciliation and the reconvening of parliament. Ever the perfect diplomat, Dayal fumbled a little in these early days of Mobutu's rise. "The Western embassies and press hailed the military takeover enthusiastically," he later recalled, "glorifying Mobutu as the 'strong man of the Congo.' When asked by the Western media for my perception of the 'strong man,' I could not help saying that he was the weakest 'strong man' I knew, a remark widely reported and resented."[140] Lumumba's reckless deployment of murderous troops in Kasai Province now came back to haunt him. Going out to speak with Mobutu at his home on a nearby military base the day after the coup, he ran afoul of Baluba soldiers, tribal kinsmen of those who had been massacred in Kasai. Trapped in a mess hall, he was confronted by raging soldiers and the building was soon surrounded by a torch-bearing mob. Dayal was notified by UN soldiers on duty at the base—they were doing their best to avert the worst—and he drove at once to the scene. Many senior UN people in the Congo encountered mortal danger. It was Dayal's turn. Shouting at the mob to make way, which to his surprise they did, he passed through UN soldiers holding the crowd at bay with fixed bayonets and entered the mess hall. "The din was indescribable," he later wrote. "The scene inside will always live in my memory. There was Lumumba in his shirt sleeves in a chair in a corner while a seemingly demented Baluba soldier was shouting and stamping in front of him. A couple of Ghanaian officers, a Moroccan captain, and some other military personnel were there to prevent any physical harm. . . . Lumumba was shouting out his replies in a Congolese language, obviously without carrying much conviction with his angry questioner. It was impossible to do anything in that bedlam and I ordered the Baluba to be taken away. He was bodily carried out, struggling vigorously." Dayal realized he would have to act quickly. An instant plan: he would go out the front door "with much noise and ceremony to divert the attention of the besiegers while Lumumba would be spirited away by a back door through the kitchen." It worked nicely.[141] Receiving Dayal's account of this adventure late in the day, Hammarskjöld cabled back to him: "We have followed with crossed fingers and deep engagement your road through another day of sound and fury."[142]

Lumumba was nearly finished. Within a few days he had withdrawn to his palatial home in voluntary isolation to evade arrest by Mobutu's men. Like Kasavubu and other senior figures, he had been receiving home protection from UN troops since early September; it had now become even more crucial. For the next ten weeks, two rings of soldiers surrounded the building: an inner ring of UN peacekeepers preventing an outer ring of Congolese troops from entering and arresting him, with who knows what quick consequences. He wasn't entirely cut off from communications and political activity; by a circuitous route he could telephone Kanza and others and send written messages through sympathetic soldiers. He somehow found his way out for an evening of dancing and political talk at a café in late September and held an impromptu press conference at his friend Kashamura's house, despite the danger of arrest.[143] Meanwhile Dayal was working on his behalf in the sense that UN policy was to promote the reconvening of parliament as the key to whatever reconciliation and effective government might now be possible, and Lumumba had a strong following in parliament. As well, he had an effective ally in Antoine Gizenga, the deputy prime minister who had hosted that difficult dinner for Hammarskjöld. Gizenga was beginning to organize an alternative power base and possible seat of government for Lumumba at Stanleyville (now Kisangani) in northeastern Orientale province.

On his side, Devlin was doing his shadowy best to prevent parliament from meeting. The undeclared US policy toward Lumumba hadn't changed. Even now he was feared. On the day after Kasavubu deposed Lumumba, Devlin had cabled to CIA headquarters, "Lumumba in opposition is almost as dangerous as in office," and headquarters soon concurred:

LUMUMBA TALENTS AND DYNAMISM APPEAR OVERRIDING FACTOR IN REESTABLISHING HIS POSITION EACH TIME IT SEEMS HALF LOST. IN OTHER WORDS EACH TIME LUMUMBA HAS OPPORTUNITY HAVE LAST WORD HE CAN SWAY EVENTS TO HIS ADVANTAGE.[144]

And it looks to have been true that he only needed to speak to persuade; despite his failings and errors he was, as Madame Blouin knew, an apostle for a vision larger than himself. In the truncated language and oversized type of a cablegram, the message from Washington is almost wistful: What can we do to stop this unstoppable man?

To Devlin's excruciating discomfort, an assassination plot was taking shape. In later years he said repeatedly and with evident candor that he hadn't joined the CIA to assassinate political leaders, but headquarters gave him the assignment—not of pulling the trigger but managing the process. He reluctantly accepted the task and exploited its inherent difficulties to take "exploratory steps" that caused delays. On September 26th a disconcerting fellow arrived in Léopoldville. "Joe from Paris" was his cover name. He was a CIA scientist, Joseph Scheider (known also as Sidney Gottlieb), carrying deadly biological materials to be used to poison Lumumba, who would appear to die of natural causes. The investigating Church Committee heard from Scheider—many years after the fact—that "the toxic material was to be injected into some substance that Lumumba would ingest: 'It had to do with anything he could get to his mouth, whether it was food or a toothbrush.'"[145] The defender of the free world, the United States, was balefully eyeing Lumumba's toothpaste. The overriding issue was to assassinate him in a way that couldn't be traced back to an American or to the US government; a shooting would also do. Devlin deliberately fumbled on, thought about the possibility of introducing an agent into Lumumba's household—what did it matter that he was under UN protection? But no, that couldn't be worked out: "[have] not been able penetrate entourage," he cabled to headquarters, where his superiors were already contemplating other methods. "Possibility use commando-type group for abduction (Lumumba). Either via assault on house up cliff from river or, more probably, if (Lumumba) attempts . . . breakout into town. Request your views."[146] Not too good an idea, either. In a few weeks, headquarters sent another agent to Léopoldville to focus solely on assassinating Lumumba, as Devlin let it be known that he had too many projects to give it his full time. To push the enterprise forward, the second agent in turn recruited a European criminal with some connection to the CIA. Years later the Church Committee asked the second agent about his new hire: "So he was a man capable of doing anything?" "I would think so, yes."[147]

This nauseating Keystone Kops episode, which fortunately failed in all respects, illustrates the hidden forces against which the UN and Hammarskjöld were pitted, and it puts us on notice that thugs were for hire in the Congo. One would think and hope that an unbridgeable distance separated UN people and their efforts from those who were "capable of doing anything." But it wasn't so; at times they drew close.

Whose saint is he?

Meeting for three days prior to the opening of its regular session on September 20th, the emergency session of the General Assembly was a curtain raiser to the intensely dramatic session lying just ahead, which would be attended by many heads of state. Although a curtain raiser, its agenda was significant: to debate and very likely pass the resolution that had foundered in the Security Council and to admit fifteen new member nations, all but one African and including both Congo (Léopoldville) and Congo (Brazzaville), so that they could promptly take part in debates on the Congo. This last didn't work out: to spite the United States, the Soviet Union argued for a more ceremonious admission at the start of the regular session. But a debate on the resolution, shifting in tone from ferocious to sensible, got under way with Hammarskjöld's frequent participation.

We can pick out both grave and colorful threads from these few days. The US ambassador, James Wadsworth, was operating in blessed ignorance of the CIA program in the Congo. "We have sent no troops and no weapons to the Congo," he said. "We have not taken one single step in the Congo independent of the United Nations."[148] For the Soviet Union, Mr. Zorin delivered one of his slash-and-burn speeches targeting the United States and its NATO allies, the UN command in the Congo, and Hammarskjöld. Other delegates sprang to the support of the operation and the secretary-general. Not unreasonably, the Brazilian delegate praised Hammarskjöld for his "handling [of] one of the most difficult tasks ever conferred upon a man."[149] The astute Argentine ambassador said, among other things, "Truly we do not understand the Soviet Union's position. . . . We do not know what it is driving at by its attacks on the Secretary-General."[150] A day earlier, Hammarskjöld had expressed his own puzzlement: "The representative of the Soviet Union used strong language which, quite frankly, I do not know how to interpret." He recognized that the Soviets were inching toward a demand for his resignation. "The General Assembly knows me well enough," he said, "to realize that I would not wish to serve one day beyond the point at which such continued service would be, and would be considered to be, in the best interests of this Organization."[151]

On the 18th he chose to set the record straight again and methodically, touching on the main points of criticism now familiar to us. "I excuse myself for such repetition," he added. "It is rendered necessary by the fact that so many errors in the way of writing history . . . have been repeated."[152] At times he broke from his orderly review of facts, and of facts distorted, to speak from just anger.

> It has . . . been said that we are not helping the government. Well, there are ways and ways of helping a government. There are ways which are in keeping with the rules of the United Nations; there are ways which are not in keeping with such rules. No sovereign government, as an act of sovereignty, can turn the United Nations Force into a national force which it uses for its own purposes. That is what I refused to do, and if that is wrong I do not understand the Charter and I do not understand the rules applied to the United Nations Force.[153]

Similarly, at the end of his talk he dwelt on the gap between the expectations he was carrying and the resources at his disposal.

In a speech made yesterday . . . , it was said that the Secretary-General has all powers to implement the Belgian withdrawal. All powers! The Security Council itself has not resorted to any decision regarding enforcement measures. . . . So much less have they delegated to the Secretary-General any right to take any decision on enforcement measures. The power of the Secretary-General in such circumstances resides exclusively in the moral and legal weight of the decisions of the Security Council itself. If that weight in this case, in the view of some, has proved insufficient, it seems to me to be not the first case in the history of the United Nations.[154]

In the evening session, the Pakistani ambassador warmly endorsed Hammarskjöld's view: "We consider," he said, "that it is not the Secretary-General who has failed the United Nations; it is rather the Security Council which has not fully measured up to its responsibilities and has sometimes taken refuge in resolutions which fail to clarify the mandate which the Secretary-General was expected to carry out." Late in the day, Hammarskjöld cabled a brief commentary to Dayal. "GA tonight was quite frankly a rotten show. Washington tried to be smart and trapped themselves by trying to get admission of new fifteen states in emergency session. Zorin was worse than on Wednesday in Secco [the Security Council], which must mean that I am enough of a stumbling block for their African policy to make them go for my head. . . . To represent reason and decency against such odds is certainly fun for everybody who cares for those forgotten values."[155]

There was such fine intelligence among many delegates and such dogged refusal on the part of the Soviet bloc to allow that intelligence to shape attitudes and actions without hindrance. The Soviets had become a street bully or daft relative, and there was worse to come. In its UN version, the Cold War was akin to mental illness. Many delegations were concerned. The Nepalese ambassador—representing a small, even diminutive power—expressed with exceptional grace and clarity a wish shared by many: "In examining the question of the Congo, as in considering any other problem, delegations must show a degree of objectivity, calm, and moral dignity, for otherwise it is to be feared that the prestige of our Organization may be permanently lowered among the people whose cause we defend and whose confidence we seek. . . . We have the right, I believe, and the duty to ask that our Organization should preserve intact all the human values which it symbolizes for us."[156]

The meeting wore on. The Soviets tried to introduce a revised resolution that explicitly criticized Hammarskjöld; it found few takers. U Thant of Burma, Hammarskjöld's successor as secretary-general, rose to issue a serious warning: "This . . . session of the General Assembly may well be historic," he said, "in the sense that the survival of the United Nations itself is at stake. . . . All of us assembled here today should remember that our decision on the Congo can either strengthen the hands of the United Nations or pave the way for its tragic disintegration and demise."[157] At very last, just after 1:00 a.m. on September 20th, with the regular session set to begin that afternoon, the Assembly passed the resolution that had occasioned the emergency session. It was logical to do so and expected by all, but Hammarskjöld spoke briefly afterward to acknowledge the good sense of what had occurred and the role of African member nations in achieving the result. The UN effort in the Congo would receive urgently needed funds, all member nations were reminded to provide aid, including military aid, exclusively through the UN, all prior resolutions on the Congo were confirmed, and the secretary-general was "request[ed] to continue to take vigorous action."[158] Despite the Soviets' best efforts, the session had ended with strong support for Hammarskjöld and his management of the Congo Crisis.

Nikita Khrushchev arrived in New York on the 19th after a sea voyage, rough at first, later pleasant. A seaworthy fellow, he had had a good time on board. Among other things he had discovered shipboard shuffle board, which he described in his autobiography as if he were an alien coming upon the customs of earthlings. "I remember one game involved sliding a large puck across the deck with a stick and trying to make the puck come to rest in a grid, divided into numbered squares, each representing a different number of points. We couldn't get enough of this game."[159] His first opportunity to address the General Assembly fell on Friday, September 23rd, and he took full advantage by delivering a speech of two and a half hours' length, two hours longer than President Eisenhower's the day before. (Fidel Castro would enter and win this competition a few days later with a speech exceeding four hours.) Khrushchev's topics were disarmament, the misdeeds of the United States, the progress of the Soviet Union, the Congo and colonialism, and the secretary-general. We can safely skip over much of this, even much that he said about the Congo; Soviet-bloc diplomats had been delivering the message for months, he was for the moment delivering it in a more statesman-like manner. "While granting independence in form," he said, "the colonialists do their utmost to maintain colonial oppression." With this he naturally associated the secretary-general: "Unfortunately . . . they have been doing this unseemly work through the United Nations Secretary-General, Mr. Hammarskjöld and his staff. . . . The Assembly should give a rebuff to the colonialists and their stooges and call Mr. Hammarskjöld to order so that he should not abuse his position as Secretary-General."[160]

Toward the end of his speech Khrushchev made a proposal that surely awakened all delegates.

> The Soviet Government has come to a definite conclusion. . . . Conditions have obviously matured [to the point that] the post of the Secretary-General—who alone governs the staff and alone interprets the decisions of the Security Council and . . . General Assembly—should be abolished. It is expedient to renounce the system under which all the practical work in the period between General Assembly sessions and Security Council meetings is determined by the Secretary-General alone.
>
> The executive body of the United Nations should reflect the actual situation that obtains in the world today. . . . We consider it reasonable and just for the executive body . . . to be constituted not as one person . . . but as three representatives. . . . This executive body should represent . . . the Western powers, the socialist states, and the neutralist states. . . . In brief we consider it expedient to set up . . . a collective executive body . . . comprising three persons, each of whom would represent a certain group of states. . . . Then the United Nations executive will really be a democratic body, it will really safeguard the interests of all United Nations member states irrespective of [their] social and political systems.[161]

The following day in a press conference at the Soviet delegation's spacious "dacha" in suburban Long Island, Khrushchev clarified a point. "My speech was not directed against Mr. Hammarskjöld personally," he said. "It is not a matter of his person, but the fact that he expresses the position only of that group of countries which is headed by the USA."[162] Hammarskjöld would prove to agree with the first thought and rigorously reject the rest.

Khrushchev had added to the targets of Soviet attack the leadership structure of the UN and the Charter defining that structure. Hammarskjöld could not let that pass. He had the weekend to collect his thoughts. When the Assembly reconvened on Monday morning, he was the first speaker. "The General Assembly is facing," he said,

> a question not of any specific action but of the principles guiding United Nations activities. In those respects it is a question not of a man but of an institution. . . .

It is common experience that nothing, in the heat of emotion, is regarded as more partial by one who takes himself the position of a party than strict impartiality. . . . Use whatever words you like, independence, impartiality, objectivity—they all describe essential aspects of what, without exception, must be the attitude of the Secretary-General. Such an attitude . . . may at any stage become an obstacle for those who work for certain political aims which would be better served or more easily achieved if the Secretary-General compromised with this attitude. But if he did, how gravely he would then betray the trust of all those for whom the strict maintenance of such an attitude is their best protection in the worldwide fight for power and influence. Thus, if the office of the Secretary-General becomes a stumbling block for anyone, be it an individual, a group, or a government, because the incumbent stands by the basic principle which must guide his whole activity, and if, for that reason, he comes under criticism, such criticism strikes at the very office and the concepts on which it is based. I would rather see that office break on strict adherence to the principle of independence, impartiality, and objectivity than drift on the basis of compromise. . . .

One last word. Sometimes one gets the impression that the Congo operation is looked at as being in the hands of the Secretary-General, as somehow distinct from the United Nations. No: this is *your* operation, gentlemen. . . . It is for you to indicate what you want to have done. As the agent of the Organization I am grateful for any positive advice, but if no such positive advice is forthcoming . . . , then I have no choice but to follow my own conviction, guided by the principles to which I have just referred.[163]

A remarkable statement. It is indirect: it doesn't confront in so many words the "troika" concept (as it quickly came to be called) under which the office of the secretary-general would be trisected but looks instead at why the concept was introduced. It isn't ad hominem: it looks at principles, not persons. It relies on the bedrock of the Charter: Hammarskjöld seems to have always had near at hand his oath of office, which restates with little change Article 100 requiring the secretary-general and his staff neither to seek nor to receive instructions from any government or other authority external to the United Nations. And it finds bedrock even deeper, in its recognition of the international network of trust centered on the secretary-general. Networks of that kind rely in the end on conscience, on the probity and goodwill of their participants. As

Hammarskjöld would say in the spring of 1961, in a speech deliberately assembling lessons from the Congo Crisis, "Finally, we . . . deal here with a question of integrity or with, if you please, a question of conscience."[164] And in "one last word" he reaffirms an attitude we have heard him express several times since his reelection.

Some years earlier in a press conference, Hammarskjöld improvised a striking metaphor that reflects his preference for a light touch in political processes. We looked at it in an earlier chapter. He said, "A good driver makes only slight movements of the wheel in order to give direction at the critical moment. . . . It is a question of remaining wide awake and . . . saying our word in the way which seems . . . appropriate to give that touch to the wheel which helps to keep the car on the road."[165] In the coming days and months, as Khrushchev and his allies intensified their attack, that preferred light touch would no longer be adequate to every circumstance. At times he would need to turn with defiance toward his adversaries.

On his side, Mr. Khrushchev's manners were deteriorating. By his own cheerful admission, he had no experience of parliamentary procedures and customs, although what he was witnessing in the Assembly recalled youthful impressions of the prerevolutionary Russian Duma. It interested him, as shuffleboard had interested him. He also recalled how rudely members of the Duma had sometimes behaved with one another. That gave him an inspiration. According to his memoirs, when the Spanish ambassador replied furiously to his verbal attack on Franco's fascist government, Khrushchev and his delegation began "making noise, shouting, and yelling. I even took off my shoe and pounded on the desk. Needless to say, this caused quite a reaction among the journalists, the cameramen, and others. Our friends used to joke about it whenever we met, although some people did not seem to understand this unparliamentary method. Nehru, for instance."[166] There are several other versions of when and why, the most authoritative likely to be by Khrushchev's son, who blamed the whole affair on a clumsy journalist (crowding close and causing shoe loss as Khrushchev entered the hall) and a polite UN usher (returning the shoe later on a tray discreetly covered by a napkin). As he had too large a waistline to negotiate the narrow space available for him to put his shoe on, it remained in sight for some time and found a new use.[167] Whatever specifics may apply, it was an oafish sort of theater, and Khrushchev and his colleagues took to it: they continued pounding their desks and stamping on the floor from time to time, even—and especially—in response to Hammarskjöld. Khrushchev was hugely entertaining, and dangerous. He controlled a vast conventional military and a nuclear arsenal, he was ideologically driven, and he had a fondness for risk: consider his defiant gift of aircraft and ground transportation to Lumumba. He had both the alert political instincts of a survivor of Stalin's regime and the cunning of a peasant elder. Belligerently beating the air with his fist as he spoke in Assembly sessions to come, he was frightening. But he was also, and obviously, overacting—chewing the scenery. The UN had seen nothing like it.

On October 1st, in a speech mainly concerned with advocating UN admission for the People's Republic of China, Khrushchev bared in passing a theme he would now pursue. He spoke of "Mr. Hammarskjöld, who is the Secretary-General of the United Nations (although I think this injustice will be rectified)."[168] On the morning of October 3rd, he warmed to the theme. Hammarskjöld was at his customary place on the high dais, to the right of that year's president of the General Assembly, Frederick Boland, a veteran Irish diplomat whom he had once described as "one of the best diplomatic technicians in the business."[169]

"Now one man is the interpreter and executant of all the decisions of the Assembly and the Security Council," Khrushchev said.

> But an old saying has it: there are no saints on earth and there have never been. Let those who believe that there are saints keep their belief. We have no faith in such fables. . . . This one man, Mr. Hammarskjöld . . . , must interpret and execute the decisions of the Assembly and the Security Council with due consideration for the interest of the countries of monopoly capital, the interests of socialist countries, and the interests of the neutralist countries. But this is impossible. Everyone has seen how vigorously the imperialist countries have been defending the position of Mr. Hammarskjöld. Is it not clear whose interests he interprets and executes, whose "saint" he is? . . . The developments in the Congo, where he played a most unseemly role, were but the last straw that has exhausted our patience. . . . Unfortunately, in the United Nations the Congolese people did not find a protector of their interests. . . . To avoid any misunderstanding, I want to repeat: we do not and cannot trust Mr. Hammarskjöld. If he himself does not muster up enough courage to resign, so to say in a chivalrous manner, we shall draw the necessary conclusions. . . . A man who has trampled upon elementary justice is not fit to occupy such an important post as that of the Secretary-General.[170]

And he went on, as you might expect, to repropose the troika. Toward the end, he renewed his direct attack: "Do not fall for the high-sounding phrases pronounced here by Mr. Hammarskjöld and the representatives of colonial powers who are trying to justify the bloody deeds committed against the people of the Congo. . . . We are convinced that the seeds of truth will reach the minds of the peoples to whom we are appealing."[171]

Urquhart tells us that Hammarskjöld, "although outwardly calm, was so enraged" that he leaned toward Boland and asked for the floor at once to reply. But he accepted Boland's sound advice to wait until the afternoon session when he would surely have better collected his thoughts.[172] At 3:00 pm Boland pronounced, "I call now on the Secretary-General," and Hammarskjöld entered on what much of the diplomatic community came to regard as the most memorable speech and moment of his UN years.

The Head of the Soviet Delegation to the General Assembly, this morning, . . . said . . . that the present Secretary-General has always been biased against the socialist countries, that he has used the United Nations to support the colonial powers fighting the Congolese government and parliament in order to impose "a new yoke on the Congo"; and, finally, that if I myself "cannot muster the courage to resign in, let us say, a chivalrous way, we [the Soviet Union] shall draw the inevitable conclusions from the situation." In support of his challenge the representative of the Soviet Union said that there is no room for a man who has "violated the elementary principles of justice in such an important post as that of Secretary-General."

Later on he found reason to say to the representatives at this session that they should not "be deluded by the high-flown words used here" by me "in an attempt to justify the bloody crimes committed against the people of the Congo." . . .

The Assembly has witnessed over the last weeks how historical truth is established. Once an allegation has been repeated a few times it is no longer an allegation, it is an established fact even if no evidence has been brought out to support it. However, facts are facts and the true facts are there for whomsoever cares for truth. . . .

I have no reason to defend myself or my colleagues against the accusations and judgments to which you have listened. Let me say only this: that you, all of you, are the judges. No single party can claim that authority. . . .

I regret that the intervention to which I found it necessary to reply has again tended to personalize an issue which, as I have said, in my view is not a question of a man but of an institution. The man does not count; the institution does. A weak or nonexistent executive would mean that the United Nations would no longer be able to serve as an effective instrument for active protection of the interests of those many Members who need such protection. The man holding the responsibility should leave if he weakens the executive. He should stay if this is necessary for its maintenance. This and only this seems to be the substantive criterion that has to be applied.

I said the other day that I would not wish to continue to serve as Secretary-General one day longer than such continued service was considered to be in the best interests of the Organization. The statement this morning seems to indicate that the Soviet Union finds it impossible to work with the present Secretary-General. This may seem to provide a strong reason why I should resign. However, the Soviet Union has also made it clear that if the present Secretary-General were to resign now, it would not wish to elect a new incumbent but insist on an arrangement which . . . would make it impossible to maintain an effective executive. By resigning I would, therefore, at the present difficult and dangerous juncture throw the Organization to the winds. I have no right to do so because I have a responsibility to all those Member states for which the Organization is of decisive importance—a responsibility which overrides all other considerations.

It is not the Soviet Union or indeed any other Big Powers which need the United Nations for their protection. It is all the others. In this sense, the Organization is first of all their Organization and I deeply believe in the wisdom with which they will be able to use it and guide it. I shall remain in post during the term of office as a servant of the Organization in the interest of all those other nations as long as *they* wish me to do so. [*Here the speech was interrupted for several minutes by a standing ovation, while Khrushchev and his entourage drummed extravagantly on their desk.*]

In this context the representative of the Soviet Union spoke of courage. It is *very* easy to resign. It is not so easy to stay on. It is *very* easy to bow to the wish of a Big Power. It is another matter to resist. As is well known to all members of this Assembly I have done so before on many occasions and in many directions. If it is the wish of those nations who see in the Organization their best protection in the present world, I shall do so again.[173]

It was their wish. A second ovation, accompanied by Soviet pounding, lasted as long as the first. In the interval since Khrushchev's denunciation earlier in the day, Hammarskjöld had succeeded in bringing the issues to a sharp focus. Khrushchev's demands cancelled each other out: even if, like his predecessor Trygvie Lie, he were willing to resign in response to Soviet pressure, he could not and would not do so because yielding to the demand for a troika at the top would destroy the executive capacity of the UN. It would "throw the Organization to the winds."

Hammarskjöld sent a discreet note to Ralph Bunche: "Did I read it all right?" Bunche wrote out his reply on the same sheet of paper and saw to it that it promptly reached him: "Perfectly. The voice was the most resonant I have ever heard from you; the pace was measured and the enunciation crystal-clear—all of which did full justice to the superb text. Thus the greatest—& most spontaneous—demonstration in UN annals. Congratulations."[174] Hammarskjöld's lightly written words above Bunche's bold scrawl survive as a relic of that moment.

The "conference machinery," as Hammarskjöld sometimes called the UN without pleasure, ground on. The next scheduled speaker was János Kádár, the Hungarian Communist who had acceded to power after the Soviets crushed the 1956 revolution. Pure anticlimax, he went to the rostrum to deliver a speech essentially identical in length and content to many others from the Soviet bloc, apart from pleading for the legitimacy of his regime before an audience most of whom had been appalled by Soviet violence in Hungary. Other delegates intelligently came to the defense of the secretary-general's office. Speaking for Venezuela and many other member nations, a future president of the General Assembly, Carlos Sosa Rodriguez, said that the troika notion would "write into the very Charter of the United Nations the division of the world into hostile blocs of nations. This would be against the spirit of the Charter, which was designed to bring individual nations of the world together without any distinction regarding their political or social systems. If such a tripartite body were set up to replace the Secretary-General, the highest administrative office of the United Nations would lose all of its flexibility and efficacy."[175]

Meanwhile Hammarskjöld received a puzzling invitation from the Soviet embassy to join Mr. Khrushchev and his colleagues for cocktails the following evening. He checked: in light of everything that had occurred, was the invitation still intended? It was, and he decided to attend in the interest of . . . what? Some years earlier he had told an audience of American students how important it is to remember that "your adversaries of today were your friends of yesterday and will have to be your friends of tomorrow."[176] He must have attended in that spirit. After the cocktail party, someone overheard Kádár asking Khrushchev why he had so warmly welcomed Hammarskjöld. "Do you know the tradition of the mountain people of the Caucasus in our country?" Khrushchev asked him. "When an enemy is inside your house, sharing your bread and salt, you should always treat him with the greatest hospitality. But as soon as he steps outside your door, it is all right to slit his throat."[177]

In the event, no throats came to harm. Over the coming days Khrushchev realized that he had been unable to carry the Afro-Asian bloc and its influential leaders with him—Nehru and Nasser among others. Both were there, listening carefully. He softened his remarks without recanting. Among many other opinion makers, the New York Times did its best to interpret Khrushchev's motives for attacking not only Hammarskjöld but the office he held. In that paper's view, he had indeed wanted to position the Soviet Union as the most valuable friend of newly independent countries, did indeed want to lay the groundwork for disarmament talks—and apart from that was making a display of toughness to impress his own Soviet bloc and Mao's China, with which there were increasing difficulties.[178] Some thought that Khrushchev blamed the UN for the humiliating expulsion of the Soviet and Czech embassies from the Congo. Hammarskjöld also was reaching for an interpretation that looked past the obvious; a few months later he would write his findings confidentially to Östen Undén, the Swedish foreign minister and a trusted friend. For the moment, as he cabled to Dayal, it was clear to him that Khrushchev had "paid the greatest compliment so far paid to UN in recognizing that we now were the main obstacle to an expansion of empire into Africa. . . . The very venom of certain statements is a recognition of defeat, which . . . is of interest for ONUC as it means that it is our duty to continue in the interest of those who wish only the best for the people of the Congo."[179]

In the remaining days until his departure by air on October 13th, Khrushchev continued to bat away at his chosen topics. "Wake up, gentlemen," he admonished the General Assembly, "pinch yourself where it hurts if you find it difficult to stay awake. Many have become accustomed to hearing unctuous words here. I will not be sly with them or pat them on the back now that the world is on the brink of catastrophe. If my words are not pleasing to someone, then I have achieved my goal—that is what I wanted to do."[180] In his last speech before the Assembly, he again had something to say about the secretary-general. The Black Sea rowboat drifted back into view:

> Gentlemen, speaking personally about Mr. Hammarskjöld, I am not fighting him. I have met him and we had a very courteous conversation. I think that Mr. Hammarskjöld owes me a debt because he exploited me when we entertained him on the Black Sea coast. I took him rowing and he did not work off the debt, did not repay me in kind.
>
> This is not a personal issue. The point is that I am a Communist and he represents big capital. It is immaterial what capital he actually has in his pocket because . . . it is often easier to come to terms with a capitalist than with his lackey.[181]

There is more than enough here for a sharp reaction; no one takes to being called names. But surely to his delight, another approach occurred to Hammarskjöld, and he replied at the first opportunity.

> I ask the indulgence of the General Assembly in order to say just a few words to the spokesman of the Soviet Union. I do so because he addressed me so personally.
>
> I was very happy to hear that Mr. Khrushchev has good memories of the time when I had the honor to be rowed by him on the Black Sea. I have not, as he said, been able to reply in kind. But my promise to do so stands, and I hope that the day will come when he can avail himself of this offer. For if he did I am sure that he would discover that I know how to row—following only my own compass.[182]

The tormenter and the tormented, the proletarian statesman and the aristocratic chief of the UN, had one possession in common: their naval expedition. Alone with one another on a storied sea, limited to simple expressions of pleasure and interest in the absence of an interpreter, they had been content. It was perhaps their one moment of undefended humanity with each other.

"Despite buffetings from various quarters, there is no alternative for us except to pursue the laws of the compass . . . ," Hammarskjöld wrote to an acquaintance that fall.[183] As the first debate on the Congo in the General Assembly was nearing its conclusion on October 17th—more would follow—he was meeting privately with key leaders. His cable to Dayal about Nasser's attitudes, and his own, is memorable:

> My guest of honor at dinner tonight obviously has been vaccinated against Lumumbism and may have infection but it has not given him

any fever. In fact all he now wants is a strong government without East or West influence, irrespective of who the top man is. I replied that I would be happy enough if there would be any government at all, provided of course that there was no East or West influence. . . . We . . . sit on a volcano—with the pleasant quality that, if it erupts, even the Organization is likely to disappear underground. This may be meager consolation but it creates the right kind of philosophical approach.[184]

He somehow found time to meet, as well, with at least a few people outside of UN circles. A fragment of remembered conversation with an unnamed American editor addresses in its own way "the right kind of philosophical approach." The editor recalled saying to him that "after Khrushchev had turned against him, proposed the troika, etc. . . , he had no reason to be surprised. . . . He belonged to the West, and at a certain moment the Russians had come to recognize it. He looked at me with those friendly eyes I will never forget, and said that we who have been shaped by the spirit of Pascal cannot help becoming intolerable to them."[185] A stunning remark in light of the pressure on him of current events, it unexpectedly returns us to the origins of Hammarskjöld's mind and sensibility in authors—teachers, really—who never lost their authority for him. Pascal was a discerner, a subtle psychologist and observer of society, a mathematician of genius, a man of faith who steadily questioned his faith. He understood both how to measure and how to dwell in experience. What part of all this would Hammarskjöld have had in mind?

On October 17th, closing the Assembly's month-long debate, Hammarskjöld devoted a talk of some length to the forgotten participants in the turmoil of the Congo and the challenge of sustaining the UN's work. Yet another effort to share what he read on his own compass, no matter what guided other parties, it was an extraordinarily good statement. It restored order and decency. If words could still move minds, these words would do. "Much has been said which has been ill-founded," he said.

Whether this has been the result of misinformation, of an emotional engagement, or of tactical considerations but flimsily related to the interests of the Congo, I leave to others to consider. . . . In the confusing fights and conflicts which have now been going on for more than three months in the Congo among political dignitaries of that country, an impression has grown that few have realized that to lead and govern is not a privilege to be sought but a burden of responsibility to be assumed. . . . That work has been undertaken by many who are nameless, by Congolese officials who are never mentioned and whose names will probably never be known to the world. . . . May I pay tribute to these men and to what they have done to give life and sense to the independence of the Congo. . . .

About UN people in the Congo, he offered an equally rich and felt tribute:

> Those many men, from very many nations in Africa, Asia, Europe, and the trans-Atlantic countries who are serving the United Nations in the Congo, why are they there? They have left their families. . . . They work against the heaviest odds under a continuous nerve strain, they have endless working days, they do not know whether all that they do will not be swept aside one of these days by new waves of political unrest. . . . May I pay them a tribute. . . . Blame them for their shortcomings, if you will; say that they should do more, if you believe that you are entitled to say so; . . . but do not throw doubt on their honesty and seriousness, do not impugn their motives and, especially, do not try to depict them as enemies of the very cause—the well-being of the Congolese people . . . —for which they are giving so much. . . .
>
> When we could not find those whose support we wished to have, we had to act as responsible human beings facing a desperate emergency. You try to save a drowning man without prior authorization and even if he resists you; you do not let him go even when he tries to strangle you. I do not believe that anyone would wish the Organization to follow other rules than those you apply to yourself when faced with such a question. . . .

And he concluded by warning against substituting means for ends, putting the interests of a specific political leader or group ahead of the needs of the Congolese people.[186]

His advice to Dayal in the Congo shifted the metaphor from threatened death by drowning to threatened death by mushrooms. "As regards political situation," he cabled during these days,

> one major difficulty is that we can never get inside the skin of our Congolese friends or disentangle outsider maneuvers. For that reason we are constantly under handicap which we cannot overcome. For that reason also I find it dangerous to base our actions on anything but rather general concepts as to interplay of forces to extent we find our analysis supported by confirmed facts. Believe that on the whole we will get safer results with this skeptical approach. Believe also that this may save us from danger of getting tied up in Congo-type intrigues which grow like mushrooms and die like mushrooms and mostly, like mushrooms, are rather poisonous.[187]

A musical interlude

One of the charms of annual festivities is that they come along no matter what mischief or agony has also come along, and for that reason impose a discipline. For United Nations Day, October 24th as always, Hammarskjöld and all combatants lay down arms to celebrate again the signing of the UN Charter in 1945. The concluding choral movement of Beethoven's Ninth Symphony had become a tradition at these celebrations; this year the Philadelphia Orchestra, under the baton of Eugene Ormandy and with full chorus, performed the entire symphony. Also in keeping with tradition, Mr. Hammarskjöld spoke briefly, on this occasion interpreting Beethoven's music in terms of the drama faced by the UN. His words were recorded.[188] There is no need to include the full text here, but a few lines should find a place. "On his road from conflict and emotion," Hammarskjöld said,

> to reconciliation in [the] final hymn of praise, Beethoven has given us a confession and a credo which we, who work within and for this Organization, may well make our own. We may take part in the continuous fight between conflicting interests and ideologies which so far has marked the history of mankind, but we may never lose our faith that the first movements one day will be followed by the fourth movement. In that faith we strive to bring order and purity into chaos and anarchy. Inspired by that faith we try to impose the laws of the human mind and of the integrity of the human will on the dramatic evolution in which we are all engaged and in which we all carry our responsibility. . . . And may now the symphony develop its themes, uniting us in its recognition of fear and its confession of faith. . . .[189]

With a mountaineer's skill, he had regained the heights. One could say that his remarks applied to nothing, that they were too pure and remote. Or one could say that they applied to everything because they captured essential characteristics even of the harsh events and debates then in motion. Like the concert itself, which reached many parts of the world by radio, Hammarskjöld's words circulated widely in the commonplace form of a press release. His exquisite assertions raise questions both intimate—necessarily worked out for oneself—and broadly communal. What, after all, are the laws of the human mind, and the laws of the integrity of the human will? Is integrity subject to laws? What laws, then, and how to discover them for oneself? What is faith, understood not as consoling belief but as a robust agent for the good in the face even of terrible difficulties? Looking now, long after his death, we can see that he was returning politics to a discipline of awareness and inquiry—to the way of the statesman so evident in *Markings*.

He must have approached the task of speaking at UN Day, and interpreting Beethoven's transcendently powerful music, with a degree of irony. How could he possibly do so, in light of what he described to a colleague as "this perpetuum mobile of crises and quarrels" in and concerning the Congo?[190] He did so.

The Congo needs martyrs

There was the unfinished business of seating one of the two competing Congolese delegations. To oppose the effort of Ghana, India, and other nations friendly to Lumumba, President Kasavubu flew to New York to address the General Assembly on November 8th. In the debate that followed, he came under heavy fire from the Soviet bloc. Zorin described the circle of younger commissioners around Mobutu and Kasavubu as "a band of half-developed adolescents with Fascist tendencies"—this was his best for the day.[191] The United States pulled out all stops to ensure enough votes for the Kasavubu delegation in preference to Lumumba's, and so it was. Hammarskjöld had done his best to avoid that outcome. Although the UN consulted with authorities in the Congo "to all the extent there was anybody who could be consulted," as he once put it, he dearly wanted to keep this particular matter in suspension, not favoring either side, until a process of reconciliation could be set in motion and even succeed. But US policy was now openly declared against Lumumba, and Hammarskjöld's Congo policy, doggedly implemented by Dayal from Léopoldville, was coming under criticism from nearly all sides. Hammarskjöld cabled his views to Dayal: "Results of credentials maneuver is so far strengthening of Kasavubu's hand here and probably a creation of great resistance against all UN efforts. . . . You will be best judge of repercussions in Léo." From his perspective on the spot in "Léo," Dayal wrote later that he saw no good coming of it: "The patient work of . . . ONUC to hold the scales even, and by insulating the situation to make it more amenable to correction by legitimate parliamentary means, was undone. This was the harvest reaped by the maneuver to force the seating of Kasavubu's delegation. The seeds carried by the winds from New York produced an even more bitter crop of violence, disorder, and bloodshed in the Congo."[192]

Kasavubu returned to the Congo on November 27th in a mood of triumph. It may have been his departure, and some brief drop in tension at the UN, which for the first time in months gave Hammarskjöld the impulse to open his journal to a fresh page. He would have been in Brewster for the weekend; the opening lines of the poem suggest that. What he wrote was infinitely lonely. And for those who suspect that Dag Hammarskjöld had a "messiah complex," that he thought of himself and his role as Christlike in some sense, this is the poem to bring to court. For the first time, and not the last, the hard path he had been treading struck him as a Way of the Cross. The torches, the kiss would not be those Jesus had experienced; they would, of course, be different and no doubt disguised. But they would also be the same: that is the last burden of the *imitatio Christi*, the imitation of Christ which he still meditated in the pages of Thomas à Kempis and increasingly knew in his own life.

> The winter moon
> Was caught in the branches.
> Heavy with my blood was the promise.
>
> Naked against the night
> The trees slept. "Nevertheless,
> Not as I will. . . ."
>
> The burden remained mine:
> They could not hear my call,
> And all was silence.
>
> Soon, now, the torches, the kiss:
> Soon the gray of dawn
> In the palace.
>
> What will their love help there?
> There, the question is only
> If I love them.[193]

During that weekend in Brewster, he also tasted the pleasure, rarer now, of reading good literature. He made light of how difficult it was to find time in a note to Eyvind Johnson, whose latest novel he was reading: "With really good books it's good to be forced to read slowly; the old technique—one chapter a day, read aloud by the 'evening lamp'—wasn't so bad, it created the right forum for the joy of storytelling."[194]

In the Congo, Kasavubu emerged from his plane in a dazzling white military uniform, so like the one worn by King Baudouin at the independence ceremonies a half year earlier, and made his way into the city. Despite a heavy tropical storm that evening, a pleasant banquet in his

honor saw him home. Elsewhere in the city, hard events were taking
shape. For some time, Lumumba had been telling Dayal that he needed
to connect with his political base and wasn't taking well to being cooped
up, and Dayal had been telling Lumumba that UN protection necessarily ended at the door of his mansion. UN peacekeepers couldn't follow him wherever he might go; he would be on his own. Some weeks
earlier Lumumba had arranged to send his oldest children safely and
clandestinely to Cairo, where President Nasser had assured him of their
well being. Because the Kasavubu government now enjoyed the open
support of the West and had prevailed in the UN seating controversy,
Lumumba's future had dimmed. He decided to make a breakout. He
would go to Stanleyville in the northeast and assume leadership of a
nascent Lumumbist government then forming around his loyal ally, Antoine Gizenga. In their last conversation, by telephone, Thomas Kanza
recalls that he begged Lumumba to be patient. "Things won't stay like
this forever; even if you have to stay in your house for years, I am convinced that sooner or later you will emerge victorious. Your enemies will
be forced to appeal to you under the pressure of those who still have
faith in you."[195] Such things have proved to be true—witness Aung San
Suu Kyi's fifteen years of house arrest in Burma and Václav Havel's years
of imprisonment in Czechoslovakia. They emerged from their ordeals
as trusted leaders, like Hammarskjöld politically astute and spiritually
alive—Suu Kyi drawing on Buddhist tradition, Havel on intuitions of
Being and conscience that gave Christian warmth to contemporary European philosophy. But Lumumba had, of course, his own mind.

In the stormy night of November 27th, a limousine passed without
incident through the rings of UN and Congolese soldiers. It carried
Lumumba. He collected his wife Pauline and one of their children, Ro-
land, from the safety of the Ghanaian embassy and moved on. A convoy
of cars, eventually nine, made its way toward the border of Orientale
Province, some six hundred miles distant, where a protective escort of
soldiers loyal to Gizenga and himself would await Lumumba's arrival.
In his joy to be free at last, he stopped with reckless generosity to speak
with people, accepted invitations from villages to linger for a word or a
meal, held impromptu rallies, even spoke with Europeans encountered
on the road. His open pilgrimage to the northeast made him an easy
enough target for the Mobutu-Kasavubu search party that had begun to
track him. Dayal reports that the US ambassador lent a hand by person-

ally arranging with President Youlou, across the river in Brazzaville, to borrow a helicopter, which was turned over to a particularly unattractive character, a Congolese security officer named Gilbert Pongo.[196] Dayal recalled that Pongo would repeatedly show up at UN headquarters, armed with a pistol, with the stated intention of assassinating Dayal's military adviser. He would be turned away; the UN had no authority to arrest him. He may also have been among the sources of anonymous telephone calls and written messages threatening Dayal with "the fate of Count Bernadotte."[197] Such was the Congo. After consulting with Hammarskjöld, Dayal announced that the UN would protect Lumumba if his life was known to be in danger or he reached Stanleyville and requested house protection. But for the moment his location was unknown.

Kanza heard later about the arrest from an eyewitness. On December 1st, Lumumba and his party had reached a ferry crossing on the Sankuru River, due east from Léopoldville. The safety of Orientale province lay on the far shore. He had already crossed the river with some of his companions when Pongo's men caught up with his wife and child, who were waiting with others of their party for the return of the small ferry. Lumumba's entourage begged him not to cross back to rescue his family—things would work out, they wouldn't be harmed—but he felt compelled to return to defend them.[198] He was easily arrested together with two companions. His family members were apparently unmolested, although memories differ on this point like so many others. The episode of the river arrest is told in a different way by one of Lumumba's close allies, but the outcome is the same.[199]

He and his companions returned by air to Léopoldville with Pongo and his troops a few days later. There is newsreel footage of Lumumba's arrival: beaten up, hands bound with rope, his glasses long since gone, shoved and lifted like livestock onto the back of an open military truck. A soldier tries to force him to eat a shredded copy of a speech he had given; he refuses. He casts his eyes around. His expression conveys startling dignity. Though flawed, he was an essential man in Africa. That is what the newsreel shows.[200] And then, it gives rise to mental double exposures or ghost images: the truck uncannily recalls the tumbrel or peasant cart that carried the condemned to their deaths in the French Revolution, the soldier trying to stuff his prisoner's mouth with paper uncannily recalls Matthew 27:34—"They offered him wine to drink, mingled with gall; but when he tasted it, he would not drink it." How strange that this African tragedy moved at moments along tracks laid long before.

Lumumba and his companions were shown to Mobutu as if they were trophies, and they were beaten in front of him. Later they were taken to a military prison at Thysville (now Mbanza-Ngungu), some one hundred miles from Léopoldville. Separately arrested, two prominent members of his government—the former minister of youth, Maurice Mpolo, and former senate vice president, Joseph Okito—and four other Lumumba loyalists were also confined at Thysville. The UN community and the world public heard without delay of Lumumba's arrest, abuse, and imprisonment. Hammarskjöld immediately wrote to Kasavubu to make him understand that many delegations had expressed profound concern and to appeal for due process and humane treatment. "This is of special significance now," he wrote, "when you personally are the recognized head of the Congo delegation to the United Nations." Two days later, a second letter: "I am sure," he wrote, "you will already have given your closest examination to the effect upon world opinion of any departure from the observance of the principles of the United Nations Charter concerning 'respect for human rights and for fundamental freedoms for all.' . . . I wish to invite your attention also to the reports of a number of independent eyewitnesses, which give ground for fearing that the detainees, in particular Mr. Lumumba, have suffered physical violence and degrading treatment."[201] He did his best to catch and hold the vigilante style of the Mobutu-Kasavubu government in the network of constitutional and international obligations that should have been observed and might still be. Kasavubu and his colleagues replied with defiance.

Late in the day he had learned of Lumumba's capture, when Hammarskjöld again opened his journal, a ghost image or double exposure came to mind. The news of Lumumba's flight and capture with his close companions evoked both the menacing atmosphere of Joseph Conrad's *Heart of Darkness* and his own unforgotten theme of sacrifice for the good of others. Among its lines, these are the center of the poem he wrote that evening:

> Night flared.
> Phosphorescent,
> The jungle wailed in the fierce grip of the storm.
>
> They paid
> The full price of love
> That others might enjoy a victory.[202]

It is true that he thought Lumumba out of his depth as prime minister and thought him both naïve and careless at crucial turning points, but the poem shows something other than that: it shows fellow feeling. From a political perspective, Hammarskjöld must already have understood that Lumumba's fall could set in motion a causal chain that might defeat the UN effort in the Congo and defeat him as secretary-general. But the poem isn't political, and there is a further ghost image in it—of Hammarskjöld himself, no less at bay than Lumumba and in much the same way.

Just days before his flight, one of Lumumba's allies asked him for his sense of things. Lumumba knew that once he was at large he would be in danger. "If I die, *tant pis*," he said, "the Congo needs martyrs."[203]

Like fighting an avalanche

It will come as no surprise that the Soviet Union circulated a long written denunciation to members of the Security Council and called urgently for a meeting. It convened on December 7th. Mr. Zorin was Council president that month; over US objections, he was both managing the Council's process in a statesmanlike manner and, in his other role, calling down hellfire on Hammarskjöld and the colonialists. Updated to include Lumumba's arrest and mistreatment, the charges were familiar. Hammarskjöld was condemned as "a lackey of the colonialists" playing a "base role" in collaboration with "Mobutu's gangs."[204]

Hammarskjöld judged it necessary to respond in the late afternoon session by making the first of several Zorin-length statements. If Zorin was tireless in bringing Soviet condemnations, Hammarskjöld had evidently decided that he too must be tireless. For the moment, he confined his comments on Lumumba to a few concluding sentences. "The facts are known: it is for everybody to put them into the total perspective of the tragic and confused history of the Congo. . . ." He didn't want at this point to be drawn into judgments; a few days later he would say that Kasavubu as head of state and head of the Congolese delegation to the UN had signed or at least approved the writ of arrest, with the implication that this was as much legality as could currently be had. For the moment he had in mind to restate the UN mandate in the Congo and vigorously defend his approach against the latest round of criticism coming now not only from the Soviet bloc but from all sides. The Congo effort was in danger, its fate very possibly tied to Lumumba's fate. He spoke of the immense difficulty of impartial, compassionately intended service under conditions in which nearly everyone had a furious agenda. "There have been no shifts in policy or changes of approach," he said.

Nor have we been "lackeys" of anybody or shown "servility" to any interest. Of course, we have been accused of all this, and from all sides
. . . . What is more natural? By maintaining our aim, and by being faithful to the principles of the United Nations, we were bound to cause
disappointment to those who have wished to abuse the Organization,
and we were bound to be regarded also as enemies or obstacles by those
who found that the very neutrality of the United Nations represented
an obstacle to their aims. . . . That does not mean, of course, that I claim
any infallibility for what the United Nations has done in the Congo—
naturally, mistakes have been made. . . .

We have been accused of servility in relation to the West, of soft-
ness in relation to the East, of supporting this or that man in the Congo
whom one group or another on the world scene has chosen to make
its symbol. . . . However, this is no excessive price to be paid for avoiding the thing for which no one in my position should be forgiven: to
compromise, in any political interest, with the aims and principles of
this Organization. It has not been done and it will not be done with my
knowledge or acquiescence. I can only repeat what I said in the General
Assembly, that I would rather like to see the office of the Secretary-
General break on this principle than drift on compromise. . . .

What is now laid at the doorstep of the United Nations as a failure
is the failure of the political leaders of the Congo and of its people to
take advantage of the unparalleled international assistance for the creation of normal political life within the country. These are harsh words
and I hesitate to pronounce them but I do believe that this Organization is too often and too easily used as a whipping horse. . . . Putting
responsibility . . . where it properly lies, I do not wish to criticize any
individual or to pass judgment, I only wish to fulfill my duty to this
Organization which, in the best interest of all its Member nations, also
has a claim to fair judgment and to justice.[205]

In the course of Council meetings over the next week, new threats and dis-
locations developed both at the UN and in the Congo. A number of member nations, predominantly Afro-Asian, which had contributed forces to
ONUC, declared that they might withdraw them because they believed that
the forces had not been used aggressively enough to shut down Katanga, free
Lumumba, and more still. Those nations included the United Arab Republic whose foreign minister and UN head of delegation, Mahmoud Fawzi,
had long been among Hammarskjöld's most intelligent allies in the diplo-

macy of peace and reason. Competing resolutions proposed to the Council by the Soviet Union, the Western members, and the Afro-Asian bloc all failed to survive in debate or vote. When Fawzi supported the Soviet resolution, which included references to "the armed bands of Mobutu" and other inflammatory language, Hammarskjöld noticed. Meanwhile, in the Congo, the nascent Lumumbist government at Stanleyville so intimidated Belgian civilians in the region that they asked for and were granted UN protection in a school building. It would not be the last protective encampment. Antoine Gizenga soon proclaimed his government at Stanleyville as the only legitimate government of the Congo, and the Soviet bloc instantly voiced its support. There were now four governments: Kasavubu-Mobutu at Léopoldville, Tshombe in Katanga, Kalonji in South Kasai, and the newcomer Gizenga. A genius for fragmentation was at work both in New York and in the Congo. Years later, Dayal offered a brilliant perspective: "Big powers became hostage to the fortunes of ephemeral Congolese politicians, the Congolese finally reversing roles and turning their patrons into clients. Thus, if Lumumba fell, it became a rebuff for the Soviet Union; if Mobutu was held in check, the United Kingdom felt offended; if Kasavubu was not seated at the UN, the United States would be affronted; if Tshombe was pressured, Belgium would be infuriated. It was like a three-legged race in which a great power was linked to a Congolese politician, with the diverting quality that if the pigmy fell, he brought his giant partner down with him."[206] Anyone who has heard the music of the Congolese pygmy peoples knows that they are giants—giants of another kind. But Dayal's analogy is in substance both colorful and exact.

Hammarskjöld spoke from time to time in the Security Council, and at length in the concluding meeting of December 13th, just prior to the year-end session of the General Assembly. Under his implicit policy of correcting misleading statements as soon as possible, he affirmed to the Council on the 8th that in speeches of recent days "it has been very difficult to recognize historical realities. . . . We have not 'paid Mr. Mobutu,' we have not 'fought for Mr. Tshombe,' and we have had no 'complicity' in the arrest of Mr. Lumumba."[207]

In the midst of his struggle to keep the Congo effort on course, Hammarskjöld had one cause for happiness and one for thoughtful communication. On December 10th, the poet and friend he had championed for the Nobel Prize in Literature, Saint-John Perse, was in Stockholm to accept the award. "I will miss you in Stockholm," Perse had written some weeks earlier. "It will be to you, invisible and present, that I will secretly address my speech at the Nobel banquet."[208] He sent an advance copy of the speech in French to Hammarskjöld with a veiled request that he arrange for an English translation. Fulfilling that request was widely beyond the call of duty, but Hammarskjöld had a resource—the poet W. H. Auden, who gamely agreed to draft a rapid translation. Sending his version to Hammarskjöld at the end of November, Auden expressed his support in this time of trial. "My opinions are of no importance, but I cannot refrain from taking this opportunity to express my unbounded admiration for the integrity, courage, and practical finesse you have displayed during the past six months, qualities which are as rare in public life as they are the hallmarks of greatness." To this typed message he added an earthy handwritten PS: "Really! This sounds like a Frog Orator. Let me revert to my native Limey rhetoric: 'Jolly good show, Hammarskjöld!'"[209] Strange that Auden was still fighting the Napoleonic wars, but no matter—Hammarskjöld surely enjoyed his note. Perse's banquet speech, a statement of the vocation of poetry in our time, echoed Hammarskjöld's own convictions. "Astronomers have been bewildered," Perse said, "by the theory of an expanding universe, but there is no less expansion in the moral infinite of the universe of man. . . . Since even the philosophers are deserting the threshold of metaphysics, it is the poet's task to retrieve metaphysics."[210] Hammarskjöld's beautifully designed, bilingual edition of Perse's long poem *Chronique* had been published in Sweden just in time for the occasion.[211] The poem was of deepest interest to him; to his friends Leif and Greta Belfrage he had sent the draft in October with a note that "it states better than I could dream of doing in my own words [the] perspective of our generation and a revolution that now seems to be entering its crucial stage."[212]

There was a second occasion, also falling on Saturday, December 10th; the day must have felt like a sabbath. For the annual celebration of the 1948 signing of the Universal Declaration of Human Rights, Hammarskjöld gave a short pre-concert statement that reflected the ordeal of the United Nations in the strong light of free thought. "The General Assembly is now engaged," he said toward the end of his talk, "in a debate on the colonial issue. It is significant for the present international revolution. The progress toward self-determination and self-government for all peoples is truly an encouraging translation into political action of the concept of human rights. . . . But let us not forget that there is a colonialism of the heart and of the mind, which no political decision can overcome and against which the battle must be waged within ourselves, without any exception."[213] He was speaking with the mind of *Markings*. He seems never to have lost from sight the battle to be waged within ourselves, in this instance to scour away vestiges of colonial smugness or, among the formerly colonized, a reflexive sense of inferiority and resentment. Thomas Kanza later rephrased this insight as "mental decolonization," applicable equally to the colonizer and the colonized.[214]

Hammarskjöld's extended statement in the Security Council on December 13th was yet another tireless effort to clarify the debate and point toward issues genuinely needing the Council's attention. Unwilling to permit the UN effort or himself to be whipping horses, he gave as good as he got in forceful, often eloquent language. It was political speech at a very high level, comprehensive and forward looking. He deployed a large vocabulary and literary care, as if fine shades of meaning needed just the right words. As before, he must have known that some were listening appreciatively while others were taking notes toward their next attack. "If the United Nations operations were, for whatever reason, to be forced out of the Congo," he began,

> I am convinced that the consequence would be immediate civil war, degenerating into tribal conflicts fought in the most uninhibited manner . . . . It would also mean the complete disintegration of whatever fabric of national unity still remains. . . . It can be safely anticipated that the outside world would not stand aside in such a situation. . . . If and when that were to happen, the world would be facing a confused Spanish-war situation, with fighting going on all over the prostrate body of the Congo and pursued for nebulous and conflicting aims. Could such a situation be contained? And if not contained, how would it influence peace and war in the world? . . . These, gentlemen, are the stakes. . . .
>
> [The UN operation] cannot continue if it is being pushed around by various leaders and factions in the Congo, able to activate, against the United Nations, this or that member country, or group of member countries, willing, for whatever reason, to keep the operation under a fire of criticism and suspicion. It cannot continue if it is enfeebled from within by divisions, or by withdrawals, or by a lack of financial and material support. . . . The Organization might still stop complete chaos from developing in the Congo but it might itself get corroded, saddled as it would be with grave responsibilities, while powerless to act beyond the insufficient capabilities open to it in view of the actions of its own Member nations.
>
> From some speeches in the Council a listener might have been tempted to draw the conclusion that he was attending a lawsuit against

the Organization by its own Members, with the Secretary-General and his collaborators in the dock. . . .

[There is a] desperate need for an unemotional, unpolitical, clear-headed analysis of the sickness from which the Congo is suffering; short of such an analysis, how can this body hope to find a remedy? . . .

Blamed repeatedly for working hand in glove with the Belgian government, Hammarskjöld offered the original insight that Belgium's actions represented a failure of friendship. He may well have had in mind the irony of the General Treaty of Friendship, Assistance, and Cooperation signed by Belgium and the Congo on the eve of independence.

I may . . . be permitted to express my hope that the Belgians show the first and most essential quality of friendship: that in their actions they put the interests of the Congo before their own interests, and also that they realize that a people, like an individual, has problems into which especially a friend knows that he should not permit himself to intrude.[215]

Expressing the issue in intimate, human terms, he did what he could to distance it from the impersonal realm of national and economic interests.

He concluded by asking the Security Council to provide a wider mandate for the UN operation in the Congo, if that was their wish. It couldn't do so. When the General Assembly resumed session a few days later, it was as unable as the Security Council to enact a resolution. However, the Assembly's debate and several sensible resolutions that fell short of passage gave Hammarskjöld what amounted to talking points with all concerned parties. As in the Council, he spoke with stinging forthrightness. Responding to a long series of accusations from the Polish delegate, he observed that "the concentration on my activities is such that for a moment even the imperialists and colonialists seem to fade out of the picture. . . . As I have not been willing to pave the way for reforms of the Secretariat, . . . the desired result has to be achieved in a way the least weakness of which is that it is not chivalrous."[216] He conveyed his best hope for the Congo:

The overriding consideration must be one of . . . return to constitutionality and . . . national reconciliation. With this background I feel that the United Nations should exercise its influence in favor of the restoration of parliament to its proper position in the constitutional scheme. . . . Combined with that, I feel that it is necessary to work in the direction of a reduction of the army to its constitutional place as a subordinate instrument for the national executive in the maintenance of law and

order. . . . Naturally, the development I envisage would require the establishment of a certain balance between various factions in Congolese
political life. . . . The secessionist tendencies must in this context be
broken if we are to be entitled to hope for future stability in the area.[217]

Difficult to fault him for being soft on Tshombe in light of such words,
but no words of his, no clarity, was sufficient to stop the torrent of invective from the Soviet bloc and the uneasiness of many in the Afro-Asian
bloc, the largest contributor of troops to the peacekeeping force, now
numbering eighteen thousand.

A few days later, Hammarskjöld warned the General Assembly that in
the event of civil war in the Congo, almost inevitably involving foreign
support on all sides, he would feel obliged to ask the Security Council to
withdraw the UN operation. "Everything should be done by the Organization and its representatives to forestall such a crisis," he said, "but if our
efforts are of no avail it is better for the future of the Organization to look
the situation in the eye and to draw the conclusions." He asked also for the
main organs of the UN to come to the aid of the Secretariat by taking a
greater share of responsibility for the Congo operation. "I hope everybody
understands that . . . decisions of the type which we have to take daily . . . go
beyond what reasonably should be put on the shoulders of any one man and
his collaborators." However, he said, were there no change in the allocation
of responsibility, he would continue "to rely on the Advisory Committee,
which, with all its high competence, has after all only limited authority."[218]
On December 20th, when the General Assembly was about to take a holiday
break, he didn't hesitate to record his dissatisfaction: "Just as a short time
ago the Security Council, so now after a long debate the General Assembly
has failed to reach a positive decision regarding the problem of the Congo,
further developing the stand of the Organization. . . . Naturally the operation will be continued under the previous decisions with all energy, within
the limits of the law. . . . However, the outcome here . . . has not given us the
moral or political support of which the operation is in need."[219]

It was time to wrap up this most difficult of years. On the 21st he sent
off two letters, one for UN purposes to Kasavubu, the second privately
to his brother Bo. To Kasavubu he outlined the highlights of the General
Assembly resolutions that had won considerable support, if not enough
to pass. Many in the Assembly wanted to see parliament reconvene and "a
return to democratic practice." They wanted the human rights of prisoners
to be respected and "the immediate release of all political prisoners under

detention and particularly of those enjoying parliamentary immunity"—
referring to Lumumba and his companions. They hoped for a good result
from a planned roundtable scheduled to convene under Kasavubu's auspices, and they expected the Congolese government to cooperate with a
Conciliation Commission, appointed by Hammarskjöld's advisory group
and due to reach the Congo quite soon. They also expected the Armée Nationale Congolaise to stop interfering in politics and no longer to accept
aid other than through UN channels. Hammarskjöld warned Kasavubu
of the possibility of civil war and the disastrous consequences were that
to occur. "I am deeply convinced," he concluded, "that it is imperative to
reach a clear understanding concerning the conditions under which the
United Nations can usefully remain and serve in the Congo."[220]

At the close of the year, this was not a letter of closure: every issue
remained an open threat. Lumumba was in prison under conditions that
changed from easy to appalling and back again. There were four governments in the Congo, supported from abroad in a complex pattern of
Cold War and economic interests. There were episodes of merciless tribal
warfare. The UN peacekeeping force, already small for its mission, was
threatened with withdrawals. Oscillating between political wisdom and
verbal violence, meetings of the Security Council and General Assembly
were incapable for the moment of generating guidance in the form of resolutions. The Soviet bloc had retreated but not abandoned its campaign
to introduce what amounted to a Soviet veto at the top of the Secretariat
by means of a troika. Relations with the Western powers were troubled.
On this score, Urquhart heard Hammarskjöld remark that "if his difficulties with the Russians seemed greater than with the Americans, it was
only because the former had been publicized, as had been his one-month
quarrel with Lumumba, to the almost total exclusion of his three-month
struggle with the Belgians."[221] And Hammarskjöld was under personal attack. "As I have told you," he wrote to his brother on the 21st,

> recent times have been unusually difficult. At the same time that the Con-
> go operation is becoming increasingly complicated and has to be handled
> with hopelessly inadequate personnel resources, during the last few weeks
> I've been fighting a one-man battle against the Soviet bloc and some of its
> Afro-Asian parrots. The traces you will find in the speeches I've sent over.
>
> Now we will get a short respite, I suppose, since the Assembly early
> this morning packed up. . . . But the battle from the Russian side is
> planned on a long view and the pause will therefore not be long. So far

so good: on the whole I'm quite pleased with the position to which I've maneuvered myself, even if it forces me to continue offensive tactics in the Congo as well as here. . . .

Christmas will not give me any break, and the many books that are waiting to be read I will have to put in my suitcase when I fly to Africa in the first days of January. I must go for a few days to Léopoldville—a city I honestly dislike unusually much, even apart from the political difficulties—and later to Johannesburg. The reason for this trip is primarily that I need to negotiate about apartheid. So you see, I get a pleasant start to the New Year.[222]

Two days later, he put a note in the mail to his artist friend, Bo Beskow: "In a few days I am off to Africa again. It is a bit hard after this autumn death-dance and without any rest, but necessity knows no law and developments are not waiting for my convenience."[223] To a Norwegian minister and friend he wrote in a similar vein at the turn of the year. "The job has become a bit like fighting an avalanche; you know the rules—get rid of the skis, don't try to resist but swim on the surface and hope for a rescuer. (Next morning historians will dig up the whole rotten mess and see how many were buried.) A consolation is that avalanches, after all, automatically always come to a stop and that thereafter you can start behaving like an intelligent being again—provided you have managed to keep afloat."[224]

At last he had time to himself—too much. Christmas Eve dinner with Bill Ranallo and his family must have been warming, safely distant from the avalanche. At some point that day, he reflected on the birth and death of Jesus, noted down (surely from memory) a valiant verse from an old Swedish hymn, and read in his beloved Psalms. He found in Psalm 4 a most beautiful reassurance: "I will lay me down in peace, and take my rest; for it is thou, Lord, only that makest me dwell in safety." And found in Psalm 60 a mirror of his experience in recent months: "Thou hast showed thy people heavy things: thou hast given us a drink of deadly wine." But as a man of living faith, he recorded the next verse also: "Thou hast given a token for such as fear thee: that they may triumph because of the truth."[225]

On Christmas morning he asked Heinz Wieschhoff, his leading expert on Africa, whether he would care to take a walk. Wieschhoff understood how lonely holidays could be. He drove in from Bronxville, just outside New York City, to pick him up, and after a good walk Hammarskjöld accepted his invitation to stay for dinner with the family.[226]

Whenever it was in the coming year that he edited and partially retyped the manuscript of *Markings*, Hammarskjöld exercised author's

license by putting two poems from early December out of sequence so
that the year ends on their note, rather than on the heartening language
of Psalms. The first of those poems we have seen; it is what I take to be
his oblique homage to Lumumba and his companions, and to Conrad's
Heart of Darkness. The second is a set of dark promises and premonitions.

> The way,
> You shall follow it.
>
> Happiness,
> You shall forget it.
>
> The cup,
> You shall empty it.
>
> The pain,
> You shall conceal it.
>
> The answer,
> You shall learn it.
>
> The end,
> You shall endure it.[227]

If there were to be readers someday of his private journal, this is what
he wanted them to know of himself at year end. The deliberate skew in
dating emphasizes all the more his sense of loss and stoic acceptance, his
promises not only to himself but to the Elder Brother who prayed in the
garden of Gethsemane, "My Father, if it is possible, may this cup be taken
from me. Yet not as I will, but as you will" (Matthew 26:39).

It would be so easy to overlook this moment and others like it—to
construct from Hammarskjöld's writings a generally sunny architecture
of ideas and practices. And we would err. The way of the statesman and
stateswoman is unlikely to be free of anguish.

16

Have Mercy upon Our Efforts

"This has now developed into a [chess] problem...," he would write to the Swedish foreign minister in mid-March. "The Soviets have not even managed to convince themselves . . . that there has been . . . any lack of objectivity on my side. It is funny when time in this way, even among those responsible, eliminates even the last vestige of an emotional involvement in the coldly calculated tactical moves in so-called politics. I am afraid I am [enough] of an intellectual . . . to take a certain pleasure in the game when it is scaled down to these terms of an abstract problem concerning the right way to get or avoid 'checkmate in three moves.'"[1] Hammarskjöld's verve and lean into events reasserted themselves in the months ahead, although entries in *Markings* for 1961 reflect his presentiment that he too could fall victim to violence in the Congo or the artillery of words at the UN. In public statements he was altogether himself: superbly lucid, forward looking, crisply defiant in defense of the UN at home and in the Congo, resourceful in planning and diplomacy. In deep privacy and correspondence it was sometimes otherwise. The first lines of an entry in *Markings* for July 6th reflect a recurrent state of mind and heart:

> Tired
> And lonely,
> So tired
> The heart aches
> . . .
> It is now,
> Now, that you must not give in.[2]

In early January Hammarskjöld spent two days in Léopoldville before flying on to South Africa to engage with government leaders on apartheid. Welcoming him after the long flight, Dayal found him confident and seemingly unaffected by the avalanche of criticism at UN headquarters. As it happens, nothing much came of those few days in the Congo: he met with members of the central government and they complained bitterly, met also with the newly arrived Conciliation Commission to help set their work in motion; they too had complaints. Asked by Dayal how things had changed since his last visit to the Congo in August, he nonetheless replied, "Then we were all full of confidence in New York, but things here were panicky. Now we are panicky in New York, but here in ONUC I find a mood of confidence."[3] Though his visit was low-key, UN staff members recalled years later a notable event. Hammarskjöld had become more demanding, and often enough irritable, as the Congo Crisis made its way on. Staff members stoically endured his impatience. Heinz Wieschhoff's wife, Virginia—who like Dayal's wife, Susheela, had no fear of the great secretary-general and boundless affection—let him know that he would do well to make a sign to the staff while in the Congo. Why not a gala picnic? John Olver, a colleague of Urquhart's, tells the story. Hammarskjöld gave him a guest list and remarked that it was an unusual one, not to be tampered with. The next day his guests gathered at the Dayals' home for a few hours far from "the horrors," as Olver put it, "that lay just beyond the neatly manicured lawns." Hammarskjöld took aside many members of staff for private talks. "So much was happening," he told Olver, "that I didn't realize until recently how some of you were being pressed beyond the limit. . . . I know that sometimes I was unreasonably hard on you, and I just hope that you didn't take it personally."[4]

In South Africa, the Sharpeville massacre of March 21st, 1960, marked a turning point in international opposition to the government's policy of apartheid. The incident is inscribed in the history of the Republic of South Africa, which celebrates Human Rights Day on March 21st. A large, essentially peaceful demonstration against the pass laws, which required nonwhite Africans to carry internal passports and limited their freedom of movement, became a bloodbath when the police opened fire: 69 killed, 180 wounded, including women and children. The Security Council responded vehemently ten days later, the United States and Soviet Union for once agreeing on a resolution that "deplore[d] the policies and actions of the Government of the Union of South Africa" and called upon it "to initiate measures aimed at bringing about racial harmony based on equality . . . and to abandon its policy of apartheid and racial discrimination. . . ."[5] As so often, the resolution requested the secretary-general to carry the message, in this instance to a founding member nation whose elder statesman, Jan Smuts (1870–1950), had exercised a large influence on the concepts and language of the Charter.

Hammarskjöld had hoped to call much earlier on the prime minister of South Africa, Hendrik Verwoerd, a principal creator of apartheid. At last there was time in early January.

As expected, the visit yielded no change and no promise of change. Before Hammarskjöld's arrival, Verwoerd had made a speech asserting that, in response to international pressure, South Africa would have to be "as unyielding as walls of granite." He was true to form in that regard, although he found Hammarskjöld interesting, "a person he could engage with."[6] The visit was a managed sequence of official meetings and events, including time with harmless, state-approved black leaders; the genuine leaders were "outlaws" whom it would naturally be inappropriate for him to meet. When Hammarskjöld stopped his limousine in a black township and popped out for a visit, the world's newspapers considered that at last they had an unscripted event. "Mr. Hammarskjöld went into one of the houses and spoke with the housewife as she was busy with her chores. Hundreds of African children gathered in the street and surrounded Mr. Hammarskjöld when he emerged. He shook their hands and laughed at their excited cries."[7] Returning directly to New York and Security Council meetings, he could report only that both he and Mr. Verwoerd were open to further discussions. And yet his visit, much publicized, marked a new stage of concerted international pressure on South Africa.

At headquarters more than enough needed time and attention: outrageous collusion between Mobutu and the Belgians, hot Security Council meetings, withdrawals from the peacekeeping force, reports from the opening days of a meeting of African heads of state at Casablanca. They had the Congo and Lumumba much in mind; Thomas Kanza was among them as an unofficial delegate. Like a sign from a cancelled world, *National Geographic* published that month an article Hammarskjöld had prepared some time ago on Mount Everest and Nepal, illustrated with his own color photographs taken from the air.[8] It conveyed his love of the mountains and reverent curiosity about the religions and sacred imagery of Asia. How strange it must have been for him to look at those pages—and set them down again.

Needless to say, he had reason to worry about Lumumba. "There was no prison in Kasavubu's Congo secure enough to contain him," Dayal has written.[9] At times Lumumba was mistreated and tortured, at times treated well enough to recover and resume his mission. He would speak with the soldiers as only he could about the future of the nation. He spent Christmas Eve freely at table with the commander of the Congolese garrison. During his weeks of incarceration a series of mutinies over pay alarmed Lumumba's enemies in Léopoldville, who feared that if discipline broke down he might charm his way out of prison. Kasavubu and Mobutu with senior colleagues went out to Thysville to calm or replace the erring troops and unexpectedly offered Lumumba a post as a deputy minister in the government then weakly taking shape around the nominal prime minister, Joseph Iléo. He refused. After Christmas, his treatment must have worsened. On January 4th he smuggled a letter to Dayal to say that he and his companions were living "in absolutely impossible conditions. . . . The food we receive is bad and insufficient, I often eat nothing but a banana over three or four days. . . . I ask you to acquaint the secretary-general . . . with my situation and thank him for intervening on my behalf."[10]

The authorities in Léopoldville and Brussels had another kind of intervention in mind. Like the CIA, Belgium had been working for some months toward the *élimination définitive* of Lumumba; that was how they put it.[11] Imprisoned, Lumumba remained a political force. Free, he could return to power. Close to Léopoldville, he made his keepers violently uneasy. They decided to send him to one of two places—either Bakwanga, capital of the seceded state of South Kasai where he was hated, or Elisabethville, capital of the seceded state of Katanga where he was feared and hated. After a brief negotiation in which the Belgians' views weighed heavily, it was agreed that Lumumba and his two unfortunate companions, Mpolo and Okito, would be secretly sent by air to Elisabethville, where Moïse Tshombe and his Interior Minister, Godefroid Munongo, would await them.

On January 8th, Lumumba smuggled a letter to his wife, Pauline. His last political testament, it reads like the reflection in a mirror of his Independence Day speech only six months earlier. "I am writing this without knowing whether you will ever get it, or when, or whether I shall be still alive when you read it." He reaffirmed his vision of the Congo and assigned blame for all that had occurred to Belgium, the West, the United Nations, and those of his countrymen whose minds had been corrupted or who had simply been bought. "Dead or alive, free or imprisoned . . . , it is not I who matter. It is the Congo and our people whose independence has been transformed into a sad farce. My faith remains unshaken." He thought of his children. "Don't tell everything to the children," he wrote. "Just tell them that I came fifty years too early. I want my children to be told that the future of the Congo is beautiful. . . ." He wrote about his attitude in the face of his sufferings. "Brutality, agony, torture have never driven me to beg for mercy. I would rather die with my head high, my faith unshaken, and profound trust in the destiny of our country . . . . History will one day pronounce its judgment. . . . Africa will write its own history. . . ."[12] Africa remained a tangible presence to him, a promise to be kept. He asked his wife not to weep.

A little more than a week later, January 17th, Lumumba was approached in his prison cell by a young man he knew and rather trusted, Jonas Mukamba, a member of Mobutu's College of Commissioners. Mukamba and a few companions told him that there had been a revolution in Léopoldville, the populace was calling for him, it was time to return in triumph to the city. And Lumumba believed him. Accompanying Mukamba to a local airport for the short flight home, he and his companions were taken into custody by a Mobutu official and soldiers of the Baluba tribe that had suffered near-genocide at the hands of Lumumba's troops. Forced into an aircraft, the prisoners departed not for Léopoldville but for Elisabethville. En route they were beaten so atrociously by their guards that the civilian pilots were nauseated. Unable to persuade the guards to stop, they locked their cabin door. They landed in Elisabethville and taxied to a part of the airport unsupervised by UN peacekeepers, who saw from the distance what occurred. Battered, half dead, Lumumba and his companions were hustled into heavily guarded vehicles that immediately quit the airport. Their destination was an isolated house at no great distance.

Hammarskjöld had written a few weeks earlier about the "autumn death-dance" he was so glad to see end. Learning of Lumumba's transfer with his companions to Katanga, he immediately wired Tshombe and Kasavubu to urge humane treatment and the return of the prisoners to Léopoldville—naturally, to no avail. What took place was a death-dance in the rainy season, hidden from all but a few conspirators in the Congo and Belgium. Thanks to two sources mentioned in the previous chapter—the investigative work of a Belgian author, Ludo De Witte, published only in 2001, and the government inquiry and report of several years later—we know what occurred.[13] In and around the bungalow there were Belgian members of the Katangan gendarmerie, military police, and Katangan troops. Guards outdoors were under orders to shoot to kill any UN peacekeepers who might somehow find their way to the bungalow. The three prisoners were tied up indoors and mercilessly beaten. Lumumba said to someone that he was thirsty. A soldier brought a pail of water and threw it in his face. A Belgian lieutenant saw Lumumba when he had been separated from the others and tied up in a bathroom. "I remember being struck by his dignity."[14] Early that evening, Tshombe, Munongo, and other Katangan ministers paid visits. Some of them participated in brutalizing the prisoners. A witness recalled that by 7:00 p.m. the prisoners were "tied up in a bundle, theirs faces swollen by the blows. . . . They were no longer talking, they were inert."[15] Tshombe and his ministerial accomplices left to counsel with each other at the presidential palace. They drank quite a lot. After dinner at a restaurant, they returned at about 9:30. The prisoners were brought into the living room and again beaten by some of the ministers. Tshombe's butler recalled that Tshombe's suit was "stained with blood."[16] At about 10:00 p.m. the prisoners were taken to a convoy of cars and driven some thirty miles to a clearing where shallow graves had already been dug. Led out of a car, Lumumba said to one of the Belgians, "You're going to kill us, aren't you?" They were escorted one by one to a tree in front of a firing squad, Okito first. "I want my wife and children in Léopoldville to be taken care of." One of the executioners replied, "We're in Katanga, not Léo!" A rain of bullets. Mpolo was next. And then Patrice Lumumba. A rain of bullets. He was not quite thirty-six years old. Kasavubu heard later that he had lived his last hours "with supreme contempt and extraordinary courage."[17] He must have asked. His suit also was stained.

In the Congo inferno it was not enough to murder; the remains had to vanish. As there was a good deal of improvisation in all this, it took the Katangan ministers and their Belgian advisers some hours to work out what to do next. The day after the executions they dispatched a squad of Belgians and Katangese police to recover the bodies and rebury them more than a hundred miles away, near the border with Northern Rhodesia in a region where Munongo had hereditary prestige. Within a few days that solution came to be viewed as inadequate. The executioners wanted to eliminate the possibility of a future shrine. Another team, described by De Witte as two Europeans in uniform and their black assistants (their names are known), was dispatched with suitable tools and a barrel of sulphuric acid. They retrieved the bodies, cut them into pieces, and dissolved them in acid. They also were drinking; this wasn't a task for sober men. What didn't dissolve they ground up and scattered as they returned to Elisabethville.

Over the next days and weeks, the government in Katanga offered assurances that Lumumba and his companions were being treated humanely. Here there is a gap in the gruesome tale. Although the Katangan assurances held public concern at bay for some weeks, Thomas Kanza knew two days after the executions that Lumumba had died. A Guinean friend in Léopoldville had seen a few words of Swahili in a written message he wasn't supposed to have seen: *Patrice akufi*. He asked Kanza what they meant. Patrice dead. Shouldn't that have been enough to ignite newspaper inquiries or a rapid sequence of communications reaching the UN without delay? Dayal wrote later that there were rumors in Léopoldville, but "even the most polite inquiries evoked angry rejoinders about keeping ONUC's nose out of the Congo's internal business."[18] Hammarskjöld cabled to Dayal that there were rumors also at UN headquarters; meanwhile Tshombe had told Hammarskjöld that he thought it best to isolate Lumumba from all contact.

On February 10th, more than three weeks after the murders, Munongo announced on Radio Katanga that Lumumba and his companions had escaped, and he posted large rewards for their recapture. Few believed him. Three days later he called a press conference to announce that the fugitives had been killed by unidentified villagers and their bodies buried in a location that would remain secret "if only to prevent pilgrimages being made there in the future." About the fictive villagers, Munongo said, "we cannot honestly blame them for having rid Katanga, the Congo, Africa, and the world of a problem. . . . I should be lying if I were to say that I was sorry that Lumumba is dead. You know my feelings: he was a common-law criminal. . . . I realize of course that the UN will say the whole thing was a plot, and that we killed him ourselves. . . . My answer will be: 'Prove it'. . . ."[19]

Throughout this long engagement with the Congo Crisis, I have searched periodically for the enduring Congolese identity—the hidden truth of this people or collection of peoples, undisturbed by the chaos of their tragic effort at nation building. I looked in music, dance, art, and proverbs, in early photographs of regional royalty seated at ease among courtiers and wives, in African histories written by Africans as Lumumba had foreseen. Somewhere there would be firm signs of a culture *not* deranged by the slave trade in centuries past, by Léopold II at the turn of the twentieth century, by colonial condescension and exploitation in the decades before independence. Mobutu Sese Seko had the same idea; he launched in later years a policy of *retour à l'authenticité*, return to authenticity—but he had political motives. It was a substitute for progress. I found treasures, carved images of remarkable dignity, dances that make one feel wooden in comparison, proverbs that catch the mind. "One finger cannot extract a thorn," "No dew falls at midday": calls to cooperation and realism, virtues mostly lacking in what we have seen of the Congo. But once, at the center of this narrative, the fullness of Congolese identity made itself known. There was no need to search; she came forward. The word belongs to Ambassador Dayal:

> Shortly after the news of his death, the widow of the slain leader came to ask for ONUC's intercession with Tshombe for the body of her husband. It was a moving occasion. When Mme Lumumba had seen me after Lumumba's transfer to Elisabethville to ask about his welfare, she was well-dressed in European clothes and high-heeled shoes. This time she came bare-breasted and with shaven head, with a cloth around her waist and she sat on the floor in the traditional manner of African mourning. Her young son, carrying marks of beatings received at the hands of Mobutu's soldiers, accompanied her.... She was a picture of sorrow and despair. I could do little to comfort her except to arrange for her safety and that of her children....[20]

As a young man, Lumumba once shared a dream. "I will write a novel," he said, "to express the black soul, the true face of Africa, described by an African...."[21] He did not live to write it, but his life embodied it. One could say, with a little generosity, that he fulfilled his dream.

Patrice akufi

In late January and early February, before the revelation of Lumumba's death, Hammarskjöld was asking the Security Council to strengthen his mandate in the Congo. "The Organization could well be blamed if, at the present juncture, it did not reassess its policy in the light of experience and consider whether . . . more far-reaching measures are not now called for . . . , even if such measures by some might be felt as coming close to a kind of interference."[22] This was, in fact, the direction that would emerge out of the sharp controversy that lay just ahead. Privately, Hammarskjöld confided to friends in the distance what he could say to very few in New York: he was suffering. "My comments of today would be very bitter," he wrote to Beskow, "and this goes for both East and West, and for both Africa and Asia. We are far from a world where even a true national interest leads to the individual subordinating himself, not to mention how far we are from the stage where a question of vital international interest is given superiority over a national one."[23] To another friend he wrote—again, before the news broke—that

> the Congo crisis continues its wild course of events, with frightening elements of irresponsibility, intrigues, untruthfulness, and cruelty. This really is a history that soon must be written, written by a cold head and a sharp pen, as a frightening picture of our world and of our present-day humanity. Not least outrageous is the way almost all parties blame the UN as its scapegoat in total forgetfulness of the fact that by doing so they try to save their own hides at the expense of common values that are to be the heritage of the future; what does X [a prominent diplomat] care about the success of this desperately necessary experiment in rational international politics and international cooperation when his personal position ... is in jeopardy—and he is typical of too many, if not most.[24]

When the Security Council received the news of Lumumba's death on February 13th, the intended agenda was set aside and there was an intense exchange—furious, saddened, thoughtful, depending on the speaker—before the delegates dispersed for forty-eight hours to consult with their governments. Hammarskjöld limited his remarks to recognition of the tragic nature of the event and a call for an international investigation; Zorin declared that his government could "no longer have any confidence in the Secretary-General and his staff"; and the US head of delegation, Adlai Stevenson (appointed days earlier by the new US president, John F. Kennedy), joined several others in defending the Congo operation and Hammarskjöld's leadership. "We believe," said Stevenson, "that the only way to keep the cold war out of the Congo is to keep the United Nations in the Congo. . . ."[25] Adlai Stevenson (1900–65), twice a presidential candidate, a man of keenest intelligence and refreshing wit, would bring to the United Nations both candor and courage. Kennedy found Stevenson, if anything, too effective: he once described himself as "the ambassador's special representative in the White House."[26]

In the Congo, Dayal faced many difficulties. Conditions in Léopold-ville approached civil war. The Kasavubu-Mobutu regime was terrorizing opposition leaders, who flocked to Dayal for protection. As in Stanleyville, the UN set up a protective camp for them. Kasavubu objected that this was done without consulting him. The Western embassies objected that the camp would expose the government in Léopoldville to criticism. Dayal himself was coming under increasingly heated criticism from Kasavubu and others. Already in early January Kasavubu had formally asked Hammarskjöld to recall him; Hammarskjöld had refused. As when Bunche was on duty in the Congo, relationships were going bad. A little later that winter, Hammarskjöld reported to Dayal: "I said yesterday to one of the Soviet people, 'Kasavubu has again broken with Dayal and your Government has broken with me; are there any relations left but those between Dayal and me?'"[27]

In the evening of February 13th Hammarskjöld opened his journal and began a short sequence dated February 13th through March 13th, to which he must have returned from time to time that month. He recorded only quoted texts that spoke to him; there are no direct words until mid-May, but each quotation conveys a state of mind and heart. On that devastating day when the news reached the UN, he copied out a prayerful passage in Saint-John Perse's *Chronique*, which asks the Lord who has "brought us to this naked life of the soul" to consent to be among us some evening to tell the ancient tale of the Shirt of Nessus—the poisoned, burning shirt sent unknowingly by Heracles's wife to her husband. When Heracles donned the shirt, invisibly stained with the magical tears of his enemy, the centaur Nessus, the poison caused such agony that he threw himself on a pyre and ended his life. Hammarskjöld must have felt that shirt nearby. He copied out, as well, a few lines from Djuna Barnes's *Antiphon*, soon to have its theatrical premier in Stockholm—lines including this: "We're about a tragic business."[28] However, he wasn't confined to the Shirt of Nessus; he was nothing if not a fighter of a refined but powerful kind, ready to begin again in the most dismal of circumstances. You may recall from chapter 1 a note he sent to a senior British diplomat in mid-March that reflects his stamina and good humor: "I don't think it will surprise you to hear that we all manage to remain in good health and in good heart, catching as they pass those bricks which can be built into the structure and dodging, if we can, those that we fail to catch."[29]

On the following day, February 14th, the Soviet Union filed a letter with the president of the Security Council and requested distribution to all delegations. Its furious attack on Hammarskjöld and the UN presence in the Congo surpassed all previous language.

> Everyone knows that the Governments [of the major Western powers] had only to give their henchman Hammarskjöld the word and . . . the life of the modern hero of the Congolese people would have been saved. . . . The murder of Patrice Lumumba and his comrades-in-arms in the dungeons of Katanga is the culmination of Hammarskjöld's criminal activities. It is clear to every honest person throughout the world that the blood of Patrice Lumumba is on the hands of this henchman of the colonialists and cannot be removed. . . . His actions place a dark stain on the whole United Nations. Not only can such a man not enjoy any confidence; he deserves only the contempt of all honest people. There is no place for Hammarskjöld in the high office of Secretary-General of the United Nations and his continuance in that office is intolerable. . . . The Soviet Government, for its part, will not maintain any relations with Hammarskjöld and will not recognize him as an official of the United Nations. . . .[30]

The letter called for the withdrawal of UN troops in the Congo within one month, the arrest of Tshombe and Mobutu, and responsiveness from "all freedom-loving States" if help was requested by the lawful government of the Congo (which it located in Stanleyville, not Léopoldville).

Over the coming days there were street demonstrations in cities of the Soviet bloc but also in London, Vienna, and elsewhere, and demonstrators attacked the Belgian embassy in Moscow. When the Security Council reconvened on the morning of February 15th, a well-planned riot broke out in the visitors' gallery, set in motion by a number of delegations through an underhanded use of guest passes. Urquhart reports that twenty unarmed UN guards were seriously injured by people armed with brass knuckles, spiked heels, and who knows what else. When Hammarskjöld's security guard heard shouts of "Get Hammarskjöld," he persuaded the secretary-general to leave the Council chamber, and Hammarskjöld learned later that a woman from the Ghanaian mission had been overheard elsewhere in the building saying that she hoped the rioters had killed him.[31] Order was eventually restored; the Council reconvened in the afternoon for what would prove to be a harsh session. Years later, Hammarskjöld's successor, U Thant, recalled Hammarskjöld telling him that "during his tenure as secretary-general, he had never received as much hate mail on any issue as he had on the Congo."[32] One such was from Sékou Touré, president of the West African Republic of Guinea, who sent what Hammarskjöld described "as a 'straightforward go to hell message,' accusing him of personal responsibility for Lumumba's murder."[33]

February 15th and days following were hard fought. Introducing a resolution that demanded among other things Hammarskjöld's dismissal, Zorin took his time to convey the Soviets' indignation in lurid language modeled on that of the letter he had circulated. His resolution was fully supported by Guinea and Mali, and received support in some respects, though not against Hammarskjöld personally, from the United Arab Republic. This was a source of unhappiness for Hammarskjöld, who counted on Nasser and his ambassadors by and large to work with him. Insofar as words can rescue, some delegates came to his rescue. The Chinese ambassador declared that "the Soviet Union denounces the Secretary-General in language which can only be characterized as indecent. . . . My delegation regards this new accusation . . . as fantastic, irresponsible, and dangerous, that is, dangerous to the United Nations and dangerous for the peace of the world. . . . In the Congo Mr. Hammarskjold has done his best to prevent politics from becoming mere brutality. He has not always succeeded. . . . He has had a limited mandate with even more limited means. . . ." Even the French ambassador, serving a head of state with no regard for the UN or Hammarskjöld, declared that "the violence of today's accusations seems to exceed all bounds and we can only condemn it formally. The Soviet delegation is not only attacking a policy; it is attacking in this case a man and his dignity. . . ."[34]

Hammarskjöld must have been grateful to his defenders. He responded to Zorin in what had become his customary fashion, at length, restating the long path from early July to Lumumba's death and the limitations placed by the Security Council and General Assembly on UN initiative in the Congo. He was again ironic about the rewriting of history and the Soviet demand that he use the peacekeepers as a fighting force without a mandate to do so.

> It does not seem to me to be asking too much if those who now talk about the responsibility of the United Nations, and more especially of its Secretary-General—in language which only emotion could excuse but which may be inspired by cold calculation—are requested to state clearly when and how representatives of the Organization did not use all the means put at their disposal. . . . It seems to me to be fair to point out that it is not the Secretary-General who has determined the mandate. . . . There is no escape from the responsibility which flows from this. . . . In the pres-

ent effort in some quarters to blacken the Organization and discredit its representatives, irrespective of the validity of the reasons and irrespective of the facts of the case, the real victim is the future.[35]

He spoke also, with feeling, about the strains placed on the UN and its people by the Congo Crisis.

> For seven or eight months, through efforts far beyond the imagination of those who founded this Organization, it has tried to counter tendencies to introduce the Big-Power conflict into Africa and put the young African countries under the shadow of the cold war. It has done so with great risks and against heavy odds. It has done so at the cost of very great personal sacrifices and for a great number of people. . . . We effectively countered efforts from all sides to make the Congo a happy hunting ground for national interests. To be a roadblock to such efforts is to make yourself the target of attacks from all those who find their plans thwarted. In the case of some, the opposition to the United Nations line was for a while under the surface, but it was not long before it broke out in the open.[36]

Hammarskjöld finished out his comments by asking the Council for a widened mandate and detailed the points he thought most important. "[The Security Council] cannot shirk its responsibilities by expecting from the Secretariat action on which it is not prepared to take decisions itself."[37]

He had a wry moment on the 16th, the eve of the premier of Djuna Barnes's *Antiphon* in Stockholm. He had hoped to spend the evening in New York with Ms. Barnes but that was not to be, as he explained ruefully in a cable to his co-translator, Karl Ragnar Gierow, who had also directed the production. "Although security measures intervene with plan to have DB at home tomorrow, thoughts of both of us will be with you and actors in this pioneer venture. Sure you will put up a play which may even compete with ours, with decisive difference that yours will lead to catharsis for which there is no hope outside the closed world of mature art."[38] Even in this witty, kind note to Gierow in a world far off, his unhappiness is evident. It was generally a time of cancelled pleasures. To W. H. Auden he sent a cable a few days later: "Everything geared for me finally to present personally my birthday greetings when not unexpectedly I was called to order by Khrushchev's men. Thus no birthday party for me. All good wishes."[39]

Though there was noise, as Hammarskjöld would say, the Council responded to his request for a strengthened mandate through a resolution adroitly drafted by Ceylon, Liberia, and the UAR, members of the Afro-Asian bloc on which he relied for non-aligned common sense. As this initiative was making its way, news reached the Council and the world that the Kasavubu-Mobutu government had sent six prominent Lumumba allies to their deaths in Bakwanga, capital of the secessionist province of South Kasai. A season of assassinations had arrived; it had nearly reached the Security Council chamber. Speaking to the Council on February 20th, Hammarskjöld expressed what almost everyone felt: "I bring this news to the knowledge of the Council with revolt and shock . . . . It should be inconceivable for personalities with whom the United Nations has to deal—in a country to which it has tried its utmost to bring assistance—to flout in this way basic values upheld by the Organization."[40] The miserable event gave further impetus to Resolution 161, adopted the next day. It included important guidance for the months ahead: "The Security Council . . . urges that the United Nations take immediately all appropriate measures to prevent the occurrence of civil war in the Congo, including arrangements for cease-fires, the halting of all military operations, the prevention of clashes, and the use of force, if necessary, in the last resort."[41] This was the first authorization of military force. Its oddly halting words—"force, if necessary, in the last resort"—would both serve and haunt the UN operation. The resolution was definite about the need for "the immediate withdrawal and evacuation from the Congo of all Belgian and other foreign military and paramilitary personnel and political advisers not under the United Nations Command, and merce-naries"—in other words, a thorough house cleaning of Belgian elements, from high-level advisers in presidential palaces to hired soldiers of for-tune in improvised command centers. Three further points: the Council called for an "immediate and impartial" investigation of the deaths of Lumumba and his colleagues, reorganization of the Congolese army and its removal from political roles, and "the convening of parliament and the taking of necessary protective measures in that connection." As a conces-sion to the Soviet Union, there was no mention of the secretary-general's leadership. In exchanges surrounding the resolution, the United States and others made clear that prior resolutions placing responsibility in the secretary-general's hands remained in force. In public Hammarskjöld made no reference to the omission. He spoke at session's end to welcome the resolution and again set facts straight. He seems to have been either infinitely patient about doing so again and again or infinitely sure that the record should be restored to factuality as soon as possible after distortions had been introduced. But he was not above expressing bitterness: as he corrected the delegates' memories concerning his introduction of UN peacekeepers into Katanga—you will recall that brave adventure—he didn't refrain from saying that "even the implementation of a request of the Council can obviously be held against me."[42]

A few days after passage of the resolution, Hammarskjöld wrote a letter to Kasavubu that called him to task with dry fury. Given the willful difficulties encountered, he wrote, "the work of the United Nations has been kept down to a difficult holding operation while, with loyalty and cooperation, it could long ago have been a full success in the best and widest interest of the people of the Congo and of the world." His colossal disappointment couldn't be more plainly stated. The envisioned goodness of the intervention had slipped entirely away. He described the new Security Council resolution as "a unanimous decision to cut through all that has hampered the United Nations effort. . . . The world is no longer willing . . . to accept the consequences of the continued splits, abetted by outside interests, which divide the country. Reconciliation on a nationwide scale is, therefore, imperative, and anyone in a responsible position refusing to make his full and selfless contribution to such a reconciliation shoulders a heavy responsibility. . . ." He made clear that the UN in the Congo would act more forthrightly than in the past "to prevent developments toward civil war and to counteract all forces which upset law and order." It would do so not to establish a trusteeship, as Kasavubu had recently prophesied, but "to give to the sovereignty and independence of the country its full meaning. . . ." A few paragraphs on in the letter, his language perhaps unconsciously echoed Shakespeare: "It would be idle to expect world opinion to accept things to continue as they have been. Either the will manifested by the world community will be respected, or chaos will come about. . . ."[43] *Othello* 3:3: "Chaos is come again." Terrifying words resonating down to our time from the tragedy of a bold African deluded by a European intriguer.

There can be no mistaking Hammarskjöld's public position on the political murders and their consequences for UN policy in the Congo. What was his private position? And how, privately, did he take the Security Council's omission of his role from the new resolution? As it happens, the day after he dispatched his letter to Kasavubu, he sent a thoughtful note to the novelist John Steinbeck, who had posed this question in a recent letter: "When a murder has been committed by a person or persons unknown the first question asked is—who stands to gain by this death— who profits by it?"[44] Steinbeck offered the tentative hypothesis that only the Soviets might profit because Lumumba's murder added fuel to their attack on the secretary-general. Hammarskjöld replied:

> Your approach to the Lumumba tragedy—his murder was, in Talleyrand's words, "more than a crime, it was a major stupidity"—is unique; no one in these parts, at least, has suggested it, and it invites thought. I suppose there are many possible answers to the question you pose, but I incline to the conclusion that *no one*, in the long pull, will really profit from Lumumba's death; least of all those outside the Congo who now strain to do so but should one day confront a reckoning with truth and decency. There may be immediately some propaganda exploitation of this blunder; indeed, we have been seeing it in staged bursts in many parts of the world, but to what avail, really, and even those efforts have required unbridled distortion. It is, I imagine, at its earliest that the big lie shines brightest; does one ever endure? Events in the Congo move quickly and, it seems, so far always badly or in bad directions; memories, even of ghosts and legends and certainly of synthetic martyrs, are short and everything soon gets swallowed up in the confusions, frustrations, and sheer imbecilities of that arena.[45]

In a cool-minded way he was thinking of consequences along the causal chain. The assassination was worse than a crime, Lumumba was a "synthetic martyr" who might prove to be little remembered in a context where events and people tumbled over one another.

A letter of two months later to Jytte Bonnier, wife of a major publisher and newspaper owner and an author in her own right, had a different tone. She had written critically to him about what she took to be the UN's role in the death of Lumumba. He didn't let that pass—and added a biting commentary.

> I was interested to see that you share the very common reaction to the assassination of Lumumba. What that story tells about the UN is only that this Organization, unlike the God of classical theology, is neither omnipresent, omniscient, nor omnipotent. To have, over a territory which is five times as large as France, soldiers less numerous than the policemen in Manhattan does not make us more efficient than the New York police in the prevention of murder, rape, and similar time-honored ways for man to realize himself.

No, in spite of Lumumba, the UN as a live reality—which is not what you read about in the newspapers—has in no way failed. However, these last few months have shown that a dangerous erosion is going on in the world in which we believe and for which the Organization should be an expression and an instrument. Alas, that erosion has its main center in the West. If you permit me to make a comparison about the world body-politic, I might say that while the East tries in an old-fashioned way to murder international cohesion with fists, daggers, and poison, we may in fact, due to developments on the other side, find it quietly dying from cancer—or is it perhaps advanced arteriosclerosis of the heart and brain?[46]

Mrs. Bonnier had her views, but so too did some of Hammarskjöld's closest colleagues and genuine well-wishers, who had lost patience with the UN policy of nonintervention in Congolese politics and were dismayed—who wasn't?—by the collision between the "S-G" and major powers in the Security Council. Writing years later, Dayal recalled that he tried to persuade Hammarskjöld in November, when Kasavubu was at the UN, to push for a more aggressive mandate. "The principle of non-intervention," he had argued, "should not be carried beyond the point at which the UN Force became the laughing-stock of the world."[47] Also writing years later, U Thant remained uneasy about the circumstances surrounding Lumumba's transfer to Thysville and imprisonment. "To my knowledge," he wrote, "there was no rational explanation why ONUC troops failed to intervene. If they had attempted to do something, then I cannot trace any official record to that effect. Perhaps in strict legal terms, intervention would have meant an interference in the domestic affairs of the Congo, but I felt then, and I still feel now, that . . . protection of Patrice Lumumba by the United Nations might have been justified, since it would have had the effect of preserving the status quo ante. . . . The United Nations contributed, perhaps inadvertently, to [his] tragic end. . . ."[48] Dayal records that Ayub Khan, president of Pakistan and a military man, expressed a hard view that occurred to some at the time and recurs even today in interpretations of the first year of Congolese independence. "The United Nations had been toying with a situation which needed drastic measures," said the field marshal. "The Congolese were obviously quite incapable of governing themselves and the United Nations must assume responsibility for running the country for a period of ten years."[49]

This climate of opinion even among close colleagues helps explain the rift that appeared between Hammarskjöld and Mahmoud Fawzi, the foreign minister of the UAR who, with Nasser, determined the line followed by their UN ambassador, Omar Loutfi. Needing to clear the air after the resolution that omitted mention of the secretary-general, Hammarskjöld wrote at length to Fawzi. "Recent developments," he began, "have shed a cruel light on the standards of integrity and courage in present international life."

> It is not only a question of distorting facts as soon as you believe that they may be forgotten, but also a question of picking up old correct facts to which previously there has been no reaction, and fitting them into a totally new picture so as to make them take a totally new and utterly unjustified significance. That of course is combined with intimidation based on the experience that few countries and few persons are guided by so strong inner criteria that they will not give in to pressure, continued for a sufficient time and concentrated on their feeling of safety and self-respect....
>
> I feel . . . strongly the absence of support from quarters who, of course, know the full story.
>
>   Naturally I understand why it was considered wise not to mention the Secretary-General in the UAR-sponsored resolution—although I think that it was a great tactical mistake—and, naturally, I understand that Loutfi. . . found it difficult to say anything when Zorin in the debate interpreted this omission as an expression of no confidence. But it must be sad to have to bow in this way, with fresh memory of your own experiences. For me, your doing so is still something I have to get over.
>
>   The world goes on . . . and we have to try to mend fences and to stop gaps and to forget in order to permit things to move forward. I am certain that you are aware that only an ultimate and hard-tested sense of duty not to desert the ship in a storm keeps me prisoner here. But even a prisoner in that position should have access to sporadic radio communication, and that is really the reason for this message. . . .[50]

A few days later, in a further note to Fawzi, he acted on his desire to mend fences. "I promise you," he wrote, "to remember the good things achieved and forget the wounds."[51] There had been many good things— above all, concerted action to end the Suez Crisis in a way that saved face for all concerned and permitted things to move forward.

    The nightly cable traffic between Hammarskjöld and Dayal—intensely practical, always inquiring—came to an end on March 1st, when Dayal returned to UN headquarters at Hammarskjöld's request. In part he was needed to reinforce Hammarskjöld's approach to the General Assembly, which would soon reconvene. But he had left the Congo for other reasons. Kasavubu and his government had refused to have anything more to do with him and threatened to break entirely with the UN if he remained. The Americans considered him left leaning, biased toward the Lumumbist element in the Congo and likely to help Lumumba's man, Antoine Gizenga, become prime minister. Others had their complaints. Hammarskjöld didn't wish to yield to pressure, nor did Dayal, but even Frederick Boland, the very sensible president of the 15th General Assembly, advised against Dayal's further service in the Congo. Boland felt that if Dayal and his wife were to return to the Congo it would mean "certain death." Hammarskjöld couldn't help but agree. Mobutu had let it be known with casual malevolence that if Dayal returned to the Congo he would be assassinated.[52] Assassination had become easy "in a world of stupidity abused by evil," as Hammarskjöld once said of the Congo.[53] Was Dayal wholly without responsibility for the nasty way his service ended? Linnér thought that he brought a certain Brahmin haughtiness to his relations with Congolese leaders and offended them.[54] But Dayal knew that there was blood on the hands and nonstop plots in the minds of key Congolese politicians with whom he had to deal from day to day. That can produce aversion in the best of diplomats. This he undoubtedly was.

Rather than appoint a new special representative, in the course of the spring Hammarskjöld named Sture Linnér as officer in charge of the overall mission in the Congo, in cooperation with three Africans—among them the Tunisian Mahmoud Khiari—as well as the Irish military commander General Sean McKeown and his Ethiopian chief of staff. A preeminent historian of the first years of Congolese independence, Catherine Hoskyns, makes the point that Linnér was not a politician by nature and tended to delegate political responsibilities to Khiari.[55] This would prove to be consequential. With the addition in mid-June of the Irish diplomat and author Conor Cruise O'Brien as the UN representative based in Elisabethville, an essentially new team would be in place. After considerable negotiation between Hammarskjöld and Nehru, one further problem was solved: Nehru proved willing to send five thousand additional Indian troops to the Congo, crucially important at a time when some other countries had withdrawn. "Nehru insisted," Dayal recalled, "that he would not allow [the troops] to be pushed around and further insisted on their being used effectively and given the requisite powers to do so."⁵⁶ Nehru's view reflected the consensus: the Congo mission had gone badly in many respects, and "if necessary, in the last resort," military force under Hammarskjöld's guidance could set things right.

Political and moral striptease

Congolese politicians of nearly all stripes were united in their dislike of the Security Council resolution of February 21st. Reorganize, discipline, and depoliticize the army? Convene and protect parliament? *All* Belgians to go, even "our" Belgians, the ones we like? Investigate the deaths of Lumumba and his allies? Throughout the month of March the politicians mounted resistance of various kinds, from slander to military assaults on UN positions. The 130-member UN contingent guarding the port of Matadi was forced to surrender, and there were other incidents. At a nearly all-Congo emergency gathering of political leaders at Tananarive, in Madagascar, Tshombe persuaded Kasavubu to work toward a loose confederation of partially independent states. Under such an arrangement, they hoped to achieve enough order across the country to dismiss the UN, now regarded quite generally as the common enemy. Arriving home to Léopoldville, Kasavubu realized he had sold his constitutional birthright for pottage and disavowed the agreement.

Soon after the General Assembly resumed its sessions on March 7th—they would continue until April 22nd—Hammarskjöld received an encouraging note in the mail and responded in a way that reassures concerning his state of mind and heart. "At moments like these," he wrote in reply, "when one happens to be standing in the middle of crossroads along which an abnormally high level of political traffic is pressing, it is good . . . to have such warm expressions of friendship."⁵⁷ Vivid and interesting, these are the words of someone who could withstand oncoming political traffic. He spent the month of March in attendance at the General Assembly and writing a stream of formal notes to Kasavubu and the Belgian government—often enough beginning "I have the honor to protest. . . ." With the support of the Congo Advisory Group he also dispatched two highly competent African members of the Secretariat to work with the Kasavubu government toward implementing the Council's resolution and sent an equally able Tunisian diplomat to work toward the same goal with the authorities in Brussels. Urquhart writes that both diplomatic initiatives would prove helpful.⁵⁸

On March 20th the Assembly received the report of the Conciliation

Commission, now returned from the Congo. Though the commission had thoroughly explored the situation, it had been unable to move matters forward, owing to "the uncooperative and intransigent attitude of certain leaders and the constantly deteriorating situation."[59] In Dayal's view, the commission's visit had inadvertently made matters worse because it was ineffective: "The Congolese had realized the impotence of the sovereign organs of the UN, the Security Council and General Assembly, to do anything to deflect them from the unbridled pursuit of their personal ambitions. In fact, the situation at the time of the Commission's departure was far worse than it had been on its arrival."[60]

The Congo was briefly on the agenda when the Assembly reconvened, and violently on the agenda from March 21st forward when the Soviet foreign minister took the rostrum. A leading figure in Soviet diplomacy from Stalin to Gorbachev, Andrei Gromyko (1909–89) had an asymmetrical, pouchy face not easily forgotten. In the early years of the UN as chief of his nation's delegation, he earned a *Time* cover story (August 18th, 1947) depicting him in the company of a horned serpent spelling "veto" with its coils. Known, not among his friends, as "Mr. Nyet," he was a formidable partisan of his country's international agenda and a formidable obstacle to everything else. On March 21st he hoped to slay once for all Hammarskjöld's reputation. He gave a Zorin-like speech covering every familiar point but lied more brazenly and lashed out in language still more extreme. One wouldn't have thought that possible.

> Mr. Hammarskjöld. . . .and those who guided his actions wrought havoc [in the Congo]. . . . Without any legal title he took the entire matter into his own hands and began to decide what should and what should not be undertaken; in fact he reduced everything to turmoil and barren correspondence. . . . The troops whom he sent to the Congo brought with them not only sky-blue helmets and military equipment but also a policy of virtual cooperation with the aggressor and his agents. . . .
>
> The Soviet Government has already stated that it holds Hammarskjöld responsible for the murder of Patrice Lumumba and his comrades-in-arms. . . . We cannot be content that a permanent post in the United Nations should be occupied by a man who has sullied himself with this murder. The murderer is not only the person who has wielded the knife or revolver; the chief criminal is he who placed the weapon in his hand. . . .
>
> If he is allowed to go on as he is going, he will probably soon fancy that he is Prime Minister of the World Government and, given half the

chance, will assert, "L'Organisation, c'est moi.". . .

We are calling for the removal of Hammarskjöld from the post of Secretary-General. . . . Those who sympathize with him can give him a farewell dinner. . . . But you will not see us there. . . .[61]

And he reasserted Khrushchev's demand for a troika at the top of the Secretariat to remedy what he called the "lopsided, crazy structure both of the Secretariat and of the other organs of the United Nations." This proposal would not prevail; few member nations thought it sensible. But it was persistently thrown on the path by the Soviet bloc, and just as persistently pushed aside by others.

Hammarskjöld kept his counsel for the moment—he would speak some days later—but various delegates, notably Adlai Stevenson, sprang to the defense of the man and the operation. Stevenson somehow managed to speak as if in conversation with the assembled delegations; one hears that even now. "After listening to the Soviet speech," he said,

I have concluded that there are two Congo problems, one in Africa and one in New York, and that the one in New York is, if anything, the more serious . . . . I was frankly astonished to hear the Soviet representative open the first debate of this resumed session with a speech which, to say the least, is in the worst and most destructive traditions of the cold war. . . . We have not even been spared the charge of being an accomplice to murder. . . . We consider [the Secretary-General] a dedicated, impartial, and scrupulously honest official of unimpeachable integrity, and we are fortunate to have such a man in this most difficult post at this most critical time. . . .[62]

Debates tend to move slowly in the General Assembly because so many speakers take part. It was only on March 28th, a full week later, that Frank Aiken of Ireland—we know him from the Tibetan debate—had his opportunity. His voice was unique. "There has been an . . . insidious . . . attack of a defeatist character," he said, "to the effect that the United Nations has failed in the Congo. We do not believe that the United Nations has failed. . . . It is true that the outcome is still unknown to us but there is no reason for despair. . . ." And he added, if anyone was likely to miss the point, that "[Dag Hammarskjöld] will be honored as long as men strive for peace and brotherhood. . . ."[63]

Hammarskjöld listened to words kind and unkind, truthful and deceiving, from his high seat in the General Assembly alongside that year's president—with much the same attitude, one hand often cupping his chin, the other perhaps holding a pencil, his expression impossible to read. But we know through relics saved by Andrew Cordier, his chief of staff seated on the president's other side, that there was no lack of response behind that impassive façade. You may recall that they would occasionally pass notes back and forth. "What an absolutely despicable fellow that Romanian is!" Hammarskjold once wrote surreptitiously to Cordier. To which the latter replied: "He is completely irresponsible." And the traffic of messages flowed in the opposite direction. Cordier to Hammarskjöld: "This is gross interference in internal affairs." To which Hammarskjöld replied: "Of course, but have these boys ever hesitated when it suited *them*?"[64] Both truth and decorum were served.

In correspondence with Östen Undén, Hammarskjöld had elaborated a theory concerning the Soviet bloc's attack on his person and the office of the secretary-general. It turned on the notion that the attack had little or nothing to do with the Congo, which served only as a pretext, and everything to do with Khrushchev's disarmament proposal. Were the proposal to make its way, Khrushchev wanted to be sure that an international police force could act only if the Soviet Union agreed—hence the need for a troika, a built-in veto, and the stipulation of unanimous decision making. "With his notion of tactics and psychology," Hammarskjöld wrote, "what followed is quite logical once he got the anti-colonial chance and the Congo windfall."[65] This is only the minimal core of Hammarskjöld's reasoning, his effort to anticipate and prevent "checkmate in three moves." The analysis gives little weight to the Soviet self-image as leading friend of the newly independent nations and leading adversary of colonialism. As well, it doesn't take into account Khrushchev's love of revolutionary theater: his performance in the General Assembly had a revolutionary flavor, as if October 1917 were being dusted off. In the course of that spring, however, Khrushchev did mention the link between disarmament and the proposed troika.

The Soviet bloc continued to gnaw away at Hammarskjöld, the structure of his office, and the Congo operation, and he continued to listen and attend as needed to other business until the sessions of March 29th and April 5th, when he chose at last to speak. On the 29th, replying on matters of detail to the Congolese ambassador, who had just spoken, he also offered a broad perspective that drew on the metaphor he had much in mind: avalanche.

> It has been said that the United Nations operation in the Congo is disappointing or even a failure. It seems reasonable to ask those who say so whether the reason for their disappointment is that the Organization has done anything less than it could do, or that elements beyond

the control of the Organization have created difficulties which at the present stage of its development are insuperable. . ., even when [the Organization] is strained to its utmost capacity. One can blame a mountain climber for his failure to reach the summit when his road has been blocked by an avalanche, but to do so is an irresponsible play on words.[66]

It was effective public speech. Who wouldn't be struck by the metaphor? But privately the theme was also in his thoughts. The day after this talk in the Assembly—Maundy Thursday in the Christian calendar, commemorating the Last Supper—he took time to write out in his journal a few lines from Ibsen's play *Brand*, which ends dramatically with an avalanche.[67] A mysterious voice speaks from beyond and above the avalanche that takes the hero's life: *Han er Deus Caritatis*—He is the God of Love. Hammarskjöld's perceptions of the chaos and menace of the Congo Crisis flowed alongside a determined effort to remember that there is more to reality than chaos, menace, and slander.

This dividing line between divine truth and power and the world's appears again in verses from Psalm 73 he wrote into his journal at some point in the next five weeks. The few words he noted down are in the nature of an aide-mémoire pointing to the text as a whole, to which he returned from time to time in the remaining months of his life. One of the great laments in biblical poetry, it records a sudden shift in perspective with psychological realism. The psalmist recognizes with physical revulsion—one can still sense it—the power, freedom of action, and deceptiveness of harmful people:

> Their eyes swell with fatness: and they do even what they lust. They corrupt others, and speak of wicked blasphemy: their talking is against the most high.
> For they stretch forth their mouth unto the heaven: and their tongue goeth through the world. . . .
> Lo, these are the ungodly, these prosper in the world: . . . And I said,
> Then have I cleansed my heart in vain and washed my hands in innocency. . . .
> All the day long have I been punished: and chastened every morning.

These are not yet the lines Hammarskjöld wrote out, though he surely had them much in mind. Their horrified, surreal imagery of mouths and tongues reached him from ancient times as the perfect evocation of the ordeal in which he and so many others were immersed. A few lines later, the psalmist acknowledges that he cannot understand why evil prevails. Utterly lost, he takes refuge in the Lord. It was these lines Hammarskjöld chose to record:

Then thought I to understand this:
but it was too hard for me;
Until I went into the sanctuary of God.

Here the theme of sanctuary recurs with all possible urgency. This book began with it and we encountered it again when Hammarskjöld was redesigning the Room of Quiet. *Markings* was a sanctuary. The psalm continues:

. . . then understood I the end of these men.
Namely, how thou dost set them in slippery places: and castest them down and destroyeth them.
Oh, how suddenly do they consume: perish, and come to a fearful end!
Yea, even like as a dream when one awaketh; so shalt thou make their image to vanish out of the city. . . .
My flesh and my heart faileth: but God is the strength of my heart, and my portion for ever.[68]

Through these magnificent lines, Hammarskjöld was looking at the extremes in his life—his grappling with adversities in New York and the Congo, of which there seemed to be no end, and the moments, however brief, when he found his way into the sanctuary of God. Rarely in his UN years, perhaps never, was the distance between his inner life and outer circumstances so vast, or the need so great for faith at more than one level. In mid-May, he wrote to John Steinbeck about "all those compromises which we fool ourselves into calling small," and hoped to see him soon. "I might feel like telling you about a few of the things *I* see happening and which really make continuing faith as necessary as it makes it difficult."[69]

On April 5th in the General Assembly, Hammarskjöld spoke at length to answer the charges brought by Gromyko. He was aware as he did so that Kasavubu had recently used the radio to rally the Congolese against the UN. "Let the leopard, symbol of the Congo, show his claws, make his mighty voice resound, and leap forward towards the foe."[70] Both in the Congo and at UN headquarters, absurdity had reached a culminating point. In response, Hammarskjöld exercised meticulous rationality—but not without sharp turns toward his adversaries and appeals to the conscience of all delegations. Referring to the many charges made against him, he said, "Members of the Assembly will have noted that these accusations, couched in the most general and condemning terms, were put forward without attempts to give them credence by the indication of any single substantive fact on which they might be based. . . ." So far, so composed.

But what followed is a cry to heaven, to history, to conscience—quietly spoken, no doubt, and closely reasoned, but white-hot.

> Where, in any parliament, jealous of its democratic traditions, its integrity, and its respect for the human person, could such allegations be made without those making them trying to justify their case or, especially, without the parliamentary body requesting them to do so? The United Nations General Assembly has been called a parliament of nations. Are the peoples of the world less jealous of the integrity of the General Assembly than the members of a nation are of the integrity of its democratic institutions? . . .
>
> When we come under responsible criticism, we accept it as a valuable contribution to the common effort, aimed at improving its quality. However, when criticism takes such a direction as to negate the very ideals for which the Organization stands and for which we consider it a privilege to work, one may be led to ask whether the spirit of this Organization will justify for long the faith on which the efforts are and must be based. . . .[71]

He expressed his firm refusal to resign at the request "of a Big Power and its like-minded supporters." On the other hand, he continued, "I regard the will of the General Assembly in this respect as my law, and the General Assembly may thus consider itself as seized with a standing offer of resignation, were the Assembly to find it to be in the best interest of the Organization that I leave."[72] Momentous words: he put himself wholly and squarely in the hands of the General Assembly. He was confident of his standing with the majority, but it was nonetheless a sincere act of trust. The Assembly finished out the week in the manner to which it had now become accustomed, with attacks by Zorin (again on the job) and his bloc allies, rejoinders as needed from Hammarskjöld, and statements from less embattled nations' delegates, which cleared the air for a short nonce.

That weekend, April 8th through 9th, Hammarskjöld probably took refuge in Brewster. There was time for correspondence. To his friend Beskow he confessed, "You will understand that when I get off the hook, I kind of sink back into passivity, which in due time, I hope, will be reasonably fertile, but which for the moment represents a somewhat barren land as human contacts and correspondence go."[73] To Uno Willers, the library director in Stockholm who discreetly helped him stay in touch with Chinese diplomats, he wrote an unexpectedly optimistic note:

> Tactically I am very satisfied with the situation here, as the third Russian assault seems to have been broken quite successfully. Of course they

will come back, but I guess they have to rearrange their forces and arguments a bit before starting it all over again, and in the meanwhile things may have changed also on my side.

The Congo continues extremely confused with some quite dangerous elements, but if my instincts are correct, the pattern which has been in the back of my mind is slowly beginning to emerge in the field. And if this is so, we might be in calmer waters before too long. . . .[74]

His friends were justifiably worried about him—how long could he withstand the avalanche of personal attacks, the ceaseless demand for analysis, decision, communication, and action in the chaos of the Congo? Alexis Leger (the poet Saint-John Perse) wrote from his home in Washington, DC, in these mid-April days to express his concern.

My dear Dag,

I can't open the newspapers anymore without being moved by friendly thoughts of you. The ordeal whose heavy burden you carry alone is too cruel. In the long run, it is beyond human measure. And I worry about the limits of your physical resources—but certainly not spiritual!

. . . Your servitude is more exhausting than that of any statesman, of any chief in combat or any captain at his bridge. But when the storm lasts so long, one really must take a break from the watch . . . . Perhaps I am annoying you with my little sermon. But I can't stop thinking about the kind of life I have seen you lead for so long, which is too close to being superhuman. I follow all this with such anxiety and such apprehension. . . .[75]

Well said, sir, and true. But the next week would bring Hammarskjöld considerable satisfaction and vindication.

Vindication took the form of three resolutions successfully sponsored by coalitions of Afro-Asian member nations, among which one in particular, not quite deliberately, became a vote of confidence in the secretary-general and a welcome cure of the wound inflicted by the Security Council. The resolutions overall were sensible reinforcements of the Council's resolution on the departure of Belgians no matter what their roles, steps to avoid civil war, and steps toward national reconciliation. There was greater emphasis than before on the necessity to reconvene parliament under the safe-conduct and protection of UN peacekeepers. A brief resolution established by name a four-person, international commission to investigate promptly the deaths of Lumumba and his colleagues. The vote of confidence came about in the second resolution where it stipulated the need to "prevent the introduction of arms, military equipment, and supplies into the Congo, except in conformity with the resolutions of the United Nations."[76] Who was to do this? The original draft assigned the task to the secretary-general. The Guinean delegate demurred: reference to the secretary-general should be replaced by the words "all authorities concerned." A debate ensued in which the majority of African delegates argued for the original language. There was a vote—which language was it to be? The result was a formidable vindication: eighty-three in favor of specifically mentioning the secretary-general, eleven against, and five abstentions (including France, with which a separate, unhappy drama would soon unfold). Had Hammarskjöld any doubt that he had survived the campaign of denigration waged by the Soviet Union and its allies, this vote must have laid doubt to rest. The Congo Crisis was grievously unresolved, but he knew that he had a strong constituency behind him as he and his Secretariat colleagues set out to try again, under their wider mandate, to bring peace with justice to the Congo.

Three days later in the Assembly, Mr. Zorin took his last opportunity to attack—the 15th General Assembly was winding down—and Hammarskjöld took his last opportunity to speak immediately afterwards. In the battle of words with Khrushchev a subcurrent of humor had occasionally surfaced, recognition on both sides that Khrushchev had taken matters "over the top" into a zone of political burlesque that was nonetheless deadly serious. With Zorin there was nothing of the kind: he was a sullen fellow. Hammarskjöld met his charges without a good-natured smile and managed to lodge a dazzlingly clear point in the minds of Assembly delegates. "In considering the whole question of the implementation of the resolutions," he said,

> I think it would be appropriate to make a distinction between demands, authority, and means. I believe that all through the history of the Congo operation demands have gone far beyond authorization and authorization far beyond means. That is the only comment I would like to make on the new complaints.[77]

Ite missa est. The horrendous 15th General Assembly, an ordeal from start to finish, concluded on April 22nd with a predawn vote, of course bitterly debated, about funding the Congo operation. Later that day Hammarskjöld put a note in the mail to Beskow.

Six o'clock this morning we buried the 15th session of the General Assembly after various political and moral striptease acts—performed by less than well-shaped personalities. Now I guess I should "relax" for some 24 hours before trying to tidy up everything that has been deranged during this strange session which, anyway from my point of view, was fruitful since the wear and tear process, which the Russians tried on me and my position, did not work while it proved highly effective with regard to their own impact on the Afro-Asians. This showed up just as well yesterday night as Saturday a week ago when they tried a vote of confidence which flopped hopelessly. . . .[78]

You must not flinch

Politics in the Congo now varied from respectable and responsible to the disconcerting blend of Gilbert and Sullivan and Grand Guignol that Hammarskjöld had detected some years earlier in the Lebanon-Jordan crisis. In the realm of respectable and responsible, Kasavubu had rethought his violent opposition to the UN ("Let the leopard show his claws!") and made the decision to negotiate and sign an utterly sensible agreement to cooperate with the UN.[79] The two diplomats sent to the Congo by Hammarskjöld had established a good rapport with Kasavubu; his change of heart and direction was largely their work, although Kasavubu and others in Léopoldville had been appalled by recent reports of atrocities committed by mercenaries in Katanga and realized that it was time to give UN policies a better chance.[80] The agreement underscored the sovereignty of the republic but invited UN cooperation on many key issues, from eliminating "deleterious foreign influence" to technical aid and training and the reorganization of the army. Receiving from Kasavubu the negotiated agreement for his signature, Hammarskjöld was particularly gracious in the note of reply accompanying his approval. "May I say that I have been encouraged by the results of the discussions which took place between you and your colleagues and my representatives in terms not only of the substance of the agreement itself, but also of the spirit of constructive cooperation and mutual trust which my representatives have reported to me. . . ."[81] This was a spectacular advance, bearing out Hammarskjöld's comment that "we might be in calmer waters before too long."

Where dangerous comedy was concerned, on April 24th many though not quite all Congolese leaders reconvened at Coquihatville

(now Mbandaka), a city some four hundred miles northeast of Léopoldville on the Congo River, to reconsider the political order planned at
Tananarive and disavowed shortly after. There were some two hundred
participants, including European advisers. Mr. Kasavubu again faced
Mr. Tshombe across the table. In the first session Tshombe insisted that
Kasavubu rescind the new agreement with the UN. Kasavubu refused.
Tshombe then insisted that he abide by the Tananarive agreement,
which gave Katanga and other potential states of the Congo a high
degree of autonomy under a weak central authority. Kasavubu refused.
Whereupon Tshombe and his entourage (in part Belgian advisers) left
the meeting in anger though it had scarcely begun and went out to
the airport—where Congolese troops loyal to Kasavubu and Mobutu
wouldn't allow him to board and depart. Hoskyns writes that it is unclear whether the soldiers acted under orders or without orders, but
there was a general conviction in the city and region that the politicians
should together accomplish something for the country rather than go
their separate ways.[82] Tshombe and his comrades spent that night in
the airport lounge and the following night also—it can't have been
pleasant—while Kasavubu and his comrades decided what to do. Their
decision was to place Tshombe under house arrest and to expel at once
his Belgian advisers. The conference continued without Tshombe to
its conclusion on May 28th and, in the new climate of reasonableness
that had blown into the Congo, it reached a good deal of clarity about
convening parliament, selecting a new government of greater national
unity, revising the flawed Loi Fondamentale in a joint Congolese-UN
task force, better managing the army, and much else.

Tshombe's arrest of course created a fraught situation. As we know,
the arrest of senior Congolese politicians had a miserable track record.
Elisabethville was covered with posters saying, "He is suffering for us.
Be worthy of him."[83] He wasn't treated as an out-and-out enemy—he
was comfortable and regularly saw other politicians, Mobutu would
drop by with an offering of whisky—but he was nonetheless detained
and under threat of trial for treason. In mid-June a deal was worked out:
released from custody on June 22nd, two days later he signed a "protocol
of agreement" based on the decisions reached at Coquilhatville in his
absence.[84] Returning home to a hero's welcome, he debated for some days
with his ministerial colleagues and Belgian advisers what to do next,
then publicly abrogated his agreement with the explanation that it had

been obtained under duress. "*Vive le Katanga indépendant!*"—this from a speech he gave on the 28th. By this time he and his colleagues had assembled, and would continue to assemble, a gendarmerie officered by Belgian, French, South African, and British mercenaries who came to be known as *les affreux*. The word is strongly idiomatic. To say that they were fearsome or frightening isn't saying enough; "dreadful" is closer. Urquhart had direct experience of them and didn't like what he saw. In the oral history project he gave his assessment. "A great number of [exiled French paratroopers] showed up in Katanga as military advisers to Tshombe. They were very bad stuff. The ordinary mercenaries were a bunch of clapped-out British, South Africans, . . . mostly adventurers; this lot were . . . professional soldiers [with] huge battle experience. They had been in Dien Bien Phu, Algeria, and God knows where else. They were very, very good officers and fanatical, all-white, anti-black, right-wing. . . . They were real trouble. . . ."[85]

The carousel continued whirling. However, not with quite the same abandon. A new government in Brussels, in which the well-regarded Paul-Henri Spaak was foreign minister, promised at least incremental change in Belgian policy. And the will to reconvene parliament and restore constitutionality was firm. Defended with arms by *les affreux*, with political know-how by Belgian advisers, and with funding by entrenched business interests, Katanga was the unyielding problem.

We should turn back now to Hammarskjöld in mid-April. At that time he found food for thought in a newly published interview with Nikita Khrushchev conducted by Walter Lippmann (1889–1974), the distinguished American journalist who was among Hammarskjöld's firm friends. Lippmann invariably understood what Hammarskjöld was doing and in his widely read column provided thoughtful, often eloquent support. Their relation reached past politics; together they were inspectors of humanity. "I would love to roam around with you and Walter," Hammarskjöld wrote to Helen Lippmann that summer, "talking about essentials of life at a place like yours, so infinitely much more real than most of the things with which we have to deal professionally and, therefore, so likely to put them in the right perspective."[86] Published in the *New York Herald Tribune* on April 17th, the interview took place at Khrushchev's Black Sea dacha, site of the great rowboat incident of a few years earlier. A point from the interview, altogether thought provoking, found its way into the opening lines of a major talk

Hammarskjöld may already have begun preparing in thought if not on paper. Scheduled for May 30th at the University of Oxford, it was to be a talk on the role of the international civil servant. There he hoped to stand back from the turmoil of the Congo and the incessant hectoring he had been experiencing as the world's foremost and most exposed international civil servant. He had in mind to reason freshly about this still novel role, detached from ideological, national, and partisan passions, attached to a Charter, a Declaration of Human Rights, and a heritage of sound diplomatic practice. The talk would not and could not be an act of revenge for the misery he and his colleagues had suffered; it would have no taste of that. It would nonetheless state his understanding freely and restore the complex goodness of the role he and other members of the Secretariat had made the center of their working lives.

Exploring various topics in succession, the Lippmann interview looked at the obstacles to Khrushchev's disarmament proposal. Were it to be adopted, who would oversee a disarmament agreement? Khrushchev's response supports Hammarskjöld's theory about the purpose of Soviet attacks on his office. "[Khrushchev] was vehement and unqualified," reported Lippmann. "He would never accept a single neutral administrator. Why? Because, he said, while there are neutral countries, there are no neutral men. . . . We cannot have another Hammarskjöld, no matter where he comes from among the neutral countries." Lippmann continued, "I found this enlightening. It was plain to me that here is a new dogma, that there are no neutral men. . . . The Soviet Government has now come to the conclusion that there can be no such thing as an impartial civil servant in this deeply divided world, and that the kind of political celibacy which the British theory of the civil service calls for is in international affairs a fiction. This new dogma has long consequences . . . ."[87]

Hammarskjöld would work into the Oxford talk the charming notion of political celibacy. "It seemed almost axiomatic," he said of the League of Nations, "that the civil service had to be 'politically celibate' (though not perhaps politically virgin)"[88]—a remark remembered, surely with delight, by later generations at the UN. But what most provoked his interest was Khrushchev's confident formulation: there are no neutral men. In cooperation with Oscar Schachter, his senior legal counselor and later a celebrated professor of law at Columbia University, he began constructing an extended exploration of the international civil servant with May 30th, Oxford, in mind.[89] It was to be both a statement of professional identity and a matrix of ideas for future generations. Khrushchev had contributed a gem.

The Oxford talk occupies the center of a period of weeks when Hammarskjöld at last had time to turn inward. From time to time in recent years he had experienced and welcomed waves of retrospection. While the Swedish Academy address of 1954 about his father had met an institutional obligation, the haiku poetry in *Markings* through the summer and fall of 1959 was a spontaneous and richly felt exercise in recovering youthful memories of Uppsala. Something now prompted him again to review his life and restate its guiding principles, to formulate his concerns in austere lines of poetry, to put into words his acceptance of whatever fate might have in store. It was as if well-chosen words signed a contract with himself and his Lord. That spring he had also accepted a commission from the Swedish Touring Association, of which he remained an officer, to contribute an essay to the club's yearbook. This too would be part of his remembering. At some point he began writing an account of the cycle of seasons, events, and moods associated with the Vasa castle in Uppsala, the home of his youth. By mid-July he had a draft to send to his friend Gierow, whose literary judgment he trusted. Needless to say, throughout this period he remained engaged in political and administrative challenges, but the notes we should listen for are internal.

One of the most powerful entries in *Markings* is dated Pentecost according to the calendar of Christian festivals, Sunday, May 21st that year. It is also the first original entry in *Markings* for the year—the first not quoted from elsewhere. Had he not written these lines, there is much we would not know. They virtually summarize his inner life since entering UN service. That he felt moved at Pentecost to cast his experience in terms of hearing a call and responding cannot be accidental: Pentecost celebrates a fiery call and the disciples' initially confused, primal response (Acts 2:1–6).

> I don't know who—or what—put the question, I don't know when it was put. I don't even remember answering. But at some moment I did answer *yes* to someone—or something—and from that hour I was certain that existence is meaningful and that, therefore, my life, in self-surrender, had a goal.
>
> From that moment I have known what it means "not to look back," and "to take no thought for the morrow."
>
> Led by the Ariadne's thread of my answer through the labyrinth of life, I came to a time and place where I realized that the way leads

to a triumph which is a catastrophe, and to a catastrophe which is a triumph, that the price for committing one's life would be reproach, and that the only elevation possible to man lies in the depths of humiliation. After that, the word "courage" lost its meaning, since nothing could be taken from me.

As I continued along the way, I learned, step by step, word by word, that behind every saying of the hero of the Gospels stands *one* man and *one* man's experience. Also behind the prayer that the cup might pass from him and his promise to drink it. Also behind each of the words from the Cross.[90]

I circle this statement most respectfully. When a person speaks his or her truth with utter concentration, without a wasted word, there is an instinctive recoil from interpretation. Of course, one could say something about the breadth of his perception of the divine at this time in his life: it is both "someone" or "something" and also precisely incarnate in Jesus. One could reason about that—but I won't. One could recall the power of his *yes*, sustained over so many years. One could argue with Hammarskjöld's extreme view that "the only elevation possible to man lies in the depths of humiliation"—but why would we do so after what we have witnessed of his experience in the Congo Crisis? He has earned his extreme view. We could also recall his discovery years ago in the Swedish far north of the primacy of the present moment and recognize how steadfastly he has lived by that insight. But that is obvious in the words he set down here; we needn't linger over it. There is more still to notice and savor, including his insistence on the singular humanity of Jesus. Committed to the Imitation of Christ taught by Thomas à Kempis, he had touched in his life and trials something of that singularity: the story told just one way, not abstract in the least but vividly particular, with just this pain, just these thoughts and responses, just this devoted intention to see the story through to the end.

Well, I have interpreted a little, but in the manner musicians call "cancrizans"—crab-like, backing away, largely unwilling.

From early July 1960, when the situation in the Congo first reached the UN, to what he broadly dated as "spring 1961," he had a dark poem in progress in the pages of his journal. He must have started and reworked it from time to time as the first ten months or so of the crisis unfolded. A troubling poem, not a masterpiece, it is biographically revealing. He imagines himself as an early Christian preparing for martyrdom in an arena, a Colosseum of some kind. He is courageous, he defends himself in gladiatorial battle. Abruptly the metaphor shifts to something like an Aztec sacrifice: he is "strapped fast to the altar," silent as his body is "slit up and the live heart plucked out."[91] It is not the only poem of its kind. In early June there is another, again stoic, in which he accepts to die in a hail of arrows from unnamed executioners. "What have I to fear? . . . What is there in that to cry about?" he asks. "Others have gone before, others will follow."[92] On June 18th there is another quite like it. "He will come out between two warders . . . He has not betrayed us. He will meet his end without weakness. . . ."[93] On July 30th there is another, this time seemingly the record of a dream in which neither victim nor assailant has clear identity: "Who the quarry, who the silent hunter . . . ?"[94] Were these poems of the Congo, of the UN, or of both?

That was one mood. But he cannot be understood narrowly through these months, as if one mood or attitude prevailed. He experienced and recorded other states of mind and heart—cheerful, prayerful, questioning, free and well. One such, of June 8th, possesses great charm. It is a call to his body for courage.

> Body,
> My playmate!
> Neither the master
> Nor the slave,
> A buoyant mind
> Shall bear you along,
> While you cheer my way
> With your lively flame.
>
> But body,
> My playmate,
> You must not flinch
> Nor fail me when
> The moment comes
> To do the impossible.[95]

Responsibilities cannot be laid aside

There is a pleasant photograph of Hammarskjöld at Oxford. Wearing a Tudor bonnet and academic gown, with a sheaf of papers in hand, he looks like Henry the Eighth's slim brother.[96] On the occasion of receiving an honorary doctorate in law at the beautiful Sheldonian Theatre in

Oxford, he delivered an exacting lecture under the title "The International Civil Servant in Law and in Fact."[97] Oscar Schachter, who helped him
write it, recalled years later that "the lecture was not a purely theoretical exercise. . . . Underlying the carefully worded analysis of history and
ideas . . . was a poignant personal drama. . . . But, characteristically, he
also saw the issues as transcending his personal position. . . ."[98] Occupying
an important place in Hammarskjöld's thought, the lecture has a juridical
flavor as if its purpose is to rebuild, brick by brick, a damaged structure of
ideas and values. Within its history of the international civil service from
Sir Eric Drummond and the League of Nations to the United Nations,
and its account of stresses and grey areas of authority and responsibility
in recent years, certain reflections deserve a place here. He began with the
Lippmann-Khrushchev interview. "Were it to be considered," he said of
the international civil service, "that . . . this radical innovation in international life rests on a false assumption because 'no man can be neutral,'
then we would be thrown back to 1919, and a searching reappraisal would
become necessary." After some pages of historical and legal analysis, he
turned to circumstances in which "the Secretary-General was confronted
with mandates of a highly general character, expressing the bare minimum
of agreement attainable. . . . That the execution of these tasks involved the
exercise of political judgment by the Secretary-General was, of course, evident to the Member states themselves." Among various instances, naturally
he spoke of the Congo Crisis. "These recent examples," he continued,

> demonstrate the extent to which the Member states have entrusted
> the Secretary-General with tasks that have required him to take action
> which unavoidably may have to run counter to the views of at least some
> Member states. . . . A simple solution for the dilemmas thus posed for
> the Secretary-General might seem to be for him to refer the problem
> to the political organ for it to resolve the question. . . . But the serious
> problems arise precisely because it is so often not possible for the organs
> themselves to resolve the controversial issue. . . . The required majority
> in the Security Council or General Assembly may not be available. . . .

He weighed various options which could follow from that point, including
refusal to implement a resolution that leaves so much in doubt. And just
there he spoke resolutely, though indirectly, of his own decision process.

> For the Secretary-General this course of action—or more precisely, non-
> action—may be tempting; it enables him to avoid criticism by refusing

to act until other political organs resolve the dilemma. An easy refuge may thus appear to be available. But would such a refuge be compatible with the responsibility placed upon the Secretary-General by the Charter? Is he entitled to refuse to carry out the decision properly reached by the organs, on the ground that the specific implementation would be opposed to positions some Member states might wish to take, as indicated, perhaps, by an earlier minority vote? Of course the political organs may always instruct him to discontinue the implementation of a resolution, but when they do not so instruct him and the resolution remains in effect, is the Secretary-General legally and morally free to take no action, particularly in a matter considered to affect international peace and security? Should he, for example, have abandoned the operation in the Congo because almost any decision he made as to the composition of the Force or its role would have been contrary to the attitudes of some Members as reflected in debates, and maybe even in votes, although not in decisions?

The answers seem clear enough in law; the responsibilities of the Secretary-General under the Charter cannot be laid aside merely because the execution of decisions by him is likely to be politically controversial. . . .

In my opinion and on the basis of my experience, . . . it is possible for the Secretary-General to carry out his tasks in controversial political situations with full regard to his exclusively international obligation under the Charter and without subservience to a particular national or ideological attitude. This is not to say that the Secretary-General is a kind of Delphic oracle who alone speaks for the international community. . . .[99]

In the last paragraphs of his talk, Hammarskjöld drew even closer to his own experience and practice. Several lines here we have seen before; this is their context.

It is obvious from what I have said that the international civil servant cannot be accused of lack of neutrality simply for taking a stand on a controversial issue when this is his duty and cannot be avoided. But there remains a serious intellectual and moral problem as we move within an area inside which personal judgment must come into play. Finally, we have to deal here with a question of integrity or with, if you please, a question of conscience.

The international civil servant must keep himself under the strictest observation. He is not requested to be a neuter in the sense that he has to have no sympathies or antipathies, that there are to be no interests which are close to him in his personal capacity or that he is to have no ideas or ideals that matter for him. However, he is requested to be fully aware of those human reactions and meticulously check himself so that they are not permitted to influence his actions. . . .

If the international civil servant knows himself to be free from such personal influence in his actions and guided solely by the common aims and rules laid down for, and by the Organization he serves and by recognized legal principles, then he has done his duty, and then he can face the criticism which, even so, will be unavoidable. As I said, at the final last, this is a question of integrity, and if integrity in the sense of respect for law and respect for truth were to drive him into positions of conflict with this or that interest, then that conflict is a sign of his neutrality and not of his failure to observe neutrality—then it is in line, not in conflict with his duties as an international civil servant.[100]

And so he had, after all, spoken his mind. Although he had immersed the argument in useful preliminary pages of historical and legal context, it came in the end to this: a statement for all to hear of integrity and exquisite caution in his exercise of leadership in the Congo Crisis. Mr. Zorin could not rise to contradict him; Mr. Gromyko was presumably in Moscow; Mr. Khrushchev and his shoe were nowhere to be seen. Hammarskjöld had spoken for the principles guiding the UN and for the enduring status of the office of the secretary-general. It was his last major speech.

The poem of unanswerable questions

Before setting out for Oxford, Hammarskjöld had been in touch with the superb British sculptor Barbara Hepworth and arranged to meet her in London on May 31st at an exhibition of her work. She had in mind to offer him a sculpture, and he set himself the pleasant task of finding which sculpture it was without a hint from her. He easily succeeded. A gallery assistant recalled later that when he arrived and scanned for the intended sculpture, she had never witnessed such tangible attention. Hammarskjöld and Hepworth had corresponded and occasionally met since late 1956. Her letters always spoke from the heart. In fall 1960, when the Soviet campaign against him was advancing nicely, she had written the most encouraging of notes: "Almost everybody I meet is completely aware of the fact that you are the only living person both able & willing to help humanity—everywhere the *gratitude* for this & for your strength is profound."[101] He owned several works by her, both sculpture and drawings; her work epitomized the spare elegance and spiritual atmosphere of the contemporary art to which he felt akin. As Martin Buber was the living philosopher to whom he felt most akin, she was the artist. Upon his return from London, he put a note in the mail to her about their meeting: "It was a sunny moment, full of impressions of perfect beauty, but beauty used as a road to some very fundamental experiences and, if I may say so, expressions of faith. . . . I hope that . . . I shall have the great pleasure of seeing you here. In the meanwhile I promise you that we shall, for our part, continue as well as we can to model in actions and words what you are so fortunate to express, to perfection, visibly and tangibly."[102] One can see why some commentators have detected between them signs of a late romance. It was probably better than romance: it was sincere love and care, seeing with the same eyes.

At the first press conference after Oxford, journalists were naturally interested to follow up with Hammarskjöld, and he proved willing to speak in what he called "more personal terms." "It may be true," he said,

> that in a very deep, human sense there is no neutral individual, because . . . everyone, if he is worth anything, has to have his ideas and ideals— things which are dear to him, and so on. But what I do claim is that even a man who is in that sense not neutral can very well undertake and carry through neutral actions, because that is an act of integrity. That is to say, I would say there is no neutral man, but there is, if you have integrity, neutral action. . . . I am not neutral as regards the Charter; I am not neutral as regards facts. But that is not what we mean. What is meant by "neutrality" in this kind of debate is, of course, neutrality in relation to interests; and there I do claim that there is no insurmountable difficulty for anybody with the proper kind of guiding principles in carrying through such neutrality one hundred percent.[103]

Home from Oxford within a very few days, Hammarskjöld found time over the weekend of June 3rd to see to correspondence. He wrote to Barbara Hepworth and Karl Ragnar Gierow, and at length to his brother Sten. This last, a spirited letter, ranged in theme from weary reflections about diplomacy and a swipe at Khrushchev to a distinctly unfavorable comparison between biblical prophets and contemporary journalists. He was relaxing.

> As usual, there is both too much and too little to tell from here, too much in terms of noise and events, too little in the sense that even big noises and supposedly important events by sheer repetition get solidly deflated into monotony. Poor boys and girls who, when entering politics

and diplomacy, expect something adventurous and glamorous, when for those who have a sense of responsibility it is just another "corvée" [chore], as in fact all other decent work is, with the added disadvantage of alternatively too hot and too cold winds of publicity.

The big shoe-thumping fellow continues as a dark thunderhead to threaten all unrepentant "non-communists" with hail and thunder and probably also locusts and other plagues traditionally favored by tribal gods, if we are to believe what we were told in school. Some believe in umbrellas and some in propitiating sacrifices and some go for a holiday. The classic role of the prophets has been taken over by the newspapermen but they prophesy for profit and in that respect—as well as in the question of prose style—they differ from Jeremiah. To continue with these free associations to the Bible, I am in this situation constantly reminded of the good old story about Jehovah's willingness to save the "cities of the plain" if he could find ten righteous men.

I apologize to characterize the situation from my angle in terms such as those I use, but they really give the best summing up, short of a boring enumeration of moves and counter-moves and threats and intrigues.[104]

Early summer brought something like a surcease in the tragic course of events in the Congo. The authorities in Léopoldville and Stanleyville and the United Nations team were cooperating on preparations to reconvene parliament at the University of Lovanium in a near suburb of Léopoldville. Tshombe had removed Katanga from the picture but events moved on without him. Hammarskjöld also experienced surcease, in some respects to very positive effect. He found time to advance the project for a mural decoration in the new UN library (Bo Beskow, artist) and arranged for Beskow to spend a week as his guest in mid-June. The unexpected calm also left time to look back.

> Sleepless questions
> In the small hours:
> Have I done right?
> Why did I act
> Just as I did?
> Over and over again
> The same steps,
> The same words:
> Never the answer.[105]

I showed these lines to a friend. She was overwhelmed with admiration that the harshness of events, the hard sequence of decisions, the abuse he had taken from so many at such length had not hardened him inside. He could doubt himself, he was uneasy. She felt that his vulnerability crowned his greatness.

On Sunday June 11th, Hammarskjöld recorded in his journal a complex vision. Was it of the kind that flashes through the mind, whole in that instant but later needing a sequence of thoughts and words to capture it? The early lines recall a slender column of language we have seen, from the end of 1960 ("The way, / you shall follow it . . ."), but later lines open out into an enigmatic, radiant vision of release.

> Summoned
> To carry it,
> Alone
> To assay it,
> Chosen
> To suffer it,
> Free
> To deny it,
> I saw
> For one moment
> The sail
> In the sun storm,
> Alone
> On a wave crest,
> Far off,
> Bearing from land.
>
> For one moment
> I saw—[106]

I don't think anyone reads "it" as the sail; the reference must be to the "it" with which he had been confronted in the past year and for which he carried a lonely burden of leadership, however much helped by coworkers. That is the context for what follows: a vision of freedom, a departing sailboat far at sea, sighted only for a moment "in the sun storm," *i solstormen*. The phrase can refer to solar storms of the kind astronomers track, but that is surely not the meaning. Are we to imagine a majestically active sun, its aureole enveloping the sailboat, not just a light in the sky but the icon of a realm beyond? For once Hammarskjöld's aloneness seems not a personal misery or burden of office but natural, desirable, restful. However, the poet's closing insistence on "one moment" resituates him, and us, on this Earth.

Bo Beskow didn't neglect to record in later years an account of his mid-June visit. "I found him changed," he wrote.

> More tired, restless, and pessimistic than I had ever seen him. . . . The last year had left a mark on him.
>
> I asked as I used to do on meeting him again, "Do you still have faith in man?" Meaning the individual on his own, not in mobs or masses or political parties. Dag had always up to then answered positively, but this time he looked sad and pensive and he said, "No I never thought it possible, but lately I have come to understand that there are really evil persons—evil right through—only evil."[107]

Driving from Manhattan to Brewster for the weekend, they had a consequential conversation. "If I have only *one* unsolvable problem to think of night and day," Hammarskjöld was saying, "I can manage, and even if I have two or three at the same time—but when they keep multiplying, my brain starts to boil. I simply have to find something to translate. But what?"[108] The intimate exercise of translation was still his preferred counterbalance to politics. They considered various options: Beskow could recall discussion of Julien Gracq and Martin Buber, and surely Hermann Hesse came to mind (Hammarskjöld intended to send a copy of Hesse's marvelous short novel, *The Journey to the East*, to Barbara Hepworth). But the urgency of finding something perfect to translate slipped away until mid-August, when he resumed correspondence with Buber and efficiently arranged with Bonnier in Stockholm to publish a translation of Buber's *I and Thou*. Estimating that final manuscript might be ready by January, he must have felt that the Congo Crisis would no longer command every hour of the day.

The hawks are hungry

"It is too early to say anything definite," he wrote to his brother Bo on June 22nd, "but things in Congo are finally moving as planned—in fact, as planned for something like ten months—and if we can keep up the momentum, they may be brought to a point where we can readjust our presence and our work to a more normal operation. However, you never know with the Congolese, who are unsurpassed in their mastery of the absolutely irrational."[109] With a staff member in Geneva a few weeks later, he was even more reassuring: "I have the definite feeling that we are beginning to get the Congo situation under control."[110] He was in Geneva for a regularly scheduled meeting but also conferred with the new Belgian foreign minister about affairs in Katanga, particularly the needs to replace Belgian political advisers with UN representatives and to do something about the mercenaries under Tshombe's command. Some progress was achieved, but on the military side Hoskyns records that more than five hundred foreign officers and enlisted men remained in Katanga in early August.[111] We know Urquhart's assessment of the top echelon.

The parliamentary assembly at Lovanium opened on July 16th under the protection of UN peacekeepers. Policies and safeguards were in place for a successful meeting: an electrified fence with a single guarded gate; no money, arms, or stray visitors; no one to leave until all business was transacted; all interested parties represented except Katanga; and a general understanding that the prime minister would be either Antoine Gizenga, favored by the Lumumbist faction, or Cyrille Adoula, a moderate favored by the Western embassies. The gathering seemed sheltered from external influence or corruption; some delegates complained that it was monastic. However, the UN authorities had overlooked a number of details that would have occurred to any reader of spy novels. Mr. Devlin, the CIA station chief, had discovered a sewer pipe large enough for a man to walk or wriggle through, which allowed his agents to bypass the fence and security checks. He had also arranged for a two-way radio in the car of at least one of his high-level sympathizers among Léopoldville politicians. In consequence, he was able to follow the proceedings, able also to send cash and buy votes in order to promote an Adoula victory.[112] Other agents of other countries were engaged in similar mischief, but the Americans apparently outbid them. Linnér himself, despite the policy of nonintervention in domestic politics, is said to have persuaded Kasavubu to take various measures.[113] In the end, the outcome was reasonable: Adoula, widely respected, became prime minister; Gizenga accepted a post as first deputy prime minister and in September, after some hesitation, took up his duties; and Mobutu and the army for the moment fell in line. Albert Kalonji agreed to dissolve his secessionist state in South Kasai. Kasavubu's presidency was never in question. The Congo, without Katanga, had at last restored constitutional government. On August 2nd at UN headquarters Hammarskjöld circulated a report on the meeting and its outcomes, including the texts of two resolutions unanimously passed at Lovanium. The first expressed gratitude to the United Nations for the security it had provided; the second proclaimed the new government as the sole legitimate authority in the republic. The fundamental, and dangerous, opposition between Léopoldville and Elisabethville continued without remedy.

Hammarskjöld was of course pressed for time, but by mid-July he was sufficiently confident of his essay for the Touring Association to send it to Gierow and others for comment. From its opening lines, he was re-membering: "June evening. The migratory flocks of students have left." The accompanying letter to Gierow began with a practical discussion of how to fund performances by Gierow's Swedish National Theater at the 1962 World's Fair in Seattle. Hammarskjöld was always interested in arts patronage; like translation, it was a counterpoint and it united people in a festive spirit. Then he turned to the matter at hand. "From my angle," he wrote about the essay in progress,

> it is very much an experiment. The stuff, of course, is more personal, under the surface, than most readers will see. It has had to be written in a form which, for me at least, is rather untried. . . . As I have very little time to get a cold perspective myself. . . , I would be very happy if . . . you would run over the text and put your question marks where you think I may have slipped off the rails. . . . Petrén has sent me some rather stimu-lating notes. . . . [He] is amused but, it seems, also a little bit worried by my increasing tendency to use a slightly anglicized syntax. You may well be the same. I am not aware of it anymore.

And at the end he returned to the symbol they shared: the skylarks at Brewster.

> Ornithological reports from Brewster indicate that the skylarks are in very good shape, but that the hawks are hungry and spend the summer stretch-ing their wings, sharpening their beaks and letting their claws grow.[114]

That summer's hawk was Charles de Gaulle, president of the French Re-public since January 1959. Hammarskjöld had done his best to forge a relation with him that might stand them both in good stead. Naturally he was aware of de Gaulle's predisposition where the UN was concerned—"*ce machin*," that *thing*, he would call it in a speech of September 1960. He would also have been aware of de Gaulle's attitude toward him as secretary-general. In Urquhart's view, de Gaulle considered him "an international interloper attempting under false pretenses to gain admission to the hallowed fraternity of leaders of powerful sovereign states."[115] Suez was not long past, and the French-Algerian conflict had occasioned periodic debate and resolutions in the General Assembly that offended French diplomacy as violations of Article 2.7, noninterference in domestic affairs. By what right did the General Assembly in February and December 1957 (and again in December 1960) call for a "peaceful, democratic, and just solution" in Algeria?[116] And what right did the UN have to question French nuclear tests in the Sahara? When the time came, the French joined the Soviets in refusing to participate in funding the Congo operation. It was all rather a mess, but Hammarskjöld was nothing if not game. Why should a working relation with de Gaulle be more difficult than his relation with Ben-Gurion, for example, who was an equally strong-minded nationalist leader and intellectual?

After meeting de Gaulle in Paris, in August 1959, Hammarskjöld wrote a thoughtful note to Alexis Leger about his search for relationship with him. "Naturally," he wrote of his days in Paris,

> the main human experience was the long time I spent together with de Gaulle. In one way he surprised me—by a kind of warm simplicity which was in no way immediately visible, but could be elicited by a refusal from my side to treat either him or myself as an official personality. In everything he struck me as a very lonely man, far more used to listen to himself than to others. This left me with a great uncertainty regarding the extent to which I managed to get across to him what I wanted to say. This, also, in a way explains the discrepancy between the liberal and nearly Goethean philosophy of French politics which he developed and the realities of the policy of France as apparent to the world.[117]

And here he recounted an exchange that still leaves one dumbfounded.

> When I pointed out to him [this discrepancy] he did not understand me, but said that there could be no such discrepancy since—and this without any irony and quite unselfconsciously—"la France *c'est* moi."
> I believe that what may have resulted from the visit is a thin link of mutual human sympathy which may come to be needed with the strains on France-UN relations which undoubtedly are in front of us.[118]

He would have been thinking of Algeria and of tension between France and its former colony, Tunisia.

Anticipating a visit by de Gaulle to New York in March 1960, Hammar-skjöld cordially invited him to lunch at UN headquarters. De Gaulle replied by letter in a deliberately tone-deaf manner that left no doubt of his attitude:

> Mr. Secretary-General,
>
> I have received your letter and can tell you that in the course of my com-ing visit to New York it is not my intention to visit the United Nations. Furthermore, this organization will not, as far as I know, be in session at the time of my visit to New York. How would I be able to meet it?
>
> It will, on the other hand, Mr. Secretary-General, be entirely agree-able to me to receive you. . . .[119]

A month earlier, in a note circulated in the French government if not more widely, de Gaulle referred to "Mr. Hammarskjöld's ambition and vanity" with regard to the nations of French-speaking Africa. It was clear, he continued, that "the African leaders with whom Mr. H. was in touch immediately recognized that he could be for them a dispenser of gifts requiring no quid pro quo except, of course, contributions to his pretensions and pride."[120] Hardly preparation for a pleasant lunch. A few months later, on April 11th, he would again lay into the UN and Hammarskjöld at a press conference in Paris: "As the United Nations becomes a scene of disturbance, confusion, and division, it acquires the ambition to intervene in all kinds of matters. This is especially true of its officers. . . . It carries to the local scene its global incoherence [and] the personal conceptions of its various agents. . . ."[121]

Such was the troubled political and human background to an encoun-ter in summer 1961 that had nothing to do with petty one-upmanship or lofty condemnation. It had to do with aggression and bloodshed. Three years earlier, Hammarskjöld had played a part in calming a vio-lent dispute between France and Tunisia over Tunisian aid to Algerian independence fighters and French access to military bases it had retained in Tunisia. The issue of the continuing and unwelcome French military presence in Tunisia resurfaced in July when president Habib Bourguiba (1903–2000) communicated to the French government with consider-able force his government's wish for the French to withdraw from their base at Bizerte, a coastal city with a spacious harbor, and from one other site. Generally regarded as a patient negotiator, in this case Bourguiba was responding to various signals in his political environment, not least French-Algerian negotiations that could indirectly make it more difficult later to send the French home from Bizerte. De Gaulle refused to negotiate under conditions he described as a threat, and he regarded the base at Bizerte as essential to the security of France and the Western alliance. Bourguiba immediately lengthened the causal chain by ordering a naval blockade and deploying around the base both Tunisian troops and civilians under their protection. There was an exchange of fire, perhaps started by Tunisian fire on a French helicopter. De Gaulle ordered armored units to occupy the city with the help of seven thousand paratroopers airlifted from France. Both sides rapidly added to the scale and intensity of the encounter. The ensuing three-day battle was bloody and damaging to the city. Tunisia called for a meeting of the Security Council on charges of French aggression. France countercharged that it had done only what was necessary to defend the base and had already sought a cease-fire. The Council met on the 21st, Hammarskjöld in his usual place at the horseshoe table. The Tunisian chief of delegation, Mongi Slim, had been invited to attend though, as customary with such invitations, he did not have the right to vote.

The conflict at the UN and in Tunisia put to the test Hammarskjöld's thinking about neutral men and neutral action. President de Gaulle was deliberately rude to him, and French policy toward the Congo operation was dismissive. At the opposite pole of relationship, President Bourguiba and Mongi Slim were loyal to the UN and intelligently helpful to Hammarskjöld in his efforts to untangle Middle Eastern and postcolonial issues. He relied on them. Now it was their turn to rely on him. As he would later make clear in private correspondence, he was critical of both parties to this crisis and as a matter of principle followed the middle way of neutral action, but the French were quick to tell the world that he was acting on behalf of Tunisia. In part their own actions made it seem so.

On July 22nd, Hammarskjöld invoked his duty under Article 99 to advise the Council of the urgent need for a resolution, if possible that very day. He suggested that it contain a call for cease-fire and the return of armed forces to their original positions before the outbreak of violence. It should also explicitly state that the Security Council debate would continue. Led by Liberia, the Council adopted the resolution, with France pioneering a new pattern: refusing even to abstain. Away from the conference table, Slim asked Hammarskjöld for an observation team like the one that had been effective several years earlier on the Lebanon-Syria border, but to do so would have needed a Security Council mandate and unlikely French agreement. As prompt action of some kind was needed to insert the tangible influence of the UN into a conflict with unpredictable consequences, Hammarskjöld advised Bourguiba that if he were to invite him to Tunis for an exchange of views, that would fall within allowable boundaries and he would immediately respond. Without delay Bourguiba cabled the request. Hammarskjöld planned his departure, informed the French government through the French diplomat on duty that weekend in New York, and offered to stop in Paris after Tunis. He expected a response from Paris but, receiving none, left for Tunis in the evening of Sunday 23rd by way of Zurich, where he was joined by Piero Spinelli (whom we last knew as his special representative in the Middle East). Hammarskjöld had made clear to all concerned that a "direct and personal exchange of views" with Bourguiba and later, as he hoped, with de Gaulle, might be helpful but should not be construed as a substitute for the Security Council's continuing debate.[122]

In Tunis Hammarskjöld found the situation alarming. On the 25th he sent a letter to the French foreign minister, Maurice Couve de Murville, to state his concerns and ask for compliance with the Security Council resolution as a basis for further developments. More than twenty-four hours later he received a reply that dismissed his efforts, passed over in silence his offer to confer in Paris, and accused him of advocating the views of the Tunisians.[123] Given the day-long gap between communications, he decided to see Bizerte for himself and sent word to the commander of the French forces to expect a small convoy of cars. Flying the UN flag, his convoy passed through two French roadblocks but was stopped at a third where, despite Hammarskjöld's indignant protest, French paratroopers insisted on searching for weapons. Hammarskjöld later wrote that news cameras and reporters were already there to record the incident. It was a deliberate affront, stage-managed from Paris. Eventually an officer came by, casually identified the secretary-general, and let the convoy through. Hammarskjöld's tour of the wounded city appalled him. Later in the day, again at Tunis, the French commander refused his invitation to confer. His treatment from start to finish had been an erasure, less vulgar and shrill than the Soviets', different from the Belgians' subversion and reluctant compliance in the Congo, but no less an erasure of Hammarskjöld's person and office, and of the authority of the UN itself. That Hammarskjöld had wished to visit the war zone demonstrated again his personal courage, but that was hardly the point.

The parallels with Suez weren't lost on him. A few days into August, when he was again in New York, he wrote as much to Mahmoud Fawzi:

> Bizerte has given us a new Port Said, and forced me into a very exposed position. To you I need not explain why I did what I did, or why I did it in the way I did it. You know my philosophy so well and you know how I interpret it in action, from our shared experience during the Suez Crisis. The French are pleased to say that I side with the Tunisians. As in the Suez case, I retorted to the press that I side with the principles of the UN. And if that displeases any big power, that is their business and not mine. However, it is sad to see men, whom I would like to be able to respect, believing that you are great if you are conceited and that you are strong if you isolate yourself.[124]

The isolation he had in mind would have been the unwillingness of the French to negotiate with their Tunisian adversary or receive him in Paris. This is an apt moment to recall how much of French culture Hammarskjöld had adopted as his own. He belonged as much to Blaise Pascal as to Carl Linnaeus. He read his revered Thomas à Kempis in antique French as a matter of preference. He had successfully championed a French poet for the Nobel Prize and translated one of his major works into Swedish. He was rejected by Charles de Gaulle. There is a greater irony than this one in the narrative we are exploring, but the flavor of irony is unmistakable here too. The greater irony is that the lesson of Suez had not been learned.

In New York on July 28th, Hammarskjöld responded to the request of the Liberian delegate to report on his mission to the Security Council. The French were again on strike, refusing to participate. He carefully stated the limited scope of his mission and emphasized both the absence of communication between France and Tunisia and the instability of the cease-fire so far achieved. He urged the two parties to negotiate. Committing himself to state facts only, he did introduce a fact he had encountered. "By personal experience I can . . . confirm that [French paratroopers], at the time of the visit, exercised functions for the maintenance of law and order in the city which normally belong to organs of the sovereign government."[125] In a note to a Swedish friend some days later, he was more forthright. Speaking of Bill Ranallo, who had accompanied him to Bizerte, he commented: "Bill took a *very* dim view of the paras. He is now on vacation but fully ready for fighting at the prospect of new attacks on the S-G."[126] Who can doubt that Hammarskjöld also took a *very* dim view?

More political distress lay ahead, but on the ground in Bizerte the situation gradually calmed. When the Security Council failed to pass any further resolution, diplomatic efforts shifted to the General Assembly. Meeting in emergency session between the 21st and 25th of August, the Assembly succeeded in adopting a resolution that recognized Tunisia's right "to call for the withdrawal of all French armed forces present on its territory without its consent."[127] That had moral force, though unlike a Security Council resolution it wasn't binding on France under the Charter. De Gaulle soon had second thoughts about defying the will of Francophone Africa, uniformly aligned with Tunisia. By the fall of 1963, French forces had fully withdrawn from Bizerte. The General Assembly passed a further judgment on the Bizerte affair, and sent a stunning message to France, by electing the Tunisian Mongi Slim to be president of its sixteenth session, scheduled to begin in mid-September.

Hammarskjöld's rough journey to Tunisia seemed a failure, but in point of fact he was right when he wrote shortly after that "it was a useful move in a sense which will never reach the press, as it gave both the people in Tunis and in particular the poor devils in Bizerte a badly needed booster. . . . I shall continue to see what I can do, but I fear that I have played my cards now. . . ."[128] Urquhart provides a graceful valediction: "Six years later, Bourguiba told Spinelli that Hammarskjöld's visit had bolstered the morale of the Tunisian population at a critical time and had never been forgotten by them, and that it had also helped him in his later negotiations with de Gaulle. Certainly his courage in standing up to a great power and in at once going to the scene of conflict did not pass unnoticed among the majority of small nations in the UN."[129] For his part, President de Gaulle remained on his lofty perch. In a press conference on September 11th, he said, "It seems that the so-called 'United' Nations discussed and voted a resolution on the subject [of Bizerte]. . . . We do not recognize its having any right of arbitration or jurisdiction. . . ."[130]

Hammarskjöld experienced the Bizerte affair as compressive, to judge by the number of letters he wrote in its aftermath to friends and family with whom he could safely release pressure. Bo Beskow, Sture Petrén, his brothers Bo and Sten, his French confidant Alexis Leger—all heard from him within the same few days. Beskow had written that in his opinion generals without exception could go to hell. In his reply, Hammarskjöld translated that sentiment unchanged into proper diplomatic language: "There would be much to write about Bizerte and about the standards of those who pretend to be

our leaders. . . . I can agree with your colorful and strong exclamations."[131]
For Sture Petrén he essayed a highly original portrait of de Gaulle. "From the
somewhat questionable peace at 73rd Street," he wrote,

> warm thanks go to the peace at Örnahusen [on the southern coast of
> Sweden]. . . . With special interest I have read about your German ex-
> periences and their lingering echoes in the summer tranquility. I have
> for my part had reason for serious contemplation of another cultural
> heritage: the French in the peculiar incarnation that is called Charles
> de Gaulle. We talked about our friend Gripenberg [G. A. Gripenberg,
> Finnish ambassador to the UN] as an elk that has gone astray out of the
> big forest. De Gaulle seems to me an example of another very noble sort
> of big game, directly from one of the caves his early forefathers deco-
> rated with such ample fantasy. . . .[132]

De Gaulle recast as "a very noble sort of big game" whose image could be
found on the walls of Lascaux—this is fun. Hammarskjöld was using wit
and his license as an undeclared poet to free himself from the lingering
tarnish of difficult people and events.

With his brother Bo he worked through more detail and consequence
from Bizerte. As we know, Bo had business interests in Liberia. "It will
amuse me to hear of your experiences in Liberia with the excellent Tub-
man," Dag wrote.

> (By the way, Swiss and Belgian papers, with a rather typical mixture
> of misunderstandings and spontaneous venom, have launched the the-
> ory that "the brother of the Secretary-General" is the head of a newly
> founded Swedish-American mining company for the exploitation of the
> mineral deposits of Katanga).
>
> Whatever happens, I hope that the trip to the US will come about,
> and if so—if I manage to get through the General Assembly—April,
> from all that I know, would be a very good time. . . .
>
> The Congo development—which I hope will prove stable—has
> given us a very good political card. On the other hand, the Bizerte story
> is frankly rotten and demonstrates a sickly attitude of "ci-devants" unable
> to face the realities of the world of the next generation. How ironic that
> those who speak with the loudest voice and a beautiful tremble about
> Europe should rally with the Soviets against what, if anything, is a Euro-
> pean legacy to the world, the idea of an international discipline imposed
> on all countries in the common interest. That France tries to reserve for

itself a useless base may be their affair, but if they do it at the cost of a new serious drop in the faith of other peoples in the integrity of Western Europe, this is a matter of concern to all. Also, without any Security Council decision requesting their withdrawal to the base from the city of Bizerte, which they have highhandedly occupied, the French would be in flagrant violation of international law in upholding such an occupation by force; it would have shown at least good taste to straighten this out without provoking and necessitating international intervention.

For the moment I have a fairly quiet time, but it will certainly not be of long duration and a week or so from now we have again the General Assembly. I shall be as lazy as I can during the fairly quiet days which we may get. . . .[133]

"It would have shown at least good taste. . ." He was applying French values to French misconduct. To describe de Gaulle as a *ci-devant*, a political leader with outworn ideas, was apt under the circumstances. The resolution of the Algerian crisis, in which de Gaulle took great risks and exercised high political intelligence, still lay ahead.

To his brother Sten, Dag wrote more briefly on the same day and again balanced Bizerte against the Congo. "Until the last few days," he wrote,

my time has continued to be rather dramatic, but now suddenly there is a kind of pause, which may last even up to the Assembly some ten days from now. But I cross my fingers because here the unexpected is the rule and you never know what strange crises people suddenly cook up—as they did, for example, in the case of Bizerte. On the other hand, as the Congo shows, the unexpected may sometimes come also in favorable directions. . . .[134]

The longest letter, something of a masterpiece of political sensibility and analysis, was reserved for Alexis Leger, who had had his differences with de Gaulle.[135] Because the letter is published in full elsewhere, here we need only take note of a few key passages. "It is a relief for me to be able to talk to you," Hammarskjöld wrote—without question, this cycle of correspondence was a healing. He speculated that when Tunisia became independent, France had had in mind "an independence somewhat in the Indo-Chinese style, that is to say, with enough troops remaining, in several places, to ensure this pied-à-terre for France in the event of war." Though his sympathy lay with Bourguiba and the Tunisians, he took Bourguiba to task for the show of force he had organized from land and sea around the French base. "He shouted without realizing that above him piles of snow would be shaken loose in an avalanche by his shout. . . . So that's the story, so typical of zealous men and nations—and perhaps of us all. In the legal sense, everyone is wrong. In the moral sense, France. In the sense of political wisdom, Bourguiba—and, also, de Gaulle. . . ."[136] The overall experience had been a severe disappointment. "But, my dear Alexis," he continued, "I don't want to prolong this sad story. It is not necessary to believe the accounts of atrocities to feel an extreme bitterness when one sees such a reaction against the United Nations and against those poor people for whom this organization seems to be the last recourse before they turn to the Soviets."[137] In closing, Hammarskjöld paid the poet of *Chronique* a compliment that reflected on them both: "This time around, I have not found any encouragement or any way to escape toward a purer world by translating another *Chronique*, but how visionary your poem remains. . . . I apologize for this enormous letter, but I needed to talk to someone who, for me, represents unambiguously Eternal France and the Europe that must survive."[138]

Charles de Gaulle began his most famous book with the words, "All my life I have had a certain idea of France." So did Hammarskjöld.

A tone poem and an annual report

> Weep
> If you can,
> Weep,
> But do not complain.
>
> The way chose you—
> And you must be thankful.[139]

These are lines from *Markings*, early July. Beskow was right that Hammarskjöld was weary, although he rose to all occasions. The positive turn of events in the Congo that summer, which genuinely cheered him, was countered by the violence in Bizerte and, for a time, the dearth of political wisdom on both sides of that conflict. On the day war broke out in Bizerte, he wrote into his journal a touching prayer. It has the pace of slowly spoken language. Referring to no current event, though it may in part respond to Bizerte, it exists in the privacy where he could hear his own voice and sense his full identity without interference. He was writing on a Wednesday, not the weekend when he more often had private time; there must have been an urgency. The distance is vast between the place and moment of this prayer and the United Nations, the Congo, Bizerte. Yet the prayer is for "us," not only for himself. It asks for mercy upon our efforts. In that sense it is the prayer of a man of action in community with others, asking that action be guided by goodness. The closing lines, reflecting some of the largest paradoxes of religious life, have a different nature. Through briefest words they evoke the poet's faith that God is unknown yet we belong to Him, beyond comprehension yet He takes a hand in our destinies and we can speak with Him intimately as Thou. Like other entries in *Markings* through these months, the prayer is a column of words, few at a time. It stops and starts, advancing carefully. It speaks of silence. It still carries silence with its words. This is Hammarskjöld's *Kyrie eleison*.

> Have mercy
> Upon us.
> Have mercy
> Upon our efforts,
> That we
> Before Thee,
> In love and in faith,
> Righteousness and humility,
> May follow Thee,
> With self-denial, steadfastness, and courage,
> And meet Thee
> In the silence.
>
> Give us
> A pure heart
> That we may see Thee,
> A humble heart
> That we may hear Thee,
> A heart of love
> That we may serve Thee,
> A heart of faith
> That we may live Thee,
>
> Thou
> Whom I do not know
> But Whose I am.

Thou
Whom I do not comprehend
But Who hast dedicated me
To my destiny.
Thou—[140]

Throughout the summer, and through thick and thin so far as political events were concerned, he must have been perfecting his essay on Castle Hill.[141] It could be called a tone poem, though that is a musical term. A sustained exercise of memory, it draws into a refined whole his recall of people, seasons, places, sounds, ceremonies, customs, even plants and birds and bugs at the Vasa castle in Uppsala where he grew up. He had no reason to think of its composition as a leave-taking from Sweden. On the contrary, it might foreshadow a homecoming. Some around him believed that he was at last preparing to resign his office. A few more good turns of fortune in the Congo, a little more common sense between Paris and Tunis, and he might come to feel that he could safely leave his office in other hands. The Soviet notion of the troika had nearly died off; no one took it seriously except its originators, and even they now beat the drum weakly. Gromyko had made up a little jingle about it in English for the benefit of journalists.[142] That is not robust advocacy. Were Hammarskjöld to resign, naturally he would return to Sweden. He had in mind to write, to spend time at Backåkra, the farmhouse by the sea he scarcely knew. It goes without saying that he would return on occasion to Uppsala; the university would have much to interest him, and he to interest it. Therefore, *Castle Hill*, his exquisite reminiscence, was nothing more than a pleasant gesture toward the Swedish Touring Association. Yet it was and is obviously more than that. How strange, one might even say kind, that the pattern of events led to this lovely reminiscence in the summer of 1961.

Castle Hill is more important to us musically than as a text for thorough exploration. We should hear it advancing through the summer, a private melody shared with a handful of friends. He had a copy with him in mid-September when he returned to the Congo—it must have still been on his mind, not quite settled. Hammarskjöld's almanac, his round of the year, was written, as he put it, "in the present [tense]—the present of immediate experience, of what is still here or of what, deep down, never changes."[143] We have spoken once in this book of the scent of forever. Here it is again in the cycle of life at Uppsala. Of winter and early spring he wrote:

Just as age in a human face can chisel out what is permanent under what is temporary, so winter clarifies the features, restoring what summer hid . . . . Now farmers and Lapps from the north put up their stall in the yards by Svartbäcken and a brisk trade is done in reindeer meat and skin rugs. About this time, too, the bullfinches, and perhaps waxwings, come sweeping along in great flocks. . . . A few days later they have gone again, and with them red berries. . . .

The March sun thaws the banks of snow. . . . In the evenings the sky glows as red as a rebellion above the woods away towards Läbyvad. . . . One morning—it may have been already round about Lady Day—the first violets bloom in the round bed in the courtyard. . . . Then the celandine awakes. The earth is thin. It is quickly warmed by the sun. . . .[144]

This is autobiography of an unusual kind, beautifully characterized by Karl Ragnar Gierow in a mid-August letter. "One is simply not used to a style of autobiography in which the memories really stand out and the one who remembers voluntarily steps back, half-hidden behind his words. The opposite happens more often—he gets in the way and with ardent gestures blocks the view. But certainly he is there in your description, on the spot every second. And I think it's precisely that which gives your essay its special inner tension. . . ."[145] The text ends—of course—on a nostalgic note: the encounter of new doctoral graduates looking toward their life's work and "jubilee doctors" returning to the university fifty years after earning their degrees. As Sweden was and is a nation of customs, the jubilee doctors he describes wear laurel wreaths on their brows.

In an essay Hammarskjöld had published several years earlier in a Swedish photography magazine, he wrote that "the camera taught me to see. . . . The camera becomes a means to learn to see 'in pictures,' but also to see and commit to memory the play of lines, the distribution of light, the balance between detail and the whole. . . ."[146] He had written *Castle Hill* in this mode: it was much like a linked series of photographs imagined and set to words.

A poet died on July 19th: Hjalmar Gullberg, whom Hammarskjöld had profoundly admired and, more simply, liked. A member of the Swedish Academy for decades, he had steadily published and drawn the country's radio listeners into the world of theater through a program he oversaw. Suffering in his very late years from a painful degenerative disease and no longer willing to accept life on those terms, he had chosen to drown. On Sunday August 6th, Hammarskjöld found time to acknowledge reflectively his passing. To Beskow he described Hjalmar Gullberg in words that would be later redirected toward Hammarskjöld himself. "There has not for a long time been a death which I believe has been more strongly felt by Swedes of our generation than that of Hjalmar's. He was indeed one of the few and perhaps last representatives of a spiritual standard, a natural nobility, a warmth of heart and an iron-clad integrity, which is more necessary than ever in the present period of growing darkness and decay. . . ."[147] On the same day Hammarskjöld also mentioned the poet's passing to Erik Lindegren, himself a poet. In that letter he spoke of "the sadness which I and so many of us feel at the passing of Gullberg. But how grateful we should be for the miracle of his three last collections of poems, torn from his vision and his suffering with lame and bleeding hands."[148] There is large quality in Hammarskjöld's words on this day of reflection and mourning. He was living with enriched awareness.

On a day of mourning. Greenback had died. You will recall Hammarskjöld's monkey, living in his apartment, a favorite. On this Sunday in early August Hammarskjöld wrote into his journal an elegy for Greenback, who had strangled in the vine-like rope suspended from the top of the stairs between floors. Hammarskjöld had sensed Greenback's difficulties.

> Who had ever understood
> His efforts to be happy,
> His moments of faith in us,
> His constant anxiety,
> Longing for something. . . .[149]

The death of Greenback can't help but leave us uneasy. He was Africa, its lively symbol. He was a fellow you could look at when confused. It would have been better, had he lived.

There was more still in this day of vivid feelings. In the letter to Lindegren that spoke of Gullberg's passing, Hammarskjöld gave some thought to what he called "the industrialization of literature" and moved on to a theme at the center of his life: contemplation and action.

Sten Selander—who, as you know, never outgrew the adventurous explorer spirit of a boy—wrote me once with an accent of envy about those who create poetry by action. It is a beautiful concept and there may be some little element of truth in it but basically it is an illusion. We all remain free to form our personal life in accordance with standards which otherwise may find their expression in poetry. But obligation to action, especially in the political field, is more of a danger than a privilege. At the present phase events on all levels and the basic stone-age psychology of men make it rather difficult to translate contemplation into action and to make action the source material for contemplation. However, we do not ourselves choose the shelf on which we are placed.

I regret losing practically completely the personal contacts with my friends in Sweden to which you very much belong. Let us at least keep the bridge of letters.[150]

That weekend he must have been in Brewster because he found time to hike in the highlands overlooking the Hudson River, some thirty miles west from his home. Perhaps on Sunday evening he wrote a poem in which, toward the end of day, he is looking out from a height of land. The sun is setting

> In a haze of heat
> Over Poughkeepsie.

A true son of Linnaeus, he recognizes by name the flowers in a distant meadow and admires what he calls Indian corn ripening in the fields below. The scene is perfectly lovely. As in *Castle Hill*, he imagines the passage of time—and recalls a moment at the summer solstice, known to Swedes as midsummer, when he experienced at that very place a unique joy. We are not told more.

> Seven weeks have gone by,
> Seven kinds of blossom
> Have been picked or mowed. . . .
> Was it here,
> Here, that paradise was revealed
> For one brief moment
> On a night in midsummer?[151]

As in his poem of June 11th, in which he tells us that he saw "For one moment / The sail / In the sun storm," we are not going to know more. But this much we can know: this man had moments, even in this long period of difficulty and uncertainty, effort and risk, release from grave events and recapture in further grave events, when he was all joy, all freedom. He could hardly believe it—was it here, here?—but it was so.

One of Hammarskjöld's summer duties was to write the introduction to the sixteenth annual report, completed on August 17th and released a week later. As in the past, he used the report as a teaching occasion for the UN community as a whole and strategically put the most important thoughts in the first paragraphs where even impatient readers would find them. Some regard the UN, he wrote, as "a static conference machinery for resolving conflicts of interests and ideologies," served by a Secretariat in which continued loyalty to those interests or ideologies need not be set aside. Others, he continued, "conceive of the Organization primarily as a dynamic instrument of governments . . . through which they should seek . . . reconciliation but through which they should also try to develop forms of executive action . . . in a spirit of objectivity and in implementation of the principles and purposes of the Charter."[152] There is no question where he stood. The second view, he wrote, "opens the road towards more developed and increasingly effective forms of constructive international cooperation," while the first view remained bound to "the time-honored philosophy of sovereign national states in armed competition of which the most that may be expected in the international field is that they achieve a peaceful coexistence. . . ."[153] Abiding by the service ethic of his office, he wrote that it was for the member nations to choose their concept and path, but he would nonetheless explore the issue in further pages—and went on to do so with rigor.

Toward the end he turned to current issues, primarily the Congo. "Throughout the first year of its work in the Congo," he wrote,

> up to the point when Parliament reassembled and invested a new national government, [the UN] has refused—what many may have wished—to permit the weight of its resources to be used in support of any faction so as thereby to prejudge in any way the outcome of a choice which belonged solely to the Congolese people. It has also had to pursue a line which, by safeguarding the free choice of the people, implied resistance against all efforts from outside to influence the outcome. In doing so, the Organization has been put in a position in which those within the country who felt disappointed in not getting the support of the Organization were led to suspect that others were in a more favored position and, therefore, accused the Organization of partiality, and in which, further, such outside elements as tried to get or protect a foothold within the country, when meeting an obstacle in the United Nations, made similar accusations. If, as it is sincerely to be hoped, the recent national reconciliation, achieved by Parliament and its elected representatives of the people, provides a stable basis for a peaceful fu-

ture in a fully independent and unified Congo, this would definitely confirm the correctness of the line pursued by the United Nations in the Congo. In fact, what was achieved by Parliament early in August may be said to have done so with sufficient clarity. It is a thankless and easily misunderstood role for the Organization to remain neutral in relation to a situation of domestic conflict and to provide active assistance only by protecting the rights and possibilities of the people to find their own way, but it remains the only manner in which the Organization can serve its proclaimed purpose of furthering the full independence of the people in the true and unqualified sense of the word.[154]

In all respects—as an invitation to rethink the United Nations and confirm its dynamic role in the world, and as a startlingly brief but satisfactory summary of fourteen months of conflict in the Congo and at the UN—Hammarskjöld's introduction possessed a certain finality. He was the first to recognize that. When he gave Andrew Cordier a draft for review, he said, "I don't see what I can write after this one."[155] Casual though it was, his comment suggests again that he may have been thinking that conditions would soon allow him to resign without, as he once put it, deserting the ship in a storm.

There were signs of peaceful consolidation in the Congo and signs of trouble. Prime Minister Adoula was successfully establishing his new government and cooperating with the UN. As Hammarskjöld wrote to him in early September, "The excellent relations which exist, and the fruitful consultations initiated by your government with the representatives of the Organization, are a subject for congratulation."[156] Antoine Gizenga was coming forward to cooperate with Adoula, though he retained a fall-back position in Stanleyville in case of need. All to the good. The same could not be said of Katanga. The arrival of hardened French officers, some of whom had staged an unsuccessful revolt against de Gaulle's policy in Algeria, had strengthened Tshombe's belief that Katanga could defend its independence by force of arms if necessary. Katanga now possessed the only fighter jet in the Congo, a French Fouga Magister. Those words, Fouga Magister, have long since become part of the legend of the Congo Crisis. It was just a trainer jet, not advanced for its time. But it could be handy. Tshombe's Belgian advisers saw every reason for Katanga to remain independent and, despite UN resolutions, there was no lack of support for that position in the West. Conor Cruise O'Brien, who had taken up his post in Elisabethville in early June as the senior UN leader, had come to believe that forceful measures would be needed to eliminate mercenaries and Belgian advisers from Katanga. Negotiation hadn't achieved a great deal, piecemeal police actions had achieved only piecemeal results, and Tshombe wouldn't budge from Elisabethville to confer with Adoula. In this view that more forceful action was needed he was joined by Mahmoud Khiari, the UN head of civilian operations based in Léopoldville, and by Sture Linnér, the officer in charge after Dayal's departure. The Adoula government wanted nothing so much as to end the secession, by force if necessary, and many African member nations shared that stand. In the course of August O'Brien and his colleagues obtained Hammarskjöld's approval to stage a surprise roundup and expulsion of mercenaries toward the end of the month. Meanwhile, at Hammarskjöld's urging, they would strengthen UN forces in Katanga so as to have the strongest possible position when the time came—a position so strong that armed resistance could be avoided. The notion of "force, if necessary, in the last resort" was poised to become operational. The roundup, called Rumpunch, was set for August 28th.

We should pause over C. C. O'Brien (1917–2008). He had not been Hammarskjöld's first choice for the highly sensitive and responsible role he came to play, but Hammarskjöld was confident in him. O'Brien had been a member of the Irish mission to the UN for some years; though there seems to have been little or no direct contact between them, Hammarskjöld had heard him speak. When O'Brien flew from Ireland to New York to be briefed on his new role, they had their first long talk. Urquhart knew O'Brien well and considered him a friend—and was beside himself when Hammarskjöld told him about the appointment. "I had rather a special relationship with Conor," Urquhart recalled in the oral history project.

> He was a very old friend of mine before all this. . . . I was horrified when Hammarskjöld appointed him to Katanga because I didn't believe he was a suitable personality to send there. Conor was a brilliant man, a remarkable writer, highly imaginative, a rather subjective man, with a very large ego. It didn't seem to me that in the kind of mess in which we were in Katanga he was necessarily the person who would last very well. . . .
>
> Hammarskjöld was a very bad judge of character. He was easily swayed by extraneous factors. He had greatly admired Conor's writing and especially a book about French Catholic writers . . . , and he had heard that Conor was in the Irish Foreign Service, a marvelous

sort of renaissance diplomat. He thought he was like Saint-John Perse, in fact—which he wasn't—and so he appointed him. . . . I remember, because I rode down in the elevator with Hammarskjöld one day and he said, "I think at last we've got the right man for Katanga." And I said: "Oh really. Who's that?" He said: "You wouldn't know him. He is an Irishman called Conor Cruise O'Brien." I said "Good God! Not Conor—it can't be. You must be joking." And he got furious. I said: "Well, I know him extremely well. You shouldn't send him there." And he said: "Do you often speak like that of your friends?" I said: "Most of my friends I wouldn't make a doorman in this building. That isn't the point. The point is that he is temperamentally unsuited to that climate; most people are. He is a wonderful man. I know him very well." . . . O'Brien never understood Hammarskjöld . . . and Hammarskjöld didn't know O'Brien. That was, I think, primarily Hammarskjöld's fault; he should have known better what he was doing. But he was very vague about personalities. He always was. I think that was a great pity. . . .[157]

General I. J. Rikhye, Hammarskjöld's Indian military adviser—acerbically but no doubt accurately described by Urquhart as "a very good soldier, which most people in the Secretariat were not"[158]—had a rather different view. He believed that Hammarskjöld deliberately chose "an Irish anti-colonial. . . . His own strategy had to be . . . to win the Belgians and Belgium's Western friends to his side. So he wanted . . . checks and balances . . . to project an image . . . more acceptable to the UN's wider membership. The purpose of his selection was correct, but he found that O'Brien was less manageable than he had anticipated. . . ."[159] O'Brien himself agreed with the first lines in this analysis.[160] He was known to be radically anticolonial. Anyone hiring him was hiring *that*. And hiring a wit who could simultaneously entertain and demolish. In the year after O'Brien's service in Katanga had ended in bitterness, he offered a description of Hammarskjöld's executive suite on the top floor of UN headquarters: "Zoologists tell us of tiny mammals who manage to exist in the high Himalayas 'exclusively on a diet of wind-blown debris.' Such a diet should not be expected, however, to keep body and soul together at the altitude of the 38th floor."[161] It was mean, it was funny, and in its implications untrue.

It would be nearly as important to characterize Mahmoud Khiari but the evidence for doing so is sparse and contradictory, and his career after the Congo, unlike O'Brien's, seems not to have been in the public eye. In the oral history project, Urquhart described him with distaste: "Khiari was an extremely Machiavellian and dishonest man who had a very firm view of his own about how things ought to be done in the Congo...."[162] That can't be good. O'Brien's deft characterization of the man sheds another light on the same traits: "He had no patience at all with the theory ... that the United Nations must refrain from interfering in the internal affairs of the Congo. 'What are we here for then?' he would ask. '*Il faut faire de la politique!*' And on the word *politique* his brown eyes, usually ... disconcertingly blank, would flash."[163] But Khiari was entrusted by the UN to negotiate a cease-fire with Tshombe in the days after Hammarskjöld's death, and Ralph Bunche—than whom no one was more devotedly loyal to Hammarskjöld—appears to have accepted Khiari as a colleague and worked with him in the Congo in late 1961.

Hammarskjöld planned to visit the Congo in early September before the opening of the next session of the General Assembly on the 19th. He had two purposes in mind: attempting to bring Adoula and Tshombe together for a start toward reconciliation, and conferring with Adoula about a possible reduction in the size of the UN mission, which then stood at nearly seventeen thousand troops from twenty different countries and a substantial civilian element.[164] He was quite hopeful about the possibilities. As late as September 11th he wrote to a member of his family that on the following day he would "have to go for a couple of days to the Congo. If all works out as we may hope, it is more or less the epilogue of the political operation."[165] If all were to work out as hoped, the next session of the General Assembly would be more civilized.

Publicly unavowable

In the late days of August and early September, the Congo operation was much on Hammarskjöld's mind and in his calendar, but less oppressively so than in months past. At the end of August he put a note in the mail to Mekki Abbas, an Ethiopian colleague who had served in the Congo. He must have been responding to a letter. "I see that the Congo continues to be very active in your mind," Hammarskjöld wrote, "as it does in the minds of all of us here. It is the sort of problem-challenge that does stay in one's blood once there has been exposure."[166] Reflecting the breadth of his relationships and concerns, his correspondence in those weeks is rich in his characteristic flicker of wit and warming thought; despite the "problem-challenge," he had time. In a note to Karl Ragnar Gierow he followed up on the question of raising funds for his theater to perform at the Seattle World's Fair. "I shall write to X," he began (referring to a wealthy industrialist), "whose qualities of evasion, when it comes to spending money in ways not of his own invention, may well make my effort vain. Alas, I am not in the favorable position of the great archbishop of Uppsala who, talking about an unwilling donor, said that to his regret he would find it necessary to 'tickle him with eternal damnation.'"[167] On the same day, he dared to send a word of literary advice to John Steinbeck. He knew that Steinbeck had a work in progress and was perfectly aware that advising a novelist of worldwide fame was a bit much. "If you permit me to be terribly preposterous," he inched toward his topic, "I hope that you will manage to make the architecture of your work, and its unavoidable ornaments, so invisible or translucent as to make your strong inner light shine forth and illuminate the simplest of human relations and the simplest of human characters. . . ."[168] It won't be lost on us that he was describing his own aesthetic and values. He had no doubt that Steinbeck would understand.

Preposterous as he may have been, Hammarskjöld had a stake in Steinbeck's continuing excellence: he was discreetly championing him for the Nobel Prize. Some weeks earlier he had indirectly opened the topic with Anders Österling, permanent secretary of the Swedish Academy. "I sent you Steinbeck's new novel," he wrote, "first of all because I really regarded it in most respects as a very perfect little piece of story-telling, entertaining but with great mastery of form, an incredibly fine ear for nuances of the language of this part of the world, and an unusual ability to raise very serious issues in an everyday form, which is in a most modern sense classical. . . ."[169] In early September, when Steinbeck was preparing to take his two sons on a world tour, Hammarskjöld sent letters of introduction to a number of world leaders and friends in which he compactly characterized Steinbeck in terms that could be applied to himself. Despite their wholly different backgrounds, there was considerable brotherhood between them. "He is . . . one of those observers of life in our generation," he wrote to David Ben-Gurion and others, "who feel that its survival will depend on our ability to know ourselves and to stick to basic human values with the will to pay what it may cost. . . ."[170] John Steinbeck would be awarded the Nobel Prize in Literature in 1962. "Man himself," he would say in his acceptance speech, "has become our greatest hazard and our only hope."[171]

Hammarskjöld took time on August 24th to send a congratulatory cable to Östen Undén on the occasion of his seventy-fifth birthday. Still in office, Undén was the long-serving Swedish foreign minister to whom he had turned earlier in the year to reason through the motives behind the Soviet attacks on his person and office. It was a gracious note to a mentor and friend.

> Happy to know that you are still at your post with the entire experience of age but without its burdens, I send you warmest congratulations. It is tempting this day to think back over the forty years I have been allowed to know you. They have taken me from the student's reverence for the respected professor and politician, through the undergraduate's respect for an excellent teacher and the civil servant's trust in his upright chief of staff, to a friend's warm gratitude for a forerunner and fellow fighter on the same front lines.[172]

Hammarskjöld had a way of setting traps for himself in the form of literary challenges that he knew—as he said of Steinbeck—would cost something to accomplish. Creating a private world of thought distant from day-to-day politics, his chosen traps required concentration and contact with all of the resources of language and sensibility—and for that reason refreshed him. His Swedish translations of two formidably difficult texts, Saint-John Perse's *Chronique* and Djuna Barnes's *Antiphon*, from French and English, respectively, were of this kind. The trap wasn't simply the decision to translate, it was also the commitments he made: to circulate *Chronique* in translation to his Nobel Prize–conferring colleagues in the Swedish Academy, to arrange for performance of *Antiphon* at the Swedish National Theater. Martin Buber's *I and Thou* was to be next in the series.[173]

He had known the book for some years. First published in 1923 in German, it is Buber's poetic and intellectually demanding exploration of the life of dialogue with one's fellow human beings and with God. It is one of those books that more people know of than read. Perfect for Hammarskjöld. In an exchange of letters in mid-August, the first contact between them in two years, Hammarskjöld essentially left to Buber the choice of which work to translate; he seems not to have had a specific work in mind. Early in the letter that reopened their correspondence, he expressed how much he appreciated Buber's essay collection, *Between Man and Man*, which he had recently come across.[174] "You have formulated shared experiences in ways which made your studies very much what you would call a 'sign' for me. It is strange—over a gulf of time and a gulf of differences as to background and outer experience—to find a bridge built which, in one move, eliminates the distance. . . ." And he broached the idea of translation. "I still keep in mind the idea of translating you so as to bring you closer to my countrymen, but it becomes increasingly difficult to choose. . . . Also, the more I sense the nuances in your German, the more shy I become at the thought of a translation. . . ."[175] Buber replied without delay: "If I were asked which of my books a Swede ought to read first, I would answer: 'The most difficult one of all, but one that is most suited to introducing the reader to the realm of dialogue, namely, *I and Thou*.'"[176] He arranged at once for Hammarskjöld to have the latest German edition, which included a new afterword by the author. Hammarskjöld willingly entered the trap, now perhaps more formidable than he had anticipated. In his prompt reply to Buber, he obviously delighted in the German word *Aufruf*, call or summons, as if he were already translating. "Yesterday I got your kind letter," he wrote, "and also the last German edition of *Ich und Du* with the postscript. I am certain that I am reading you correctly if I see reflected in your reply a silent 'Aufruf' that I try a translation of the key work, as decisive in its message as supremely beautiful in its form. This decides the issue. . . ."[177]

On the very day he accepted the *Aufruf*, he sent a note to Jytte Bonnier, whom we know as an author married to Tor Bonnier, owner of Sweden's most important publishing house.

> May I ask you for a service which, I believe, is within your sphere of interests? You may know that for quite some time I have played with the idea to translate some of the key parts of Martin Buber's work. It is at least as exacting from the point of view of form as Perse or Barnes. . . . However, it has been a most challenging thought. Now Buber himself has, so to say, pushed me over the brink, as I have just received a letter from him which I may regard as a "call" to me to translate *Ich und Du*, which of course is the culminating crystallization of his mystical thought and, from the point of view of both form and content, not only a key work in modern philosophy but moreover one of the few great poems of this age. To such a "call" I feel that I should respond, and for some time ahead I shall therefore, in odd hours, instead of reading, try to make this translation.
>
> A book like that one is the very opposite to "box office," and I guess most publishers would look at it with considerable skepticism, especially as I would not like it published as a philosophical or theological

work but as a work of pure literature. However, Buber is Buber, and while [Thomas] Mann and [Hermann] Hesse are well known in Sweden, Buber, as the third and in some sense the greatest one in Germany of that generation, has been left aside. . . .[178]

Hammarskjöld relished the challenge of translating what he has just called "one of the few great poems of this age." His enthusiasm is evident in a note of early September to Georg Svensson, a senior executive at Bonnier, who had just confirmed Bonnier's interest in publishing his translation. "Buber's prose is exceedingly difficult," Hammarskjöld wrote, "and I shall have to make a first version which makes the sense crystal-clear and a second version representing a maximum approximation to his intensely beautiful, intensely personal, but also intensely Old-Testament-German prosody." He promised to deliver final manuscript in January, as we know, and closed on words that echo strongly to this day. "I may end by saying," he wrote, "that this is really something I am very happy to do—also for the publicly unavowable reason that this translation in a certain sense is a personal declaration."[179]

What caused his excitement, so poignant in light of circumstances? Through fall and early winter he was poised to express in Buber's recondite yet touching words much of what he himself had understood about dialogue, the central practice of diplomacy and the basis of prayer. Nearly any page of *I and Thou* answers the question, but a forceful statement from an early page will do, the German original first because its term *Grundwort* is so memorable:

> *Das Grundwort Ich-Du kann nur mit dem ganzen Wesen gesprochen werden.*
>
> *Das Grundwort Ich-Es kann nie mit dem ganzen Wesen gesprochen werden.*[180]
>
> The primal word I-Thou can only be spoken with one's whole being.
>
> The primal word I-It can never be spoken with one's whole being.

The text would convey some part of Hammarskjöld's own *Grundwort*, the word preceding all others, spoken from his depths and refined over many years of service. This was the nature of the trap he created and invited in late summer before leaving for the Congo.

He promptly started his translation and had twelve pages in typed draft by the time of his departure.

Is it a new country?

In this magical late summer when Hammarskjöld was reaching out in many directions with keenest intelligence and sensitivity, he awoke one morning in New York on a remarkable dream. He didn't fail to record it in his journal. Because these are the last words of *Markings*, for that reason alone they have weight, but they also possess finality, as if he might well have left this poem in place as the concluding note, however much he would add in years to come. Surely not by chance, his words echo the opening poem of *Markings* in which a young man, questing in high terrain, is "driven forward into an unknown land." That young man expectantly senses a promising wind "from my unknown goal," and asks himself if he is capable of finding the way to the place where "life resounds, a clear simple note in the silence." In the dream we now hear of, the setting is "a new country in another world of reality," yet strangely familiar. If this is the "unknown land" toward which the young man, unsure of his ability, was questing, the older man writes a song of recognition: he knows where he is, he has seen this land before, he has not mastered its every feature but he belongs. It is a heartening poem, as if Hammarskjöld has come full circle; he is again trekking in the far north, again dreaming wisely and richly, again finding in dream both insight and solace of undeniable power.

> Is it a new country
> In another reality
> Than today's?
> Or did I live there
> Before this day?
>
> I awoke
> To an ordinary morning with gray light
> Reflected from the street,
> But still remembered
> The dark-blue night
> Above the tree line,
> The open moor in moonlight,
> The crest in shadow.
> Remembered other dreams
> Of the same mountain country:
> Twice I stood on its summits,

I stayed by its remotest lake,
And followed the river
Toward its source.
The seasons have changed
And the light
And the weather
And the hour.
But it is the same land.
And I begin to know the map
And to get my bearings.[181]

Four days after Hammarskjöld wrote these lines, Operation Rumpunch was launched in Katanga.

17

Far Away a Heart Stops

"This is excellent, if it's true; but is it not too simple?"[1] The speaker was a participant in the advisory committee working through the long crisis with Hammarskjöld. In mid-August Hammarskjöld endorsed his colleague's skeptical wit, but he also had new hope that the crisis might wind down. Operation Rumpunch made sense to him as a step in that direction. By design it was forceful but nonviolent. Not a shot was fired; the show of force was enough. Somehow kept secret in a city and province where everyone had sources, it expressed in utterly concrete terms the Security Council's resolution in February to expel the mercenaries from Katanga. They had done great harm by strengthening Tshombe's resolve, helping local white "ultras" organize into armed militias, and contributing to an exterminatory war against Baluba tribal villages in northern Katanga that had remained loyal to the central government. By mid-September, some thirty-five thousand or more Baluba refugees had gathered in protective camps under UN care. O'Brien recalled that this huge population included not only villagers but also good citizens of Elisabethville who had been persecuted by Munongo's forces. "They now came to squat on the ground around our camps in conditions of the greatest misery and squalor."[2] The burden of responsibility carried by the UN was nearly overwhelming.

Rumpunch was planned by O'Brien with the top UN military leader in Katanga, brigadier K. A. S. Raja. It focused on key places and people. Before dawn on August 28th, UN forces in Elisabethville surrounded or occupied the radio station, post office, telephone center, and gendarmerie headquarters. In a surprise maneuver, they also surrounded the residence of the interior minister, Munongo, the most aggressive of Tshombe's ministers, to cut him off from command. Tshombe remained at liberty: once the UN had demonstrated its ability to arrest and expel his mercenaries, he would be the crucial negotiating partner. In the course of the day, eighty-one European officers were arrested without struggle in Elisabethville and elsewhere in Katanga and sent off to the vast military base at Kamina for return to their home countries.

The 28th was also a day for diplomacy. O'Brien and Raja met with Tshombe that morning and secured his agreement, long sought, to dismiss all foreign officers—an agreement he announced rather docilely by radio later in the day. His quid pro quo was the release of Munongo and the withdrawal of UN forces from the sites they had occupied. Meanwhile the Western consular corps, Belgian, British, and French, requested a meeting with O'Brien and Raja. It was ill-starred. Owing to a naïve concession by O'Brien at the meeting, the coherence of the well-launched operation began to fall apart. In an interview for the United Nations Oral History Project, Urquhart comments that O'Brien "had no idea of military affairs at all" and relied on "a very inefficient military opposite number."[3] Perhaps that is enough to explain the error he fell into. When the Belgian consul offered to take over the assembling and repatriation of mercenary officers, most of whom were Belgian, O'Brien relinquished control to him. The consul explained that "the arrests were an unnecessary humiliation imposed on officers who had orders from their own government never to fire on UN troops. These officers were willing, indeed anxious, to leave Katanga. . . ."[4] Brigadier Raja didn't like the offer one bit, but O'Brien accepted because, as he later explained, it ensured that the operation would remain nonviolent from start to finish. It must also have been in his interest to maintain give-and-take with the consulates. Later he acknowledged that it had been a "*sottise*," a stupidity. He borrowed his French from a report on Operation Rumpunch in a Belgian newspaper.[5]

Unsurprisingly, from one day to the next the repatriation process broke down. While the more cooperative mercenaries headed for home, the ruthless core—*les affreux*—went into hiding, regrouped, and revised its strategy. At UN headquarters, Hammarskjöld had mixed feelings. He sent O'Brien a witty, jubilant congratulatory cable. "Congo Club in congress assembled passed unanimous vote of congratulations gratification and sincere respect for an exceedingly sensitive operation carried through with skill and courage. . . ."[6] Notwithstanding, he worried that the operation had ended too soon.[7]

The days following in Katanga were full of turmoil. Heartened by his advisors, Tshombe turned loudly against the UN with covert encouragement from some of the Western consuls and bellicose encouragement from the neighboring Rhodesian Federation, a white supremacist nation with a brawling prime minister, Sir Roy Welensky. Northern Rhodesia—

one of three territories in the federation—was a British protectorate with uneasy ties to Britain, mining wealth, and as O'Brien put it, "an acute and passionate community of interest" with independent Katanga.[8] Their common border allowed for traffic of all kinds. From O'Brien's perspective, Welensky's encouragement was crucial to Tshombe's renewed resolve. The rumor was put about that Katanga's military, some fifteen thousand strong and now with fewer Belgian officers, was restive and poised to revolt—a rumor apparently with its grain of truth.[9] The UN was blamed for the unrest. There was worse still. O'Brien heard from a mercenary who had changed sides that Munongo was contracting out the assassination of UN personnel, including a senior official briefly arrested by Munongo's security police at the post office. Outraged by the broad threat and the specific arrest, he demanded that Tshombe suspend Munongo from his cabinet—of course, to no avail. Renewed efforts to persuade Tshombe to meet in Léopoldville with Adoula came to naught; among other things, were he to absent himself from Elisabethville he feared a coup by Munongo. Tshombe refused, as well, to agree to meet Hammarskjöld a little later in Léopoldville—he was expected on the 13th. On his side, Adoula or those around him had lost patience. If no solution short of war was effective, he had the support of parliament to send the army against Katanga. His government's credibility depended in some good measure on ending the secession.

The UN leaders in the Congo had also lost patience. They began framing out a plan to complete Rumpunch, go well past it, and set things right at last. Hammarskjöld was aware of the developing plan and wary of it. He hadn't failed to notice that his representatives in both contesting cities, Léopoldville and Elisabethville, were nearing their rope's end. How much confusion and adversity could they withstand without losing their good judgment? He would have preferred, as he put it in a cable to Linnér, to "remain strong but to sit tight and to let the medicine do its work without, if possible, new injections."[10] But the plan communicated to him in early September by Linnér and Khiari was sensibly staged. It called for a linked series of diplomatic and political actions: persuading the Western consulates to rally to the UN and calm Tshombe, parallel activities by Hammarskjöld among delegations in New York, a lightning trip by Linnér to Brussels to explain the situation from direct experience and secure agreement to necessary measures, an end to anti-UN propaganda in the Katangese media, the curbing of Munongo's security forces who were justly feared, a near deadline—a matter of days—for the voluntary expulsion of all mercenaries. And if all this were to yield no significant result, paragraph 9(c) of the proposed plan would be set in motion: recapture of key sites in the city; arrest and expulsion of the remaining mercenaries, the arrest of key ministers—among them Munongo—and the introduction of a state commissioner dispatched from Léopoldville to represent the central government. In the view of Linnér and Khiari, the alternative to what they were suggesting was civil war, the worst of outcomes in the long effort to reunite the country.

Hammarskjöld took the precaution of asking Oscar Schachter, the legal adviser who had helped him think out his Oxford lecture, for his assessment of the legality of the proposed plan.[11] Schechter's carefully crafted memo in response reiterated the limitations on the use of offensive force by the UN and answered questions Hammarskjöld must specifically have asked—for example, under what conditions the UN could make arrests. The gist of what Schachter wrote is that arrests were justified only when individuals were directly engaged in military action "or otherwise *in flagrante delicto* . . . or clearly engaged in incitement to immediate violence." If both the central and provincial governments authorized an arrest, that would be a legally acceptable basis for the UN to act, but if the central government independently authorized arrests, the UN should take no part.

An exchange of cables with Khiari and separately with Linnér seemed to settle the matter. Khiari wrote on September 10th that he had given instructions to O'Brien matching those to which Hammarskjöld had agreed, "*avec toutefois réserve d'application après entente avec vous-même à Léo.*" The phrase is important: Khiari offered his assurance that the plan would not be set in motion without further discussion with Hammarskjöld in Léopoldville a few days later. "The means foreseen . . . in 9(c)," Khiari continued, "will only be applied as a last resort, but we have no hesitation about the necessity to apply them if the other means yield no result. . . ." He was detectably proud of the forceful plan: "The 9(c) measures are applicable as a whole and the fragmentation or partial deployment of these measures risks subjecting us to nearly certain failure. If the whole of 9(c) is set in motion, that will not fail among other things to create a psychological shock in the population, which will reduce possibilities of armed opposition."[12] Khiari here was distant from Hammarskjöld; we have never known

Hammarskjöld to interest himself in anything resembling a "*psychose de choc*," as Khiari put it. Hammarskjöld never spoke of terrifying and subduing an entire population.

At some point that day, September 10th, Hammarskjöld cabled to Linnér his overall assessment:

> The speed of developments and the stage reached means that short of a change for the better in Katanga we are beyond the point of no return as regards our plan under 9-C. You are therefore authorized to pursue the policy outlined by you also to the central government, but we must impress on you the necessity in the course of its implementation to keep in mind the various views we have found necessary to express in the course of our exchange, views of principle which we know from your own cables that you share.[13]

The cable implies that Hammarskjöld lacked confidence in the judgment of some of his representatives. It wasn't Linnér who concerned him; Linnér was a loyal and cautious colleague whom he was essentially asking to keep an eye on the others. It must have been Khiari, with his ambition to inflict "shock and awe" on Katanga, and perhaps by now also O'Brien. Many years later in the oral history project, Linnér remarked that Hammarskjöld had begun to lose faith in O'Brien's tact and judgment some time before the events we are now exploring.[14]

What were Hammarskjöld's expectations at this point? What were his orders? He expected his team in the Congo to wait for his arrival to revisit their options. Subject to that timing, he favored another roundup of mercenaries, more thorough than Rumpunch but, as before, nonviolent. He was aware of the plan to introduce a state commissioner representing the central government and had tried unsuccessfully to substitute a reasonably neutral figure for the person actually chosen by Adoula for the role, a Gizenga ally regarded by the Western consuls as from the Lumumba camp, therefore dubious. That was a difficulty, not intolerable. This much is evident: to bring Tshombe and Adoula together for reconciliation talks, he needed peace, not war.

A few days before this exchange of cables Hammarskjöld met in the General Assembly hall with what must have been the entire Secretariat staff. It was Staff Day, an occasion neglected in the past two years. Though nearly every chair was filled in the vast hall, he spoke with warmth, as among friends, but also comprehensively on a wide range of issues from the demands of the Congo to salary and assignments. "Those of you who have responded to the call to go out to the Congo," he said, "have displayed your readiness often despite considerable personal and family inconvenience. . . . Tribute is due equally to those who stayed behind and did the backstopping from Headquarters. I . . . take this opportunity to record, and express, a deep gratitude to all of you. . . ."[15] It was in character that he spoke of "a" not "my" gratitude. An insight he had written down in the summer of 1957 comes to mind: "You will know life and be acknowledged by it according to your degree of transparency, your capacity, that is, to vanish as an end, and remain purely as a means."[16] He must have been practicing that as he spoke—practicing vanishing. The gratitude due was larger than himself; he could only point to it.

He went on to restate for his colleagues the opening theme of his introduction to that summer's annual report: what was the Secretariat to be, an "intergovernmental" organization serving a "conference machinery" or a truly international force dedicated to peace and development, its members owing no allegiance to any national government? He acknowledged that this was a decision for the member nations, not the Secretariat, but "the quality and spirit of our work will necessarily greatly influence the reply." He also acknowledged that in light of the immense burdens they had carried in recent years, "it is understandable that staff members should sometimes feel frustrated and even depressed." But he read out of his own experience a simple maxim: "Dejection and despair lead to defeatism—and defeat."

Reaching the end of his talk, Hammarskjöld offered a large vision in muted tones. "The role of the Organization is necessarily a modest one," he said, "subordinated as it must be to governments, and through governments to the will of the peoples. . . . It would be too dramatic to talk about our task as one of waging a war for peace, but it is quite realistic to look at it as an essential and—within its limits—effective work for building dams against the floods of disintegration and violence. . . . Short of the heavy work in which you, all of you, have had his or her part, the Congo would by now have been torn to pieces in a fight which in all likelihood would not have been limited to that territory, but spread far around. . . ." And here he shared his own hard-earned insight into the difference between personal vanity and proper satisfaction. "It is false pride . . . to boast to the world about the importance of one's work, but it is false humility, and finally just as destructive, not to recognize—and recognize with gratitude—that one's work has a sense. Let us avoid the second fallacy as carefully as the first, and let us work in the conviction that our work *has* a meaning beyond the narrow individual one and *has* meant something for man." There he closed his remarks.

There was time in the early days of September for dinners at home with guests, among them John Steinbeck and perhaps his wife, who spent a Sunday evening with him. This was the occasion for certain words we first read many pages ago in chapter 2. The Steinbecks were preparing to take their sons on a world tour. "I asked him what I could do for him," Steinbeck recalled, "and he said, 'Sit on the ground and talk to people. That's the most important thing.' And I said, 'You keep well. That's the *most* important.' He said, 'I'm all right. Don't worry about me.' And as I was leaving he repeated that—'I'm all right! Don't you worry!'"[17] At a time when Hammarskjöld was soon departing for the Congo and what was sure to be an intricate negotiation to bring Tshombe and Adoula together, his advice is striking. Perhaps in the end it sums up diplomacy. It's a matter of sitting on the ground and talking with people.

A favorite and distinguished visitor was expected in New York—Carl Nordenfalk, director of the Swedish National Museum since 1958, an art historian of widely acknowledged excellence. I don't know what Nordenfalk's primary mission in New York might have been, but with Hammarskjöld he had been in correspondence for some months concerning a project that keenly interested him: commissioning a portrait of Hammarskjöld by the American artist, Ben Shahn, for the national collection. Since January Nordenfalk had been trying without success to get artist and sitter in the same room. "I am quite convinced," he had written Hammarskjöld in January, "that you and Ben Shahn would get on very well together, since he is a very pleasant man, and finely educated. . . . Of course, I am aware that you have difficulties finding time, but perhaps it would be easier for you now than later, in March, when Khrushchev is prepared to put on his shoes again for another trip to the UN. There are, of course, more important things in the present situation than portrait painting! But with your wonderful capacity to combine an ability to perform great deeds with artistic hobbies, it might still not be totally impossible."[18] This was charming, and Hammarskjöld had agreed in principle to the portrait if time and artist could be found. Ben Shahn (1898–1969) was a truly notable artist with a strong social conscience rooted in his Eastern European Jewish background and his experience in federal arts programs during the Depression. His later style, with debts to Paul Klee and German Expressionism, drew on his remarkable drafts-manship and ability to characterize. He was a very good choice.

In early August, Hammarskjöld had written an amused word to a Swedish friend who moved in the same circles as Nordenfalk. "Send my regards to Carl and Cecilia. You can tell Carl that Ben Shahn after an earlier visit during the spring and a couple of telephone contacts has been quite invisible. But he will, no doubt, sooner or later, be seized by zest for work."[19] Ten days later in a note to Nordenfalk he returned to the issue with zest of his own. Though he was not on summer holiday, there is holiday spirit in his words. Shahn was still elusive. "Under the cir-cumstances, we can both just as well wait to get in touch again with Ben Shahn, although the boy certainly missed a chance when he has not used the last few weeks, during which I could really have put in the necessary time for him. However, all this is more easily straightened out once you come. I was rather amused to hear that he has back of him two portraits (which I would really like to see) of such distinguished 'loners' as Freud and Hemingway. What a 'troika.'"[20]

Nordenfalk and Shahn came to dinner at Seventy-Third Street on September 11th, the eve of Hammarskjöld's departure to the Congo. It must have been a cheerful occasion. The portrait was executed in 1962 from memory and UN photographs, rather than sittings. We'll return to it in a few pages. "I knew Dag Hammarskjöld," Shahn wrote a few years later. "I knew him personally, but even more, in a certain spiritual way. I am not a portrait painter, and I should never have wanted to paint a por-trait of this man had I not been so deeply moved by what he was. . . ."[21]

The day after, Hammarskjöld boarded a flight to the Congo. Some of his closest colleagues accompanied him to the airport. "Well, Dag," Cordier said, "I believe this . . . is going to be your most pleasant trip to Léopoldville."[22]

It belongs to history

Khiari had, in effect, the run of the Congo while Linnér made a hurried round trip to Brussels, and in that interval seems to have revised the ob-jectives of 9(c) without fully notifying his immediate superior, Linnér, or Hammarskjöld. The notion of mutiny comes to mind; it was some-thing like that. Khiari and O'Brien shared the view that larger measures should be taken, to which Brigadier Raja contributed a situation analysis and military plan. O'Brien was especially concerned to reduce Munongo's influence. "It was at the center," he wrote later, "that action should be taken. Munongo was the center and symbol of the whole system."[23] He should be removed from power or arrested. The operation they developed in cooperation with Raja was code named Morthor. A Hindi word variously translated over the years, it meant "smash" or "twist and break." The name itself, like "*psychose de choc*," could not be more distant from Hammarskjöld's humane diplomacy. No one in New York is said to have been aware of this dark code name until some hours after the operation began. In Linnér's absence and as Hammarskjöld flew to the scene from New York, a new attitude had gained control of events.

The concealed goal of Morthor was to end the secession, if possible without violence. Khiari's orders to O'Brien and Raja were to seize the key points targeted in Operation Rumpunch plus several more, most significantly the headquarters of Munongo's security police. He had obtained from the central government warrants for the arrest of Tshombe, Munongo, and three other ministers on charges of torture and assassination and, despite the Schachter memo, was willing to apply them. "As regards Tshombe," O'Brien wrote later, "we were to arrest him only in the last resort. . . . I was to parley with him, making it clear that his only hope lay in cooperating with the United Nations, and in peacefully liquidating the secession of Katanga. . . ."[24] The strategy called for the state commissioner dispatched from Léopoldville to assume authority, preferably in cooperation with Tshombe, in the name of the central government. As a sign to all, the flag of the central government was to be raised on public buildings. In that strident city there were many flags. "*Surtout pas de demi-mesures*," Khiari cautioned—above all, no half-measures. He had learned from Rumpunch.

Khiari had presented his aggressive plan as approved from the top of the chain of command, and O'Brien took him at his word. It was nothing of the kind, although O'Brien maintained in later years, against strong currents in the opposite direction, that Hammarskjöld had indeed approved it. Hammarskjöld's instructions and their timing have legitimately puzzled some later interpreters: he left more to the judgment of his representatives in the Congo than might be expected in this tense situation.[25] Close witnesses to the events that followed have puzzled over the motives of the troika Khiari, O'Brien, and Raja. Their impatience and urgent desire to change the miserable state of affairs were evident—but there was something more that remains at the level of surmise. Urquhart has described it as wanting "to present Hammarskjöld with a kind of 'apple to the teacher' when he arrived in the Congo,"[26] the vast problem of Katanga solved at last. Dayal said much the same thing: "Perhaps it was hoped that a swift and sudden action would produce the desired results, which would then be presented to the Secretary-General as a *fait accompli*."[27] However that may be, they were poised to exceed their authority and defy the principles governing the Congo operation for a result that would justify the liberty taken. Their timing, so incredibly odd, fits into this rationale: Raja had assured them that the military aspects of the operation would take two hours and meet little resistance. On that basis they decided to launch Morthor before Hammarskjöld's arrival. All or most of the difficulties would be behind them before his plane touched down. Early on September 13th, UN forces deployed.

They were expected. Instead of a more rigorous but nonviolent repetition of Rumpunch, they encountered determined defenders at the post office and radio station. The first shot was apparently fired by a mercenary sniper in an upper story across the street from the post office. The Belgian consulate occupied lower floors. An Indian soldier fell dead, the Indian troops returned fire, and the first skirmish began. The eight-day, episodic war that followed was destined to cost more dead and wounded than any past UN engagement in the Congo. Raja had grievously underestimated the opposing forces. They were well equipped and officered with flair both in Elisabethville and elsewhere in the province where troops clashed. And he had grievously overestimated the fighting capability and available arms of his UN forces. One telling asymmetry was the Katangan forces' possession of a jet fighter-bomber, the Fouga Magister, while the UN had no combat aircraft whatever. It entered battle unopposed.

Tshombe telephoned O'Brien—"What does this mean? What does this mean?"—and was easily persuaded to order a cease-fire. But for some reason UN troops hadn't shown up yet to encircle his residence and pin him down. Within a short time, he had second thoughts. Instead of ordering a cease-fire, he vanished. There was no need for sophisticated methods; he climbed over a wall to the safety of the adjoining British consulate, where the consul later said they spent a pleasant hour talking about everything except politics. He was then spirited away under a rug in the back of the consul's car to greater safety at Katanga's border with Northern Rhodesia. Within a few hours he was calling on his fellow citizens over Rhodesian radio to wage total war against the UN. Soon after, he went into hiding on the Katangan side of the border. In his sparkling and, where most needed, self-exonerating account of his experience in Katanga, O'Brien acknowledged that the failure to hold Tshombe within reach was another lapse on his part.[28] "By this time," he wrote in a second and later account, "Morthor had definitely gone off the rails. That was how things stood when Hammarskjöld arrived in Léopoldville."[29]

In a cable to Ralph Bunche two days later, Hammarskjöld wrote, "It belongs to the history re consultations that the first I knew about this development I learned by a tendentious Reuters report on my way to Léo."[30] This is more packed with detail than the memorable phrase often associated with this moment—"It belongs to history . . ."—but we can hear that phrase inside the rest and also realize that he was reassuring Bunche, and those at the UN and the US State Department with whom Bunche was speaking, that he hadn't been consulted about the timing and final purpose of Morthor. He had been approached for comment by reporters during a refueling stop in Accra, capital of Ghana, and dismissed their information about the battle in Elisabethville as one more rumor; there were so many. Urquhart brilliantly, and sadly, characterized the situation that awaited Hammarskjöld in Léo: "Fighting broke out, and it broke out when Hammarskjöld was literally flying over the Atlantic for this supposedly triumphal, last visit to the Congo to patch the whole thing up. So, instead of arriving as a sort of *deus ex machina* and arranging a reconciliation between Tshombe and the central government, he arrived to find a very nasty little war going on in Elisabethville in which his own people were on the ropes. . . ."[31]

In the afternoon of September 13th, it wasn't yet evident to O'Brien that Morthor was leading to days of warfare in Katanga and a chaotic diplomatic crisis for the UN and Hammarskjöld personally. He called a press conference in Elisabethville to announce that "the secession of Katanga was at an end."[32] Hammarskjöld could not believe that any such thing had been said to the media. "It is obviously intolerable," he cabled O'Brien on the 17th, "to read that UN was resolutely decided to carry out the operation it has launched in order to put an end to the Katanga secession, to quote only one of the many erroneous and damaging judgments and statements. Will you please instruct [name omitted] that as long as UN has anything to do with running station, news reporting has to be conducted in as impartial and accurate repeat accurate manner as possible."[33] His wording seems to bypass O'Brien, as if he weren't directly responsible. In general, Hammarskjöld was intent on rescuing the situation without assigning blame. That could be sorted out later.

Hammarskjöld's priorities were to locate Tshombe and, wherever it could be arranged, invite him to a cease-fire negotiation. UN forces in Katanga were on the defensive: the Fouga Magister piloted by a Belgian mercenary was strafing and bombing at will; a contingent of Irish troops was besieged and forced to surrender; there had been hand-to-hand combat in the streets of Elisabethville; O'Brien himself was deliberately attacked from the air and ducked for cover during a small press conference some days later. The hatred of the UN in Katanga among some ministers and virtually all of the local white "ultras" and fanatical mercenaries was driving the battle, as if revenge had at last found its moment. Vehement questioning and criticism from all sides were reaching Hammarskjöld in Léopoldville. The British asked for an explanation, threatened to withdraw support from the Congo operation as a whole, and refused Hammarskjöld's request for fly-over rights in British East Africa for Ethiopian jet fighters offered as reinforcements to even the balance in the air war. They took the view, unpersuasive to UN peacekeepers running for cover, that more jets in the Congo would only escalate the battle (two days later, after tragedy had struck, they relented).[34] The US secretary of state wanted to know why the United States hadn't been consulted before such a consequential operation and just what Hammarskjöld had in mind: didn't he realize that replacing Tshombe with that Communist state commissioner from Léopoldville was unacceptable? The Rhodesian Federation sent troops and armored vehicles to the border with Katanga, ready to defend itself and cross over if need be. Following up on a conversation between Hammarskjöld and the British ambassador in Leopoldville, Britain hurried Lord Lansdowne, an undersecretary of state, from London to the Congo to carry a message from the prime minister, Harold Macmillan. Lansdowne reported later to Parliament that Hammarskjöld made clear his dismay over the fighting and his intention to seek a cease-fire. Their meeting must have been difficult. Soon after,

Hammarskjöld's senior African expert, Heinz Wieschhoff, is said to have thrown up his hands: "All is finished, all is finished."[35]

Hammarskjöld didn't think so. Communication had again been established with Tshombe, and he knew that O'Brien had proposed to meet him in Northern Rhodesia to negotiate a cease-fire. He decided to keep that appointment himself, without O'Brien. Linnér recalled asking him whether he felt that, if he met Tshombe, he could convince him. Hammarskjöld replied, "I want to explore that possibility because, with the prestige of the office of the Secretary-General being as high as one can go, if that doesn't help then nothing would help."[36] The plan to meet Tshombe worked a welcome change in him. Bill Ranallo wrote to his wife on September 17th that "the boss has been in such a depressed mood— worse than any time I have known him. . . . He was much better last night because he's set up a parley with Tshombe in Ndola for some time today."[37]

Through intermediaries Hammarskjöld sent a note to Tshombe laying out methodically the common ground between them despite the current situation. "You yourself accepted the objectives of the United Nations mission . . . , that is to say, the maintenance of public order, the prevention of civil war, and the evacuation of all the personnel referred to by the Security Council. There should therefore be no difference of opinion between the Organization and you as to the framework within which ways must be sought of putting an end to the present armed conflict." This was somewhat tough and systematic; much of the letter had that character. But as he proposed to meet with Tshombe, the tone changed: he again had in mind the larger reason for his presence in the Congo. He wasn't there to quell an unexpected war, although he accepted responsibility for doing so. He was there to bring Tshombe and Adoula together and reduce the need for the UN in the Congo. "I suggest that I should meet you personally, so that together we can try to find peaceful methods of resolving the present conflict, thus opening the way to a solution of the Katanga problem within the framework of the Congo. . . ."[38] Ndola would be the meeting place. There were difficulties to overcome: Tshombe accepted only on condition of a cease-fire that disadvantaged the UN forces, Hammarskjöld replied that an even-handed cease-fire would first have to be agreed—and Tshombe failed at that point to reply. Hammarskjöld nonetheless decided to keep the appointment on the assumption that Tshombe would find his way there. That was so—he arrived by air, with an honorific escort of Rhodesian fighter jets, at 5:00 p.m. Somewhat surprisingly, he was accompanied by leading Katangese ministers but not one Belgian adviser to a meeting that was sure to be consequential.[39]

Either Lansdowne or Hammarskjöld had suggested the Rhodesian mining city of Ndola for the rendezvous. It was scarcely ten miles over the border from Katanga with a modern airport: easily reached by Tshombe, not easily reached by Hammarskjöld who would have to fly some hours, but it was arguably a safe site under the dual aegis of the Rhodesian Federation and Britain. On the 17th, at Hammarskjöld's request, Lansdowne flew to Ndola in advance to ensure that conditions were prepared for the meeting, which was to be in the plain but serviceable airport manager's office. Lansdowne also agreed to leave Ndola before Hammarskjöld's arrival later in the day to avoid even the appearance of member-nation influence on the negotiation to follow. However, Britain would be represented at Ndola by Lord Alport—Cuthbert, or "Cub" Alport, high commissioner to the Rhodesian Federation—who had flown in from Salisbury, the capital of Southern Rhodesia (future Zimbabwe) and of the federation. It seems that Alport was expected to hover and ensure that all went as planned. Britain had retained control over the international affairs of the Federation; he was the point man. Later Alport wrote that he had met Hammarskjöld just once, in London. "My recollection of Hammarskjöld is of a small, fair, dapper little man, very incisive in his speech, very frank and sophisticated in his manner. He obviously possessed great charm and conveyed instinctively an impression of common sense and integrity."[40] It's a pleasant description, but if I'm not mistaken he has called Mr. Hammarskjöld both "small" and "little" in a single sentence, betraying an attitude otherwise undeclared.

Through much of the afternoon of the 17th, Hammarskjöld was winding up business in Léopoldville. Ralph Bunche at New York headquarters received from him a coolly thoughtful cable. Bunche had managed to calm the US State Department, which now better understood both the difficulties and hope attending Hammarskjöld's days in the Congo. Hammarskjöld's cable was rather complex, as if he needed to step back from his own dismay and the waves of criticism and emotion to which he had been subject to reestablish the ordering power of reason. "[Various signs] amply prove that our evaluation of the civil war risks has been correct," Hammarskjöld wrote to his old companion-in-arms. "These risks, of course, may have been or may yet be activated either by [an army] intervention or by a break-up of the cabinet, the [Gizenga] group returning to its base, short of a tangible and explicable trend in the direction of a resolution of the Katanga problem, at least in the form of discussions between the parties. . . . Our gradual response to the situation by measures tending to set Tshombe free from domination by foreign elements or ultra while at the same time keeping him under pressure, which should convince him about the impossibility to hold out with Katanga separatism, has been an absolute condition for the staving off so far of aforementioned risks. . . ."[41] It was in search of a "tangible and explicable trend" that Hammarskjöld would soon leave for Ndola.

Hammarskjöld, Linnér, and his travel party reached the airport in the late afternoon. Passengers and crew—sixteen in all—included Heinz Wieschhoff, Vladimir Fabry (a UN legal adviser on assignment to the Congo), Alice Lalande (Linnér's multilingual secretary), Bill Ranallo, a number of additional security personnel and Swedish soldiers, and a veteran Swedish crew of six, flying a comfortable DC-6 leased to the UN by a Swedish company, Transair. Typically used by General McKeown, the senior military commander in the Congo, the airplane was known as the Albertina. It had come under fire as it took off from Elisabeth-ville earlier in the day, but the few needed repairs had been made on the tarmac at Léopoldville. Linnér expected to fly with the party, but as he and Hammarskjöld sat in the airplane before the door closed Linnér noticed him nervously jiggling his foot, a familiar sign. Something was troubling him. "What's wrong?" Linnér asked. Hammarskjöld replied that he didn't feel comfortable with both of them away from Léopold-ville—he should stay behind.[42] Linnér of course agreed. Hammarskjöld accompanied Linnér down the boarding steps; there is film footage of them reading last-minute telex tapes before Hammarskjöld reboarded. It may have been while they were sitting together that Hammarskjöld invited him to look at the twelve initial pages of his Swedish transla-tion of Martin Buber's *I and Thou*, which he had left in the guest room at Linnér's residence. They would discuss them when he returned in a few days. Hammarskjöld mentioned that Buber's thought brought to mind the medieval mystics whom he had been reading for so many years. "Love, for them," he said, "was a surplus of power which they felt completely filled them when they began to live in self-forgetfulness."[43] Those were the last words Linnér could recall of their conversation. They are hauntingly close to Hammarskjöld's homage to his medieval religious masters near the beginning of his years of UN service. In the radio address of November 1953, he had said: "'Love' ... for them meant simply an overflowing of the strength with which they felt themselves filled when living in true self-oblivion." In my first meeting with Sture Linnér in Stockholm—he was then in his nineties—I didn't miss the opportunity to ask whether this was well and truly what Hammarskjöld had said. Perhaps there was some blurring between the early memorable text and this late memorable moment? He replied without hesitation that it was precisely what Hammarskjöld said. As the cable to Bunche implicitly reestablished reason, this conversation seems in retrospect to have reestablished his values, his inner life and willing openness to others. To state such a serious thing is to recommit to it.

He has gone elsewhere

Later in the day, after Hammarskjöld's departure at 4:45 p.m., Linnér dropped by for a word with the prime minister. Adoula said that, had he known the secretary-general was flying to Ndola, he would have stopped the plane.[44] What did he have in mind? It goes without saying that he didn't trust the white supremacist Rhodesian regime and resented its support of independent Katanga. Perhaps that was all.

At this point in expositions of the journey to Ndola, which has some qualities of legend, it is customary to show a map with two flight paths: Lansdowne's route due southeast direct to the destination, Hammarskjöld's eastbound at length, turning south toward Ndola over Rhodesian territory. With a Fouga Magister in the skies over Katanga and operating at will, the decision had been made to cloak Hammarskjöld's flight path and destination in secrecy. There was to be no radio contact with ground stations until necessary toward the end of the flight. A radio frequency was kept open and reserved for the Albertina only in case of need, but it wasn't used. In spite of the effort to maintain secrecy, word got out that Hammarskjöld was expected at Ndola, and reporters found their way there, as did a friendly crowd of Africans hoping to catch sight of a great champion of African independence. Arriving without incident, Lansdowne oversaw preparations on the ground. Hammarskjöld's flight is said to have reached Ndola air space shortly before midnight. It's a good surmise that in the long course of those hours he discussed the impending negotiation with Wieschhoff and Fabry, chatted with Bill Ranallo and Alice Lalande, had the pleasure of speaking Swedish with soldiers in the security detail, perhaps went forward to have a word with

Captain Hallonquist and the flight crew. But that is all surmise. What we do know is that he continued translating *I and Thou*, more than five pages of the printed text. Using Buber's German and an English transla- tion, he had picked up the thread at the bottom of page 16 (English) and, writing out his draft on a yellow legal pad, worked through to mid-page 22.[45] These observations can't help but seem like an inventory of things that don't matter until one reads the text to which he was giv- ing concentrated thought while in flight. Buber's words are in part so abstract and intellectually challenging that he surely spent hours with them. To understand anew the flight to Ndola, we need to impress on our minds the image and content of this long moment of translation. Hammarskjöld was neither in Léopoldville with its anguish and passions nor in Elisabethville with its anguish and passions. He was nowhere pre- cise, free for a few hours to resume contact through Buber's thought with some of the foundation elements of his own perspective on life.

The section he translated begins with reflections about an unstable zone in human experience where the purity of encounter between I and Thou inevitably falters. "This is the exalted melancholy of our fate," he would have read in the English version he had at hand, "that every *Thou* in our world must become an *It*. . . . Love itself cannot persist in direct relation. It endures, but in interchange of actual and potential being. . . ." (The closing phrase is needlessly obscure. Kaufmann's more recent trans- lation is better: "It endures, but only in the alternation of actuality and latency.") Buber writes that we inevitably categorize one another, find uses for one another, become again for one another "a *He* or a *She*, a sum of qualities," and lose awareness of the uncoercive dialogue at the very base of relationship. But the encounter of I and Thou can be renewed. "In the beginning is relation," Buber writes, as if revising the opening words of *Genesis*. Hammarskjöld must have paused over this grand asser- tion; so much in his working life relied on this truth of feeling, even if the mind can deprecate it. He had said to Steinbeck, "Sit on the ground and talk with people. That is the most important thing." Is there a dif- ference in meaning? He asked Steinbeck to discover Thou, a thousand Thou's, as he traveled.

The pages Hammarskjöld was translating turn at this point toward reflections about the consciousness and symbols of so-called primitive societies, in which Buber discovers the central concern of his book: direct relationship—or dialogue—with fellow human beings, God, and the natural world. The quality of awareness of tribal humanity immersed in nature and interpreting its powers fascinates him. Flying over the vast landscape of the Congo with its hundreds of tribes and ancient living cultures, Hammarskjöld had every reason to share that fascination. He had had so little opportunity—likely none at all—to make contact with what was grandly called "the bush," where complex indigenous cultures had somehow survived.[46] One of Buber's themes in these few pages is the aboriginal perception of causality. We know the extent to which Hammarskjöld's diplomatic life had to do with breaking the tyranny of causal chains in international life, and we have heard him reflect on and pray for providential guidance that obeys another law. He must have paused with interest over these lines: "Causality in [aboriginal peoples'] world-image is no unbroken sequence but an ever new flashing forth of power . . .; it is a volcanic movement without continuity. . . ." The discovery in political processes of a better way sometimes has that quality: discontinuous with what has come before, with the prevailing logic. Hammarskjöld had often lived that. He counted on living it again at Ndola. Flying toward his appointment, he was immersed in the spare thought of a spiritual kinsman about the primacy of relationship. In the beginning is relation.

My understanding of the events at Ndola is guided by an extraordinary book published only a few months before this chapter was written: Susan Williams's *Who Killed Hammarskjöld? The UN, the Cold War and White Supremacy in Africa.*[47] A Senior Research Fellow at the Institute of Commonwealth Studies, University of London, she had written extensively on Africa and decolonization before taking up this topic. In the course of five years of research, she functioned as both scholar and sleuth, discovering, exploring, and authenticating archives that had long escaped attention, finding leads in unlikely places, fearlessly meeting with figures from murky worlds who might just know something more. As well, and equally important, she reevaluated eyewitness testimony that had been willfully ignored or undervalued in early investigations because it was the testimony of Africans, men and women of dark skin, participating in the formal inquiries of a white supremacist government. She met and spoke with some—young then, old now—who had testified at the time or out of fear refrained from testifying, and in the months following publication of her book additional eyewitnesses have stepped forward to set in place their pieces of the puzzle. The humble charcoal burners who pursued their livelihood in the forests surrounding Ndola are among the indisputable heroes in what follows. As is Dr. Williams.

What follows is the most consistent narrative *currently* available. However, some of its elements—even fundamental elements—may well be revised in the second edition of Dr. Williams's book, in which her further research, together with documentation assembled and interpreted by Hans Kristian Simensen and others, is sure to shed further light. Reinvestigation of the tragedy at Ndola a half century after the event bears some resemblance to the rediscovery of the *Titanic*: the object is fragmented, encrusted, in the dark. But it is not entirely out of reach.

As the Albertina flew south over Rhodesian territory, the pilot broke radio silence several times to contact ground control at Salisbury and entered Ndola airspace just before midnight. Conditions were normal, the half-moon setting but visible. At ten minutes after midnight, the Albertina radioed to Ndola ground control, "Your lights in sight overhead Ndola, descending," and was advised to descend to a certain altitude and report in again. There was no further word from it. It had seemingly disappeared. After some minutes, Lord Alport calmly suggested to the air traffic team that Hammarskjöld must have "gone elsewhere," perhaps to Elisabethville to get a direct report on conditions there. He appeared to be undisturbed, in contrast to Lord Lansdowne who left by air for Salisbury soon after hearing that the Albertina had fallen silent. He was honoring the agreement with Hammarskjöld not to be at Ndola for his arrival, but he was worried. He had his pilot try repeatedly to contact the Albertina. At 2:20 a.m., Ndola airport sent an uncertainty signal to Salisbury—by the book, it should have been sent considerably earlier—and shortly after 3:00 a.m., with Alport's agreement, closed down for the night. His prestige as British High Commissioner carried more weight than standard procedure, and he was willing to wait until morning to sort things out on the premise that the secretary-general's flight must have gone elsewhere. However, there were stirrings in the night; a policeman had seen "a tremendous flash of light in the sky," heard the sound of a small jet overhead, and a few minutes later saw a second flash. He and a colleague scared up the airport manager at his hotel and awakened him to tell him what he had seen, but Red Williams—that was his name—said that there was nothing to be done until first light. In any case, he said, "VIP planes don't crash."[48]

The next morning there were attempts to clarify the situation, none as important as the dispatch at 10:00 a.m.—hardly first light—of search aircraft. However, owing to a thoughtless application of standard procedure, they were sent in all directions except the one from which flights normally approached Ndola airport. From Alport's comment that Hammarskjöld must have gone elsewhere to the dispatch of air search in pointless directions at midmorning the next day, something indecipherable hung over Ndola airport, a lassitude or thickness. In the early afternoon the search from the air by UN, US, and Rhodesian flight crews intensified. That broke the spell. The crash of the Albertina was sighted at 3:10. As Williams writes, "It had taken more than fifteen hours for the Albertina to be found—nine hours after first light on 18 September. This was all the more surprising, given that the plane lay . . . just eight miles away."[49]

Rhodesian police and firefighters rushed to the crash site, followed by reporters and press photographers. The plane was 70 to 80 percent incinerated. With the exception of two among them, its passengers were severely burned and unrecognizable, some reduced to the size of children. Hammarskjöld had been thrown clear of the crash. Dead but unburned, he was found on his back beside a massive ant hill. He disliked seatbelts; that probably explains why he was thrown clear. A single survivor, the UN security officer Harold Julien, had lain under the hot sun with severe burns for many hours while the airport authorities dawdled and the air search fanned out in irrelevant directions. He was in misery and delirious but able to give his name and ask that his wife be notified. He died six days later in the hospital, not before saying what he could about the crash. It wasn't a great deal, but it mattered a great deal. The crash site was secured, bodies removed and taken to a morgue. An autopsy of the secretary-general's body identified fatal internal injuries that were presumed to have killed him instantly, though there is said to have been discussion as to whether he might have lived a little longer, had medical help arrived sooner. His body was taken in a coffin to a Protestant chapel in Ndola, where it was draped with the flag of Sweden and overspread with flowers. Moïse Tshombe came to pay his respects and left flowers. He "stood still for a moment, bowed slightly, then turned away."[50] On the following day Hammarskjöld's nephew Knut arrived to represent the family, accompanied by Dag's close colleague Piero Spinelli representing the UN. Dag and Knut had been close: after the early death of Dag's brother Åke, Knut found in his uncle a devoted surrogate father.[51]

How did this happen? About the ground controllers' conduct, there has never been any question. Had they acted immediately, following international norms and the promptings of compassionate concern, Sergeant Julien's life might have been saved—the doctor who treated him thought so—and his unique knowledge of the crash would not have been lost. About Alport's conduct, despite his low-key account written years later and his high station, there has accumulated the conviction that he was inexcusably casual. About the cause of the crash, the obvious question has never quite disappeared, though three formal investigations soon after the event seemed to settle the question: while there was some possibility of foul play, pilot error was the likely cause owing to weariness, unfamiliarity with the airport, possible misreading of the altimeter. A wingtip caught in treetops on a rise of land. The plane sheared a long path through the trees, spun around, broke up, and burst into flames on the ground. It was an accident.

Many accepted this explanation at the time and since, though some felt uneasy or refused it because the timing was so strange. Hammarskjöld's death at a time when the Katanga secession seemed closer to resolution could have served *someone's* imagined interest—but who precisely? And would that *someone* or consortium of interests—again, who?—resort to murder? There were those who felt it might be so, but feelings are one thing and evidence another. A Swedish investigator who reopened the inquiry in 1993 at the request of the Swedish government reaffirmed pilot error as the least improbable cause.[52] Pilot error was the only acceptable explanation for Brian Urquhart, who expressed impatience in the 1972 biography—and in the years since its publication—with conspiracy theories and theorists. That understanding of the event is clean and clear. It attributes to Hammarskjöld dreadful luck, but he leaves this world untouched by evil. A martyr, surely, but martyred by the hazards of life.

There is another version, in fact multiple versions; none has yet eliminated the others. (That may change as the UN or governments follow up on the research of Dr. Williams and H. K. Simensen.) What they all have in common is that the circumstances are not clean and clear. They suggest assassination, planned and carried through by the darkest elements in central Africa. In all of these versions Hammarskjöld descends into a trap laid for him and his companions with the same attitude of remorseless hatred that led to the death of Patrice Lumumba. In all such versions he falls victim to conspirators and their mercenary agents who perceived in him an effective enemy of their plan for Katanga, for Rhodesia, for white supremacy elsewhere in Africa—there isn't enough information yet to know where to set the boundary. He had foreseen something like this; the poems of 1960–61 return repeatedly to the theme of execution. Insofar as one can tell, he had made his peace with it. Lines come to mind from a poem he completed in spring 1961:

> Asked if I have courage
> To go on to the end,
> I give an irreversible
> Answer.[53]

While he was merely a human being—one of us, as his preferred author Joseph Conrad would say, and a near contemporary—in my mind's eye, when I think of Hammarskjöld's death, I sometimes see a terrifying image. It is an image from early Flemish art, depicting repulsive faces crowding in on the face of Jesus as he toils toward Golgotha. Years earlier, Hammarskjöld had weighed the idea that imagery of this kind offered a likeness to the UN at its worst—and rejected it. "If I were [Hieronymus] Bosch," we have heard him say to his friend Beskow, "I could paint a beautiful triptych in the colors of Hell. . . . But why be bitter."

The charcoal burners

Several years ago I asked Linnér what he thought about the crash. "I have an idea," he responded, "but I have no facts to stand on. I can only give you what I intuitively felt about it. I went to Katanga immediately, and what I found was hatred in the highest places—hatred against the UN, hatred against Dag Hammarskjöld, a feeling of joy and relief that he was no longer alive. That much I can say. When I returned to Léopoldville I received one invitation after another from Belgian families to celebrate his death. Of course, underneath it all they hated me even more than Hammarskjöld. Can you imagine—celebrating the death of Hammarskjöld?"[54] Within days of the crash, Prime Minister Adoula voiced a severe accusation that found echoes—typically with less fervor but no less conviction—in many parts of the world. "Katanga is in the hands of capitalist imperialism," he charged. "It is in this net of capitalist imperialism, in which the traitor Tshombe is hopelessly enmeshed, that the real causes of the disappearance of Mr. Hammarskjöld can be found. How ignoble is this assassination, not the first of its kind perpetrated by the monied powers. Mr. Hammarskjöld was the victim of certain financial circles for whom a human life is not equal to a gram of copper or uranium."[55] Urquhart summarized attitudes at the time: "There was an immediate and widespread assumption that foul play had caused the disaster, with the British, the Rhodesians, Tshombe, the Belgians, and the mercenaries being credited singly or collectively with the deed."[56]

In rather rapid succession there were three investigations.[57] The first was instituted immediately after the crash by the Rhodesian authorities, as required by international convention, with observers joining the investigation from the UN, Sweden, international aviation organizations, and Transair, the Swedish company that flew the Albertina. The two primary Swedish observers, one of whom was a criminal investigator, annoyed the Rhodesian team by insistently searching the wreckage for signs of "bullet holes . . . , parts of grenades, rocket parts," and they noted with alarmed interest that the body of one of the security guards, a French-speaking Haitian, had been found in the cockpit. Had he seen something outside a cabin window, was he alerting or consulting with the crew, was he needed for unusual radio communications?[58] At the time, these questions didn't have much staying power. The board of inquiry interviewed some eyewitnesses and their testimony was taken but not taken seriously. It also questioned Red Williams, who said among other things that he had discounted the importance of the policemen's urgent visit in the middle of the night because there are brush fires all the time at that season; he assumed that the fellow had seen the light of one in the sky. Harold Julien's testimony was also considered. Here we encounter words central to the drama. According to Julien, Hammarskjöld had called out "Go back, go back," and there had been "sparks, sparks in the sky."[59] The board of inquiry nonetheless concluded after more than six weeks of investigation that the probable cause was pilot error: the Albertina had been on a correct approach but 1,700 feet too low. The board recorded that foul play could not be entirely ruled out but, based on Williams's reading of disregarded testimony, it chose to emphasize pilot error despite suggestive testimony to the contrary from both white and black witnesses.

A few days after the first Rhodesian inquiry got under way, a second Rhodesian inquiry was set in motion by a different government agency. The first investigation was predominantly technical, focused on the crash site and air traffic control; this was to be a Commission of Inquiry taking testimony under oath and conducting its proceedings openly in the public interest. Attorneys representing the Rhodesian Federation, the UN, Sweden, and Great Britain interrogated witnesses—but the white supremacist norms of Rhodesia prevailed in both the treatment of witnesses and the weighting of their testimony. Europeans were addressed as "Mister," others as "African." Again there was testimony to events in the sky above Ndola suggesting an attack on the Albertina by a smaller plane or pair of planes. The commission listened to further evidence from Sergeant Julien, a tape recording made on the way to the hospital in an ambulance, and interviewed the nurses who had cared for him. They had the assurance of the doctor who looked after him that he had lucid moments; there was no medical reason to disregard his testimony, brief as it was. Here again we encounter words central to the drama. In the ambulance he had said that the plane "blew up." "Was this over the runway?" asked the police interviewer. "Yes . . . There was great speed. Great speed . . . Then there was the crash. . . ."[60] Timothy Kankasa testified for the second time. A municipal administrator in the township of Twapia near the airport, he had seen a smaller airplane "beaming lights on the bigger plane."[61] His testimony was rejected: "Completely unacceptable . . . You made a mistake"—this from a Rhodesian attorney. The commission also heard from charcoal burners. In the report later issued, the charcoal burners from the forests surrounding Ndola are made to seem the humblest of folk, looking up into the sky with smudged faces, incapable of understanding what they might have seen, easily mistaking one thing for another. That they lived and worked near the airport and had observed thousands of aircraft coming and going was of no account. Decades later, Williams discovered that some of these smudged charcoal burners and officials of local black townships, and some of their wives, had risen to prominence in independent Zambia and Malawi, successors in 1964 to the Rhodesian Federation. The late Mr. Kankasa had been a minister of state in Zambia and ambassador to the Congo, then known as Zaire. His spirited wife, who became in later years the formidable Mama Kankasa, was a freedom fighter as a young woman and in independent Zambia the long-serving minister for women's affairs (1969–88). When they met not long ago, she told Williams that her husband had immediately informed Rhodesian authorities about what he had seen in the sky. No action was taken, as we know, until midmorning.

In Williams's account, Dickson Buleni testified as follows: "He was sitting outside his home in the charcoal burners' compound that night with his wife when they were surprised to see a large plane with a small plane flying above it. He saw a 'fire' coming from the small plane to the roof of the big plane, when he heard the sound of an explosion. Then the big plane fell down and crashed. After circling once, he said, the small plane flew off . . . to the west."[62] Other Africans offered comparable testimony, all of which was challenged and ultimately ignored by the commission. Buleni was described in the final report as "not a reliable witness," in part because he had been to a "beer drink" that night—but factually he never took alcohol. Similar evidence given by whites received the same treatment. There were other featured witnesses. A Belgian officer in the Katangan air force testified as if he were the pilot of the feared Fouga Magister. In reality he occasionally occupied the second seat in the aircraft, while its pilot—a Belgian mercenary who did not appear before the commission—did the driving. The officer's testimony was understood to prove that the Fouga Magister could not have been operating that night in Ndola airspace and that may have been so, though we'll soon come to curious evidence to the contrary. Sergeant Julien's words were again considered, but the commission decided that "no attention need . . . be paid to remarks about sparks in the sky. They either relate to the fire after the crash or to a symptom of his then condition."[63] Despite their flourish of legal procedure and open inquiry, the proceedings were pitiful: the pursuit of a foregone conclusion. Eliminating the previous board's mention of the remote possibility of foul play, the commission's concluding report attributed the crash exclusively to pilot error. The only concession was criticism of Ndola airport management.

On October 26th the General Assembly passed a resolution calling for "an international investigation into the conditions and circumstances resulting in the tragic death of Mr. Dag Hammarskjöld and of members of the party accompanying him."[64] General Assembly resolutions are often dry objects, but this one has an undercurrent of sorrow and urgent questioning. It lists by name all of Hammarskjöld's fellow victims and specifically asks hard questions—for example, "why the flight had to be undertaken at night without escort," and "whether . . . the fact of [the Albertina's] having crashed did not become known until several hours afterwards, and . . . why," and more still. Five "eminent persons" were to lead the investigation and report to the president of the General Assembly within three months. The persons chosen owed nothing to local African regimes or the great powers: they were from Sweden,

Nepal, Argentina, Yugoslavia, and Sierra Leone. The new commission held hearings in Léopoldville, Salisbury, and Ndola in early 1962, and later met in Geneva to take further testimony. Williams reports that it heard ninety witnesses, some of whom had not dared to come forward earlier out of fear of the Rhodesian regime. New evidence tumbled out. Among the most important witnesses was another smudged charcoal burner, later a political leader in Malawi. Mr. Mpinganjira testified that he and a fellow worker had seen two small aircraft in the sky that night pursuing a larger plane. "The lower of the small aircraft overtook it, flying just above—and then there was a red flash on the big plane, which dipped down to the sound of a loud explosion and then a series of smaller ones. The little plane circled and flew off."[65] About a half hour later he and his companion saw two Land Rovers rush by on a bush road. Ten or fifteen minutes later they saw "a sudden, huge burst of flames," and the Land Rovers soon drove past again at top speed. "I have no doubt," Mr. Mpinganjira said, "that they had something to do with increasing the flames."[66] A Rhodesian official who interrogated him later told a Northern Rhodesian newspaper that "all the evidence about jets firing at a large plane proves that there is an organized attempt by a political group to discredit the Federation."[67] Since the publication of Susan Williams's book, another witness has come forward to amplify Mr. Mpinganjira's testimony. He was a miner traveling to work by motorbike "when he heard the . . . Albertina come down and went to investigate. Simultaneously, six to eight men he describes as paramilitary . . . arrived in two Jeeps 'as if prewarned.' He was about twenty meters from the aircraft and, before he was ordered away, noted fist-sized holes from the wing to the fuselage, 'as if it had been sprayed by bullets,' and the fact that the wreckage was unburned."[68]

Khiari's testimony to the UN commission is interesting.[69] At the request of his superiors at UN headquarters, he had gone at once to Ndola after the crash to negotiate a cease-fire with Tshombe. "I did oppose Mr. Hammarskjöld's journey to Ndola," Khiari testified,

> but not on the grounds of danger. I opposed it on political grounds
> . . . . I was convinced that if Mr. Hammarskjöld went to Ndola and saw
> Tshombe, Tshombe would become quite a different man. He would
> think he was victorious and become impossible. [Mr. Hammarskjöld]
> saw the problem from a higher position, and he knew more aspects than
> I . . . . He felt he had a political and moral obligation to go there. . . .

At Ndola Khiari had spoken with Alport informally about reports he had heard that

> several people saw a plane on fire in the sky, then heard an explosion. But the High Commissioner did not seem to attach any great importance to this. Either he did not answer or said 'So many people see so many things.' He gave me the impression that he did not want to discuss the matter. . . . I had the impression that the Europeans, the white population, did not want to speak about the death of Mr. Hammarskjöld, and the white officials . . . gave me the impression that they had received definite instructions not to discuss the question. . . . The Africans, on the other hand, were very desirous of discussing the problem, they gave us a lot of theories and wanted to discuss it freely. . . .

Earlier in his testimony that day, Khiari made clear that it hadn't been easy to speak with Africans.

> Many people told us that around midnight, maybe a quarter past . . . , a large number of Africans in the neighborhood of the airport saw a high flame and heard the noise of an explosion. We had this information from a few people we could get to because . . . our movements were restricted. We got this information in the hotel, from taxi drivers, waiters. Many saw the flame and heard the explosion. I must point out that the High Commissioner told us that . . . no flame had been seen from the control tower. I find it strange that a large number of people at the airport saw this flame while people in the control tower, which I think is about 70 feet high, and on which they could see much better, say they saw nothing.

In Ndola there were two racial realms and two conversations. In the white realm, Hammarskjöld's death was a controlled topic—best to say little. In the African realm, people were speaking of nothing but. Hammarskjöld may not have been aware of what he meant to the African population of Northern Rhodesia. Mama Kankasa put it movingly: "When we heard that Dr. Hammarskjöld was coming for peace talks in Ndola we were very happy. We looked on him as a peacemaker coming to see what to do about . . . Mr. Welensky and Tshombe. . . ."[70] To this day many Zambians esteem Hammarskjöld, not only as a peacemaker, but as a man of spirit, one with "eyes to see."

While the UN commission's report (April 1962) acknowledged that attack or sabotage could not be ruled out, it reached "an open verdict," as Williams puts it.[71] However, the report added a previously unexplored scenario to the range of possibilities. When the Albertina had undergone repairs at Léopoldville airport, after sustaining light damage from gunfire as it flew out of Elisabethville early on September 17th, it had been left locked but unattended for some hours on the tarmac. While the main cabin and cockpit had been secured, the undercarriage, hydraulic compartment, and heating equipment remained accessible. This raised the possibility that a bomb with a timing device could have been planted. It may seem unlikely, but Williams's pursuit of evidence led to this scenario as yet another version of what may have happened. Archbishop Desmond Tutu's Truth and Reconciliation Commission, in South Africa, surfaced papers in the late 1990s from an extremely shady organization that appear to document a successful attempt to plant and detonate a bomb in the Albertina. When he announced their existence, the archbishop commented that while the papers may be an exercise in disinformation for motives unclear, "things of that sort have happened in the past"; the papers were worth a closer look.[72] Williams has so far been able to document the organization—it is not an invented figment—but the originals of the incriminating documents have disappeared, and with photocopies only at her disposal has been unable to confirm their authenticity.[73]

There is much more detail in Williams's account of the three investigations conducted soon after the catastrophic crash. Even the abridged summaries here make clear that radically different and troubling versions of the crash emerged from the hearings but remained at the margin, disparagingly recorded or simply omitted by the early pair of investigations, respectfully recorded by the third but exercising little influence. Despite the passage of decades, Williams's further investigations uncovered much more.

At this point we need Hammarskjöld back. We need his breadth of mind to hearten us because some of the findings are sickening. You may recall that he once wrote to Pär Lagerkvist about rare occasions when "the distinction between triumph and tragedy is totally obliterated in a victorious and affirmative humanity." In his reflections at Pentecost, less than a half year before his death, he returned to that theme in lines we have paused over. "I came to a time and place," he wrote then, "where I realized that the way leads to a triumph which is a catastrophe, and to a catastrophe which is a triumph, that the price for committing one's life would be reproach, and that the only elevation possible to man lies in the depths of humiliation. After that, the word 'courage' lost its meaning, since nothing could be taken from me." These thoughts are needed because, in one recurrent version of how Hammarskjöld's body was found, it had been treated violently and contemptuously by thugs. Concerning which, he might remind us that such things are only to be expected. "Blood, grime, sweat, earth—where are these in your world of will?" he asked in 1954. "Everywhere," he answered, "—the ground from which the flame ascends straight upwards." That his body may have been, and probably was, subjected to humiliation finds its place in this austere pattern.

Williams discovered in the archived papers of Sir Roy Welensky photographs of the dead at the Ndola crash site and later in the morgue. For some reason—it is a serious gap—there was no photo of Hammarskjöld where found at the crash site, but in photos of his body about to be transferred to an ambulance and at the morgue itself, two features particularly drew her attention: an area around the right eye and mid-forehead seemed to have been retouched, and in the crash site photograph a playing card is tucked into his collar. A playing card? Ian Black, currently Middle East editor for *The Guardian*, was nearby at the time of the crash and saw photographs taken at the site by the young Rhodesian policeman, Adrian Begg, who had gone to Red Williams's hotel to alert him and went out the following afternoon to the site. "The body of Dag H. was the only one that did not have any visible burns," Black has written, "and very strangely had the Ace of Spades playing card stuck in his collar. I have seen the photo but have been unable to ascertain if this was done as some kind of a joke."[74] His innocence is our own: he had encountered a symbol from an unfamiliar, violent subculture. In the company of a forensic expert, Williams has directly examined the photographs. She writes that "there is an object—which looks like a playing card—protruding from the ruffled tie . . . around Hammarskjöld's neck . . . . It is not possible to identify the card as the Ace of Spades on the basis of the photograph, but a civilian photographer at the scene claimed years later to have seen it. 'Yes! D. H. did have the Ace of Spaces in his shirt collar—no comment,' he recalled. 'It was requested at that time not to mention this.'"[75]

I dwell on the playing card because it is a tangible sign of the clash between all that Hammarskjöld was and represented, and the forces to which he was vulnerable at Ndola. The Ace of Spades is known as the death card. US soldiers in Vietnam would sometimes put it on the bodies of enemy dead as a warning—that is well documented. But where did they get the idea? It seems to have passed through the military and perhaps underworld organizations from a folkloric source in eighteenth-century piracy. How can we piece all this together? Are we to imagine that a mercenary, arriving in one of two vehicles soon after the crash "as if prewarned," ensured that the secretary-general was dead and by means of the card left a signature? Is that correct?

There is likely to have been a second signature. Williams writes:

> In 2005, Major General Bjørn Egge, a Norwegian who had been the UN's head of military information in the Congo in 1961 . . . suggested that Hammarskjöld had a round hole in his forehead that was possibly consistent with a bullet hole. . . . He explained . . . that he had been sent to Ndola to collect the Secretary-General's cipher machine and his briefcase and had been allowed to see his dead body in the mortuary. The body seemed to have a hole in the forehead. . . . "On photos taken of the body, however, the hole has been removed. I have always asked myself why this was done. Similarly, the autopsy report has been removed from the case papers. Again, I ask why?" . . . He said there was no tangible evidence that Hammarskjöld's death was the result of a conscious act by a third party, but that circumstantial evidence pointed in that direction.[76]

Should we take it that the paramilitary who rushed to the scene soon after the crash fired a shot to ensure that the secretary-general was dead, set the taunting card in place, and in one way or another caused the near-total incineration of the Albertina?

While there is no need to reproduce here all of Williams's findings—her book is available to all, and there is surely more to come—we should be aware of three further elements she has uncovered. The first concerns Godefroid Munongo, Tshombe's minister of the interior, conspirator in the death of Lumumba, and apparently also Tshombe's bête noire—he feared the man. At about 3:00 p.m. on September 18th, Munongo was overheard by a military clerk saying to a colleague "with a look of satisfaction": "I must inform you that Mr. H. has been struck down. We'll teach them!"[77] The crash was only discovered at 3:10 p.m. What are we to think? That Munongo knew in advance? There is an utterly curious incident at his life's end. Munongo lived on, rich, generally successful in both government and business, and honored as a hereditary ruler of his tribe. In May 1992, he announced that he would break his decades-long silence about the death of Patrice Lumumba, but on the very day he intended to do so, he died abruptly of a heart attack. His family's website implies that it was not a natural death.[78] What more did he know?

Others seem to have known in advance. There is disquieting testimony from a retired US Naval intelligence officer, who recalled an incident at a secret naval listening station in Cyprus just after midnight on September 18th. He was at home that evening when he received a call from a colleague in the other service that used the listening station, the CIA: "Hey! Get yourself out here tonight! Something interesting is going to happen." He drove back to the Naval Communications Facility. Williams continues:

> Shortly after midnight, he and about four or five other officers found themselves clustered round a loudspeaker, listening to a recording. They heard the rushing noise of an aircraft engine and the commentary of the pilot: "I see a transport plane coming now. All the lights are on. I'm going down to make a run on it. Yes, it is the Transair DC6. It's the plane." The pilot's voice was "cool and professional." Then they heard gun cannons firing—and the pilot exclaiming: "I've hit it. There are flames! It's going down. It's crashing!" . . . He had the impression that the pilot was "expecting the plane." . . . Somebody made the point at the time . . . that the recording was only seven to eight minutes old when it came through—it was "history in the making."[79]

The pilot would have been talking with a ground station, although the other voice is absent from the recording. The team on Cyprus thought they recognized his voice. It was the Lone Ranger—their name for the Belgian pilot of the Fouga Magister, who had acquired some notoriety. The Fouga Magister was supposedly unable to operate offensively at night, but there were other warplanes on the ground at Ndola and mercenaries to fly them. Williams has documented that a surprising number of mercenaries from across the border were drinking and swapping stories at the airport bar that night. As well, she writes that Rhodesian Air Force jets and de Havilland Doves were at hand. The latter were small passenger planes, some of which had been adapted to drop bombs through an improvised hole in the fuselage. Apparently the mercenaries were good at it. There are still more questions. What does the listening station team's foreknowledge of the event imply? Was the United States involved? Was the CIA running its own foreign policy? Larry Devlin, so to speak the sole CIA contact for this book, rehearses in his memoir a suite of possible causes of the crash and settles on "pilot error that may have resulted from fatigue."[80]

That night a Swedish flight instructor in Ethiopia picked up by chance a similar conversation on shortwave radio. "All of a sudden," he later reported, "I hear a conversation in English, obviously from an airport control tower. I also hear the name 'Ndola'. . . . The voice says, 'He's approaching the airport, he's turning . . . he's leveling'—where the pilot is approaching the actual landing strip. Then I hear the same voice saying, 'Another plane is approaching from behind, what is that?'"[81]

What is this, all of this? It is time for a new investigation by the UN and the governments involved: at a minimum the Democratic Republic of the Congo, Zambia, Belgium, Great Britain, and of course Sweden. Susan Williams has discovered and assembled masses of evidence, but her question remains: Who killed Hammarskjöld? "There are compelling grounds," Williams writes in her conclusion, "for arguing that, as in the case of Lumumba, there should be a further, transparent, public inquiry into the death of Dag Hammarskjöld. . . . Hammarskjöld's untimely death was different in many ways from that of Lumumba, but there was a shared context: the decolonization of central Africa and the self-interest of the Western powers and the multinationals operating in the region. . . . Patrice Lumumba and Dag Hammarskjöld were both killed because they sought to protect the integrity of the Congo and the self-determination of its people—free from the greed and interference of foreign powers."[82] The same call has been heard in Sweden: in their book published shortly before Williams's, Rembe and Hellberg insisted that "it is late in the day for the government to demand that all documentation about Dag Hammarskjöld and Ndola be made public. This is what Sweden owes history and the memory of Hammarskjöld."[83] Retired from his post as archbishop and head of the Church of Sweden, K. G. Hammar made the same demand emphatically in a major Swedish newspaper after he visited and spoke at Ndola during the fiftieth anniversary commemoration of the tragedy.[84]

Responding to Susan Williams's book and these individual expressions of concern, in July 2012 a distinguished international Commission of Jurists began meeting under private auspices to review all evidence, old and new, about the fatal crash at Ndola and its aftermath. If they see fit, they will recommend to secretary-general Ban Ki-Moon that the UN reopen its investigation. And events tumble on. Retired Swedish diplomat Bengt

Rösiö, leader of the 1993 Swedish review of the air crash evidence, which reaffirmed pilot error as the cause, told the press in mid-September 2012 that he now has doubts; there may have been foul play. To mark the fifty-first anniversary of the events at Ndola, the Swedish newspaper *Aftonbladet* published photographs of Hammarskjöld's bloodied body, sourced who knows where—no image of its kind had seen the light of day before. He is scarcely recognizable. It is a profoundly distressing photograph. However, if it helps to drive home in decision-making circles that Hammarskjöld's death cannot be viewed abstractly as a near-forgotten episode in the history of the Cold War or a martyr's icon on the wall, but was a miserable and likely murderous end inflicted on a very great individual, then the provocation of publishing the death photographs will have served to good purpose.[85]

You may remember that in the summer and fall of 1959 Hammarskjöld was writing brief haiku poems about his early years in Uppsala and much else. A poem from that time comes to mind. I don't know why he wrote it.

> While the shots echoed
> He sought the life of words
> For the sake of life.[86]

Though we may never know to whom it refers, it foreshadows the flight to Ndola. There is another, equally mysterious.

> A warm autumn evening,
> Moonlight on the path –
> Far away a heart stops.[87]

Trauer und Sorge

On the day of Hammarskjöld's death, Konrad Adenauer, chancellor of the Federal Republic of Germany, sent word to the president of the General Assembly. Among the many words received and spoken at the UN that day and in days to come, some very touching, Adenauer's simple, felt message is among the most memorable. "*Sein Tod erfüllt alle Menschen guten Willens mit Trauer und Sorge*," he had written: his death fills all men of good will with grief and concern.[88] Adenauer incarnated the gravity, the tormented past and hope of Europe. Now of advanced years, he had experienced everything that life can throw our way. His words are the first strike of a bell that would ring out for days and months to come.

"News of D. H.'s death so devastating it's hard to think," Steinbeck wrote to one of his oldest friends after hearing the news. "Two weeks ago last night I had dinner with him. My hand is shaking pretty badly, isn't it? Guess Dag's death hit hard. I'm all shaky inside. Have been reading the appraisals of his character in the paper and I guess I knew a different man than they did. He was neither cold, cool, dispassionate, nor neutral. He was a man passionate about what he was doing. . . . I just can't seem to write a coherent letter today. I'll do better later. I'm all shook up."[89]

Brian Urquhart of course vividly remembered the first days after. "It was absolutely devastating," he recalled in the United Nations Oral History Project.

> It was terrible. Hammarskjold . . . was not somebody one got to know very well. He was extremely aloof. . . . If you were on trips . . . you would have a marvelous evening with him and he'd be simply enchanting, but the next day he would be the same old, slightly Garboesque Swede. He was very impressive. It was his personality and it was a great strength for him. So we were all quite surprised at what an enormous emotional shock it was, that this absolutely extraordinary person should have simply gone in that grotesque way. It was a terrible blow. I think it was felt to an extraordinary extent throughout the Secretariat and the delegations. Even people who didn't like Hammarskjöld very much suddenly realized that they'd seen the last of someone who was totally unique; that there was never going to be anybody like that again.[90]

"At headquarters in New York," a senior security officer recalled,

> "I watched the world body go into total shock. . . . The entire staff, delegates from all over the world, the public—all were affected. People were crying openly in every office, on every staircase. I had never seen so much sadness . . . disbelief . . . sheer grief. . . . Numb for hours, I could barely cry until the tears came down before my anguished staff. . . ."[91]

In Katanga, C. C. O'Brien was working through his own reactions. "In these days immediately after Hammarskjöld's death, I felt, not personal grief but an obscure sense of misunderstanding mingled with, not exactly guilt but uneasiness. I knew that my pressing for renewed action in Elisabethville—following up Rumpunch—my emphasis on urgency, leading to the timing of the action for the morning of his arrival in the Congo, and my failure to avert certain errors in execution, were among the links in the chain that led to his death. . . ."[92] Later, after his forced resignation from the Secretariat and voluntary resignation from the Irish Foreign Service, his attitude changed. He would angrily assert that Hammarskjöld had approved Operation Morthor and, when it went bad, betrayed his own people by misrepresenting it, bowing to British pressure, and abjectly seeking a cease-fire. His attitude would change again by 1968, when he published *Murderous Angels*, a slanderous theater piece in which he rewrote Hammarskjöld to suit himself.[93] At least he had the grace to write years later, "My tenure of this post, for less than a year, was to alter the course of the rest of my life."[94] Socrates warned long ago not to offend a writer.

It is the duty of survivors to inventory and safeguard the belongings of the dead. This was promptly accomplished, although Bjørn Egge and Piero Spinelli had some difficulty extracting the secretary-general's briefcase from the Rhodesian police. Thrown clear of the crash, it is now preserved with its contents in the Swedish Royal Library. Were any items removed by the police before surrendering the briefcase? It now contains a copy of a letter from Lord Lansdowne dated September 17th; a readable small edition of the New Testament; a fresh edition in German of Rilke's *Duino Elegies* and *Sonnets to Orpheus*; an uncut, unread copy of *Noé* by the lyrical French author Jean Giono; his copies of Martin Buber's *I and Thou* in German and English, with markers placed at the same paragraph in each just after "In the beginning is relation," and the seven pages of his Swedish translation. A large library for a two- or three-day trip, but he was an efficient reader and may have wanted a selection on hand; he didn't need much sleep in times of crisis. There were a few stray items: personal stationery, a roadmap of southern New England, other things.

At Sture Linnér's residence in Léopoldville, he left a good deal more. As we know, there were the typed pages of his Swedish draft of *I and Thou*. He left behind, as well, two typed copies of his other work in progress, *Castle Hill*, with handwritten corrections. His edition of the *Imitation of Christ* with the oath of office of the secretary-general serving as a bookmark. Two miniature copies of the UN Charter. And his wallet. The wallet proved to be a revealer of good and charming things. Wallets, as you know, are both temporary cash depositories and time capsules where one puts intriguing items and forgets them. Mr. Hammarskjöld's wallet fits this description. Our aloof world diplomat seems to have enjoyed newspaper cartoons that poked fun at him. One of the cartoons folded into his wallet shows a huge gorilla perched on a chair behind a desk—he is identified as "King Kongo"—with a hapless UN official saying to reporters, "As far as I can make out, he says he's arrested Lumumba, Kasavubu, Iléo, Colonel Mobutu, General Victor Lundula, and Dag Hammarskjöld." A second cartoon shows a group of disgruntled baseball players surrounding a home plate umpire as he gets a dressing down from another umpire: "You're not expected to be Dag Hammarskjöld, Potts. Just call them as you see them." The wallet time capsule also has a scrap of printed paper with the first few verses of a popular song of the mid-1950s, "Be-Bop-Alula," first recorded by Gene Vincent and His Blue Caps. The Elvis Presley version is inscribed in the nervous systems of Americans who passed through adolescence in the 1950s. What can a shattered biographer say about this discovery? Probably—but who knows?—it recalls a conversation with the teenage children of one of the families Hammarskjöld saw regularly. The children of Bill and Toddy Ranallo, or perhaps the Wieschhoff children, were doing their best to educate the great man about a few basic essentials of life in their time, and he found the boomingly rhythmic lyrics interesting enough to store in his wallet for further study.

There is another stunning item in the wallet storage area, clipped from some larger document. This is the text in full:

> "What I have said has demonstrated that it is very difficult to find an answer to that question, but if I were pressed for an answer I would say that, so far as we can see, taking it rather by and large, taking one time with another, and taking the average of Departments, it is probable that there would not be found to be very much in it either way." —Sir Thomas Padmore, reported in *Minutes of Evidence to Royal Commission on the Civil Service*

Delicious. There could be no better example of bureaucratic vapor. Sir Thomas Padmore, GCB, was a twentieth-century British civil servant who held greater and lesser posts for decades. As we know, Hammarskjöld was famous for saying nothing much at some length when discretion served his diplomatic purpose. Urquhart delighted from time to time in describing how he went about it: "Over the years," Urquhart has written, "he perfected a technique of escaping into a cloud of metaphor or abstraction, with a style at the same time articulate and obscure, brilliant but hard to grasp, apparently forthright but often uninformative. . . ."[95] Now we know that he could laugh about it.

A few days before his last departure to the Congo, Hammarskjöld had asked a trusted friend and younger colleague, Per Lind, to take responsibility in the event of his death for his papers at the apartment, his UN office, and Brewster. Lind said later that Hammarskjöld's secretary had insisted on him making sensible arrangements of the kind. Assigned to the office of Andrew Cordier and serving as Hammarskjöld's personal aide in the first three years, 1953–55, Lind had seen a great deal of him, including family weekends at Brewster. At the end of 1955, he and his wife chose to return to Sweden for the sake of their children's education, but he remained on the best of terms with Hammarskjöld and from the Swedish Foreign Office stayed in touch with UN affairs. Their correspondence, though sparsely represented at the Royal Library, reflects Hammarskjöld's regard for him. "It is a pity that you are not around," we have heard Hammarskjöld write during the Suez Crisis. "It would have been refreshing to have you in the 24-hour working team which has been running this show. . . ."

After Hammarskjöld's death, Lind spent four weeks in New York. At the UN he worked with Brian Urquhart to collect and, in a preliminary way, order the secretary-general's papers. It was during this process that Urquhart conceived of writing the biography. Accompanied by an attorney, Lind also visited Hammarskjöld's apartment and, as he has said, "found on his bed table a file with typewritten pages headed *Vägmärken* [*Markings*], which I had never seen or heard of before. Attached to the file was a small envelope addressed to a mutual friend in Sweden, Leif Belfrage, containing the letter quoted on the first page of all editions of *Markings*, in which Dag Hammarskjöld asked Belfrage to decide whether it should be published."[96]

As a permanent record, photographs were taken throughout the apartment.[97] The images tell many stories, many more than we can interpret and, no doubt, many more than can ever be interpreted because the keys to them were lost with the man. His bedroom was as austere as one would expect of a person of monastic temperament: a single bed, spare Scandinavian furniture and little of it, a nondescript bedside table on which he had left his journal in a stiff cardboard folder. However, the art and artifacts he chose to live with are surprising. There is a framed Tibetan or Nepalese thangka on the wall—an image of the seated Buddha and attendants, richly painted on canvas. There is an ink rubbing from what appears to be a South Asian low-relief sculpture, again of a sacred subject. There is a small Himalayan bronze, apparently a dancing *apsara*—a celestial maiden. There is what appears to be an Indian stone carving, perhaps a female head or torso. A little horse, Indian or

African folk art. A Chinese vase in the fireplace. And a lovely, watery ink drawing of a figure standing before a high Christian cross in a wooded setting. All of which, taken together, demonstrates that he was a man of Christian faith who loved the tranquility and contained dynamism of Asian art. It made a sanctuary.

There was much to do in the days after the deaths of Hammarskjöld and his companions. In the saddest of marathons, their bodies were flown in a chartered airplane from city to city in Europe and North America to be returned to their families. The sixteen coffins were transported to Salisbury Airport and loaded into a nearly empty cabin, where each was draped with the appropriate national flag. John Olver, whom we have encountered in Léopoldville, was responsible for the flight onward, which left Salisbury on Tuesday 19th, stopped in Léopoldville for a mournful acknowledgment of the dead, and continued on to Geneva, Malmö in southern Sweden, Stockholm, Dublin, Montreal, and New York.[98] Piero Spinelli and Knut Hammarskjöld were on board; they needed to reach Stockholm with Dag's body by the 21st, when there would be a reception ceremony. Sture Linnér joined the flight at Léopoldville. "I sat beside him," Olver has written, "wondering whether there was any comfort I could bring. . . ."[99] There was to be a state funeral at the cathedral in Uppsala on the 29th, an honor not accorded even to Count Bernadotte ten years earlier.

As the plane approached Stockholm, three Swedish fighter jets eased into formation on each side. Olver wrote later that "King Gustaf Adolf had sent a special escort for the arrival home of Sweden's outstanding son. . . ." This was the beginning of ceremony, so urgently needed to make the transition from a life lived to a life remembered. As the larger plane began its descent, the fighters dipped their wings and withdrew. Olver continued,

> The city below was an unusual sight, as all traffic had been stopped; cars, trucks and buses were lined up motionless on streets and highways of the busy capital. Activity at the airport was also in suspension. . . . Dozens of large and small aircraft stood waiting on the tarmac, silent and still.
>
> We touched down precisely at high noon and came to a halt in a vast square created by throngs of mourners, military and police units, officials of the Government, and representatives of most countries of the world. Members of the Hammarskjöld family formed a small group at the center. . . . To the slow, solemn beat of drums, we were slowly escorted around the plane to take part in the ceremonial handing over

of the remains of Dag Hammarskjöld and the two Swedish soldiers of ONUC who had accompanied him on his final flight. . . .[100]

When Olver and Spinelli walked through the city that night, they noticed that "store and bank windows displayed [Hammarskjöld's] black-draped portrait." It was the same in Uppsala a few days later.

Hammarskjöld had hoped to bring good news to the sixteenth General Assembly, which met as scheduled in the afternoon of September 19th—but for a very few minutes. Hammarskjöld's friend and colleague, Frederick Boland, serving his last day as president, was the only speaker.

> The sixteenth session of the General Assembly meets today in the shadow of an immense tragedy, in the midst of deep and heartfelt mourning which extends far beyond the walls of this chamber to millions of men and women throughout the world.
>
> This is not the moment to speak of the loss which we have sustained, or to recount the high qualities and the virtues which gave those who have died so firm a hold on our respect and admiration. There will be opportunities for that later. For the moment, I would simply propose that, as a tribute to the memory of the late Secretary-General and of the devoted officers of the United Nations who died with him, and as a mark of our profound condolence with their families and relatives, we should stand and observe a minute of silence, after which this meeting should be adjourned until 10:30 tomorrow morning.[101]

The chair at Boland's right on the high dais was empty. I do not much like learned play with the notions of absence and presence—the "presence of absence" and such things. But at that time and place there was unmistakably the presence of absence. *Time* magazine's superb portrait artist Boris Chaliapin was among many who noticed: his September 29th cover shows the careworn face of Mongi Slim, the Tunisian president of the sixteenth session, with the seal of the United Nations and an empty chair. Even today, when one has the privilege of witnessing a session of the General Assembly, the chair can seem not unoccupied but abandoned, until the current secretary-general takes his place.

The fifth-grade class of an elementary school in Scarsdale, New York, bestirred itself to write to the president of the General Assembly. Some of the children's letters captured the feelings of much older people. "Dag Hammarskjöld I think was a great man because he wanted peace. He was indeed a brave man. He risked his own life almost every trip he made.

Dag Hammarskjöld went on a trip a week ago. People told him not to go but he went and was killed."

Another child wrote: "Secretary-General Dag Hammarskjöld a man dedicated to world peace sacrificed his life that we may live in peace. There is little we can do though." And a third: "Dag Hammarskjöld liked a lot of people but it's a question if a lot of people liked him. I myself think a lot of them didn't."[102]

At the final last

The General Assembly has rarely been more tribal than in the afternoon of September 20th, when all delegations gathered to praise Dag Hammarskjöld. His friend and trusted colleague, Mongi Slim, was now presiding. "On behalf of the General Assembly," Slim opened the session, "I should like to pay tribute to this messenger of peace...."[103] As delegates one after the other came to the front to speak, the chartered aircraft carrying the bodies of Hammarskjöld and his companions was still making its way from Africa across Europe to Stockholm.

Speaking for the Scandinavian countries (though Sweden's representative would reply at the end of this ceremony of words), the Danish ambassador established the tone of much to follow. "Never before in the history of international organizations," he said, "has one single man played so central a role as did Dag Hammarskjöld or, at his death, left a political vacuum and a grief embracing the globe.... He devoted his life and his brilliant mind to the cause of peace and justice, and he proved what a dedicated mind can achieve even when faced with superhuman burdens...." The delegate from the Congo (Léopoldville), next to speak, nearly and quite beautifully offered citizenship to Hammarskjöld: "I declare that Dag Hammarskjöld ... is a martyr of peace.... He died on our own soil of Africa, for peace in my country. I declare that Dag Hammarskjöld will remain in Congolese hearts as the best friend of our Republic." The Nigerian ambassador, who had chaired the ill-fated conciliation commission to the Congo, was first but not last to acknowledge the empty chair. As a courtesy, speakers in the Assembly turn before and after speaking to acknowledge the president and secretary-general above and behind them on the high dais. "None of us expected that we would stand here to speak and would look back, as we used to do, only to find an empty chair in the place of the Secretary-General." V. K. Krishna Menon, the Indian ambassador who had sometimes helped and sometimes immeasurably irritated Hammarskjöld, gracefully described him as "a great world statesman . . . and a friend of us all." "If it is an accident," he said of Hammarskjöld's death, "it is a great international tragedy; if it is something else, it will become an international crime. It is the desire of my Government and people that there should be a complete investigation. . . ." Krishna Menon was among those mentioning that a cease-fire had just been achieved in Katanga.

Speaking for the Soviet Union and the Soviet bloc, Ambassadors Zorin and Winiewicz (Poland) were less generous than Nikita Khrushchev. Making a condolence call at the Swedish Embassy in Moscow, Khrushchev had said, "Our relations were somewhat special, but I am now having regard to the humanitarian aspect. This is not the way to solve problems. Hammarskjöld was a great man."[104] Something of his folk wisdom came forward: he was simple, he spoke from the heart. In New York, the two representatives expressed sympathy without much warmth and reviewed in brief the difficulties they had had with Mr. Hammarskjöld.

Speaking for the Arab countries, Hammarskjöld's friend Mahmoud Fawzi recalled in passing "what some of us consider to have been his mistakes." He was undoubtedly thinking of the circumstances surrounding Lumumba's death and the stalemate with Katanga. But he focused on Hammarskjöld's brilliant leadership in the Suez Crisis. "With countless others," he said, "we shall always hold his name and his record in high and affectionate esteem." And then he centered himself in Muslim tradition to state a keenly felt truth: "God gave the world Dag Hammarskjöld. God has taken him away. God alone is eternal. A great friend of peace has departed—a great friend indeed, a shining symbol of integrity, a glorious flag." The closing metaphor immerses Hammarskjöld in Muslim history, as if he were another Saladin setting order in the world.

There seems to have been scarcely enough time, but Hammarskjöld's personal aide in the later years has recorded that Adlai Stevenson, who reached the UN in February 1961, was "his favorite among the ambassadors. . . . Dag found him easygoing and humorous, like himself. . . . Others were Tunisia's Mongi Slim and Burma's U Thant. . . ."[105] His regard for Stevenson was reciprocated. Stevenson's eulogy cast the widest net.

> In his passing the community of nations has lost one of the greatest servants it ever had—a brilliant mind, a brave and compassionate spirit. I doubt if any living man has done more to further the search for a world in which men solve their problems by peaceful means and not by force than this gallant friend of us all. . . .

Dag Hammarskjöld was the very embodiment of the international civil servant—as the Secretary-General of the United Nations should ideally and always be. He was resolutely impartial, resolutely even-handed and resolutely firm in carrying out the mandates with which he was entrusted. He never swerved from what he conceived to be his duty to the United Nations and to the cause of peace. He never wavered under irresponsible invective and unjust criticism. Mr. Hammarskjöld's skill as a diplomatist was admired in every chancellery of the world and it was attested to many times, when leaders who could not bring themselves to confide in each other were glad to confide in him. . . .

The memory of this one man, humane, cultured, judicious, possessed of a poetic and philosophic vision, free of passion—other than a passion for the rule of reason and of decency—modest and brave, this memory will always be with us as a reminder of the best that the United Nations can be and of the qualities which it demands of us all. . . .

There is a good deal more in his speech, which has become something of an anthologized model, but we have heard enough to know that Stevenson had not missed the man. His call toward the end of his speech for a memorial to provide "a permanent tangible tribute" was joined by others'. It would have good consequences.

After well more than three hours, the Swedish ambassador responded and the meeting rose. "I have been deeply moved by the expressions of sorrow and appreciation," Agda Rössel said, "which members of the Assembly have devoted to a great citizen of the world. I shall convey these messages to my Government."

It was a time when people reached out to one another. Probably after seeing the text of Stevenson's eulogy in the newspaper, John Steinbeck wrote to him from London. "I had a letter from a friend today," he wrote, "which ended thus—'Poor Mr. Stevenson—he must feel like God's Last Good Man. Wish I could send him a word of cheer.' And so do I. And so I try. You must have awakened with a sentence in your mind as though it had been spoken. The night after the crash I had such an experience and the words were odd—'Baldur is dead! Loki has won again—but Baldur does not remain dead. . . .'"[106] Norse myth had spontaneously occurred to him: the cunning murder of noble Baldur by his enemy Loki, in a myth that promises Baldur's rebirth on an Earth redeemed and more beautiful. Steinbeck writes as author to author, attributing to Stevenson some part of his own creative process.

The days between the eulogies of September 20th and the funeral in Uppsala on the 29th belonged to Hammarskjöld. The mood of eulogy was evident in nearly all public media worldwide. Even *Dagens Nyheter*, Tingsten's paper, relented. "Swedes can proudly see him as an outstanding representative of the Swedish principles of a society under the rule of law. . . . He was a man who grew with difficulties. . . . His clear and quick intelligence based on a self-evident inner harmony, a lack of tension, . . . proved an asset in periods of great strain." *Svenska Dagbladet* recalled an utterly interesting comment Hammarskjöld had made a year earlier to one of its reporters: "Khrushchev made two mistakes when he began his attack on me. He underestimated the immense role the UN plays in the consciousness of the young nations, and he did not understand the extent to which those countries identify the UN with me."[107] On the 24th, the *New York Times* made its statement. "How can the power of this irreplaceable man be analyzed?" asked its editorialist. "It rose from patience, from an inherited wisdom, from a profound experience, from the ability to detach himself from the deep traditions of his native land and to be first of all an international statesman. In an age of violence, he had gentleness. He never rose in a public meeting to say that he loved humanity, but he evidently did. What he said was the same thing—that he loved justice."[108] There was considerable tension around the speech expected the following day in the General Assembly from President Kennedy. The *Times* editorialized again on the morning of Kennedy's appearance, as if beseeching him to rise above the American objections to what had occurred in Katanga and say what truly mattered. "This is a time to speak and be bold. . . . The UN is in danger. It was in danger before Hammarskjöld died. It is in greater danger now. Let us rally to its defense. . . ."[109] Kennedy did not disappoint in his nearly forty-five-minute speech. "We meet in an hour of grief and challenge," he began. "Dag Hammarskjöld is dead. But the United Nations lives. His tragedy is deep in our hearts, but the task for which he died is at the top of our agenda."[110]

Bunche, Cordier, and Urquhart understood that something more was needed, a powerful ceremony turned inward for all members of the Secretariat and delegations, and it was needed soon. All three were still terribly shaken. They must have read out of their own need the needs of the UN community. "[Hammarskjöld]," Urquhart later wrote, "had come to occupy a unique place in our lives, thoughts, and affections by the nature of his leadership and his character. For a long time it was hard to think of him without tears. . . ."[111] Urquhart proposed a memorial occasion, at once accepted by the others: a perfect replica of the United Nations Day concert a year earlier, when at Hammarskjöld's invitation Eugene Ormandy had conducted the Philadelphia Orchestra and a university chorus in the last section of Bach's St. Matthew Passion and Beethoven's complete Choral Symphony. Ormandy and all concerned responded with unstinting generosity. On the 28th, three thousand UN people gathered in the General Assembly hall for an occasion which the three grieving UN leaders had respectfully foreseen as a shared experience that was certain to break hearts but also make an orienting mark in time. Mongi Slim opened the occasion with further words of praise. Then the chorus and orchestra performed the magnificent finale from the St. Matthew Passion, large enough in spirit and genius to catch up misery and place it in God's world. *Ruhe sanfte*—rest gently, they sang. Then a recorded voice resounded in the hall: Hammarskjöld's commentary on the Ninth Symphony, delivered a year earlier. "We strive to bring order and purity into chaos and anarchy," he had said. "We try to impose the laws of the human mind and of the integrity of the human will on the dramatic evolution in which we are all engaged. . . ."[112] Urquhart later wrote that "this was an unbearably emotional moment, ended only by the first notes of the symphony, which Ormandy conducted with tears streaming down his face."[113]

After this collective experience of grief, Urquhart felt that the Secretariat "got down to business again with perhaps a new sense of purpose," without forgetting for a moment what had occurred.[114] That evening in Stockholm there was another collective experience: a torchlight procession of some eight thousand people to the huge open field known as Gärdet in the eastern part of the city, where one hundred thousand eventually gathered to hear words of praise and mourning from speakers who had been close to Hammarskjöld.[115] Östen Undén was among them; he was the Swedish foreign minister to whom Hammarskjöld had turned privately to put a reasoned frame around Khrushchev's attacks. "International problems seemed for him," Undén said, "to have become at the same time a science and a passion." Karl Ragnar Gierow, with whom Hammarskjöld had had such satisfactory adventures—midwifing the first production of a Eugene O'Neill masterpiece, bringing Djuna Barnes's *Antiphon* to the Swedish stage, listening to the message of the skylark in Brewster—spoke with overwhelming sadness, partly in the poets' code they shared. He spoke of "an unexplained catastrophe in enigmatic darkness over a foreign continent. There is in that darkness one single shining light, himself. . . ." He recalled Hammarskjöld's bond with Carl Linnaeus. "There existed between him and the uncrowned ruler of the united realm of flowers a very profound relationship. He was, like the young Linnaeus, a lucid genius, life's good friend, the most luminous human being I have known. . . ." Sture Linnér recalled the moment before the doomed flight when Hammarskjöld spoke of love as an overflowing of strength that fills those who act entirely for the benefit of others. "Still he stands in this moment vividly before me."

The following morning, a procession of cars and other vehicles made its way to Uppsala for the state funeral in the cathedral, seat of the Church of Sweden and royal burial. As in the General Assembly the day before, music was at the center of that service. Bach's organ fantasy in C minor, Gabrieli's Agnus Dei, hymns from the Swedish hymnal, Handel's "I Know that My Redeemer Liveth" sung by Elisabeth Söderström, a Swedish star of the international operatic stage. Then a Schütz motet and the closing chorale of Bach's St. John Passion—quiet and foursquare, all brilliance set aside as the singers beg the Lord to send angels to carry a soul to heaven. And "at the final last," as Hammarskjöld once said, Bach's majestic organ fugue in E-flat major, the "St. Anne," serving as the recessional. Like the last chorus of the Matthew Passion heard in New York the day before, it projects a vast order in which all things—lives and deaths—find their place. Perhaps no one was listening all that well on a day of such sorrow and leave taking, but the cathedral's music directors had spoken through their selections.

King Gustaf Adolf and Queen Louise were present, the cathedral filled with Swedish and foreign leaders, representatives of the United Nations, and students who played ceremonial roles throughout. Wilhelm Wachtmeister, who had served for some three years as Hammarskjöld's personal aide, recalled that "the coffin was draped in the Swedish colors and surrounded by white lilies and larkspur. [There was] a wreath of flowers from Dag Hammarskjöld's country place in the south of Sweden and one from the Lapland where he loved to wander in earlier days."[116] The service was in the care of archbishop Erling Eidem. Slender and ascetic in appearance, as if a visitor from an earlier era, he had been the immediate successor to Nathan Söderblom, young Dag's marvelous mentor. The archbishop had long since retired but willingly agreed to return to the cathedral to preside. When he had his moment to speak freely, he spoke of service. Wachtmeister recalled the archbishop saying that "to serve each other, without dividing lines or exceptions, is the innermost purpose of our life," richly fulfilled by "this faithful son of his fatherland, a faithful servant of all mankind."

After the cathedral service, the funeral cortege made its way to the nearby cemetery where Dag's father had years earlier established a family precinct. On the state catafalque the coffin was drawn by four horses along a lane formed by the university students wearing their characteristic white caps; behind them the good people of Uppsala. With due formality, hymn, and prayer, the coffin was lowered into the grave. The archbishop read the words of a medieval hymn: "Let us praise and pray to our God when the moments change and move on. The day is never so long that its end does not come." There was a minute of silence across the entire nation, from Lapland in the north to the southern coast where Hammarskjöld had wished to have a farmhouse retreat.[117] I do not know whether the family's floral wreath had been displayed in the cathedral, but it commanded attention in the bright sunlight. Its inscription could not have been starker: "Why?"[118]

A few days after the funeral, George Ivan Smith sent a note to Max Ascoli, a journalist whom Hammarskjöld had particularly respected. "I have just returned from Stockholm and Uppsala," he wrote.

> The service in the cathedral was magnificent, but the walk through the cobbled streets of Uppsala and through the ranks of university students who lined the route to the graveyard was quite the most moving experience of all. The utter simplicity, the quiet dignity and the intense depth of feeling in the audience made the final moment at the church-yard the most memorable of my life. At the very end, when the representatives of kings and governments were dispersing, I caught sight of a man in highly colored folk dress standing under the shadow of the nearby chapel from where he had watched the service. I made my way to him and through an interpreter discovered that he was a guide from northern Lapland who had been with Dag on many northern journeys. He had made his own way south for the funeral. The sorrow expressed in that man's face is something else I shall not forget. . . .[119]

The Sami mourner was Andreas Labba, the guide and herdsman whom Hammarskjöld had persuaded in the mid-1930s to write the lives of his

people. They had made five treks together, "and it was during these ex-
cursions that Dag took it upon himself to convince me that I should
learn to write without worrying about correctness of language. He practically forced me to write short letters and note down my memories.
Little by little I learned not to make any difference between an ordinary
tourist and a reindeer herdsman. I began to understand that we walk
the same earth with the same troubles and the same right to live. And
without this confidence in myself, which I owe to Dag's friendship, I
would never have dared to write the tales and narratives I have from the
elders."[120] Labba's book *Anta*, of 1969, fulfilled its author's dream, and
Dag's. As noted many pages ago, Labba had spent a week in New York
at his friend's invitation in 1958. They must have had a spectacular time.

The day after the funeral, it occurred to Labba to build a commemorative chapel in Dag's honor on the summit of Sweden's highest peak,
Kebnekaise. "I recalled the image of Dag," he wrote, "reading the Bible
outside our kota [tent] during a mountain trek. My mother had asked
him whether he wanted to become a minister. 'No,' Dag had answered,
'but I like to read the Bible.'" A few years later the chapel was indeed
completed—at a somewhat lower elevation, in the forested region
of Kaitum. At its informal consecration, Labba read aloud lines from
Markings: "A landscape can sing about God."[121]

Swedish burial custom often refers to the Norse past, to endless time
and unbroken connection—hence the massive, nearly uncarved block like
an ancient stele, bearing the name of Hammarskjöld's father, which dominates the family plot. Dag's own stone is simple, flat, like his mother's and
brothers'. I was searching for his grave one winter in foot-deep snow. A
young woman walking her dog nearby noticed me trailblazing somewhat
blindly in approximately the right direction. "That's the one," she said.

A surprisingly considerable success

On December 10th in Oslo, the Nobel Peace Prize for 1961 was conferred posthumously on Dag Hammarskjöld. At the family's request,
Rolf Edberg, Swedish ambassador to Norway, offered the acceptance
speech. It was both informed and sensitive. Putting himself in the position of a participant in the General Assembly, Edberg asked,

> What does he represent, that slender man up there behind the green
> marble desk? A tradition of polished, quiet diplomacy, doomed to

drown in the rising tide of the new clamor? Or is he, with his visions of a world community, a herald of the future? The latter is what we would like to believe. He himself had no doubt about the convincing force of his ideals. . . . Such a conviction must be based on a determined philosophy of life. No one who met him could help noticing that he had a room of quiet within himself. Probably no one was ever able really to reach into that room. . . .[122]

There were further tributes to "the devoted chief executive of the world" in the months after his death—among them Urquhart's extraordinary, felt interview in *The New Yorker*, Max Ascoli in *The Reporter*, Auden in *Encounter*, and Buber's talk on Swedish radio, later converted into an essay.[123] To this roster belongs the poet Erik Lindegren's compelling address of December 1962 about his predecessor in Seat No. 17 of the Swedish Academy.[124] One homage, personally delivered, must be noted. On March 14th, 1962, Sture Linnér "was summoned to a meeting with President Kennedy." He continued:

> The meeting—which took place in the Oval [Office] . . . —started with Kennedy explaining the background to his actions. . . . He had, for his own political survival, felt obliged to heed the deep aversion towards communism or extreme left views in general, which even long after McCarthy's hysterical heyday played an important role in domestic American politics. He had gradually come to realize how unjustified it was to oppose the UN Congo policy for that reason, and since it was now too late to express his apology to Dag Hammarskjöld, he wanted to do so to me. And the most powerful man in the world added: "I realize now that in comparison to him, I am a small man. He was the greatest statesman of our century."[125]

Though there was understandable anxiety at the UN concerning the election of a new secretary-general, the actual process was reasonably straightforward. The main points of contention were how many advisers he might possibly tolerate and whether to name a secretary-general to a new full term or designate an acting secretary-general to complete Hammarskjöld's term through April 1963. The latter course was adopted as a means of sidestepping the Soviet demand for a troika, which in time many hoped would vanish. That proved to be true. Three candidates stood out: Frederick Boland, Mongi Slim, and U Thant. Boland felt that it was time for a non-Western secretary-general; Slim didn't want the position though he would have responded to a draft, and Thant was both willing and widely respected. The editors of his *Public Papers* make the point that his well-argued, thoughtful views had at one time or another offended nearly all of the great powers—and no one seemed to hold it against him. He was unanimously nominated by the Security Council and welcomed by the General Assembly in an unrecorded ballot on November 3rd. U Thant was an interesting man. Burmese, moderate in height, quiet in manner, formidably intelligent, he was a practicing Buddhist in his country's Theravada tradition who occasionally wrote on Buddhist values. He was also decisive and, though fundamentally opposed to violence in every form, wasn't squeamish about the use of military force in circumstances that undeniably called for it.

The Congo did not grant a long honeymoon. Thant's own account of the next sixteen months' drive toward resolution in the Congo is all that one could hope for: clear, sensible, detailed but to the point.[126] Eight days after he took office, UN airmen arriving at an airport serving the central Congolese city of Kindu were brutally murdered in the airport mess hall by regular Congolese troops, dismembered by a crowd of armed civilians—and the rest, though it is remembered, cannot be said. The airmen had been mistaken for Belgian paratroopers in Tshombe's pay. This was the Kindu atrocity.

The Security Council responded with the resolution of November 24th, declaring "full and firm support for the Central Government of the Congo," condemning "all secessionist activity," and authorizing the secretary-general "to take vigorous action, including the use of the requisite measure of force, if necessary," to rid the Congo of mercenaries, foreign political advisers, and other obstacles to peace and reconciliation.[127] It was a resolution that would have served Hammarskjöld well, but it took catastrophes—Lumumba's death, Hammarskjöld's death, the Kindu atrocity—to lurch UN policy forward. Tshombe responded to the resolution by taking to the radio and calling, not for the first time, for all-out war. "Let Katanga fighters arise in every street, . . . in every village. You cannot all have automatic weapons or rifles. But we still have our poisoned arrows, our spears. . . ."[128]

Fighting broke out in early December in Elisabethville and elsewhere in Katanga, and continued through the 19th, the UN forces gradually gaining control. On the 20th, at a meeting with Prime Minister Adoula, Tshombe capitulated and agreed to end the secession. However, upon returning to

Elisabethville, he and his ministers displayed only the most superficial interest in abiding by his agreement and that summer again sponsored an independence celebration in the streets of Elisabethville. There were graver provocations. Thant writes that Tshombe organized crowds of women and children to "curse, abuse, and spit upon" UN troops, who exercised remarkable restraint. It was U Thant's turn to be fed up. At a press conference in Helsinki on July 20th, he described Tshombe and his ministers as "a bunch of clowns." The *New York Times* and other papers duly reported his choice of words. When he returned to New York, Ralph Bunche asked him whether he had said that. The phrase was new to diplomacy.

At the end of December 1962, Thant consulted widely at the UN and authorized major military action despite the trepidations of Belgium and Britain and Tshombe's routine threat that, if the UN attacked, refineries and other precious resources in Katanga would be deliberately destroyed. Bunche was deeply involved in the politics and planning that preceded the action and spent some days in the Congo at Thant's request. "The object of the operation," Thant wrote later, "was to remove the gendarmerie and the mercenaries from the Elisabethville area and to establish complete freedom of movement in the whole of Katanga."[129] The operation was considerably and easily more successful than expected, with more far-reaching consequences. On January 14th, Tshombe again capitulated, this time without recourse. The secession of Katanga was over on condition of a general amnesty, which the central government saw fit to grant. Bunche was especially struck by the peaceful entry of UN troops on January 21st into the mining city of Kolwezi, described by Urquhart as "Tshombe's last stronghold." Bunche's notes for that day read: "Big day for the Congo operation. Peaceful entry into Kolwezi . . . That about winds up the military phase and takes us over the big hump—after two and a half years! We ought to breathe a bit easier now. I feel that I've done something for Dag now."[130]

The last contingent of UN peacekeepers left Léopoldville on June 30th, 1964. After which, as Thant puts it, "the situation in the Congo rapidly deteriorated."[131] The Adoula government folded in the face of two opposition movements, one led by Tshombe, who had been freed by the general amnesty to remain in political life. Mr. Tshombe became prime minister, though a miserable one. He was unacceptable to other African states and unable to prevent the renewed breakup of the country into warring factions. He fled the country in the fall of 1965. He had only a few more years to live. In late November 1965, the future Mobutu Sese Seko deposed Kasavubu as president and declared himself head of state. The long and bloody saga of the Congo had just begun.

Among other close witnesses and interpreters, Dayal and Urquhart did their best to sum up what had occurred both in Hammarskjöld's lifetime and in the years just following. The long crisis had been a dizzying, disastrous spectacle involving millions of Congolese lives, tens of thousands of UN personnel, and a destructive conflict of ideas and interests, backed by force and subterfuge, that had left the world no peace for years. It had caused the deaths of two outstanding leaders, one mature in his authentic greatness, the other immature but full of potential that would never be realized. For his part, Dayal was critical of elements of Hammarskjöld's management of the Congo Crisis but warmly appreciative in final judgment. Hammarskjöld could have had better relations with the Soviets, Dayal believed, had he made a greater effort before things got rough. He could have agreed to an advisory committee, appointed by the Security Council, to work side by side with his senior representative in the Congo; it would have slowed decisions but distributed responsibility and spared him unmerited criticism.[132] All this said, Dayal recognized the accomplishment of Hammarskjöld in the Congo:

> Despite occasional failings and misjudgments, history will record the heroic and selfless nature of Hammarskjöld's final service to world peace in the Congo. The consequences of what would inevitably have occurred, had the Secretary-General quailed before the task, baffle the imagination. . . . The great powers would not have left the Congolese to tear each other apart but would have intervened on opposite sides, bringing the entire world to the verge of a general war.[133]

Urquhart was asked to take over O'Brien's role in Katanga in November 1961. Though he nearly lost his life within days of his arrival in a grotesque beating at the hands of Tshombe's gendarmerie, he lived to tell the story with exemplary black humor.[134] His credentials to sum up the Congo Crisis are sound. "The only question to be asked," he has said,

> is whether it was smart ever to have got into it in the first place. But if we hadn't got into it, supposing then a vacuum had been left which the United States and the Soviet Union both tried to fill, how far would that have taken everybody? So I think one has to admit that it had to be done. . . . Though it was very costly and we lost a lot of people, in

fact it was, in the circumstances, a surprisingly considerable success. We actually kept that country going and we preserved it as a country, which is certainly a good deal more than I thought we'd ever be able to do . . . . It was a remarkable effort which deserved to succeed better than it did, and in fact did succeed quite a bit. And I doubt we shall ever do anything like that again.[135]

Urquhart was hardly alone in his view that "the following years would largely belie Hammarskjöld's vision of a newly free continent marching into the future under able young leaders, helped and advised by the UN."[136] However, if the Congo failed to prosper, there was nonetheless a gain for the world at large. Writing at the time as UN Under-Secretary-General for Peacekeeping Operations, Jean-Marie Guéhenno offers a key insight:

Abused, hated, humiliated, and mocked, the mission in Congo succeeded. And in large part it succeeded because of the power of Hammarskjöld's intellect and of his will—including the will to stand up to the world's most powerful men. . . . Had his will been less and the experiment in Congo failed, as almost everyone predicted—often gleefully— that it would, peacekeeping would likely have ended. The peacekeeping interventions, which have played a major part in reducing . . . worldwide conflict fatalities by almost 90 percent in a decade, may never have happened. And in that sense, his legacy must be counted in the numbers of lives that have since been saved by peacekeeping.[137]

This great incantation

Hammarskjöld's love of literature, music, theater, and the visual arts, though glimpsed in passing, has been evident throughout these pages. His response to works of art was artistic in itself. Writing to Saint-John Perse in the summer of 1956, for example, about a section of Perse's long poem *Amers*, he said, "what I hesitate to put on paper concerning my reactions to *Étroits sont les vaisseaux*, I may have a chance to tell you when we meet. This great incantation has been a counterpoint to what I have had to deal with recently, maintaining a balance which we too easily lose without the firm hand and the open eye of great art."[138] His own great incantation is the private journal that became *Markings*.

We have heard Per Lind's account of its discovery. A letter clipped to the typescript of *Markings* was addressed to a close friend, the Swedish diplomat Leif Belfrage. Its text is memorable—pure Hammarskjöld:

Dear Leif:

Perhaps you may remember I once told you that, in spite of everything, I kept a diary which I wanted you to take charge of some day. Here it is.

It was begun without a thought of anybody else reading it. But, what with my later history and all that has been said and written about me, the situation has changed. These entries provide the only true "profile" that can be drawn. That is why, during recent years, I have reckoned with the possibility of publication, though I have continued to write for myself, not for the public.

If you find them worth publishing, you have my permission to do so— as a sort of *"white book"* concerning my negotiations with myself— and with God.

Dag

Leif Belfrage (1910–90) and his wife Greta had been warm friends; there is extensive correspondence between them in the UN years, Hammarskjöld often addressing them both. The couple shared the worry and need for care occasioned by their friend's charge. They understood that, were the book to be published, it would change the world's view of Dag Hammarskjöld in ways that could not be anticipated. And of course they felt compelled to publish: they also understood that the book was an immeasurably important element in the true profile of a man who had changed the world. A pair of dissimilar letters from the two-year interval between the discovery of the typescript and its publication in Sweden conveys a rich sense for that period and its concerns. The first was written by Greta to George Ivan Smith just prior to the book's appearance in Sweden.[139] Felt and wise, it is one of the most beautiful letters in the Hammarskjöld archive. The second, professional and discerning, was written by Georg Svensson, whom we know as a senior figure at Bonnier, long Hammarskjöld's contact in Swedish publishing and publisher of the Swedish edition of *Markings*. It is a sales letter to Alfred A. Knopf, the American publisher, whom he wants to persuade to buy rights to the book. First her letter:

Dear George

For about two years we have known that one day we would have to face the heavy responsibility of publishing the papers Dag left to Leif with a letter, leaving to him to decide about publication or not, but giving to understand that during the last years before his death he had himself counted with this.

. . . These papers were found on Dag's night table by Per Lind and his lawyer, and since the day they were brought to us, we have never been free of worry as to the right thing to do about them. Then, at last, we have considered that enough time had passed, time enough for the hysteria and the reaction to this to have ebbed out, but not too long a time for all those who worked with him, who thought that they knew him, and loved him. He does not here show the profile he turned to the world and it is not in the least what is usually meant by a "diary." Political events or people he met are never mentioned, but those who followed his work closely and know the dates of certain happenings might get more out of a reflection than the ordinary reader. It is shattering reading, of his struggle with himself, of the strong belief he has in himself as having been "chosen," of his never-faltering will to be led in his life and his work only by this God, who once spoke to him and called him. Aphorisms, ethical reflections, but also nature descriptions and lyrics, of sometimes such a beauty and so loaded with meaning that it will go to the heart of even the coldest reader. The last page bears the date August 24th 1961 and is a poem about a land he has often seen in his dream, a mountain land where he knows his way, where he has followed the river towards its source. . . .

It is a book of someone who knows of his extraordinary gifts, which give him outward satisfaction but inner isolation and emptiness, up till the day where his cup brims over for joy, the day when he sees that his God can use him. From that moment he stands in readiness, and for him it is a natural thing, something he is prepared for and familiar with, the acceptance of the utmost sacrifice.

I am relating all this to give you an idea of the line of his thoughts because you might hear people talking of it before it has been translated to English (which I suppose they will do, sooner or later), and some people might react in the wrong way to his mystic belief in a road leading him to martyrdom. But we, who knew him and knew his many other "profiles," will never forget those when reading of his bitter loneliness in the middle of action and friends. It gives also, in a kind of inner dialogue, his moral and aesthetic standards, and will, I am absolutely convinced, become a book that many will turn to for help and support, even if Dag's life and integrity were unique.

This book will appear on the 17th of October and as soon as it is in our hands, we will let you have a copy, even if the text will be unreadable to you. It makes me cry, the idea that you cannot read it until the translator has been found that will do it justice.

This "profile" that Dag himself thinks is the only adequate one will add something to your picture of him, but it certainly is not the whole truth, impossible as it is for us all to see ourselves from all angles, sincere though we may be.

Leif is just now writing a preface to the volume and that cannot be anything like this emotional description that I give you. I look at your photos from Ndola and of course we know, even if we will never say so to anybody else, that he was a saint.

Yours affectionately,

Greta

Just three days later, Svensson wrote to Alfred Knopf a cool assessment nonetheless fully confident in the future of the book. "We are later this autumn," he wrote,

> publishing a book that we think will be of worldwide interest. It is a posthumous book by Dag Hammarskjöld in the form of a personal diary that was found after his death. . . . I do not want to anticipate the critical reaction to this book but can only say as my private opinion that this is a very remarkable human document that will give a very interesting and impressive picture of the personality behind it. We at least think that the book will be read by many for a long time to come, and that many of those who read it will be strongly influenced by it. . . .[140]

In the weeks after the publication of *Markings* in Sweden, critics and editorial writers struggled to make sense of it, and many failed. Olof Lagercrantz, Herbert Tingsten's successor as editor in chief of *Dagens Nyheter*, led off with a long, mean-spirited article on the day after publication, October 18th, under the abrasive title "Hammarskjöld, Jesus, and the Truth."[141] What he couldn't swallow or abide—not in the least— was Hammarskjöld's religious sensibility. In recent decades Sweden had become one of the most secularized nations of Europe. The foundation for understanding Hammarskjöld's perspective on life had gone missing in many people, including journalists. *Markings*, Lagercrantz wrote, "is about life in the service of God and *as* Jesus. . . ." He was willing to praise the more literary passages, but the inedible object was the striving to be a faithful disciple. Lagercrantz needed to misread to get where he was going. For example, toward the end of 1955 Hammarskjöld wrote into his journal a quite perfect and touching text about service to the United Nations. He described the UN as "a jealous dream . . . the greatest creation of mankind . . . Therefore: gladly death or humiliation if that is what the dream demands. Therefore: how easy to forgive."[142] What a warmly felt movement from abstraction to living gesture, from the jealous dream to forgiveness. Lagercrantz read differently: "Hammarskjöld's role is to suffer for this dream," he wrote. "He identifies himself to a higher and higher degree with Jesus. The certainty as well as the exaltation rises in every year that passes. . . ." And in the end Lagercrantz wrote what seems to me a blasphemy. "Roughly expressed, [Hammarskjöld] means that Jesus, had he lived in our days, would have been Secretary-General of the United Nations and worked for the creation of an efficient world government. . . ." Lagercrantz's judgment on Hammarskjöld—he felt authorized to judge—was categorically negative: "Here is a tragedy. . . . Hammarskjöld . . . lost contact with reality and no longer could be reached or saved. . . . In the end the Secretary-General stands alone with his God. He becomes the Prince of Peace, the Prince of the World, the Savior. . . ."

It leaves one speechless. In summer 1958, Hammarskjöld said to a colleague, "Only one member government has ever betrayed me, and that is my own."[143] The circumstances are different but the taste is the same. It is far easier now to understand why Hammarskjöld was rigorously discreet about his religious life. He had spoken freely once, in the Edward R. Murrow credo, and spoken once more through the design of the Room of Quiet and its accompanying text. Beyond that, nothing really—occasional remarks with audiences that shared his religious perspective.

A few weeks later the same newspaper ran an editorial, "The Hammarskjöld Myth," unsigned but probably by Herbert Tingsten. Its tone is somewhat less strident but the message unchanged. The editorialist lingers over a massively negative article published a few days earlier in a Norwegian newspaper by Eyvind Bertels, the Norwegian ambassador to France, who had described Hammarskjöld as "a poor, miserable aesthete, a despairing man," and written that "[Hammarskjöld] wanted us to believe that behind the skilled diplomat and eminent thinker was a powerful personality, guided by God towards a destiny that could be entered into the holy book. . . . But in this endeavor [he] faced defeat and not victory. . . ."[144] Tingsten, or whoever was writing, used the strategy of disagreeing a little with Bertels as a means of making Bertels's points.

The battle of critics was joined on terrain that many educated Swedes thought settled: the place of religion in contemporary culture. In Hammarskjöld's lifetime some had attacked him for his politics. Now some attacked him for who he was.

A brilliant champion arose not merely to defend him but to mock his attackers: Kerstin Anér (1920–91). She was interesting. After earning a doctorate in literature at the University of Gothenburg in 1948, she had a first career in high-level print and radio journalism. In later years as a member of the Swedish parliament, she involved herself in many new issues—environmental policy, the impact of computer technology, still others—while maintaining a full schedule as a sought-after speaker in churches and other venues. Some of her poetry, in the form of modern psalms, found its way into the standard Swedish hymnal. This was a person for whom Christianity was integral to her thought and feeling, as natural as breathing, and like Hammarskjöld she experienced religion as the basis for a personal quest, a way of keeping deep curiosity, ready love, and conscience alive.

Writing in *Aftonbladet*, a newspaper that competed with Lagercrantz and Tingsten's *Dagens Nyheter*, she spoke her mind after reading a negative editorial published a little earlier by *Aftonbladet*. She must have had Lagercrantz and Tingsten in mind, as well.

Hammarskjöld as a Christian mystic must irritate all our atheists

No one understands better than I that it must be utterly annoying to all our atheists when Dag Hammarskjöld proves to be a Christian mystic. You cannot say that he was stupid—you cannot say he was immoral—you cannot say he was confined to a small-town environment and influenced by its narrow-minded values. Instead you choose to say that his own, innermost outlook on life didn't have the slightest bit to do with his lifework. . . .

If you translate his words into plain language, the editorial writer of *Aftonbladet* says: I do not understand one word of Hammarskjöld's mysticism, so therefore I understand it completely. He dismisses the fact that you need a certain degree of expert knowledge and professional education to be able to read the book correctly. . . . Is that a reason to allow only ignorance to have its say?

Because ignorance it is, and nothing but, if you read *Markings* in such a way that you believe you find in it tendencies toward dictatorship. The book is about something quite different: self-criticism concerning the highest moral norms. A perpetual road toward greater and greater devotion to truth, compassion, insight, in the face of a model that is unattainable and certainly never identified with Hammarskjöld. . . .

Reading *Markings* as if it were a manual for monomaniacal dictators is to characterize yourself, not the author of the book. But I understand . . . the editorial writer. *Markings* is a book that burns you, a book that has an effect like the antique torso of Apollo in Rilke's poem:

> . . . here there is no place
> that does not see you. You must change your life.

No wonder that you would rather deal with it wearing asbestos gloves and blackened glasses.[145]

She was keenly aware of the existential challenge implicit in *Markings*: you must change your life—or at very least witness Hammarskjöld's and let its influence play over you and into you. Her choice of metaphor at the end is perfect, as if *Markings* were a red-hot object in a forge. Reading her, we can be certain that Hammarskjöld's fellow Swedes would, in time if not at once, better understand him. In the course of the 1960s, two Swedish authors published very good books on Hammarskjöld's spirituality. Sven Stolpe, his friend from university years and a prominent Catholic writer, published *Dag Hammarskjölds andliga väg* (Dag Hammarskjöld's spiritual way) in 1965—reaching the English-speaking world a year later as *Dag Hammarskjöld: A Spiritual Portrait*. In 1969, bishop Gustaf Aulén published directly in English his *Dag Hammarskjöld's White Book: The Meaning of* Markings, with a Swedish edition in 1970.[146] Both were, and remain, important books. And if finding readers is the best revenge, or at least satisfactory revenge, Hammarskjöld had his revenge: the *New York Times* reported sales of 95,000 copies of the Swedish edition in the first eight months or so, equivalent to the sale of 2.5 million copies in the United States.[147] The editorial writers had had their day; now readers had theirs, and they were showing appreciation.

Some Swedish venom found its way into American media, notably in an article by John Lindberg, "The Secret Life of Dag Hammarskjöld," in the popular magazine *Look* for June 30th, 1964, a few months before *Markings* was published in English. Lindberg was a diplomat and economist, sometimes at the UN, who must secretly have found Hammarskjöld unbearable. "The arrogance, the awful pride of the man," he had written; "the sacrificial, self-destructive Messianic role" of the man. He delivered the same message a year later to *Der Spiegel*, the leading German news magazine, in an interview entitled "He believed he was Christ: The Swedish diplomat John Lindberg on Hammarskjöld."[148] Was it envy speaking, or obsession? Ralph Bunche couldn't bear to let the American article go unquestioned. In a letter to the editor he wrote, "I am simply appalled by the characterization of the late Secretary-General . . . in this article. The man Mr. Lindberg describes, or more accurately invents and dissects . . . has little or no resemblance to the man I knew. . . . I cannot think of anything more despicable than to engage in character assassination against a dead man. . . ."[149]

John Steinbeck, in an undated letter, also gave his appraisal. He quotes *Markings*; it must have recently been published. "This man was writing poetry with his life. It makes me angry to see these shoddy Swedes taking revenge on his greatness. . . . But I love his words —'Don't measure the height of a mountain until you have climbed it and then you will see how low it is.' And I loved him."[150]

Despite the furious attempt by a handful of writers in Sweden to spoil readers' receptiveness, the book sailed on, free of their misrepresentations and contempt. Lines from *Markings* come to mind: "You wake from dreams of doom and—for a moment—you *know*: beyond all the noise and the gestures, the only real thing, love's calm unwavering flame in the half light of an early dawn."[151]

Knopf told Urquhart that he was willing to publish in the United States if a celebrated author collaborated on the translation—he had that much faith, and that much doubt, as to the market for the book. Urquhart understood what to do: he invited Auden to dinner and successfully drafted him. Auden knew no Swedish, but as it happens he was already in touch with Leif Sjöberg, professor of Swedish and Scandinavian literature at Columbia University, concerning an unrelated translation project. Sjöberg proved to be a skilled partner for the Hammarskjöld project—and one who found the working process with Auden so interesting that he wrote an account of it more than a decade later.[152] As they advanced, they received good press from time to time, rare for a book that had not yet appeared. There was a report in the *New York Times* for January 12th, 1964, that the first draft was in Auden's hands, he was making good progress and would soon go to Sweden. He did find his way there in the spring and shared with Leif Belfrage his draft introduction to the book. Andrew Cordier had seen the draft in April.

Behind scenes, in a courteous, distressed exchange of letters in various directions, Auden's troubles began.

The difficulty was that Auden had absorbed some of the Swedish journalists' venom in dilute form—or had reached those views on his own. In late April Cordier wrote to William Koshland, a senior executive at Knopf and later president. "Auden has done a very perceptive piece of work on the foreword," Cordier began,

> although I feel that he has over-stressed several points that will leave a regrettably negative distortion in the minds of people regarding Dag Hammarskjöld. I refer particularly to . . . the . . . paragraph . . . regarding his alleged narcissistic tendencies, and later his obsession with death and suicide; and finally, the problem of identification with God. Rather than meeting these issues head on, Mr. Auden has added fuel to the fire. Having been his closest and most intimate associate for eight and a half years, I feel that it would be in the interest of truth and accuracy to engage in some modification of these three points in the introduction. May I add that I feel the other parts of the introduction are really splendid.[153]

A few months later, Auden himself got off a resentful note to Koshland. "The truth is," he wrote, "that DH's Swedish friends have been much more shocked by the book than they dare admit to themselves, so that the shock is turned on me."[154]

Everyone involved was qualifying remarks through this prepublication period. No one wanted to offend, yet everyone was offended. Auden was no exception: in the controversial foreword he qualified some of his remarks. At its very end, for example, he grumbled that Hammarskjöld would have been better off, had he regularly attended church—because "introverted intellectuals" benefit from "ecclesiastical routine." He was drawing on his own experience. "But how frivolous all such misgivings look," he continued, "in the light of the overall impression which the book makes, the conviction when one has finished it, that one has had the privilege of being in contact with a great, good, and lovable man."[155] This was a lovely, memorable conclusion—but the damage had been done pages earlier.

Auden had a pleasant spring visit to Sweden. He met "Hammarskjöld people" and did some useful digging to identify Swedish authors cited in *Markings*. Some time after he left Sweden for his second home in Austria, Leif Belfrage sent him a five-page, typed response to the foreword, prepared jointly with Per Lind and other unnamed "friends of DH whom you met here in Sweden." "Whatever you may think of our observations," Belfrage wrote, "I wish to emphasize that it is not our purpose to try to persuade you to change your introduction into a glorification of DH. The absurd idea of Mr. Auden in the role of a hagiographer has certainly never entered our minds. . . . Please be assured that I do submit the enclosed paper in all humility and respect . . . ."[156] Just past this courteous disclaimer begins a scorching examination. Belfrage and his colleagues did not want Auden to play armchair psychiatrist: "Especially in an introduction which is so important for the future comprehension of DH as a person, it seems to us quite daring to lose oneself in a very personal interpretation of the psychological make-up of this man. . . . As a matter of fact, none of us recognized DH from the picture you have drawn here, neither from what we read in *Markings* nor from our knowledge of the man. . . ." They also took issue with Auden's remark that, by his personal definition, Hammarskjöld was not a genius and with his treatment of Hammarskjöld's insistence on searching for the will of God. Especially in that regard, Auden echoed the furious Swedish journalists. "The man who says, 'Not I, but God in me,'" Auden wrote, "is always in great danger of imagining that he *is* God, and some critics have not failed to accuse Hammarskjöld precisely of this kind of megalomania." Belfrage and his colleagues found this unendurable on Auden's part. "To consider oneself a son of God," they wrote, "and by His Grace an instrument of God, could also be argued as rather . . . a basic element of the Christian faith. . . . Furthermore, to be such an instrument of God seems exactly the opposite of 'being God.'" In his excellent book, Sven Stolpe made the same point: "This is no mannered aestheticism, no narcissism in disguise: it is classical Christianity."[157]

There is much more in the sadly accusatory letter, but just one further point calls for a place here. "Our views on DH's religion differ from yours," Belfrage wrote. "While keeping his roots in the Christian faith, we think that DH may have 'out-winged' what is usually described as religion, reaching a point where it does not matter anymore what label you give it. That needs, we think, just as much, and perhaps even more, discipline than any ecclesiastical routine may be able to give. . . ." The agony of Dag's friends is poignantly evident—particularly Leif Belfrage's agony. He felt responsible for the life of the book wherever it appeared in the world, and in his view Auden was—in a most civilized, literate way—betraying it. *Markings* was published in October 1964 in the United States with Auden's foreword unchanged. It said much that was true, and much that was terribly questionable.

George Ivan Smith naturally read the book as soon as it appeared. To Max Ascoli, his friend as much as Hammarskjöld's, he wrote that

> [Auden's] essay (it was not an introduction in the strictest sense) angered me. As a prelude to a work that concerned itself with self-surrender, it jerked over the surface of life and lost itself in . . . theories. . . . Privately and frankly, Auden scarcely knew Dag at all. They dined together very occasionally. I believe I may have been present on the majority of occasions. Dag enjoyed the crackle of Auden's mind, his imagery and his concern with words and forms. . . . But not by the wildest stretch of the imagination would I have turned to [him] to write an introduction to such a book. My choice would have been Martin Buber or Saint-John Perse.[158]

In the event, Auden's foreword did no harm. *Markings* at once found a very large and appreciative audience. The *New York Times* noted with precision that in its first six months in bookstores 184,712 copies had sold in the United States, and it received thoughtful reviews from literary critics, theologians, and Brian Urquhart, who wrote in *The New Yorker* a few weeks after publication.[159] His review article should be anthologized some day with others of its quality; it offers permanent food for thought. Urquhart was by no means hagiographic in his approach to this utterly surprising, revelatory document. But he left no doubt, as he put it, that

> an extraordinarily wide range of public figures in many countries, and countless millions of ordinary people as well, felt instinctively that [Hammarskjöld] could be trusted and could help them. He himself felt that he, lacking some ordinary capacity for private life, had been given the greatest boon of all in this opportunity to serve others, and that he must repay the debt with all his spirit, his intellect, and his energy, and even with his life. He repaid it handsomely.[160]

Urquhart's reference to instinctive trust is key here: few had the slightest notion of Hammarskjöld's inner life, but many sensed something unusual and unusually reliable in him.

Auden's biographer offers a glimpse into the personal consequences of the foreword for its author. Of course, he had been a candidate for the Nobel Prize in Literature. His works over a long career—poetry, essays, criticism, even the libretto for an opera now standard in the repertory—

were acknowledged for their intelligence, originality, and grasp of the resources of contemporary English. His biographer writes, "Before the typescript [of *Markings*] had gone to press, Auden was warned by a high Swedish official that his criticisms would prejudice the members of the Swedish Academy . . . but he would not modify his phrases. 'Well, there goes the Nobel Prize,' he said glumly at dinner with Lincoln Kirstein....."[161] Both Auden and Kirstein had been Hammarskjöld's friends. He might have enjoyed the scenario and found more to laugh about than lament.

After a wish of Dag Hammarskjöld

Two works of art came to be the most vivid and poignant memorials to Hammarskjöld. They could not be more different. The first is familiar to every visitor to the United Nations in Manhattan: the monumental bronze sculpture by Barbara Hepworth in the forecourt of the Secretariat building. Its title is *Single Form*, its base records that it was created and placed "after a wish of Dag Hammarskjöld," and it is an inexhaustibly beautiful, speaking work of art (fig. 18). The second memorial is little known, probably little liked, and relatively inaccessible—yet it is quite perfect. It is the portrait of Hammarskjöld by Ben Shahn, completed in 1962, now in the Swedish National Portrait Collection housed some forty-five miles west of Stockholm in Gripsholm Castle (fig. 19). By experiencing these two works in relation to each other, we may assemble an original memorial of our own. The first is a blissful thing—lofty, shaped by ideals. In Hammarskjöld's lexicon, it is "the flame that ascends straight upward." The second is dark, haunted—touched by the chaos inflicted by the Congo Crisis and Hammarskjöld's tireless efforts to set things right. It is "blood, grime, sweat, earth," and a sign of the focused human will to resist disorder and evil.

It was not difficult, and entirely fitting, for the General Assembly on October 16th to confer on the new UN library the name it carries to this day: the Dag Hammarskjöld Library. But the circle closest to him—Ralph Bunche, Andrew Cordier, Brian Urquhart, joined by Secretary-General U Thant—knew that some larger memorial was needed. Several of them could recall a stroll with Hammarskjöld, after a working lunch, around the forecourt of the Secretariat building, which at the time had a rather plain reflecting pool. They were in the company of the American industrialist and diplomat Jacob Blaustein (1892–1970) who, with his father, had built the extremely successful Amoco oil company and related businesses and, in later years, served as a US delegate to the UN while pursuing philanthropic work. During that stroll, Blaustein later recounted, "the Secretary-General . . . had expressed . . . once again the opinion that something aesthetic and impressive, in keeping with the importance of this area, should be added to the pool—perhaps a large sculpture such as could be created by Barbara Hepworth, whose work Hammarskjöld greatly admired. . . ."[162] Bunche wanted to ask Blaustein at once to consider financing the project, but Hammarskjöld restrained him: he didn't want in any way to exploit his friendship with Jacob Blaustein.

But the situation was now different, and Blaustein agreed at once, as did Barbara Hepworth, to realize the vision sketched by Hammarskjöld. The architects of the UN complex were engaged to redesign and enlarge the reflecting pool to accommodate a major sculpture.[163] On June 11th, 1964, the sculpture in its impressive new setting was unveiled in a ceremony given sparkling life by words from U Thant, Jacob Blaustein, Barbara Hepworth, and the director of the Museum of Modern Art, René d'Harnoncourt. Hepworth spoke briefly but unforgettably. She recalled conversations with Hammarskjöld about her series of works all carrying in some version the title *Single Form*. He had owned one for some years and cared so much for it that he had written a sequence of haiku poems under that title.[164] She seems to have had no doubt about what was needed: it would be a monumental reinterpretation of *Single Form*. She continued:

> Dag Hammarskjöld had a pure and exact perception of aesthetic principles, as exact as it was over ethical and moral principles. I believe they were, to him, one and the same thing, and he asked of each one of us the best we could give.
>
> The United Nations is our conscience. If it succeeds it is our success. If it fails it is our failure. Throughout my work on the "Single Form" I have kept in mind Dag Hammarskjöld's ideas of human and aesthetic ideology and I have tried to perfect a symbol that would reflect the nobility of his life, and at the same time give us a motive and symbol of both continuity and solidarity for the future.[165]

René d'Harnoncourt offered an initial interpretation of the massive sculpture, "rising before us," he said, "like a great cliff or prow or gigantic living being . . . ," and he quoted a talk at the Museum of Modern

Art given by Hammarskjöld years earlier. "Modern art teaches us to see by forcing us to use our senses, our intellect, and our sensibility," Hammarskjöld had said, "to follow it on its road of exploration. It makes us seers—and explorers—these we must be if we are to prevail."[166]

What is this sculpture? It is the single form of many different things, to borrow words written long ago about symbols by Ananda Coomaraswamy. It is an archaic standing stone, a most ancient and venerable object. It is very young, just born. It is a standing human figure purified to essentials. It insists on openness, on receptivity and welcome. It is what Mahmoud Fawzi said of Hammarskjöld himself: a flag of glory.

Certain things are best hidden. While the plinth of the sculpture displays an open message—the artist's and donor's names, the title of the work, the melancholy and touching phrase "After a wish of Dag Hammarskjöld"—a hidden message is inscribed in Hepworth's hand aloft in the rim of the circle. "To the Glory of God and the memory of Dag Hammarskjöld. Ndola 17–9–61."[167]

Ben Shahn's portrait inhabits a different world. It is tied to time, its themes are suffering and resistance. Drawing on his direct familiarity with Hammarskjöld and on characteristic photographs, particularly of Hammarskjöld cradling his chin as he listened to Nikita Khrushchev in the General Assembly, Shahn chose to create what he called "a portrait about, rather than of a man."[168] He wrote to Carl Nordenfalk about his vision for the painting at a time when Swedish critics were saying, correctly, that the portrait was not a good likeness. "I did not like the notion of a conventional portrait," he wrote.

> That seemed to me a commonplace. I wanted to express Hammarskjöld's loneliness and isolation, his need actually, for such remoteness in space that he might be able to carry through, as he did, the powerful resolution to be just. His unaffiliated kind of justice, it seems to me, held the world together through many crises that might have deteriorated into world conflicts. I have a truly profound feeling for this man, and I hope it will be felt in the painting. I must mention, too, the threat that hung over him as it hung over the world, and does still.[169]

The calligraphy on the tabletop in front of the figure of Hammarskjöld records his words in reply to Khrushchev's demand for his resignation— "I shall remain at my post. . . ." The chaotic swirl above and behind, with the sorrowful face of a prophet just visible in it, reflects the nuclear catastrophe that Hammarskjöld had given his all to prevent. The face of Hammarskjöld is darkly thoughtful, compositionally and emotionally midway between the firm courage of the written text and the chaos behind him. In this harsh context, the compressed image of sky and bridge on the right (the bridge combines features of two East River crossings) gives a welcome suggestion of movement and, as Shahn wrote, some small promise of spaciousness. This is a *difficult* work. It isn't easily likable. But as Nordenfalk wrote, "it will have something to tell future generations about what our life was like. . . ."

It is just and sensible to remember these works together as a composite memorial to Hammarskjöld. But we need an inscription to complete our memorial. Consider this tribute from a UN official in Geneva, who knew Hammarskjöld well.

> *Il était comme la Bize du Nord—qui balaye tout ce qui est mauvais et assure le beau temps.*[170]

He was like the north wind that sweeps away everything bad and brings good weather. This speaks to his buoyant spirit. But consider also Hammarskjöld's own tribute to the first UN High Commissioner for Refugees at a ceremony honoring his memory:

> He thrust the love of man into vigorous battle against indignity to man.[171]

This speaks to his dedication. Can we allow a third? You may recall these few words from a letter of 1957:

> I take pride in belonging to the family of grasses, and I remain quite green in spite of a lot of trampling.[172]

This speaks to Dag Hammarskjöld's permanence.

Afterword

The Spirit in Public Life

"One with your task, whole in your duty of the moment," he wrote in his journal in the fall of 1957.[1] To this day there is a rush of good energy in these words, which capture his way of engaging. They are a mandate, not a description: for this he would strive. It is a value.

Consider other words he wrote that year: "We all have within us a center of stillness surrounded by silence"—this from the text distributed at the entrance to the Room of Quiet.[2] These words whisper. There is no rush of energy but something more like a settling. Yet he is just as certain, and this too is a value.

Hammarskjöld knew two unlike worlds very well. The world of politics and political leaders, deception and honesty, violence and kindness, reflection and the search for solutions. And another world: of inwardness and prayer, of self-scrutiny and ancient wisdom, of periodic return to a "center of stillness surrounded by silence" that nourishes, situates, and restores. In the first world he was nearly always with people. In the second, nearly always alone with his own person and his God. In both worlds he was a lifelong inquirer with initiative; it wasn't enough to pass through, contributing cautious splashes of oneself here and there. In the world at large he strove to summon the best of himself, look carefully and imaginatively, and act as wisely as possible. We have seen how closely he studied situations and sought to conceive his role and deploy the resources of the United Nations without a shred of self-concern. He asked for providential help but left nothing to chance. In his inner world we have seen how closely he scrutinized his experience and faithfully gave himself to prayers that inch along the page, leading he knew not where but often to necessary truths.

Early in the UN years he spoke of "the laws of inner life and of action."[3] This unusual thought—who else would have said this?—captures his respect for both worlds and his conviction that they can be deciphered by patient engagement. Strikingly, the notion of laws implies both science and obedience. There was something to know and, once known, something to obey. He acknowledged that the direction is not always evident. "Thy orders are given in secret," he wrote in 1956. "May I always hear them—and obey."[4]

It can't always have been easy to move between his inner world and world affairs. As he wrote to a friend in August 1961, "[The] obligation to action, especially in the political field, is more of a danger than a privilege. At the present phase, events on all levels and the basic stone-age psychology of men make it rather difficult to translate contemplation into action and to make action the source material for contemplation. . . ."[5] Nonetheless, he was able to do so, and he was convinced to his marrow that "in our era the road to holiness necessarily passes through the world of action."[6]

He spoke in different ways of this road between worlds. At times, and I think often, he experienced what he called moments of intuitive rediscovery when he would know in some large sense and also know the most promising direction. Even for him, an exacting writer, it was difficult to find the right words. In the following entry from *Markings*, he resorted to quotation marks to blur somewhat the certainty surrounding a key word choice: "In this intuitive 'rediscovery' which has become my Ariadne's thread through life—step by step, day by day—the end is now as real to me as tomorrow morning's foreseen task."[7] Intuitive rediscovery must be the opposite of formulated knowledge; it is a readiness, not a rule book; a sudden recognition of something one knew all along though it hadn't declared itself. He once wrote an amazingly complex entry in his journal headed "In self-defense— against the system-builders."[8] In his working life, intuitive rediscovery was likely to have been an unsystematic, spontaneous arrival of knowledge summoned by circumstances. But it was far from groundless: it drew upon and expressed the fullness of his identity, the long search for self-knowledge, the values by which he lived, the intricate experience of international life, the discipline of awareness and empathy to which, insofar as possible, he held himself. Following his Ariadne's thread in this way, he could travel light.

Many entries in *Markings* make clear that intuitive rediscovery applied not only to political life but to himself—to knowledge *and* self-knowledge. Men and women who follow spiritual disciplines somewhat like his know that they lose touch with themselves, become creatures of habit, but a fresh, more rooted sense of self returns in moments of rediscovery or remembering. In Hammarskjöld's spiritual vocabulary, intuitive rediscovery is likely to point toward renewed awareness of the presence of "someone or something" of another order in our lives, which both sustains us and makes demands. That this recognition is "intuitive" may indicate that one approaches it with all of one's perceptive powers functioning as a kind of radar looking out into a darkness it can penetrate.

Now that we have tried to understand him, we can surely sympathize with his use of quotation marks around "rediscovery." This isn't easy, but for him it was crucial; it was the Ariadne's thread.

A discipline of awareness and empathy? I have no better words for the approach he spontaneously described to a UN journalist. You may recall that conversation as he later relayed it to a friend: "The other day I was forced by a journalist to try to formulate my views on the main requirements of somebody who wishes to contribute to the development of peace and reason. I found no better formulation than this: 'He must push his awareness to the utmost limit without losing his inner quiet, he must be able to see with the eyes of others from within their personality without losing his own.'"[9] Without explicitly saying, he makes clear here that disciplines he valued privately for his inner life contributed in essential ways to the working day. Despite the stone-age psychology of humankind and the often senseless nature of events, there are still creative possibilities. Ariadne's thread doesn't go around in circles, it leads on.

What does it mean to push awareness to the utmost limit? Among other things, it would mean to refuse distraction, to be glisteningly available, to empty oneself of personal concerns so that all features of the present conversation can be received. It defines diplomacy, or relationship, as first an act of attention; the rest follows. Rajeshwar Dayal observed in Hammarskjöld the radiance and effectiveness of this approach. "Hammarskjöld excelled at face-to-face encounters," he wrote. "He carried an air of total attention, alert to the slightest nuance of word or gesture. He seemed able to sense what was in one's mind and to provide the answer even before a thought was fully formulated."[10]

We should ask a further question: what makes it possible to see with the eyes of others from within their personality without losing one's own? In his original conversation with the UN journalist, Hammarskjöld shared an insight: "A certain humility . . . helps you to see things through the other person's eye, to reconstruct his case, without losing yourself, without being a chameleon, if you see what I mean."[11] And then, it relies on receptivity and listening. "To remain a recipient," he wrote in his journal, "—out of humility. And preserve your flexibility. To remain a recipient—and be grateful. Grateful for being *allowed* to listen, to observe, to understand."[12] What he writes here about gratitude reminds us that he was religious; no picture was complete if it excluded the presence of "someone or something," of God close and distant simultaneously.

We are looking at markings on Hammarskjöld's compass. Empathy, receptivity, listening—couched in a certain reserve ("without being a chameleon, if you see what I mean")—are linked to one another as distinct shades of experience in the movement between worlds, inner and outer. To these elements of his unseen discipline should be added another: a certain emptiness that paradoxically allows life to flourish. His teachers in this regard were the medieval mystics he revered and early Chinese texts that confirmed their teachings and demonstrated their universality. In his introduction to *Markings* Auden touches absurdity where he writes that Hammarskjöld "lacks originality of insight" and "one has read it all before somewhere."[13] Of course, one has read it all before! That is the very nature of traditional religious and spiritual teachings. That is why we write things down in one century and read them in the next and the next. But teachings change and enrich in the lives of men and women who explore them as direct experiences in current contexts. For that reason it's worthwhile to write them down again. Hammarskjöld's understanding of emptiness and participation is vividly new and blessedly old. "Each day the first day," he wrote in *Markings*. "Each day a life. Each morning we must hold out the chalice of our being to receive, to carry, and give back. It must be held out empty—for the past must only be reflected in its polish, its shape, its capacity."[14] It is a restatement in different terms of the direction toward intuitive rediscovery, toward traveling light.

Not so many of us are able to convert written text into lived teaching, but Hammarskjöld had the right sort of workshop inside to make that possible. In this instance, he had heard from the legendary Chinese sage Tsze Sze that "he who can totally sweep clean the chalice of himself can carry the inborn nature of others to its fulfillment . . . unseen it causes harmony; unmoving it transforms; unmoved it perfects."[15] It brings *la Bize du Nord*—the cleansing north wind. He had heard much the same from Meister Eckhart who wrote, "You must have an exalted mind and a *burning* heart in which, nevertheless, reigns *silent* stillness."[16] In such sources he also found hints about the value, even the necessity, of intuitive rediscovery as a means of knowing and participating. Tsze Sze put it this way: "The sincere man finds the axis without forcing himself to do so. He arrives at it without thinking and goes along naturally in the midst of the process. . . ."[17]

We shouldn't emphasize one world and disregard the other. Hammarskjöld was not a Confucian sage, a medieval monk, or a shy visitor in the world of action. He had integrated depth of inner life with mastery of political processes. He had done so as a man of the modern West, a Christian and humanist open to the world's political wisdom and spiritualities. This was his astonishing achievement and contribution. "The UN . . . is an operation where you have to work on the basis of very great realism," he said on *Meet the Press*, a classic American television program.[18] He insisted on the need for realism—and for action. In another passage transcribed from Tsze Sze into his journal, he underscored the need to root action in self-knowledge. The italics here are his own, not in the original text: "Who has this great power to see clearly into himself without tergiversation, *and act thence*, will come to his destiny."[19] In his view, it isn't enough to see clearly into oneself without evasion; that is preparation for one's destined role, however small or great, among other people in the world at large. In public talks, he expressed this balance from time to time in ways that didn't ask his listeners to become sages or monks—but did ask them to recognize the imperative need for contact and coherence between their inner and outer worlds. "Our work for peace must begin within the private world of each one of us," he said in his year-end radio message in 1953. "To build for man a world without fear, *we* must be without fear. To build a world of justice, *we* must be just. And how can we fight for liberty if we are not free in our own minds? How can we ask others to sacrifice if *we* are not ready to do so? Some might consider this to be just another expression of noble principles, too far from the harsh realities of political life. . . . I disagree. . . ."[20]

Hammarskjöld had thought about indirection and disguise. To give peace and reason their best chance, he recognized that a light but persistent touch serves better under most circumstances than righteous determination. An exalted mind and burning heart need not make a display. The movement between worlds asks for something else. "In many matters," he wrote, "profound seriousness can only be expressed in words which are lighthearted, amusing, and detached; such a conversation as you may expect to hear from someone who, while deeply concerned for all things human, has nothing he is trying to gain or defend."[21] This expresses, I think, a preference; this approach was in character. For the rest, he was willing to disguise: "While performing the part which is truly ours, how exhausting it is to be obliged to play a role which is not ours: the person you must really be in order to fulfill your task, you must not appear to others to be, in order to be allowed by them to fulfill it. How exhausting—but unavoidable, since mankind has laid down once and for all the organized rules for social behavior."[22] Something of this kind led to Auden's ambiguity: in

Markings he saw Hammarskjöld's "true profile," undisguised by urbanity and wit around the dinner table—and he resisted.

To live in two worlds was a struggle, sometimes sharp, sometimes scarcely evident, but the struggle conferred strength and creativity in both worlds. "Out of myself as a stumbling block, into myself as fulfillment," he wrote in the spring of 1957.[23] The drama of a living, questing identity is implicit in these words, which again have a forward rush. He worked with his own person as an instrument for the good. He knew himself to be both flawed and capable of immensely effective service to high ideals. He was never invulnerable, and that wasn't needed. On the contrary. In the late fall of 1955, no doubt at his country home, he had a surprise: "The light died in the low clouds. Falling snow drank in the dusk. Shrouded in silence, the branches wrapped me in their peace. When the boundaries were erased, once again the wonder: that *I* exist."[24] He was tirelessly interested in what it is to live, to be aware, to carry a world within, to belong to God and one's fellow human beings, to be responsible for nearly impossible tasks, to bring what light and goodness he could. It was the best of struggles. Its results were shared in his lifetime through his work at the UN, and later through *Markings*.

I never tire of his clarity about values and attitudes that make sense of the world and help to set one's course in it. "A task becomes a duty," he wrote in 1955, "from the moment you suspect it to be an essential part of that integrity which alone entitles a man to assume responsibility."[25] The words preserve an atmosphere, as if just spoken.

I never tire of his distillations of experience, in which he accomplishes with ease what he said is rarely accomplished: to make action the source material of contemplation.

> Beyond obedience, its attention fixed on the goal—freedom from fear.
> Beyond fear—openness.
> And beyond that—love.[26]

I never tire of the moments he recorded when he came to rest in his inner world and, as William Blake said long ago, "the doors of perception were cleansed." An exceptional passage in *Markings* will allow us to acknowledge this aspect of his nature and experience.

> To have humility is to experience reality, not in relation to ourselves, but in
> its sacred independence. It is to see, judge, and act from the point of rest in
> ourselves. Then, how much disappears, and all that remains falls into place.

> In the point of rest at the center of our being, we encounter a world
> where all things are at rest in the same way. Then a tree becomes a mys-
> tery, a cloud a revelation, each man a cosmos of whose riches we can
> only catch glimpses. The life of simplicity is simple, but it opens to us a
> book in which we never get beyond the first syllable.[27]

In the fall of 1960, when he was under nearly intolerable pressure from
all sides, Hammarskjöld received a letter from the virtuoso Austrian pianist, Paul Badura-Skoda, who was performing in New York at the time.
They had been in touch some months earlier when the pianist had been
trying to trace a lost Mozart manuscript across Cold War borders. Badura-Skoda inquired whether a recital for the United Nations community
might be welcome. It happens that Hammarskjöld responded to his kind
offer just after the UN Day celebration at which he had memorably interpreted the musical narrative in Beethoven's Ninth Symphony. "Yesterday, United Nations Day," Hammarskjöld wrote, "we honed our faith in
humanity and human brotherhood by listening again to the message of
Beethoven's Ninth. It would have been lovely to have an evening devoted
to a quiet celebration of those values, as you put it, which make existence
worth the price we all pay as human beings."[28] He was unable to organize
it on such short notice. Perhaps another time.

Perhaps another time . . . I salute the United Nations and its people.
You were the ground and height where all this proved to be possible.
Dag Hammarskjöld was yours, as much as the United Nations in that
era was very considerably his. It is not old magic. This story, this adept
human being, and these swarms of ideas are integral to the story and
humanity and intellectual substance of the United Nations itself. "This
great dream is exacting," he once said to you in a year-end message.[29]
The words preserve an atmosphere, as if just spoken to us all. Implicitly
they measure the distance between the ideals he so cared for and the
realities that he, like us all, addressed from day to day. "Seers—and explorers—these we must be if we are to prevail."[30] Seers are not wholly of
this world; they know another and draw from it for the benefit of their
fellow human beings. Explorers belong to this world; they like maps and
terrain and challenges. Dag Hammarskjöld was both seer and explorer.
Without "noise," as he liked to say—without calling attention to it—he
brought spirit into public life and learned through public life to care still
more for the point of rest at the center of our being. The two worlds fit.

Abbreviations in the Endnotes

In the notes, translations by Daniel von Sydow are attributed to DvS. Frequently cited works are identified by the following abbreviations.

Beskow — Bo Beskow. *Dag Hammarskjöld: Strictly Personal— A Portrait.* Garden City, NY: Doubleday, 1969.

Dayal (1) — Rajeshwar Dayal. *Mission for Hammarskjold: The Congo Crisis.* Princeton, NJ: Princeton University Press, 1976.

Dayal (2) — Rajeshwar Dayal. *A Life of Our Times.* New Delhi: Orient Longman, 1998.

DH — Dag Hammarskjöld

Erling — Bernhard Erling. *A Reader's Guide to Dag Hammarskjöld's Waymarks.* Translation with a commentary. St. Peter, MN: privately published, 1999. Available online at www.dhf.uu.se.

Kanza (1) — Thomas Kanza. *The Rise and Fall of Patrice Lumumba: Conflict in the Congo.* Rochester, VT: Schenkman, 1972.

Kanza (2) — Thomas Kanza. *Evolution and Revolution in Africa.* London: Rex Collings, 1971.

Kelen — Emery Kelen. *Hammarskjöld.* New York: Putnam, 1966.

KB — Kungliga biblioteket (National Library of Sweden)

Markings — Dag Hammarskjöld. *Markings.* Translated by Leif Sjöberg and W. H. Auden. New York: Knopf, 1964.

PP I — Andrew W. Cordier and Wilder Foote, ed. *Public Papers of the Secretaries-General of the United Nations.* Vol. 1, *Trygve Lie 1946–1953.* New York: Columbia University Press, 1969.

PP II — Andrew W. Cordier and Wilder Foote, ed. *Public Papers of the Secretaries-General of the United Nations.* Vol. 2, *Dag Hammarskjöld 1953–1956.* New York: Columbia University Press, 1972.

PP III — Andrew W. Cordier and Wilder Foote, ed., *Public Papers of the Secretaries-General of the United Nations.* Vol. 3, *Dag Hammarskjöld 1956–1957.* New York: Columbia University Press, 1973.

PP IV   Andrew W. Cordier and Wilder Foote, ed. *Public Papers of the Secretaries-General of the United Nations*. Vol. 4, *Dag Hammarskjöld 1958–1960*. New York: Columbia University Press, 1974.

PP V   Andrew W. Cordier and Wilder Foote, ed. *Public Papers of the Secretaries-General of the United Nations*. Vol. 5, *Dag Hammarskjöld 1960–1961*. New York: Columbia University Press, 1975.

Thelin (1)   Bengt Thelin. *Dag Hammarskjöld: Barnet, Skolpojken, Studenten*. Stockholm: Carlssons, 2005.

Thelin (2)   Bengt Thelin. *Dag Hammarskjöld: FN-chefen och människan*. Stockholm: Carlssons, 2010.

Urquhart (1)   Brian Urquhart. *Hammarskjold*. New York: Knopf, 1972.

Urquhart (2)   Brian Urquhart. *A Life in Peace and War*. New York: Harper & Row, 1987.

Urquhart (3)   Brian Urquhart. *Ralph Bunche: An American Life*. New York: Norton, 1993.

Williams   Susan Williams. *Who Killed Hammarskjöld? The UN, the Cold War and White Supremacy in Africa*. London: Hurst, 2011.

Endnotes

Chapter 1

1. Urquhart (1), 321.

2. Manuel Fröhlich, *Political Ethics and the United Nations: Dag Hammarskjöld as Secretary-General*, the abridged version of his *Dag Hammarskjöld und die Vereinten Nationen: Die politische Ethik des UNO-Generalsekretärs* (Paderborn, Germany: Schöningh Ferdinand, 2002).

3. DH letter to Eyvind Johnson, 31 January 1958, KB (trans. DvS).

4. Henry Adams, *The Education of Henry Adams*, 975.

5. *PP II*, "International Service," Address at Johns Hopkins University Commencement Exercises, 14 June 1955, 507.

6. *PP II*, Address at the Annual Meeting of the Association of American Colleges, 13 January 1954, 248.

7. *PP II*, Address at Luncheon Given by the American Political Science Association, 11 September 1953, 85.

8. United Nations Oral History Collection, interview with George Sherry, 12 July 1990, 4–5.

9. *PP II*, Address at Dinner in His Honor Given by the American Association for the United Nations in Cooperation with the New York University Institute for Review of United Nations Affairs, 14 September 1953, 88.

10. *Markings*, 1955, 114. The first edition is Dag Hammarskjöld, *Vägmärken*, published in English as *Markings*, trans. Leif Sjöberg and W. H. Auden. Two further editions are especially useful: Bernhard Erling, trans. and commentary, *A Reader's Guide to Dag Hammarskjöld's* Waymarks; and Anton Graf Knyphausen, trans., *Zeichen am Weg: Das spirituelle Tagebuch des UN-Generalsekretärs*. Erling offers a highly literal translation and often useful background; Knyphausen/Fröhlich has an excellent introduction and a consistently more accurate translation than Sjöberg/Auden. Readers may want to look at the Italian translation, Guido Dotti, trans., *Tracce di Cammino;* and the French, C. G. Bjurström and Philippe Dumaine, *Jalons*.

11. DH letter to Sir Pierson Dixon, 10 March 1961, KB.

12. *Markings*, v (following the title page).

13. *PP II*, Address at Commencement Exercises of Amherst College, 13 June 1954, 303–4.

14. *Markings*, 1955, 119.

15. *PP V*, "The International Civil Servant in Law and in Fact," Lecture Delivered in Congregation at Oxford University, 30 May 1961, 488.

16. DH letter to George Ivan Smith, 23 September 1957, in the Papers of George Ivan Smith, the Bodleian Library, University of Oxford. See Lucy McCann, *Catalogue of the Papers of George Ivan Smith, 1888–1995*, Bodleian Library, University of Oxford, available online at www.bodley.ox.ac.uk/dept/scwmss/. The first, and excellent, account of these papers is Manuel Fröhlich, "'The Unknown Assignation': Dag Hammarskjöld in the Papers of George Ivan Smith," *Critical Currents*, no. 2 (March 2008), 9–35, available online at www.dhf.uu.se.

17. DH letter to Bo Beskow, 16 March 1957, KB.

18. DH letter to Sture Petrén, 9 April 1961, KB (trans. DvS).

19. *PP II*, Statement to the Press on Arrival at International Airport, New York, 9 April 1953, 29.

20. DH letter to David Ben-Gurion, 31 July 1956, KB.

21. DH letter to Ahmed S. Bokhári, 9 September 1953, KB.

22. A facsimile of Frost's letter to Bokhári appears at http://patrasbokhari.com/content/patras-bokhari-robert-frost. The letter itself is in the Stanley Burnshaw archive (24.3), Harry Ransom Center, University of Texas, Austin.

23. *Markings*, 1955, 110.

24. See also *PP IV*, Words Spoken at Services for Ahmed S. Bokhári, UN Under-Secretary for Public Information, Pakistan House, New York, 6 December 1958, 305–6.

25. Eric Lindegren, *Dag Hammarskjöld*, trans. Thord Palmlund, 5. DH had mentioned to Beskow that he hoped to write in retirement; see Beskow, 17.

Chapter 2

1. *Markings*, 1959, 185.

2. DH letter to Jytte Bonnier, 26 August 1961, KB. DH's phrase in German, "und der Teufel steckt darin" (and the Devil is in it) is a variation on a familiar proverb: "Der Teufel steckt im Detail" (the Devil is in the details).

3. *Markings*, 1959, 175.

4. *PP II*, "Old Creeds in a New World," written for Edward R. Murrow's radio program *This I Believe*, November 1953.

5. DH letter to Georg Svensson (a senior executive at leading Swedish publishing house Bonnier), 25 January 1954, KB (trans. DvS).

6. Karl E. Birnbaum, ed., *Dag Hammarskjöld: Ungdomsårens vittnesbörd—*

brev och uppteckningar 1925–1931, 91 (trans. DvS).

7. Stig Holmqvist, *Visions of a Secretary-General: Dag Hammarskjöld and the United Nations 1953–1961*.

8. Kelen, 34.

9. Birnbaum, *Dag Hammarskjöld*, 91 (trans. DvS).

10. *PP II*, Address at Dinner in His Honor Given by the American Association for the United Nations in Cooperation with the New York University Institute for Review of United Nations Affairs, New York, 14 September 1953, 95.

11. Marie-Noëlle Little, *The Poet and the Diplomat: The Correspondence of Dag Hammarskjöld and Alexis Leger*.

12. "An Interview with the Secretary-General," *Secretariat News*, 14 February 1958, 3.

13. *PP II*, Inaugural Address upon Taking His Seat as a Member of the Swedish Academy, Stockholm, 20 December 1954, 409.

14. Ibid., 412. In a letter to his friend Bo Beskow, in which he shared the Swedish text of his Academy address, DH commented on what the address did and did not cover: "The Academy speech is not attacking any myths. But it is strictly honest—an attempt at an all-through subjective analysis of motives. The picture is true—from a clearly stated aspect, that *also* is mine. Of course I have other aspects, where I myself stand in the center in a perpetual conflict with a dominating father-image (in many ways deeply unlike me) whose pressure I hated and whose weaknesses I consequently saw very clearly. But that picture tells more about me than about him and is in this connection outside the lighted area"; see Beskow, 33. Sven Stolpe, an accomplished author and friend from Dag's student days, also received a copy of the text. Stolpe later wrote that "when Dag gave me the manuscript of his Academy speech, he said in a quiet, diffident voice: 'Well, you know me—you'll realize that I never knew my father as well as this during his lifetime....'" See Stolpe, *Dag Hammarskjöld*, 20.

15. See Hjalmar's letter to Nathan Söderblom on this topic in Bengt Sundkler, *Nathan Söderblom: His Life and Work*, 388–89.

16. See G. K. A. Bell, ed., *The Stockholm Conference 1925: Being the Official Report of the Universal Christian Conference on Life and Work Held in Stockholm, August 19–30, 1925*, 747–50.

17. Cf. Ephesians 6:5–9; I Peter 2:18–20.

18. *PP II*, Inaugural Address upon Taking His Seat as a Member of the Swedish Academy, Stockholm, 20 December 1954, 406.

19. Per Lind and Bengt Thelin, "Nature and Culture: Two Necessities of Life," in Sten Ask and Anna Mark-Jungkvist, ed., *The Adventure of Peace:*

Dag Hammarskjöld and the Future of the UN, 91.

20. Thelin (1), 109 (trans. R. D. Deroche).

21. Ibid., 176 (trans. R. D. Deroche).

22. Stolpe, *Dag Hammarskjöld*, 17.

23. Ibid., 24.

24. Ibid., 25.

25. Thelin (1), 188.

26. Ibid., 171–72 (trans. R. D. Deroche).

27. Elaine Steinbeck and Robert Wallsten, ed., *Steinbeck: A Life in Letters*, 715.

28. Dag Hammarskjöld, *Castle Hill*, 20.

29. *Markings*, 1959, 177.

30. Ibid., 178.

31. *PP III*, "The Linnaeus Tradition and Our Time," Presidential Address at the Annual Meeting of the Swedish Academy, Stockholm, 20 December 1957, 701–9.

32. Ibid., 703.

33. *Markings*, 1956, 140 (trans. slightly revised). Sjöberg/Auden gives the devise entirely in italics, although the typescript of *Markings* and editions in other languages italicize only *semper*, always. The small typographic difference preserves a large difference in meaning.

34. C. G. Jung, another shaper of twentieth-century culture, had a nearly identical devise engraved above a doorway used routinely by his patients: *Vocatus atque non vocatus, Deus aderit* (Called or uncalled, God will be present). The routing from ancient literature to modern doorway is similarly elaborate, from Thucydides via Erasmus to Jung.

35. See Birnbaum (1) and (2); and Thelin (1). See also Frank A. Wollheim, "Jan Waldenström and Dag Hammarskjöld: A Friendship between Two Swedish Humanists," *Hektoen International, A Journal of Medical Humanities* 3:3 (September 2011), available online at www.hektoeninternational.org.

36. DH Letter to D. Allanson, 6 August 1961, KB.

37. Thelin (1), 139.

38. This copy of the book is preserved in the Dag Hammarskjöld Collection, KB.

39. Birnbaum (2), 78 (trans. R. D. Deroche).

40. Steinbeck and Wallsten, *Steinbeck*, 715.

41. Stolpe, *Dag Hammarskjöld*, 60–61.

42. Claes Grundsten, *Swedish Wilderness: The Mountain World of Dag Hammarskjöld*, with a foreword by Sverker Åström, includes DH's

wilderness writings in English translation.

43. Gösta Lundquist, *Lappland*, with a foreword by Dag Hammarskjöld; an English translation (see the bibliography) was issued by the same publisher in 1960.

44. Grundsten, *Swedish Wilderness*, 38.

45. Andreas Labba, *Anta: Mémoires d'un Lapon*, trans. Vincent Fournier.

46. *Markings*, 1951, 72. The Sjöberg/Auden translation of the last lines in the original Swedish—*lever tinget, / äro vi*—is a good solution but something of a rewrite. The published French translation is closer: *l'objet vit / et nous sommes*. The published German is closer still: *lebet das Ding, / sind wir*.

47. Ibid., 79, 80.

48. Grundsten, *Swedish Wilderness*, 143.

49. Dag Hammarskjöld, *Från Sarek till Haväng*.

50. *PP II*, Remarks at the United Nations Press Club, 9 April 1954, 280.

51. Birnbaum (1), 107 (trans. R. D. Deroche).

52. Birnbaum (2), 20 (trans. R. D. Deroche).

53. Birnbaum (1), 63 (trans. R. D. Deroche).

54. Axel Hägerström, *Philosophy and Religion*, trans. Robert T. Sandin. See also Patricia Mindus, *A Real Mind: The Life and Work of Axel Hägerström*.

55. Hägerström, *Philosophy and Religion*, 215–16.

56. Ibid., 296.

57. Birnbaum (2), 75.

58. Ibid., 16.

59. Stolpe, *Dag Hammarskjöld*, 22–23.

60. Sundkler, *Nathan Söderblom*, 403.

61. Ibid., 397, citing a German newspaper article of 1926.

62. Ibid., 366–67.

63. Ibid., 258.

64. Ibid., 376.

65. Nathan Söderblom, *Christian Fellowship, or The United Life and Work of Christendom*, 89.

66. Henry P. Van Dusen, *Dag Hammarskjöld: The Statesman and His Faith*, 22.

67. Sundkler, *Nathan Söderblom*, 80.

68. For Söderblom's own account of the 1893 experience, see Eric J. Sharpe, *Nathan Söderblom and the Study of Religion*, 44.

69. Ibid., 124.

70. Sundkler, *Nathan Söderblom*, 71.

71. Ibid.

72. Söderblom, *Christian Fellowship*, 150.

73. Stolpe, *Dag Hammarskjöld*, 30.

74. *PP III*, "On the Uppsala Tradition," From Address after Receiving Honorary Degree at Upsala College, East Orange, NJ, 4 June 1956, 164–65.

Chapter 3

1. While the great majority of DH's personal library is housed in the National Library of Sweden (Kungliga Biblioteket), with volumes available upon request to researchers, the Hammarskjöld Museum at Backåkra in southern Sweden also has a significant collection.

2. Sveriges Riksbank, *Sveriges Riksbank Economic Review*, special issue, *Dag Hammarskjöld 100th Anniversary* 2005:3.

3. Scott, *Sweden*, 488.

4. Hans Landsberg, "Time for Choosing: Dag Hammarskjöld and the Riksbank in the Thirties," *Sveriges Riksbank Economic Review*, special issue, *Dag Hammarskjöld 100th Anniversary* 2005:3, 19.

5. Ernst Wigforss, in Uno Willers, ed., *Dag Hammarskjöld: En minnesbok*, 98, 100 (trans. DvS).

6. Ernst Wigforss, *Minnen I – Före*, 198 (trans. DvS).

7. Stolpe, *Dag Hammarskjöld*, 38–39.

8. Landsberg, "Time for Choosing," 21.

9. Ibid., 22.

10. Ibid.

11. Wigforss, *Minnen I*, 197.

12. Assar Lindbeck, "Dag Hammarskjöld as Economist and Government Official," *Sveriges Riksbank Economic Review*, special issue, *Dag Hammarskjöld 100th Anniversary* 2005:3, 9.

13. Örian Appelqvist, "Civil Servant or Politician? Dag Hammarskjöld's Role in Swedish Government Policy in the Forties," *Sveriges Riksbank Economic Review*, special issue, *Dag Hammarskjöld 100th Anniversary* 2005:3, 35.

14. Wigforss, *Minnen I*, 198 (trans. DvS).

15. Ibid., 201.

16. Ibid., 198.

17. Ibid., 202.

18. Göran Ahlströhm and Benny Carlson, "Hammarskjöld, Sweden and Bretton Woods," *Sveriges Riksbank Economic Review*, special issue, *Dag Hammarskjöld 100th Anniversary* 2005:3, 57.

19. Hammarskjöld's library in the KB has a volume of poetry by T. S. Eliot, *Dry Salvages,* inscribed "Dag Hammarskjöld London 43" and a copy of *Ten Principal Upanishads* inscribed "Dag Hammarskjöld London 44"— evidence of two official visits during the war years and of his unflagging interest in both modern literature and the classics of world religion. A third volume of Eliot, *Four Quartets,* is inscribed with his name and London 43/44, followed by Marstrand 51; he must have been rereading the *Quartets* in 1951 during a holiday on the coastal island of Marstrand in the North Sea—and trying to remember just when he had acquired his copy.

20. Ahlströhm and Carlson, "Hammarskjöld, Sweden and Bretton Woods," 52.

21. Ibid.

22. Exchange of notes between DH and Sture Petrén, KB (trans. DvS).

23. Ahlströhm and Carlson, "Hammarskjöld, Sweden and Bretton Woods," 76.

24. Lars Heikensten and Björn Hasselgren, "Foreword," *Riksbank Economic Review*, 7.

25. Joseph P. Lash, *Dag Hammarskjöld: Custodian of the Brushfire Peace*, 41.

26. Sture Linnér, interview with the author, August 2008.

27. Lash, *Dag Hammarskjöld*, 42–43.

28. Henrik Klackenberg, *Dag Hammarskjöld: En minnesbok*, 59.

29. Kelen, 44.

30. Ibid., 57.

31. Klackenberg, *Dag Hammarskjöld: En minnesbok*, 50–51 (trans. R. D. Deroche).

32. Lindbeck, "Dag Hammarskjöld as Economist and Government Official," 12.

33. Wigforss, in Willers, *En minnesbok*, 99.

34. Ibid.

35. DH letter to Ernst Wigforss, 7 April 1953 (trans. DvS).

36. *Markings*, 1953, 89 (punctuation revised to conform with Swedish original).

37. In Sjöberg/Auden the epigraph is incorrectly attributed to Meister Eckhart.

38. *Markings*, 1925–30, 5 (trans. slightly revised). Sjöberg/Auden has "a clear pure note" for Sw. *en klar enkel ton*. Because DH periodically reflects in

Markings on the meaning of purity, it is preferable here to avoid confusion by translating *enkel* literally as "simple."

39. Ibid., 8 (trans. slightly revised).

40. The gift copy, inscribed to her son by Agnes, is preserved at Backåkra.

41. *Markings*, 1955, 103, citing Thomas à Kempis 3:33. DH's eighteenth-century French translation of Thomas's Latin reads "l'oeil de l'intention," yet "attention" is preferable here. The Latin dictionary gives both translations, presumably context dependent.

42. Ibid., 1925–30, 8 (trans. slightly revised in light of Bernhard Erling's version).

43. Ibid., 1941–42, 13.

44. Ibid., 15.

45. Ibid., 12, 14.

46. Ibid., 13.

47. Ibid., 17 (trans. slightly revised in light of Erling).

48. Ibid., 16.

49. Ibid., 11, 12.

50. Ibid., 15.

51. Ibid., 16.

52. Ibid.

53. The etching is now in the collection of the Hammarskjöld Museum, Backåkra.

54. *Markings*, 1941–42, 13.

55. Ibid., 1945–49, 19 (trans. slightly revised).

56. Dag Hammarskjöld, "The camera taught me to see," in Kai Falkman, ed., *To Speak for the World: Speeches and Statements by Dag Hammarskjöld, Secretary-General of the United Nations, 1953–1961*, 221–24.

57. *Markings*, 1945–49, 34.

58. Kelen, 40–41.

59. *Markings*, 1945–49, 24–25.

60. "Force has tied its endless chain around nothing"—a striking phrase, perhaps reflecting a line in Goethe taken up by Schubert in his remarkable song "Grenzen der Menschheit" (The limits of humanity), which evokes the "endless chain of Being." However that may be, the phrase ironically reflects the traditional notion of the Great Chain of Being.

61. This portion of the translation is from Erling, 21; Sjöberg/Auden departs too far from the Swedish original.

62. Markings, 1945–49, 28 (trans. slightly revised in light of Erling).

63. Ibid., 1952, 86 (trans. slightly revised in light of Erling).

64. Ibid., 1957, 159 (trans. slightly revised in light of Erling's discussion of Sw. *förintelsen*, annihilation).

65. Ibid., 1945–49, 33.

66. Ibid., 20.

67. Ibid., 35 (trans. slightly revised).

68. Ibid., 36.

69. Ibid (trans. slightly revised). Sjöberg/Auden reads "O Caesarea Philippi: to accept condemnation of the Way as its fulfillment, its definition, to accept this both when it is chosen and when it is realized." This has many problems for such a short passage. There is no literal mention of "the Way"; the Swedish word translated as "definition" is better rendered as "presupposition" (Ehrling, Aulén) or "premise"; and the last phrase is better translated in the active voice than in the passive. Finally, Sw. *insats*, translated by Sjöberg/Auden as "the Way," is a multivalent word cognate with German *Einsatz*—"effort," "commitment," even "task"—and perhaps best translated here as "the work ahead."

Chapter 4

1. See Official Records of the General Assembly, 7th Session, beginning 14 October 1952 at the new headquarters building in New York; xxiv notes that "during the absence of the Minister for Foreign Affairs, H. E. Mr. Dag Hammarskjöld, Minister of State, acted as Chairman of the Delegation." The minister for foreign affairs was Östen Undén, DH's superior in the Swedish government and, as correspondence testifies during the UN years, a trusted friend.

2. Dag Hammarskjöld, "Att välja Europa" (To choose Europe), *Svensk Tidskrift* 38, (1951), 442–59; Dag Hammarskjöld, "Statsjänstemannen och samhället" (The civil servant and society), *Tiden* 43 (1951), 391–96; Dag Hammarskjöld, "Politik och ideologi" (Politics and ideology), *Tiden* 44 (1952), 6–17. English translations available in the Andrew W. Cordier Papers, Columbia University Libraries (see online finding aid).

3. *PP V*, "The International Civil Servant in Law and in Fact," Lecture Delivered in Congregation at Oxford University, Oxford, England, 30 May 1961, 471–89.

4. Dag Hammarskjöld, "The Civil Servant and Society," typescript translation in the Andrew W. Cordier Papers, Columbia University Libraries. An entry in *Markings* for the same year (1951, 77) looks at the middle ground from the perspective of what DH calls "a revolutionary." As so

often, the privately written passage has a literary flair and compactness missing from the public writings of this time: "To separate himself from the society of which he was born a member will lead the revolutionary, not to life but to death, unless, in his very revolt, he is driven by a love of what, seemingly, must be rejected, and therefore, at the profoundest level, remains faithful to that society."

5. *PP III*, From Transcript of Press Conference, Moscow, 5 July 1956, 172.

6. Dag Hammarskjöld, "The Civil Servant and Society," typescript translation in the Andrew W. Cordier Papers, Columbia University Libraries.

7. *PP II*, "Old Creeds in a New World," Written for Edward R. Murrow's Radio Program *This I Believe*, November 1953, 194–96.

8. Dag Hammarskjöld, "The Civil Servant and Society," typescript translation in the Andrew W. Cordier Papers, Columbia University Libraries. This passage is also cited in Stolpe, *Dag Hammarskjöld*, 59–60.

9. *PP II*, From Message to New York Herald Tribune Forum on "Patterns for Peaceful Change," New York, 18 October 1953, 98.

10. Ananda K. Coomaraswamy, "On Translation: Māyā, Deva, Tapas," *Isis* 19 (1933), 85.

11. *Markings*, 1950, 45 (trans. slightly revised). What is the source of his metaphor here? Perhaps a refining process noticed as a young man at a mine owned by his father?

12. Dante Alighieri, *The Divine Comedy: Inferno*, trans. Charles S. Singleton, 2–3.

13. Blaise Pascal, *Memorial* (trans. of its opening lines by the author), available in the original French and Latin online at www.users.csbsju.edu/~eknuth/pascal.html. DH echoes it at the end of an important entry in *Markings*, 1955, 110.

14. *Markings*, dated entry for Whitsunday (21 May) 1961, 205.

15. Ibid., 1950, 43. Sjöberg/Auden accurately translates Sw. *igenkännande självsyn* as "conscious self-scrutiny." A more literal translation of the adjective might be "cognizant" or even "re-cognizant," but "conscious" best captures the root cognate with Eng. "knowledge, knowing."

16. Ibid., 39.

17. Ibid. (trans. slightly revised).

18. Ibid.

19. Ibid., 41.

20. Ibid., 43 (trans. slightly revised). Sjöberg/Auden renders Sw. *tjädertupp* accurately as "cock capercailzie," but this creature of the northern forests

will be unfamiliar to many readers; hence the revision to "mountain cock."

21. Ibid., 37.

22. Ibid., 38 (trans. slightly revised). Sjöberg/Auden introduces here a phrase—"transcendental co-inherence"—quarried by Auden from the religious philosophy of Charles, which had long interested him. Wherever the term "co-inherence" appears in Sjöberg/Auden, there is invariably a better translation. For an introduction to Williams, see Barbara Newman, "Charles Williams and the Companions of the Co-inherence," *Spiritus* 9:1 (Spring 2009), 1–26.

23. *Markings*, 38 (trans. slightly revised).

24. Ibid., 40.

25. Ibid., 47.

26. Ibid.

27. Ibid., 55.

28. Ibid., 45 (trans. slightly revised).

29. Ibid., 56.

30. Ibid., 55.

31. Ibid., 51.

32. Ibid.

33. Ibid., 58 (trans. slightly revised in light of Erling).

34. Beskow, 32.

35. *Markings*, 1950, 57.

36. Ibid. Sjöberg/Auden introduces for clarity the word "now", although it doesn't actually appear in the Swedish text, which begins "*Det är detta ögoblick*": It is *this* moment.

37. Ibid., 59.

38. Ibid., 1951, 72.

39. Ibid., 61.

40. Ibid., 67 (trans. slightly revised).

41. Ibid., 76 (trans. slightly revised). This is in part a difficult passage to translate. In Sjöberg/Auden, DH's botanical reference to the flowering white wintergreen (Sw. *vita skogsstjärna*), is literally (and opaquely) rendered as "a forest star," and his resonant word Sw. *samhörighet* is translated "affection," though it means kinship, solidarity, belonging; the thoughtful Italian translator opted for "una nuova comunione." Where Sjöberg/Auden has "the depths" at the close of the sentence, DH's Sw. *kaos* suggests the literal translation "chaos." Finally, the descent is characterized by DH as Sw. *att*

formande stiga ned, literally a "shaping step down" or downward step of one who is equipped with form-creating, organizational ability. Erling's translation, "as a shaping agent," seems best and is adopted here.

42. Ibid., 1950, 55.

43. Ibid., 1952, 82.

44. Ibid., 1951, 63.

45. Ibid., 1952, 82.

46. Ibid., 1951, 73.

47. Ibid., 78. Sjöberg/Auden's "perplexing mystery" has literary flair and is generally correct, but DH's Swedish, *oroande okände*, could be translated more literally to make a better tie with key word choices elsewhere in *Markings*. The nominal root of *oroande* is Sw. *oro*, meaning "uneasiness, disquiet"; *okände* could be more simply and literally translated as "the unknown."

48. Ibid., 65.

49. Ibid., 1955, 105.

50. Ibid., 1951, 64.

51. Ibid., 1952, 84.

52. Ibid., 1951, 65.

53. Ibid., 64.

54. Ibid., 67.

55. Ibid., 70.

56. Ibid. (trans. slightly revised). The phrase "fellowship transcending the individual" translates Sw. *gemenskap över individen*, where Sjöberg/Auden again introduces the anomalous phrase "transcendental co-inherence" (see above, note 27).

57. Ibid., 67.

58. Ibid., 68–69, citing John 13:14.

59. Hans Küng, *Why I Am Still a Christian*, 40.

60. *Markings*, 1951, 69.

61. Ibid., 1956, 123.

62. Ibid., 1951, 74.

Ibid., 76 (trans. slightly revised). "A yes to the unknown" is a literal rendering of Sw. *ett ja till det okände*, in preference to Sjöberg/Auden's "an assent to the unknown." DH's magnificent discovery of deep willingness at the beginning of the UN years, which he experienced as an unconditional "Yes," is foreshadowed here and should not go unnoticed in translation.

"Desire is purified into openness" is a more literal and, I think, more appropriate translation than Sjöberg/Auden's "Desire is purified and made lucid," which loses DH's reference to Sw. *öppenhet*. One could debate the rendering, retained from Sjöberg/Auden, of Sw. *längtan* by "desire." Appearing elsewhere in *Markings*, *längtan* is cognate with Eng. "longing."

63. Ibid., 79.
64. Ibid., 80.
65. Ibid., 78 (trans. slightly revised).
66. Ibid., 1952, 83.
67. Ibid., 86.
68. Ibid.
69. Ibid., 84.
70. Ibid., 85.

Chapter 5

1. Kelen, 153.
2. For the anecdote about the UN photographer, see Kelen, 56–57; for the society journalist, Betty Pepes, "Scandinavian Import," *New York Times*, 1 August 1954, NYTimes.com archive. DH's elegant duplex apartment had a separate gated entrance on Seventy-Third Street.
3. George Ivan Smith Letter to Tristram Powell, 29 May 1976, cited in Fröhlich, "'The Unknown Assignation,'" 19.
4. James Barros, *Trygve Lie and the Cold War: The UN Secretary-General Pursues Peace, 1946–1953*, 341.
5. Brian Urquhart, interview with the author, November 2010.
6. Urquhart (1), 27.
7. Van Dusen, *Dag Hammarskjöld: The Statesman and His Faith*, 83.
8. Transcript of a Swedish television program regarding DH with Brian Urquhart, George Ivan Smith, Bo Beskow, and others, including Victor Noble who recorded this memory, n.d., 15, in the library of the Dag Hammarskjöld Foundation.
9. George Ivan Smith, letter to the editor of the *Times* (London), 31 August 1984. See McCann, *Catalogue of the Papers of George Ivan Smith*.
10. Roger Peyrefitte, *Tableaux de chasse ou la vie extraordinaire de Fernand Legros*, 11–13.
11. James Kirkup, obituary in *The Independent*, Tuesday Review, 7 November 2000, 6.

12. United Nations Oral History Collection, interview with Pauline Frederick, 11 July 1986, available online at www.un.org, 7.

13. "New U.N. Hostess Must Be Married," *New York Times*, 11 May 1953.

14. W. H. Auden, "Dag Hammarskjöld," in *Encounter* 17:5 (November 1961), 4.

15. A small but formidable literature critiquing the Sjöberg/Auden translation has run parallel to the book itself for many years. Initiated in Gustaf Aulén, *Dag Hammarskjöld's White Book: An Analysis of* Markings, it was forcefully and persuasively taken up in Kai Falkman, "Signposts in the Wrong Direction: W. H. Auden's misinterpretations of Dag Hammarskjöld's *Markings*," *Times Literary Supplement*, 10 September 1999, 14–15. An exchange of letters between Falkman and Auden's biographer, Richard Davenport-Hines, appeared in *Times Literary Supplement*, 1999: 24 September, 8 October, 29 October, and the topic resurfaced, again at Falkman's urging, during the Hammarskjöld birth centenary; see Warren Hoge, "Swedes Dispute Translation of a U. N. Legend's Book," *New York Times*, 22 May 2005, available at the NYTimes.com archive. Endnotes in this book continue the critique.

16. DH letter to Folke Isaksson, 10 December 1959 (trans. DvS). "Searching discussion" translates Sw. *naken diskussion*, literally "naked discussion." The word "naked" is not to be taken in the erotic sense; DH means serious discussion rather than pleasant, learned repartee.

17. Sverker Åström, interview with the author, Stockholm, 2008.

18. DH letter to Sture Petrén, 26 March 1956, KB (trans. DvS).

19. Sverker Åström, foreword, in Grundsten, *Swedish Wilderness*, which publishes in English translation many of DH's previously scattered writings on wilderness, including his foreword to Lundquist. Readers of Swedish will enjoy an interview with Åström that goes further into the ascent of Sulitälma, at www.fjallklubben.se/fjallet/artiklar/1-05art1.htm.

20. There was an English-language edition: Gösta Lundquist, *Lapland: Reindeer, Lapps and Midnight Sun* (Stockholm: Bonniers, 1960).

21. DH letter to Sture Petrén, 1 November 1956, KB (trans. DvS). DH makes an ironic reference to *The Praise of Folly*, a work published in 1511 by the Dutch humanist Erasmus. A French edition dated 1716, now in the KB, was in DH's library. The speech to which he referred is more than likely to have been his courageous statement about principle and expediency, *PP III*, 1. Suez Crisis, New York, 31 October 1956, 309–10.

22. *Markings*, 1959, 193 (trans. slightly revised). In the effort to preserve the seventeen-syllable pattern of haiku, Sjöberg/Auden translates Sw. *pervers* as "abnormal." Restoring the literal translation makes sense here.

23. Ibid., 190.

24. Stolpe, *Dag Hammarskjöld*, 47–48.

25. *Markings*, 1950, 53.

26. Ibid., 42 (trans. slightly revised).

27. Ibid., 1952, 85.

28. Ibid., 1951, 77.

29. Thomas Merton, *Day of a Stranger*, 49.

30. *Markings*, 1956, 139.

31. Ibid., 1954, 98.

32. Beskow, 37, citing Matthew 12:46–50.

33. Charmingly, there is a photograph of the photographer photographing, published by Bo Beskow in *Strictly Personal*, 116: DH is on one knee perhaps ten feet from his subject, focusing his camera under a brilliant summer sun. Greta could not be more pleased or poised.

34. *Markings*, 1955, 120 (trans. slightly revised). The compact phrase Sw. *en okänd insats möjlighet*, literally "an unknown achievement's possibility" or "unknown effort's possibility," is probably better served in this slight revision than by Sjöberg/Auden's "the call of the Way of Possibility."

35. Marc E. Vargo, *Noble Lives: Biographical Portraits of Three Remarkable Gay Men—Glenway Wescott, Aaron Copland, and Dag Hammarskjöld.*

36. Sture Linnér, interview with the author, April 2008. Conor Cruise O'Brien refers in passing to Linnér in New York on August 20th, in his *To Katanga and Back: A UN Case History*, 206.

37. *Markings*, 1952, 82.

38. *Ibid.*, 1950, 42.

39. W. H. Auden, book review of 1941, cited in Katherine Bucknell and Nicholas Jenkins, ed., *"In Solitude, for Company": W. H. Auden after 1940*, 155. Tracy Cochran quoted this passage in one of our many discussions of DH.

40. *Markings*, 1950, 55.

41. Thomas Merton, *Learning to Love: The Journals of Thomas Merton, Volume Six, 1966–1967*, ed. Christine M. Bochen, 108.

42. *Markings*, 1952, 86.

43. *PP II*, "The United Nations in the Modern World," *Journal of International Affairs*, Columbia University, 1955, 539. After writing this chapter, I came across its theme in Kelen, 249: "Hammarskjöld was a worldly monk."

Chapter 6

1. Barros, *Trygve Lie*, 335.

2. *PP II*, Statement in the General Assembly after Taking the Oath of Office, 10 April 1953, 31.

3. *Punch*, 29 September 1943, in Helena Walasek, ed., *Punch Goes to War 1939–1945*, 184.

4. Bruce Munn, president of the United Nations Correspondents Association, introductory remarks, 9 April 1958, later issued as a press release by the UN, United Nations Archive.

5. *PP II*, Address at Dinner in His Honor Given by the American Association for the United Nations in Cooperation with the New York University Institute for Review of United Nations Affairs, New York, 14 September 1953, 88.

6. DH communication to Östen Undén, 1 April 1953, KB (trans. DvS). The abstention was from the Republic of China (Taiwan), which objected to the fact that Sweden—unlike many countries—had recognized the People's Republic of China.

7. Irresistible to mention here a little known, remarkable book, Vijaya Lakshmi Pandit, *The Scope of Happiness: A Personal Memoir*.

8. United Nations Oral History Collection, interview with Brian Urquhart, 30 May 1984, 20.

9. Kelen, 27.

10. Urquhart (1), quoting Carl Schürmann, 15.

11. United Nations Oral History Collection, interview with Pauline Frederick, 20 June 1986, 1–2.

12. United Nations Oral History Collection, interview with Brian Urquhart, 30 May 1984, 21–22.

13. *PP II*, Statements on Assumption of Office, April to May 1953, 27.

14. Gladwyn Jebb, speech to the General Assembly, 10 April 1953, par. 37, in Official Records of the United Nations General Assembly, available online at www.un.org.

15. *PP II*, Statements on Assumption of Office, April to May 1953, 27.

16. Beskow, 12.

17. Ibid., 14.

18. Ibid., 14–15.

19. DH letter to Sture Petrén, 13 August 1955, KB.

20. Sverker Åström, interview with the author, April 2008.

21. Sverker Åström, *Ögonblick*, 66 (trans. Thord Palmlund).

22. Urquhart (1), 13.

23. Wigforss, in Willers, *En minnesbok*, 100 (trans. DvS).

24. *PP III*, Address on Human Rights and the Work for Peace at the Fiftieth Anniversary Dinner of the American Jewish Committee, New York, 10 April 1957, 554; DH recalling four years later the election process of 1953.

25. A. M. Rosenthal, "New U.N. Secretary Cautious On Issues," *New York Times*, 10 April 1953.

26. *PP II*, Statement for United Nations and Swedish Radio on Departure from Stockholm for New York, 8 April 1953, 28.

27. *PP II*, Statement to the Press on Arrival at International Airport, New York, 9 April 1953, 29.

28. Ibid., 30.

29. *PP II*, From Transcript of Press Conference at the Swedish Foreign Office, Stockholm, Sweden, 19 May 1953, 42.

30. *PP II*, Statement to the General Assembly after Taking the Oath of Office, 10 April 1953, 31.

31. Ibid., 31–32; DH recalls the closing lines of "Inför freden" (In the presence of peace), a poem published in 1927 by Erik-Axel Karlfeldt (1864–1931), posthumous recipient of the Nobel Prize in Literature, 1931. For the Swedish text, see http://runeberg.org/hosthorn/6_02.html.

32. Trygvie Lie, *In the Cause of Peace: Seven Years with the United Nations*, 417—this among many other sources for his memorable remark.

33. *PP II*, From Transcript of Press Conference, New York, 12 May 1953, 41.

34. *Markings*, 1953, 89.

35. Ibid., dated entry for 7 April 1953, 91.

36. Hammarskjöld, *Vägmärken*, 1953, 74.

37. *Markings*, 1953, 89.

38. Ibid., 90.

39. Ibid., 89 (trans. slightly revised). Sjöberg/Auden translates Sw. *raffine-mang* as "irony"—valid as an interpretation of DH's meaning but unnecessarily distant from the Swedish original. The concluding quoted phrase, "who abases him whom He raises up," occasions a scholar's hunt. It is cited by DH in German: "welcher den Menschen zermalmt, wenn er den Menschen erhebt." Several commentators give the source as Friedrich Schiller's poem "Shakespeares Schatten" (Shakespeare's shade), relayed to DH via Bertil Ekman's published journal *Strödda blad ur Bertil Ekmans*

efterlämnade papper (Stockholm: Norstedt, 1923), 79, which he read and
valued over the years. Schiller's lines concern the workings of Fate in a
Greco-Roman cultural setting, but Ekman draws them into a Christian
context. DH's overall thought, coherent with much in Thomas à Kempis,
reflects Proverbs 3:12 and Hebrews 12:6.

40. *Markings*, 1953, 91.

41. Ibid.

42. Ibid., 93.

43. Ibid.

44. Ibid., 91.

45. *PP II*, From Statement on the Occasion of the Rededication of the Memorial Plaque for Count Folke Bernadotte, New York, 24 July 1953, 78–79.

46. Ibid.

47. *PP IV*, At UN Staff Meeting at the Beginning of His Second Term, New York, 10 April 1958, 66.

48. *Markings*, 1953, 91.

49. Ibid., 92.

50. Ibid., 89.

51. Ibid., 90.

52. DH Letter to Sten Selander, 27 December 1956, KB (trans. DvS).

53. *Markings*, 1953, 93 (trans. slightly revised). To Sjöberg/Auden's pleasant translation I have added the words "in the moment" to capture DH's phrase *i ögonblicket*, which relates this entry to many others, earlier and later, in which he explores the here and now as a source of stability. "Radiant serenity" more closely translates DH's *ljusa lugen* than Sjöberg/Auden's otherwise attractive "unclouded happiness."

54. *PP II*, Transcript of Background Press Conference on Reports on Personnel Policy and Administrative Tribunal Awards, New York, 3 November 1953, 149.

55. Ezra Pound, trans., *Confucius: The Great Digest; The Unwobbling Pivot; The Analects*, 59–61.

56. *PP II*, Introduction to the Eighth Annual Report, 15 July 1953, 68.

57. DH letter to Pär Lagerkvist, 31 January 1958 (trans. DvS), KB.

58. *PP II*, "The Weapons of the Secretariat," From Message for United Nations Staff Day at Geneva, 4 December 1953, 193.

Chapter 7

1. DH letter to Leif Belfrage, 9 May 1953, KB (trans. DvS).

2. DH letter to Bo Hammarskjöld, 3 May 1953, KB (trans. DvS).

3. Charles P. Henry, *Ralph Bunche: Model Negro or American Other?*, 178.

4. Urquhart (3), 257.

5. Ibid., 295.

6. In addition to Urquhart's biography of Bunche and Henry's study (see note 3), see Charles P. Henry, ed., *Ralph J. Bunche: Selected Speeches and Writings.*

7. George Ivan Smith letter to Andrew Cordier, 3 February 1975, cited in Fröhlich, "'The Unknown Assignation,'" 20.

8. DH memorandum to Andrew Cordier, 21 April 1956, KB.

9. DH letter to Bo Hammarskjöld, 16 January 1954: "May I first of all send my best wishes for the New Year. My own Christmas was short and formless but was followed by 6 days in and on the waters of Florida. At my return it all started in a way that quickly eliminated my tan. And now the storm is on with Korea and Palestine as low-pressure centers." KB (trans. DvS).

10. *Markings*, 1954, 95–96 (trans. slightly revised). In the first passage, Sjöberg/ Auden has "lack of faith," for Sw. *misstron*, literally "mistrust." In light of DH's frequent and explicit references to faith, it's preferable to avoid the term except where he explicitly uses it. Sjöberg/Auden unnecessarily complicates the second sentence by adding "with the measure"; here it has been dropped. There is little to query in the translation of the second passage. "Pure" translates Sw. *friska*, meaning "sound" in the sense of healthy and robust, but there is no reason to meddle with a translation lovely overall.

11. *PP II*, Address at Dinner in His Honor Given by the American Association for the United Nations in Cooperation with the New York University Institute for Review of United Nations Affairs, New York, 14 September 1953, 87.

12. *PP II*, Address at a Public Meeting Organized by the United Nations Association at the Royal Albert Hall, London, 17 December 1953, 203.

13. William O. Douglas, "The Black Silence of Fear," *New York Times Magazine*, 13 January 1952, 37–38, reprinted in the excellent Ellen Schrecker, ed., *The Age of McCarthyism: A Brief History with Documents*, 271–74.

14. Two films, Emile de Antonio's *Point of Order* (1964) and George Clooney's *Good Night, and Good Luck* (2005), effectively supplement the extensive bibliography on Joseph McCarthy. Publications of particular value are Ellen Schrecker, cited in the previous note, and David M. Oshinsky, *A Conspiracy So Immense: The World of Joe McCarthy.*

15. Both references were cited verbatim in major UN meetings—the first with some approval by the newly appointed US ambassador Henry Cabot Lodge on 28 March 1953 in the General Assembly, the second with utter distaste by Trygve Lie in his final, comprehensive account of the loyalty issue before the General Assembly on 10 March 1953. For Lie, see *PP I*, Statement on Personnel Policy before the General Assembly, United Nations, NY, 10 March 1953, 498.

16. DH letter to Stig Sahlin, 1 December 1959, KB.

17. DH letter to Herbert Tingsten, 4 January 1954, KB (trans. DvS).

18. Ralph Bunche, "Marxism and the 'Negro Question,'" 1929, in Henry, *Ralph J. Bunche: Selected Speeches and Writings*, 35–45.

19. William E. Jenner, "Let's Put America First," address of 14 February 1955, available online at http://history.hanover.edu/hhr/09/americafirst.pdf.

20. Urquhart (3), 248.

21. Ibid., 249.

22. Oshinsky, *A Conspiracy So Immense*, 192.

23. Ibid., 252.

24. Press release, Address of the Secretary-General at the United Nations Day Observance at UN Headquarters, 24 October 1953. United Nations Archive. Since there can be at least two views on earth about everything without exception, there were even two views about the appropriateness of concerts for UN Day. Pauline Frederick recounts, "[Hammarskjöld] once told me that when he decided to introduce concerts into the UN, someone said that Trygvie Lie had remarked that this was 'profaning the parliament of man.' Hammarskjöld responded, I'm told, that if this was profanity, he was prepared to make the most of it." United Nations Oral History Collection, interview with Pauline Frederick, 20 June 1986, 12.

25. *PP II*, Introduction to the Eighth Annual Report, 15 July 1953, 68–69.

26. Press conference, 14 February 1956, Canberra, Australia. United Nations Archive.

27. *PP II*, Statement at Meeting of European Office Staff, Geneva, 26 May 1953, 49.

28. *PP II*, Statement at a General Meeting of the Staff, New York, 1 May 1953, 32.

29. *PP II*, from Transcript of Press Conference, Geneva, 22 May 1953, 45.

30. *PP II*, Address at Luncheon Given by the American Political Science Association, Washington, DC, 11 September 1953, 82.

31. DH letter to Pär Lagerkvist, 7 August 1958, KB (trans. DvS).

32. DH letter to Herbert Tingsten, 25 August 1953, KB (trans. DvS).

33. *PP II*, Statement at Meeting of European Office Staff, Geneva, 26 May 1953, 50.

34. *PP II*, Introduction to the Eighth Annual Report, 15 July 1953, 69–70.

35. *PP II*, Statement on Personnel and Staff Policies at General Meeting on Staff Day, New York, 8 September 1953, 117.

36. *PP II*, From Transcript of Press Conference, New York, 12 May 1953, 40.

37. *PP II*, Press Conference, 12 May 1953, 39–40.

38. *PP II*, From Transcript of Press Conference, New York, 19 May 1955, 487.

39. *PP IV*, From Transcript of Press Conference, New York, 4 February 1960, 524.

40. DH's use of the expression "this house" for UN headquarters was noticed by others. Pauline Frederick, a leading journalist, sent a note to DH after a reception he hosted for the UN Correspondents Association, 19 February 1959, KB: "I want to express our appreciation for last night's hospitality in 'your home' in This House." The capitalizations are hers.

41. *PP II*, Address at Dinner in His Honor Given by the American Association for the United Nations in Cooperation with the New York University Institute for Review of United Nations Affairs, New York, 14 September, 1953, 92.

42. Press release, Welcome by the Secretary-General on Opening the General Staff Day Meeting Tuesday, 8 September 1953. United Nations Archive.

43. For the full text of the UN Charter, see www.un.org/en/documents/charter/index.shtml.

44. *PP II*, Address at a Public Meeting Organized by the United Nations Association at the Royal Albert Hall, London, 17 December 1953, 206.

45. See Virginia Crocheron Gildersleeve, *Many a Good Crusade: Memoirs* (New York: Macmillan, 1954); and the excellent biography at the Columbia University website, www.columbia.edu.

46. *PP II*, Address at Luncheon Given by the American Political Science Association, Washington, DC, 11 September 1953, 84.

47. Transcript of Press Conference, Geneva, 22 May 1953, United Nations Archive. This passage is not included in *PP II*, 42–45, where other parts of the press conference are reproduced.

48. *PP II*, Address at Dinner in His Honor Given by the American Association for the United Nations in Cooperation with the New York University Institute for Review of United Nations Affairs, New York, 14 September 1953, 94.

49. Ibid.

50. Kelen, 110.

51. *PP IV*, At UN Staff Meeting at the Beginning of His Second Term, New York, 10 April 1958, 68.

52. *PP II*, From Address at Commencement Exercises of University of Pennsylvania, Philadelphia, Pennsylvania, 13 February 1954, 256.

53. *PP III*, Message to the United Nations Emergency Force, UN Headquarters, New York, 10 December 1956, 405.

54. *PP III*, From Transcript of Press Conference, UN Headquarters, New York, 22 June 1956, 170.

55. *PP IV*, From Transcript of Press Conference, New York, 5 February 1959, 329.

56. *PP III*, Remarks at Luncheon of the United Nations Correspondents Association, New York, 8 August 1957, 618.

57. *PP II*, Address at Annual Dinner of the Advertising Council, New York, 17 November 1954, 387.

58. Urquhart (1), 254; cited also in part in *PP II*, "An International Independent Responsibility," from Transcript of Remarks to a Meeting of International Nongovernmental Organizations, London, 19 March 1954, 278.

59. *PP II*, Introduction to the Eighth Annual Report, 15 July 1953, 71.

60. *PP II*, Remarks at Luncheon of the United Nations Correspondents Association, New York, 10 July 1953, 58, 63.

61. *PP II*, Address at a Public Meeting Organized by the United Nations Association at the Royal Albert Hall, London, 17 December 1953, 203.

62. *PP II*, Address at Luncheon Given by the American Political Science Association, Washington, D.C., 11 September 1953, 84–85.

63. *PP II*, Transcript of Press Conference, New York, 14 January 1955, 448.

64. *PP II*, Speech to the Foreign Policy Association at a Dinner Given in His Honor, New York, 21 October 1953, 102.

65. Ibid., 102–04.

66. *PP II*, Address at a Public Meeting Organized by the United Nations Association at the Royal Albert Hall, London, 17 December 1953, 202.

67. Ibid.

68. Kanza (1), 200.

69. *PP II*, Address at Dinner in His Honor Given by the American Association for the United Nations in Cooperation with the New York University Institute for Review of United Nations Affairs, New York, 14 September

1953, 92–93.

Chapter 8

1. Press release of 14 August 1953, KB.
2. See www.americanrhetoric.com, where Eisenhower's speech is available in both print and audio files.
3. DH letter to Dwight Eisenhower, 11 December 1953, KB.
4. A. M. Rosenthal, "Dag Hammarskjöld Sizes Up His U.N. Job," *New York Times*, 18 August 1953, NYTimes.com archive.
5. DH letter to Sture Petrén, 22 May 1954, KB (trans. DvS).
6. DH letter to Bo Hammarskjöld, 21 August 1953, KB (trans. DvS).
7. DH letter to Bo Hammarskjöld, 19 September 1953, KB (trans. DvS).
8. DH letter to Sture Petrén, 17 October 1953, KB (trans. DvS).
9. *PP II*, Remarks during the Intermission of United Nations Day Concert by the New York Philharmonic Orchestra, New York, 25 October 1953, 107–09.
10. *PP II*, Address at Freedom House Dinner, New York, 22 November 1953, 198.
11. DH letter to David Ben-Gurion, 31 July 1956, KB.
12. *PP II*, From Transcript of Background Press Conference, New York, 20 April 1954, 290.
13. *PP II*, Address at Dinner in His Honor Given by the American Association for the United Nations in Cooperation with the New York University Institute for Review of United Nations Affairs, New York, 14 September 1953, 91.
14. *PP II*, From Transcript of Press Conference, New York, 22 December 1955, 631.
15. *PP II*, From Statement at the Opening of the Merrill Center of Economics, Southampton, New York, 28 June 1953, 56.
16. *PP II*, Address at Dinner in His Honor Given by the American Association for the United Nations in Cooperation with the New York University Institute for Review of United Nations Affairs, New York, 14 September 1953, 95.
17. *PP II*, Address at a Public Meeting Organized by the United Nations Association at the Royal Albert Hall, London, 17 December 1953, 205.
18. Kelen, 130.
19. *PP II*, Address at Luncheon Given by the American Political Science Association, Washington, DC, 11 September 1953, 85.

20. *PP II*, Address at Dinner in His Honor Given by the American Association for the United Nations in Cooperation with the New York University Institute for Review of United Nations Affairs, New York, 14 September 1953, 89–90.

21. *PP II*, From Message to New York Herald Tribune Forum on "Patterns for Peaceful Change," New York, 18 October 1953, 98–99.

22. *PP II*, From Transcript of Background Press Conference, New York, 10 February 1954, 225.

23. *PP II*, Introduction to the Eighth Annual Report, 15 July 1953, 72.

24. *PP II*, From Broadcast on United Nations Radio Program "On The Record," New York, 26 June 1953, 53–54.

25. See www.korean-war.com/swedishhospital.html.

26. *PP II*, Address at Freedom House Dinner, New York, 22 November 1953, 198.

27. Press release, from a talk at the City Hall of New York, 23 October 1953, United Nations Archive.

28. *PP II*, From Message to New York Herald Tribune Forum on "Patterns for Peaceful Change," New York, 18 October 1953, 99.

29. *PP II*, Address at a Public Meeting Organized by the United Nations Association at the Royal Albert Hall, London, 17 December 1953, 201, 203.

30. *Markings*, 1953, 92 (trans. slightly revised).

31. Ibid.

32. *PP II*, "Old Creeds in a New World," written for Edward R. Murrow's radio program *This I Believe*, November 1953, 195–96. The recording of DH giving this talk is available at http://thisibelieve.org/essay/16608/. He appears to have added one sentence to the printed text; otherwise, the two are identical.

33. Where DH writes, "all men [are] equals as children of God, and should be met and treated by us as our masters in God," he may be taking the word "masters" literally, but perhaps also in its meaning "teachers." Somewhat related New Testament passages are Matthew 23:8, Ephesians 6:5–9, and Colossians 3:22–25. In his Swedish Academy address of late 1954, DH spoke of his mother as endowed with "a radically democratic view of fellow humans." I am grateful to Father Mark Scott for exploring this text with me. He is innocent of my conclusions.

34. Jan van Ruysbroek, *The Spiritual Espousals*, trans. Eric College (New York: Harper, 1947), 128–30. This is the edition read by DH; his copy in the KB is inscribed with his name and "Marathon Key, New Year 1954."

About DH's term "singleness of mind," consider Ruysbroek, 97, 149.

35. Stolpe, *Dag Hammarskjöld*, 65.

36. DH letter to Bo Hammarskjöld, 21 February 1954, KB (trans. DvS).

37. Beskow, 32.

38. *PP II*, From New Year's Message as Broadcast over United Nations Radio, New York, 31 December 1953, 209.

Chapter 9

1. DH letter to Herbert Tingsten, 4 January 1954, KB (trans. DvS); "messages" and "statements" are originally in English.

2. Documentation in the Andrew W. Cordier Papers, Columbia University Libraries.

3. DH letter to Bo Hammarskjöld, 24 January 1954, KB (trans. DvS).

4. DH's desk calendar and a parallel calendar kept by his secretary are preserved in the KB.

5. *PP II*, Introduction to the Ninth Annual Report, 21 July 1954, 327.

6. Urquhart (1), 83.

7. I. I. Rabi speaking at the Salazar Atomic Centre, Mexico, October 1972, available online at http://www.iaea.org/Publications/Magazines/Bulletin/Bull151/15105083134.pdf.

8. DH letter to Greta Garbo, 25 April 1959, KB, thanks her for coming to dinner with Mrs. O'Neill, Dr. Gierow of the leading Swedish theater, and himself. The letter identifies this as their first meeting; he had first expressed interest in meeting her in 1954.

9. United Nations Oral History Collection, interview with Brian Urquhart, 30 May 1984, 42.

10. DH letter to Uno Willers, 10 May 1955, KB. There is one further though minor treasure with regard to G. Garbo. Asked by Carl Nordenfalk, an illustrious Swedish art historian and later director of the National Museum, to join a commemorative committee in 1954, DH responded: "I am sure you understand my attitude, dictated by my office. But since you have managed to persuade Greta Garbo to join, you won't be needing another international name!" DH letter to Carl Nordenfalk, 1 April 1954, KB.

11. DH letter to Per Lind, 13 August 1955, KB.

12. Henry, *Ralph J. Bunche: Selected Speeches and Writings*, 190.

13. *PP II*, "An International Independent Responsibility," from Transcript of Remarks to a Meeting of International Nongovernmental Organizations,

London, 19 March 1954, 278.

14. *PP II*, Address at the Annual Meeting of the Association of American Colleges, Cincinnati, Ohio, 13 January 1954, 248. *PP III*, Address on Human Rights and the Work for Peace at the Fiftieth Anniversary Dinner of the American Jewish Committee, New York, 10 April 1957, 554, citing Arthur Waley, *The Way and Its Power* (London: Allen and Unwin, 1934), 90.

15. This I Believe website, http://thisibelieve.org/essay/16608/.

16. *Markings*, 1955, 112 (trans. slightly revised), citing Matthew 12:36.

17. *PP II*, Address at the Annual Meeting of the Association of American Colleges, Cincinnati, Ohio, 13 January 1954, 249.

18. Ibid., 250–51.

19. Ibid., 251–52.

20. Ibid., 254.

21. DH letter to Bo Beskow, cited in Beskow, 146. Urquhart (1), 375–76, points to a related and very good statement by DH: "'Underdeveloped countries' is a rather curious term . . . if you realize that a few of them have civilizations dating back far beyond anything we know of; they have attained a maturity of the individual which makes you feel rather humble. They are underdeveloped only in the economic sense."

22. *PP II*, From Address at Commencement Exercises of University of Pennsylvania, Philadelphia, Pennsylvania, 13 February 1954, 256–57.

23. *PP II*, Address at University of California Convocation, Berkeley, California, 13 May 1954, 296.

24. Ibid., 297.

25. Ibid., 297–98.

26. Ibid., 300–1.

27. *PP II*, Address at Commencement Exercises of Amherst College, Amherst, Massachusetts, 13 June 1954, 303.

28. Ibid., 305.

29. Ibid., 303–4.

30. Ibid., 305–6.

31. Ibid., 306. Edgar Lee Masters, "Lucinda Matlock," in *Spoon River Anthology* (New York: Macmillan, 1915).

32. *PP II*, Address at the Charter Day Dinner of the Columbia University Bicentennial Year, New York, 30 October 1954, 379.

33. Ibid., 380.

34. *Markings*, 1954, 95.

35. Ibid., 101; Sw. *andliga disciplin*.

36. Ibid., 100.

37. Ibid., 97 (trans. slightly revised).

38. Ibid., 97 (trans. slightly revised). Retained here is Sjöberg/Auden's "see, hear, and attend," which solves the problem of style posed by Sw. *lyssna och se*, two verbs not three, meaning "to listen and see."

39. *Secretariat News*, 14 February 1958, United Nations Archive.

40. DH letter to Eyvind Johnson, 31 January 1958, KB (trans. DvS).

41. *Markings*, 1951, 80.

42. Ibid., 1954, 96 (trans. slightly revised). "Surrendered" is written in English in an otherwise Swedish entry. It would tell us something more about DH's reading if we knew why. Is he recalling lines from the Book of Common Prayer or from T. S. Eliot, *The Dry Salvages*? Impossible to know.

43. Ibid., 99 (trans. slightly revised). Sjöberg/Auden has "the world you desire" for Sw. *din värld av vilja*. Though their version is beautiful and offers an intelligent commentary on the original, it strays too far from the Schopenhauer-like rigor of DH's text.

44. Ibid., 1955, 122.

45. See Thomas Merton, *The Wisdom of the Desert: Sayings from the Desert Fathers of the Fourth Century* (New York: New Directions, 1960).

46. *Markings*, 1954, 100. The Sjöberg/Auden translation of Sw. *det enda förblivande i ditt liv* as "all that remains for you to live for" leaves me uneasy but without a better solution. Erling offers "the only permanent thing in your life." Knyphausen/Fröhlich benefits from the similarity of German to Swedish in its translation, *an dieses einzig Bleibende in deinem Leben*, where *Bleibende*—that which remains—captures the bareness of DH's *förblivande*.

47. Ibid., 101 (trans. slightly revised).

48. Press conference, Headquarters, New York, 24 March 1954, United Nations Archive.

49. DH letter to Bo Hammarskjöld, 27 March 1954, KB (trans. DvS).

50. DH letter to W. D. Matthews, minister of Canada to Sweden, 15 April 1954, KB.

51. DH letter to Sten Selander, 12 April 1954, KB (trans. DvS); consider also DH letter to Yngve Brilioth, archbishop of Uppsala (1950–58), 29 April 1954, KB (trans. DvS). An author on Christian topics, Brilioth was the

son-in-law of Nathan Söderblom, DH's early mentor: "Warm thanks for your very kind letter occasioned by my election to the Swedish Academy. I can't quite get used to the thought of belonging to this circle, where I would instead have been happy to see you in Chair no. 17. It might interest you that my father on one or two occasions when he happened to touch on the subject said that the one he hoped to be his successor indeed was you. I quite share your feelings that it's peculiar that the Academy, with its missions and traditions, lacks a representative of the Church. It should always have its man in that circle, both because of the spiritual heritage the Church represents and in view of its traditions of the spoken and written word."

52. DH letter to Sture Petrén, 22 May 1954, KB (trans. DvS).

53. *PP II*, Inaugural Address upon Taking His Seat as a Member of the Swedish Academy, Stockholm, 20 December 1954, 400.

54. DH letter to Sture Petrén, 30 December 1954, KB (trans. DvS).

55. Herbert Tingsten, "Hammarskjöld as a way of life," *Dagens Nyheter*, late December 1954.

56. DH letter to Herbert Tingsten, 28 December 1954, KB (trans. DvS).

57. DH letter to Sture Petrén, 30 December 1954, KB (trans. DvS). If this was the second time in his life, what was the first? He may have been thinking of the moment late in his Swedish career when the Soviet Union shot down Swedish military aircraft over international waters. Or was he thinking of the need to rid the UN of the influence of McCarthyism?

58. *PP II*, Speech at National Press Club Luncheon, Washington, DC, 14 April 1954, 286.

59. Urquhart (1), 97.

60. *PP II*, Address before Second Assembly of the World Council of Churches, Evanston, Illinois, 20 August 1954, 353.

61. Ibid., 355–56.

62. DH letter to Sverker Åström, 6 October 1954, KB (trans. DvS).

Chapter 10

1. Philippe Lecomte du Nouy, "An Actor Observes," in Mary-Lynn Henley and Henning Melber, ed., *Dag Hammarskjöld Remembered: A Collection of Personal Memories* (Uppsala, Sweden: Dag Hammarskjöld Foundation, 2011), 18.

2. DH letter to Sture Petrén, 13 August 1955, KB.

3. The General Assembly resolution is available in full online at www. un.org.

4. See the comment of an eyewitness and later biographer of DH in Joseph Lash, *Custodian of the Brush-Fire Peace*, 58.

5. *PP II*, editors' introduction, "The Imprisoned American Flyers [*sic*]—Mission to Peking," December 1954, January 1955, 419.

6. *PP II*, From Transcript of Press Conference at the Swedish Ministry for Foreign Affairs, Stockholm, 17 December 1954, 426–27.

7. Ibid., 427.

8. *PP II*, From Transcript of Press Conference, New York, 22 December 1954, 428–29.

9. Ibid., 433.

10. *Markings*, 1954, 102.

11. DH letter to George Ivan Smith, 24 August 1955, cited in Manuel Fröhlich, "'The Unknown Assignation,'" 15n16. I have edited slightly: DH's "spiritualism" can't be what he meant, and the line from Psalm 139 is written a little more correctly here than in DH's original.

12. DH letter to Sten Selander, 27 December 1954, KB (trans. DvS).

13. DH letter to Leif and Greta Belfrage, 29 December 1954, KB.

14. Engström is sparsely translated into English, but his observant eye and blithe style are evident in Harold Borland, trans., *Twelve Tales by Albert Engström* (London: Harrap, 1949), a bilingual edition. I am grateful, as so often, to Daniel von Sydow for informing me about Engström.

15. DH letter to Bo Hammarskjöld, 30 December 1954, KB (trans. DvS).

16. I have mislaid the specific source for Kissinger's evaluation, but similar remarks are found in Henry Kissinger, *On China* (New York: Penguin, 2011).

17. Although contemporary China has established Confucius Institutes—analogous to Germany's Goethe Institutes—around the world, the status of China's great sage and social thinker remains controversial within the country. See Andrew Jacobs, "Confucius Stood Here, but Not for Very Long," *New York Times*, 22 April 2011, NYTimes.com archive.

18. Gao Wenqian, *Zhou Enlai: The Last Perfect Revolutionary*, trans. Peter Rand and Lawrence R. Sullivan (New York: Perseus, 2007), 299.

19. *Markings*, 1954, 102, citing Psalm 139:8–9.

20. See Urquhart (1), 104–12; and *PP II*, editors' introduction, "The Imprisoned American Flyers [*sic*]—Mission to Peking, December 1954, January 1955," 415–59.

21. Urquhart (1), 112.

22. See Qu Xing, "International Negotiator: Mission Beijing," in Sten Ask and

Anna Mark-Jungkvist, ed., *The Adventure of Peace: Dag Hammarskjöld and the Future of the UN*, 48–63.

23. Urquhart (1), 110.

24. Ibid., 112.

25. Marie-Noëlle Little, *The Knight and the Troubadour: Dag Hammarskjöld and Ezra Pound*, 111, available online at www.dhf.uu.se.

26. *PP II*, Transcript of Press Conference, New York, 14 January 1955, 441.

27. Ibid., 441.

28. Ibid., 450.

29. Ibid., 446, 448.

30. Urquhart (1), 114, for both quotations.

31. Ibid., 119fn.

32. DH letter to Uno Willers, 31 January 1955, KB.

33. DH letter to Leif Belfrage, 19 February 1955, KB (trans. DvS).

34. DH letter to Bo Beskow, 12 February 1955, KB; a slightly edited version of this letter appears in Beskow, 36.

35. Bill Ranallo letter to DH, 29 July 1954, KB.

36. DH letter to Bo Hammarskjöld, 17 February 1955, KB (trans. DvS).

37. *Markings*, 1955, 103.

38. Ibid., 104 (trans. slightly revised). Sjöberg/Auden's "peace" for Sw. *stillhet* obscures DH's reasonably frequent references to stillness throughout the later years of *Markings*.

39. *PP II*, From Transcript of Press Conference, New York, 5 April 1955, 471.

40. *Markings*, 1955, 110 (trans. slightly revised). Sjöberg/Auden softens some of the sharp edges of this entry.

41. *PP II*, From Transcript of Press Conference, New York, 19 April 1955, 479.

42. Press conference 5 May 1955, partially reproduced in *PP II*, From Transcript of Press Conference, New York, 5 May 1955, 480–83; however, this witty exchange is preserved in the KB collection of complete press releases.

43. "Swedish Envoy Sees Zhou in China Visit," *New York Times*, 20 May 1955, NYTimes.com archive.

44. DH letter to Leif Belfrage, 20 May 1955, KB; Hameln is the German spelling of the town known in English as Hamelin, home of the legendary pied piper. Bandung refers to the meeting of nonaligned nations at Bandung, Indonesia.

45. DH letter to Rolf Sohlman, included with previous letter (trans. DvS).

46. Vijaya Lakshmi Pandit, *The Scope of Happiness: A Personal Memoir*, 286–

87. Rajeshwar Dayal, who may have had no score to settle, held a similar view: "For all his cleverness and subtlety, Menon lacked finesse, nor did he show good judgment. . . . Speculation about how and why Menon had such a hold on Nehru has never ceased." Dayal (2), 202–03.

47. Krishna Menon had his moment on the cover of *Time*—2 February 1962—during important Indian elections.

48. *PP II*, editors' note, 491.

49. DH to Alva Myrdal, 15 August 1956 (trans. DvS).

50. *PP II*, Address at the Opening of the San Francisco Tenth Anniversary Meetings, San Francisco, 20 June 1955, 515.

51. DH letter to Bo Hammarskjöld, 13 August 1955, KB (trans. DvS).

52. *PP II*, From Transcript of Press Conference, New York, 12 August 1955, 574.

53. *Markings*, dated entry for 29 July 1955, 107.

54. DH letter to Sture Petrén, 13 August 1955, KB (trans. DvS).

55. Urquhart (1), 126.

56. United Nations Oral History Collection, interview with Brian Urquhart, 6 January 1984, 24.

57. DH letter to Andrew Cordier, 3 August 1955, KB.

58. *PP II*, From Transcript of Press Conference, New York, 12 August 1955, 580.

59. DH letter to Sten Selander, 13 August 1955, KB.

60. DH letter to Ernst Wigforss, 13 August 1955, KB (trans. DvS).

61. Urquhart (1), 544.

62. Stolpe, *Dag Hammarskjöld*, 35–36. DH also quotes these lines from Ekman in a letter to Leif Belfrage, 22 May 1956, KB.

63. *Markings*, 1955, 108–9.

64. Ibid., 1956, 128; see also 1956, 143, "Your own efforts . . ."

Chapter 11

1. *PP II*, From Transcript of Press Conference, New York, 19 May 1955, 488.

2. *PP II*, Statement at the Opening of the International Conference on the Peaceful Uses of Atomic Energy, Geneva, 8 August 1955, 571.

3. Urquhart (3), 260.

4. *PP II*, Remarks at United Nations Day Concert in the General Assembly Hall, New York, 24 October 1955, 620–21.

5. DH letter to Leif and Greta Belfrage, 21 November 1955, KB (trans. DvS).

6. Year-end message, 22 December 1955, United Nations Archive.

7. *PP II*, From Transcript of Press Conference, New York, 22 December 1955, 637.

8. DH telegram to Karl Ragnar Gierow, 24 August 1955, KB.

9. Karl Ragnar Gierow letter to DH, ca. September 1955, KB (trans. DvS).

10. Karl Ragnar Gierow letter to DH, 2 February 1956, KB.

11. DH letter to Erik Lindegren, 17 May 1956, KB (trans. DvS). On DH's relation with Saint-John Perse and his successful campaign to see to it that the poet received the Nobel Prize in Literature (1960), the primary source is Little, *The Poet and the Diplomat*. For further background and a different perspective, see Saint-John Perse and Henri Hoppenot, *Correspondance 1915–1975*, ed. Marie France Mousli (Paris: Gallimard, 2009), s.v. indexed references to Hammarskjöld.

12. DH letter to Sten Selander, 6 January 1956, KB (trans. DvS).

13. *PP II*, From Transcript of Press Conference, New York, 22 December 1955, 632.

14. DH letter to Sten Selander, 14 January 1956, KB (trans. DvS). "Fun" properly translates Sw. *kul*.

15. *PP II*, Transcript of Press Conference, New York, 27 February 1956, 684.

16. Urquhart (1), 150.

17. Benny Morris, *Righteous Victims: A History of the Zionist-Arab Conflict, 1881–2001*, 311, citing a member of the Knesset in 1967.

18. Gamal Abdel Nasser, *The Philosophy of the Revolution*.

19. Mohamed Hassanein Heikal, *The Cairo Documents: The Inside Story of Nasser and His Relationship with World Leaders, Rebels and Statesmen*, 160.

20. *PP II*, Transcript of Press Conference, New York, 27 February 1956, 688.

21. *PP II*, "The United Nations—Its Ideology and Activities," Address before the Indian Council of World Affairs, New Delhi, India, 3 February 1956, 658.

22. Ibid., 660, 662. See www.un.org for an overview of UN aid programs today.

23. *PP II*, Transcript of Press Conference, New York, 27 February 1956, 681.

24. Ibid., 682–83.

25. Ibid., 697–98.

26. *Markings*, 1955, 111 (trans. slightly revised). Cf. Hjalmar Gullberg, *Dödsmask och lustgård*, 9–10. See also Hjalmar Gullberg, *Gentleman, Single, Refined and Selected Poems, 1937–1959*, trans. Judith Moffett.

27. *PP III*, Address at Celebration of the 180th Anniversary of the Virginia Declaration of Rights, Williamsburg, Virginia, 15 May 1956, 139.

28. DH letter to Leif Belfrage, 22 May 1956, KB (trans. DvS).

29. *PP III*, Address at Celebration of the 180th Anniversary of the Virginia Declaration of Rights, Williamsburg, Virginia, 15 May 1956, 141–42.

30. Ezra Pound, *The Cantos of Ezra Pound*, Canto XC, 609. Pound describes Elektra as "the dark shade of courage . . . bowed still with the wrongs of Aegisthus"—taking "shade" in the sense of the afterlife presence of Elektra.

31. *PP III*, Report to the Security Council Pursuant to the Council's Resolution of April 4, 1956, on the Palestine Question, New York, 9 May 1956, 111.

32. DH letter to Sten Selander, 21 May 1956, KB.

33. DH letter to Bo Hammarskjöld, 24 May 1956, KB (trans. DvS). The one chain broken may refer to his temporary success in restoring the consent of all parties to adhere to the terms of the armistice agreements. The larger context of Middle Eastern affairs remained unstable and threatening, and border violence soon recurred despite his efforts.

34. DH letter to Eyvind Johnson, 24 April 1958, KB (trans. DvS). See also DH letter to Mahmoud Fawzi, 11 June 1956, KB, referring to "the need for the strongest to break the chain and start a development in a new direction"; and DH to Gamal Abdel Nasser, 8 April 1956, cited at *PP III*, Communications Circulated by the President of the Security Council at the Request of the Secretary-General, New York, 12 April 1956, 78: "I wish to draw your attention to the vital need of breaking the present chain of actions and reactions."

35. *PP III*, Address before the International Law Association at McGill University, Montreal, 30 May 1956, 157.

36. Press conference, Geneva, 24 July 1956, United Nations Archive.

37. *PP III*, Statement of August 17 (on Further Palestine Incidents), UN Headquarters, New York, 16–17 August 1956, 231.

38. DH letter to David Ben-Gurion, 26 September 1956, KB.

39. Heikal, *Cairo Documents*, 175.

40. Press conference, 5 April 1956, UN headquarters before leaving for Middle East, United Nations Archive.

41. DH letter to Sture Petrén, 26 March 1956, KB (trans. DvS).

42. Kelen, 83.

43. *PP III*, From Press Conference Transcript, New York, 5 April 1956, 76.

44. E. L. M. Burns, *Between Arab and Israeli*, 112–13.

45. Ibid., 142.

46. Ibid., 140–41.

47. Ibid., 41.

48. Ibid., 151.

49. *PP III*, From Transcript of Press Conference, New York, 7 June 1956, 133.

50. Burns, *Between Arab and Israeli*, 143.

51. Urquhart (1), 148.

52. Ibid., 146.

53. DH letter to Selwyn Lloyd, 24 January 1956, KB.

54. Brian Urquhart interview with the author, February 2011.

55. United Nations Oral History Collection, interview with I. J. Rikhye, 26 March 1990, 24–25.

56. See Fröhlich, "'The Unknown Assignation,'" 14.

57. Urquhart (1), 143–44. See also United Nations Oral History Collection, interview with Brian Urquhart, 30 May 1984, 42: "A lot of people said [to DH], 'You can't do that, you'll get killed!' and he said, 'I don't care, I'm going to do it. I just want to prove a point, that this is what it is: this is an armistice demarcation line.'"

58. Ibid., 145.

59. *Markings*, dated entry for 8 April 1956, 126; DH would have found the Eckhart passage in the German edition he regularly used—he probably had it with him. Herman Büttner, trans., *Meister Eckhart Schriften*, 204 (reference provided by Erling, 146). In English the passage can be found in Edmund Colledge, trans., *Meister Eckhart: The Essential Sermons, Commentaries, Treatises, and Defense*, 276. In the Scholastic lexicon, "habitus" denotes ingrained virtue rather than routine behavior.

60. DH letter to George Ivan Smith, 24 May 1956, KB.

61. *Markings*, dated entry for 22 April 1956, 127 (trans. slightly revised). Sjöberg/Auden's "conquer" for Sw. *vinna* is coarse in this context, which hardly has to do with conquest. The passage from Eckhart falls toward the end of "Qui audit me." DH would have transcribed from Büttner, *Meister Eckhart Schriften*, 224. In English it is easily found in "Distinctions Are Lost in God," trans. Raymond P. Blakney, in *Meister Eckhart: A Modern Translation*, 206.

62. This good translation is from Oliver Davies, trans., *Meister Eckhart: Selected Writings*, 179.

63. *Markings*, 1956, 127 (trans. slightly revised). Where I revise to "coherence" for Sw. *sammanhang*, Sjöberg/Auden has "co-inherence," a recurrent

usage previously critiqued.

64. Ibid., 128.

65. DH letter to Bo Beskow, 4 June 1956, KB (trans. DvS). Gustaf Fröding (1860–1911) was a Swedish poet.

66. *Markings*, 1956, 128 (trans. slightly revised), citing John 3:8 and 1:5. Sjöberg/Auden replaces the powerful—and necessary—phrase "even though bound to the earth" with the lovely, incorrect "even when it is bent flat." As well, it drops the concluding phrase "to new strength," which reflects DH's faith in the possibility of positive change.

67. George Ivan Smith letter to Brian Urquhart, n.d., in Fröhlich, "'The Unknown Assignation,'" 26.

68. Lincoln Kirstein letter to DH, 4 May 1956, KB.

69. PP III, Report to the Security Council Pursuant to the Council's Resolution of April 4, 1956, on the Palestine Question, New York, 9 May 1956, 111.

70. PP III, Statement in the Security Council, 29 May 1956, 124.

71. DH letter to Östen Undén, 10 May 1956, KB.

72. Urquhart (1), 151n.

73. Ibid., 144.

74. DH letter to David Ben-Gurion, 26 June 1956, KB.

75. DH letter to David Ben-Gurion, 3 October 1956, KB.

Chapter 12

1. Sir John Bagot Glubb, *A Soldier with the Arabs* (1957), 265.

2. Anthony Nutting, *No End of a Lesson: The Story of Suez*, 34–35.

3. David A. Nichols, *Eisenhower 1956: The President's Year of Crisis—Suez and the Brink of War*, 140.

4. *Markings*, 1956, 142; Erling, 168–69. Though both Erling and Sjöberg/Auden put quotation marks around the words beginning "I believe," DH doesn't. I have left them in place because they serve much the same function as a language difference in the original: the first line is in DH's Swedish, the next in English, clearly implying that DH is recording words spoken by someone else.

5. Nasser's speech of 26 July 1956 is available online in French at www.ena.lu.

6. *PP III*, From Transcript of Press Conference, UN Headquarters, New York, 22 June 1956, 170–71.

7. Ibid., 171.

8. *PP III*, From Transcript of Press Conference, Vienna, 10 July 1956, 179.

9. *PP III*, From Transcript of Press Conference, Geneva, 24 July 1956, 180.

10. Glubb, *A Soldier*, 426.

11. Nutting, *No End*, 14–15.

12. Donald Neff, *Warriors at Suez: Eisenhower Takes America into the Middle East*, 161.

13. Nichols, *Eisenhower 1956*, 13.

14. Neff, *Warriors at Suez*, 262.

15. Nichols, *Eisenhower 1956*, photo caption facing 205.

16. See Heikal, *Cairo Documents*, 86ff., for an account of Nasser's thought process as he considered the nationalization.

17. Excerpt translated by the author.

18. *PP III*, From Transcript of Press Conference, UN Headquarters, New York, 2 August 1956, 225.

19. *PP III*, From Transcript of Remarks at UN Correspondents Luncheon, New York, 8 March 1956, 53.

20. *Markings*, 1956, 136, citing Sir Thomas Browne, *Religio Medici* 2:6, 63; 1:15, 15 (citations specified by Erling, 159).

21. *PP III*, From Transcript of Press Conference, UN Headquarters, New York, 16 May 1957, 578.

22. DH letter to Bo Beskow, 15 September 1956, KB (trans. DvS); DH's word "frustrating" is in English in the original.

23. *PP III*, Introduction to the Eleventh Annual Report, 4 October 1956, 270.

24. *PP III*, Six Principles for Settlement of the Suez Canal Dispute, UN Headquarters, New York, 13 October 1956, 297–98.

25. DH Letter to Bo Beskow, 20 October 1956, cited in Beskow, 62–64.

26. Michael Bar-Zohar, *Ben-Gurion: A Biography*, trans. Peretz Kidron, 241.

27. Press release, Statement of the Secretary-General at the United Nations Day Concert, 24 October 1956, KB.

28. *PP III*, Exchange of Correspondence on Steps toward a Settlement of the Suez Canal Question with the Foreign Minister of Egypt, UN Headquarters, New York, 3 November 1956, 298–303.

29. Nichols, *Eisenhower 1956*, 201.

30. *PP III*, Suez Crisis, New York, 31 October 1956, 309–10.

31. United Nations Oral History Collection, interview with Brian Urquhart, 20 July 1984, 7.

32. Neff, *Warriors at Suez*, 385.

33. Ibid., 366.

34. Nichols, *Eisenhower 1956*, ix.

35. *PP III*, Statement to the Press after General Assembly's First Cease-fire Resolution on Middle East, UN Headquarters, New York, 2 November 1956, 317.

36. Lester B. Pearson, *Mike: The Memoirs of the Rt. Hon. Lester B. Pearson*, ed. John Munro and Alex I. Inglis, 3 vols., 2:241.

37. Nichols, *Eisenhower 1956*, 207.

38. Urquhart (1), 194.

39. Ibid.

40. Ibid., 176.

41. *Markings*, initial entry in a series dated 1–7 November 1956, 139 (Psalms 4:9 and 37:7, 8). Though DH recorded only the first and last words of 37:7–8, the full text is so relevant to this moment in his experience that I'm led to think he used the ellipsis for convenience but had the full text in mind: "Hold thee still in the Lord, and abide patiently upon him: but grieve not thyself at him whose way doth prosper, against the man that doeth after evil counsels. / Leave off from wrath, and let go displeasure: fret not thyself, else shalt thou be moved to evil."

42. Ibid., 1956, 140 (trans. slightly revised). Where I revise to "looks on," Sjöberg/Auden literally translates Sw. *överser* as "overlooks," a choice that generates ambiguity. The semicolon in my version, replacing DH's comma, dispels possible confusion by showing the parallel structure of the two phrases beginning with "which."

43. DH letter to Ben-Gurion, 19 April 1957, KB.

44. Pearson, *Mike*.

45. Pearson, *Mike*, 2:246.

46. Ibid., 247.

47. Ibid., 251.

48. *PP III*, Statement to the Press after General Assembly's First Cease-fire Resolution on Middle East, UN Headquarters, New York, 2 November 1956, 320.

49. Urquhart (1), 181.

50. Urquhart (3), 268.

51. United Nations Oral History Collection, interview with Brian Urquhart, 20 July 1984, 13–14.

52. *PP III*, Statement in the General Assembly Introducing Second Report on

UN Emergency Force, UN Headquarters, New York, 7 November 1956, 352.

53. *PP III*, Further Statement in the General Assembly during Debate on UN Emergency Force, UN Headquarters, New York, 7 November 1956, 354.

54. Urquhart (3), 267.

55. *Markings*, 1956, 140 (trans. slightly revised in light of Erling, 165). Sjöberg/Auden reads "Without our being aware of it, our fingers are so guided that a pattern is created when the thread gets caught in the web." Erling does better by translating Sw. *omärkligt* (cognate to Eng. "unmarked" in the sense of "unnoticed") by a single word, and avoids the ambiguity of "caught in the web," which many readers today, apart from weavers, will find confusing.

56. Ibid., 141.

57. Christian Pineau, *1956 Suez*, 176–77 (trans. by author).

58. *PP III*, editors' note, 360.

59. United Nations Oral History Collection, interview with Brian Urquhart, 20 July 1984, 12 [Suez Crisis].

60. *PP III*, From Transcript of Press Conference, UN Headquarters, 12 November 1956, 368–69; the pundit in question was Walter Lippmann.

61. *PP III*, Private *Aide-Mémoire* on Conditions that Should Govern the Withdrawal of the United Nations Emergency Force, UN Headquarters, New York, 5 August 1957, 379.

62. Urquhart (3), 269–70.

63. *PP III*, Private *Aide-Mémoire* on Conditions that Should Govern the Withdrawal of the United Nations Emergency Force, UN Headquarters, New York, 5 August 1957, 382.

64. *Markings*, 1956, 141.

65. *New York Times*, 20 November 1956, NYTimes.com archive.

66. DH letter to Arthur H. Sulzberger, 24 November 1956, KB.

67. DH letter to Max Ascoli, 29 November 1956, KB.

68. *PP III*, Message to the United Nations Emergency Force, UN Headquarters, New York, 10 December 1956, 405.

69. DH letter to Uno Willers, 19 December 1956, KB (trans. DvS).

70. DH letter to Sten Selander, 19 December 1956, KB (trans. DvS).

71. DH letter to Hjalmar Gullberg, 28 May 1957 (trans. DvS).

72. United Nations Oral History Collection, interview with Brian Urquhart, 20 July 1984, 18–19.

73. *Time*, 7 January 1957, *Time* online archive.

74. Burns, *Between Arab and Israeli*, 250–51.

75. Bar-Zohar, *Ben-Gurion*, 258.

76. DH letter to Bo Beskow 5 January 1957, KB (trans. DvS). The phrase beginning "You should be grateful" is in English, in the original.

77. DH letter to Per Lind, 16 March 1957, KB.

78. DH letter to Bo Beskow, 16 March 1957, KB.

79. Urquhart (3), 289, 297.

80. Lester B. Pearson, Nobel Lecture, 11 December 1957, available online at http://nobelprize.org, with a brief audio excerpt.

81. See www.un.org/en/peacekeeping/contributors/2011/jun11_1.pdf.

82. DH letter to Sten Selander, 6 April 1957, KB (trans. DvS). Tingsten pursued his unflagging criticism of DH throughout the year. In a year-end 1957 letter to Hjalmar Gullberg, DH expressed his nostalgia for Sweden—and then remembered Tingsten: "The contact with the home environment is a vital necessity. It contains a lot that is good—but also some that is bad. Even if rationally I can totally neglect such writing as Tingsten's, it does hurt emotionally when you see something so obviously inspired by ill will. . . . What confusion of values must in the end come about when the tone is set by those who are noisiest [and] most ignorant, because the wise ones are too clever to waste time replying. However, that sort of noise is forgotten when the last sound wave has died away. What is left is what is essential." DH letter to Hjalmar Gullberg, 31 December 1957, KB (trans. DvS).

83. DH letter to Bo Hammarskjöld, 30 May 1957, KB (trans. DvS).

84. *PP III*, From Transcript of Press Conference, 6 June 1957, 589.

85. *PP III*, From Transcript of Remarks at Luncheon of the United Nations Correspondents Association, New York, 19 June 1957, 596.

86. DH letter to Per Lind, 15 November 1957, KB.

87. *PP IV*, From Transcript of Press Conference, New York, 2 April 1959, 344.

88. *Markings*, 1956, 146 (trans. and punctuation slightly revised).

Chapter 13

1. George Ivan Smith, from the transcript of a Swedish television program with Brian Urquhart, Bo Beskow, and others speaking (Dag Hammarskjöld Foundation Archive: n.d.), 8.

2. U Thant, quoted in Andrew W. Cordier and Max Harrelson, ed., *Public*

Papers of the Secretaries-General of the United Nations, vol. 6, *U Thant 1961–1964*, Address at Uppsala University, 6 May 1962, 110.

3. *PP IV*, Address to a Meeting of Members of Both Houses of Parliament under the Auspices of the British Group of the Inter-Parliamentary Union, London, 2 April 1958, 55.

4. DH letter to Östen Undén, 16 May 1957, KB (trans. DvS).

5. The UN provides a transcript of the reelection session speeches at www.un.org/depts/dhl/dag/docs/apv690e.pdf. This phrase is at par. 77.

6. *PP III*, Statement in the General Assembly on His Reappointment—for a Second Term, UN Headquarters, New York, 26 September 1957, 662–63.

7. As for note 5, par. 162.

8. Urquhart (1), 252–53.

9. *PP III*, Statement in the General Assembly on His Reappointment—for a Second Term, UN Headquarters, New York, 26 September 1957, 663–65.

10. *PP IV*, From Transcript of Press Conference, New York, 30 June 1960, 638.

11. *Markings*, dated entry for 26 September 1957, 156 (trans. slightly revised). Erling locates the passage from Eckhart at Büttner, *Meister Eckhart Schriften*, 67. Sjöberg/Auden disregards DH's use of the Swedish for "your" or "thy" in both, not just one, of the passionate promises here (they render: "*Now* into the storm."). DH's unusual choice of image, Slinger (Sw. *Slungare*), asks for interpretation. He may be recalling the combat of David and Goliath in I Samuel 17—therefore viewing himself as the stone projectile in David's sling. However, the context is likely to be not just scriptural but also literary, leading from T. S. Eliot's translation of Saint-John Perse's long poem *Anabase* to the pages of *Markings*. Where Perse has (in canto 3) "Va! nous nous étonnons de toi, Soleil! . . . ô Frondeur! fais éclater l'amande de mon oeil!" Eliot translates "Come, we are amazed at you, Sun! . . . O slinger! Crack the nut of my eye!" DH was, from his youth, a close reader of T. S. Eliot's poetry, and Perse was one of his most valued friends during the UN years. This passage seems to unite by allusion his two preferred poets. I would have been unaware of these threads of possible connection without Satwana Haldar, *T. S. Eliot: A Twenty-first Century View*, 90.

12. *Markings*, 1956, 145.

13. DH letter to Pär Lagerkvist, 11 October 1957, KB (trans. DvS).

14. DH letter to Eyvind Johnson, 12 March 1958, KB (trans. DvS).

15. Much of the detail in this overall discussion of the early background of the Room of Quiet derives from a booklet published in 1977 as a supplement

to the United Nations Meditation Group Bulletin under the title *20th Anniversary of the United Nations Meditation Room*, available online at www.worldharmonyrun.org. For discussion of the aesthetics of the Room of Quiet and further detail about its history, see Roger Lipsey, *An Art of Our Own: The Spiritual in Twentieth-Century Art*, chapter 23, "Enlightened Patronage: Dag Hammarskjöld at the UN," 444–60.

16. Summary of DH remarks, 12 August 1953, United Nations Archive.

17. DH letter to Weyman G. Huckabee, 19 April 1957, KB.

18. DH on modern art will be found in *PP II*, Address at the Inauguration of the Twenty-fifth Anniversary of the Museum of Modern Art, New York, 19 October 1954, 372–75.

19. *PP III*, A Room of Quiet (The United Nations Meditation Room), December 1957, 710–11.

20. Beskow, 104. Writing some years after the fact, Beskow seems to have confused Krishna Menon's eight-hour speech and fainting spell in the Security Council with whatever speech the gentleman gave in the General Assembly. See Shashi Tharoor, *The Elephant, the Tiger, and the Cell Phone: Reflections on India—The Emerging 21st-Century*.

21. *PP III*, "The Linnaeus Tradition and Our Time" (Presidential Address at the Annual Meeting of the Swedish Academy), Stockholm, 20 December 1957, 704.

22. Ibid., 702.

23. Ibid., 703, 705; DH recalls here the language of Rudolf Otto in *The Idea of the Holy*, trans. John W. Harvey, which influenced his early thinking.

24. Ibid., 703, 704.

25. Ibid., 707–8.

26. DH letter to Eyvind Johnson, 12 March 1958, KB (trans. DvS).

27. *Markings*, dated entry for 22 December 1957, 161.

28. DH letter to Eyvind Johnson, 31 December 1957, KB (trans. DvS); "Tingsten's scribblings" is from DH letter to Pär Lagerkvist, 31 December 1957, KB (trans. DvS). See Herbert Tingsten, "Hr Hammarskjöld festtalar" (Mr. Hammarskjöld holds forth), *Dagens Nyheter*, 22 December 1957: "Wherever you try to touch the Hammarskjöld tangles of thought, you find the same emptiness and lack of insight. . . . Later, a complete little army of admonitions marches on." (trans. DvS).

29. *Markings*, dated entry for 24 December 1957, 161. DH's few days in Gaza must have had extraordinary moments. Upon his return to New York, he wrote to Lagerkvist: "The short Stockholm visit again gave me

a feeling of how much I lose by being away. All the same, the result is worth the prize: the latest example being Gaza where I had a rich and fine experience of how international cooperation can create new human values. When it is convenient I hope to be able to tell you some details from the trip that are among the most beautiful things I have experienced." DH letter to Pär Lagerkvist, 31 December 1957, KN (trans. DvS).

30. DH letter to Pär Lagerkvist, 31 January 1958, KB (trans. DvS).

31. DH letter to Pär Lagerkvist, 7 August 1958, KB (trans. DvS).

32. *PP IV*, Press Conference, New York, 2 January 1958, 16.

33. DH letter to Eyvind Johnson, 31 January 1958, KB (trans. DvS).

34. See Lou Marin, "Can We Save True Dialogue in an Age of Mistrust? The Encounter of Dag Hammarskjöld and Martin Buber," *Critical Currents*, no. 8 (2010), with extensive bibliography. Available online at www.dhf.uu.se.

35. *PP IV*, "The Element of Privacy in Peacemaking," Address at Ohio University, Athens, Ohio, 5 February 1958, 25.

36. *PP IV*, At UN Correspondents Association Luncheon in His Honor at the Beginning of His Second Term, New York, 9 April 1958, 62–64.

37. Cited in Urquhart (1), 522. I note with relief that a word I often use to describe DH—"verve"—occurred to those who worked with him at the time.

38. *PP IV*, UN Staff Meeting at the Beginning of His Second Term, 10 April 1958, 66.

39. Ibid., 68.

40. *Markings*, dated entry for 10 April 1958, 165 (trans. slightly revised). DH's own punctuation of this passage, with commas linking most of the elements in a single run of perception, has been altered here for the sake of clarity. The ellipsis at the end is his; the entry ends in that way.

41. Otto, *The Idea of the Holy*, 30.

42. Farid Ud-Din Attar, *The Conference of the Birds*, trans. C. S. Nott (Boulder, Colo.: Shambhala, 1954).

43. Thomas J. Hamilton, "Hammarskjöld's View of His U.N. Role Today," 13 April 1958, *New York Times*, NYTimes.com archive.

44. DH letter to David Ben-Gurion, 31 July 1956, KB.

45. *PP IV*, From Address at the Fiftieth Annual Meeting of the United States Governors' Conference, Miami, Florida, 19 May 1958, 89.

46. Martin Buber, *Pointing the Way*, ed. and trans. Maurice Friedman.

47. DH letter to Eyvind Johnson, 24 April 1958, KB (trans. DvS).

48. *PP IV*, Statement on Disarmament in the Security Council, New York, 29 April 1958, 70–71.

49. DH letter to Bo Beskow, 29 April 1958 (trans. DvS).

50. DH letter to George Ivan Smith, 29 April 1958, cited in Fröhlich, "'The Unknown Assignation,'" 16.

51. *PP IV*, "The Walls of Distrust," Address at Cambridge University, Cambridge, England, 5 June 1958, editors' note, 94–95.

52. *PP IV*, From Transcript of Press Conference, New York, 1 May 1958, editors' note, 80.

53. DH letter to Bo Beskow, 3 May 1958, KB.

54. DH letter to Bo Hammarskjöld, 3 May 1958, KB (trans. DvS).

55. DH letter to Erik Lindegren, 3 May 1958, KB (trans. DvS).

56. *PP IV*, "The Walls of Distrust," Address at Cambridge University, Cambridge, England, 5 June 1958, 90–95 passim.

57. DH letter to Sir Dennis Robertson, 19 January 1959, KB.

Chapter 14

1. *PP IV*, Transcript of Remarks at Luncheon of United Nations Correspondents Association, New York, 11 December 1959, 506.

2. DH letter to Erik Lindegren, 28 July 1958, KB (trans. DvS). DvS comments that DH's term Sw. *rövardrama*, robbers' drama, is his own coinage. It may refer obliquely to Friedrich Schiller's play of 1781, *Die Räuber*, said to be the prototypical melodrama.

3. *PP IV*, Editors' introduction, 98.

4. *PP IV*, From Transcript of Press Conference, New York, 12 June 1958, 102.

5. *PP IV*, From Transcript of Press Conference, New York, 3 July 1958, 122.

6. *PP IV*, Declaration in the Security Council of His Intentions in the Lebanon Affair, New York, 22 July 1958, 144–45.

7. Ibid., editors' note, 146.

8. DH letter to Bo Hammarskjöld, 31 July 1958, KB (trans. DvS).

9. *PP IV*, Statement in the General Assembly before Beginning of the Debate, New York, 8 August 1958, 162.

10. United Nations General Assembly, 733rd Plenary Meeting, 13 August 1958, available online at www.un.org. All further citations from the session are from this source.

11. *PP IV*, Statement in the General Assembly before Beginning of the

Debate, New York, 8 August 1958, editors' note, 165–70.

12. *PP IV*, From Transcript of Press Conference, New York, 22 August 1958, 171–72.

13. Ibid., 174.

14. Kelen, 80–81.

15. Cited in Fröhlich, "'The Unknown Assignation,'" 21–22. For Ralph Bunche's thoughtful definition of UN presence, see Urquhart (1), 294–95.

16. Urquhart (1), 295.

17. *PP IV*, Report on the Withdrawal of United States and British Troops, New York, 10 November 1958, 218.

18. United Nations Oral History Collection, interview with Brian Urquhart, 1 June 1984, 28.

19. DH letter to Bo Beskow, 24 August 1958, KB (trans. DvS).

20. DH letter to Erik Lindegren, 27 September 1958, KB (trans. DvS).

21. *PP IV*, Report to the General Assembly on Developments under Its Middle East Resolution of August 21, New York, 29 September 1958, 203–17; and editors' introduction, "The UNEF Experience Report, October–November 1958," 227–95. Urquhart's remarks on the genesis of the UNEF report are especially interesting: Urquhart (1), 228–30.

22. DH letter to Eyvind Johnson, 4 October 1958, KB. DH's reference to the High Priest recalls John 18:14, "It was Caiaphas who had given counsel to the Jews that it was expedient that one man should die for the people."

23. *Markings*, dated entry for 5 October 1958, 167 (trans. slightly revised). Sjöberg/Auden's effort to duplicate in English DH's syllable count generates unfortunate results here: Sw. *bryter genom*, break through, is not as dramatic as Sjöberg/Auden's "shatters to pieces"; and their "Autumn's clear eye" replaces with a somewhat awkward image DH's straightforward *höstens klarhet*.

24. Ibid., dated entry for 29 July 1958, 166.

25. Ibid., 1958, 166. Here we can be grateful to Auden: his rendering of the very beautiful Sw. *kärlekens svala, raka låga* (love's calm, unwavering flame) is perfect.

26. Ibid., 170.

27. Ibid., dated entry for 19 October 1958, 172. DH's desk calendar at the KB records the evening with the Rockefellers.

28. Lincoln Kirstein letter to DH, 10 November 1958, KB.

29. Lincoln Kirstein letter to DH, 12 April 1959, KB.

30. *PP IV*, Words Spoken at Services for Ahmed S. Bokhári, UN Under-Secretary for Public Information, Pakistan House, New York, 6 December

1958, 305–6.

31. *PP IV*, From Transcript of Press Conference, New York, 16 January 1959, 322.

32. *PP IV*, Address at the Opening of the First Session of the Economic Commission for Africa, Addis Ababa, 29 December 1958, 311.

33. Press conference, 16 January 1959, United Nations Archive.

34. *PP IV*, From Transcript of Press Conference, New York, 5 February 1959, 327.

35. Urquhart (1), 467.

36. *PP IV*, From Transcript of Press Conference, New York, 16 April 1959, 353.

37. Press conference, UN Archive, 8 April 1959

38. *PP IV*, Dictated Version of Extemporaneous Remarks in Reply to a Speech by the Foreign Minister of Mexico, Dr. Manuel Tello, at Official Luncheon, Mexico City, 8 April 1959, 350.

39. *Markings*, 1955, 117.

40. Address at an international YMCA gathering, Cleveland, Ohio, 4 February 1958, United Nations Archive.

41. *PP IV*, From Transcript of Press Conference, New York, 30 April 1959, 360.

42. Remarks at Luncheon of United Nations Correspondents Association, 11 December 1959, UN Archive. A portion of this transcript appears in *PP IV*, Transcript of Remarks at Luncheon of United Nations Correspondents Association, New York, 11 December 1959, 502–9.

43. *PP IV*, "Asia, Africa, and the West," Address before the Academic Association of the University of Lund, in Lund, Sweden, 4 May 1959, 380–87. Where Asia is concerned, DH would have been thinking of recent admissions—Cambodia, Laos, and Nepal in 1955—rather than of the vast nations of India and Pakistan, which were already deeply integrated in world affairs and UN operations, or of the People's Republic of China, which remained for several more decades outside the UN circle.

44. *PP II*, Address at the Annual Meeting of the Association of American Colleges, Cincinnati, Ohio, 13 January 1954, 248.

45. *PP IV*, Extemporaneous Remarks at Inauguration of the Congress for International Cooperation in Africa at the University Institute of Somalia, Mogadiscio, Somalia, 14 January 1960, 515.

46. DH letter to Bo Hammarskjöld, 28 September 1959, KB (trans. DvS).

47. Urquhart (1), 367.

48. *PP IV*, Proposals Submitted to the General Assembly for the Continua-

tion of United Nations Assistance to the Palestine Refugees, New York, 15 June 1959, 414–36.

49. *PP IV*, From Transcript of Press Conference, New York, 23 July 1959, 444.

50. *PP IV*, Statement on the Continuation of UNRWA in the Special Political Committee of the General Assembly, New York, 10 November 1959, 492.

51. DH letter to Saint-John Perse, 23 August 1959, quoted in Little, *The Poet and the Diplomat*, 95.

52. *PP IV*, From Transcript of Press Conference, 2 April 1959, 343, and UN Archive.

53. Tenzin Gyatso, *Freedom in Exile: The Autobiography of the Dalai Lama*, 144.

54. See *Tibet in the United Nations 1950–1961*, a verbatim record of all debates in the United Nations on "the Question of Tibet," published by the Bureau of His Holiness the Dalai Lama. Both the Kashag's letter of 1950 and the Dalai Lama's letter of 1959 are included, respectively, 1–4 and 17–19. Other important sources include Anne-Marie Blondeau and Katia Buffetrille, ed., *Authenticating Tibet: Answers to China's 100 Questions*; Melvyn C. Goldstein, *A History of Modern Tibet*; and Tsering Shakya, *The Dragon in the Land of the Snows: A History of Modern Tibet since 1947*.

55. Bureau of His Holiness the Dalai Lama, *Tibet in the United Nations*, 11.

56. Ibid., 15.

57. Ibid., 17.

58. Conor Cruise O'Brien, a member of the Irish delegation, discusses his country's participation in *To Katanga and Back: A UN Case History*, 193–95. "Tibetans didn't expect much from the UN and of course they got very little. But they did get—mainly through us—a hearing of their case. . . ."

59. Bureau of His Holiness the Dalai Lama, *Tibet in the United Nations*, 20.

60. Ibid., 25.

61. Ibid., 28–29.

62. Ibid., 96.

63. Ibid., 223.

64. Ibid., 230.

65. Shakya, *The Dragon in the Land of the Snows*, 221–22.

66. *Markings*, dated entry for 8 February 1959, 173 (trans. slightly revised).

67. Crosscurrents Press, *Khrushchev in New York: A Documentary Record of Nikita S. Khrushchev's Trip to New York, September 19th to October 13th, 1960, including All His Speeches and Proposals to the United Nations and Major Addresses and News Conference*, 196.

68. Bureau of His Holiness the Dalai Lama, *Tibet in the United Nations*, 250–51.

69. Ibid., 311.

70. Remarks at Luncheon of United Nations Correspondents Association, 11 December 1959, UN Archive. A portion of this transcript appears in *PP IV*, Transcript of Remarks at Luncheon of United Nations Correspondents Association, New York, 11 December 1959, 502–9.

71. Rajeshwar Dayal, *Mission for Hammarskjold: The Congo Crisis*, 305.

72. *PP IV*, Statement at the Second Session of the Economic Commission for Africa, 26 January 1960, Tangier, 517.

73. Ibid., 519.

74. *PP IV*, Airport Statement on Return from African Trip, New York, 31 January 1960, 522.

75. *PP IV*, From Transcript of Press Conference, New York, 4 February 1960, 526–28.

76. *PP IV*, "Know Yourself, Know Your World," Address at the Seventy-fifth Anniversary Meeting of the Swedish Tourist Association, Stockholm, 27 February 1960, 548–49.

77. Ibid., 549.

78. *PP IV*, "The Development of a Constitutional Framework for International Cooperation," Address at the University of Chicago, Chicago, Illinois, 1 May 1960, 592.

79. Harold G. Henderson, *An Introduction to Haiku: An Anthology of Poems and Poets from Bashō to Shiki.*

80. One answer to the pleasant mystery of how DH found time for translation appears in a letter to Leif and Greta Belfrage, where he refers to "a translation of Perse's *Chronique* that I did before the Congo crisis but finished during its first stage (with a last finishing touch, as a matter of fact, during translations in the Security Council)." DH to Leif and Greta Belfrage, 15 October 1960, KB (trans. DvS). See also DH letter to Georg Svensson, 20 November 1960, KB, which refers to participation by Erik Lindegren, the Swedish poet who vetted the translation: "And so, with the American expression, the text has been put to bed. It could be better and it could be worse. Of course one never reaches the bottom in this kind of transposition or re-creation where the original phrases and words lend themselves to long meditation and often suddenly, after a long time, reveal new facets and overtones."

81. Léo Sauvage, "M. Hammarskjold quitte la séance de l'ONU et nous parle des bienfaits de la Poésie en diplomatie," *Le Figaro*, 30 October 1960

(trans. by the author).

82. *PP IV*, Message on the Occasion of the Attainment of Independence by the Congo, Léopoldville, The Congo, 30 June 1960, 636.

83. *PP IV*, From Transcript of Press Conference, New York, 30 June 1960, 638.

84. Ralph J. Bunche, "The UN Operation in the Congo," quoted in Henry, *Ralph J. Bunche: Selected Speeches and Writings*, 190–91.

85. Toddy Ranallo letter to DH, n.d., KB.

Chapter 15

1. *Markings*, 1954, 99.

2. For a brilliant introduction to this topic, see Adam Hochschild, *King Leopold's Ghost: A Story of Greed, Terror, and Heroism in Colonial Africa*.

3. On Morel, see Hochschild, *King Leopold's Ghost*, 177ff.; for Casement, see Séamas Ó Síocháin and Michael O'Sullivan, ed., *The Eyes of Another Race: Roger Casement's Congo Report and 1903 Diary*.

4. Hochschild, *King Leopold's Ghost*, 182, referring to Arthur Conan Doyle, *The Crime of the Congo*.

5. Mark Twain, *King Leopold's Soliloquy: A Defense of His Congo Rule*.

6. Joseph Conrad, *Heart of Darkness*, 22–23.

7. The portrait of Conrad is now in the collection of the Hammarskjöld Museum, Backåkra, Sweden.

8. Lieve Spaas, *How Belgium Colonized the Mind of the Congo: Seeking the Memory of an African People*, 47.

9. See Hergé, *Archives Hergé*, vol. 1. This edition reproduces without alteration the 1930 comic strip and book *Tintin au Congo*. While European children were reading this, generations of American schoolchildren were being introduced to Vachel Lindsay's poem, "The Congo" (1922), with its mixed message of "darkest Africa" ("Mumbo-Jumbo will hoo-doo you") and renewal ("Pioneer angels cleared the way / For a Congo paradise, for babes at play").

10. *PP IV*, "The Walls of Distrust," Address at Cambridge University, Cambridge, England, 5 June 1958, 91.

11. United Nations Oral History Collection, interview with Sture Linnér, 8 November 1990, 2, with additions from an interview with the author, December 2008.

12. The tune in a 1960 performance may be found online at www.youtube.com/watch?v=reModLpEloc.

13. Kanza (1), 155.

14. Ibid., 149.

15. Spaas, *How Belgium Colonized the Mind of the Congo*, 165.

16. Jean Van Lierde, ed., trans. Helen R. Lane, *Lumumba Speaks: The Speeches and Writings of Patrice Lumumba, 1958–1961*, 221–24. Van Lierde has "trivial" where the version published here has "tribal," in keeping with the French text published by Anicet Kashamura, *De Lumumba aux colonels*, 31. "Tribal" seems more likely, and the difficulties caused by tribal competition and enmity were not trivial.

17. Patrice Lumumba, *Congo, My Country*, 3.

18. For a thoughtful brief biography of Lumumba, see Dayal (1), chapter 17, "Lumumba: Dream and Reality."

19. Bunche, *Selected Speeches and Writings*, 193–94.

20. Crawford Young, "Ralph Bunche and Patrice Lumumba: The Fatal Encounter," in Robert A. Hill and Edmond J. Keller, ed., *Trustee for the Human Community: Ralph J. Bunche, the United Nations, and the Decolonization of Africa*, 142.

21. Dayal (1), 55.

22. Andrée Blouin, *My Country, Africa: Autobiography of the Black Pasionaria*, 227.

23. Ibid., 263, 270. The original Pasionaria was Dolores Ibárruri, a Spanish Republican leader of fame and influence in her era.

24. Kanza (1), 104.

25. Carl von Horn, *Soldiering for Peace*, 181.

26. Dayal (2), 402; Kanza (1), 258.

27. Dayal (1), 296.

28. *Time*, 22 December 1961, 16.

29. Urquhart (2), 184–85.

30. O'Brien, *To Katanga and Back*, 121.

31. Larry Devlin, *Chief of Station, Congo: A Memoir of 1960–67*, 77.

32. Kanza (1), 119, 151.

33. See Kashamura, *De Lumumba aux colonels*, 90–94, for an account of Janssens's attitudes and a précis of his words to the troops.

34. Urquhart (3), 308.

35. Van Lierde, *Lumumba Speaks*, 235–36.

36. *PP V*, Editors' introduction, "The United Nations Operation in the Congo Begins," 18–19.

37. Kelen, 186.

38. *PP II*, From Transcript of Press Conference, Djakarta, Indonesia, 12

February 1956, 678.

39. United Nations Oral History Collection, interview with F. T. Liu, 23 March 1990, 15–16.

40. United Nations Oral History Collection, interview with Brian Urquhart, 19 October 1984, 2.

41. *PP V*, Opening Statement in the Security Council, New York, 13 July 1960, 23.

42. "Khrushchev Backs Congo Mutineers," *New York Times*, 13 July 1960, NYTimes.com archive.

43. *PP V*, Third Statement in the Assembly, New York, 19 December 1960, 285.

44. *PP V*, Second Statement in the Security Council, New York, 13 July 1960, 25.

45. Official Records of the United Nations Security Council, 14 July 1960, par. 247.

46. Urquhart (1), 400n.

47. Dayal (2), 391–92.

48. Kanza (1), 207.

49. *PP V*, Statement in the Security Council Introducing His Report, New York, 20 July 1960, 43.

50. Kanza (1), 227.

51. For the resolution, see *PP V*, Statement in the Security Council Introducing His Report, New York, 20 July 1960, 44; for the commendation of DH, see Security Council transcript, 22 July 1960, par. 154.

52. Kanza (1), 238.

53. Madeleine G. Kalb, *The Congo Cables: The Cold War in Africa—from Eisenhower to Kennedy*, 34.

54. Kanza (1), 241. The anecdote about Lumumba's press conference is in Thomas Kanza, *Sans rancune*, 18–19.

55. Kanza (1), 243.

56. Ibid., 106.

57. Ibid., 248.

58. Beskow, 167 (DH letter dated 20 December 1960).

59. Urquhart (3), 322.

60. Sture Linnér interview with the author, January 2010.

61. *PP V*, Statement at Dinner Given by the Vice-Premier of the Republic of the Congo, Antoine Gizenga, Léopoldville, The Congo, 31 July 1960, 51–52.

62. *PP V*, Statement at Dinner for President Joseph Kasavubu of the Republic

of the Congo, Léopoldville, The Congo, 1 August 1960, 54–55.

63. *PP V*, Second Report on the Implementation of the Security Council Resolutions of July 14 and 22 on the Congo, New York, 6 August 1960, 61.

64. Kalb, *The Congo Cables*, 40.

65. *Markings*, 1955, 114.

66. *PP V*, Second Report on the Implementation of the Security Council Resolutions of July 14 and 22 on the Congo, New York, 6 August 1960, 65–66.

67. *PP V*, Exchange of Messages with Sékou Touré on Use of Guinea's Troops in Katanga, New York, 7 August 1960, 69.

68. Ibid.

69. *PP V*, First Statement in the Security Council Introducing His Second Report, New York, 8 August 1960, 71–75.

70. *PP V*, Second Statement in the Security Council, New York, 8 August 1960, 78–79.

71. *PP V*, First Statement in the Security Council Introducing His Second Report, New York, 8 August 1960, 75–76.

72. James Reston, *New York Times*, 10 August 1960, NYTimes.com archive.

73. *PP V*, Interpretation of Paragraph 4 of the Security Council's Third Resolution on the Congo, Léopoldville, The Congo, 12 August 1960, 87.

74. Eyewitness account in United Nations Oral History Collection, interview with F. T. Liu, 23 March 1990, 21–22.

75. Urquhart (1), 426fn.

76. Eyewitness account by major general Indar Jit Rikhye, *Trumpets and Tumults: The Memoirs of a Peacekeeper*,142–43. Another participant who could see the occasional humor of life in the Congo was Linnér. For the United Nations Oral History Collection (8 November 1990, 18) he told the following story: "One day a Congolese came saying, 'I want to repair your telephone.' I said, 'It is working a bit haphazardly. Do what you can. As a rule, though, I can at least talk locally without interruptions.' And he worked and worked and worked and then said, 'I can't manage it.' I said, 'What are you doing?' He said, 'I am supposed to put in one of these listening devices, but I can't get it screwed in in the right way.'"

77. United Nations Oral History Collection, interview with Pauline Frederick, 11 July 1986, 23.

78. Urquhart (1), 427–28.

79. This and the following citations are from Security Council Official Records,

Fifteenth Year, Supplement for July, August, and September 1960, Document S/4417/Add. 7.

80. Lash, *Dag Hammarskjöld*, 240.

81. *PP V*, Opening Statement in the Security Council, New York, 21 August 1960, 101–02.

82. Ibid., 104.

83. Ibid.

84. All citations other than of DH are from Security Council Official Records, 888th Meeting, 21 August 1960, available online.

85. *PP V*, Third Statement during Council Debate, New York, 21 August 1960, 118.

86. Ibid.

87. DH Letter to Uno Willers, 10 February 1961, KB (trans. DvS).

88. Kalb, *The Congo Cables*, 121.

89. Dayal (1), 103.

90. DH letter to Eyvind Johnson, 18 September 1960, KB.

91. Source reference mislaid; the context is the Bizerte incident of midsummer 1961.

92. Karl Ragnar Gierow letter to DH, 2 August 1960, KB (trans. DvS).

93. Karl Ragnar Gierow cable to DH, 21 September 1960, KB (trans. DvS).

94. DH cable to Karl Ragnar Gierow, 21 September 1960, KB.

95. DH cable to Karl Ragnar Gierow, 29 December 1960, KB (trans. DvS).

96. Urquhart (3), 331.

97. United Nations Oral History Collection, interview with Brian Urquhart, 19 October 1984, 9.

98. *PP II*, "An International Independent Responsibility," From Transcript of Remarks to a Meeting of International Nongovernmental Organizations, London, 19 March 1954, 278.

99. *PP V*, Introduction to the Fifteenth Annual Report, New York, 31 August 1960, 124.

100. Ibid., 131–32.

101. Little, *The Poet and the Diplomat*, 109.

102. Dayal (1), 52.

103. *PP V*, Opening Statement in the Security Council, New York, 9 September 1960, 167.

104. Kanza (1), 274.

105. Dayal (2), 417–19. Dayal is referring to two primary sources. The first consists of reports published in 1975 by the Senate Select Committee to Study Governmental Operations—known as the Church Committee for its chairman, Senator Frank Church. The most relevant section is *Alleged Assassination Plots Involving Foreign Leaders*, III. Assassination Planning and Plots, A. Congo (S. Rep. No. 94-465, 1975; hereafter cited as Church Committee). The text is available online at www.aarclibrary.org. The second source he would have had the opportunity to read is Kalb, *The Congo Cables*.

106. A series of reports issued by the Belgian government is available online at www.lachambre.be, accessed by a search on "Lumumba." The most comprehensive is identified as *Compte rendu integral – Séance plénière 50/ip205.pdf*. See also Ludo De Witte, *The Assassination of Lumumba*, trans. Ann Wright and Renée Fenby.

107. See note 106.

108. Devlin, *Chief of Station*, 28.

109. Ibid., 47–48.

110. Ibid., 54.

111. Church Committee, *Alleged Assassination Plots*, 15.

112. Devlin, *Chief of Station*, 66.

113. Kanza (1), 283.

114. Devlin, *Chief of Station*, 67.

115. United Nations Oral History Collection, interview with Sture Linnér, 8 November 1990, 22–23.

116. Kanza (1), 287.

117. Kanza (1), 288.

118. Ibid., 160.

119. Urquhart (1), 446; Dayal (1), 46.

120. Dayal (1), 46.

121. *PP V*, Opening Statement in the Security Council, New York, 9 September 1960, 164–65.

122. Ibid., 165.

123. Ibid., 166–67.

124. Ibid., 169.

125. Dayal (1), 308–09; *Time*, 24 February 1961.

126. United Nations Oral History Collection, interview with Brian Urquhart, 6 January 1984, 28.

127. *PP V*, Second Statement after Soviet Demand for His Dismissal, New York, 15 February 1961, 343.

128. Security Council minutes, 901st Session, 14 September 1960, par. 2–70 passim.

129. *PP V*, Fourth Statement during Security Council Debate, New York, 14 September 1960, 180.

130. Ibid., par. 4.

131. Ibid., par. 20.

132. Ibid., par. 73.

133. Dayal (1), 83.

134. Kanza (2), 111.

135. Dayal (1), 62ff.

136. United Nations Oral History Collection, interview with Brian Urquhart, 19 October 1984, 15.

137. Devlin, *Chief of Station*, 86.

138. Dayal (2), 416.

139. Ibid., 414.

140. Dayal (1), 72–74.

141. Ibid., 75.

142. Kashamura, *De Lumumba aux colonels*, 156–57.

143. Church Committee, *Alleged Assassination Plots*, 17.

144. Ibid., 25.

145. Ibid., 32.

146. Ibid., 48.

147. General Assembly, Fourth Emergency Special Session, 17 September 1960, par. 127.

148. General Assembly, Fourth Emergency Special Session, 18 September 1960, par. 7.

149. Ibid., par. 46–47.

150. *PP V*, First Statement in the Assembly after Soviet Attack on His Policies, New York, 17 September 1960, 186.

151. *PP V*, Second Statement during Debate, New York, 18 September 1960, 187–90.

152. Ibid., 188.

153. Ibid., 190.

154. DH cable to Rajeshwar Dayal, 18 September 1960, KB.

155. General Assembly, Fourth Emergency Special Session, 18 September 1960, par. 118.

156. General Assembly, Fourth Emergency Special Session, 19 September 1960, par. 185.

157. For the text of this resolution as considered by the Security Council, see *PP V*, Fifth Statement during Security Council Debate, New York, 16 September 1960, 184–85; it passed without modification in the General Assembly.

158. Nikita Khrushchev, *Khrushchev Remembers: The Last Testament*, trans. and ed. Strobe Talbott, 465.

159. Crosscurrents Press, *Khrushchev in New York*, 20–22.

160. Ibid., 52–53.

161. Ibid., 99.

162. *PP V*, Statement of Reply to Khrushchev and Others during General Debate, New York, 26 September 1960, 196–98.

163. *PP V*, "The International Civil Servant in Law and in Fact," Lecture Delivered in Congregation at Oxford University, Oxford, England, 30 May 1961, 488.

164. *PP II*, From Transcript of Background Press Conference, New York, 10 February 1954, 225.

165. N. Khrushchev, *Khrushchev Remembers*, 473.

166. Sergei Khrushchev, "Nikita Khrushchev and Dag Hammarskjöld," in Sten Ask and Anna Mark-Jungkvist, eds., *The Adventure of Peace*, 71–72.

167. Crosscurrents Press, *Khrushchev in New York*, 125.

168. Sean Finn, "Promotion Prospects," in Mary-Lynn Henley and Henning Melber, ed., *Dag Hammarskjöld Remembered: A Collection of Personal Memories* (Uppsala, Sweden: Dag Hammarskjöld Foundation, 2011), 23.

169. Crosscurrents Press, *Khrushchev in New York*, 130–32.

170. Ibid., 137, 139.

171. Urquhart (1), 462–63.

172. *PP V*, "I Shall Remain in My Post . . .," Second Statement of Reply, New York, 3 October 1960, 199–201. Italics added to reflect his delivery of certain words; video available online at www.daghammarskjold.se.

173. Urquhart (1), 465, where their handwritten exchange is reproduced.

174. General Assembly Official Records, Fifteenth Session, 883rd Plenary Meeting, par. 130.

175. *PP II*, From Statement before New York Herald Tribune Youth Forum, New York, 26 March 1955, 465.

176. Lash, *Dag Hammarskjöld*, 272–73.

177. "Khrushchev in the U.N.: The Shouts and the Pounding Are Seen as a Soviet Cry to Change the World," 4 October 1960, NYTimes.com archive.

178. Dayal (1), 93.

179. Crosscurrents Press, *Khrushchev in New York*, 197.

180. Ibid., 237.

181. *PP V*, Third Statement of Reply, New York, 13 October 1960, 202.

182. DH letter to Jean-Flavien Lalive, 14 November 1960, KB.

183. Dayal (1), 98.

184. Van Dusen, *Dag Hammarskjöld: The Statesman and His Faith*, 153.

185. PP V, Statement on United Nations Operation in the Congo at End of General Debate, New York, 17 October 1960, 202–7.

186. Urquhart (1), 473.

187. The audio recording is available online at www.unmultimedia.org.

188. PP V, Remarks at United Nations Day Concert, New York, 24 October 1960, 224–25.

189. Urquhart (1), 485, citing a DH letter to the Egyptian foreign minister, Mahmoud Fawzi.

190. "Kasavubu Insists on a Seat in U.N.; Asks Early Vote," 9 November 1960, NYTimes.com archive.

191. Dayal (1), 125.

192. *Markings*, 1960, 199, dated entry for 26 November 1960 (trans. slightly revised). In the first stanza, Sjöberg/Auden's "Bound by its vow, / My heart was heavy" for Sw. *Tungt av mitt blod band löftet* ignores the reference to blood. Wiser to reinstate. This difficult line was translated by Thord Palmlund.

193. DH letter to Eyvind Johnson, 28 November 1960, KB (trans. DvS).

194. Kanza (1), 312.

195. Dayal (2), 436–37.

196. Dayal (1), 136.

197. Kanza (1), 318ff.

198. Kashamura, *De Lumumba aux colonels*, 164–71.

199. The film footage is available online at www.youtube.com/ watch?v=JGnGFaJqmzU.

200. *PP V*, Letters to President Kasavubu, Letter Dated December 3, 1960, 238–39.

201. *Markings*, 1960, dated entry for 2 December 1960, 200.

202. Kalb, *The Congo Cables*, 157, citing a direct witness.

203. Security Council Official Records, 6 December 1960, Document S/45673, par. 15–16.

204. *PP V*, Opening Statement in the Security Council, New York, 7 December 1960, 242–54 passim.

205. Dayal (2), 439.

206. Security Council Official Records, 8 December 1960, par. 152–53.

207. Little, *The Poet and Diplomat*, 115.

208. W. H. Auden letter to DH, 28 November (year unspecified, but circumstances impose 1960), KB .

209. Saint-John Perse, Speech at the Nobel Banquet, 10 December 1960. Available online at www.nobelprize.org.

210. Saint-John Perse, *Chronique/Krönika*, trans. Dag Hammarskjöld (Stockholm: Bonniers, 1960).

211. DH letter to Leif and Greta Belfrage, 15 October 1960, KB (trans. DvS).

212. *PP V*, Statement at the Human Rights Day Concert, New York, 10 December 1960, 296–97.

213. Kanza (1), 220–21; Kanza (2), 115.

214. *PP V*, Concluding Statement in the Security Council, New York, 13 December 1960, 256–68 passim.

215. *PP V*, Second Statement in the Assembly, New York, 17 December 1960, 276.

216. Ibid., 279.

217. *PP V*, Third Statement in the Assembly, New York, 17 December 1960, 285–86.

218. *PP V*, Concluding Statement in the Assembly, New York, 20 December 1960, 287.

219. *PP V*, Letter to President Kasavubu, New York, 21 December 1960, 288–93.

220. Urquhart (1), 475.

221. DH letter to Bo Hammarskjöld, 21 December 1960, KB (trans. DvS).

222. Beskow, 175.

223. Urquhart (1), 492–93.

224. *Markings*, dated entry for Christmas Eve 1960, 198.

225. Urquhart (1), 491.

226. *Markings*, dated entry for 3 December 1960, 201 (trans. slightly revised). Sjöberg/Auden's "road," in the first couplet, deprives DH's *vägen* of religious content. Their "fun" for DH's *lyckan*, happiness or success, is an unhappy choice. Finally, it is not precisely the "truth" that he will be told, in the penultimate couplet; better to translate literally "the answer" for DH's *svaret*, therefore (and literally) "learn" for his *lära*. In the choice of "fun" for *lyckan*, is there unstated resistance to the poem?

Chapter 16

1.   DH letter to Östen Undén, 18 March 1961, KB.

2.   *Markings*, dated entry for 6 July 1961, 213.

3.   Dayal (1), 172. An important source for this period is a UN document dated 11 November 1961, entitled "Items in Peacekeeping Operations— United Nations Operations in the Congo—Lumumba—Reports on his Death," available online at http://archives-trim.un.org.

4.   John Olver, "Under Fire with Dag Hammarskjöld," in Henley and Henning Melber, *Dag Hammarskjöld Remembered*, 56–57.

5.   See www.un.org/documents/scres.htm, entry for 1 April 1960.

6.   Chris Saunders, "Dag Hammarskjöld and Apartheid South Africa," in *Development Dialogue* no. 57, December 2011, 71. See also African Centre for the Constructive Resolution of Disputes (ACCORD), *African Journal on Conflict Resolution* 11:1 (2011), dedicated to the theme of Southern Africa fifty years after Hammarskjöld.

7.   NYTimes.com archive, 12 January 1961, item 102.

8.   DH, "A New Look at Everest," *National Geographic* 119:1 (January 1961), 87–93.

9.   Dayal (1), 190.

10. G. Heinz and H. Donnay, *Lumumba Patrice: Les cinquante derniers jours de sa vie*, 75 (trans. by the author).

11. De Witte, *The Assassination of Lumumba*, 71.

12. As with so much in the Congo narrative, several versions of this letter have been published. The translation here (by the author) draws on

Kanza (1), 377–78; Kashamura, *De Lumumba aux colonels*, 173–75; and Spaas, *How Belgium Colonized the Mind of the Congo*, 181.

13. A series of reports issued by the Belgian government is available at www.lachambre.be, accessed by a search on "Lumumba." The most comprehensive is identified as *Compte rendu integral – Séance plénière 50/ip205.pdf.*

14. De Witte, *The Assassination of Lumumba*, 106.

15. Ibid., 107.

16. Ibid., 121.

17. Dayal (1), 193.

18. Kanza (1), 375–76.

19. Dayal (1), 197–98.

20. Kashamura, *De Lumumba aux colonels*, 4.

21. *PP V*, Appeal in the Security Council, 1 February 1961. 332.

22. DH letter to Bo Beskow, 27 January 1961, in Beskow, 169.

23. DH letter to Uno Willers, 10 February 1961, KB (trans. DvS).

24. Security Council Official Records, session of 13 February 1961, par. 39.

25. Richard D. Mahoney, *JFK: Ordeal in Africa*, 75.

26. Urquhart (1), 511.

27. *Markings*, dated entry for 13 February–13 March, 1961, 203. The French edition of the DH-Perse correspondence (see bibliog.) includes book dedications each made to the other. DH's dedication of his elegant bilingual edition of *Chronique* cites in French the lines about the Shirt of Nessus, 241.

28. DH letter to Sir Pierson Dixon, 10 March 1961, KB.

29. Security Council Official Records, Document S/4704, Letter dated 14 February 1961, par. 7–15.

30. Urquhart (1), 506–7.

31. U Thant, *View from the UN: The Memoirs of U Thant*, 109.

32. Kalb, *The Congo Cables*, 229.

33. Security Council Official Records, 935th Session, 15 February 1961.

34. *PP V*, Second Statement after Soviet Demand for his Dismissal, 15 February 1961, 346–47.

35. *PP V*, Second Statement after Soviet Demand for his Dismissal, 15 February 1961, 349–50.

36. *PP V*, Second Statement after Soviet Demand for his Dismissal, 15 February

1961, 352.

37. DH cable to Karl Ragnar Gierow, 16 February 1961, KB.

38. DH cable to W. H. Auden, 21 February 1961, KB.

39. Statement in the Security Council after Summary Executions in Bakwanga, 20 February 1961, 356.

40. *PP V*, 356–58.

41. *PP V*, Statement in the Security Council after Adoption of Afro-Asian Resolution, 21 February 1961, 364.

42. *PP V*, Letter Dated 27 February 1961 to the President of the Republic of the Congo (Léopoldville), 371–76 passim.

43. Hovde, "The Dag Hammarskjöld–John Steinbeck Correspondence," 123.

44. Ibid., 124 (DH letter to John Steinbeck, 28 February 1961).

45. DH letter to Jytte Bonnier, 24 April 1961, KB.

46. Dayal (1), 115.

47. Thant, *View from the UN*, 122–23, 126.

48. Dayal (1), 240. For a recent echo of this view, see Lord Skidelsky, "Dag Hammarskjöld's Assumptions and the Future of the UN," in Ask and Mark-Jungkvist, *The Adventure of Peace*, 387. "Authorizing a temporary trusteeship . . . was never suggested, out of pusillanimous concern for African sensibilities. . . ."

49. DH letter to Mahmoud Fawzi, 25 February 1961, cited in Urquhart (1), 509–10.

50. DH letter to Mahmoud Fawzi, 1 March 1961, KB.

51. Dayal (1), 261.

52. Urquhart (1), 421n.

53. Sture Linnér interview with the author, January 2010.

54. Hoskyns, *The Congo Since Independence*, 365–66. Hoskyns may be echoing O'Brien, *To Katanga and Back*, 70.

55. Dayal (2), 454.

56. DH letter to unknown recipient, 10 March 1961, KB.

57. Urquhart (1), 514.

58. See the 1961 United Nations Yearbook online for a summary of the Conciliation Commission's findings, at http://unyearbook.un.org.

59. Dayal (1), 176.

60. United Nations Official Records, General Assembly, Fifteenth Session, 21 March 1961, par. 9–82 passim.

61. Ibid., par. 104–9.

62. United Nations Official Records, General Assembly, Fifteenth Session, 28 March 1961, par. 10–12.

63. Andrew W. Cordier Papers, Columbia University Libraries.

64. DH letter to Östen Undén, 18 March 1961, KB.

65. *PP V*, First Statement during Renewed Congo Debate in the General Assembly, 29 March 1961, 420.

66. *Markings*, dated entry for Maundy Thursday, 1961 (30 March), 204.

67. This version of Psalm 73 is from the antique edition of *The Book of Common Prayer* read by DH.

68. DH letter to John Steinbeck, 20 May 1961, in Hovde, "The Dag Hammarskjöld–John Steinbeck Correspondence," 125.

69. Cited by V. K. Krishna Menon in United Nations Official Records, General Assembly, 5 April 1961, par. 128.

70. *PP V*, Second Statement, 5 April 1961, 423.

71. Ibid., 430.

72. Beskow, 178.

73. DH letter to Uno Willers, 9 April 1961, KB.

74. Alexis Leger letter to DH, 11 April 1961, in Little, *The Poet and the Diplomat*, 121–22.

75. *PP V*, editors' note, 433–36.

76. *PP V*, Fourth Statement, New York, 18 April 1961, 437.

77. Beskow, 179 (DH letter to Bo Beskow, 22 April 1961).

78. *PP V*, Agreement on General Principles Between the President of the Republic of the Congo (Léopoldville) and the Secretary-General of the United Nations, 451–53.

79. Hoskyns, *The Congo Since Independence*, 393–94.

80. *PP V*, Final Text of a Letter Dated April 26, 1961, from the Secretary-General to the President of the Republic of the Congo (Léopoldville) Concerning the Agreement Relating to Security Council Resolution S/4741, 452–53.

81. For a full account of Coquilhatville and its aftermath, see Hoskyns, *The Congo Since Independence*, 359–74.

82. O'Brien, *To Katanga and Back*, 100.

83. See *PP V*, Document S/4841/ADD.2, 504–06.

84. United Nations Oral History Collection, interview with Brian Urqu-

hart, 19 October 1984, 27–28. For the mercenaries' view of themselves, see Colonel Trinquier, Jacques Duchemin, and Jacques Le Bailly, *Notre guerre au Katanga.*

85. DH letter to Mrs. Walter Lippmann, 1 July 1961, KB.

86. Walter Lippmann, "An Interview with Khrushchev on World Political Issues," 17 April 1982, in Heinz-Dietrich Fischer, ed., *The Pulitzer Prize Archive*, vol. 1, *International Reporting 1928–1985*, 192–96.

87. *PP V*, "The International Civil Servant in Law and in Fact," Lecture Delivered in Congregation at Oxford University, Oxford, England, 30 May 1961, 473.

88. See Oscar S. Schachter, "The International Civil Servant: Neutrality and Responsibility," in Robert S. Jordan, ed., *Dag Hammarskjöld Revisited: The UN Secretary-General as a Force in World Politics*, 39–63.

89. *Markings*, dated entry for Pentecost 1961 (21 May), 205 (trans. slightly revised). Sjöberg/Auden has "every saying in the Gospels," a reductive rendering of DH's "every saying of the hero of the Gospels" (this is Erling's preferable translation of Sw. *var sats av evangeliernas hjälte*).

90. Ibid., dated entry for 7 July 1960–Spring 1961, 206–7. In this and the following few citations from DH's poetry, I have taken the liberty of not showing where lines divide for the sake of more clearly presenting his words.

91. Ibid., 1961, 210.

92. Ibid., dated entry for 18 June 1961, 212.

93. Ibid., dated entry for 30 July 1961, 216.

94. Ibid., dated entry for 8 June 1961, 208 (trans. slightly revised). Sjöberg/Auden has "heart" for Sw. *sinne*, more likely "mind."

95. See Sten Söderberg, *Hammarskjöld: A Pictorial Biography*, 98.

96. *PP V*, "The International Civil Servant in Law and in Fact," 471–89.

97. Schachter, "The International Civil Servant: Neutrality and Responsibility," in Jordan, *Dag Hammarskjöld Revisited*, 40.

98. Ibid., 486–87.

99. Ibid., 488–89. "At the final last" is an unusual locution, somewhat biblical in resonance ("the last trump"), but to my knowledge rare in English. DH may be recessively hearing a Danish expression common in Swedish, *til syvende og sidst*, which has something of the same weight. This note written with thanks to Thord Palmlund.

100. Manuel Fröhlich, "A Fully Integrated Vision: Politics and the Arts in the Dag Hammarskjöld—Barbara Hepworth Correspondence," *Development Dialogue* 2001:1, 52.

101. Ibid., 54 (letter dated 3 June 1961, like the letters to Sten Hammarskjöld and Karl Ragnar Gierow cited several paragraphs later).

102. *PP V*, From Transcript of Press Conference, New York, 12 June 1961, 492.

103. DH letter to Sten Hammarskjöld, Saturday 3 June 1961, KB. DH reused the paragraph about Khrushchev in a letter written the same day to Karl Ragnar Gierow, cited in Urquhart (1), 531.

104. *Markings*, 1961, 209. The entry falls between 8th and 11th June.

105. Ibid., dated entry for 11 June 1961, 211 (trans. slightly revised). One can argue with Sjöberg/Auden over the early lines of this translation. Sw. *Kallad/att bära den* could be translated to cognate "Called to bear it," and Sw. *avskild/att pröva den* might be clearer if *avskild*, separated, isolated, were translated "set apart." Rendering *pröva* as "assay" is correct and sonorous in context, but other solutions would be worth a try. However, these considerations don't infringe the basic good sense of the existing translation.

106. Beskow, 181.

107. Ibid., 184.

108. DH letter to Bo Hammarskjöld, 22 June 1961, KB.

109. Olver, "Under Fire with Dag Hammarskjöld," in Henley and Melber, *Dag Hammarskjöld Remembered*, 58.

110. Hoskyns, *The Congo Since Independence*, 399.

111. See Dayal (2), 467–68, for the tale of the sewer pipe and a view of foreign interference at Lovanium; and Devlin, *Chief of Station*, 156–58. Devlin does not divulge the tale of the sewer pipe.

112. Kalb, *The Congo Cables*, 272–73.

113. DH letter to Karl Ragnar Gierow, 18 July 1961, KB.

114. Urquhart (1), 534.

115. General Assembly Official Records, Resolutions 1012 (15 February 1957) and 1184 (10 December 1957), followed on 19 December 1960 by Resolution 1573 "deeply concerned by the continuance of hostilities."

116. DH letter to Alexis Leger (Saint-John Perse), 23 August 1959, in Little, *The Poet and the Diplomat*, 95.

117. Charles de Gaulle letter to DH, 26 March 1960, cited in Urquhart

(1), 535, and footnote.

118. Charles de Gaulle, *Lettres, Notes et Carnets, Juin 1958–Decembre 1960*. Document dated 4 February 1960, 325 (trans. by the author).

119. Fourth Press Conference Held by General de Gaulle as President of the French Republic in Paris at the Elysée Palace, 11 April 1961, in *Major Addresses, Statements and Press Conferences of General Charles de Gaulle*, 19 May 1958–31 January 1964, 120–21.

120. *PP V*, editors' note, 530.

121. Urquhart (1), 537–38.

122. DH letter to Mahmoud Fawzi, 4 August 1961, KB.

123. *PP V*, Oral Report to the Security Council on His Initiative, New York, 28 July 1961, 536.

124. DH letter to Sture Petrén, 9 August 1961, KB. *Para* is colloquial French for paratroopers.

125. *PP V*, editors' note, 537.

126. DH letter to Mahmoud Fawzi, 4 August 1961, KB.

127. Urquhart (1), 541.

128. Fifth Press Conference Held by General de Gaulle as President of the French Republic in Paris at the Elysée Palace, 5 September 1961, in *Major Addresses*, 149.

129. DH letter to Bo Beskow, 6 August 1961, cited in Little, *The Poet and the Diplomat*, 135n1.

130. DH letter to Sture Petrén, 9 August 1961, KB.

131. Ibid.

132. Ibid.

133. See Saint-John Perse, "Réponse à un historien allemand," in *Oeuvres complètes*, 632–34.

134. DH letter to Alexis Leger, 31 July 1961, in Little, *The Poet and the Diplomat*, 126–37 (trans. slightly revised by the author).

135. Ibid., 131.

136. Ibid., 132.

137. *Markings*, dated entry for 6 July 1961, 213.

138. *Markings*, dated entry for 19 July 1961, 214–15.

139. Hammarskjöld, *Castle Hill*. First published in *Svenska Turistföreningens Årsskrift 1962*, an annual publication of the Swedish Touring Association.

140. "United Nations: Battlefield of Peace," *Time*, 29 September 1961,
141. Ibid., 9.
142. Ibid., 17–18.
143. Karl Ragnar Gierow letter to DH, 10 August 1961, KB (trans. DvS).
144. DH, "The Camera Taught Me to See," in Falkman, *To Speak for the World*, 221–22. First published as "Kameran har lärt mig att se," in *Foto: Tidskrift för Foto och Film*, no. 12, 1958, 21ff.
145. DH letter to Bo Beskow, 6 August 1961, in Beskow, *Strictly Personal*, 191, with a one-sentence addition from the original in KB.
146. *Markings*, dated entry for 6 August 1961, 219–20.
147. DH letter to Erik Lindegren, 6 August 1961, KB.
148. *Markings*, dated entry for 6 August 1961, 221.
149. *PP V*, Introduction to the Sixteenth Annual Report, New York, 17 August 1961, 542.
150. Ibid., 543.
151. Ibid., 559–60.
152. *PP V*, editors' note, 542.
153. *PP V*, Letter to Prime Minister Adoula, 10 September 1961, 568.
154. United Nations Oral History Collection, interview with Brian Urquhart, 19 October 1984, 33–37.
155. Brian Urquhart, quoted by Adam Bernstein in an obituary, "I. J. Rikhye; Indian Major-General Oversaw UN Peacekeeping Efforts," *Washington Post*, 25 May 2007, available online at www.washingtonpost.com.
156. United Nations Oral History Collection, interview with I. J. Rikhye, 26 March 1990, 29–30.
157. For O'Brien's discussion of his selection, see O'Brien, *To Katanga and Back*, 41–45.
158. Ibid., 55.
159. United Nations Oral History Collection, interview with Brian Urquhart, 19 October 1984, 33.
160. O'Brien, *To Katanga and Back*, 189.
161. Urquhart (1), 565n.
162. DH letter to Peder Hammarskjöld, 11 September 1961, KB.
163. DH letter to Mekki Abbas, 30 August 1961, KB.
164. DH letter to Karl Ragnar Gierow, Saturday 19 August 1961, KB.

165. DH letter to John Steinbeck, in Hovde, "The Dag Hammarskjöld–John Steinbeck Correspondence," 127.

166. DH letter to Anders Österling, 8 July 1961, KB. The novel was probably *The Winter of Our Discontent* (New York: Viking, 1961).

167. DH letter to Martin Buber, 5 September 1961, in Hovde, "The Dag Hammarskjöld–John Steinbeck Correspondence," 129. Buber, Ben-Gurion, and others in other countries received the same letter of introduction.

168. John Steinbeck, Nobel Prize Acceptance Speech, available online at www.nobelprize.org.

169. DH cable to Östen Undén, 24 August 1961, KB (trans. DvS).

170. Martin Buber, *Ich und Du* (1923). See also Ronald Gregor Smith, trans., *I and Thou* (the edition used by DH alongside the German); and the more recent Walter Kaufmann, trans., *I and Thou*.

171. Martin Buber, *Between Man and Man*, trans. Ronald Gregor Smith.

172. DH letter to Martin Buber, 17 August 1961, in Nahum N. Glatzer and Paul Mendes-Flohr, ed., *The Letters of Martin Buber: A Life of Dialogue*, 640–41.

173. Ibid., 641.

174. DH letter to Martin Buber, 26 August 1961, cited in Lou Marin, "Can We Save True Dialogue in an Age of Mistrust? The Encounter of Dag Hammarskjöld and Martin Buber," in *Critical Currents* no. 8, January 2010, 59–60.

175. Ibid., DH letter to Jytte Bonnier, 26 August 1961, 61.

176. DH letter to Georg Svensson, 12 September 1961, KB.

177. Martin Buber, *Ich und Du*, rev. ed. (Heidelberg: Lambert Schneider, 1983), 3. Trans. by the author in dialogue with Jacob Needleman.

178. *Markings*, dated entry for 24 August 1961, 222.

Chapter 17

1. DH letter to Bo Beskow, 19 August 1961, cited in Van Dusen, *Dag Hammarskjöld: The Statesman and His Faith*, 167.

2. Conor Cruise O'Brien, *Memoir: My Life and Themes*, 220. For a vivid account of the suddenly mushrooming refugee camp, see David Halberstam, "A Refugee 'City' Rises in Katanga," *New York Times*, 10 September 1961, NYTimes.com archive.

3. United Nations Oral History Collection, interview with Brian Urquhart,

19 October 1984, 31.

4. O'Brien, *To Katanga and Back*, 221.

5. Ibid., 221.

6. Ibid., 219.

7. Kalb, *The Congo Cables*, 290.

8. O'Brien, *Memoir,* 209.

9. O'Brien, *To Katanga and Back,* 224–27.

10. *PP V*, editors' note, 568.

11. Oscar Schachter, Memorandum of 7 September 1961, "Observations on the Legal Aspects of the Present Katanga Situation," available in *The Guardian* online archive, www.guardian.co.uk, accessed through a search on "Hammarskjöld." This document is also summarized in Urquhart (1), 561–62.

12. Mahmoud Khiari, cable to DH, 10 September 1961, available in GNM Archive, www.guardian.co.uk/gnm-archive, accessed through a search on "Hammarskjöld" (trans. by the author).

13. DH cable to Sture Linnér, 10 September 1961, available in GNM Archive, www. www.guardian.co.uk/gnm-archive, accessed through a search on "Hammarskjöld."

14. United Nations Oral History Collection, interview with Sture Linnér, 8 November 1990, 36.

15. PP V, Last Words to the Staff—from Remarks on Staff Day, New York, 8 September 1961, 562–66.

16. Markings, 1957, 156.

17. Steinbeck and Wallsten, *Steinbeck*, 715–16.

18. Carl Nordenfalk letter to DH, 31 January 1961, KB (trans. DvS).

19. DH letter to Sture Petrén, 9 August 1961, KB.

20. DH letter to Carl Nordenfalk, 19 August 1961, KB.

21. Frances K. Pohl, *Ben Shahn, with Ben Shahn's Writings*, 149. A good color reproduction of the Ben Shahn portrait is on the facing page.

22. Urquhart (1), 566.

23. Ibid., 248.

24. Ibid., 249.

25. See the recent book by Rolf Rembe and Anders Hellberg, *Midnatt i Kongo: Dag Hammarskjölds förlorade seger* (Midnight in the Congo: Dag Hammarskjöld's lost victory), chapter 17.

26. United Nations Oral History Collection, interview with Brian Urquhart,

19 October 1984, 31.

27. Dayal (1), 269.

28. O'Brien, *To Katanga and Back*, 255.

29. O'Brien, *Memoir*, 225.

30. DH cable to Ralph Bunche, 15 September 1961, available in GNM Archive, www.guardian.co.uk/gnm-archive, accessed through a search on "Hammarskjöld."

31. United Nations Oral History Collection, interview with Brian Urquhart, 19 October 1984, 28–29.

32. O'Brien, *To Katanga and Back*, 266.

33. Urquhart (1), 583.

34. From a retrospective debate in the House of Commons, 14 December 1961, the Lord Privy Seal Edward Heath speaking: "We were asked late on 16th September for overflying rights. . . . This was at the same time as Mr. Hammarskjöld told us that he would do his best to organize a cease-fire. Lord Lansdowne was, therefore, asked to inquire of Mr. Hammarskjöld whether he wished to risk air warfare at the same time as he was trying to organize cease-fire talks. We for our part said that we would use any influence we had on Mr. Tshombe to ground the Fouga. . . ." The full debate on British interests and conduct in the Congo can be accessed online at www.theyworkforyou.com via a search on the debate date. I am grateful to Hans Kristian Simensen for alerting me to this remarkable online resource, a verbatim collection of Commons debates.

35. Dayal (1), 273.

36. United Nations Oral History Collection, interview with Sture Linnér, 8 November 1990, 34–35.

37. William Ranallo letter to his wife, 17 September 1961, cited in Urquhart (1), 584.

38. *PP V*, First Message to Mr. Tshombe, 16 September 1961, 570–71.

39. Williams, 63.

40. Lord Alport, *The Sudden Assignment: Being a Record of Service in Central Africa during the Last Controversial Years of the Federation of Rhodesia and Nyasaland 1961–1963*, 94.

41. DH cable to Ralph Bunche, 17 September 1961, KB. In a handwritten note dated 6 November 1961, which accompanies this document as archived, Bunche recorded that "This was the last cable sent from Léopoldville by Mr. Hammarskjöld."

42. United Nations Oral History Collection, interview with Sture Linnér,

8 November 1990, 35.

43. George Ivan Smith letter to Martin Buber, 3 October 1961, cited in Fröhlich, "'The Unknown Assignation,'" 34.

44. Urquhart (1), 585.

45. Sources for this discussion are the 1958 German edition, and the 1958 and 1970 English translations (see bibliog.).

46. For insight into the diversity of tribal cultures and regions in the Congo, see Angelo Turconi and François Neyt, *Infini Congo / Eternal Congo*.

47. See note 38.

48. Adrian Begg, "Crash of Hammarskjöld's Plane in 1961: 'VIP planes don't crash...,'" 27 January 2012, available online at www.hurstblog.co.uk.

49. Williams, 75, 186–89.

50. Ibid., 86, citing the Rhodesian press.

51. See Knut Hammarskjöld, "'Leave it to Dag'—A Personal Experience," in Henley and Melber, *Dag Hammarskjöld Remembered*, 102–3.

52. Ibid., 4.

53. Markings, dated entry for 7 July 1960–Spring 1961, 206 (trans. slightly revised). Sjöberg/Auden has "I answer Yes without / A second thought" for Sw. *ger jag svaret utan / återvändo*. The difficulty is that it introduces DH's Yes where in point of fact it isn't present, and by doing so will confuse readers of English interested enough in DH's thought to assemble all occurrences of Yes throughout *Markings*. Better to translate differently.

54. Sture Linnér interview with the author, January 2010.

55. "Adoula Pledges Move on Katanga," New York Times, 21 September 1961, NYTimes.com archive.

56. Urquhart (1), 591.

57. In point of fact there were four investigations. An immediate investigation by the Royal Swedish Board of Aviation resulted in a report, dated 18 December 1961, which was kept secret until the early 1990s. Its conclusion raised the possibility of interference by other aircraft: "Disturbance of SE-BDY during landing from one or several unfamiliar aircraft, without SE-BDY being shot at, could have caused the crew to have taken evasive action. In this situation SE-BDY could have lost altitude and collision with the ground was unavoidable." Again thanks to H. K. Simensen for informing me about this little-cited document.

58. Williams, 90–91.

59. Ibid., 94.

60. Ibid.

61. Ibid., 96.

62. Ibid., 97.

63. Ibid., 100. The treatment of a witness named Simango, quite typical, remains a shock. He acquitted himself courageously under the circumstances. Mr. Adams (interrogating): "You say you saw a flash, then you saw the airplane crash, and then you heard the explosion?" Mr. Simango: "I beg your pardon?" Mr. Adams: "That first you saw a flash, then you saw the airplane go down, and I think you used the word 'crash,' and then you heard an explosion—is that right?" Mr. Simango: "It is a bit right." Mr. Adams: "Well, what is wrong with it?" Mr. Simango: "I said I saw a flash and the flash was even coming down with the airplane, and I heard a crash, and after a few moments explosives. . . ." *Report of the Rhodesian Commission*, 30. Document kindly provided by H. K. Simensen.

64. United Nations General Assembly Resolution 1628, 26 October 1961, available online at www.un.org.

65. Williams, 104.

66. Ibid., 104–5.

67. Ibid., 105.

68. "New Clues to 1961 Death of Hammarskjöld," at www.hurstblog.co.uk, reproducing an article from a South African news site, The Witness, 14 March 2012.

69. All citations are from the UN document designated A/AC.107/Hearing 6, 29 January 1962, a session in Léopoldville. Thanks to Hans Kristian Simensen for providing this significant document.

70. Mama Kankasa interview with KG Hammar and H.K. Simensen, Lusaka (Zambia), 16 December 2011. Transcript obtained through the kindness of H. K. Simensen.

71. Ibid., 108. For further details, see the official United Nations document: *Report of the Commission of Investigation into the Conditions and Circumstances Resulting in the Tragic Death of Mr. Dag Hammarskjöld and of Members of the Party Accompanying Him*, A/5069, 26 October 1962.

72. For a contemporaneous account, see "Letters Say Hammarskjöld Death Western Plot," Reuters, 19 August 1998, available online at www.globalpolicy.org/secgen/pastsg/murder.htm.

73. See Williams, 193ff.

74. See www.greatnorthroad.org/bboard/message.php?id=13454.

75. Williams, 7.

76. Ibid., 5.

77. Ibid., 155.

78. See www.kingmsiri.com/eng/kings/king6.htm.

79. Williams, 142–43.

80. Devlin, Chief of Station, 167–68.

81. Williams, 151–52.

82. Ibid., 236–37. Dr. Williams's description of the context echoes words spoken soon after Ndola. In the long debate about the Congo in the House of Commons, 14 December 1961, the Labour leader Harold Wilson, a future prime minister, eloquently described—and condemned—the influence of major corporations in central Africa: "Cecil Rhodes has been dead these sixty years. . . . But if the day of Rhodes is buried with the past, so is the day of the charter company, of powerful corporations who regard themselves as being above the law, as a State within a State, as a State above any national or international disciplines. This is the problem—the influence, in Africa and here in London, the power, highly organized and secretly and subtly exercised, of powerful and unscrupulous corporations, notably Union Minière and Tanganyika Concessions and, linked with them, the British South Africa Company. Let no one underrate the power of these pressures which have been brought to bear, directly or indirectly, on Westminster. They permeate the Establishment—£145 million of assets, with their full power mobilized and deployed against the United Nations. . . . All money talks and big money talks loudest of all." Available online at www.theyworkforyou.com, accessed by a search on the date. I thank H. K. Simensen for pointing to this memorable statement.

83. Rembe and Hellberg, *Midnatt*, 259.

84. K. G. Hammar, "Utred Hammarskjölds död igen," *Svenska Dagbladet*, 29 January 2012, published in translation as "I am convinced! Hammarskjöld did not die in an air accident," available online at www.hurstblog. co.uk. Eyewitnesses to the event in the sky and the crash survive to this day. In a recorded interview in the region of Ndola with K. G. Hammar and H. K. Simensen, the elderly Johnny Ngongo said that it was "God's will that he had lived to this time to testify truthfully that he witnessed the crash. . . . The crash happened only about 500 meters away. . . . As the plane was descending it came down on one side and it was burning . . . . It crashed into a tree." Ngongo and a fellow charcoal burner explored the crash site early the next morning and saw the secretary-general where he lay dead against the ant-hill; they may have been the first to reach the site. K. G. Hammar and Simensen were led to surviving witnesses by two compelling articles published a month prior to their

days in Ndola. The first was written by a Swedish aid worker stationed in Africa who, with an African colleague Jacob Phiri, had searched for witnesses over a period of three years; see Göran Björkdahl, "I Have No Doubt Dag Hammarskjöld's Plane Was Brought Down," *The Guardian*, 17 August 2011. See as well an article by *Guardian* reporters who presented Björkdahl's findings in greater detail: Julian Borger and Georgina Smith, "Dag Hammarskjöld: Evidence Suggests UN Chief's Plane Was Shot Down," *The Guardian*, 17 August 2011.

85. See Raphael Satter (Associated Press), "New Inquiry into Death of Dag Hammarskjöld," available online at www.publicopiniononline.com; also Staffan Lindberg, "De hemliga bilderna på Dag Hammarskjöld" (The secret pictures of Dag Hammarskjöld), *Aftonbladet*, 19 September 2012, and related articles.

86. *Markings*, 1959, 195 (trans. slightly revised).

87. Ibid., 188 (trans. slightly revised). It is just possible that DH was thinking of his admired friend, the poet Hjalmar Gullberg, whose grave illness had intensified that fall. In a letter of 26 October 1959 to Erik Lindegren, DH wrote, "I hope to be able to come home in December for the usual flying visit. This year there will be a shadow over December 20th, due to the depressing development of Hjalmar's disease. It has now reached a degree of tragic atrocity I have seldom encountered." KB (trans. DvS).

88. Konrad Adenauer, cable to the president of the General Assembly, 18 September 1961, KB.

89. Steinbeck and Wallsten, *Steinbeck*, 715–16.

90. United Nations Oral History Collection, interview with Brian Urquhart, 19 October 1984, 38.

91. Cecil T. J. Redman, "A Haunting Memory," in Henley and Melber, *Dag Hammarskjöld Remembered*, 28.

92. O'Brien, *To Katanga and Back*, 304–5.

93. Conor Cruise O'Brien, *Murderous Angels: A Political Tragedy and Comedy in Black and White* (Boston: Little, Brown, 1968). In his *Memoir*, 207, O'Brien stated his purpose in writing the play: to show "the interaction between Hammarskjold's spiritual aspirations and his Machiavellian course in practical political decisions."

94. O'Brien, *Memoir*, 201.

95. Urquhart (1), 56.

96. United Nations Oral History Collection, interview with Per Lind, 7 November 1990, available online at www.unmultimedia.org. See also Per Lind, "An Unusual Letter," in Henley and Melber, *Dag Hammarskjöld Remembered*, 94–97.

97. Photographs of DH's New York apartment are preserved in the KB collection.

98. See Olver, "Under Fire with Dag Hammarskjöld," in Henley and Melber, *Dag Hammarskjöld Remembered*, 59–69. Photographs and word-portraits of the UN members who died with DH will be found in *Secretariat News* 15:17 (16 October 1961), with statements by Andrew Cordier and other colleagues.

99. Ibid., 63.

100. Ibid., 66.

101. Official Records of the United Nations, United Nations General Assembly, Sixteenth Session, 19 September 1961.

102. From a collection of twenty-one letters written by the children of Grade Five, Greenacres Elementary School, Scarsdale, New York, accompanied by a $6 contribution to UNICEF. KB.

103. All texts cited from this session appear in Official Records of the United Nations, United Nations General Assembly, Sixteenth Session, 20 September 1961.

104. Urquhart (1), 472.

105. Wilhelm Wachtmeister, "Leader–Statesman–Friend," in Henley and Melber, Dag Hammarskjöld Remembered, 85.

106. Steinbeck and Wallsten, Steinbeck, 716.

107. These and other newspaper articles will be found in Svenska Folkets Historia, *Dag Hammarskjöld: En minnesbok*, 151–53 (trans. Thord Palmlund).

108. "A Voice That Will Be Heard," *New York Times*, 24 December 1961, NYTimes.com archive.

109. "A Day for Plain Speaking," *New York Times*, 25 December 1961, NYTimes.com archive.

110. "JFK Address at UN General Assembly, 25 September 1961," available online as a video and in print at www.jfklibrary.org.

111. Urquhart (2), 175.

112. PP V, Remarks at United Nations Day Concert, 24 October 1960, 225.

113. Urquhart (2), 176.

114. Ibid.

115. Description of the Gärdet gathering and citations from eulogies will be found in Svenska Folkets Historia, *Dag Hammarskjöld: En minnesbok*, 105–12 (trans. Thord Palmlund).

116. Wilhelm Wachtmeister, "On the 29th of September," Secretariat News 15:17 (16 October 1961), 5.

117. Details recorded in Svenska Folkets Historia, *Dag Hammarskjöld: En minnesbok*, 126–31.

118. Williams, 87.

119. George Ivan Smith letter to Max Ascoli, 3 October 1961, in Fröhlich, "'The Unknown Assignation,'" 34n107.

120. Labba, *Anta*, 420 (trans. by the author). KB preserves a letter from Labba to DH, dated 11 February 1940: "Old brother, [I] hope you have not forgotten your good friend in the mountains. I must write some lines from the mountains now and thank you for your hospitality. In Stockholm I lived the most fun-filled days in my life. Maybe I won't be able to come down again to have such fun. Anyway, thank you very much for all the time I could spend with you, dear brother. . . ." (trans. DvS).

121. Labba, 427–28. See also Stephan Mögle-Stadel, *Dag Hammarskjöld: Visionary for the Future of Humanity*, 94ff., for discussion and photographs of the chapel at Kaitum.

122. Rolf Edberg, Nobel Peace Prize acceptance speech on behalf of DH, 10 December 1961, available online at http://nobelprize.org.

123. Alfred Luthuli, the South African anti-apartheid leader and 1960 Nobel Peace Laureate, was responsible for the memorable phrase "devoted chief executive of the world." He is cited in Tor Sellström, "Hammarskjöld and Apartheid South Africa: Mission Unaccomplished," *African Journal on Conflict Resolution* 11:1 (2011), 59. See also Tor Sellström, ed., *Albert Luthuli and Dag Hammarskjöld—Leaders and Visionaries* (a joint publication of the Nordic Africa Institute, the Dag Hammarskjöld Foundation, and the Luthuli Museum, 2012, available online at www.dhf.uu.se). Key reflections in the aftermath of DH's death will be found in Lillian Ross, "Dag Hammarskjöld," *The New Yorker*, 30 September 1961, 35ff.; Max Ascoli, "Dag Hammarskjöld," *The Reporter*, 12 October 1961, 12; W. H. Auden, "Dag Hammarskjöld," *Encounter* 17:5 (November 1961), 3–4; Martin Buber, "Memories of Hammarskjöld," in *A Believing Humanism: My Testament 1902–1965*, ed. and trans. Maurice Friedman, 57–59.

124. Lindegren, *Dag Hammarskjöld*.

125. Sture Linnér, "Dag Hammarskjöld and the Congo crisis, 1960–61," in Sturé Linnér and Sverker Åström, *UN Secretary-General Hammarskjöld: Reflections and Personal Experiences*, The 2007 Dag Hammarskjöld Lecture, booklet published jointly by the Dag Hammarskjöld Foundation and Uppsala University, 26.

126. Thant, *View from the UN*, 134ff.

127. Security Council resolution of 24 November 1961, available online at

www.un.org.

128. Thant, *View from the UN*, 136.

129. Ibid., 142.

130. Urquhart (3), 360.

131. Thant, *View from the UN*, 149.

132. For Dayal's critique, see Dayal (1), 308–10.

133. Dayal (1), 311.

134. Urquhart (2), 180–83; United Nations Oral History Collection, interview with Brian Urquhart, 19 October 1984, 40ff. "It certainly messed up the dinner party. Everybody was a little disconcerted by the whole thing."

135. United Nations Oral History Collection, interview with Brian Urquhart, 22 October 1984, 15ff.

136. Urquhart (3), 303.

137. Jean-Marie Guéhenno, "The Peacekeeper," in Ask and Mark-Jungkvist, *The Adventure of Peace*, 189–90.

138. DH letter to Saint-John Perse, 30 August 1956, in Little, *The Poet and the Diplomat*, 56.

139. Letter from Greta Belfrage to George Ivan Smith, 14 September 1963. Original in the Papers of George Ivan Smith, Bodleian Library, University of Oxford; photocopy in the collection of the Dag Hammarskjöld Foundation.

140. Georg Svensson letter to Alfred A. Knopf, 17 September 1963, in Alfred A. Knopf, Inc. Records, Harry Ransom Center, University of Texas at Austin.

141. Olof Lagercrantz, "Hammarskjöld, Jesus, and the Truth," *Dagens Nyheter*, 18 October 1961 (trans. DvS).

142. *Markings*, 1955, 115.

143. Sverker Åström, "The Swedish Government and Secretary-General Dag Hammarskjöld," in Ask and Mark-Jungkvist, *The Adventure of Peace*, 79.

144. "The Hammarskjöld Myth: Hammarskjöld's Intimate Diary Must Be Looked upon as a Central Document in Forming the Judgment of His Achievement," unsigned editorial, *Dagens Nyheter*, 10 November 1963 (trans. DvS). See also Oliver Clausen, "Clues to the Hammarskjöld Riddle," *New York Times*, 28 June 1964, NYTimes.com archive.

145. Kerstin Anér, writing in *Aftonbladet*, 29 December 1963.

146. Stolpe, *Dag Hammarskjöld*; and Aulén, *Dag Hammarskjöld's White Book*.

147. The third book of importance in that season of reception and assimila-

tion of *Markings* was Van Dusen, *Dag Hammarskjöld: The Statesman and His Faith*. All three continue to reward the reader.

148. Clausen, "Clues to the Hammarskjöld Riddle."

149. Lindberg's interview is available online at http://www.spiegel.de/spiegel/print/d-46273583.html.

150. Ralph Bunche letter to the editor of *Look*, in an issue postdating 30 June 1964.

151. John Steinbeck, undated letter, offered for sale in the online autograph market, 2009.

152. *Markings*, 1958, 166.

153. Leif Sjöberg, "Translating with W. H. Auden: Gunnar Ekelöf's last poems," in Elinor Shaffer, ed., *Comparative Criticism: A Yearbook*, 185–97. Though Sjöberg's focus is Ekelöf, there are quite a few remarks about working with Auden on *Markings*.

154. Andrew Cordier letter to William A. Koshland, 29 April 1964, in Alfred A. Knopf, Inc. Records, Harry Ransom Center, University of Texas at Austin.

155. W. H. Auden letter to William A. Koshland, 14 August 1964, in Alfred A. Knopf, Inc. Records, Harry Ransom Center, University of Texas at Austin.

156. *Markings*, xxii.

157. Leif Belfrage letter to W. H. Auden, 29 May 1964, photocopy in the collection of the Dag Hammarskjöld Foundation, Uppsala, Sweden.

158. Stolpe, *Dag Hammarskjöld*, 114.

159. George Ivan Smith letter to Max Ascoli, 16 June 1965, cited in Fröhlich, "'The Unknown Assignation,'" 17.

160. The statistic is from "Other Side," *New York Times*, 25 April 1965, NYTimes.com archive. Brian Urquhart's review, "The Still Point," appeared in *The New Yorker*, 31 October 1964, 232–44.

161. Urquhart, "The Still Point," 244.

162. Richard Davenport-Hines, *Auden*, 304.

163. United Nations, *The Unveiling of Single Form by Barbara Hepworth, Gift of Jacob Blaustein, after a wish of Dag Hammarskjöld*, 11 June 1964, United Nations, New York (a commemorative booklet), 12.

164. Hepworth's correspondence with Ralph Bunche and some part of her creative process are recorded in Manuel Fröhlich, "A Fully Integrated Vision: Politics and the Arts in the Dag Hammarskjöld–Barbara Hepworth Correspondence," *Development Dialogue* 2001:1, 17–57.

165. *Markings*, 1958, 171.

166. United Nations, *The Unveiling of Single Form*, 4.

167. Ibid., 5; see also *PP II*, Address at Inauguration of the Twenty-Fifth Anniversary of the Museum of Modern Art, New York, 19 October 1954, 372–75. For an additional interpretation of the memorial sculpture and exploration of DH's approach to art, see Roger Lipsey, "Enlightened Patronage: Dag Hammarskjöld at the UN," in *An Art of Our Own: The Spiritual in Twentieth-Century Art* (Boston and Shaftesbury: Shambhala Publications, 1988), 444–60.

168. Lipsey, *An Art of Our Own*, 458. There was always a little confusion about that date—midnight on the 18th in Ndola was 6 in the evening, New York time.

169. Cited in Frances K. Pohl, *Ben Shahn, with Ben Shahn's writings* (Pomegranate Artbooks: San Francisco, 1993), 149. A color print of the portrait is on the facing page. For a second reproduction of the portrait see James Thrall Soby, *Ben Shahn: Paintings* (New York: Braziller, 1963), fig. 75.

170. Cited in Carl Nordenfalk, *Ben Shahn's Portrait of Dag Hammarskjöld* (7 pp., a publication of the National Portrait Collection).

171. Urquhart (1), 33.

172. DH, ceremony honoring Dr. G. J. Van Heuven Goedhart, Geneva, 2 May 1958, United Nations Archive.

173. DH letter to Bo Beskow, 16 March 1957, KB.

Afterword

1. *Markings*, 1957, 158.

2. *PP III*, A Room of Quiet (The United Nations Meditation Room), December 1957, 710–11.

3. *PP II*, "Old Creeds in a New World," Written for Edward R. Murrow's Radio Program *This I Believe*, November 1953, 196.

4. *Markings*, 1956, 145.

5. DH letter to Erik Lindegren, 6 August 1961, KB.

6. *Markings*, 1955. 122.

7. *Markings*, 1955, 107 (trans. slightly revised). Sjöberg/Auden has the learned and interesting term "anamnesis" for Sw. *återfinnande*, translated here as "rediscovery." "Anamnesis" recalls New Testament Greek—Luke 22:19, where Jesus commands the disciples at the Last Supper to "do this in memory (anamnesis) of me." It also evokes the Platonic theory of knowledge as a remembering. I don't think we need to disregard either of these associations, but DH is re-

porting in this passage on direct experience, better reflected in simple language.

8. Ibid., 1956, 130–31.

9. DH letter to Eyvind Johnson, 31 January 1958, KB (trans. DvS).

10. Dayal (1), 302–3.

11. *Secretariat News*, 14 February 1958, 3–4.

12. *Markings*, 1955, 120.

13. Ibid., xx.

14. Ibid., 1957, 147.

15. Ibid., 1956, 134, citing Pound, Confucius, 173.

16. *Markings*, dated entry for Christmas Eve 1956, 143 (trans. slightly revised to conform with DH's original italics).

17. Pound, *Confucius*, 167–69.

18. Transcript of Meet the Press, 18 September 1955, KB.

19. *Markings* 1956, 133, citing Pound, *Confucius*, 135.

20. *PP II*, From New Year's Message as Broadcast over United Nations Radio, New York, 31 December 1953, 209.

21. *Markings*, 1955, 121.

22. Ibid., 1955, 112.

23. Ibid., 1957, 152.

24. Ibid., dated entry for 19–20 November 1955, 113.

25. Ibid., 1955, 111.

26. *Markings*, 1956, 129 (trans. slightly revised). Where DH has simply Sw. *öppenhet*, openness, Sjöberg/Auden has "openness to life"—logical but restrictive.

27. Ibid., dated entry for 4 August 1959, 174.

28. DH letter to Paul Badura-Skoda, 25 October 1960, KB (trans. from French by the author). DH's phrase "la célébration recueillie" is in part marvelously untranslatable. *Recueilli* means collected, gathered, contemplative—and not quite any of these things separately. For simplicity's sake, I've chosen "quiet."

29. Year-End Message of the Secretary-General, 22 December 1955, United Nations Archive.

30. *PP II*, Address at Inauguration of the Twenty-Fifth Anniversary of the Museum of Modern Art, New York, 19 October 1954, 375. For a discussion of DH's approach to art, see Lipsey, "Enlightened Patronage: Dag Hammarskjöld at the UN," in *An Art of Our Own*, 444–60.

Bibliography

Adams, Henry. *The Education of Henry Adams*. Edited by Ernest Samuels and Jayne N. Samuels. New York: Library of America, 1983.

African Centre for the Constructive Resolution of Disputes (ACCORD). *African Journal on Conflict Resolution*. Special issue, *Southern Africa —50 Years after Hammarskjöld* 11:1 (2011). Umhlanga Rocks, South Africa: ACCORD, 2011.

Ahlströhm, Göran, and Benny Carlson. "Hammarskjöld, Sweden and Bretton Woods." *Sveriges Riksbank Economic Review*. Special issue, *Dag Hammarskjöld 100th Anniversary* 2005:3, 50–77.

Alighieri, Dante. *The Divine Comedy: Inferno*. Translated by Charles S. Singleton. Princeton, NJ: Princeton University Press, 1970.

Alport, Lord. *The Sudden Assignment: Being a Record of Service in Central Africa during the Last Controversial Years of the Federation of Rhodesia and Nyasaland 1961–1963*. London: Hodder and Stoughton, 1965.

Amadi, Karl, and Michael H.-Froehlich. *Dag Hammarskjöld: His Death, Legacy and Vision—An Appeal / Dag Hammaskjöld: Sein Tod Vermächtnis Vision —ein Appel*. Basel, Switzerland: AAP-Verlag, 2011. English, German.

Amiel, Henri-Frédéric. *Fragments d'un journal intime*. 11th ed. 2 vols. Geneva: Georg, 1911.

Annan, Kofi. "Dag Hammarskjöld and the 21st Century." Lecture delivered 6 September 2001, at Uppsala University. Available as a booklet from the Dag Hammarskjöld Foundation and online at http://www.dhf.uu.se/pdffiler/Kofi%20Annan.pdf.

Appelqvist, Örjan. "Civil Servant or Politician? Dag Hammarskjöld's Role in Swedish Government Policy in the Forties." *Sveriges Riksbank Economic Review*. Special issue, *Dag Hammarskjöld 100th Anniversary* 2005:3, 33–49.

Ascoli, Max. "Dag Hammarskjöld." *The Reporter*, 12 October 1961, 12.

Ask, Sten, and Anna Mark-Jungkvist, ed. *The Adventure of Peace: Dag Hammarskjöld and the Future of the UN*. New York: Palgrave Macmillan, 2005.

Åström, Sverker. *Ögonblick*. Stockholm: Bonnier Alba, 1992.

Attar, Farid Ud-Din. *The Conference of the Birds*. Translated by C. S. Nott. Boulder, CO: Shambhala, 1954.

Attié, Caroline. *Struggle in the Levant: Lebanon in the 1950s*. London: Tauris, 2004.

Auden, W. H. "Dag Hammarskjöld." *Encounter* 17:5 (November 1961), 3–4.

Aulén, Gustaf. *Dag Hammarskjöld's White Book: An Analysis of* Markings. Philadelphia: Fortress, 1969.

Balandier, Georges. *Daily Life in the Kingdom of the Kongo: From the Sixteenth to the Eighteenth Century.* New York: Pantheon, 1968.

Barnes, Djuna. *The Antiphon.* Copenhagen: Green Integer, 2000.

Barros, James. *Office without Power: Secretary-General Sir Eric Drummond, 1919 –1933.* Oxford, England: Oxford University Press, 1979.

Barros, James. *Trygve Lie and the Cold War: The UN Secretary-General Pursues Peace, 1946–1953.* DeKalb: Northern Illinois University Press, 1989.

Bar-Zohar, Michael. *Ben-Gurion: A Biography.* Translated by Peretz Kidron. New York: Adama, 1977.

Bell, G. K. A., ed. *The Stockholm Conference 1925: Being the Official Report of the Universal Christian Conference on Life and Work Held in Stockholm, August 19–30, 1925.* London: Oxford University Press, 1926.

Ben-Gurion, David. *Memoirs: David Ben-Gurion.* Compiled by Thomas R. Bransten. Cleveland: World, 1970.

Bergson, Henri. *Creative Evolution.* Translated by Arthur Mitchell. Mineola, NY: Dover, 1998.

Bergson, Henri. *The Two Sources of Morality and Religion.* Translated by R. Ashley Audra and Cloudesley Brereton. Notre Dame, IN: University of Notre Dame Press, 1977.

Berridge, G. R. *Diplomacy: Theory and Practice.* 2nd ed. New York: Palgrave, 2002.

Berridge, G. R., and Alan James. *A Dictionary of Diplomacy.* 2nd ed. New York, Palgrave Macmillan, 2003.

Beskow, Bo. *Dag Hammarskjöld: Strictly Personal—A Portrait.* Garden City, NY: Doubleday, 1969.

Birnbaum, Karl E., ed. *Dag Hammarskjöld: Ungdomsårens vittnesbörd—brev och uppteckningar 1925–1931.* Stockholm: Kungl. Samfundet för utgivande av handskrifter rörande Skandinaviens historia, 2001.

Birnbaum, Karl E. *Den unge Dag Hammarskjölds inre värld—inblickar i en människas tillblivelse.* Ludvika, Sweden: Dualis, 1998.

Blakney, Raymond P., trans. *Meister Eckhart: A Modern Trnaslation.* New York: Harper & Row, 1941.

Blondeau, Anne-Marie, and Katia Buffetrille, ed. *Authenticating Tibet: Answers to China's 100 Questions*. Berkeley: University of California Press, 2008.

Blouin, Andrée. *My Country, Africa: Autobiography of the Black Pasionaria*. New York: Praeger, 1983.

Bregman, Ahron. *Israel's Wars: A History since 1947*. Oxon, England: Routledge, 2000.

Buber, Martin. *A Believing Humanism: My Testament, 1902–1965*. Translated and edited by Maurice Friedman. New York: Simon & Schuster, 1967.

Buber, Martin. *Between Man and Man*. Translated by Ronald Gregor Smith. New York: Macmillan, 1947.

Buber, Martin. *Ich und Du: Um ein Nachwort erweiterte Neuausgabe*. Heidelberg: Verlag Lambert Schneider, 1958.

Buber, Martin. *I and Thou*. Translated by Ronald Gregor Smith. 2nd ed. New York: Scribner's, 1958.

Buber, Martin. *I and Thou*. Translated by Walter Kaufmann. New York: Simon & Schuster, 1970.

Buber, Martin. *Pointing the Way*. Translated and edited by Maurice Friedman. New York: Harper & Row, 1957.

Bucknell, Katherine, and Nicholas Jenkins, ed. *"In Solitude, for Company": W. H. Auden after 1940*. Oxford, England: Clarendon, 1995.

Bureau of His Holiness the Dalai Lama. *Tibet in the United Nations: 1950–1961*. New Delhi: Bureau of His Holiness the Dalai Lama, n.d.

Burns, Lt.-Gen. E. L. M. *Between Arab and Israeli*. New York: Obolensky, 1963.

Butcher, Tim. *Blood River: A Journey to Africa's Broken Heart*. London: Chatto & Windus, 2007.

Büttner, Herman, trans. *Meister Eckhart Schriften*. Jena, Germany: Eugen Diederichs, 1943.

Césaire, Aimé. *Une saison au Congo*. Paris: Seuil, 1973.

Church of England. *The Book of Common Prayer, and Administration of the Sacraments, and Other Rites and Ceremonies of the Church, according to the Use of the Church of England; Together with the Psalter or Psalms of David, Pointed as They Are to Be Sung or Said in Churches*. Cambridge, England: Bentham, 1762.

Clausen, Oliver. "Clues to the Hammarskjöld Riddle." *New York Times,* 28 June 1964.

Colledge, Edmund, trans. *Meister Eckhart: The Essential Sermons, Commentaries, Treatises, and Defense.* New York: Paulist, 1981.

Colvin, Ian. *The Rise and Fall of Moise Tshombe.* London: Frewin, 1968.

Conrad, Joseph. *Heart of Darkness.* New York: Penguin, 1999.

Cordier, Andrew W., and Kenneth L. Maxwell, ed. *Paths to World Order.* New York: Columbia University Press, 1967.

Cordier, Andrew W., and Max Harrelson, ed. *Public Papers of the Secretaries-General of the United Nations.* Vol. 7, *U Thant 1965–1967.* New York: Columbia University Press, 1976.

Cordier, Andrew W., and Wilder Foote, ed. *Public Papers of the Secretaries-General of the United Nations.* Vol. 1, *Trygve Lie 1946–1953.* New York: Columbia University Press, 1969.

Cordier, Andrew W., and Wilder Foote, ed. *Public Papers of the Secretaries-General of the United Nations. Vol. 2, Dag Hammarskjöld 1953–1956.* New York: Columbia University Press, 1972.

Cordier, Andrew W., and Wilder Foote, ed. *Public Papers of the Secretaries-General of the United Nations.* Vol. 3, *Dag Hammarskjöld 1956–1957.* New York: Columbia University Press, 1974.

Cordier, Andrew W., and Wilder Foote, ed. *Public Papers of the Secretaries-General of the United Nations.* Vol. 4, *Dag Hammarskjöld 1958–1960.* New York: Columbia University Press, 1974.

Cordier, Andrew W., and Wilder Foote, ed. *Public Papers of the Secretaries-General of the United Nations.* Vol. 5, *Dag Hammarskjöld 1960–1961.* New York: Columbia University Press, 1975.

Cordier, Andrew W., and Max Harrelson, ed. *Public Papers of the Secretaries-General of the United Nations.* Vol. 6, *U Thant 1961–1964.* New York: Columbia University Press, 1976.

Cordier, Andrew W., and Wilder Foote, ed. T*he Quest for Peace: The Dag Hammarskjöld Memorial Lectures.* New York: Columbia University Press, 1965.

Crosscurrents Press. *Khrushchev in New York: A Documentary Record of Nikita S. Khrushchev's Trip to New York, September 19th to October 13th, 1960, Including All His Speeches and Proposals to the United Nations and Major Addresses and News Conferences.* New York: Crosscurrents Press, 1960.

Dag Hammarskjöld Foundation. *Critical Currents: Beyond Diplomacy: Perspectives on Dag Hammarskjöld. Occasional Paper Series,* no. 2. Uppsala, Sweden: Dag

Hammarskjöld Foundation, 2008.

Dag Hammarskjöld Foundation. *Critical Currents: Can We Save True Dialogue in an Age of Mistrust? The Encounter of Dag Hammarskjöld and Martin Buber.* Occasional Paper Series, no. 8. Uppsala, Sweden: Dag Hammarskjöld Foundation, 2010.

Daun, Åke. *Swedish Mentality.* Translated by Jan Teeland. University Park, PA: Pennsylvania State University Press, 1989.

Davenport-Hines, Richard. *Auden.* New York: Pantheon, 1995.

Davies, Oliver, trans. *Meister Eckhart: Selected Writings.* London: Penguin, 1994.

Dayal, Rajeshwar. *A Life of Our Times.* New Delhi: Orient Longman, 1998.

Dayal, Rajeshwar. *Mission for Hammarskjold: The Congo Crisis.* Princeton, NJ: Princeton University Press, 1976.

Development Dialogue, 1987:1. Articles relevant to DH, passim.

Development Dialogue 1987:2. Articles relevant to DH, passim.

Development Dialogue 2001:1. Articles relevant to DH, passim.

Development Dialogue, no. 57, December 2011. Articles relevant to DH, passim.

Devlin, Larry. *Chief of Station, Congo: A Memoir of 1960–67.* Cambridge, MA: Perseus, 2007.

de Gaulle, Charles. *Lettres, Notes et Carnets, Juin 1958–Décembre 1960.* Paris: Plon, 1985.

De Witte, Ludo. *The Assassination of Lumumba.* Translated by Ann Wright and Renée Fenby. London: Verso, 2001.

Dil, Anwar, ed. *On This Earth Together: Ahmed S. Bokhari at UN, 1950–1958.* San Diego, Bookservice, 1994.

Doyle, A. Conan. *The Crime of the Congo.* 1909. Honolulu: University Press of the Pacific, 2004.

Dugauquier, D. P. *Congo Cauldron.* London: Jarrolds, 1961.

Eden, Anthony. *The Memoirs of Sir Anthony Eden: Full Circle.* London: Cassell, 1960.

Edgerton, Robert B. *The Troubled Heart of Africa: A History of the Congo.* New York: St. Martin's, 2002

Eisenhower, Dwight D. *Waging Peace, 1956–1961; The White House Years.* Garden City, NY: Doubleday, 1965.

"The Empty Chair of Mr. U.N." *Life*, 29 September 1961, 42–53.

Engström, Albert. *Twelve Tales by Albert Engström.* Translated by Harold Borland. London: Harrap, 1949.

Erling, Bernhard. *A Reader's Guide to Dag Hammarskjöld's* Waymarks. Translation with a commentary. St. Peter, MN: privately published, 1999. Available online at www.dhf.uu.se.

Falkman, Kai, ed. *Ringar Efter Orden— femton röster kring: Dag Hammarskjölds* Vägmärken. Lund, Sweden: Ellerströms, 2005.

Falkman, Kai. "Signposts in the Wrong Direction: W. H. Auden's misinterpretations of Dag Hammarskjöld's *Markings.*" *Times Literary Supplement,* 10 September 1999, 14–15.

Falkman, Kai. *A String Untouched: Dag Hammarskjöld's Life in Haiku and Photographs.* Winchester, VA: Red Moon, 2006.

Heinz-Dietrich Fischer, ed. *The Pulitzer Prize Archive.* Vol. 1, *International Reporting 1928–1985.* Munich: K. G. Saur, 1987.

Foote, Wilder, ed. *Servant of Peace: A Selection of the Speeches and Statements of Dag Hammarskjöld, Secretary-General of the United Nations, 1953–1961.* New York: Harper & Row, 1962.

Friedman, Maurice S., ed. *Pointing the Way: Collected Essays by Martin Buber.* New York: Schocken, 1974.

Fröhlich, Manuel. "A Fully Integrated Vision: Politics and the Arts in the Dag Hammarskjöld–Barbara Hepworth Correspondence." *Development Dialogue,* 2001:1, 17–57. Available online at www.dhf.uu.se.

Fröhlich, Manuel. *Political Ethics and the United Nations: Dag Hammarskjöld as Secretary-General.* London: Routledge, 2008.

Fröhlich, Manuel. "'The Unknown Assignation': Dag Hammarskjöld in the Papers of George Ivan Smith." *Critical Currents,* no. 2, March 2008, 9–35. Available online at www.dhf.uu.se.

Fröhlich, Manuel, Helmut Klumpjan, and Henning Melber. *Dag Hammarskjöld (1905–1961): Für eine friedliche Welt—Ideen und Impulse des zweiten UN-Generalsekretärs.* Frankfurt am Main, Germany: Brandes & Apsel, 2011.

Gavshon, Arthur L. *The Mysterious Death of Dag Hammarskjöld.* New York: Walker, 1962.

Gérard-Libois, Jules, Jean Kestergat, Jacques Vanderlinden, Benoît Verhaegen, and Jean-Claude Willame. *Congo 1960: Échec d'une décolonisation.* Edited by André Versaille. Brussels: GRIP, 2010.

Giampiccoli, Franco. *Dag Hammarskjöld: Un credente alla guida dell'ONU.* Turin, Italy: Claudiana, 2005.

Glatzer, Nahum N., and Paul Mendes-Flohr, ed. *The Letters of Martin Buber: A Life of Dialogue.* Translated by Richard and Clara Winston and Harry Zohn. New York: Schocken, 1991.

Glubb, John Bagot. *A Soldier with the Arabs.* London: Hodder & Stoughton, 1957.

Goldstein, Melvyn C. *A History of Modern Tibet.* 2 vols. Berkeley: University of California Press, 1989, 2007.

Gracq, Julien. *Le rivage des Syrtes.* Paris: José Corti, 1951.

Grundsten, Claes. *Swedish Wilderness: The Mountain World of Dag Hammarskjöld.* Stockholm: Bokförlaget Max Ström, 2007.

Gullberg, Hjalmar. *Dödsmask och lustgård.* Stockholm: Norstedt & Söners, 1952.

Gullberg, Hjalmar. *Fem kornbröd och två fiskar.* Stockholm: Norstedt & Söners, 1948.

Gullberg, Hjalmar. *Gentleman, Single, Refined and Selected Poems, 1937–1959.* Translated by Judith Moffett. Baton Rouge: Louisiana State University Press,1979.

Gustafsson, Lisbeth, ed. *Möten med Dag Hammarskjölds* Vägmärken: *En bok för reflektion och samtal.* Örebro, Sweden: Cordia, 2005.

Gyatso, Tenzin. *Freedom in Exile: The Autobiography of the Dalai Lama.* New York: Harper, 1990.

Hägerström, Axel. *Philosophy and Religion.* Translated by Robert T. Sandin. London: Allen & Unwin, 1964.

Haldar, Satwana. *T. S. Eliot: A Twenty-first Century View.* New Delhi: Atlantic, 2005.

Hammarskjöld, Dag. *Castle Hill.* Uppsala, Sweden: Dag Hammarskjöld Foundation, 1977.

Hammarskjöld, Dag. *Från Sarek till Haväng.* Stockholm: Svenska Turistföreningen, 1962.

Hammarskjöld, Dag. *Jalons.* Translated by C. G. Bjurström and Philippe Dumaine. Paris: Plon, 1966.

Hammarskjöld, Dag. "Kameran har lärt mig att se." Foto: *Tidskrift för Foto och Film,* no. 12, 1958, 21ff.

Hammarskjöld, Dag. *Markings.* Translated by Leif Sjöberg and W. H. Auden. New York: Knopf, 1964.

Hammarskjöld, Dag. "A New Look at Everest." *National Geographic* 119:1 (January 1961), 87–93.

Hammarskjöld, Dag. *To Speak for the World: Speeches and Statements by Dag Hammarskjöld.* Edited by Kai Falkman. Stockholm: Atlantis, 2005.

Hammarskjöld, Dag. *Tracce di cammino.* Translated by Guido Dotti. Magnano, Italy: Qiqajon, 2005.

Hammarskjöld, Dag. *Vägmärken.* Stockholm: Bonniers, 1963.

Hammarskjöld, Dag. *Zeichen am Weg: Das spirituelle Tagebuch des UN-Generalsekretärs.* Translated by Anton Graf Knyphausen, revised, with a new introduction by Manuel Fröhlich. Stuttgart, Germany: Freies Geistesleben & Urachhaus, 2011.

"The Hammarskjöld Myth: Hammarskjöld's Intimate Diary Must Be Looked upon as a Central Document in Forming the Judgment of His Achievement." *Dagens Nyheter*, 10 November 1963.

Heikal, Mohamed Hassanein. *The Cairo Documents: The Inside Story of Nasser and His Relationship with World Leaders, Rebels, and Statesmen.* Garden City, NY: Doubleday, 1973.

Heikensten, Lars, and Björn Hasselgren. "Foreword." *Sveriges Riksbank Economic Review.* Special issue, Dag Hammarskjöld 100th Anniversary 2005:5–9.

Heinz, G., and H. Donnay. *Lumumba Patrice: Les cinquante derniers jours de sa vie.* Brussels: CRISP, 1966.

Henderson, Harold G. *An Introduction to Haiku: An Anthology of Poems and Poets from Bashō to Shiki.* Garden City, NY: Doubleday, 1958.

Henley, Mary-Lynn, and Henning Melber, ed. *Dag Hammarskjöld Remembered: A Collection of Personal Memories.* Uppsala, Sweden: Dag Hammarskjöld Foundation, 2011.

Henry, Charles P. *Ralph Bunche: Model Negro or American Other?* New York: New York University Press, 1999.

Henry, Charles P., ed. *Ralph J. Bunche: Selected Speeches and Writings.* Ann Arbor: University of Michigan Press, 1995.

Hergé (pseud. Remi, Georges). *Archives Hergé.* Vol. 1. Tournai, Belgium: Casterman, 1973.

Hill, Robert A., and Edmond J. Keller, ed. *Trustee for the Human Community: Ralph J. Bunche, the United Nations, and the Decolonization of Africa.* Athens: Ohio University Press, 2010

Hilson, Mary. *The Nordic Model: Scandinavia since 1945.* London: Reaktion,

2008.

Hochschild, Adam. *King Leopold's Ghost: A Story of Greed, Terror, and Heroism in Colonial Africa.* New York: Mariner, 1999.

Holmqvist, Stig. *Visions of a Secretary-General: Dag Hammarskjöld and the United Nations 1953–1961.* Lidingo, Sweden: Athenafilm, 2005.

Hoskyns, Catherine. *The Congo since Independence: January 1960–December 1961.* London: Oxford University Press, 1965.

Hoskyns, Catherine. "Sources for a Study of the Congo since Independence." *Journal of Modern African Studies* 1:3 (1961), 373–82.

Hovde, Carl F. "The Dag Hammarskjöld–John Steinbeck Correspondence." *Development Dialogue*, 1997:1–2, 97–129.

Jordan, Robert S., ed. *Dag Hammarskjöld Revisited: The UN Secretary-General as a Force in World Politics.* Durham, NC: Carolina Academic Press, 1983.

Kalb, Madeleine G. *The Congo Cables: The Cold War in Africa—from Eisenhower to Kennedy.* New York: Macmillan, 1982.

Kanza, Thomas. *Evolution and Revolution in Africa.* London: Rex Collings, 1971.

Kanza, Thomas. *The Rise and Fall of Patrice Lumumba: Conflict in the Congo.* Rochester, VT: Schenkman, 1972.

Kanza, Thomas. *Sans rancune.* Paris: L'Harmattan, 2006.

Kashamura, Anicet. *De Lumumba aux colonels.* Paris: Buchet/Chastel, 1966.

Kelen, Emery. *Hammarskjöld.* New York: Putnam, 1966.

Kennedy, Paul. *The Parliament of Man: The Past, Present, and Future of the United Nations.* New York: Random House, 2006.

Kille, Kent J. *From Manager to Visionary: The Secretary-General of the United Nations.* New York: Palgrave Macmillan, 2006.

Khrushchev, Nikita. *Khrushchev Remembers: The Last Testament.* Translated and edited by Strobe Talbott. Boston: Little, Brown, 1974.

Küng, Hans. *Why I Am Still a Christian.* Nashville, TN: Abingdon, 1987.

Labba, Andreas. *Anta: Mémoires d'un Lapon.* Translated by Vincent Fournier. Paris: Plon, 1989. First published Stockholm: Bonniers, 1969.

Lacouture, Jean. *Une adolescence du siècle: Jacques Rivière et la NRF.* Paris: Gallimard, 1994.

Lagercrantz, Olof. "Hammarskjöld, Jesus, and the Truth." *Dagens Nyheter*, 18 October 1961.

Lambert, Lars. *Dag Hammarskjölds Uppsala*. Uppsala, Sweden: Kornhuset, 2005.

Landsberg, Hans. "Time for Choosing: Dag Hammarskjöld and the Riksbank in the Thirties," *Sveriges Riksbank Economic Review*. Special issue, *Dag Hammarskjöld 100th Anniversary* 2005:3, 13–32.

Lash, Joseph P. *Dag Hammarskjöld: Custodian of the Brushfire Peace*. Garden City, NY: Doubleday, 1961.

Leach, Henry Goddard, ed. *American Swedish Historical Museum: Yearbook 1962*. Bridgeport, PA: Chancellor, 1962.

Leavitt, David. *The Man Who Knew Too Much: Alan Turing and the Invention of the Computer*. New York: W. W. Norton, 2006.

Levine, I. E. *Dag Hammarskjöld: Champion of World Peace*. New York: Messner, 1962.

Lie, Trygve. *In the Cause of Peace: Seven Years with the United Nations*. New York: Macmillan, 1954.

Lin, Nancy T., trans. *In Quest: Poems of Chou En-lai*. Hong Kong: Joint, 1979.

Lindbeck, Assar. "Dag Hammarskjöld as Economist and Government Official." *Sveriges Riksbank Economic Review*. Special issue, *Dag Hammarskjöld 100th Anniversary* 2005:3, 9–12.

Lindegren, Erik. *Dag Hammarskjöld*. Stockholm: Norstedts, 1962.

Linnér, Sture, and Sverker Åström. *UN Secretary-General Hammarskjöld: Reflections and Personal Experiences*. Uppsala, Sweden: Dag Hammarskjöld Foundation, 2008.

Lippmann, Walter. *Public Persons*. Edited by Gilbert A. Harrison. New York: Liveright, 1976.

Lipsey, Roger. *An Art of Our Own: The Spiritual in Twentieth-Century Art*. Boston and Shaftesbury: Shambhala Publications, 1988.

Lipsey, Roger. "Blessed Uneasiness: Dag Hammarskjöld on Conscience." *Parabola* 22:3 (August 1997), 47–57.

Lipsey, Roger. "Dag Hammarskjöld and *Markings*: A Reconsideration." *Spiritus* 11:3 (Spring 2011), 84–103.

Lipsey, Roger. "Desiring Peace: A Meditation on Why Dag Hammarskjöld Matters." *Parabola* 35:3 (Fall 2010), 20–29.

Lipsey, Roger. "For the Other Mahatma." *Parabola* 21:3 (August 1996), 12–17.

Lipsey, Roger. "Freedom in the Midst of Action: United Nations Leader Dag Hammarskjöld and Buddhism." *Tricycle,* Fall 2012, 80–83.

Little, Marie-Noëlle, *Alexis Leger, Dag Hammarskjöld: Correspondance,*

1955–1961. Paris: Gallimard, 1993.

Little, Marie-Noëlle. *The Knight and the Troubadour: Dag Hammarskjöld and Ezra Pound.* Uppsala, Sweden: Dag Hammarskjöld Foundation, 2011. Available online at www.dhf.uu.se.

Little, Marie-Noëlle. *The Poet and the Diplomat: The Correspondence of Dag Hammarskjöld and Alexis Leger.* Syracuse, NY: Syracuse University Press, 2001.

Lloyd, Selwyn. *Suez 1956: A Personal Account.* New York: Mayflower, 1978.

Lumumba, Patrice. *Congo, My Country.* New York: Praeger, 1962.

"Lumumba's Legacy: Troubles All Over." *Life,* 24 February 1961, 16–21.

Lundahl, Anders. Dag Hammarskjöld: *En vilja bortom stigarna.* Nora, Sweden: Nya Doxa, 2006.

Lundquist, Gösta. *Lappland.* With a foreword by Dag Hammarskjöld. Stockholm: Bonniers, 1954. Translated by Ebba de Dardel as *Lapland: Reindeer, Lapps and Midnight Sun.* Edited by Olof Thaning. Stockholm: Bonniers, 1960.

Mahoney, Richard D. *JFK: Ordeal in Africa.* New York: Oxford University Press, 1983.

Major Addresses, Statements and Press Conferences of General Charles de Gaulle, 19 May 1958–31 January 1964. New York: French Embassy.

Malloch-Brown, Mark. *The Unfinished Global Revolution: The Pursuit of a New International Politics.* New York: Penguin, 2011.

Marin, Lou. "Can We Save True Dialogue in an Age of Mistrust? The Encounter of Dag Hammarskjöld and Martin Buber." *Critical Currents* no. 8, January 2010, 59–60.

McCann, Lucy. *Catalogue of the Papers of George Ivan Smith, 1888–1995.* Bodleian Library, University of Oxford. Available online at www.bodley.ox.ac.uk/dept/scwmss/.

Melber, Henning, ed. *Dag Hammarskjöld and Global Governance.* Uppsala, Sweden: Dag Hammarskjöld Foundation, 2011.

Melber, Henning, ed. *The Ethics of Dag Hammarskjöld.* Uppsala, Sweden: Dag Hammarskjöld Foundation, 2010.

Meredith, Martin. *The Fate of Africa: A History of Fifty Years of Independence.* New York: Perseus, 2005.

Merton, Thomas. *Day of a Stranger.* Salt Lake City, UT: Gibbs M. Smith, 1981.

Merton, Thomas. *Learning to Love: The Journals of Thomas Merton. Vol. 6, 1966–*

1967. Edited by Christine M. Bochen. San Francisco: HarperSanFrancisco, 1997.

Mindus, Patricia. *A Real Mind: The Life and Work of Axel Hägerström*. Dordrecht, Netherlands: Springer, 2009.

Mögle-Stadel, Stephan. Dag Hammarskjöld: *Visionary for the Future of Humanity*. Capetown: Novalis, 2002.

"Monsieur 'H' mort pour l'O.N.U." *Paris Match,* 30 September 1961, 56–61.

Montgomery, Elizabeth Rider. *Dag Hammarskjöld: Peacemaker for the UN*. Champaign, IL: Garrard, 1973.

Morris, Benny. *Righteous Victims: A History of the Zionist-Arab Conflict, 1881–2001*. Expanded ed. New York: Vintage, 2001.

Nasser, Gamal Abdel. *The Philosophy of the Revolution*. Washington, DC: Public Affairs Press, 1955.

Ndaywel é Nziem, Isidore. *Histoire du Zaïre: De l'héritage ancien à l'âge contemporain*. Louvain-la-Neuve, Belgium: Duculot, 1997.

Neff, Donald. *Warriors at Suez: Eisenhower Takes America into the Middle East*. New York: Simon & Schuster, 1981.

Nelson, Paul R. *Courage of Faith: Dag Hammarskjöld's Way in Quest of Negotiated Peace, Reconciliation and Meaning*. Frankfurt am Main, Germany: Peter Lang, 2007.

Nichols, David A. *Eisenhower 1956: The President's Year of Crisis—Suez and the Brink of War*. New York: Simon & Schuster, 2011.

Nutting, Anthony. *Nasser*. New York: Dutton, 1972.

Nutting, Anthony. *No End of a Lesson: The Story of Suez*. London: Constable, 1967.

Nzongola-Ntalaja, Georges. *The Congo from Leopold to Kabila: A People's History*. New York: St. Martin's, 2003.

O'Brien, Conor Cruise. *Memoir: My Life and Themes*. New York: Cooper Square, 2000.

O'Brien, Conor Cruise. *Murderous Angels: A Political Tragedy and Comedy in Black and White*. Boston: Little, Brown, 1968.

O'Brien, Conor Cruise. *To Katanga and Back: A UN Case History*. London: Hutchinson, 1962.

Oshinsky, David M. *A Conspiracy so Immense: The World of Joe McCarthy*. New York: Oxford University Press, 2005.

"Other Side." *New York Times*, 25 April 1965.

Otto, Rudolf. *The Idea of the Holy*. Translated by John W. Harvey. London: Oxford University Press, 1958.

Pandit, Vijaya Lakshmi. *The Scope of Happiness: A Personal Memoir*. New York: Crown, 1979.

Pearlman, Moshe. *Ben Gurion Looks Back: In Talks with Moshe Pearlman*. London: Weidenfeld & Nicolson, 1965.

Pearson, Lester B. *Mike: The Memoirs of the Right Honourable Lester B. Pearson*. Edited by John Munro and Alex I. Inglis. 3 vols. Toronto: University of Toronto Press, 1972–1975.

Perse, Saint-John. *Chronique / Krönika*. Translated by Dag Hammarskjöld. Stockholm: Bonniers, 1960.

Perse, Saint-John. *Oeuvres complètes*. Paris: Gallimard, 1972.

Peyrefitte, Roger. *Tableaux de chasse ou la vie extraordinaire de Fernand Legros*. Paris: Albin Michel, 1976.

Pineau, Christian. *1956 Suez*. Paris: Laffont, 1976.

Pohl, Frances K. *Ben Shahn, with Ben Shahn's Writings*. San Francisco: Pomegranate, 1993.

Pound, Ezra. *The Cantos of Ezra Pound*. New York: New Directions, 1970.

Pound, Ezra, trans. *Confucius: The Great Digest; The Unwobbling Pivot; The Analects*. New York: New Directions, 1951.

Rembe, Rolf, and Anders Hellberg. *Midnatt i Kongo: Dag Hammarskjölds förlorade seger*. Stockholm: Bokförlaget Atlantis, 2011.

Rikhye, Indar Jit, Michael Harbottle, and Bjørn Egge. *The Thin Blue Line: International Peacekeeping and Its Future*. New Haven, CT: Yale University Press, 1974.

Rikhye, Indar Jit. *Trumpets and Tumults: The Memoirs of a Peacekeeper*. New Delhi: Manohar, 2002.

Rivière, Jacques. *A la trace de Dieu*. Paris: Gallimard, 1925.

Roberts, Ivor, ed. *Satow's Diplomatic Practice*. 6th ed. Oxford, England: Oxford University Press, 2009.

Röhlin, Ruth, and Röhlin, Karl-Heinz. *Dag Hammarskjöld: Mystiker und Politiker*. Munich: Kösel, 2005.

Rosenthal, A. M. "New U.N. Secretary Cautious On Issues." *New York Times*, 10 April 1953.

Ross, Lillian. "Dag Hammarskjöld." *The New Yorker*, 30 September 1961, 35.

Saunders, Chris. "Dag Hammarskjöld and Apartheid South Africa." *Development Dialogue* 57, December 2011, 61–76.

Sauvage, Léo. "M. Hammarskjold quitte la séance de l'ONU et nous parle des bienfaits de la Poésie en diplomatie." *Le Figaro*, 30 October 1960.

Schlesinger, Stephen C. *Act of Creation: The Founding of the United Nations—a Story of Superpowers, Secret Agents, Wartime Allies and Enemies, and Their Quest for a Peaceful World.* Boulder, CO: Perseus, 2003.

Schrecker, Ellen, ed. *The Age of McCarthyism: A Brief History with Documents.* 2nd ed. Boston: Bedford/St. Martin's, 2002.

Schweitzer, Albert. *The Mystery of the Kingdom of God: The Secret of Jesus' Messiahship and Passion.* Translated by Walter Lowrie. Amherst, NY: Prometheus, 1985.

Schweitzer, Albert. *Out of My Life and Thought: An Autobiography.* 60th anniversary edition. Baltimore: Johns Hopkins University Press, 2009.

Schweitzer, Albert. *The Quest of the Historical Jesus.* Edited by John Bowden. Minneapolis: Fortress, 2001.

Scott, Franklin D. *Sweden: The Nation's History.* Carbondale: Southern Illinois University Press, 1988.

Sellström, Tor. "Hammarskjöld and Apartheid South Africa: Mission Unaccomplished." *African Journal on Conflict Resolution* 11:1 (2011), 35–62. Available online at www.accord.org.za.

Settel, T. S., ed. *The Light and the Rock: The Vision of Dag Hammarskjöld.* New York: Dutton, 1966.

Sjöberg, Leif. "Translating with W. H. Auden: Gunnar Ekelöf 's last poems," in Elinor Shaffer, ed., *Comparative Criticism: A Yearbook,* Cambridge: Cambridge University Press, 185–97.

Shakya, Tsering. *The Dragon in the Land of the Snows: A History of Modern Tibet since 1947.* New York: Columbia University Press, 1999.

Sharpe, Eric J. *Nathan Söderblom and the Study of Religion.* Chapel Hill, NC: University of North Carolina Press, 1990.

Síocháin, Séamas Ó, and Michael O'Sullivan, ed. *The Eyes of Another Race: Roger Casement's Congo Report and 1903 Diary.* Dublin: University College Dublin Press, 2003.

Snow, C. P. *Variety of Men.* New York: Scribner, 1966.

Soby, James Thrall. *Ben Shahn Paintings.* New York: Braziller, 1964.

Söderberg, Sten. *Hammarskjöld: A Pictorial Biography.* New York: Viking, 1962.

Söderblom, Nathan. *Christian Fellowship, or the United Life and Work of Christendom*. New York: Revell, 1923.

Spaas, Lieve. *How Belgium Colonized the Mind of the Congo: Seeking the Memory of an African People*. Lewiston, NY: Edwin, 2007.

Steinbeck, Elaine, and Robert Wallsten, ed. *Steinbeck: A Life in Letters*. New York: Viking, 1975.

Stolpe, Sven. *Dag Hammarskjöld: A Spiritual Portrait*. Translated by Naomi Walford. New York: Scribner, 1966.

Suffran, Michel. *Jacques Rivière, ou la conversion à la clarté*. Paris: Wesmael-Charlier, 1967.

Sundkler, Bengt. *Nathan Söderblom: His Life and Work*. Lund, Sweden: Gleerups, 1968.

Svegfors, Mats. *Dag Hammarskjöld: Den Förste Moderne Svensken*. Stockholm: Norstedts, 2005.

Svenska Folkets Historia. *Dag Hammarskjöld: En minnesbok, del. 1*. Malmö, Sweden: Världslitteraturens, 1961.

Sveriges Riksbank. *Sveriges Riksbank Economic Review*. Special issue, *Dag Hammarskjöld 100th Anniversary* 2005:3. Stockholm: Sveriges Riksbank, 2005.

Talbott, Strobe, trans. and ed. *Khrushchev Remembers*. Boston: Little, Brown, 1970.

Talbott, Strobe, trans. and ed. *Khrushchev Remembers: The Last Testament*. Boston: Little, Brown, 1974.

Thant, U. *View from the UN: The Memoirs of U Thant*. Garden City, NY: Doubleday, 1978.

Tharoor, Shashi. *The Elephant, the Tiger, and the Cell Phone: Reflections on India —The Emerging 21st-Century Power*. New York: Arcade, 2008.

Thelin, Bengt. *Dag Hammarskjöld: Barnet, Skolpojken, Studenten*. Stockholm: Carlssons, 2005.

Thelin, Bengt. *Dag Hammarskjöld: FN-chefen och människan*. Stockholm: Carlssons, 2010.

Thiong'o, Ngũgĩ wa. *Something Torn and New: An African Renaissance*. New York: Perseus, 2009.

Thomas à Kempis. *L'Imitation de Jésus-Christ*. Translated by Sieur de Beuil, Prieur de Saint-Val. Paris: 1761.

Thorpe, D. R. *Selwyn Lloyd*. London: Cape, 1989.

Torén, Gunnel, compiler. *Dag Hammarskjöld on the 50th Anniversary of His Death: A Compilation Based on the Collections of the Dag Hammarskjöld Library, Uppsala.* Uppsala, Sweden: Dag Hammarskjöld Library and Dag Hammarskjöld Foundation, 2011.

Trinquier, Colonel, Jacques Duchemin, and Jacques Le Bailly. *Notre guerre au Katanga.* Paris: Pensée Moderne, 1963.

Turconi, Angelo, François Neyt. *Infini Congo / Eternal Congo.* Milan: Silvana Editoriale, 2010.

Turner, Barry. *Suez 1956: The Inside Story of the First Oil War.* London: Hodder & Stoughton, 2007.

Twain, Mark. *King Leopold's Soliloquy: A Defense of His Congo Rule.* Boston: Warren, 1905.

United Nations. Oral History Collection of the United Nations, Dag Hammarskjöld Library. Multiple online interviews and interviewees with relevance to DH. Available online at: http://www.unmultimedia.org/oralhistory/. (The frequently cited Urquhart interviews may no longer be available online.)

United Nations. *The Unveiling of "Single Form" by Barbara Hepworth, Gift of Jacob Blaustein after a Wish of Dag Hammarskjöld.* New York: United Nations, 1964.

United Nations General Assembly. *Report of the Commission of Investigation into the Conditions and Circumstances Resulting in the Tragic Death of Mr. Dag Hammarskjöld and of Members of the Party Accompanying Him,* 26 October 1962. A/RES/1759. Available online at http://www.unhcr.org/refworld/docid/3b00f06b6a.html

United Nations General Assembly Official Records. *Resolutions Adopted by the General Assembly during Its Fourth Emergency Special Session, 17–19 September 1960.*

"United Nations: Arms & the Man." *Time,* 26 November 1956, 27–33.

"United Nations: Battlefield of Peace." *Time,* 29 September 1961, 21.

"United Nations: Quiet Man in a Hot Spot." *Time,* 22 August 1960, 18–22.

"United Nations: World on Trial." *Time,* 27 June 1955, 20–24.

United States Senate (Church Committee). *Alleged Assassination Plots Involving Foreign Leaders.* Senate Report No. 94-465. Washington, DC: GPO, 1975.

Urquhart, Brian. *Hammarskjold.* New York: Knopf, 1972.

Urquhart, Brian. *A Life in Peace and War.* New York: Harper & Row, 1987.

Urquhart, Brian. *Ralph Bunche: An American Life.* New York: Norton, 1993.

Urquhart, Brian. "The Still Point." *The New Yorker,* 31 October 1964, 232–44.

Van Dusen, Henry P. *Dag Hammarskjöld: The Statesman and His Faith.* New York: Harper & Row, 1967.

Van Lierde, Jean, ed. *Lumumba Speaks: The Speeches and Writings of Patrice Lumumba, 1958–1961.* With an introduction by Jean-Paul Sartre. Translated by Helen R. Lane. Boston: Little, Brown, 1972.

Van Ruysbroek, Jan. *The Spiritual Espousals.* Translated by Eric College. New York: Harper, 1947.

Varble, Derek. *The Suez Crisis 1956. Essential Histories.* Oxford, England: Osprey, 2003.

Vargo, Marc E. *Noble Lives: Biographical Portraits of Three Remarkable Gay Men—Glenway Wescott, Aaron Copland, and Dag Hammarskjöld.* Binghamton, NY: Haworth, 2005.

Von Horn, Carl. *Soldiering for Peace.* New York: McKay, 1966.

Walasek, Helena, ed. *Punch Goes to War 1939–1945.* London: Prion, 2010.

Waley, Arthur. *The Way and Its Power: A Study of the Tao Të Ching and Its Place in Chinese Thought.* London: Allen & Unwin, 1949.

Welensky, Roy. *Welensky's 4000 Days: The Life and Death of the Federation of Rhodesia and Nyasaland.* London: Collins, 1964.

Wenqian, Gao. *Zhou Enlai: The Last Perfect Revolutionary.* Translated by Peter Rand and Lawrence R. Sullivan. New York: Perseus, 2007.

Wigforss, Ernst. *Minnen I – Före 1914.* Translated by Daniel von Sydow. Stockholm: Tidens, 1950.

Willers, Uno, ed. *Dag Hammarskjöld: En minnesbok.* Stockholm: Bonniers, 1961.

Williams, Susan. *Who Killed Hammarskjöld? The UN, the Cold War and White Supremacy in Africa.* London: Hurst, 2011.

Wrong, Michela. *In the Footsteps of Mr. Kurtz: Living on the Brink of Disaster in Mobutu's Congo.* New York: HarperCollins, 2001.

Zacher, Mark W. *Dag Hammarskjöld's United Nations.* Edited by Leland M. Goodrich and William T. R. Fox. New York: Columbia University Press, 1970.

Acknowledgments to Rights Holders

Every effort has been made to contact rights holders.

Literary and photographic documents publicly available in the Swedish National Library (Kungliga biblioteket), Stockholm, are published in this book in conformity with the Swedish Copyright Act, Chapter 2, Article 22.

Columbia University Press, publisher of the Public Papers of Dag Hammarskjöld, does not assert copyright over the wealth of United Nations documents on which this book draws. The author nonetheless wishes to express most sincere thanks for access to the documents collected in the meticulous editions issued by Columbia University Press.

Grateful thanks are due to publishers, archives, and estates for permission to cite from sources crucial to the documentation of this book:

Markings, trans. W. H. Auden and Leif Sjöberg (New York: Knopf, 1964); translation copyright © 1964, copyright renewed 1992 by Alfred A. Knopf, a division of Random House, Inc., and Faber & Faber Ltd. Used by permission of Alfred A. Knopf, a division of Random House, Inc.

Brian Urquhart, *Hammarskjold* (New York: Knopf, 1972); used by permission of Curtis Brown Ltd.

For certain correspondence of W. H. Auden and Andrew W. Cordier: The Harry Ransom Center, Austin, Texas ; the Auden material is reproduced with the kind permission of the Estate of W. H. Auden.

For access to the Papers of Andrew W. Cordier: The Rare Book & Manuscript Library, Columbia University in the City of New York

For permission to cite Susan Williams, *Who Killed Hammarskjöld? The UN, the Cold War and White Supremacy in Africa* (London: Hurst, 2011): C. Hurst & Co. (Publishers) Ltd.

The United Nations Photo Library

For permission to publish fig. 13, kind thanks to Greta Beskow Wernstedt.

For permission to publish fig. 18, kind thanks to Sophie Bowness and the Hepworth Estate.